WITHDRAWN

FREE TRADE

AGREEMENTS

US Strategies and Priorities

FREE TRADE AGREEMENTS

US Strategies and Priorities

Edited by **Jeffrey J. Schott**

INSTITUTE FOR INTERNATIONAL ECONOMICS
Washington, DC
April 2004

Jeffrey J. Schott, senior fellow, was a senior associate at the Carnegie Endowment for International Peace (1982–83) and an international economist at the US Treasury (1974–82). He is the author, coauthor, or editor of *Prospects for Free Trade in the Americas* (2001), *Free Trade between Korea and the United States?* (2001), *The WTO after Seattle* (2000), *NAFTA and the Environment: Seven Years Later* (2000), *Launching New Global Trade Talks: An Action Agenda* (1998), *Restarting Fast Track* (1998), *The World Trading System: Challenges Ahead* (1996), *WTO 2000: Setting the Course for World Trade* (1996), *The Uruguay Round: An Assessment* (1994), *Western Hemisphere Economic Integration* (1994), *NAFTA: An Assessment* (rev. ed. 1993), *North American Free Trade: Issues and Recommendations* (1992), *Economic Sanctions Reconsidered* (2d ed. 1990), among others.

INSTITUTE FOR INTERNATIONAL ECONOMICS
1750 Massachusetts Avenue, NW
Washington, DC 20036-1903
(202) 328-9000   FAX: (202) 659-3225
www.iie.com

C. Fred Bergsten, *Director*
Valerie Norville, *Director of Publications and Web Development*
Edward Tureen, *Director of Marketing*

Typesetting by BMWW
Printing by United Book Press, Inc.

Printed in the United States of America

06 05 04   5 4 3 2 1

Library of Congress Cataloging-in-Publication Data

Free trade agreements : US strategies and priorities / Jeffrey J. Schott, editor.
    p. cm.
    Includes bibliographical references and index.
    ISBN 0-88132-361-6
    1. Free trade—United States.
I. Schott, Jeffrey J., 1949–

HF1756.F728 2003
392′.9′0973—dc22   2003060419

Contents

Preface

The United States has recently initiated or agreed to pursue free trade negotiations with a broad range of countries in the Western Hemisphere, Asia, Africa, and Oceania. A large number of additional countries are seeking to launch similar talks with the United States in the near future. All these initiatives, under the banner of "competitive liberalization," are intended to complement ongoing multilateral trade negotiations under the auspices of the World Trade Organization (WTO) and the super-regional creation of a Free Trade Area of the Americas (FTAA).

The sheer number of these bilateral and regional initiatives is unprecedented for the United States. These initiatives raise important questions concerning US interests and priorities in negotiations with key trading partners in each region and concerning the objectives of those countries in concluding deals with the United States. They may also have important implications for the ongoing negotiation of the Doha Round in the WTO and the FTAA and for the global trading system more broadly.

This Institute publication examines the role of free trade agreements (FTAs) in US trade policy. The first section analyzes why FTAs have become more prominent and their implications for the Doha Round and the FTAA. The second section draws lessons from existing US FTAs to date. The next three sections then examine existing or potential new initiatives in the Asia Pacific (Australia, Korea, Taiwan, and ASEAN, especially Thailand), Latin America (Brazil and Central America), and Africa (the Southern African Customs Union) and the Middle East (Egypt and Morocco). All these discussions address the economic and political objectives of the partner countries in engaging in free trade talks with the United States and the implications for other regional trade talks that they may be conducting as well as for their participation in the Doha Round. The final section draws conclusions from this extensive menu of trade policy possibilities regarding the benefits and drawbacks of the proposed initiatives, the sequencing of the negotiations, and their importance for the Doha Round.

One important objective of the volume is to identify criteria that might govern the selection and prioritization of FTA partners by the United States. Over 20 countries have already indicated an interest in launching such negotiations, and the list is growing steadily and rapidly. Should the United States respond on the basis of the economic potential of the respective agreements? their implications for US security relationships? with an eye to their prospects for promoting economic (and thus perhaps political) reform in the partner country? From a broader systemic perspective, should the United States consider prospective FTA negotiations based on the contribution they could make as models for subsequent multilateral or broader regional agreements? as spurring the process of competitive liberalization among the large and growing array of bilateral, plurilateral, subregional, regional, and superregional as well as multilateral negotiations?

The topic of FTAs has been a major interest of the Institute for some time. We did much of the original analytical work on both the Canada–United States Free Trade Agreement and NAFTA. In late 1988, we held a two-day conference on "More Free Trade Areas?" that produced a policy analysis with that title and a conference volume *Free Trade Areas and US Trade Policy*, both by Jeffrey J. Schott. We have more recently produced extensive analyses of the key superregional trade initiatives that have been undertaken by the United States: the Free Trade Area of the Americas and the pursuit of "free and open trade and investment in the Asia Pacific region" by the Asia Pacific Economic Cooperation (APEC) forum. My own paper on "Competitive Liberalization and Global Free Trade: A Vision for the Early 21st Century" and its subsequent version entitled "Globalizing Free Trade" in *Foreign Affairs*, inaugurated discussion of those concepts in 1996.

The conference on which this volume is based, held in May 2003, is part of a broad ongoing Institute program on "Free Trade Agreements and US Trade Policy." Its initial publication, by Inbom Choi and Jeffrey J. Schott in 2001, was *Free Trade between Korea and the United States?* which has become something of a model for our subsequent country studies. The conference papers on Egypt and Taiwan have subsequently been expanded into more comprehensive analyses of the prospects with those countries. We are now conducting similar studies on Colombia and Sri Lanka.

This project has been organized by a small steering committee at the Institute. Jeffrey J. Schott has taken the lead in developing the program and arranging for the individual analyses. Dean DeRosa has managed the day-to-day preparations as well as some of the important substantive portions of the papers. Gary Hufbauer and Howard Lewis advised throughout. I have personally chaired the committee.

This publication is being made possible by the generous support of a number of donors with keen interest in the topic. The Ford Foundation is providing major funding for the Institute's ongoing program in this area. The GE Fund and Merck and Co., Inc. are contributing to that program. The US-Egypt Business Council and the US-Taiwan Business Council supported both the conference and our further work on the countries of particular interest to them.

In addition, Hunton & Williams provided major support for the conference in May 2003. The Government of Australia, the Korea International Trade Association, and the Government of New Zealand contributed to it. We deeply appreciate the assistance of each of these donors and hope that the new volume will add usefully to the domestic and international debate on free trade agreements.

C. FRED BERGSTEN
April 2004

Acknowledgments

Special thanks are due for the hard work of many of my colleagues at the Institute in organizing the conference in which the papers in this volume were first presented, and in preparing the revised manuscripts for publication. Helen Hillebrand, Katharine Keenan, Yvonne Priestley, and Shannon Skupas ensured that the conference ran smoothly and efficiently. Valerie Norville, Marla Banov, and Madona Devasahayam then undertook the unwieldy task of editing the manuscript and managing the publication process. In addition, I would like to thank Paul Grieco and Yee Wong for their invaluable research assistance in preparing the overview and concluding chapters of this volume.

OVERVIEW

1

Free Trade Agreements: Boon or Bane of the World Trading System?

JEFFREY J. SCHOTT

Economists have long argued the costs and benefits of preferential trading arrangements (PTAs)—notably customs unions and free trade agreements (FTAs)—and their impact on the world trading system. Jacob Viner (1950) sparked this debate with his classic study, *The Customs Union Issue*; subsequently, James Meade, Richard Lipsey, Paul and Ronald Wonnacott, Jagdish Bhagwati, and others have built an extensive literature on the complex effects of PTAs on economic activity both within and between countries.[1] This chapter is not meant to survey this rich body of work. But it is worth noting that the general conclusion from these economic studies is that it is clearly preferable to negotiate in a multilateral forum and implement reforms on a most favored nation (MFN) basis. Moreover, unilateral liberalization of trade is usually even better, even without reciprocal "concessions" from trading partners.

At first blush, PTAs seem antithetical to the core principles of the postwar multilateral trading system. The General Agreement on Tariffs and Trade (GATT) has a golden rule, set out in Article I, to "do unto others as you do to your best trading partner." In GATT jargon, this obligation requires a country to accord unconditional MFN treatment to the trade of all other contracting parties to the GATT. However, the original drafters of the GATT carved out specific exceptions from the MFN obligation for

---

Jeffrey J. Schott is a senior fellow at the Institute for International Economics.

1. For a political economy survey of the key findings in this area, see Bhagwati (1993) and Frankel (1997).

existing preference schemes, such as the British system of imperial preferences (dating back to the Ottawa Agreements of 1932) and the special US tariff arrangements with Cuba and the Philippines (GATT Article I:2), and for customs unions and free trade areas (GATT Article XXIV).[2] More recently, the General Agreement on Trade in Services (GATS) established comparable exceptions for service industries in regional integration arrangements (GATS Article V).

In fact, the postwar trade regime—reflecting a lingering mercantilist ethic—sanctions discriminatory treatment via a number of policy instruments. Some GATT provisions allow members to impose selective protection to counter "unfair" trade practices such as subsidies and dumping; others permit preferences for intraregional trade covered by customs unions and FTAs that eliminate barriers on "substantially all" trade between the partner countries. However, the GATT requirements that allow MFN exceptions are vague and have been abused. For example, agreements notified under GATT Article XXIV often exclude important sectors like agriculture, or overlook increased protection against third-country suppliers via restrictive rules of origin. Under both the GATT and the World Trade Organization (WTO), monitoring of such agreements has been notoriously lax. Indeed, a large number of FTAs receive no scrutiny at all because the agreements have not been notified to the GATT/WTO.

GATT negotiators attempted to rectify these shortcomings in the Uruguay Round but failed. The current Doha Round is again charged with this task. To date, however, little has been done. Reform proposals have been inhibited by what I call the "glass house syndrome"—virtually all WTO members are party to some type of regional agreement, and thus don't want to throw stones at other pacts lest their own preferential deals come under attack. As a result, the trading system has treated FTAs with benign neglect. GATT/WTO obligations regarding regional arrangements continue to be dead letters.

Have trade officials been too complacent in their handling of FTAs in the GATT and WTO? Or have economists been too harsh in critiquing regional trading blocs and their threat to the multilateral trading system? Or have both practitioners and academics been too inflexible in their approaches?

To put it another way, are FTAs a boon or are they a bane for the WTO? Do they promote trade liberalization and reinforce multilateralism, or do they detract from and obstruct WTO initiatives and present an alternative to the WTO regime?

Not surprisingly, I find that there are no definitive answers to the questions posed above. The assessment depends importantly on how the FTAs

---

2. Interestingly, the original draft of the GATT covered exceptions only for customs unions and did not mention FTAs, which were added to the GATT during a substantial rewriting of these provisions at the 1946–47 Havana Conference (GATT 1994, 785–88).

are crafted and the volume of trade covered, who participates, and whether significant progress on multilateral reforms proceeds in tandem in the WTO.

In the following sections, I first examine the growing number of FTAs in the world trading system. I then assess whether concerns about the impact of proliferating regionalism on the WTO are justified, weighing the benefits and drawbacks of these preferential trading arrangements to the multilateral system. I conclude with a few concrete recommendations for WTO reforms that would mitigate some of the potential WTO problems posed by FTAs and, I hope, ensure that FTAs are compatible with and reinforce the objectives of the multilateral trading system.

FTAs in Current Context

Over much of the 55-year history of the GATT and WTO, regional trading arrangements have been a sideshow in international trade relations (with the notable exception of the agglomeration of the European Union). Until the 1980s, such pacts were a distinctly European neighborhood affair, with a few notable and mostly failed ventures at regional integration by small groups of developing countries.[3] None of these arrangements was constrained by GATT obligations. The European deals were accepted in deference to broader security concerns, because they helped to build a stronger and more unified European Community against the Soviet threat; the developing-country pacts didn't matter, because those countries didn't undertake significant GATT obligations. Of the pacts notified to the GATT, only a few were deemed consistent with GATT obligations, but none was ruled inconsistent. Most were put in an obscure legal limbo in which countries reserved the right to take future action against alleged abuses.

Overall, European integration has been a resounding success. The European Community has gradually expanded from 6 to 15 countries (and will increase to 25 in May 2004), deepened its integration to develop an as yet incomplete single market, and extended trade preferences to a large number of neighboring countries and former colonies. In contrast, South-South regional pacts generally failed—in part because of their focus on import-substitution policies.

Over the past two decades, regionalism has changed dramatically—involving more countries (especially the United States), linking developed and developing countries in reciprocal trading arrangements, and spreading beyond local neighborhoods to connect trading partners across continents. The biggest policy shift has occurred in East Asia, where until

3. These PTAs took various forms—from "simple" cooperation arrangements, which covered the regulation of border barriers to trade, to FTAs and customs unions.

recently Japan, South Korea, and China had totally abstained from regional trade arrangements. These countries are now engaged in talks with each other and with the members of the Association of Southeast Asian Nations (ASEAN). In addition, South Korea has negotiated an FTA with Chile, and Japan has concluded an FTA with Singapore and is finalizing a pact with Mexico.

Several factors explain this new interest in regionalism by East Asian countries. First, the incremental integration of China into the regional economy has simultaneously created new opportunities for trade and investment in a huge, underdeveloped market and fierce new competition from China-based producers. China is rapidly becoming Korea's top trading partner and hosts substantial Korean and Japanese foreign direct investment. Second, Korean and Japanese trade initiatives reflect growing concerns in those countries about the drift in multilateral negotiations and the prospects for achieving their objectives in the Doha Round without a significant change in their protectionist farm policies. Third, the Asian financial crisis of 1997–98 demonstrated the economic linkages between the countries in the region, as well as each country's vulnerability to economic problems that beset its neighbors.

In addition, the past decade or so has seen the launch of new negotiations toward what I have called "superregional" pacts—pacts that seek to integrate already existing trading blocs. The most notable examples of these initiatives are the ongoing negotiations on a Free Trade Area of the Americas (FTAA), the EU-Mercosur FTA, and the long-term effort to achieve free trade and investment in the Asia-Pacific region.

Perhaps the biggest change over the past two decades, however, has been the global economic environment in which FTAs and other regional pacts operate. Globalization of economic activity has encouraged new alliances between developed and developing countries, sharpened the competition for foreign investment, and placed a high premium on outward-oriented policies. Concerns about insular trading blocs do not square with the market imperatives of the new global economy. Market forces now discipline discriminatory trade practices far more quickly and effectively than in the past; and government policies that raise the cost of doing business by imposing excessive trade, tax, or regulatory burdens often find their companies retrenching and investors relocating elsewhere.

Table 1.1 reports the FTAs and customs unions that are in effect or under negotiation as of May 2003. It includes those that have been notified to the WTO, those concluded but not notified to the WTO, and those under negotiation, as best can be discerned from public and private sources.[4] The totals underestimate the number of active regional negotiations; many

---

4. I appreciate the help provided by Clemens Boonekamp and Carmen Pont-Vieira of the WTO Secretariat in compiling information on regional pacts from published and unpublished sources for this table.

Table 1.1 Regional trade agreements in effect or under negotiation (as of May 2003)

Country/region	Notified to WTO[a]	Concluded but not notified	Under negotiation[b]	Total	Share (percent)
Agreements					
involving	155	83	46	284	100
United States	3	2	6	11	4
Canada	4	0	5	9	3
European Union or EFTA	59	6	6	71	25
Japan	1	0	1	2	1
Intra-FSU/CIT	41	48	6	95	33
Intradeveloping countries	27	26	23	76	27

EFTA = European Free Trade Association
FSU/CIT = former Soviet Union and other countries in transition

a. Agreements are counted only once, even if they are notified to the WTO under both GATT Article XXIV and GATS Article V. However, the North American Free Trade Agreement is counted twice, as US-NAFTA and Canada-NAFTA.
b. Current negotiations on a Free Trade Area of the Americas are counted twice as US developing countries and Canada developing countries; similarly, the Canada-EFTA FTA is counted under Canada and under EFTA.

Sources: WTO Web site, Trade Topics, www.wto.org/english/tratop_e/region_e/region_e.htm, and unpublished data sheets from the WTO.

new initiatives were launched in the second half of 2003, particularly in East Asia and Latin America, and several more have been vetted since the collapse of the WTO ministerial in Cancún in September 2003. Overall, these new initiatives reinforce the general trends reflected in the table and discussed below. The numbers differ somewhat from those reported by the WTO; I have corrected for double counting of regional pacts and for a few other classificatory abnormalities in the WTO data to provide a better breakout on who is doing business with whom.[5]

The table confirms that regional pacts have proliferated; almost all WTO members participate in one or more of the nearly 300 agreements in effect or under negotiation (WTO 2003). When these are taken together, one can understand why concerns arise that discriminatory trade preferences created by these pacts could threaten to fragment the multilateral trading system and to undermine its core principle of MFN treatment. Care should be taken, however, in drawing general conclusions from this seemingly vast pool of agreements.

First, the table groups together regional pacts that differ widely in terms of content and participants.[6] Some, such as the Closer Economic

---

5. For example, the WTO database double counts agreements containing goods and services that have been notified under both the GATT and GATS.

6. Seventy-seven percent of the regional pacts in force "are intended to be" FTAs or customs unions; 27 of these pacts cover goods and services. The other 23 percent are "partial scope agreements" (WTO Secretariat 2003).

Relations trade agreement between Australia and New Zealand, or the North American and Chile-US FTAs, are comprehensive FTAs. Others simply reduce or eliminate tariffs, subject to extensive sectoral or product exceptions; such pacts are the rule among developing countries. Some are notable for the volume of trade eligible for preferences; others apply to very little trade. Their trade impacts and implications for the world trading system vary accordingly. So beware comparing acorns and oak trees!

Second, many of the agreements that have been recorded so far have been neighborhood affairs. About one-quarter of the total agreements involve European countries; most of these pacts contributed to the incremental development of the European Union and the European Free Trade Association. Another one-third of the agreements are among countries that formerly were part of the Soviet Union and other countries in transition. These pacts sought to reestablish trade ties that formerly existed in the socialist bloc among countries that are now returning to a market-oriented trading system. In addition, a little more than one-quarter of the total are agreements among developing countries, seeking to link together their small fragmented markets into an integrated regional economy. Together, these neighborhood deals account for 85 percent of all regional pacts covered in table 1.1.

Third, new negotiations represent about 16 percent of the agreements listed in table 1.1, and this sum does not include negotiations launched since mid-2003 by the United States, Japan, India, Thailand, and others. Conservatively, I estimate that there are more than 60 FTAs under negotiation as of January 2004. FTA negotiations have accelerated in response to and in tandem with the drift in WTO talks since the failed Cancún ministerial in September 2003.

Fourth, the United States has to date been a very small part of the story, accounting for only 4 percent of the total agreements. While the US share of FTAs under negotiation is significantly higher, it still represents less than 20 percent of new FTA talks around the globe. Almost all of the new US initiatives involve developing countries and require agreement on a comprehensive agenda of market access reforms in goods, services, and agriculture (though liberalization of some farm products is subject to lengthy transition periods or outright exemptions). If all these initiatives culminate in FTAs, they will cover more than 40 percent of US merchandise trade (see chapter 13 of this volume).

While table 1.1 describes general trends over four decades, what is perhaps more interesting and more important for the trading system is the recent activity by developing countries—both among themselves and in partnership with developed countries. The totality of these initiatives is reported in table 1.2 (again as of May 2003).

Table 1.2 reports the regional pacts in which developing countries participate. The totals illustrate the active and growing role of regionalism in the developing world. Agreements involving developing countries repre-

Table 1.2   Developing-country participation in regional trade agreements (as of May 2003)

Country/region	Notified to WTO	Concluded but not notified	Under negotiation	Total	Share (percent)
Developing-country agreements					
involving	76	34	39	149	100
United States	3	2	4	9	6
Canada	4	0	3	7	5
European Union or EFTA	24	5	5	34	23
Japan	1	0	1	2	1
Intra-FSU/CIT	16	0	0	16	11
Intradeveloping countries	27	26	23	76	51

EFTA = European Free Trade Association
FSU/CIT = former Soviet Union and other countries in transition

Sources: WTO Web site, Trade Topics, www.wto.org/english/tratop_e/region_e/region_e.htm, and unpublished data sheets from the WTO.

sent more than one-half of all FTAs and customs unions (recorded in table 1.1); more than half of these are pacts among developing countries, as noted above, and about one-quarter link developing countries with European countries.

Table 1.2 also highlights the increasing participation of developing countries in new regional trade negotiations. Almost 85 percent of the agreements that are currently under negotiation worldwide involve developing countries, and more than half of these are between developing countries. Whatever one thinks about the systemic implications of this spurt of negotiating activity, the proliferating regionalism among developing countries clearly has very important consequences for development.[7]

Why are developing countries so interested in FTAs? In the past, these countries were able to obtain improved access to industrial markets through GATT negotiations that did not require them to reciprocate by opening their own markets to foreign competition. While useful, prior GATT rounds had two major shortcomings: they did not prompt policy changes in developing countries that would induce adequate flows of investment and transfers of technology (apart from extractive industries), and competitive agricultural and manufactured exports of developing countries often were excluded from the reforms. In short, developing countries were free riders on the GATT system until the Uruguay Round, but derived only modest benefits from their minimal contributions to GATT negotiations. They protected their own markets, but in turn had to accept the maintenance of high foreign trade barriers against their most competitive exports.

---

7. For a comprehensive analysis of this set of issues, see Schiff and Winters (2003).

Though such policies never yielded big economic rewards, they were politically convenient. Many developing countries relied on protected home markets and commodity exports to support modest growth; some followed a strategy of export-led growth and became platforms for the assembly and export of light manufactures. Their success in turn provoked a wave of new protectionism in developed markets via so-called voluntary export restraints, antidumping and countervailing duties, and special protection regimes like the Multi-Fiber Arrangement. This strategy of limited engagement in the world trading system became increasingly untenable over the past two decades with the globalization of economy activity, which has been punctuated by a series of financial crises, depressed commodity prices, and growing competition from China.

Countries must now adapt quickly to changing conditions in world markets or fall sharply behind in the global competition for market share and investment resources. They can no longer afford to protect their industries from foreign competitors; the world will simply pass them by. Trade and integration arrangements must be part of each country's policy response and integrally linked with its development strategy (though not necessarily the main driver of that strategy).

For developing countries, regional trading arrangements have become increasingly important components of economic policy for several reasons. First, they contribute to economic growth by spurring competition in domestic markets, dampening inflation, and promoting investment.[8] Second, they provide an "insurance policy" against new protectionism at home and abroad by substantially raising the cost of reversing the free trade reforms mandated by the regional pacts—and thus creating a more stable and attractive environment for investment. Indeed, competition for investment drives many of the FTAs in which developing countries participate. If the country maintains high levels of protection, costly regulations, or discriminatory standards, investors generally will opt to locate in other countries that have policies more conducive to production and investment.

That said, trade pacts are not magic potions that automatically create economic prosperity (even if they are often sold to the public on that promise). Countries can take full advantage of the new trading opportunities created by trade accords only if they pursue domestic economic policies—in conjunction with their trade reforms—that provide a stable macroeconomic climate for investment and job creation, and that command sufficient political support to ensure their durability. Thus, one of the most important aspects of FTAs is that they encourage developing countries to liberalize their own trade and regulatory barriers in order to

---

8. Much of the benefit derives from the removal of restrictions to economic activity in their own markets, but countries also gain by being able to trade and invest across a broader regional market.

attract foreign investment. Developing countries face tough competition for investment and therefore have to engage in a process of competitive liberalization to secure the capital inflows needed to finance their development as well as to import needed technologies and management skills. Competitive liberalization is what differentiates current integration policies from past episodes among developing countries where import-substitution policies supported defensive fortress strategies that did not seek to improve the efficiency and competitiveness of their economies in contending with the outside world.

FTAs: Balancing Benefits and Costs

Lowering intraregional trade barriers expands trade among partner countries and encourages economies of scale of production together with intra- and interindustry specialization. But do FTAs generate *net* trade creation? and *net* welfare gains for both the FTA members and their third-country partners? If the FTA preferences shift imports from suppliers in third countries to less efficient regional firms (i.e., trade diversion), then the pact may increase costs and reduce welfare. A lot depends on the impact on productivity in the partner economies, as well as on the conditions applied to qualify for the trade preferences (e.g., rules of origin) that may increase transaction costs and reduce economic benefits.[9] Thus, determining whether FTAs help or hinder the multilateral trading system requires a complex calculus.

On the positive side, FTA advocates cite four main advantages of pursuing regional pacts in tandem with multilateral reforms: advancing trade liberalization, establishing useful precedents for WTO talks, locking in domestic reforms, and bolstering alliances among trading partners. On the negative side, critics of FTAs generally cite four sets of problems created by the negotiation and implementation of regional trade agreements: trade and investment diversion (which may also create disincentives to advance WTO talks), overlapping and conflicting trading rules and regulations, attention and resource diversion from WTO talks, and bad precedents for other trade accords. The following subsections summarize the main points on each side.

Benefits of Pursuing FTAs

The first and most important benefit of FTAs is the depth of trade reform to which the partner countries aspire. If they are true to their name, FTAs seek to eliminate barriers on "substantially all" trade between the partner

---

9. For a fuller discussion of these issues, see Wonnacott and Lutz (1989).

countries (some are obviously less perfect in this regard than others). In contrast, WTO negotiators pursue incremental reforms in each trade round, leaving substantial barriers in place after the accords are fully implemented. The difference can be put simply: deeper cuts, but by fewer countries, and applied on a discriminatory basis. FTAs achieve deeper cuts in trade protection than WTO reforms but the FTA liberalization is accorded to only a few countries, while multilateral agreements are applied on an MFN basis to the entire WTO membership.

Advocates of FTAs argue that, on balance, the pacts are trade creating and spur positive welfare gains for participating countries as well as, over time, for third countries by stimulating growth in the FTA region. They also subscribe to the "bicycle theory" of trade negotiations, citing the systemic benefits of maintaining momentum on trade reform. Indeed, they argue that for the past four decades, GATT and WTO negotiations have been spurred by the desire to offset discrimination generated by regional pacts. Ongoing multilateral liberalization, in turn, reduces the value of regional preferences (or the amount of discrimination against third-country suppliers to the FTA region). As long as countries proceed with WTO reforms in tandem with their FTA initiatives, regional preferences will have a short "half-life" and FTA partners will lack incentives to build regional fortresses designed to shield their economies from foreign competition. Consequently, regional industries will be more likely to use the temporary period in which FTA preferences accord protection to restructure their operations so that they can compete effectively against foreign suppliers rather than lobby for continued protection.

In general, FTAs are easier to conclude than WTO accords because they require agreement among a small number of "like-minded" countries rather than among the larger and more diverse WTO membership.[10] To be sure, this ease is partly due to the limited applicability of FTA liberalization. Since the FTA reforms apply only to member countries, competition remains partially constrained; thus FTAs are easier to sell to domestic lobbies but bring fewer welfare benefits for the economy as a whole.

Second, FTAs often include rights and obligations regarding domestic regulatory practices and other "behind-the-border" measures that affect trade and investment flows—issues that had not until recently been the primary focus of multilateral talks. In several instances, FTA provisions have established precedents for broader multilateral accords in areas such as services and electronic commerce.[11] In these areas, discriminatory application of FTA rules is possible but less problematic. Usually the de-

---

10. Bhagwati (1993) disagrees, but his analysis doesn't compare the new North-South agreements against the more complex WTO process.

11. The US-Canada FTA provided very useful precedents on services that were translated into the GATS in the Uruguay Round. The US-Chile FTA may similarly affect the area of e-commerce.

mands of the marketplace (not to mention the inordinate administrative costs of implementing different standards and requirements for different countries) require convergence toward a common set of standards applied to all trade.

In addition to the value of FTAs in setting precedents, there are also important learning-by-doing effects from engaging in the negotiating process. Sitting at the negotiating table provides an education that can't be replicated in any university: officials learn to negotiate by negotiating.[12] This aspect is especially important for developing countries; FTA negotiations are helping them to educate a new class of trade negotiators to represent them in regional and WTO talks. Similarly, learning-by-doing benefits derive from the process of problem solving in new areas on the trade agenda: inevitably, the complexities of trade problems are not fully exposed until one tries to negotiate a solution.

Third, FTAs have an important lock-in effect on domestic reform: policy reversals become more costly because changes that violate the free trade obligations could trigger retaliation by trading partners. FTAs thus help governments to withstand the protectionist demands of their domestic lobbies and deflect pressure to take actions that are politically alluring but economically undesirable; in so doing, they reduce uncertainty about trade and regulatory policies and thereby facilitate business planning and investment. For many developing countries, this benefit is key to the success of their investment-led development strategies.

Fourth, FTAs strengthen trade relations among partner countries and make it easier to build alliances for WTO reforms in areas of common interest. The Doha Round itself probably would not have been launched if FTA partners (current and prospective) of the United States and the European Union had not worked in unison to craft a balanced agenda for the talks.

FTA Drawbacks

Part of the perceived advantage of an FTA is receiving preferential tariff treatment in the partner country. The higher the MFN tariff, the larger the margin of preference for suppliers based in the FTA partner countries and therefore the greater the advantage. However, the explicit discrimination also generates the key drawback of FTAs: trade and investment diversion.

Critics of FTAs decry the negative impact of regional pacts on global economic welfare as trade and investment are diverted to take advantage of the preferential trading regime, and the distraction—or even

---

12. For this reason, South Korea first entered into FTA negotiations with Chile and New Zealand to upgrade the negotiating skills of its trade officials before embarking on talks with Japan and other major trading partners.

disengagement—from multilateral trade negotiations. Richard Baldwin (1993) notes that trade diversion increases the cost of nonparticipation for third countries and spurs those that suffer trade diversion to attempt either to join the FTA or to form their own bloc. The key question is whether this "domino regionalism" fragments the trading system into protectionist blocs or spurs competitive liberalization that reinforces multilateral reforms (Bergsten 1996).

In North-South FTAs, trade diversion is often generated in sectors where MFN trade barriers are high, such as textiles, clothing, and agriculture—which also happen to be sectors of widespread export interest for developing countries. FTAs thus provide a temporary fillip to export-led growth for developing-country participants, though their gains usually come at the expense of other developing countries that are penalized by the discrimination. NAFTA caused substantial trade and investment diversion in the textile and clothing sectors from the Caribbean Basin countries as a result of the preferential treatment accorded Mexican industry. The US African Growth and Opportunity Act (AGOA) now seems to be having a similar adverse effect on nonbeneficiaries in Africa and elsewhere.

The extent of the problem caused by trade and investment diversion depends importantly on whether there is new multilateral liberalization and whether FTA partners extend similar preferences to other countries (as the United States has done with the Caribbean Basin Initiative and the Andean Trade Preferences Act, for example). Both programs dilute the value of the trade preferences of the old and new FTA partners. Unfortunately, some FTA beneficiaries try to preempt the "erosion" of their margins of preference by dragging their feet on WTO reforms (including the phaseout of the Multi-Fiber Arrangement due in January 2005).

How serious is the concern that FTAs spawn WTO foot-draggers? Some FTA critics argue that if a country cuts a trade deal with its key trading partners, it will have less interest in MFN reforms in the WTO. The classic case cited is the Common Agricultural Policy (CAP) of the European Community—the so-called glue of European integration—which arguably has made the Europeans less interested in GATT/WTO farm trade reforms (even though those policies induced the United States and others to enter into new GATT rounds in the 1960s and 1970s to try to reduce the subsidies provided and barriers erected by the CAP). FTA critics argue that European integration has made it harder to reform agriculture and that the task will become even more difficult with the expansion of the European Union in May 2004. However, European agriculture seems to be a special case that has not been replicated elsewhere to the extent of affecting GATT negotiations.

But does this hold true for North-South agreements? Some have claimed that Mexico is less interested in the FTAA because of NAFTA and doesn't want other Latin American countries to share its free access to the US market, but the facts do not seem to bear this argument out. Mexico has embarked aggressively on FTA negotiations with trading partners around the globe in parallel with its participation in the FTAA negotiations, precisely because it knows that the United States has added and will continue to add more partners, thus diluting the value of its preferences in the US market. Rather, Mexico is using its growing network of FTAs to position itself as an attractive platform for foreign direct investment to serve burgeoning Mexican and hemispheric markets. The successful conclusion of the FTAA reinforces that strategy.

To be sure, some developing countries still want to block MFN reforms to maintain their margins of preference in industrial markets; a large bloc of them voiced this position in Cancún in September 2003. Even if they succeed in blocking the WTO process, however, their protectionist efforts will fail because they cannot prevent the major industrial countries from granting unilateral trade preferences or concluding new FTAs that will diminish the value of their preferences in those markets. The policy lesson is clear: FTAs give developing countries a brief head start on competing for investment and export markets. Those that meld the trade preferences with domestic reforms can reap long-term benefits. Those that don't will find their trade gains transitory and the investment footloose.

The second major problem with FTAs is that they can create overlapping sets of trade rules and regulations that make sourcing products to different markets complicated and often more costly. Bhagwati has artfully called this mélange of different rules, procedures, and standards generated by different FTAs a "spaghetti bowl" of trade regulations.[13] FTA critics have specifically decried the imposition of restrictive rules of origin, which can be particularly distorting and can increase transaction costs.[14] Origin rules are blatant tools of discrimination, but their impact on business in terms of lost sales or increased transactions costs is unclear. Problems flourish in highly protected sectors; if MFN trade barriers are low, the protectionist effects of origin rules diminish, since importers can simply ignore the regional rules and pay the MFN tariff (as often occurs in US-Canada trade).[15] More empirical research is needed to determine how big a problem the spaghetti bowl really is.

Third, countries have limited resources to engage in trade negotiations, and FTAs clearly dilute the effort that can be directed toward WTO

---

13. See Bhagwati and Panagariya (1996) for a discussion of this problem.

14. Other nontariff barriers such as technical standards and phytosanitary measures also enter into this equation.

15. Because developing countries need to meet the standards of the dominant economy in the regional bloc to take advantage of the new trading opportunities, concerns about different standards may be overstated. More difficult is the problem of competing standards set forth by the United States and the European Union, which can be best addressed in multilateral negotiations.

initiatives. This resource scarcity problem is particularly constraining for developing countries that have only a few officials to run domestic agencies and participate in bilateral, regional, and WTO talks. But it also affects US negotiators, whose budget is inadequate to meet the extensive demands set out in US Trade Promotion Authority by their congressional masters (see Ambassador Robert Zoellick's letter appended to GAO 2004).

Fourth, regional pacts can yield both good and bad precedents (involving both rules and exceptions to trade reforms). FTA critics charge that North-South agreements are more prone to the latter owing to the asymmetric economic and political influence of the larger, industrialized countries. Here again, the prime example is the rules of origin in US FTAs, especially those regulating trade in textiles and clothing. Some critics also claim that FTAs establish bad precedents by including trade obligations in areas such as intellectual property, labor, and the environment—issues that they believe should be handled apart from trade pacts. Of course, other groups argue forcefully that these provisions are good precedents and should be incorporated into or elaborated in multilateral trading rules. In addition, some FTAs carve out important sectors like agriculture from the free trade regime, or exempt key products from the reforms (e.g., the US-Australia FTA, which excludes sugar).

In sum, FTAs can be trade creating or diverting, can build support for or divert attention from multilateral trade negotiations, can enhance or dilute (or both) negotiating resources, and can foster good and bad precedents for other trade initiatives. In addition, FTAs often can reinforce and augment domestic economic reforms in developing countries. The outcome depends on how the pacts are crafted, the commitment of the partner countries to the WTO system, and how much progress is made in parallel WTO talks.

FTA critics disagree; they remain steadfast in their commitment to the GATT/WTO process, where reforms have to be implemented (with a few exceptions) on a most favored nation basis. If WTO talks face tough sledding, their counsel is to redouble efforts at MFN reforms rather than to create new distortions via competing preferential regimes. This preference for multilateralism rings true with economic theory and arguably with the conduct of international trade negotiations throughout the GATT era. But does it fit the world of the WTO and the current Doha Round?

The new WTO does not work like the old GATT, for better or for worse, and its negotiating dynamics are much more complicated. First, conducting and concluding accords are much more complex than in prior GATT rounds. The WTO has 146 member countries; membership could increase to 170 by the end of this decade if many of the current applicants complete their accession negotiations. Most of the members are developing countries; unlike during the GATT era, many of them now have an important stake in international trade and therefore an important stake in getting something out of the trade agreements. Because each country needs to be able to bring home a trophy to justify the concessions that they make to their trading partners, WTO talks have to produce a big package of agreements that accommodates the diverse interests of its large membership. Since the WTO still operates by consensus, the task of crafting a set of agreements that meets the demands of the large and increasingly disparate membership has become much more difficult (as evidenced in Cancún).[16] WTO deliberations are now the subject of intense coalitional politics unknown in the GATT era, when the United States and European Community were the main hegemons. Members now need to build alliances by issue (the Cairns Group on agriculture) or region (the Caribbean Regional Negotiating Machinery) or groups of developing countries (the G-20 that formed before Cancún); the alliance building that takes place when one negotiates an FTA can be very helpful in pursuing common objectives in WTO talks.

The second major problem is that the United States and the European Union have very little left to offer at the negotiating table in terms of market access, except what is very difficult to give—that is, the protection in agriculture and textiles that has survived eight previous rounds of multilateral trade negotiations and that is of major export interest to developing countries. In turn, developing countries seem reluctant to lower their own generally much higher trade barriers without increased and more secure access to industrial markets. To get the United States, Europe, and Japan to commit to significant reforms in long-standing protection in agriculture and in some manufacturing sectors, other WTO members—including middle-income developing countries—need to offer concrete reductions in their protection as well. In short, the WTO talks need to produce a big deal or they may not achieve any agreement at all (see Schott 2003). That is why working out a deal in the WTO is much more complicated and why FTAs can reinforce the negotiating dynamics required for a successful WTO round.

Strengthening WTO Rules on Regional Trade Pacts

The political economy of trade liberalization and the increasing complexities of negotiating in the WTO seem to require an admixture of bilateral, regional, and multilateral trade initiatives. The following chapters in this volume will test this argument for both extant and prospective agreements between the United States and its trading partners in Latin America, Asia, and Africa and the Middle East. But if it is true, there is nonetheless a need to strengthen WTO rules to better ensure that FTAs promote

---

16. The consensus rule is still preferable to a voting scheme, but reform of the WTO's consensus-building process could make WTO decision making more efficacious and equitable (see Schott and Watal 2000).

regional deals that complement the objectives and initiatives of the multilateral trading system. There is no lack of analysis or proposals on how to redress the weaknesses of WTO obligations on regional trading arrangements (Bhagwati 1993; WTO Secretariat 1995; Lawrence 1996; Winters 1998; Schiff and Winters 2003). The following are some basic reforms that could be included in the Doha Round talks.

First, WTO members should revisit the vague and incomplete disciplines of GATT Article XXIV and GATS Article V. This task is already part of the mandate of the Doha Round, though scant progress has been made in "clarifying and improving disciplines and procedures under the existing WTO provisions" or taking account of "the developmental aspects of regional trade agreements."[17] Many proposals focus on setting some numerical definition for the GATT's "substantially all" test. While logical, such targets raise more definitional problems than they solve. In contrast, it is feasible and useful to develop indicative guidelines for rules of origin. Less is better when it comes to origin rules—the more complex and industry-specific the requirements, the more likely the rules will have a chilling effect on trade.

Second, FTA partners should commit to harmonize and lower their MFN tariffs over a 10-year period, so that there is a complementarity in the regional and multilateral reform efforts. This requirement would also mitigate problems with restrictive rules of origin by reducing the wedge between MFN and preferential tariff rates. And of course it would ensure the advance of WTO reforms, so that progress continues to be made on the path toward global free trade.

Third, the WTO should undertake more active surveillance after pacts enter into force. Most of the time, when it does take place, WTO monitoring of regional pacts examines only what was negotiated and whether it comports with GATT and GATS obligations. However, what is really important is how the agreements are implemented and what effects they have on international trade and investment. That requires ex post analysis, which should be done both by the WTO Secretariat in the trade policy reviews and by independent groups of experts. Assessments of the economic impact of FTAs and customs unions with intraregional trade exceeding $10 billion annually should be conducted every five years, starting five years after the entry into force of the agreement.

In sum, FTAs are most beneficial if their coverage is comprehensive, if origin rules are kept to a minimum, and if the members are committed to work together to advance MFN trade reforms in the WTO. For developing countries in particular, the FTA strategy works best under the umbrella of a strong rules-based multilateral trading system. New WTO rules

---

17. See paragraph 29 of the Doha Ministerial Declaration, adopted November 14, 2001, WT/MIN(01)/DEC/W/1; www.wto.org/english/thewto_e/minist_e/min01_e/mindecl_e. htm.

should be crafted to limit the downside risk of FTAs for the multilateral system as part of renewed efforts to move the Doha Round toward a successful result. The greatest risk to the WTO system is the potential failure of the Doha Round. In that event, problems with existing WTO rules would not be fixed and festering trade disputes would erode confidence and support for the multilateral trading system. Properly managed, regional pacts can be an important part of the success of, rather than a third-best substitute for, the WTO system.

References

Baldwin, Richard. 1993. *A Domino Theory of Regionalism*. NBER Working Paper 4465. Cambridge, MA: National Bureau of Economic Research.

Bergsten, C. Fred. 1996. *Competitive Liberalization and Global Free Trade: A Vision for the Early 21st Century*. APEC Working Paper No. 96-15. Washington: Institute for International Economics. Available at www.iie.com/publications/wp/1996/96-15.htm.

Bhagwati, Jagdish. 1993. Regionalism and Multilateralism: An Overview. In *New Dimensions in Regional Integration*, ed. Jaime de Melo and Arvind Panagariya. Cambridge: Cambridge University Press.

Bhagwati, Jagdish, and Arvind Panagariya, eds. 1996. *The Economics of Preferential Trade Agreements*. Washington: AEI Press.

Frankel, Jeffrey. 1997. *Regional Trading Blocs in the World Economic System*. Washington: Institute for International Economics.

General Accounting Office, United States (GAO). 2004. International Trade: Intensifying Free Trade Negotiating Agenda Calls for Better Allocation of Staff and Resources. GAO-04-233. Report to Congressional Requesters. www.gao.gov/new.items/d04233.pdf (January).

General Agreement on Tariffs and Trade (GATT). 1994. *Guide to GATT Law and Practice: Analytical Index*. Geneva: General Agreement on Tariffs and Trade.

Lawrence, Robert Z. 1996. *Regionalism, Multilateralism, and Deeper Integration*. Washington: Brookings Institution.

Schiff, Maurice, and L. Alan Winters. 2003. *Regional Integration and Development*. Washington: World Bank and Oxford University Press.

Schott, Jeffrey J. 2003. Unlocking the Benefits of World Trade. *The Economist*, November 1, 65–67. Available at www.iie.com/publications/papers/schott1103.htm.

Schott, Jeffrey J., and Jayashree Watal. 2000. Decision-making in the WTO. In *The WTO after Seattle*, ed. Jeffrey J. Schott. Washington: Institute for International Economics.

Viner, Jacob. 1950. *The Customs Union Issue*. New York: Carnegie Endowment for International Peace.

Winters, L. Alan. 1998. Regionalism and the Next Round. In *Launching New Global Trade Talks: An Action Agenda*, ed. Jeffrey J. Schott. Washington: Institute for International Economics.

Wonnacott, Paul, and Mark Lutz. 1989. Is There a Case for Free Trade Areas? In *Free Trade Areas and U.S. Trade Policy*, ed. Jeffrey J. Schott. Washington: Institute for International Economics.

WTO Secretariat. 1995. *Regionalism and the World Trading System*. Geneva: World Trade Organization.

WTO Secretariat. 2003. The Changing Landscape of RTAs. Paper prepared for the Seminar on Regional Trade Agreements and the WTO, Geneva, November 14. Available at www.wto.org/english/tratop e/sem_nov3_e/boonekamp_paper_e.doc.

Comment

RICHARD N. COOPER

I am extremely doubtful that free trade agreements make a positive contribution to overall human well-being, which is what we ought to keep our eyes on.

I want to make four substantive points and then conclude with two qualifications. The first substantive point is that one should never forget that when country A—the United States, for example—discriminates in favor of a trading partner, it discriminates *against* other trading partners. FTAs are seen as favorable agreements because the United States eliminates duties on goods from Chile or Singapore or whomever, but whenever it does that, it discriminates against everyone else. For a country that has global trade interests and pretensions of having global political interests and influence, this seems to me a thoroughly undesirable and unwise course to take. The United States thereby makes selected friends but also leaves a bad taste with other countries, which outnumber those friends by a large margin. I have nothing against Chile, but why should the United States discriminate in favor of goods from Chile as opposed to those coming, for example, from the Philippines or Thailand or India? It seems to me that US policymakers have not persuasively answered that question. Discrimination means discrimination *against* as well as discrimination *for*, and on balance such discrimination is bad politics. That is something to keep foremost in mind. Indeed, most favored nation treatment guided US trade policy for decades for just that reason.

Richard N. Cooper is Maurits C. Boas Professor of Economics at Harvard University and chairman of the Advisory Committee of the Institute for International Economics.

My second point is that unless negotiators are very careful, FTAs are also bad economics. The possibilities for trade diversion are well known. These days economists properly also worry about investment diversion because foreign direct investment, in particular, has become an important part of trading arrangements. Indeed, from the Canadian point of view investment diversion was the main point of the US-Canada Auto Pact of the mid-1960s, and the United States acquiesced in it.

Article XXIV of the General Agreement on Tariffs and Trade (GATT) provides some rules on the question of trade diversion, subsequently incorporated into the World Trade Organization (WTO). These rules were designed to minimize (but not eliminate) trade diversion by requiring that a permissible free trade area eliminate all duties and other restrictive barriers, except those that are permitted elsewhere in the GATT, "on substantially all trade between the constituent territories." The original European Community, which was a customs union, met this standard, as did the North American Free Trade Agreement (NAFTA), but most free trade areas do not. If one relaxes this Article XXIV standard that substantially all trade has to be covered, what is the likely outcome? The likely outcome, I submit, is that the exclusions in practice will take place precisely in those sectors where trade creation is likely to be most substantial. In other words, the more one backs away from the comprehensive requirement, the more likely the agreement is to involve trade diversion, so that most FTAs have a bias toward trade diversion.

The GATT also required that a free trade area have the approval of the contracting parties before it is put in place. Contracting parties were obliged to promptly notify the GATT of any FTA, specifying all of its characteristics. Then the GATT was supposed to set up panels to scrutinize the nature of the agreement to see if it was consistent with Article XXIV. If my information is correct, up until 1995—that is to say, up until the transformation into the WTO—69 cases were actually notified to the GATT. Only 6 of them actually got GATT approval; the other 63 effectively disappeared. There were no findings. They were neither approved nor formally disapproved; they were just in limbo as far as the GATT was concerned. Recall that one of the characteristics of the GATT was that a panel finding had to have unanimity, including the agreement of the parties involved. So far as I am aware, performance on this score has been no better since 1996. In my view, Article XXIV was well conceived but not well executed. There was of course the possibility, as there typically is in international agreements, for a waiver by a two-thirds vote—and the first new postwar discriminatory bloc, the European Coal and Steel Community (which certainly did not cover substantially all trade), got a GATT waiver. The issue was put, it was discussed, it was decided on balance to be a good thing. The US-Canada Auto Agreement also got a waiver, more dubiously. Most FTAs do not have waivers.

So requirements of the GATT have been all but ignored. Developing countries—most of the free trade areas are among developing countries—just used the blanket excuse that "special and differential treatment" essentially absolved them of all serious responsibility under the GATT, and the developed countries let them get away with that. I do not know what excuse Europeans used for all of their bilateral, partial-coverage free trade areas; they engaged extensively in this process. I refer here to the arrangements between the European Community and Algeria, Morocco, Israel, and other nonmember countries, not to the European Community itself. This process goes way back, but no country seriously challenged them on it. The new US free trade areas presumably meet the comprehensive standard, although the FTA with Israel, which was the first of these bilateral US agreements, falls short, as least as regards agriculture and some services.

My third point is that free trade areas, in an important difference from customs unions, require rules of origin, especially if the tariff rates differ significantly among the parties. Yet the need for rules of origin creates a playground for protectionist interests. That is the only way to describe it. Why? Because rules of origin are arcane and technical. Outsiders, such as academics or journalists, have a hard time paying serious attention to them, and even the negotiators quickly lose interest. The Polish-EU Agreement has rules of origin running to 81 pages of fine print. The rules of origin governing NAFTA cover 200 pages. You can be sure that the folks that are most intensely interested have scrutinized every line, indeed have written many lines, and they come to dominate the process. So the rules of origin often turn out to be highly protectionist. Examples in NAFTA, which is a comprehensive agreement, concern textiles and apparel, autos, processed foods, TV picture tubes, and a host of other items. A widely quoted example of trade diversion involves tomato paste from Chile, which was a major provider to Mexico before NAFTA; that paste is now provided from within NAFTA. The need for rules of origin, effectively dominated by the special interests, increases trade diversion relative to trade creation.

My fourth point concerns a claim made in support of FTAs. Jeffrey Schott argues in his overview chapter, as have others, that FTAs often lead to more general trade liberalization. I think that claim is highly dubious. It has not been put to a serious test because the great proliferation of these agreements has taken place only in the past decade, and the Doha Round is still at an early stage. There are, however, a number of examples where beneficiaries of preferential trade agreements with the European Community resisted trade liberalization in the Uruguay Round because it would reduce their margins of preference. That may have been a rational position from their perspective, particularly if they were beneficiaries of trade diversion, and it may be expected in the future also to create resistance to multilateral trade liberalization. So the claim that FTAs lead to more trade liberalization is highly dubious, but it still remains to be tested seriously.

Now let me make two qualifications to my four objections to FTAs. The first concerns NAFTA: I was and remain a strong supporter of NAFTA. It was comprehensive in coverage; it went way beyond the substantive agenda of the Uruguay Round, especially in agriculture and services. It thus encompassed a scope that was not seriously on the multilateral agenda at that time. Moreover, the Uruguay Round had hit a serious snag in 1990, and it is arguable that NAFTA did, contrary to my fourth point above, move the Uruguay Round forward, particularly in nudging the Europeans. But most important, the United States had a well-understood and easily explained strategic rationale for having a free trade area with Mexico, centering on a variety of issues, not least crime and migration. Mexico proposed an FTA to commit President Salinas de Gortari's successors to his liberal reforms, and the United States responded positively. America's strategic interest in a stable and prosperous Mexico is strong and evident. The United States has a general interest in stable and prosperous countries all around the world, but there was a special, clearly explicable case that could be made with respect to Mexico. The rest of the world could easily understand that. That case cannot be made with respect to Chile, Mercosur (the Southern Cone Common Market), Singapore, or indeed any of the other countries, except arguably those in Central America, that are now under US consideration for free trade areas. So in my mind, NAFTA stands out as a legitimate exception to the generalizations that I have made.

My final qualification concerns my presumption that negotiators can successfully move ahead in the multilateral framework, which has served the world economy extremely well during the past half century. The United States ought to devote its negotiating and political energies to getting a successful conclusion to the multilateral negotiations, currently the Doha Round and some unfinished business from the Uruguay Round. However, a serious multilateral negotiation might fail for a variety of reasons—perhaps Europe will not liberalize agriculture or India cannot agree to any further liberalization, even though India retains one of the world's highest levels of protection (there is vigorous domestic debate over the limited liberalization that India has already undertaken). Given the consensus process, it only takes one significant player to bring the whole negotiation to a halt. Should the multilateral process fail, then coalitions of the willing under those circumstances become much more attractive. FTAs are a fallback position. But my view is that they ought to be seen as just that, as fallback positions for failed multilateral negotiation, and not as the main thrust, which is what they seem to have become for the United States, emulating Europe. Now the Asian countries are in discussion about moving down the same path. As Herminio Blanco said during the conference, this is a virus and everyone has caught it. It needs to be contained.

Governments are not good at admitting that they have made mistakes. In the United States, this is a bipartisan mistake. It has occurred under several presidents, starting with Ronald Reagan. Somebody ought to say: "Well, we have looked at the matter again. We are going to put our energies in the coming years into maintenance and furtherance of the multilateral system. We will postpone further free trade areas." The United States should not be putting serious effort into negotiating FTAs at the present time.

Comment

RENATO RUGGIERO

There is a paradox in international trade policy today. Globalization is the word on everyone's lips, yet regional agreements have never been so popular. One hundred fifty-five regional trade agreements are in force around the world, half of them concluded since 1990; 83 are concluded but not notified to the World Trade Organization; and 46 are in the making. Every WTO member is part of at least one of them. Almost half of world trade now occurs between countries belonging to them. This headlong rush toward regionalism has gained new momentum in recent years. For a start, the European Union, whose long-standing commitment to regional agreements has arguably triggered this rush, is moving on with its ambitious program of announced regional deals, including with Russia. It has partnership agreements with all other European countries except Albania, Bosnia, Croatia, and Yugoslavia. It also has deals with Turkey, Israel, and Morocco. It is negotiating agreements with most other Arab countries.

Further afield, the European Union has struck deals with Chile, Mexico, and South Africa. It is pursuing agreements with the four Mercosur (Southern Cone Common Market) countries. It is also pressing 71 African, Caribbean, and Pacific (ACP) countries, mostly ex-colonies, to sign up to new regional arrangements.

Taking into account the 100 or so other poor countries covered by the Generalized System of Preferences, the European Union's network of preferences already covers most of the world. In fact there are only six

Renato Ruggiero is chairman of Citigroup Switzerland and was director-general of the World Trade Organization from 1995 to 1999.

countries—Australia, Canada, Japan, New Zealand, Taiwan, and the United States—with which it trades on a "normal" (most favored nation) basis.

The second big development is that Japan's rallying to the regional cause has sparked wider moves toward regionalism in Asia. In the aftermath of the failure to launch a new round of WTO talks in Seattle in late 1999, Japan announced that it too was going regional—and it has since concluded a bilateral deal with Singapore. Also India is proposing its own free trade agreement with ASEAN (the Association of Southeast Asian Nations).

The third and very significant development is that the United States has embraced the regional route with gusto. Spelling out America's new trade strategy, Robert Zoellick, the US trade representative, explained that President Bush has been pressing ahead with trade liberalization globally, regionally, and bilaterally. By advancing on multiple fronts, the US is creating a competition in liberalization, placing America at the heart of a network of initiatives to open markets.

The idea behind this strategy of "competitive liberalization" is that not only are US bilateral and regional agreements valuable contributions to freeing trade in themselves, they also put pressure on other countries to push forward with freeing trade multilaterally at the WTO.

Let me be clear: regional trade agreements are certainly not forbidden by the WTO and they can sometimes be very positive. The North American Free Trade Agreement has locked in Mexico's economic and political reforms. From a US perspective, it has helped stabilize a volatile neighbor with which America shares a 2,000-mile border. The European Union has cemented peace in Europe. It is building a single market with a single currency that promises huge economies of scale for companies and the benefits of increased competition, such as lower prices, for consumers. It has helped countries, such as Ireland and Spain, to make very rapid and substantial economic progress. It is a testing ground and model for other countries that want to cooperate regionally. Better still, the agreed EU membership has entrenched peace and stability in central and eastern Europe.

There are certainly other positive examples of good "regionalism." We have heard many speakers telling us the benefits of regionalism as well as its drawbacks. But this is not, I believe, the main issue. The central problem is that preferential agreements are, or should be, exceptions to the multilateral trade system and its main principle, the most favored nation clause. The very real risk is that regionalism is now becoming the preferred road to liberalization.

My concern, when I hear the announcement of a "competitive liberalization," is that we are presenting bilateralism, regionalism, and multilateralism as comparative instruments of the world trading system.

We are giving the impression that we are considering trade systems based on preferences equal to the nondiscrimination system and that we are almost indifferent if the multilateral system will not be the winner of the competition. In other words, "competitive liberalization" could mean that FTAs can become an alternative to the multilateral system and not an exception subject to some conditionality under the rules of the WTO.

We cannot forget that the foundation of our open world economy is the multilateral trading system promoted by the United States. Its underlying principles are nondiscrimination and the lowering, and then binding, of tariffs through reciprocal bargaining.

The success of this system has been extraordinary. Between 1950 and 2001, the volume of world exports rose 20-fold and the volume of world exports of manufactures 39-fold, while world output rose sevenfold. By 2001, world trade amounted to 24 percent of global output. This multilateral system is a superb product of enlightened US self-interest.

Yet it is a cruel irony that just as the multilateral trading system has scored one of its greatest successes—China's accession and the launch of the Doha Round—it seems to be at risk. In the same direction, Russia is fighting hard to become a member of the multilateral trade system, notwithstanding the regionalized perspectives offered by the European Union.

In reality, many of the arguments in favor of regionalism are far less convincing than they seem. For example, it is hard to see how achieving free trade is any easier in a vast regional arrangement like the Free Trade Area of the Americas—which covers all but one of the 35 countries in the Americas, which differ greatly in size, outlook, and level of development—than in the WTO.

It is scarcely credible that agricultural liberalization would be any easier in transatlantic talks than at the WTO. And it is not obvious how trade disputes between, say, China and the United States could be more easily managed in the Asia Pacific Economic Cooperation forum than in the WTO. Where regional agreements involve the same countries with the same interests and the same sensitivities—regardless of the context—it is arguable that overlapping rules and jurisdictions make international trade relations even harder to manage, not easier.

Competitive liberalization thus could be counterproductive. The race for regional advantage between the United States, the European Union, and others might become a substitute for, rather than a complement to, multilateral liberalization at the WTO. Negotiating bilateral and regional agreements can divert attention and effort from the Doha Round. This in turn can create a vicious cycle, whereby a lack of progress at the WTO spurs a greater emphasis on bilateralism and regionalism, which in turn further hampers efforts in Geneva. A strategy of competitive liberalization might thus in fact lead to a fragmentation of the world trade system rather than freer global trade.

As a matter of fact, the risk is that we are moving toward "competitive regionalism." The nightmare scenario could be a world split into defensive, even hostile, regional blocs. There is a political dimension in the regional blocs that must be carefully considered.

In any case, regional and bilateral deals are a poor second-best to global free trade. By definition, preferences granted to some are handicaps imposed on others. Countries that are excluded from such agreements suffer. Yet the deals create their own logic, whereby those who are discriminated against seek their own preferential deal.

The tangled web of preferential agreements that countries are weaving, each with their own differing tariff rates, rules-of-origin requirements, and industrial and health regulations, threatens to tie the world economy up in red tape, distorting the pattern of trade and creating huge new administrative burdens for exporters—not to mention opportunities for corruption.

Although WTO rules do allow regional agreements, they are supposed to meet certain conditions: they must cover "substantially all trade," eliminate internal trade barriers, and "not on the whole" raise protection against excluded countries. In other words, regional integration should complement the multilateral trading system, not threaten it.

Unfortunately, although few regional deals meet these criteria, the WTO is doing nothing about it. Since it was set up in 1995, the WTO's Regional Trade Agreements Committee has failed—because of lack of consensus—to complete any of its assessments of whether individual trade agreements conform with WTO provisions.

WTO ministers recognized this in their Doha declaration, which mandates negotiations aimed at "clarifying and improving disciplines and procedures under the existing WTO provisions applying to regional trade agreements." The problem is that this will apply only to future regional agreements—in effect, letting all the many existing agreements off the hook.

What to Do?

I have the pleasure to be a member of an informal private group called "Shadow G-8," chaired by Fred Bergsten. It is a group of very authoritative personalities that produce every year a document for the leaders participating in the summit. I can say that our work is highly regarded and that some of our ideas have been accepted by the G-8.

This year, we have produced a very good report, and I would like to tell you about one of the main messages we have sent to our leaders about the relationship between regionalism and multilateralism.

> The G-8 leaders should reaffirm their commitment to give priority to the multilateral system, seeing any regional and bilateral agreements they pursue in that

broader context and making sure that they structure those agreements in ways that are compatible with their global obligations. In addition, the leaders should agree that any Free Trade Agreements that they conclude will be comprehensive in scope, including agriculture, to assure their conformity with the WTO. They should also instruct their Trade Ministers to devise the most effective methods available, including possible amendments to the charter, to substantially strengthen the WTO rules that govern regional and bilateral agreements in order to ensure that they do not deviate importantly from the goals and precepts of the multilateral system.

This could be a commitment that, if agreed on by the leaders of the G-8 and implemented by the trade ministers, could make the idea of competitive liberalization much more acceptable and transform it into "complementary liberalization."

The responsibility for saving the multilateral system does not lie solely with the United States. In trade terms, America is not the only superpower. Europe too has a vital role to play. All too often, the European Union has been a reluctant liberalizer. Now Europe has to prove its commitment to multilateralism, the WTO, and the Doha Round and has to negotiate meaningfully on agriculture. It is the sine qua non of a successful Doha Round, even if not the only requirement—a key demand for developing countries and rich-country exporters alike, the centerpiece without which progress in other vital areas, such as services and manufacturing tariffs, is impossible.

Conversely, if agriculture is to be liberalized, this can only be at the WTO, where the European Union and Japan can trade off liberalization for greater access to all their trading partners' markets. My personal experience at the WTO has been that if Europe and the United States are divided, all the other members of the WTO are divided. If they are united, they facilitate the consensus. This is not an automatic consequence, but a precondition to a successful negotiation.

The timetable of the Doha negotiation is now very tight. All the major trading partners have to concentrate all their energies on the success of the round and on respecting the timetable, beginning at Cancun. It would be extremely important if, together with the commitment of the G8 leaders that we have proposed, there could be an informal consensus to a standstill for every new preferential agreement negotiation up to January 1, 2005. A regional peace clause!

With such a consensus, the very useful US proposal to eliminate all of the tariffs on industrial products by a certain date (perhaps 2015 or 2020) would also be seen as a real commitment to the success of the Doha Round and to the superiority of the multilateral trade system.

The economic case for the Doha Round was always compelling. But the stakes are now much higher: the future of our open world and the multilateral system.

Comment

GUY DE JONQUIÈRES

The pros and cons of free trade agreements (FTAs) are one of the most divisive topics in the trade policy world. Nonetheless, there are some points of common ground:

- FTAs are intrinsically discriminatory. But analysts sharply disagree over whether that is a plus or a minus factor from the perspective of the global trade system.

- Individual FTAs are so different that generalizations about them—except of course this one—are of very limited value.

- Politics are at least as important a driving force as economics. But there are widely divergent views on whether successful agreements depend on the political horse pulling the economic cart or the other way around.

- FTAs vary greatly in quality, in terms of both the scope of reforms and issues covered. I'll come back to that point in a moment.

It is worth asking why some FTAs achieve more integration than others. Apart from their specific provisions and the effectiveness of implementation, the evidence suggests two other factors play an important role. One is geography, the other is the relative economic development of the participants.

That is the lesson of the two most successful and largest arrangements thus far. In the European Union to date, both elements have been present;

Guy de Jonquières is the world trade editor of the Financial Times, London.

in NAFTA, economic disparities between members have been offset by their geographic proximity, which has facilitated flows of US foreign direct investment (FDI) into Mexico.

If these two elements are indeed central, they raise interesting questions about how far many FTAs currently under discussion—particularly interregional ones—will actually succeed in advancing economic integration, particularly when contending with the formidable problems of agriculture.

At the core of debate is one critical question: will bilateralism and regionalism reinforce the multilateral system—or will they undermine it?

The proposition that FTAs support multilateralism rests on two main arguments. One is that if everybody heads off in different directions, they will eventually end up in the same place. The other is that experience during the Uruguay Round suggests that bilateral or regional initiatives can jump-start multilateral negotiations.

Both arguments strike me as debatable. First, there is no compelling reason to suppose that all roads will necessarily lead back to multilateralism—unless we are prepared to undo and relearn all the lessons that led to the creation of the multilateral rules-based system in the first place.

Second, while it is true that past rounds have been launched as a US response to successive EC enlargements, times have changed. In those days, the United States regarded FTAs as the devil's work, and the General Agreement on Tariffs and Trade (GATT) as the exorcist. But today Washington is right in there, stirring the cauldron with the zeal of the recent convert.

Nor am I convinced that the creation of NAFTA and APEC (the Asia Pacific Economic Cooperation group)—and the clear implication that the United States had options if others refused to play ball in the GATT—was decisive in pushing the Uruguay Round forward. I am not saying it played no role. But what actually unblocked the Uruguay Round was the European Community's decision to move on agriculture. And it did so as much for internal reasons, arising from the unsustainable budgetary cost of the common agricultural policy, as for external ones.

What I think is not perhaps fully appreciated inside the United States is the wider global impact of its recent enthusiasm for FTAs. The United States is not just another player. It is the architect of the global trade system and by far the world's largest economy. By embracing FTAs as complementary—if not indeed an alternative—to the World Trade Organization, it sends strong political signals, particularly when Washington's commitment to other multilateral forums is in doubt. At the very least, it adds powerful impetus to the FTA bandwagon by providing further encouragement for other, smaller passengers to jump on it.

Now, I understand the reasons for this shift, though one aspect of it still puzzles me. FTAs have traditionally been tools of the weak. The European Union, for instance, has long used them as a substitute for a common foreign policy. Other, smaller and more vulnerable nations have used them to enhance their security by seeking protection under the wing of bigger and stronger countries—as many are doing today. But why does the United States feel a need for FTAs when its military, political, and economic might are unchallenged worldwide?

One answer given is that preferential trade arrangements offer a quicker route to liberalization than does the WTO. But do they—and for whose benefit, exactly? Jeff Schott argues that the United States and European Union have little left to give in terms of market access—except a few notable barriers that have survived reform in previous GATT rounds. However, many developing nations recognize that these restrictions affect their principal exports to industrialized countries.

Furthermore, even if some tariffs are reduced in FTAs, the problem pertaining to rules of origin remains. The costs of complying with these rules can be so high for many poor countries, above all for smaller exporters, that they are in fact prohibitive. As an admittedly extreme example, less than 5 percent of Albania's exports to the European Union that are eligible for preferential treatment actually receive it.

It has been suggested that the WTO should streamline the rules on rules of origin. But that would likely involve lengthy negotiations. It seems a very roundabout route to dealing with a problem that could be tackled much more directly by agreeing to scrap industrial tariffs altogether.

FTAs also discriminate between developing countries. They create not only economic but also political divisions. Just look at how the European Union is seeking to line up its African, Caribbean, and Pacific (ACP) client states against liberalization in the Doha Round, on the grounds that it would undermine their existing preferences.

Another claim for FTAs is that they push forward the frontiers by acting as laboratories for WTO-plus innovations. This is indisputable: some ideas pioneered in NAFTA and other regional agreements have been embodied in multilateral agreements. But that does not mean that WTO-plus automatically means superior—particularly in the regulatory field, where there is a danger of larger WTO members turning to bilateral trade deals to advance self-interested agendas because they have failed to get them accepted in the WTO.

The European Union is using bilateral agreements with, for instance, South Africa to entrench protection of geographical indications of wines and spirits. I doubt that the United States or most Cairns Group members regard that as a positive innovation—any more than the great mass of developing countries would welcome WTO agreements on labor standards and the environment.

Furthermore, perceptions of desirable WTO-plus provisions are highly subjective and fickle. In the Multilateral Agreement on Investment (MAI) negotiations, the United States insisted that investor-state dispute mechanisms were essential to achieve a "high-standard" investment agreement. But when it dawned on Washington that foreign companies could use those same mechanisms to override US courts, it swiftly reversed itself. And how many members of Congress who supported the creation of strong WTO dispute procedures are equally enamored of them now that other countries are repeatedly using them to challenge US laws?

Many would agree that dealing with cross-border regulatory differences, both bilaterally and in the WTO, is one of the biggest long-term challenges facing trade policy. It is not obvious, to say the least, that these differences will be any easier to resolve if the largest WTO members insist on exporting their own regulatory "models" to FTA partners—a practice that could increase friction and ultimately produce gridlock.

Renato Ruggiero argues strongly in this volume against leaping into FTAs out of a belief that the multilateral trade system has failed. I agree with him, though my perspective is slightly different.

It is at least arguable that the WTO is in difficulty because of flagging political commitment, not the other way round. The recent enthusiasm for FTAs risks accelerating that drift, and not just because they absorb so much negotiating capacity. They also divert political attention. Because FTAs appear to offer quick economic and political dividends, presidents and prime ministers of all stripes are eager to associate themselves with them, whether on golf courses in Brunei or through photo ops in the White House Rose Garden.

By contrast, achieving global liberalization is a long, grinding, and unglamorous process, littered with painful political compromises and land mines. When was the last time a world leader actually bothered to attend an important WTO meeting? As I recall, it was in 1999 when Bill Clinton visited the Seattle ministerial—and the result was hardly encouraging.

The biggest potential threat facing the multilateral trade system, it seems to me, is not that governments will deliberately spurn it, but that they will take it too much for granted and suppose that it will somehow carry on just the same. But that is a perilous assumption. There are good reasons to believe that without regular injections of political impetus and renewals of commitment, it not only will not advance but also will go into reverse. That fear was one of the most powerful drivers behind the launch of both the Tokyo and the Uruguay Rounds.

Fred Bergsten famously coined the "bicycle theory" to describe the phenomenon: if you stop pedaling, you fall off. And there is no doubt that, right at the moment, the WTO is pedaling very slowly. But it is not obvious to me that the solution is to get off your old bike—or exchange it for a tricycle—and head off in quite a different direction. Or at least before you do, you should be quite sure that the reason your new route looks easier is not because it is actually downhill.

11

LESSONS FROM US EXPERIENCE WITH FTAs

2

Lessons from NAFTA

GARY CLYDE HUFBAUER AND BEN GOODRICH

The North American Free Trade Agreement (NAFTA) broke new ground in several dimensions. Among other breakthroughs, it was the first major free trade agreement between a developing country and developed countries. FTAs between developed and developing countries are now more common, so it is logical to look to NAFTA for lessons as the United States pursues FTAs with several developing (as well as developed) countries.

NAFTA, while certainly successful, has not altogether met the optimistic predictions voiced by its sponsors. In fact, the most important lessons for the United States concern areas where NAFTA has been less successful than originally hoped. Before turning to six lessons from the NAFTA experience, we note a few essential differences between NAFTA and the FTAs now under consideration.

NAFTA Differs from the Current Batch of Potential FTAs

Foremost, both the Canada-US Trade Agreement (CUSTA), which entered into force in 1989, and NAFTA, which integrated Mexico in 1994, were far greater economic undertakings than any of the new FTAs currently envisaged.

Table 2.1 illustrates the magnitude of FTAs discussed in this volume relative to NAFTA, in terms of total trade and the stock of US foreign direct investment (FDI). The Free Trade Area of the Americas (FTAA) is the most important preferential agreement now under consideration, but most of

Gary Clyde Hufbauer is a senior fellow at the Institute for International Economics, and Ben Goodrich was a research assistant at the Institute.

Table 2.1 US exposure to current and prospective FTA partners
(millions of dollars)

	Trade			
	2002		1994	
Country/region	Trade with United States	Share (percent)	Trade with United States	Share (percent)
FTAA	685,995	38.44	404,940	35.53
Canada	353,061	19.79	232,400	20.39
Mexico	220,197	12.34	97,740	8.57
FTAA minus NAFTA	112,736	6.32	74,800	6.56
ASEAN minus Singapore	87,499	4.90	54,790	4.81
Korea	56,435	3.16	37,050	3.25
Taiwan	48,841	2.74	42,830	3.76
Singapore	28,834	1.62	27,000	2.37
Brazil	26,817	1.50	16,490	1.45
CAFTA	21,268	1.19	9,824	0.86
Australia	18,692	1.05	12,630	1.11
Israel	17,741	0.99	9,586	0.84
SACU	7,303	0.41	4,326	0.38
Chile	5,901	0.33	4,461	0.39
Egypt	4,151	0.23	3,380	0.30
Morocco	970	0.05	592	0.05
Jordan	809	0.05	316	0.03

	Foreign direct investment			
	2001		1994	
Country/region	US FDI stock in:	Share (percent)	US FDI stock in:	Share (percent)
FTAA	311,472	22.5	146,751	23.9
Canada	139,031	10.1	74,221	12.1
FTAA minus NAFTA	120,273	8.7	55,562	9.2
Mexico	52,168	3.8	16,968	2.8
Brazil	36,317	2.6	17,885	2.9
Australia	34,041	2.5	20,196	3.3
Singapore	27,295	2.0	10,940	1.8
ASEAN-9	25,684	1.9	15,600	2.6
Chile	11,674	0.8	5,062	0.8
Korea	9,864	0.7	4,334	0.7
Taiwan	8,814	0.6	3,775	0.6
Israel	4,122	0.3	1,483	0.2
Egypt	3,068	0.2	1,090	0.2
CAFTA	3,003	0.2	1,093	0.2
SACU	2,966	0.2	1,170	0.2
Morocco	55	0.0	93	0.2
Jordan	14	0.0	13	0.0

CAFTA = Central American Free Trade Agreement; FTAA = Free Trade Area of the Americas; SACU = Southern African Customs Union

Sources: For trade data: US International Trade Commission, *Tariff and Trade DataWeb,* dataweb.usitc.gov, 2003. For investment data: US Department of Commerce, Bureau of Economic Analysis, *Foreign Direct Investment (Historical Estimates),* www.bea.doc.gov, 2003.

the US trade and investment exposure within the hemisphere is already governed by NAFTA. Excluding Canada and Mexico, only 6 percent of US world trade in 2002 involved a potential FTAA partner.[1] When NAFTA came into effect in 1994, Mexico accounted for more than 8 percent of US trade. The story on FDI is similar, although not as extreme. The United States has more investment in the rest of Latin America than in Mexico, but less than in Canada.

From the US perspective, while the economic magnitude of the FTAA is similar to that of the Mexican component of NAFTA, the bilateral FTA partners identified in table 2.1 entail much smaller trade and investment ties. In 2003, the United States concluded FTAs with Singapore and Chile, which have slightly more economic importance than the previous US FTAs with Israel and Jordan.[2] The United States hopes to conclude an FTA with Australia by the end of 2003, but Australia constitutes only 1.1 percent of US trade and 2.5 percent of the US FDI stock. Some of the countries and regions listed in table 2.1 are more economically important and some are less, but none, from a US perspective, approaches the economic importance of Canada or Mexico.

The debate continues over what impact NAFTA has had, but most analysts reiterate the same story they told in 1989 and 1994: while the impact may be large relative to the size of Canada and Mexico, the impact on the United States is small relative to the size of the US economy and its workforce. The most recent estimate of the effect of NAFTA on US-Mexico trade is a gain of less than $20 billion in 2001, not counting trade diversion. The effect of NAFTA on US GDP is similarly small, perhaps on the order of $2 billion annually in a $10 trillion economy (see CBO 2003). We think the CBO's estimates are overly conservative, but even if the true trade and welfare effects are three times as large, the magnitudes remain small compared to the size of the US economy.

This message is doubly true for the FTAs contemplated in table 2.1. Individually, they will have almost no visible economic effect on the US economy. These FTAs could have measurable effects on certain companies or industries within the United States, and they may provide important precedents for the FTAA or the Doha Development Round. Taken one by one, however, their impact on US economic welfare (as classically measured) will be hard to detect.

It is questionable whether the Bush administration should characterize these potential bilateral FTAs as engines for US growth when their effects

---

1. Moreover, a relatively large sliver of US trade with FTAA countries is already covered under the Caribbean Basin Initiative and the Andean Trade Preferences Act.

2. For more analysis of the FTAs with Singapore and Chile, see chapter 4, by Sidney Weintraub, in this volume.

will be extremely small, even once the agreements are fully in effect a decade after they are signed. One of the important lessons of NAFTA, which we will discuss shortly, was that the agreement had to be oversold to ensure its passage in the US House of Representatives. NAFTA's "failure" to live up to exaggerated expectations thereafter provided ammunition for antiglobalization groups. It makes little sense to set up similar targets with the current crop of FTAs, especially when bigger fish such as the FTAA and the Doha Development Round are within sight.

If the prospective bilateral FTAs discussed in this volume make little difference to US economic welfare, then why should the United States bother with them? That is a fair question and it is discussed in detail in each of the following chapters, as well as in the overview by Jeffrey Schott. The core answer is that the benefits of FTAs go beyond narrow economic welfare calculations. They include security considerations as well as the creation of negotiating coalitions and momentum for multilateral trade liberalization.[3] Bilateral FTAs can provide a model for opening investment in sheltered industries (such as insurance and water) and more liberal US visa treatment for foreign workers. They can provide a model for overcoming entrenched interests in sensitive industries, such as sugar, dairy, steel, clothing, and footwear. These alternative considerations should be paramount, since the pure economic considerations measured in terms of GDP gains and better employment opportunities are very small. That said, it is possible to draw on the lessons learned from the NAFTA experience, bearing in mind that extrapolations to other FTAs require downsizing to match their smaller economic and political scales.

Lesson #1: Top Leadership Was Essential to NAFTA

Although CUSTA was fairly uncontroversial in the United States, it was almost derailed in April 1986 in the Senate Finance Committee until President Reagan promised to find "a rapid and effective solution to the Canadian softwood lumber problem . . . independent of the comprehensive negotiations" (Schott 1988, 12). While the negotiations were sometimes sticky (especially over trade remedies), congressional ratification was reasonably straightforward, once maritime activities and agriculture were dropped from the liberalization agenda.

By contrast, NAFTA's passage was far from a certain proposition. In 1990, President George H.W. Bush had to fight a surprisingly difficult battle in the US Congress to obtain fast-track negotiating authority, which en-

---

3. Correspondingly, the *costs* of pursuing bilateral FTAs go beyond crude mercantilist calculations, such as their effect on the US trade balance and unemployment rate. In chapter 1, Schott discusses some of the more subtle, yet more relevant, costs, such as overburdening US trade negotiators and deflecting attention from bigger fish.

abled the Bush administration to negotiate NAFTA and present the agreement to Congress for an up or down vote without amendments.

Of course, President Bush never got the chance to present NAFTA to the US Congress, because Bill Clinton took office in 1993. After putting NAFTA on the back burner for a few months, President Clinton launched negotiations with Canada and Mexico on labor and environmental side agreements. These side agreements were intended to pacify nongovernmental organizations (NGOs) and labor unions but, as we will discuss later, were much too weak to accomplish anything tangible. Canada and especially Mexico insisted that these agreements be both toothless and on the side (in the sense that the text of NAFTA was not reopened); otherwise NAFTA would have been put in severe jeopardy in Ottawa and Mexico City.

NAFTA, with its two side agreements, passed the US Congress with several votes to spare, but not without an unprecedented effort by the business community, the Mexican embassy in the United States, and other advocates. The business community had a real stake in NAFTA, actively monitored the negotiations, and directly influenced the text in several areas.[4]

Since the ratification of NAFTA in 1993 and of the Uruguay Round in 1994, the same level of political effort by the business community has been evident only in 2000, to ensure the ratification of China's accession to the World Trade Organization (WTO). Because the FTAs discussed in this volume have relatively little economic importance to the United States, it is fair to speculate that the business community may not pull out all the stops to get those agreements ratified by Congress.

Conversely, the antiglobalization lobby sees almost every battle, no matter how economically limited, in highly ideological terms. The agreement with Jordan was delayed for more than a year over the labor and environmental language in the text.[5] Once fast-track negotiating authority expired in 1994, the antiglobalization lobby was able to prevent it from being renewed until 2002 (under a new name, "trade promotion authority"), even though specific trade agreements were not at issue.

Perhaps the most bizarre trade debate in the 1990s concerned whether the United States would grant "normal trade relations," also known as "most favored nation" status to China prior to its accession to the WTO. If the United States had opted not to grant China normal trade relations, China could have maintained its high barriers against US exports. Thus, the US Congress essentially voted for China to reduce *its* trade barriers; but the vote was incredibly close because of the fervent opposition of the antiglobalization lobby to any trade liberalization initiative.

---

4. For example, see Hufbauer and Schott (forthcoming) on the NAFTA negotiations in the automobile sector.

5. One element of the fallout from the NAFTA debate is that labor and environmental groups insist that these issues be incorporated into the text rather than relegated to side agreements. This trend will continue.

The antiglobalization lobby may choose to depict some of the potential FTAs either as precursors to future global or hemispheric trade liberalization (a bad thing, from their perspective) or as successors to their favorite bugaboo, NAFTA. The Central American Free Trade Agreement (CAFTA) seems likely to be hit with both labels—as a precursor to the FTAA and as an extension of NAFTA. Strong opposition to several FTAs seems assured, and some may not pass the congressional gauntlet.

To get congressional approval, each FTA will need energetic backing from the White House and a close-knit group of supporters from the business community.[6] Foreign governments and the firms they represent—those with the largest stake in each FTA—must be geared up for a vigorous lobbying campaign.

Some countries will fare better owing to political and security considerations. The FTA with Australia is advancing rapidly because Australia supported the US war against Iraq. New Zealand's exclusion from the negotiations is attributable both to its opposition to the US war and to its break with the US security alliance in the 1980s. Conversely, an FTA with Morocco or Bahrain could advance on the back of the US need to build relations with Muslim countries.[7]

Lesson #2: Beware the *Post Hoc Ergo Propter Hoc* Fallacy

The Romans recognized that "after this" does not prove "because of this," but many analysts on both sides of the NAFTA debate uncritically attribute much that has happened in the US-Mexico bilateral relationship over the past eight years to NAFTA. For example, many credit NAFTA for the massive increase in US imports from Mexico, even though NAFTA reduced US tariffs by only 3 or 4 percent. Also, many have blamed NAFTA for Mexico's peso crisis in 1994 and 1995, even though NAFTA entailed very little change in the way Mexico conducted its finances. Zapatistas disingenuously told Western journalists that they were revolting against NAFTA, even though much of southern Mexico is isolated from international markets. Finally, some critics blame the influx in migrants from Mexico on NAFTA, even though NAFTA did not change migration rules in any meaningful way.

---

6. Some members of the business community might decide to vigorously support an agreement because it contains particular language that could serve as a precedent for more ambitious trade liberalization initiatives. One recent example was the intellectual property rights text in the US-Chile FTA.

7. In May 2003, President Bush announced plans for an FTA that would eventually encompass most of the Middle East, starting with an agreement with Bahrain. For a discussion of FTAs in the Middle East context, see chapter 11, by Ahmed Galal and Robert Lawrence, in this volume.

FTAs make no pretense at addressing the whole range of problems that developing countries face. NAFTA contributed positively to the economic development of Mexico, but Mexico has taken many positive steps on its own over the past 20 years. Moreover, Mexico will have to make many reforms over the next 20 years, independent of NAFTA, if it is to grow at a pace that will meet the demands of the Mexican population.

The process by which FTAs are ratified encourages supporting politicians to make extreme promises. In the next round of FTAs, governments should endeavor to raise the level of debate rather than attempt to "out-fallacy" their opponents. Overhyping FTAs when they are signed sets the stage for overblaming FTAs after they are implemented. If this pattern continues, the United States will find it more difficult to muster the legislative support necessary to pass big liberalization packages in the WTO and FTAA.

Lesson #3: Job Counts Are a Fool's Errand

As an example of the way in which NAFTA has been poorly analyzed, consider the obsession with "job counting." First, the media mistakes job turnover for permanent changes in the US labor market. US employment growth is largely determined by productivity and real GDP growth. The Federal Reserve attempts to tune monetary policy to balance real GDP growth against excessive inflation.[8] Exposure to the international economy affects how jobs are distributed across sectors of the economy, not the absolute number of jobs. An FTA may boost employment in one sector and diminish employment in another sector, but the net effect will be very small, *especially relative to the size of the US workforce and the normal amount of job turnover that occurs in a multitrillion-dollar economy.*[9]

The fact that the net job effects are small does not eliminate the concerns of those who lose their jobs. A worker displaced by foreign competition will almost always find another job eventually, but the pay may not be as good and the loss of wages and benefits incurred between jobs may be substantial.[10] A job "created" by exports is probably filled by someone

---

8. Beginning in May 2003, the Federal Reserve also became concerned about preventing deflation, but this is the first time since the Great Depression that deflation has been considered a serious possibility in the United States.

9. The US workforce averaged 136 million between 1999 and 2001. In that three-year period, 9.9 million workers were involuntarily "displaced." In 2001, there were 112 million hires and separations (over half of which were workers quitting). By one set of estimates (discussed below), US merchandise exports to Canada and Mexico may support 74,000 jobs annually, while job dislocation on account of imports from North America does not exceed 51,000 jobs annually.

10. See Kletzer and Litan (2001) for a wage-insurance proposal, which would go a long way toward ameliorating these two concerns. This proposal was adopted, in a very limited way, in the Trade Adjustment Assistance renewal, which was passed in August 2002.

who already had a different job. This process of musical chairs only indirectly results in an opportunity for a previously unemployed person. Thus, the emphasis in a trade agreement should be on the dynamics of job turnover, and the associated costs and benefits, rather than the aggregate level of employment.

Furthermore, only a relatively small share of job dislocations caused by trade are properly attributable to the trade induced by NAFTA or another FTA. When a US plant is in such precarious financial straits that it shuts down and moves to Mexico, it probably would have moved somewhere at some point with or without NAFTA. Thus, the plant's workers would very likely have been forced to find new jobs with or without NAFTA. If the United States had an adequate social safety net to help displaced workers manage the transition from one job to another, it should not matter whether a plant that closes moves to a neighboring state or a neighboring country, or whether, in the latter case, the country in question has an FTA with the United States. In reality, the US social safety net is inadequate, but the blame should not be placed on NAFTA or other FTAs. Labor groups should lobby Congress to fund trade adjustment assistance (TAA) programs more generously; but labor has historically been reluctant to support TAA, fearing that such programs would make trade liberalization more likely to pass Congress.

It is instructive to look back at some of the estimates of NAFTA's effect on labor markets, not because they are useful but because many of them are use*less*. For example, Ross Perot and Pat Choate (1993) predicted that 5.9 million US manufacturing jobs would be put at risk by NAFTA, thereby using the popular rhetorical technique of claiming that a large number of people *might* lose their jobs while avoiding the pesky detail of specifying the *probability* of such job loss. There was indeed a small risk that each of these 5.9 million jobs would be relocated to Mexico, and undoubtedly a small fraction of these 5.9 million jobs did in fact move to Mexico. But the "great sucking sound" was never heard. Instead, the "small sucking whisper" was drowned by the roar of the US economy as it steamed ahead during the latter half of the 1990s.

More recently, Robert Scott (2001) of the Economic Policy Institute has claimed that

> The North American Free Trade Agreement (NAFTA) eliminated 766,030 actual and potential U.S. jobs between 1994 and 2000 because of the rapid growth in the net U.S. export deficit with Mexico and Canada. The loss of these real and potential jobs is just the most visible tip of NAFTA's impact on the U.S. economy.

The footnote associated with this quotation illustrates Scott's reliance on *post hoc ergo propter hoc* reasoning. Scott admits that "[t]he total number of jobs and job opportunities is a measure of what employment in trade-related industries would have been if the U.S.-NAFTA trade balance remained constant between 1993 and 2000, holding everything else constant."

The only way to leap from the footnote to Scott's claim in the text is to assume that NAFTA is responsible for the entirety of the change in the US-NAFTA trade balance between 1993 and 2000, which is quite a stretch.

Public Citizen, an organization founded by Ralph Nader, takes note of 525,094 workers certified for assistance under the NAFTA-TAA program between January 1994 and January 2003 (Public Citizen 2003). This figure both understates and overstates the number of workers displaced by NAFTA. The understatement occurs because not all workers that are displaced by NAFTA apply for NAFTA-TAA benefits. Some may find new jobs immediately, some are not eligible, some may apply for benefits under the regular TAA program, and some are unaware of their eligibility.

The overstatement is caused by the terms of the program: to be certified under NAFTA-TAA, the worker need only show that his or her job was adversely affected by imports from Canada or Mexico or that his or her firm moved to Canada or Mexico. The worker does not have to prove that NAFTA liberalization *caused* the imports or the firm's relocation. Moreover, there is no need to establish that the job was immune to other economic forces.

In contrast to the authors of studies such as those cited above, which consider only US imports from NAFTA partners, Raul Hinojosa-Ojeda, David Runsten, Fernando Depaolis, and Nabil Kamel (2000) claim that combined US exports and imports with Mexico have a net positive effect on US employment of about 74,000 jobs annually. However, they do not attempt to specify what fraction of US-Mexico trade is attributable to NAFTA, and what fraction would have occurred without it.

Thus, it is useful to recall the words of Hufbauer and Schott (1993, 20):

> NAFTA . . . will not exert a perceptible long-run impact on overall employment levels or on the overall merchandise trade balance. In the long run, the impact of NAFTA will be offset by other changes in microeconomic policy or will be lost as noise in the background of macroeconomic events.

The same is certainly true for the FTAs considered in this volume. The lesson is that FTAs are essentially irrelevant to employment levels in the long run and that the United States is better served when FTAs are evaluated on other criteria.

Lesson #4: Paper Agreements Can't Create Social Miracles

The labor and environmental side agreements were never intended to make substantial progress in addressing labor and environmental problems.[11] The labor side agreement is little more than a toothless list of

---

11. For a more comprehensive treatment of the two side agreements, see Hufbauer and Schott (2002, 2003).

hopes and aspirations. The environmental side agreement is somewhat stronger; but no NAFTA country, especially the United States, wants intrusive surveillance of domestic environmental policies, nor is any country willing to provide large-scale funding for needed infrastructure to clean up the border zone. The two side agreements were weak by design, because Canada and Mexico would not have accepted them if they were strong enough to achieve their stated purposes.

The real purpose of the labor and environmental side agreements was to provide political cover for Democrats to support NAFTA so that they would not incur the wrath of labor unions and environmental NGOs. Viewed in these terms, the two side agreements were partially successful: NAFTA ultimately passed with the support of a fair number of congressional Democrats. However, the labor unions and NGOs have since used NAFTA "failures" as a rallying cry, and they successfully derailed substantial trade liberalization during the latter half of the 1990s.

While some in NGOs (primarily mainstream environmentalists) genuinely believe that trade sanctions can be a powerful tool to address social ills, others (in hard-core labor unions, radical environmental groups, and antiglobalization NGOs) have successfully demonstrated that social issues can be a powerful instrument to block trade agreements. The first group is wildly overambitious: they fail to take into account that long-term economic growth is the principal engine for meaningful progress on social issues. Poor countries, as a general rule, have neither the ability nor the desire to significantly address social issues before they are sufficiently developed. Once a country reaches a level of development at which it can afford to address social problems, solutions can be envisaged, but trade and investment agreements will play a minor role relative to domestic political forces.

Radical environmentalists and hard-core labor unionists in the second group seldom entertain the noble belief that trade and investment agreements can cure social ills. Radical environmentalists frequently believe that development is the cause of, not the solution to, environmental problems. Thus, their support of the environment is inseparable from their opposition to development. For their part, hard-core labor unions seek above all to reduce the chance that manufacturing firms will relocate to countries that have a comparative advantage because of low wages. Toward this goal, they champion higher wages in the export sectors of developing countries so that wage disparities might be reduced.

The goal of antiglobalization NGOs is to drive a wedge between developed and developing countries. They want developed countries to insist that trade agreements contain language on social issues that is too strong for developing countries to accept, thereby scuttling the agreement. Antiglobalization groups were able to delay NAFTA and the US FTA with Jordan, and to disrupt the WTO ministerial meeting in Seattle. But they failed to get strong language on social issues included in the Doha declaration. Since Doha, FTAs between developed and developing countries are becoming more common.[12]

These ideological battles will continue indefinitely, but the era for side agreements has passed. New trade agreements must at least pay lip service to social issues in the text itself. The challenge for trade negotiators is to find language on social issues that all parties can accept. The lesson from NAFTA, as well as from US FTAs with Jordan, Chile, and Singapore, is that agreements are possible, but they will not come easily.

Lesson #5: Dispute Settlement Mechanisms Are Good but Imperfect

NAFTA was novel in that it included a dispute settlement mechanism. Canada and Mexico were eager to rein in US antidumping (AD) and countervailing duty (CVD) actions. The dispute settlement provisions did not stop US firms from filing numerous unfair trade cases against Canada and Mexico. However, under NAFTA, national AD and CVD actions were typically vetted, after the fact, by impartial NAFTA panels.

NAFTA's dispute resolution procedures are spelled out in six different chapters. So far, there have been no disputes under Chapter 14, which pertains to financial services. By contrast, 85 cases have been handled under Chapter 19, which pertains to AD and CVD actions. With a few exceptions, notably softwood lumber and wheat, these 85 cases have been successfully handled with little fanfare.

So-called investor-state disputes under NAFTA Chapter 11 have attracted the most media attention. An impression has been created that foreign companies flagrantly abuse Chapter 11 to overturn national environmental laws. The charge is exaggerated. Of the 27 cases filed under Chapter 11, the investor has won 5 times, while the state has won (or the case has been terminated) 7 times. The remaining 15 cases remain to be concluded. The biggest controversy concerns proper interpretation of the "tantamount to expropriation" standard, and the United States has qualified this language in its recent FTAs with Chile and Singapore.

Dispute proceedings under the environmental side agreement have been mixed. A few modest decisions have been handed down, but the proceedings are hampered both by the absence of common standards and by administrative barriers. Dispute proceedings under the labor side agreement are essentially a waste of time. There are no common standards, administrative barriers create serious difficulties, and potential remedies are very weak.

---

12. See chapter 1, by Jeffrey J. Schott, in this volume for a more detailed look at the composition of FTAs.

Chapter 20, which is a catch-all provision for disputes not specifically covered in other NAFTA chapters, has also been disappointing. Panel opinions under Chapter 20 are only advisory, although they put political pressure on countries to change their ways. Of the three disputes pursued to completion under Chapter 20, the one provoked by the blatant refusal of the United States to allow Mexican trucks to carry goods beyond the border zone has been the most notable. This issue is currently thought to have been "resolved" by imposing a discriminatory safety regime on Mexican trucks and drivers.[13] However, some members of the US Congress still object to the outcome, and Mexico will, at some point, probably contest the US safety inspection regime.

NAFTA illustrates that bilateral mechanisms designed to solve commercial disputes can succeed—but only outside the realm of high-profile cases. Dispute settlement provisions of the environmental and labor side agreements have been less successful, but that was intentional. The United States seems to have learned its lesson on investor-state disputes, and future agreements will be less ambitious in this area.

Lesson #6: An FTA Is the First Step

Although NAFTA has exerted only a small impact relative to the large US economy, its effect on the Canadian and Mexican economies has been much greater. Still, NAFTA is simply one step forward for Mexico and Canada, as they attempt to grow their economies and cement their relations with the United States.

Measured in purchasing power terms, Mexico's real per capita income (in 2002 dollars) increased from $5,483 in 1993 to $6,200 in 2002. A 13 percent increase in real per capita income over the course of a decade is decent, but the average Mexican is still very poor.[14] Robert Pastor (2001) persuasively argues that the principal shortcoming of NAFTA, so far as Mexico is concerned, is the absence of funding mechanisms to promote development. He contends that the United States should make Mexico's development an explicit priority, both for the sake of Mexico and to make progress on issues that are important to the United States, especially drug trafficking and illegal immigration.

Like its predecessors, the Bush administration recognizes the importance of development but overemphasizes the role that trade and investment agreements can play in spurring economic growth. Commercial

---

13. The Bush administration's solution is now in court, challenged by NGOs on environmental grounds.

14. US real per capita income increased 21 percent over the same period (these figures are from IMF 2003).

agreements can help lock in domestic reforms, but the impetus for reforms and liberalization must come from the partner country itself. Developing countries will often require substantial financial assistance both from the United States and from multilateral institutions in order to implement ambitious visions for faster growth. The United States has not applied these lessons learned in the NAFTA context. US policy continues to emphasize the same heavy reliance on commercial agreements when negotiating FTAs with other developing countries.

Canada and Mexico are both thinking about "big ideas" to deepen their integration with the United States.[15] Most of the big ideas are well ahead of what might be contemplated in other FTAs for a decade or longer, but they are worth mentioning as possible harbingers. Mexico's main big idea is amnesty for illegal immigrants in the United States; but Mexico has little to offer in return, except expanded access to its oil sector. For political reasons, this is currently a nonstarter.

Canadians outside the government are thinking about a package that involves three big ideas:

- common defense and security initiatives,

- an energy-sector agreement, and

- renewed emphasis on economic integration.

All these topics run ahead of official thinking in Ottawa and Washington. But the important lesson for the United States is that once FTAs are put into effect, some partner governments will continue to search for ways to deepen the relationship. If the United States views FTAs solely as economic arrangements, and not as stepping-stones for progress on a wide range of issues, then potential benefits from the FTA agenda will be lost.

References

Congressional Budget Office (CBO). 2003. *The Effects of NAFTA on U.S.–Mexican Trade and GDP*. Washington: CBO. Available at www.cbo.gov/ftpdoc.cfm?index=4247&type=1 (May).

Dobson, Wendy. 2002. Shaping the Future of the North American Economic Space: A Framework for Action. C. D. Howe Institute Commentary 162. www.cdhowe.org/pdf/commentary_162.pdf (April).

Hinojosa-Ojeda, Raul, David Runsten, Fernando Depaolis, and Nabil Kamel. 2000. *The US Employment Impacts of North American Integration after NAFTA: A Partial Equilibrium Approach*. Los Angeles: North American Integration and Development Center. Available at naid.sppsr.ucla.edu/pubs&news/nafta2000.html (January).

---

15. For the genesis of "Big Idea Thought," see Dobson (2002).

Hufbauer, Gary Clyde, and Jeffrey J. Schott. 1993. *NAFTA: An Assessment*. Rev. ed. Washington: Institute for International Economics.

Hufbauer, Gary Clyde, and Jeffrey J. Schott. 2002. North American Environment under NAFTA. www.iie.com/publications/papers/nafta-environment.htm (October).

Hufbauer, Gary Clyde, and Jeffrey J. Schott. 2003. North American Labor under NAFTA. www.iie.com/publications/papers/nafta-labor.pdf.

Hufbauer, Gary Clyde, and Jeffrey J. Schott. Forthcoming. *The North American Automotive Sector*. Washington: Institute for International Economics.

International Monetary Fund (IMF), 2003. The World Economic Outlook (WEO) Database April 2003. www.imf.org/external/pubs/ft/weo/2003/01/data/index.htm (April).

Kletzer, Lori G., and Robert Litan. 2001. A Prescription to Relieve Worker Anxiety. *International Economics Policy Brief* 01-2. Washington: Institute for International Economics and the Brookings Institution.

Pastor, Robert A. 2001. *Toward a North American Community: Lessons from the Old World for the New*. Washington: Institute for International Economics.

Perot, Ross, with Pat Choate. 1993. *Save Your Job, Save Our Country: Why NAFTA Must Be Stopped—Now!* New York: Hyperion.

Public Citizen. 2003. NAFTA TAA Database. www.citizen.org/trade/forms/search_taa.cfm.

Schott, Jeffrey J. 1988. The Free Trade Agreement: A US Assessment. In *The Canada–United States Free Trade Agreement: The Global Impact*, ed. Jeffrey J. Schott and Murray G. Smith. Washington: Institute for International Economics.

Scott, Robert E. 2001. NAFTA's Hidden Costs: Trade Agreement Results in Job Losses, Growing Inequality, and Wage Suppression for the United States. *EPI Briefing Paper*. www.epinet.org/content.cfm/briefingpapers_nafta01_us (April).

3

Free Trade Agreements as Foreign Policy Tools: The US-Israel and US-Jordan FTAs

HOWARD ROSEN

The US-Israel and US-Jordan Free Trade Agreements are typically treated as footnotes in most discussions of US trade policy, owing to the small amount of trade they cover. The importance of these agreements to US trade policy goes far beyond their trade coverage, however. The agreements set several precedents for US trade policy and also provide some lessons for the broader debate over the value of bilateral free trade agreements.

First and foremost, the US-Israel and US-Jordan FTAs are clear examples of the use of trade policy—specifically bilateral free trade agreements—as a means of pursuing foreign policy objectives. The United States' foreign policy interests in these countries and the region are much more significant than its economic interests. Although the agreements serve several objectives, the primary reason the United States entered into them was to pursue foreign policy goals.

The US-Israel agreement, signed into law in April 1985, was the first free trade agreement negotiated by the United States. The US-Jordan agreement, signed into law in October 2001, is the first US trade agreement that includes specific language concerning the protection of the environment and labor. Together, the two agreements illustrate the "elastic" nature of free trade agreements. Experience now suggests that the initial

Howard Rosen was minority staff director of the Congressional Joint Economic Committee (1997–2001) and executive director of the Competitiveness Policy Council (1991–97).

US-Israel agreement discriminated against US trade with the Palestinians and with the Jordanians, precisely at a time when US policy was seeking to strengthen their economies. The US-Israel FTA was first amended, and later complemented by the US-Jordan agreement, in order to eliminate this discrimination.

The US-Israel and US-Jordan agreements are also examples of bilateral trade agreements between very small economies and a very large economy. In 2000 the US economy was 86 times larger than the Israeli economy, and more than 1,000 times larger than the Jordanian economy. By contrast, the US economy is 7½ times larger than its North American Free Trade Agreement (NAFTA) partners—Canada and Mexico—combined.

The US-Israel Free Trade Area Agreement

Although the US-Israel FTA is a by-product of the special relationship between the two countries, the agreement provides many important lessons for bilateral trade agreements between large and small countries. US goals in pursuing the agreement were:

- to demonstrate strong bilateral relations beyond military/security support;

- to counter discrimination against US exporters caused by the bilateral trade agreement between the European Community (EC) and Israel signed in 1975 (final tariff cuts were to be implemented in 1985);

- to strengthen the Israeli economy and reduce its dependence on US foreign assistance; and

- to put pressure on the major trading countries to move forward on the stalled multilateral negotiations.[1]

Israel's goals in pursuing the agreement were as follows:

- The Arab boycott made it necessary for Israel to secure access to markets outside the region.

- Given its chronic balance of payments deficits, Israel sought to expand access to markets in high-income countries, such as the United States and European nations.

---

1. Although the US-Israel FTA alone clearly would not have been sufficient to break the stalemate in multilateral talks, it was a convenient way for the United States to demonstrate that it would not wait for the rest of the world before moving ahead on trade liberalization. The prospect of the larger US-Canada agreement was also on the horizon.

- Israeli policymakers saw international obligations as a means to support internal efforts to liberalize the domestic economy.

- Israel welcomed the opportunity to strengthen its ties with the United States.

- Israel was facing possible "graduation" from the US Generalized System of Preferences (GSP) program, which afforded preferential treatment to Israeli exports to the United States.

The fundamental objective of the agreement was to eliminate all tariffs and quotas on industrial products within 10 years. There was some flexibility in the coverage of agricultural products, and services and investment were excluded from the agreement. Tariffs were reduced according to three schedules: tariffs on some products were eliminated immediately (List A); tariffs on other products were phased out over a 10-year period (List B); and tariff reductions on sensitive products were negotiated after 10 years (List C). Currently, trade in industrial products between the United States and Israel is tariff and quota free.

A key element behind the establishment of the US-Israel FTA was strong congressional support for Israel, which made it possible for this unprecedented agreement to move through Congress seemingly unaffected by the growing opposition to trade liberalization in general. Given its unique backing by US politicians, Israel was probably the best candidate to be the first partner in a US free trade agreement.

The Bumpy Road Toward Liberalization

The road to free trade between the United States and Israel was filled with obstacles thrown up by both countries. First of all, the Israeli economy is much more dependent on international trade than is the US economy. Between 1981 and 1985, total trade accounted for approximately two-thirds of Israeli GDP—Israeli imports accounted for 40 percent of GDP and exports about 23 percent. By contrast, imports and exports combined accounted for less than 20 percent of US GDP over the same period, although the United States had much lower barriers to imports than Israel. Thus, from the outset, the Israeli economy was much more sensitive to the dislocations that might result from increased import competition than the United States.

This imbalance was also present in the countries' trade policies. Prior to the signing of the US-Israel FTA, most Israeli products were already afforded preferential treatment in the US market, primarily under the GSP (though, as noted above, Israel was facing probable graduation from the program in the mid-1980s). US goods were afforded no preferential treatment in Israel.

The opening of the market to imports from Europe placed further pressure on Israeli producers. In attempting to secure export markets—an effort made necessary because of the Arab boycott and Israel's chronic balance of payments deficits—Israel entered into a free trade agreement with the European Community in 1975. Under the structure of that agreement, the European Community agreed to immediately lower its barriers to Israeli exports. In exchange, Israel agreed to lower its barriers to European exports by the end of a 10-year period. The design of this unequal schedule of tariff reductions was clearly to Israel's advantage.

In direct contrast to the EC-Israel agreement, the US-Israel agreement called on both parties to follow a schedule of *simultaneous* tariff reductions. Given the differences in the structure of the two economies, these reductions placed more pressure on the Israeli economy than on the US economy.

The bottom line is that the Israeli economy faced considerable pressure from the increased competition that resulted when barriers to exports from Europe and the United States were reduced. These two markets accounted for more than two-thirds of Israel's imports. It is therefore no surprise that the road to trade liberalization was much more bumpy in Israel than in the United States. Israeli trade negotiators had to deal with various forms of "administrative protection," including the method used by Israel in calculating the value of its imports on which it placed tariffs, as well as other import fees and licensing requirements. There was considerable delay in negotiating the removal of tariffs from the most sensitive products.

At the same time that Israel was struggling with meeting its international trade obligations, the United States began negotiating free trade agreements—first with Canada, and later with Mexico—under the North American Free Trade Agreement. Though US policymakers did draw on their experience in negotiating the US-Israel FTA, the magnitude of the issues covered by the new agreements meant that those lessons were of limited applicability. The US-Canada FTA and later NAFTA were much more far-reaching than the US-Israel agreement, going beyond trade in industrial goods to also cover agriculture, services, and investment. The US-Israel agreement quickly became obsolete—a circumstance that caused some frustration in Israel, as it wanted to ensure than its deal was as good as, if not better than, any other deal.

Although Israel and the United States met their respective obligations under the agreement, the existence of the US-Israel FTA has not removed all trade conflicts between the two countries. In addition to issues related to its implementation, a considerable amount of trade, as noted above, was not covered by the agreement. Article VI of the agreement allows both countries to maintain nontariff barriers on domestically produced agricultural products. Accordingly, in 1996 the United States and Israel signed the Agreement on Trade in Agricultural Products (ATAP), which provided for gradual and steady liberalization of trade in food and agricultural products. The initial agreement was effective for five years, through the end of 2001, and was subsequently extended for another year. Negotiations are currently under way concerning the future of the agreement.

Protection of intellectual property has long been a source of tension between the United States and its trading partners. As a member of the World Trade Organization (WTO) and the World Intellectual Property Organization (WIPO), and as signatory to several international agreements, Israel has agreed to meet certain obligations regarding the protection of intellectual property. But in Israel, as in many countries, there are numerous instances of intellectual property and copyright abuses. Although Israeli law protects intellectual property rights, the US government has complained that enforcement of those laws has been inadequate. Accordingly, the Office of the US Trade Representative (USTR) placed Israel on the Special 301 Priority Watch List. After taking some steps to address these abuses, in 2003 Israel was removed from the Priority Watch List and placed back on the Watch List.

Rules of Origin

The method used to determine a product's national identity is obviously central to any preferential trade agreement. By the terms of the US-Israel FTA, any product meeting any one of the following three criteria is considered of Israeli origin:[2]

- It is wholly grown, produced, or manufactured in Israel.

- It is "substantially transformed" in Israel into a new and different article from the article or material from which it was made.

- The sum of the cost or value of the materials produced in Israel plus the direct costs of processing operations performed in Israel is not less than 35 percent of its appraised value at the time it enters the United States. The use of US materials to produce goods in Israel has no effect on origin if their value is no more than 15 percent of the value of the article.

The rules of origin set out in the US-Israel FTA are considered to be the most liberal of those in all US trade agreements to date. The US-Israel FTA is also the only agreement that does not have special rules of origin for textiles and apparel.

---

2. I am grateful to Erik Autor of the National Retail Federation for his coherent summary of the rules of origin included in various US trade agreements.

Table 3.1   Average annual growth of Israeli exports, 1986–2000 (percent)

	1986–90	1991–95	1996–2000	1986–2000
Total	13.9	9.9	11.1	11.6
United States	10.2	10.6	15.8	12.2
European Community	15.9	7.0	7.6	10.2

Sources: US Census Bureau, Department of Commerce; and author's calculations.

Table 3.2   Average annual growth of Israeli imports, 1986–2000 (percent)

	1986–90	1991–95	1996–2000	1986–2000
Total	9.6	13.0	5.9	9.5
United States	9.9	14.5	5.1	9.8
European Community	15.7	13.5	1.3	10.1

Sources: US Census Bureau, Department of Commerce; and author's calculations.

Recent Developments in US-Israel Trade Flows

In 1985, when the US-Israel FTA was signed, the value of trade between the two countries was $4.8 billion, or less than 1 percent of total US trade. Between 1986 and 2000, total Israeli exports grew on average by a little more than 11.5 percent per year. Over the same period, Israeli exports to the United States grew on average by a little more than 12 percent per year, and Israeli exports to the European Community grew on average by a little more than 10 percent per year (see table 3.1). Israeli imports have grown on average by 9.5 percent per year since 1985. During that time, US exports to Israel grew on average by a little less than 10 percent per year, and EC exports to Israel grew on average by a little more than 10 percent per year (see table 3.2).

In 1985, the year before the US-Israel FTA was signed, US exports to Israel accounted for approximately 18 percent of the Israeli market. European exports to Israel were twice as large—almost 40 percent of the Israeli market. The US government was concerned that while it was granting Israel $3 billion in foreign assistance annually, US companies were being placed at a competitive disadvantage vis-à-vis European companies. The EC-Israel FTA intensified this concern. Under that agreement, Israel agreed to completely eliminate tariffs on EC goods by 1985, 10 years after its signing. This timetable helped to motivate the United States to negotiate the FTA, which was intended to level the playing field for US exporters.

But the existence of the US-Israel FTA does not seem to have significantly changed the market composition of Israeli imports. In 2001, US exports comprised 20 percent and EC exports almost 42 percent of Israeli imports. By contrast, Israeli exports are split almost evenly between the

Table 3.3   Market concentration of Israeli imports, 1986–2000
(annual average, percent)

	1986–90	1991–95	1996–2000	1986–2000
United States	15.7	18.1	19.3	17.7
European Community	48.2	51.6	47.9	49.2
Other	36.2	30.4	32.7	33.1

Sources: US Census Bureau, Department of Commerce; and author's calculations.

Table 3.4   Market concentration of Israeli exports, 1986–2000
(annual average, percent)

	1986–90	1991–95	1996–2000	1986–2000
United States	30.1	30.4	34.2	31.6
European Community	33.1	32.3	29.9	31.8
Other	36.9	37.3	35.9	36.7

Sources: US Census Bureau, Department of Commerce; and author's calculations.

United States and the EC market. In 1985, the United States and Europe each constituted one-third of Israel's export market; by 2001, those figures were 32 percent for the United States and a little more than 26 percent for the European Community. As tables 3.3 and 3.4 show, the agreement has made little difference in the relative dominance of EC and US trade. Israeli exports to other markets, primarily in the Far East, have increased over the past two decades.

It appears that Israeli exports to the United States have surpassed US exports to Israel since the US-Israel FTA was signed in 1985. Indeed, the United States has consistently recorded a trade deficit with Israel over the past 15 years (see figure 3.1). Various explanations have been given for this disparity:

- Israel is geographically closer to Europe.

- Consumer tastes differ (though this factor is less important today than it was 20 years ago).

- It is not profitable for US exporters to serve the Israeli market, given its small size and limited capacity to serve as a regional supplier.

- Many US firms serve the Israeli market from their European subsidiaries.

The combination of the US-Israel and EC-Israel FTAs appears to have contributed to the increase in Israeli trade. Between 1981 and 1985 Israeli exports grew on average by less than 3 percent a year. Between 1986 and 2000, Israeli exports have grown by more than 11 percent a year. And

Figure 3.1 Israel's trade with the United States, 1980–2001

billions of dollars

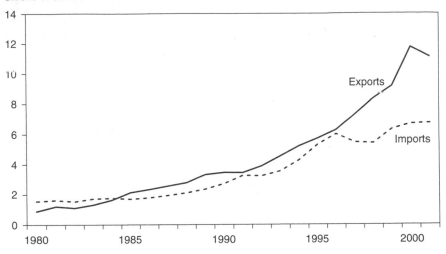

while Israeli imports grew by less than 1 percent a year between 1981 and 1985, they grew by 9.5 percent a year between 1986 and 2000.

The US-Israel FTA does not seem to have lessened Europe's dominance of Israel's import market: the modest increase in market share by US producers has not affected the ability of European producers to increase their market share. Between 1986 and 2000, the average EC share of the Israeli market remained between two and a half to three times as large as the US share of that market. However, throughout the 1990s, US exports to Israel grew faster, on average, than did EC exports.

On the export side, it appears that Israeli producers have benefited from preferential treatment in the US market. Israeli exports to the United States were a little slow to take off, but since 1990 they have been growing faster than Israeli exports to the European Community. In the late 1980s and early 1990s, most of the increase in Israeli exports went to the European Community. In the late 1990s, exports to the United States made up much of the increase in total Israeli exports. Between 1996 and 2000, Israeli exports grew twice as fast, on average, to the United States as to the European Community. As a result, by the end of the 1990s, Israel was exporting more to the United States than to the European Community.

What Do the United States and Israel Trade?

The growth in US exports to Israel seems to be concentrated in high-technology products. Table 3.5 lists the 10 products that constituted the largest

Table 3.5 Products contributing most to total growth in US exports to Israel, 1989–2000 (percent)

Standard International Trade Classification	Share of total change	Own change
79 Transport equipment	17.1	135.7
77 Electrical machinery, apparatus, and appliances	16.1	197.1
72 Specialized machinery	10.2	421.3
87 Professional scientific instruments	7.7	169.8
89 Miscellaneous manufactured articles	5.5	75.8
78 Motor vehicles	3.6	202.4
74 General industrial machinery	3.6	101.6
75 Office machines and automatic data processing equipment	3.6	49.1
33 Petroleum and chemical products	3.3	285.7
54 Medicinal and pharmaceutical products	3.0	491.9

Sources: US Census Bureau, Department of Commerce; and author's calculations.

Table 3.6 Products contributing most to total growth in US imports from Israel, 1989–2000 (percent)

Standard International Trade Classification	Share of total change	Own change
77 Electrical machinery, apparatus, and appliances	15.4	297.4
54 Medicinal and pharmaceutical products	11.8	9,340.3
76 Telecommunications equipment	9.4	254.0
93 Special transactions	9.2	686.2
87 Professional scientific instruments	7.4	258.5
89 Miscellaneous manufactured articles	6.6	121.7
84 Articles of apparel and clothing	6.4	258.9
79 Transport equipment	5.3	182.9
65 Textile yarn, fabrics	5.0	634.7
75 Office machines and automatic data processing equipment	3.3	187.1

Sources: US Census Bureau, Department of Commerce; and author's calculations.

share—taken together, three-fourths—of the *increase* in overall US exports to Israel between 1989 and 2000.

The largest gainers in Israeli exports to the United States between 1989 and 2000 were also largely concentrated in high-technology products. Most of the products are similar to those exported to Israel; the exception is textiles and apparel, which the United States does not export to Israel. The 10 products listed in table 3.6 constituted almost 80 percent of the increase in US imports from Israel between 1989 and 2000.

The "Elastic" Free Trade Agreement

One of the negative consequences of the US-Israel FTA was that it discriminated against economies that the United States was interested in assisting.

Though not much of a problem in the agreement's early years, more recently this discrimination has come into direct conflict with other US foreign policy objectives in the region.

At the time the agreement was signed in 1985, Israel exercised absolute control over territories occupied by Palestinians. A large share of Palestinians worked within Israel's pre-1967 borders, and others were employed in Palestinian-owned enterprises within the West Bank and the Gaza Strip. All Palestinian products were exported through Israel, regardless of their final destination. Under this arrangement, the US-Israel FTA technically covered Palestinian products manufactured within the existing borders of Israel.

The first intifada—the violent uprising against Israeli control of Palestinian territories—began in December 1987, two and a half years after the agreement was signed. Security concerns made it increasingly difficult for Palestinians to export their products through Israeli markets. The European Union assisted the Palestinians in setting up "direct exports"—that is, separating Palestinian from Israeli exports. The US-Israel FTA did not allow for similar treatment.

This issue took on more urgency during the Oslo peace process in the 1990s. Establishing Palestinian authority over certain territories was one of the Oslo objectives. But US law restricts the provision of trade preferences only to sovereign nations. This conundrum was particularly troublesome, since promoting Palestinian economic development became a US priority. In a great irony of economic policy, the US-Israel FTA was discriminating against the Palestinians exactly at the time US policy was aimed at promoting Palestinian economic development.

The conundrum was partially addressed in October 1996, with the establishment of the Egyptian and Jordanian-Israeli Qualifying Industrial Zones (QIZs). Like the maquiladoras that operate along the Mexican side of the US border, plants along the Egyptian and Jordanian sides of the Israeli border make products that are afforded preferential trade treatment in order to stimulate economic development. Ideally, plants operating in QIZs might cooperate to some extent with Israeli companies.

To date, fewer than a dozen industrial zones have been established, accounting for approximately $30 million in exports. Almost three-fourths of those exports have been in apparel and clothing (approximately $22.4 million). An additional $7.7 million in exports have been in leather, travel goods, and handbags. The extension of trade preferences to QIZs was a precursor to the establishment of the US-Jordan FTA.

The QIZ initiative also provided an opportunity to amend the US-Israel FTA to include articles grown, produced, or manufactured in the West Bank and the Gaza Strip. The limited availability of data makes the extent to which Palestinian trade has benefited from this arrangement difficult to judge.

Evaluation of the US-Israel FTA

The US-Israel FTA has met many of the initial goals set out by the two countries:

- It provided the United States a means to display its strong support for Israel without providing additional financial assistance. In fact, the agreement supported Israeli efforts at economic reform and liberalization, thereby strengthening the Israeli economy and reducing its long-term dependence on foreign assistance. The US-Israel FTA became an important part of Israel's efforts to liberalize its economy in the 1990s.

- Although US producers have increased their exports to Israel, the Israeli market continues to be dominated by Europe. In that regard, US efforts to level the playing field, with an eye to the EC-Israel FTA, have had little effect.

- At the same time, Israeli exporters have made significant inroads into the US market. Israeli products still constitute less than 1 percent of US imports, but Israel's share of the US market has increased by 140 percent since the agreement was signed.

- The US-Israel FTA gave the US Trade Representative an opportunity to learn about negotiating free trade agreements. However, this experience proved to be of limited value during the US-Canada FTA and NAFTA negotiations, which covered a vastly larger amount of trade and far more complicated issues.

- The signing of subsequent free trade agreements raises the question if there should be some kind of "most favored" FTA. All countries want to have the best deal (an impossible goal, unless all agreements are identical). For example, Israel continues to believe that Canada and Mexico got "better deals," and it has been asking the United States to update their agreement accordingly.

- A side benefit of the US-Israel FTA has been its use by US negotiators as a convenient tool with which to threaten other nations when multilateral negotiations seem about to stall. The United States' threat of possibly pursuing bilateral agreements, as it had done with Israel (and, more important, with Canada and Mexico), may have had some effect in pressuring others to move forward on multilateral trade negotiations. Conversely, Israeli trade negotiators firmly believe that the US-Israel FTA has strengthened their ties to the multilateral system.

- The experience of the US-Israel FTA suggests that free trade agreements may require more effort than originally anticipated. Even though Israel's economy is small and the agreement did not cover all aspects of bilateral trade, the agreement shifted a great deal of attention on trade policy issues. The US-Israel FTA therefore brought to light certain practices in the United States and Israel that might otherwise have been little heeded.

- One of the most important lessons of the US-Israel FTA is that an agreement designed to strengthen ties between two countries may unintentionally conflict with other foreign policy objectives. In this case, the US-Israel FTA discriminated against Palestinian products at just the time when the United States desired to promote Palestinian economic development. As a result, the US-Israel FTA was amended to extend coverage to the West Bank and the Gaza Strip, and later another agreement was negotiated between the United States and Jordan.

The US-Jordan FTA

The US-Jordan FTA is a direct outgrowth of the US-Israel FTA. By the end of the 1990s, the United States found itself wishing to provide assistance to Jordan for reasons somewhat similar to those that existed almost two decades earlier regarding Israel. President Clinton was looking for a way to reward King Hussein for his cooperation in the Oslo peace process—in particular, for his mediating role between Israel and the Palestinians during negotiations at Camp David. In addition, the United States wanted to keep Jordan in the peace process.

King Hussein died soon after the Camp David meeting and his eldest son, Abdullah, succeeded him. During his first official visit to Washington, on June 6, 2000, King Abdullah II and President Clinton announced the beginning of negotiations for a free trade agreement. Once again, a free trade agreement was being used primarily as a tool of foreign policy. Moreover, a full-fledged free trade agreement would remove any remaining discrimination against Jordan that had resulted from the US-Israel FTA.

Despite the clear emphasis on the foreign policy objective, economic objectives did come into play once the agreement was being negotiated. Then-US Trade Representative Charlene Barshefsky outlined the following US goals in pursuing the US-Jordan FTA:

- to encourage regional economic integration,

- to support Jordan's economic reform, and

- to develop a model for free trade agreements.[3]

---

3. Testimony by Ambassador Charlene Barshefsky before the Senate Finance Committee, March 20, 2001 (US Congress 2001, 6).

In contrast to the motivation for the US-Israel FTA, the proposed US-Jordan FTA was not seen as a wedge in the bilateral versus multilateral debate. For one thing, this time the holdup to starting multilateral negotiations was here at home—President Clinton had been unsuccessful for seven years in winning congressional authorization for entering into international trade negotiations. By contrast, in the mid-1980s, when the prospect of bilateral agreements, starting with the US-Israel agreement, was used by the United States to pressure the multilateral system, the other major trading partners were the source of the problem. In the 1990s, the holdup to starting multilateral negotiations was at home. For seven years, President Clinton was unable to win fast-track negotiating authority from Congress, which significantly contributed to the delay in starting multilateral negotiations.

To attract Democratic congressional support for further trade liberalization, President Clinton included provisions to protect the environment and labor standards in the US-Jordan FTA. His bold stroke made the US-Jordan FTA probably one of the most important trade policy precedents of his administration—and it occurred less than three weeks before the Bush administration began.

There were risks in adding provisions on the environment and labor. By doing so, the Clinton administration hoped to win back the support of Democrats who, following the president's unsuccessful attempt to win approval of fast-track trade negotiating authority in 1997, claimed to be holding trade policy "hostage" until such stipulations were made. Yet their inclusion in the agreement might have cost Republican support for this and future congressional battles. More important, a Republican move to torpedo the deal would be a great foreign policy embarrassment for the United States.

In the end, once again, foreign policy interests overshadowed the trade policy debate. By early fall of 2001, the US-Jordan FTA—with its environmental and labor provisions intact—passed both the House of Representatives and the Senate by voice vote.

The US-Jordan FTA is more comprehensive than the US-Israel FTA, covering the following areas:

- *Trade in goods:* The agreement calls for the elimination of almost all tariffs within 10 years, phased out in four stages: (1) tariffs of less than 5 percent, within 2 years; (2) tariffs between 5 and 10 percent, within 4 years; (3) tariffs between 10 and 20 percent, within 5 years; and (4) tariffs above 20 percent, within 10 years.

- *Trade in service:* The agreement aims to open the Jordanian market to US service providers.

- *Intellectual property rights:* Jordan agrees to ratify and implement the WIPO Copyright Treaty and the Performances and Phonograms Treaty within two years.

Table 3.7   US trade with Jordan, 1996–2002
(millions of dollars)

Year	Exports	Imports	Balance
1996	345.2	25.2	320.0
1997	402.5	25.3	377.2
1998	352.9	16.4	336.5
1999	275.6	30.9	244.7
2000	316.7	73.3	243.4
2001	339.0	229.1	109.9
2002	404.4	412.2	−7.8

Sources: US Census Bureau, Department of Commerce; and author's calculations.

- *The environment:* The agreement includes a specific provision linking trade liberalization to environmental protection (see below).

- *Labor:* The agreement includes a specific provision, similar to that dealing with the environment, linking trade liberalization to protection of labor standards (see below).

- *Electronic commerce:* The agreement is the first to include specific language committing both parties to promoting a liberal environment for electronic commerce.

- *Safeguard measures and dispute settlement:* Although most disputes are to be handled through direct consultations between the two parties, the agreement establishes a dispute settlement process. If consultations are unsuccessful, a dispute settlement panel can be asked to prepare a nonbinding report. The affected country can take appropriate measures if the parties are still unable to resolve a dispute after the panel has issued its report.

- *Joint committee:* The agreement establishes an organization, composed of representatives from the United States and Jordan, that is designed to supervise the implementation of the agreement.

US-Jordanian Trade Flows

In 2000, when the US-Jordan FTA was signed, total trade between the two countries amounted to $390 million. US exports to Jordan accounted for less than half of 1 percent of total US exports and a little less than 10 percent of total Jordanian imports. US imports from Jordan accounted for approximately one-tenth of total US imports and 5 percent of total Jordanian exports. The value of US-Jordanian trade was clearly very small.

Table 3.7 presents data on US-Jordan exports and imports from 1996 to 2002. The level of trade was fairly constant throughout the period, until US imports from Jordan began to sharply increase in 2001. US imports

Table 3.8   Top US exports to Jordan, 2002 (millions of dollars)

Standard International Trade Classification		Value	Share (percent)
04	Cereals	53.5	13.2
79	Transport equipment	46.4	11.5
89	Miscellaneous manufactured articles	43.1	10.7
77	Electrical machinery	27.5	6.8
76	Telecommunications	22.1	5.4
74	General industrial machinery	18.1	4.5
78	Road vehicles	16.9	4.2
87	Professional and scientific equipment	16.0	4.0
42	Fixed vegetable fats and oils	15.8	3.9
75	Office machines and automatic data processing equipment	13.9	3.4

Sources: US Census Bureau, Department of Commerce; and author's calculations.

Table 3.9   Top US imports from Jordan, 2002 (millions of dollars)

Standard International Trade Classification		Value	Share (percent)
84	Apparel	384.2	93.2
89	Miscellaneous manufactured articles	13.9	3.4
54	Medicinal and pharmaceutical products	1.9	0.5
27	Crude fertilizers	1.7	0.4
74	General industrial machinery	0.9	0.2
65	Textile yarn and fabrics	0.8	0.2
83	Travel goods and handbags	0.7	0.2
55	Essential oils	0.6	0.1
72	Special machinery	0.5	0.1
66	Nonmetallic mineral manufactures	0.5	0.1

Sources: US Census Bureau, Department of Commerce; and author's calculations.

from Jordan grew threefold between 2000 and 2001, and nearly doubled again between 2001 and 2002. Although it is impossible to draw any definite conclusions from two years of data, the US-Jordan FTA may have already begun to benefit Jordanian exports to the United States, much as the US-Israel FTA has benefited Israeli exports.

What Do the United States and Jordan Trade?

Trade between the United States and Jordan seems to be more diverse than that between the United States and Israel. Table 3.8 presents the top 10 US exports to Jordan in 2000, which account for more than two-thirds of all US exports to Jordan. The products include some food and some basic manufactured goods.

Apparel accounts for almost all of Jordan's exports to the United States (see table 3.9). This raises some concern in trade policy circles, since the US apparel industry has experienced severe dislocations—both plant closings

Box 3.1   Textile and apparel rules of origin included in the US-Jordan FTA

Basic rules
The country of origin is that country in which the textile or apparel product is wholly obtained or produced.

- For fabric, it is the oountry where the yarns, etc., are woven, knitted, or otherwise made into fabric.
- For any other textile/apparel product, it is the country where the product is wholly assembled from its component pieces.

Special rules
The country of origin is determined

- *For knit products:* by where the product is knit-to-shape.
- *For certain flat goods made from cotton, wool, or fiber blends containing 16 percent or more of cotton:* by where the fabric is made.
- *For certain flat goods made from silk, cotton, man-made fibers, and vegetable fibers:* by where dyeing, printing, and two or more finishing operations take place.

***

Source: Provided to author by Erik Autor, National Retail Federation.

and mass layoffs—over recent years. Although the volume of imports coming from Jordan remains quite small, US trade negotiators were sensitive about this issue when the US-Jordan FTA was drafted, and special rules of origin for textiles and apparel were included in the agreement.

Rules of Origin

The general rules of origin under the US-Jordan FTA are identical to those included in the US-Israel FTA, with the major exception of textiles and apparel, which follow the Breaux-Cardin rules. These also serve as the general rules of origin for all trade in textiles and apparel not covered by special agreements (see box 3.1).

Environmental and Labor Provisions

The great precedent in the US-Jordan FTA was the inclusion, in the text of the agreement itself, of specific (and parallel) provisions concerning environmental and labor issues.

At the core of the environmental provision is the recognition that "it is inappropriate to encourage trade by relaxing domestic environmental laws." At the same time, the US-Jordan FTA acknowledges the right of each country to establish its own environmental laws and policies. It goes on to state that "a Party shall not fail to effectively enforce its environmental laws, through a sustained or recurring course of action or inaction, in a manner affecting trade between the Parties" (USTR 2000, 9).

The substance of the environmental provision in the US-Jordan FTA is almost identical to that included in NAFTA. The primary difference is that the US-Jordan FTA places it in the actual body of the agreement, thereby making it subject to the general dispute settlement mechanism set out in the agreement. By contrast, under NAFTA, the environment provision is relegated to a side agreement, where it must rely on its own dispute settlement mechanism.

The dispute settlement procedure in the US-Jordan FTA sets out several steps:

1. First, both parties must attempt to resolve disputes through direct consultations.

2. If the dispute remains unresolved after 60 days, either party can refer the issue to the joint committee.

3. If the dispute is not resolved by the joint committee within 90 days, the parties can appoint a three-member panel, which can make a nonbinding recommendation.

4. Within 90 days after the panel makes its nonbinding recommendation, the joint committee "shall endeavor to resolve the dispute, taking the panel report into account, as appropriate."

5. If the joint committee's efforts do not resolve the dispute within 30 days, "the affected Party shall be entitled to take any appropriate and commensurate measure" (USTR 2000, 17–18).

Table 3.10 compares the provisions concerning the environment in the US-Jordan FTA, NAFTA, and the North American Agreement on Environmental Cooperation (NAAEC)—the NAFTA side agreement.

The provision relating to labor issues is very similar to that dealing with the environment. It, too, is included in the text of the US-Jordan FTA and is subject to the dispute settlement procedures set forth in the agreement. The labor provision sets out three requirements:

■ Each country must enforce its own labor laws in manners that affect trade, and those labor laws must reflect both "internationally recognized labor rights" as defined by the Trade Act of 1974, as amended, and core labor standards as defined by the International Labor Organization.

■ The parties agree not to relax their own labor laws in order to encourage trade with the other party.

Table 3.10 Comparison of US-Jordan FTA, NAFTA, and NAAEC: Key environmental provisions

Provision	US-Jordan FTA	NAFTA	NAAEC
Relaxation of laws to attract investment	Article 5.1. The Parties recognize that it is inappropriate to encourage trade by relaxing domestic environmental laws. Accordingly, each Party shall strive to ensure that it does not waive or otherwise derogate from, or offer to waive or otherwise derogate from, such laws as an encouragement for trade with the other Party.	Article 1114.2. The Parties recognize that it is inappropriate to encourage investment by relaxing domestic health, safety or environmental measures. Accordingly, each Party shall not waive or otherwise derogate from, or offer to waive or otherwise derogate from, such measures as an encouragement for the establishment, acquisition, expansion or retention in its territory of an investment of an investor. If a Party considers that another Party has offered such an encouragement, it may request consultations with the other Party and the two Parties shall consult with a view to avoiding any such encouragement.	No comparable provision.
Adoption of environmental measures: Levels of protection	Article 5.2. Recognizing the right of each Party to establish its own levels of domestic environmental protection and environmental development policies and priorities, and to adopt or modify accordingly its environmental laws, each Party shall strive to ensure that its laws provide for high levels of environmental protection and shall strive to continue to improve those laws.	Article 1114.1. Nothing in this Chapter (on investment) shall be construed to prevent a Party from adopting, maintaining or enforcing any measure otherwise consistent with the Chapter that it considers appropriate to ensure that investment activity in its territory is undertaken in a manner sensitive to environmental concerns.	Article 3. Recognizing the right of each Party to establish its own levels of domestic environmental protection and environmental development policies and priorities, and to adopt or modify accordingly its environmental laws and regulations, each Party shall ensure that its laws and regulations provide for high levels of environmental protection and shall strive to continue to improve those laws and regulations.

Effective enforcement of environmental laws: Obligation	Article 5.3(a). A Party shall not fail to effectively enforce its environmental laws, through a sustained or recurring course of action or inaction, in a manner affecting trade between the Parties, after the date of entry into force of this Agreement.	No comparable provision.	Article 5.1. With the aim of achieving high levels of environmental protection and compliance with its environmental laws and regulations, each Party shall effectively enforce its environmental laws and regulations through appropriate governmental action, subject to Article 37.... Article 37: Nothing in the Agreement shall be construed to empower a Party's authorities to undertake environmental law enforcement activities in the territory of another Party.
Effective enforcement of environmental laws: Exercise of discretion	Article 5.3(b). The Parties recognize that each Party retains the right to exercise discretion with respect to investigatory, prosecutorial, regulatory, and compliance matters and to make decisions regarding the allocation of resources to enforcement with respect to other environmental matters determined to have higher priorities. Accordingly, the Parties understand that a Party is in compliance with subparagraph (a) where a course of action or inaction reflects a reasonable exercise of such discretion, or results from a *bona fide* decision regarding the allocation of resources.	No comparable provision.	Article 45.1. For the purposes for this Agreement: A Party has not failed to "effectively enforce its environmental law" or to comply with Article 5(1) in a particular case where the action or inaction in question by agencies or officials of that Party: (a) reflects a reasonable exercise of their discretion in respect of investigatory, prosecutorial, regulatory or compliance matters; or (b) results from a *bona fide* decision to allocate resources to enforcement in respect of other environmental matters determined to have higher priorities.

NAFTA = North American Free Trade Agreement
NAAEC = North American Agreement on Environmental Cooperation

Source: Tiemann (2001).

- What counts as effective enforcement of labor laws allows for a "reasonable exercise of . . . discretion" and "bona fide decision[s] regarding the allocation of resources" (USTR 2000, 10).

The labor provisions are covered by the same dispute settlement procedure discussed above. Table 3.11 presents a comparison of the labor provisions in the US-Jordan FTA and in NAFTA.

The Congressional Debate

By including the articles on labor and the environment in the body of the agreement, and thereby making these provisions subject to the agreement's dispute settlement procedures, the US-Jordan FTA set two precedents. Both set off considerable controversy within Congress. Liberal Democrats, while continuing to oppose efforts to provide broader trade promotion authority (TPA) to the president, applauded the inclusion of these provisions, under the umbrella of the normal dispute settlement process, as an integral part of the US-Jordan FTA. Many Republicans, on the other hand, threatened to defeat any legislation that linked international trade to environmental and labor standards.

Because President Clinton submitted the agreement to Congress three weeks before leaving office, the Bush administration found itself in the odd position of advocating in favor of the US-Jordan FTA, despite its opposition to the agreement's inclusion of provisions on the environment and labor. In addition to threatening the administration's efforts to win congressional approval of TPA, the controversy over these provisions threatened to create an embarrassing foreign policy debacle for the United States: at one point it seemed possible that Congress might not approve the agreement already signed by President Clinton and by the Jordanian government.

A compromise was reached and on July 23, 2001, the Jordanian Ambassador to the United States and US Trade Representative Robert Zoellick exchanged identical letters. These made clear that the phrase "appropriate and commensurate measures" in the description of the dispute settlement procedures did not mean sanctions. Furthermore, the two countries agreed to settle any differences they might have through consultations, rather than through the formal dispute settlement process. The letters also stated that each government "would not expect or intend to apply the Agreement's dispute settlement enforcement procedures . . . in a manner that results in blocking trade."

Within days after the exchange of letters, the House of Representatives approved the US-Jordan FTA by voice vote. The Senate followed suit several weeks later, after debating whether the US-Jordan FTA should serve as a model for future free trade agreements.

Table 3.11 Comparison of labor provisions in the US-Jordan FTA and NAFTA

Provision	US-Jordan FTA, Article 6	NAFTA (PL 103-182) (in side agreement)
Rights of workers	"Internationally recognized labor rights" from Trade Act of 1974 (PL 93-618 as amended by sec. 503 of PL 98-573): a) right of association b) right to organize and bargain collectively c) prohibition of forced or compulsory labor d) minimum age for employment of children e) acceptable conditions re minimum wages, hours, and occupational safety and health Core labor standards from the International Labor Office (ILO): a) freedom of association b) right to organize and bargain collectively c) prohibition on the use of forced labor d) prohibition of exploitative child labor e) prohibition of employment discrimination	"Internationally recognized labor rights" from Trade Act of 1974 plus the following additions: f) the right to strike g) minimum employment standards relating to overtime pay h) elimination of employment discrimination i) equal pay for men and women j) compensation in case of occupational injuries and illnesses k) protection of migrant workers
Basic labor requirements	All countries must enforce their own labor laws and standards in trade-related situations. Each party shall strive to "not waive or otherwise derogate from" its laws as an encouragement for trade.	All countries must enforce their own labor laws and standards in trade-related situations and shall strive toward the entire list of worker rights. No comparable provision.

(table continues next page)

Table 3.11 Comparison of labor provisions in the US-Jordan FTA and NAFTA *(continued)*

Provision	US-Jordan FTA, Article 6	NAFTA (PL 103-182) (in side agreement)
Which worker rights are subject to dispute resolution?	All of them No comparable provision	Only 3 standards out of 11 (for child labor, minimum wages, and occupational safety and health) are enforceable through dispute settlement and ultimately sanctions. Dispute resolutions may be undertaken only for failure to enforce one's own labor rights laws and regulations, and if alleged failure to enforce is trade-related and covered by mutually recognized labor laws.
Enforcement body and dispute resolution procedure	Each country shall designate an office to serve as a contact point on the agreement. Any issue not resolved through consultation within 60 days may be referred to a **joint committee**, and, if still not resolved within 90 days, to a **dispute settlement panel** chosen by the parties.	Trade ministers (Ministerial Council) meet occasionally, supported by a 15-member Secretariat to resolve issues with consultation and persuasion. In each country a **national administrative officer (NAO)** oversees the law. An **evaluation committee of experts (ECE)** and subsequently an **arbitral panel (AP)** are appointed as needed to debate cases.
Ultimate penalties	If the issue is still not resolved in 30 days, after the panel issues a report, the affected party may take "any appropriate and commensurate measure."	The AP may issue a monetary assessment; and if this is not paid, issue sanctions. **Maximum penalties:** suspension of NAFTA benefits to the amount of the monetary penalty (which may be no greater than NAFTA benefits from tariff reductions) for one year.

Source: Bolle (2002).

Lessons from the US-Jordan FTA

There has barely been enough time since the US-Jordan FTA was signed in October 2000 for the ink to dry, let alone for the agreement to have had any serious impact on bilateral trade flows.[4] It is therefore premature to make any comments on the agreement's effectiveness in that regard.

Yet the US-Jordan FTA may have had a more immediate impact on US trade policy. Some argue that the passage of this agreement, with its environmental and labor provisions subject to rigorous dispute settlement, may have helped facilitate congressional passage of the Trade Act of 2002, which granted the president TPA.

The long-term impact of the US-Jordan FTA on US trade policy has yet to be seen. The US-Chile and US-Singapore FTAs, the only other bilateral agreements signed since its enactment, include similar language on the environment and labor, though their dispute settlement procedures are less stringent. Both agreements also borrow from the US-Jordan FTA and from the subsequent exchange of clarifying letters.

Conclusions and Questions for the Future

A number of conclusions and lessons can be drawn from the US-Israel and US-Jordan FTAs:

- Both the US-Israel and US-Jordan agreements unambiguously exemplify the use of free trade agreements as tools of foreign policy. In each case, the foreign policy objectives far outweighed the economic objectives as the United States entered into the agreement.

- Both agreements were used to pursue broader trade policy objectives:

  - The US-Israel agreement was the first US bilateral free trade agreement, passed largely because of the special relationship between the two countries. Yet the United States was able to use the FTA's passage—the suggestion that it could pursue other bilateral trade agreements—as leverage in stalled multilateral negotiations.

  - The US-Jordan agreement was the first to include specific provisions on labor and the environment. The US-Jordan FTA may thus have helped to win congressional passage of trade promotion authority in 2002.

---

4. Jordanian exports to the United States—which had already received preferential treatment prior to the agreement—grew threefold between 2000 and 2001. Though US exports to Jordan grew by 19 percent between 2001 and 2002, the level reached was similar to that of 1997 (well before the agreement was contemplated).

- Both Israel and Jordan, in the Middle East, rank high on the US foreign policy agenda. As the United States fashioned agreements with both, foreign policy interests far exceeded domestic economic sensitivities.

- The fact that both Israel and Jordan are small countries, accounting for a small share of US trade, raised particular issues in negotiating and implementing the agreements.

- Strong congressional support, enjoyed by both Israel and Jordan, lowered political resistance to these trade-liberalizing agreements and made them good candidates to set trade policy precedents.

- Both Israel and Jordan were undergoing internal economic reforms and trying to liberalize their economies at the time each FTA was negotiated. The US-Israel FTA provided some assistance to Israeli policymakers in overcoming domestic opposition to market liberalization, but it is too early to tell whether the US-Jordan FTA will do likewise.

- Both agreements were of more economic benefit to their partner than to the United States.

- Both agreements helped the United States to move along the FTA learning curve, although the experience it gained was of limited and short-lived value.

- Both agreements focused more attention on bilateral trade policy issues than the actual amount of trade warranted (and thus focused more attention than would have been given in the absence of the negotiations).

- Because there is very little boilerplate in free trade agreements—each FTA must take into account the nuances of the other country—they enjoy few economies of scale. In this respect, the US-Israel and US-Jordan agreements have provided little assistance in subsequent negotiations. There is one possible exception: the provisions on labor and the environment included in the US-Jordan agreement may serve as a model for future FTAs.

- FTAs are highly "USTR-intensive." Because each agreement has to take into account the nuances of the other country's situation, the USTR must start from scratch in beginning each negotiation. Because its staffing has not increased significantly over the past several years, the USTR has been forced by the increase in the number of FTAs to divert resources away from other functions. This strain is especially troubling in the functional areas, such as intellectual property rights.

- FTAs discriminate against other countries, potentially working against US efforts to assist those countries. For example, the US-Israel FTA initially discriminated against Palestinians. The later expansion of agreement to cover Palestinian trade resulted in discrimination against Jordan. The US-Jordan FTA, in turn, discriminates against Egypt and all other countries in the region and elsewhere that do not have FTAs with the United States.

■ To use a biblical metaphor, FTAs may beget more FTAs. Negotiating FTAs is an endless process. To address their inherent discrimination, the number of countries with which we have an FTA must constantly expand. For example, the US-Israel FTA contributed to the need for the US-Jordan FTA, and has set the stage for some sort of agreement with other Arab countries. This expansion further strains USTR resources.

■ One way to address the proliferation of FTAs is to use them as a first step toward regional agreements.[5] The US-Canada FTA is a case in point, paving the way for NAFTA (though NAFTA covers only three countries). Regional agreements have economies of scale and reduce discrimination—but they also run the risk of establishing regional trading blocs. In addition, a country that has signed an FTA with the United States might be reluctant to enter into a regional agreement and share its preferential treatment with its neighbors.

■ FTAs become obsolete as soon as they are signed. Most agreements look to the past and do not anticipate the future. In this regard, a ratified FTA signals not the end but rather the beginning of negotiations. Once the agreement is in place, the two countries are obligated to deal with its implementation and new issues that may arise. In addition, FTAs may need to be updated to take into account subsequent FTAs between other countries.

The lessons of the US-Israel and US-Jordan FTAs raise some very important questions:

■ What criteria should be used for choosing and negotiating FTAs?

■ Should these criteria be transparent?

■ Are FTAs deflecting scarce USTR resources away from other (and more important) functions?

■ Should all FTAs represent the same deal? Should FTAs include a clause that automatically updates the agreement when subsequent FTAs are signed?

■ Do we need an "MFFTA"—a "most favored" FTA?

---

5. In fact, a day after I presented the paper on which this chapter is based, President Bush called for the establishment of a Middle East FTA.

The limited experience of the US-Israel and US-Jordan FTAs provides only partial answers to these questions. In both cases, the agreements were primarily motivated by political, not economic, factors. Pending agreements with Bahrain and Morocco seem to follow this pattern. If it continues to hold, then we should expect these agreements to be of limited economic benefit to the United States.

Except for NAFTA, it appears that the volume of bilateral trade has not influenced the US choice of partners in negotiating an FTA. As a result, we are diverting scarce USTR resources away from issues that affect large amounts of trade and devoting them to the negotiations of FTAs, which have little potential economic payoff. From a purely economic standpoint, this strategy seems irrational.

As noted above, signing an FTA marks the beginning of continued monitoring and negotiations. And because each country entering into an FTA will want a better deal than was offered in earlier FTAs, and each signatory of an earlier FTA will want a deal as good as the latest agreement, there will be constant pressure for renegotiation. The cycle will never end unless "all FTAs are created equal"—perhaps through a standard FTA for all countries (i.e., some kind of "most favored" FTA).

Such uniformity in the agreements is unlikely; a second-best solution would be to include a clause in each FTA that calls for updating the agreement once others are signed. Some countries may be unwilling to agree to such a clause, since it would mean that other countries are in effect negotiating on their behalf.

Obviously, one way to deal with all these problems is to stop the proliferation of FTAs and concentrate solely on strengthening the multilateral trade system, affording preferential treatment to all countries on a nondiscriminatory basis and encouraging all countries to abide by internationally agreed upon standards of labor rights, environmental protection, and the like.

Are FTAs worth the effort? Is the prospect of small increases in trade worth all the time and energy spent negotiating the agreement, plus the risk FTAs pose to the multilateral trading system? Based on the limited experience to date, it appears that FTAs benefit the partner countries more than they benefit the United States. Furthermore, the risk to the multilateral system may be greater than any modest returns from FTAs.

References

Bolle, Mary Jane. 2002. *Jordan-U.S. Free Trade Agreement: Labor Issues.* Congressional Research Service, Report RS 20968. Washington: Congressional Research Service, Library of Congress.

Tiemann, Mary. 2001. *US-Jordan Free Trade Agreement: Analysis of Environmental Provisions.* Congressional Research Service, Report RS 20999. Washington: Congressional Research Service, Library of Congress.

US Congress. Senate. Committee on Finance. 2001. *Jordan Free Trade Agreement.* 107th Congress, 1st session, March 20. Available at www.senate.gov/~finance/73013.pdf.

US Trade Representative, Office of (USTR). 2000. Agreement Between the United States of America and the Hashemite Kingdom of Jordan on the Establishment of a Free Trade Area. www.ustr.gov/regions/eu-med/middleeast/textagr.pdf (October 24).

4

Lessons from the Chile and Singapore Free Trade Agreements

SIDNEY WEINTRAUB

The free trade agreement with Chile is the first bilateral FTA for the United States with a Latin American country, and that with Singapore the first FTA of any kind for the United States with an East Asian country. The two agreements are intended to be bellwethers for future FTAs in both regions, some bilateral and others plurilateral, as well as to set the substantive parameters for the hemispherewide Free Trade Area of the Americas (FTAA). Their importance, therefore, lies as much in their precedent-setting effect for future FTAs that will be undertaken as in the tangible trade benefits they will bring for the United States.

Great care was taken in choosing these two countries in order to maximize the precedential effects in their respective regions. Singapore largely practices free trade and Chile has an open economy. Both countries have solid credentials for effective macroeconomic management and both have exhibited solid economic growth during the past 15 years. Consequently, neither country has deeply entrenched or broadly based protectionist interests fighting against market opening. In this substantive sense, each country was a worthy candidate for an FTA. And, as they exploit their favored access to the large US market, this reality could be expected to set up pressures for other countries in their respective regions to seek the same.

There are both pluses and minuses for the United States in setting up this differential treatment for countries in given regions, or globally. The

Sidney Weintraub is William E. Simon Chair in Political Economy and the director of the Americas Program at the Center for Strategic and International Studies.

positive aspect is that it can lead to a clamor by countries that face discrimination in the US market to rectify their disadvantageous position by seeking an FTA of their own.[1] To highlight this point, it has been suggested that instead of calling these agreements FTAs, they should be described as bilateral preferential agreements (BPAs). The downside is that an FTA with any given country sets up political tensions with other similarly situated countries that have friendly relations with the United States; these tensions will endure until they can obtain equal treatment by means of their own BPA. Selective free trade bilateralism creates a strife-laden situation similar to that which existed under the policy of conditional most favored nation (MFN) treatment after the United States became a powerful magnet for imports. Conditional MFN was a policy of trade concessions extended only to countries with which agreements were signed—that is, these concessions were not extended automatically to other countries until they signed their own agreements with the United States. This was US policy from 1778 until 1924, when it was discarded for political reasons in favor of unconditional MFN status.[2] The United States is now repeating the process, but instead of preferential MFN status (conditional MFN and preferential MFN are oxymorons) this time its instrument is preferential free trade.

The next section of this chapter will lay out the apparent motives and objectives of the three parties to these two FTAs; it will be followed by a discussion of key elements of the two agreements. The final section will provide some judgments about the wisdom of the paths being followed by the various countries involved, particularly by the United States, and hence what lessons can be learned from these agreements.

The Motives of the Countries Involved

As background for this discussion, table 4.1 sets forth some key indicators, mostly economic, for Chile and Singapore. The data are for 2002 and don't necessarily reflect a long-term pattern. For example, annual average

---

1. For example, after the announcement that FTA negotiations would be opened with the five countries of the Central American Common Market, the Dominican Republic requested either to have its own FTA with the United States or to be included in this same negotiation. The Central American countries, on their part, have been anxious since NAFTA went into effect in 1994 to have an FTA with the United States to equalize the treatment that their goods receive with those of Mexico.

2. See Weintraub (1966). A memorandum of March 12, 1924, to the secretary of state from his economic adviser made the political point quite forcefully: "Comparatively speaking, it [conditional most favored nation treatment] arouses antagonism, promotes discord, creates a sense of unfairness and tends, in general, to discourage commerce" (quoted in Weintraub 1966, 20).

Table 4.1 Chile and Singapore economic data, 2002

Economic indicators	Chile	Singapore
Population	15 million	4 million
GDP per capita	$4,640	$22,960
GDP	$70.5 billion	$92.3 billion
Real GDP growth (percent)	1.7	2.3
Inflation (percent)	2.4	−0.5
Unemployment (percent)	8.8	4.7
Fiscal balance (percent GDP)	−0.9	1.5
Exchange rate policy	Managed float	Managed float
Current account (percent GDP)	−1.8	21.1
Merchandise exports (percent GDP)	43.0	180.0
Other FTAs	8.0[a]	10.0[b]

a. Chile has concluded or is still negotiating free trade agreements with the United States, Canada, Mexico, South Korea, Central America (ratified so far by Costa Rica and El Salvador), the European Union, the European Free Trade Association (Iceland, Liechtenstein, Norway, and Switzerland), and Bolivia.
b. Singapore has concluded FTAs with New Zealand, Japan, the European Free Trade Association, Australia, and the United States. Singapore has ongoing trade negotiations with Mexico, Canada, ASEAN and China, the Republic of Korea, and India.

Sources: IMF, Central Bank of Chile, Chilean American Chamber of Commerce, and Ministry of Trade and Industry of Singapore.

GDP growth has been much higher for both countries over the past 10 to 15 years. The average annual rate of GDP growth for Chile from 1985 through 2000 was 5.6 percent; for Singapore over the same period it was 7.3 percent (ECLAC 2002). It is evident from table 4.1 that Chile and Singapore are relatively small countries, whether measured in population or total GDP, especially in comparison with the United States. Chile's GDP is 0.07 percent and Singapore's is 0.09 percent of that of the United States.

Both Chile and Singapore are world traders, and export success is a requisite for economic growth for each of them—especially Singapore—as is evident from their export-to-GDP ratios shown in table 4.1. The United States is an important market and a significant source of imports for each country, although by no means overwhelmingly so. This can be seen in table 4.2, which shows the country composition of Singapore's exports and imports, and table 4.3, which gives this breakdown for Chile.

The main US exports to Chile are capital goods and machinery and components (about 40 percent of the total), new vehicles, aircraft, medical instruments, plastics, and organic chemicals, plus a variety of products none of which individually exceeds 1 to 2 percent of the total. The main US imports from Chile are copper, fruits, fish, lumber, wine, and some chemicals. Chile is not an important exporter of manufactured products; indeed, there is some concern in Chile about this lack of diversification (Hornbeck 2003).

The major items of merchandise trade with Singapore are machinery and transport equipment, chemicals and related products, and other man-

Table 4.2 Destination of Singapore's exports and origin of its imports, 2002

Country/region	Exports (percent of total)	Imports (percent of total)
Africa	1	1
European Union	12	12
Latin America and Caribbean	3	1
Malaysia	17	18
Oceania	4	2
United States and Canada	15	15
Other Asian countries	46	48
Rest of the world	2	3

Source: Ministry of Trade and Industry of Singapore, *Economic Survey of Singapore* (2002).

Table 4.3 Destination of Chile's exports and origin of its imports, 2001

Country/region	Exports (percent of total)	Imports (percent of total)
Asia	23	11
European Union	22	13
United States and Canada	18	23
Other Latin American and Caribbean countries	22	36
Rest of the world	15	17

Source: IDB (2002).

ufactures. These three broad areas of bilateral trade[3] constituted 87 percent of US exports to and 91 percent of US imports from Singapore in 2002. There are many variations in the products when these broad categories are more precisely defined.

One might expect some increase in US exports to Chile from the FTA insofar as it removes the discrimination that US exporters face there in comparison with countries such as Canada and Mexico that have FTAs with Chile and thus need not overcome Chile's low uniform import tariff (currently 6 percent) as it phases out under the FTAs. However, Chile's uniform MFN tariff rate may in any event be lowered in future years; and while a 6 percent tariff disadvantage may be a decisive competitive factor in some cases, exchange rate movements are often more significant.[4] US exports to Chile and Singapore in 2002 were $2.6 billion and $16.2 billion,

---

3. By "broad area" I have in mind the one-digit SITC (Standard International Trade Classification) commodity areas 7, 5, and 8, in that order.

4. The National Association of Manufacturers estimates that the discrimination inherent in the lack of a US FTA with Chile cost US exporters $800 million in lost sales in 2002. See www.nam.org.

respectively. Together the two countries were the destination of 2.7 percent of US global exports in 2002. Singapore is an important entrepôt for the shipment of goods to East Asia, and the much larger figure for exports there than to Chile reflects this fact.

What the data demonstrate is that while exports to Chile and Singapore are not negligible, trade for the sake of merchandise exports from the United States to these two countries was not the main US motive for negotiating the two free trade agreements. What, then, was? Most probably the chief factor was the desire of the authorities to demonstrate that the United States is a player in the bilateral and regional free trade game by selecting two naturals, two countries nearly ideal for this purpose, one in each region, and thereby to quietly induce other countries, especially in these regions, to seek similar agreements to avoid discrimination in exporting their products to the large US market. In the case of Chile, the FTA is intended to provide an incentive to other countries in the hemisphere heavily reliant on the US market to get on with the negotiations for the FTAA. On the potential dilemma of bilateral FTAs—that they may either stimulate third countries to seek their own agreements or arouse political resentment from them over inferior trade treatment—the first approach is clearly dominant in official US thinking.

This dominant motive goes together with fashioning agreements that include the key contents that the United States seeks in these FTAs—such as opening government procurement in the partner countries to US companies, liberalizing trade in services, protecting intellectual property, and securing national treatment for US foreign investment. Each bilateral agreement that contains provisions on these themes reinforces their inclusion in subsequent agreements. In addition, the two agreements contain formulaic commitments on labor and environmental issues, something that has become necessary to secure congressional approval.[5] Congress set forth the objectives it had in mind in its grant of trade promotion authority (TPA) and the US trade representative (USTR) worked out the benchmarks for complying with the congressional mandate. Each agreement has its own variations and innovations, but now the framework and the compulsory content from the US perspective have been established.

The motivations of the other two countries are reasonably clear, but not completely so. Both Singapore and Chile have fashioned their economic development on export expansion, as is evident from the large number of FTAs each has concluded or is negotiating (see table 4.1). The desire to include the United States in their FTA network is quite consistent with this

---

5. The earlier US FTA with Jordan, signed into law by President Bush in 2001, served as the pioneer agreement for working out labor and environmental issues, even though the Chile agreement contains some new wrinkles on these provisions (e.g., recourse to monetary fines as an enforcement measure).

reality. However, their main motivation is not to obtain reductions in US trade barriers, which already are quite low (or even set at zero for Chile for many products under the US Generalized System of Preferences), but rather to increase their attractiveness to foreign investors. US import barriers are high in agriculture, but Singapore is not an agricultural exporter. Chile did receive agricultural concessions in the FTA, but they phase in over a long period, generally 12 years for the most sensitive products. For Singapore and Chile, a legally binding agreement provides an extra degree of assurance against resort to protection at the urging of a US competitor.[6] That and the attraction of direct investment are the main motives of Singapore and Chile for wanting FTAs with the United States.

It is not an oversimplification to describe the two FTAs as deals under which the United States obtains concessions on the export of services (especially financial and telecommunications), on investment rights, on protection of intellectual property, and on the right to bid on government procurement contracts, in exchange for providing a greater degree of legal surety of access to the US market without excessive impediments. The assurances on both sides are not absolute, but they do mark a significant advance toward what the parties sought when they entered into the negotiations.

The Chile agreement had more than a decade of gestation from the time it was first suggested. The holdup ostensibly was caused by the inability of the US executive branch to obtain fast-track authority (or trade promotion authority, as it is now called) from the Congress and by Chilean unwillingness for many years to negotiate without a prior understanding that there would be no subsequent congressional review of every detail in the agreement. Fast-track (or trade promotion) authority means that the US Congress must, generally speaking, vote the agreements up or down in their entirety. Both sides have had plenty of time to consider the desirability of an FTA, and both concluded that an agreement provided more benefits than disadvantages.

The position of Singapore's ministry of trade and industry is that FTAs accelerate the liberalization of world trade and are "stepping-stones" to multilateral liberalization. The ministry also emphasizes the security that a legally binding agreement provides for Singapore's trade and investment flows.[7] The Chilean authorities make the same arguments.

---

6. The agreements do not deal with trade remedy actions of either country—that is, antidumping and countervailing duty petitions and actions—and thus omit the protectionist measure of choice for US industries. All that the agreements say on this score is the following: "Each Party retains its rights and obligations under the WTO Agreement with regard to the application of antidumping and countervailing duties" (quoted from Chapter 8 of the Chile agreement, available at www.ustr.gov).

7. See speech by George Yeo, minister of trade and industry of Singapore, on April 28, 2003, at the US Chamber of Commerce in Washington; available at www.mti.gov.sg/public/FTA/frm_FTA_Default.asp?sid=36&cid=1608.

Key Elements of the Agreements

The tariff reduction contained in the two trade agreements, at least outside of agriculture in the Chile agreement, may be their least significant aspect. Singapore will bind all its tariffs at zero on entry into force of the agreement, and the majority of US tariffs will go to zero at that time. The tariff phaseout is more differentiated in the Chile agreement, depending on the perceived sensitivity of the product to competition from the other party. According to the USTR summary of the pact (USTR 2002), duties on more than 85 percent of two-way trade will be eliminated on entry into force of the agreement, and for other products duty elimination will take 4, 8, 10, or 12 years. For the most sensitive agricultural imports, the phaseout of US duties will take 12 years; and for many agricultural products, tariff-rate quotas on imports from Chile with increase annually over 12 years. The US import duty on Chilean wine falls into the 12-year gradual phaseout category.

Chile has similar staging of tariff elimination that extends up to 12 years for the products it considers sensitive; for it, too, these tend to be agricultural.

When the agreements were concluded, the USTR, in press releases, emphasized the extent of tariff elimination on the entry into force of the agreements, but put much greater stress on provisions in other areas. The central focus of the press releases on each agreement was on the services liberalized. These include financial services, such as banking, insurance, securities, and related areas; computers; direct selling; telecommunications; audiovisual services; construction and engineering; tourism; advertising; express delivery; professional services, such as those provided by architects, engineers, and accountants; distribution, wholesale, retail, and franchising; adult education; environmental services; and energy services. It appears, however, that the opening to US banking is not as extensive in the Chile agreement as in the Singapore agreement.

The use of a negative list for determining which services are included in the agreement was a particularly notable accomplishment. A negative list signifies the inclusion of all services except those specifically excluded. Services now make up more than 75 percent of the US economy, and the United States is highly competitive in exporting sophisticated, high-value-added services such as those included in both agreements. Consequently, this area is seen as being particularly promising for future US trade, and no previous trade agreement had succeeded in employing a negative list.

The other emphases in both agreements are e-commerce, investment (emphasizing national treatment, i.e., as favorable as that of local investors, and MFN treatment, i.e., as favorable as that of any other foreign investor), intellectual property rights, government procurement, and temporary entry of personnel, which is often critical to carry on trade in services, particularly professional services. With respect to government procurement, the agreements open many more government agencies to competitive bidding by the signatories than has been the norm in past agreements. These include many state and local, as well as central government, agencies.[8] The investment chapter deals extensively with investor-state disputes and calls for consultation, negotiation, and ultimately arbitration if necessary. The procedures for arbitral proceedings are set forth in considerable detail. The handling of investor-state disputes in the North American Free Trade Agreement has been controversial; by now, there is an extensive literature, much of it polemical, on Chapter 11 disputes in that agreement. Nevertheless, the issue is included in the Chile and Singapore agreements.

Labor issues had not been included in trade agreements until US organized labor made this a point of major contention when the NAFTA negotiations were coming to a close. Approval of NAFTA was most uncertain when Bill Clinton assumed the presidency, and he promised to add separate agreements on labor and the environment to the basic NAFTA agreement; Congress then approved the NAFTA agreement and the side agreements, although not without a struggle. Subsequent labor and environment debate in the US Congress arose in connection with fast-track authority and centered on a number of related issues: Should these provisions be part of the FTA agreement, rather than set in separate parallel agreements? What labor rights and environmental protections should be covered? What should be done if a party to the agreement does not adhere to the provisions of the agreement? Chile said from the outset of its free trade negotiations with the United States that it had no objection to including these issues in the agreement or in side agreements, but would not consent to using trade sanctions as the remedy for noncompliance.

Both issues were included in both the Chile and Singapore agreements. The provisions are similar in each. Focusing for the moment on labor, the principle is that each country obligates itself to carry out its own laws on the premise that these laws are satisfactory and the problem, if any, is with enforcement. The laws relevant to the FTA deal with five areas: the right of association; the right to organize and bargain collectively; a prohibition of forced or compulsory labor; a minimum age for employment of children and the elimination of the worst forms of child labor; and acceptable conditions of work with respect to minimum wages, hours of work, and occupational safety and health.[9] There is a complaint procedure, encouragement of consultation to resolve disputes, and, if this fails, the ability

---

8. The issue of state and local procurement competition is not relevant for Singapore. Local procurement competition is relevant for Chile.

9. These are in Article 18.8 of the US-Chile FTA and Article 17.7 of the US-Singapore FTA; both available at www.ustr.gov.

to draw on a panel from a roster of eligible panelists set up in advance. If the panel concludes that the party being complained about is not living up to the terms of the agreement, the complaining party can ask the panel to impose a monetary assessment (a fine) that will go into a fund to enhance labor law enforcement. The maximum fine against any country is $15 million a year, adjusted for inflation.[10] The environmental provisions are similar.[11]

Many students of trade policy oppose including nontrade matters such as labor and the environment in trade agreements. Their argument, in part, is that there is no end to this maneuvering and the ultimate result will be to make trade agreements unmanageable (Gordon 2003). (There is further comment on this issue below, in the final section on lessons from the two agreements.) At the eleventh hour, a third nontrade issue was inserted at US insistence in the Chile and Singapore agreements: namely, a provision prohibiting the use of capital controls. This was the first time such an obligation has been included in a US trade agreement.

Both Chile and Singapore have used capital controls. Chile used its controls to make it more costly for "hot money" to enter Chile and be withdrawn before a year has passed. The law is still on the books but has not been used in recent years. Both Chile and Singapore resisted this provision but in the end had to comply because the US Treasury Department made clear that it would hold up the agreements until they did. The countries retained a right to impose controls on capital for up to a year, with some conditions, in the event of an emergency. Jagdish Bhagwati, a professor at Columbia University, told the House of Representatives Financial Services Committee, which held hearings on the issue, that the capital-flow prohibitions were unwise on financial grounds, as well as at fault for infecting trade agreements with another nongermane matter.[12] Malaysia resorted to capital controls during the Asian crisis without any apparent damage to its economy, although admittedly this action was intended to deal only with a short-term crisis.

---

10. The labor advisory committee for trade negotiations and trade policy (LAC) in the United States found the labor provisions of the two agreements unsatisfactory in that they rely on monetary assessments instead of trade sanctions and have such a low annual cap. The LAC found the labor provisions a retreat from the Jordan agreement standard, and made an additional point: the dispute settlement provisions can be brought into play only when a country is seen as not effectively enforcing its own labor laws, and these laws might not contain all five of the labor rights stated in the agreement.

11. The environment is covered in Chapter 19 of the Chile agreement and Chapter 18 of the Singapore agreement.

12. Edward Alden, "US Backs Curbs on Capital Controls," *Financial Times*, April 2, 2003; see also Jagdish Bhagwati and Daniel Tarullo, "A Ban on Capital Controls Is a Bad Trade-off," *Financial Times*, March 17, 2003.

Ten Lessons on FTAs

The foregoing discussion obviously is not a complete description of the contents of the two agreements. The devils in the details in each of the functional chapters of the two agreements are unfathomable except to experts in the particular themes covered, and even to them the full consequences will not be clear until the countries have some experience with the workings of the two agreements. The various US private-sector advisory groups generally gave high marks to the chapters they reviewed, but not without some significant, and even scathing, criticism. My commentary will focus on the policy implications of what has been done and not on how much new trade or new investment will be generated over time. The amounts may be significant for those involved in these activities, but will surely be modest in the context of the total US economy. My interest here is in the trade policy consequences of the two agreements and how they may spill over into foreign policy—perhaps even into financial policy, now that a new theme has been added to US trade agreements.

One, there has been a frenzy in concluding new FTAs during the past decade, but its ultimate effects on the world trading system are still unclear. On the positive side, trade liberalization is proceeding, new issues of much importance are being added to the trade negotiation agenda, and many smaller countries are becoming players in the world trading structure. The negative aspects are an increase in discrimination, a crazy-quilt pattern of cross-discrimination, a plethora of rules of origin such that multinational corporation exporters can shop around to choose their export source, and ultimately a situation rife with political tension as countries find themselves excluded from obtaining equal treatment in one market or another. What will this eventually do to the world trading system as embodied in the World Trade Organization? No one knows. Experts are reduced to speculating in clichés about whether the FTAs are "stepping-stones" or "stumbling blocks" to global trade liberalization, all conjectures predicated on partial evidence.

Two, large and small countries alike now find themselves free to practice self-aggrandizing trade agreements, a modern form of mercantilism based on free trade with selective countries and replete with discrimination. All of the three countries involved in the FTAs discussed in this paper—Chile, Singapore, and the United States—are important players in concluding multiple FTAs. Consequently, each of them has self-interest in defending these agreements as stepping-stones to multilateral liberalization.[13]

---

13. Singapore and Chile have been concluding multiple FTAs longer than the United States has. However, after the United States entered the game, there was no turning back. The fact that the EU is engaged in the same practice reinforces the cross-discrimination around the globe. Japan is now entering the competition, thereby making the game complete among the world's leading trading nations.

Three, for the United States, the attraction of negotiating FTAs with Singapore and Chile was that they were relatively "easy" cases, in that both have open economies that practice prudent macroeconomic policies. A key US motive for these agreements was to set a template for future US FTAs in East Asia and in Latin America and the Caribbean. The message these agreements send is that the United States is open to further bilateral FTAs, but only when based on content that meets today's US needs to cover trade in services, access to government procurement, strengthened protection of intellectual property, strong investment protection, and provisions on labor standards and environmental protection.

Four, the two agreements are comprehensive, and this should set a standard for future US FTAs.[14] Indeed, the agreements are more comprehensive than NAFTA in certain respects, including the coverage of the five areas noted in the previous paragraph as well as dealing with e-commerce and competition policy. The two agreements are also innovative in many respects, such as using conciliation and then fines instead of trade sanctions to deal with labor and environmental infractions that cannot otherwise be resolved, and defining the degree of transparency desirable in trade and regulatory proceedings.

Five, liberalization of agricultural trade remains difficult for the United States, as it does for other developed countries that subsidize their farmers either domestically, to promote exports, or both. The United States had a free ride in this sector in the Singapore case and a modestly easy time when dealing with Chile; Singapore is not an agricultural exporter, and many of Chile's products are not seasonally competitive with US products. Nevertheless, the United States found it necessary to drag out the agricultural import transition for product after product to the maximum of 12 years allowed under the agreement. The United States, in these two agreements, did not have to face the problem of significant import competition from grains and meat. Even the liberalization for the import of Chilean wines is extended over a 12-year period. This does not augur well for the degree of import liberalization the United States will concede in the FTAA negotiations.

Six, another theme that is likely to be sensitive in the FTAA discussions is the use of trade remedy procedures—that is, the US antidumping (AD) and countervailing duty (CVD) practices. Chile has experienced this form of US protection in the past as it developed its exports from salmon mariculture. The two FTAs specify nothing about AD and CVD usage other

---

14. This statement needs some qualification. In a meeting held in mid-June 2003 at the Wye Conference Center in Maryland, there was discussion among hemispheric trade ministers, including the USTR, of scaling back the substantive obligations in the FTAA on government procurement, investment, intellectual property, and services, in order to get a slimmed-down FTAA by the end of 1994 focusing on "core" objectives like market access. See "FTAA Countries Explore Lesser Commitments," *Inside U.S. Trade*, June 20, 2003, 6.

than to maintain the status quo. In response to a question as to why Chile accepted this outcome, the chief Chilean negotiator commented that it was apparent from the language used by the US Congress in granting trade promotion authority to President Bush that an agreement that weakened AD or CVD protections would not be approved.[15]

Seven, the Chile and Singapore FTAs reinforced the certainty that once nontrade issues enter into US trade agreements, they take on a life of their own in later agreements; they underscored that the likely course of events is the addition over time of further nontrade demands. This is what happened when the US Treasury insisted that the two FTAs would not be concluded until Singapore and Chile accepted a provision prohibiting capital controls.[16] The inclusion of the prohibition was an example of a nontransparent decision: it received little or no informed public debate before the agreement was set in stone. The countries managed to salvage an escape for limited capital controls for up to a year to deal with a balance of payments crisis, but this amelioration does not alter the main message that other nontrade objectives will be made part of future US trade agreements when influential groups or persons can wield enough leverage to ensure their addition. If trade agreements become repositories for one or another nontrade objective, as desirable as that objective may be in the abstract, there is considerable danger that the main purpose of expanding trade and investment will be compromised, perhaps even destroyed. US foreign aid programs went through a similar process of aggregation of objectives that severely weakened their primary purpose of promoting development.

Eight, the main trade-off in the two FTAs—under which the United States obtained broad concessions in areas it deems important, in exchange for giving legal status to US openness to products and services coming from the two countries—also meant that the United States was generally under no obligation to change its laws and regulations, other than the adjustments inherent in implementing the agreements. US tariff concessions were modest because US tariffs were already low. The United States will have to adapt to the end of the Multi-Fiber Arrangement in 2005, and preliminary steps toward this end are contained in the two agreements. In contrast, the other countries did have to change laws, such

---

15. This comment came at a conference on April 28, 2003, held at the US Chamber of Commerce in Washington and sponsored by the Chamber and the Inter-American Development Bank.

16. It is worth noting that this provision was added at the insistence of the US Treasury, not the Office of the US Trade Representative. It was Treasury this time—and the next time it can be the Treasury again, or other powerful US agencies or their congressional supporters, who can seek to insert nontrade provisions, whether they be promoting antinarcotics cooperation or democracy, fighting money laundering, or engaging with other worthy—but still nontrade—matters.

as Chile's law that permitted capital controls. The United States stood firm on AD and CVD laws and procedures. Agricultural subsidies were not addressed. Will this be the pattern of later US bilateral and plurilateral FTAs? Most probably, yes. Will it be the model for the FTAA negotiations? It is exactly this fear that concerns the Brazilians—that the United States will negotiate by seeking but not granting significant new concessions. Will it be the model for the Doha Round of negotiations in the World Trade Organization? This question is harder to answer, as the United States has submitted a proposal in Geneva for dealing with agricultural subsidies that, if accepted, will require changes in US law. If the US proposal is not accepted by the European Union and others, then it is unlikely that the United States will implement unilaterally what it seeks to accomplish through reciprocal concessions in agriculture.

Nine, it has long been evident that concluding a trade agreement is an exercise in political economy with elements of each—trade and politics—involved. The whole language of trade negotiations involving "reciprocity" and "concessions" when an import barrier is lowered reflects this reality. The United States is now most interested in these agreements to strengthen "new" issues, some introduced in the Uruguay Round, that befit its world trade and investment status—protection of intellectual property, trade in services, and the others mentioned repeatedly here. The addition of a chapter on e-commerce in the Chile and Singapore agreements is additional evidence of the intent to protect an area in which the United States is highly competitive. The handling of the Chile agreement after the negotiations were concluded introduced another political element, that of linkage. This had to do with Chilean opposition to the US position on the proposed second United Nations Security Council resolution on going to war with Iraq with or without Security Council approval. Chile, a member of the Security Council at that time, made clear that it would vote against the US-UK-Spain resolution if it came to a vote, which it did not. This Chilean stance is the only plausible explanation for the United States' delay in signing the Chile FTA while going ahead immediately with the signing of the Singapore FTA. This linkage of the two issues reflected the views of many hard-liners in the US Congress, which must pass legislation to put the Chile agreement into effect. The US government later relented and signed the Chile agreement a month after it signed the Singapore agreement.

Ten, tariff reductions took a subordinate role in the Chile and Singapore FTAs because the tariffs were not high to begin within any of the three countries. Industrial tariffs are not high in developed countries generally, and this circumstance too explains their low priority when these countries negotiate with each other. However, while tariffs are much lower in developing countries than they used to be, they are not necessarily negligible. Future trade negotiations involving these countries may therefore give attention to tariffs, but other issues are likely to play a more important role.

One can say, in summarizing this commentary on lessons from the Chile and Singapore FTAs, that future trade negotiations are more likely to be retail than wholesale, more likely to be bilateral than global, more likely to widen cross-discrimination than end it. Even as they lower impediments to trade, future bilateral FTAs are apt to complicate further the complex pattern of differentiation of countries by whether they have FTAs and with whom. Chile and Singapore have long since determined to be hubs and not spokes in trade matters, a posture that the United States has also adopted. This hub-and-spoke pattern can be lessened in the Western Hemisphere if there is a comprehensive FTAA. A successful Doha Round negotiation will ease the discrimination picture but not end it, because Doha will still leave most tariffs and other border barriers in place. The main lesson, therefore, is that the world is likely to have to live for some time with the current patchwork of trade discrimination. There may be a reduction in the degree of discrimination if the FTAs turn out to be stepping-stones to global trade liberalization in the Doha Round, an outcome that is uncertain at the moment.

References

ECLAC (Economic Commission of Latin America and the Caribbean). 2002. *Current Conditions and Outlook: Economic Survey of Latin America and the Caribbean 2001–2002*. Santiago: ECLAC.

Gordon, Bernard K. 2003. By Invitation Only: Cozy Free Trade Deals Subvert Global Integration. *YaleGlobal Online*. yaleglobal.yale.edu/display.article?id=969 (February 13).

Hornbeck, J.F. 2003. *The U.S.-Chile Free Trade Agreement: Economic and Trade Policy Issues*. Congressional Research Service, Report RL 31144. Washington: Congressional Research Service, Library of Congress.

IDB (Inter-American Development Bank). 2002. Integration and Trade in the Americas. Special Issue on Latin American and Caribbean Economic Relations with the European Union. Periodic Note (May). Washington: IDB (Integration, Trade, and Hemispheric Issues Division).

US Trade Representative, Office of (USTR). 2002. Free Trade with Chile: Summary of the U.S.-Chile Free Trade Agreement. *Trade Facts*. www.ustr.gov/regions/whemisphere/samerica/2002-12-11-chile_summary.pdf (December 11).

Weintraub, Sidney. 1966. *Trade Preferences for Less-Developed Countries: An Analysis of the United States Policy*. New York: Praeger.

NEW INITIATIVES IN THE ASIA PACIFIC

5

Australia-US Free Trade: Benefits and Costs of an Agreement

ANDREW L. STOLER

In mid-March, a team of 40 American negotiators arrived in Canberra for the first session of a bilateral negotiation that was originally expected to produce a free trade agreement with Australia by "sometime in 2004."[1] That same week, US Trade Representative Robert Zoellick and business and political members of the American-Australian Free Trade Agreement Coalition celebrated the launch of the negotiations as a "win-win" venture for both countries that would not only produce important economic gains in both markets but also contribute to the two partners' relationships with others in the Asia-Pacific region and to the successful completion of the WTO Doha Round of multilateral trade negotiations.[2] More than two hundred companies have signed on to the US-based coalition in support of the FTA. In Australia, the negotiations enjoy the strong support of the Australia–United States Free Trade Agreement Business Group (AUSTA) and are seen as central to the Commonwealth government's objective of strengthening Australia's alliance with the United States (DFAT 2003, 86–91). Two Australian studies, discussed below, have suggested that an

---

Andrew L. Stoler is executive director of the Institute for International Business, Economics, and Law at the University of Adelaide and served as deputy director-general at the World Trade Organization from 1999 to 2002.

1. Lead Australian negotiator Stephen Deady at a March 21, 2003, press conference with US lead negotiator Ralph Ives.

2. Remarks at the launch of the American-Australian Free Trade Agreement Coalition by USTR Zoellick, March 19, 2003, Washington.

FTA could produce significant economic benefits for both Australia and the United States, and both governments are actively seeking input and feedback from their private sectors in support of the negotiating effort.

The project also has important critics and detractors. In Australia, Professor Ross Garnaut of the Australian National University's (ANU) Research School of Pacific and Asian Studies argues that the completion of an FTA with the United States would not only diminish Australian economic opportunities but also weaken Australia's security. A February 2003 report prepared by ACIL Consulting for the Australian Rural Industries Research and Development Corporation downplays potential economic gains from an FTA and strongly suggests that an FTA will have a negative impact on Australian farmers (ACIL 2003). In Washington, representatives of the American dairy, sugar, and beef industries have testified that free trade with Australia would do irreparable harm to these sectors of the US economy, cutting farm incomes, forcing thousands of farmers out of business, and endangering United States security ("US Farmers See Red Over Free Trade," *Australian Financial Review*, January 22, 2003, 7).

President Bush and Prime Minister Howard have made it clear they would like to see the FTA deal done in the course of 2003; and both reiterated this objective during his October visit to Australia. In the face of this political imperative, the negotiators on both sides have now had to accelerate an already tight timetable.

Is this likely to be a good agreement or not? How will the negotiations affect the WTO's Doha Round and other strategic Australian and American interests? In this chapter, and at this early stage in the bilateral negotiations on an agreement, I propose to review the claimed benefits and costs of a free trade agreement between the United States and Australia, the core objectives of players on both sides of the Pacific, the potential trade and investment effects of an agreement, and the implications of an FTA for both countries' relations with third countries.

Although I am aware of the March 28, 2003, letter to President Bush by Senator Grassley and 17 of his Senate colleagues urging the inclusion of New Zealand in these FTA negotiations between the United States and Australia, I will not comment on that prospect in the body of this chapter other than to state the obvious: including New Zealand would clearly complicate the already politically dicey agriculture side of the negotiations, and it is difficult to see how the current US administration would put New Zealand on the same favorable political plane as Australia. American unhappiness with statements made by the New Zealand prime minister in the context of the recent war in Iraq have evidently translated into an unwillingness in Washington to include New Zealand in an FTA deal. In appendix 1, I briefly discuss how the Australia–New Zealand CER (Closer Economic Relations) Agreement might need to be factored into an Australia-US FTA and other issues relating to possible trade liberalization between the United States and New Zealand.

Objectives of an Australia-US FTA

Political leaders in the two governments and their private-sector counterparts have already commented extensively on the objectives for a bilateral FTA. In the 2003 white paper on foreign and trade policy (DFAT 2003), the Australian government signals the coming FTA as an effort to make its economic relationship with the United States commensurate to their security relationship. The Australian authorities also see clear trade and other economic benefits as flowing from the FTA, provided it offers genuine liberalization of benefit to Australian exporters. Australians have identified priorities in a number of areas where they are globally competitive. As an example of a priority on the industrial side, Australian firms have developed a well-deserved global reputation for producing high-speed catamaran ferries and they see the FTA as an opportunity to gain an exemption from US "Jones Act" limitations on their use in the American market. Priorities in agriculture include access to the highly protected sugar and dairy markets, as well as to the more open but still protected American market for beef.

In a speech delivered in late October 2002,[3] Australia's Trade Minister Mark Vaile cited as objectives *beyond those straightforwardly related to trade liberalization*

- attracting additional American investment to Australia, with consequent positive effects on employment and productivity;

- bringing about greater integration of business in the two markets and thereby enabling new synergies in areas such as research and development, materials sourcing, marketing, and use of information technologies;

- using the FTA to foster "competitive liberalization" through its demonstration effects in the WTO and other trade forums; and

- engendering a broader appreciation of the bilateral alliance and the role of the two countries in underpinning stability and prosperity in East Asia and the Pacific.

More recently, Minister Vaile added that he wants to use the FTA negotiations to discipline the extent to which food aid might be used by the United States to undercut commercial Australian agricultural exports to postwar markets in Iraq and elsewhere ("Vaile Wants Food Aid in FTA Terms," *Australian Financial Review*, April 8, 2003, 5).

---

3. "Australia and the United States: Opening Markets," speech by Vaile to the launch of American Australian Business 2003, Sydney, October 29, 2002.

The FTA negotiation with the United States also enjoys the strong support of the Business Council of Australia,[4] which sees it as enhancing the global competitiveness of Australian companies and the economy, and of the AUSTA Business Group, which set out a long list of its objectives for the FTA in a January 2003 submission (AUSTA 2003b) to the Department of Foreign Affairs and Trade (DFAT). Among other objectives, AUSTA wants to see all barriers to trade and investment removed within 10 years, a legal right to national treatment of investment, mutual recognition of professional qualifications affecting trade in services and in technical standards affecting goods trade, free movement of people, and safeguards on security of access to markets.

In his November 13, 2002, notification to the US Congress of the president's intention to enter into FTA negotiations with Australia, USTR Robert Zoellick provides considerable detail on US objectives for the FTA. On a broad political level, and much like his counterparts in Canberra, Ambassador Zoellick sees a number of objectives beyond the commercial considerations at stake in the agreement. His message makes clear that the FTA is also seen as a tool to enhance cooperation in the World Trade Organization (WTO) and to help to achieve jointly held objectives in a shared agenda. Another cited objective of the FTA is to strengthen the foundation of the security alliance and "facilitate the building of new networks that enhance our Pacific democracies' mutual interests, shared experiences, and promotion of common values so that we can work together more effectively with third countries."[5]

Ambassador Zoellick's notification letters contain nearly five single-spaced pages of detailed trade negotiating objectives for the Australian FTA. Selected examples of American objectives give a flavor of the likely approach of American negotiators. The USTR said he would seek elimination of duties and other charges affecting imports of American goods; the suppression of Australian single-desk export operations for wheat, barley, sugar, and rice; and strengthened cooperation between US and Australian authorities with responsibilities for sanitary and phytosanitary measures. The United States will be seeking to enhance the level of Australia's protection of intellectual property rights[6] and, in certain areas, will

---

4. "BCA Backs Free Trade Talks," letter to the editor from BCA CEO Katie Lahey, *Australian Financial Review*, March 24, 2003.

5. USTR Zoellick's November 13, 2002, letters to Speaker of the House Dennis Hastert and Senator Robert Byrd; see www.ustr.gov/new/fta/australia.htm.

6. USTR (2003a) expresses concern over Australian policies in respect to parallel imports (affecting CDs, books, DVDs, software, and electronic games), copyright piracy issues, a general low priority assigned to intellectual property rights enforcement, and the possibility that Australia may allow "springboarding" by generic pharmaceutical makers, enabling immediate marketing approvals on the expiration of patents held by others.

seek to have Australia apply levels of protection more in line with US law and practices. The USTR promised to pursue a comprehensive approach to market access in Australia for services and explicitly referenced financial services and telecommunications services. On the investment front, Zoellick's letters target "trade-distorting barriers to U.S. investment in Australia, including investment screening" and establish the goal of securing for US investors in Australia "important rights that would be comparable to those that would be available under U.S. legal principles and practice."

The 2003 edition of the USTR *National Trade Estimates* report on barriers to American exports reiterates concerns about aspects of the Pharmaceutical Benefits Scheme and elaborates on those areas where the United States believes Australia is lax in fighting infringement of intellectual property rights.

The timing of the FTA negotiations is felicitous for "fortune-tellers" aiming to predict the eventual content of a bilateral agreement. Considerable additional guidance on the core negotiating objectives of both the United States and Australia can be drawn from the free trade agreement each has recently separately concluded with Singapore. In fact, it seems that much of the discussion in the March and May negotiating sessions was devoted to focusing the attention of the bilateral negotiating groups on aspects of the Singapore texts. Evidently, the negotiators have found such attention to be particularly valuable in the case of the investment and services chapters of the Singapore agreement's texts. Of course, the Singapore texts are not especially instructive with respect to agriculture, one area of the US-Australian negotiation where objectives of the two sides seem certain to come into conflict (at least in the near term).

It could be that the US-Chile FTA provides insight into how Washington will handle the demands of another country with a strong interest in exporting farm products to the American market. A review of the Chilean agreement's provisions for market access in agriculture seems to have both good news and bad news for Australia's aspirations in beef, dairy, and even sugar. For beef, Chile will gain unlimited access to the US market at in-quota tariff rates after just four years. In dairy (cheese, milk powder, condensed milk, and "other" dairy products), Chile will see quantities available to its exporters increase by around 7 percent every year until limitations are fully removed in year 12. In sugar, the year-on-year increase is only 5 percent, but restrictions on quantities are again totally removed in year 12.[7] So the good news is that these sensitive products were on the table and trade will be liberalized. The bad news is that it will take a few years to get there—at least in dairy and sugar. Australians might also object to the side letter on sugar trade that is evidently part of the

---

7. See "U.S. General Notes" and "U.S. Tariff Schedule" (USTR 2003b).

Chilean deal, and may worry over Chilean and American agreement that special "snapback" safeguards are possible in these sectors.

Both the Americans and the Australians profess publicly that everything is on the table in the negotiation and that there are no a priori exceptions. Both sides say their objective is a comprehensive negotiation. "Comprehensive" in this context has to be interpreted to mean that no area is ruled out for negotiation and that requests for policy modifications and liberalization will be entertained and acted on even if a final outcome does not produce immediate free trade across the board. Politics is sure to get in the way on both sides of the Pacific. For example, to be credible Washington will need to find ways to significantly liberalize existing barriers to beef and even dairy imports from Australia. Notwithstanding industry complaints, this can likely be done without genuinely serious consequences for these sectors in the United States.

Consider the situation in the dairy sector. Following Australia's FTA with New Zealand, the Australian dairy industry successfully undertook a series of structural adjustments, the outcome of which has been the focusing of producers and processors on responding solely to market demands. In the global context, it is a "fair trader." In addition, the industry, while efficient, is small compared to other world producers and its likely focus in the US market would be on shipping increased quantities of value-added dairy products (mainly cheese), not the bulk dairy commodities (milk powder and butter) whose increased imports would burden the operation of the American support program for dairy. Seen in context, the ability of the United States to accommodate Australia in dairy seems clear: Australian dairy exports to the United States in 2001 amounted to just $84.3 million, and a fourfold increase in that trade (an amount Australia might reasonably be expected to achieve over the medium term if trade were liberalized) would put total imports from Australia at just over 1.8 percent of the gross value of producer milk receipts in 2001.[8]

Sugar is another matter. US sugar policy has fostered price levels so high that other industries (e.g., corn sweeteners) depend on the maintenance of high sugar prices for their own continued profitability. Actually, it is not at all clear that Australian sugar producers would benefit from enhanced access to the American market—particularly if the United States also liberalizes trade in sugar in the Free Trade Area of the Americas (FTAA) or US-Mercosur (Southern Cone Common Market) contexts. The Australian sugar industry is in a real mess, according to a recent report by the Centre for International Economics (CIE 2002). Though Queensland was once the competitive leader in world sugar markets, the CIE notes, Brazil is now achieving cane-growing costs 30 to 40 percent below Aus-

---

8. $18.3 billion in 2001 (US Department of Agriculture, Federal Milk Order Market Statistics, 2001 Annual Summary [Statistical Bulletin no. 979], table 2, 11).

tralia's. Australian sugar exports could benefit from enlarged quotas at high US prices in the short term (while quotas restricted competitors' access to the American market), but the Australian sugar industry would probably not gain much from US liberalization of the market over the long term unless it took drastic steps to enhance its productivity.

Australian access to the US market for fast ferries is also problematic, both because of the general political difficulty in dealing with maritime questions and (significantly) because of the peculiar way in which the Jones Act restrictions are sheltered in the WTO.[9] That said, the Jones Act might not be as serious a barrier as one would think. Australian firms have reportedly negotiated special joint venture construction and leasing arrangements that get around these restrictions to some extent. In addition, the Jones Act applies only to cabotage trade; Australian fast ferries thus can still be sold to Americans for use in transport between US and non-US destinations.

In the same vein, Australia will certainly resist anticipated US demands for radical changes in single-desk export operations, restrictions in audiovisual services, and the Pharmaceutical Benefits Scheme. But as with the anticipated situation in US agriculture, Canberra's resistance does not mean that it would be impossible to meaningfully address specific problem areas raised by the United States. Canberra might even want to use the FTA negotiation as an excuse for change in areas like single desk (which has been criticized inside Australia as anticompetitive and which was singled out as a problem for the sugar industry in the CIE report referred to above).

Notwithstanding the obviously warm bilateral relations of the post-Iraq war period, it seems clear that neither the United States nor Australia could be expected to be satisfied with a "trophy" agreement without a credible free trade outcome. This might not be an agreement to bring about completely free trade overnight,[10] but both governments share the core objective of making the coverage of this FTA as comprehensive as possible.

Potential Trade and Investment Effects of an FTA

For the United States, an Australia-US FTA clearly does not have an economic significance in the same league as the North American Free Trade

---

9. See paragraph 3 of the General Agreement on Tariffs and Trade (1994), www.wto.org/english/docs_e/legal_e/legal.htm.

10. In part because of their federal nature, neither the American nor the Australian internal markets can be said to be completely free of barriers to trade. Whether we are concerned with insurance regulation, product standards, labeling requirements, or professional qualifications, substantial barriers exist inside both countries.

Agreement or the current FTAA exercise in the Western Hemisphere. The impact of an agreement will be proportionately much more important for Australia. Considerably less than 2 percent of total American exports are destined for Australia, compared to roughly 11 percent of total Australian exports destined for the United States. Still, the numbers are large enough to make the negotiation interesting for both sides. Two-way merchandise trade exceeded $20.8 billion in 2002 (Australia recorded a deficit in goods trade of $7 billion for the year).[11]

It is very hard to come by up-to-date data on services trade that have sufficient detail to be significant for this exercise. Against this background, in 2002, bilateral services trade reached nearly $6.32 billion, with annual growth in Australia's services exports to America rising much faster than imports of services from the United States.[12] Clearly, there is already a certain amount of economic integration of the two markets. Sales of services in Australia by majority US-owned affiliates totaled $15.1 billion in 2000, while sales of services in the United States by majority Australian-owned firms totaled $8.7 billion. Total sales (goods, services, and investment income) of US affiliates in Australia amounted to $56.6 billion in 2000, with Australian affiliates in the United States recording total sales of $31.9 billion.[13] The United States is the largest recipient of Australian investment, at $70.4 billion, and Australia's largest source of investment, at $141.5 billion (DFAT 2003, 89).

Discussion in Australia of the possible economic effects of an FTA with the United States centers on three studies, two of which produced reports in mid-2001 and were undertaken at the request of DFAT (CIE 2001; AASC 2001); the third study, published in February 2003, was prepared for the Australian Rural Industries Research and Development Corporation (ACIL 2003). In addition to the reports themselves, the CIE in March 2003 issued a reaction to the ACIL report (Stoeckel and Davis 2003).

The original CIE study (2001) is the source for most of the positive economic claims made for an FTA by DFAT, AUSTA, and other proponents of an agreement with the United States. In their modeling of possible outcomes, CIE researchers made use of both the APG-Cubed model (i.e., the G-Cubed [Asia Pacific] model) and the GTAP (Global Trade Analysis Proj-

---

11. Australian Bureau of Statistics Report 5422 (December quarter, 2002). In this chapter, certain statistics emanate from US sources and others from Australian sources. For consistency, all values are shown in US dollars. The exchange rate used is that for late April 2003, reported as A$1.66 = US$1.00.

12. Statistics from the Department of Foreign Affairs and Trade (DFAT), submission by the Department of Foreign Affairs and Trade to the Senate Foreign Affairs, Defence and Trade Committee Inquiry into the General Agreement on Trade in Services and Australia-US Free Trade Agreement, Canberra, April 11, 2003, table B-1, 62.

13. US Department of Commerce, Bureau of Economic Analysis, *Survey of Current Business*, December 2002; available at www.bea.doc.gov/bea/pub/1202cont.htm.

ect) model. The CIE explains that both models were used in order to exploit the advantages of each: the APG-Cubed model provided greater information on financial flows, the timing of effects, and the macro economy; the GTAP model provided greater sector and country detail. The CIE, in its study, assumed complete removal of all identified barriers to trade between the United States and Australia. Calculations were also done on the basis of a 50 percent removal of barriers and a 25 percent removal of barriers, with the models yielding roughly proportional results in economic benefit to the participants. In all of the scenarios studied by the CIE, both the United States and Australia gained through the negotiation and implementation of an FTA. The CIE also concluded that the FTA would create more trade than it would divert and that there would be a positive economic impact on third countries (particularly for New Zealand).

Some of the figures regularly quoted by the Commonwealth government and attributed to the CIE study are:

- net economic welfare gains over 20 years of about $20.1 billion, shared evenly between the two countries;

- a 4 percent (about $2 billion) increase in Australian GDP by 2010, with a cumulative benefit over 20 years of about $15.5 billion;

- a 0.8 percent overall rise in Australian exports by 2006 (with a potentially greater than 350 percent increase in dairy exports);[14] and

- enhanced investment flows into key Australian economic sectors, such as mining and agriculture. (DFAT 2003, 91)

Central to a large proportion of the economic gains found in the CIE report are researchers' assumptions with respect to the impact of services trade liberalization. With such a large percentage of the two countries' economies now accounted for by services, it seems reasonable to assume that the removal of barriers to trade in services through the FTA would produce cost reductions contributing to economic welfare. In its study, the CIE notes the many difficulties associated with quantifying the impact of services liberalization. Research in the area to date is fairly slim, and the CIE relied primarily on estimates of the costs of trade barriers produced by staff members in various studies done at the Australian Productivity Commission. For example, these studies estimated the cost (in terms of price impact) of barriers in the Australian banking sector at 9.3 percent, and at 0.57 percent in the Australian retailing and wholesale sectors. Estimates of the price impact on professional engineering services in the

---

14. In its discussion of the sectoral changes found in the modeling, the CIE is careful to point out that certain very large percentage gains (e.g., in dairy and sugar for Australia) rise from very low bases.

United States were 3.6 percent and 2.26 percent for the American retail and wholesale sectors (cited in CIE 2001).[15] Overall, the CIE researchers appear to have taken a conservative approach—for example, they limited Australia's impact on the US services market to 1/20th of what could be the potential effect of Australia's entry (because Australia's GDP is only about 1/20th of the US GDP). Globally, (for the FTA) CIE seems to have been conservative as well, estimating the cost reduction to the economy as a result of assumed full liberalization of services trade at only 0.35 percent (CIE 2001, 58–68).

ACIL (2003) takes a different approach, and ANU's Professor Garnaut argues that the "uplift" in services productivity (the 0.35 percent) found by the CIE should be discounted because it arises out of an unrealistic assumption that all barriers to services trade would be removed by an FTA (Garnaut 2003a).[16] How services trade is treated is therefore very important, but nobody who has looked at the potential FTA so far seems to have a firm grip on what would realistically happen to trade patterns and efficiency gains in particular services sectors. This important gap in the research is a problem for the analysis of the Australia-US FTA.

As noted earlier, the CIE modeling was done on the basis of the total removal of all identified trade barriers. Under these assumptions, it is not surprising that the sectors shown by CIE as deriving the greatest benefits from the FTA are dairy and sugar. Other sectors forecast as likely to benefit from reasonably large increases in exports to the United States include ferrous metal products and motor vehicles and parts. For the United States, CIE sees the biggest potential gains in exports of motor vehicles and parts and metal products, with smaller gains for beverages and wood and paper products (CIE 2001, tables 4.5 and 4.6).

The 2001 study prepared by the Australia APEC Study Centre at Monash University (AASC 2001; hereafter referred to as "the Monash study") takes a far less quantitative approach to examining the possible benefits to Australia of an FTA; in fact, for its statements on quantifiable economic benefits it relies heavily on the slightly earlier CIE study's findings. The Monash study devotes most of its commentary to the anticipated qualitative benefits to the Australian economy over the longer term as a result of its integration with the much larger American economy. For example, the study expects that an FTA would foster greater competitiveness in the Australian economy by influencing businesses' adaptation to new information and communication technologies, by shaping business culture, and by encouraging best practices in key aspects of economic activity.

---

15. These figures were referred to on p. 61 (retail/wholesale) and p. 62 (professional engineering) of the CIE report. They refer back to Kalirajan (2000) and Nguyen-Hong (2000), respectively.

16. Garnaut (2003a) notes that, at the very least, it is hardly likely that Canberra would anytime soon remove ownership restrictions affecting Telstra and major Australian banks.

The Monash study also predicts important positive inward investment effects for Australia as a result of the FTA's contribution to improved conditions for investors and its endorsement of Australia's long-term prospects as a place for American firms to do business. Among the important qualitative benefits to Australia identified by the Monash study are FTA-inspired institutional arrangements intended to resolve problems relating to business visas, technical standards, recognition of professional qualifications, and other regulatory issues (AASC 2001, xii). The Monash researchers are right, I think, when they say that such issues, while hardly sexy, can often be serious impediments to the conduct of business across frontiers.

Coincidentally, the 2003 ACIL study began making the rounds just as those who criticize the FTA for its projected negative impact on Australia's regional and security interests were intensifying their public attacks. The ACIL report faults the "robustness" of the CIE study, finds a likely negative impact of an FTA on Australian farmers, and even postulates that complete bilateral free trade by 2010 would be "slightly detrimental" to the Australian economy. The ACIL analysis completely discounts CIE's service sector benefits analysis and assumes that the conclusion of an FTA with the United States "could undermine Australia's participation in the WTO and its multilateral negotiations" and "have a deleterious effect on the prospects for advancing other forms of trade liberalisation" (ACIL 2003, vi). ACIL states that its GTAP-type modeling was "arguably more standard" than that employed in 2001 by the CIE (ACIL 2003, 39).

The ACIL report, with its criticism of the CIE's approach, has drawn a swift and strongly argued reaction from the CIE, which calls ACIL's analysis flawed and points out that ACIL's conclusions contradict its own analysis (Stoeckel and Davis 2003). Aside from taking issue with ACIL's misrepresentations of the CIE's earlier work and discussing the errors in ACIL's treatment of trade diversion effects, the CIE criticizes ACIL for using in its modeling parameters for the elasticity of Australian export demand that are unresponsive to changes in sales. The CIE points out that the "Armington elasticities" (the degree of substitutability between locally sourced and imported products) used by ACIL in its modeling were too low and should have been doubled (as was done in the CIE study and as is recommended by the GTAP model's developers). The CIE argues that if ACIL had "corrected" the elasticities used, its analysis of the FTA's economic impact would have approximated the findings of the CIE study (Stoeckel and Davis 2003, 5).

In the context of this FTA, I think ACIL might be faulted for its presumption that free trade with the United States would lead to no productivity increases in Australia's services sector (ACIL suggests that such increases are a matter of opinion). ACIL also appears to start with a strong bias in its report. In a statement that seems to reveal much about ACIL's mind-set going in, the report categorically concludes that "bilateral free trade cannot on first principles be given a clean bill of health. The merits of a bilateral deal are difficult to estimate with confidence, but they will always hurt some trading partners and benefit others" (ACIL 2003, 48).

The ACIL study is likely to be relied on by those who are naturally critical of the FTA for other reasons and who seek to bolster their claims with studies that support their own position; however, it is unlikely to displace the CIE study as the more generally accepted basis on which to judge the probable economic effects of a bilateral FTA. There is some argument with the CIE's initial assumptions (in particular, whether they are realistic), but overall the study appears well reasoned and documented and the CIE criticism of the ACIL methodology seems justifiable.

The first US-based study of the potential trade and investment effects of a bilateral Australia-US free trade agreement seems to be John Gilbert's CGE simulation of US bilateral FTAs prepared for the conference that occasioned this volume (Gilbert 2003). The US International Trade Commission (USITC) also has a study under way of the potential impact of the FTA on United States interests, but the USITC report will be a confidential document available only to American negotiators.

Gilbert's study does not include an analysis of the impact of trade in services liberalization, and it addresses only liberalization through removal of tariffs affecting trade in goods. Even on this basis, Gilbert finds small welfare gains for both the United States (0.01 percent of GDP) and Australia (0.02 percent of GDP), which he ascribes to an expected improvement in both countries' terms of trade vis-à-vis nonmembers (Gilbert 2003, 9).

Implications of an FTA for Trade (and Other) Relations with Third Countries

There are really three issues worth discussing in this section of the chapter: (1) What could be the impact of the FTA on Australian (and to a lesser extent US) political, security, and trade interests with East Asian countries? (2) Should we expect the proposed FTA to produce important trade diversion effects? And (3) Would the negotiation of an FTA undermine the prospects for a successful WTO Doha Round?

Relations with Third Countries

In Australia, by far the greatest heat has been generated by the debate on the third of the issues raised above. Early architects of Australian policy regarding East Asia have argued that the negotiation of an FTA between Australia and the United States would be a disaster on a number of fronts. Probably the most vocal spokesman for this viewpoint is Ross Garnaut, who has stated categorically that he is opposed to the free trade agreement with the United States "amongst other things, because it is not free trade, and because it would be antithetic to continued progress towards free trade" (Garnaut 2003a, 26). Most recently, his criticism of the FTA has focused on what he believes will be the very damaging effects on trade of the American approach to rules of origin in preferential trading arrangements (Garnaut 2003b, 13). As noted above, Garnaut also doubts that there would be real benefit to Australia from an FTA—not because he disagrees with the CIE's economic analysis, but because he challenges the DFAT assumptions on which the CIE was obliged to base its analysis.

Although he is critical of the FTA on a number of counts, Garnaut's main concern seems to stem from the belief that governments in Australia's all-important East Asian markets will react to a bilateral agreement with the United States by reappraising their historical resistance to preferential trading arrangements. Having argued successfully in favor of multilateralism in trade relations and against regionalism, Australia has so far been able to avoid a situation in which these East Asian markets see it as in their interests to create their own preferential arrangement that could exclude Australia. Garnaut acknowledges that China and the ASEAN (Association of Southeast Asian Nations) countries announced in 2002 that they would seek to enter a free trade agreement, but he argues that negotiation of such an agreement "will not be a straightforward matter. The presence of trade diversion in an Australia-United States free trade agreement against East Asian countries would generate reactions that increase the probability of it happening" (Garnaut 2003a, 16). Garnaut believes that the FTA would likely create significant trade diversion, that preference margins post-FTA would disadvantage East Asian exporters, and that the global significance of the Australia-US agreement would (probably) be enough to move East Asia to create its own regional framework at the expense of Australia.

In fairness, Garnaut opposes the FTA on other counts as well, including on the theory that it would actually *worsen* relationships with the United States. First, as noted earlier, he takes issue with the assumptions underlying the economic analysis of the CIE and expresses doubt that the deal would bring real benefit to Australia. Second, he is among those who believe that the negotiation of an FTA will distract Canberra and Washington from the important WTO work in Geneva and decrease the prospects for a successful Doha Round. Third, he sees this as a dangerous time to risk souring the bilateral US-Australia alliance by placing contentious trade issues on the table. Garnaut's views are echoed by other commentators at the Australian National University.

Not surprisingly, Garnaut is on a more or less permanent collision course with Alan Oxley, a principal author of the Monash study, head of the AUSTA Business Group supporting an FTA, and Australia's former ambassador to the General Agreement on Tariffs and Trade (GATT) in Geneva. Oxley's Monash study accepts and endorses the CIE findings in respect of trade diversion from an FTA[17] and stakes out a position (already in 2001) in opposition to Garnaut's view on the East Asian dynamic:

> If the suggestion is that Australia needs to consider any proposal for strengthening its relationship with the United States, such as negotiating an FTA, in the light of its possible impact on relations with countries in East Asia, that is an altogether different proposition. Other countries in the region do not feel so constrained (Singapore is negotiating an FTA with the United States and South Korea is studying the idea). And given that the strengthening of the relationship with the US is important to Australia's economic and political interests, to suggest that actions to strengthen ties should not be pursued for their own merit must surely be to subsume Australia's national interest to that of another country's. (AASC 2001, 90)

In its recent submission to the Australian Senate, the AUSTA Business Group continues this line of reasoning, stating that "there is no evidence China considers an Australian/US Free Trade Agreement will chill Australian-China economic relations" (AUSTA 2003a). Not everyone gets the same impression, however. An article appearing in *The Australian* newspaper cited "apparent concerns in China that the free trade agreement being negotiated between Australia and the US is a signal that Canberra is placing less emphasis on its Asian trading partners" ("Beijing Vents Fury over Trade Plan Snub," March 26, 2003, 12). These "apparent concerns" were reportedly recounted by Labour's shadow minister for trade, Craig Emerson, after his return from a former visit to China. Emerson and his staff declined to elaborate when I contacted his office for comment.

What about the impact of the Australia-US FTA on the Asia Pacific Economic Cooperation group (APEC)? It seems doubtful there would be much effect either positively or negatively, as APEC seems to have lost Australian policymakers' attention as a forum for trade liberalization. Most APEC trade-related discussions these days seem either to be related to backstopping work in the WTO (e.g., APEC TEL workshops on WTO telecommunications services negotiations) or focused on regional issues, such as how to deal with the need for enhanced security requirements for containers and the like.

Trade Diversion

The CIE study found a number of cases in which an FTA between the United States and Australia could be expected to produce trade diversion, but also concluded that trade creation for Australia, the United States, and the world as a whole would outweigh the trade diversion. For example, CIE found increased American automotive exports to Australia displac-

---

17. The CIE found there would be some trade diversion but that it would be outweighed by global trade creation due to the FTA.

ing a considerable value of auto exports from Japan and Europe and increased Australian sugar and dairy exports to the United States displacing Latin American and European products. But the modeling also shows the FTA leading to considerable increases in these regions' exports of other goods to the United States. In terms of net trade creation, the CIE estimated an increase in net imports to Australia of $675 million and an increase in net US imports of $1.1 billion (CIE 2001, 42–44).

It should be pointed out that Garnaut does not accept the CIE conclusions regarding trade creation and trade diversion. He argues that "it would be possible for the total value of world trade to expand even if there were substantial trade diversion and no trade creation at all" (Garnaut 2003a, 9).

In marked contrast to the CIE study, the ACIL study asserts that one reason the proposed FTA would negatively affect Australia is "the predominance of trade diversion, especially from Asia, that such an agreement would create" (ACIL 2003, 37). As the CIE points out in its reaction to the ACIL report, no economic modeling results are offered by ACIL to explain this statement. In fact, ACIL's only basis for such a position seems to be its acceptance of the likelihood of trade diversion as articulated separately by Garnaut (ACIL 2003, 35). The CIE response to ACIL's claim makes for good reading as the authors provide a step-by-step tutorial on why ACIL's focus on potential effects in Australian export markets is misplaced (Stoeckel and Davis 2003, 10–11).

In general, I have found little reason to criticize the CIE study; however, the modeling results in respect to trade diversion produce some results that seem either counterintuitive or at odds with other CIE studies. For example, Australia is forecast to greatly expand sugar exports to the United States largely at the expense of Latin American sugar exporters, yet in its own separate study of the sugar sector in Australia (CIE 2002), the CIE notes the huge cost advantage now enjoyed by Brazil (also negotiating an FTA with the United States). Similarly, it is hard to believe that US exports to Australia of automotive vehicles and parts would actually rise more than $500 million at the expense of Japanese and European manufacturers.

WTO Negotiations and Impact on the Doha Round

Free trade agreements are not popular among certain "multilateralists" in the trade community. WTO Director-General Supachai Panitchpakdi and many academics have pointed out that the worrying tendency to negotiate FTAs has accelerated significantly in recent years; and in public remarks he has made since taking office, Supachai has been critical of FTAs as undercutting the Doha Round. A frequently voiced criticism is that FTA negotiations divert trade officials from the more important job at hand—the negotiation of multilateral trade liberalization. This view enjoys considerable support in some Australian circles.

ACIL's report strongly supports the multilateral negotiations under way in Geneva in the context of the WTO Doha Round. (Who in this debate does not?) ACIL's modeling, not surprisingly, finds full multilateral trade liberalization creating significantly greater economic benefits for Australia than a bilateral FTA or unilateral Australian liberalization. ACIL goes on from here to strongly criticize the planned FTA on the grounds that it would be a distraction, wastefully consuming officials' time and government interest. Worse still (and this is really curious), ACIL suggests that "[t]he US, for example, might feel it had done enough if it had moved somewhat to meet Australia's demands in the FTA context and might be less interested in meeting those demands in the WTO context" (ACIL 2003, vii). ACIL also sees a potential problem if Australia agreed to pursue an FTA with the United States that excluded agriculture, pointing out that this decision might undermine the credibility of Australia's position on agriculture in the WTO.

These are not plausible concerns in my opinion and, in fact, fly in the face of recent Australian government policy statements. DFAT's recent white paper makes explicit that agriculture has to be dealt with in the FTA with the United States. That same document makes clear that the Commonwealth sees the WTO Round as its best hope for major trade gains and that liberalization of agricultural markets is a priority for the country in the multilateral negotiations (DFAT 2003, 53).

In everything it has said publicly on the subject, the government of Australia, like the US government, clearly sees the negotiation of an FTA as a complement to the multilateral negotiations of the WTO. Both Washington and Canberra have used the term "competitive liberalization" to explain how the demonstration effect of an FTA could help to achieve objectives in the WTO. On this point, I cannot help but note that one of the largest FTAs, NAFTA, was concluded at a critical stage of the Uruguay Round negotiations; indeed, many commentators have credited the NAFTA negotiation with helping to push the Uruguay Round toward a successful conclusion.

Conclusions

This negotiation has only just started. It's going to be an interesting exercise, particularly in light of the political-level decision to accelerate the timetable for concluding the talks. Chief negotiators Ralph Ives and Stephen Deady and their teams have their work cut out for them. Notwithstanding the extremely friendly atmosphere that characterized the start of negotiations in Canberra in March, there are certain to be difficult discussions in the months to come.

Costs to Australia's Regional Relationships

Is Australia likely to do irreparable harm to its important political and economic relations with East Asia if it concludes an FTA with the United States? That seems very doubtful. For starters, there are probably only a very limited number of goods and services over which US and East Asian exporters are likely to be competing head-to-head in the Australian market, so the introduction by Australia of preferences favoring US suppliers is unlikely to divert importers away from Asian and toward American suppliers. The CIE study (2001) identified autos as an area where Japan could lose out to the Americans in a post-FTA world, but my observation is that there are many incentives for Japanese firms to both produce in, and export to, the Australian market. At the same time, the incentive to Ford and GM to ship large numbers of US-produced right-hand-drive vehicles to Australia is not that clear, given their important existing investments in Australian manufacturing operations, which have now been integrated into their global production plans. The new Pontiac GTO is a rebranded Holden Monaro, produced in Australia for worldwide markets.

Another reason to doubt the potential East Asian backlash predicted by some is the East Asian history of choosing deals with clear economic benefits when faced with a choice of concluding either a politically or an economically motivated trade deal. China recently faced such a choice when negotiating a long-term gas supply contract. A political choice favoring regionalism would have given the prize to Indonesia, but China chose Australia as its partner because the economics outweighed the politics.

Finally, the negotiation of an FTA with the United States is no more a sign of Australia disengaging from East Asia than it is of Australia abandoning multilateralism for bilateralism. Australia has negotiated FTAs with Singapore and Thailand. A bilateral dialogue with Japan on closer economic relations has been under way for some time, and Canberra and Beijing are in the early stages of a similar discussion.

I just don't see the big risk.

Costs to the Multilateral Trade Negotiations

What about the impact of the FTA negotiations on the WTO process? Well, where are the Doha Round negotiations in the wake of the collapse of the Cancun Ministerial? Anyone reasonably familiar with the Geneva negotiations and their prospects would say that there is currently no risk that the FTA negotiations are going to get in the way of progress in Geneva. The Geneva negotiations have slowed on their own merits. Quite predictably, the talks are stalled, awaiting one of those occasional political crises in the GATT/WTO that inspire everyone with the need to compromise and move on. Through periodic surveys of experts, the Adelaide-based Institute for International Business, Economics and Law has been collecting some fairly reliable information on attitudes to the WTO talks in Geneva and in key capitals. What the polls[18] have shown is that everyone continues to support the WTO talks as the biggest game in town, almost nobody thinks the Doha Round will finish on schedule, and most trained observers of the WTO are not worried about this scenario because it is "normal" for a multilateral trade negotiation. In the words of a good friend, "We've all seen this movie before." The professionals understand that like the war in Iraq, the Doha Round will take as long as it takes.

The round will finish eventually and it will finish successfully, because finishing successfully is important to all of the WTO's members. There is no substitute for the global system, and it will take a long time before the trend toward regional trade agreements takes (most of) us away from the belief in the primacy of the multilateral system—if for no other reason than only the WTO talks can credibly address the need to reform global trade in agriculture. This reform is important for the United States, Australia, and the Cairns Group. It is also, and perhaps more significantly, an objective that represents the only hope for many least-developed countries to trade their way out of poverty.

Director-General Supachai and his deputies at the WTO will make speeches about the threat to the organization posed by regionalism while USTR Zoellick and Trade Minister Vaile speak of their competitive liberalization efforts in the FTAs they are negotiating. Conventional wisdom in Geneva ties progress in the GATT/WTO multilateral sphere to successive EU enlargements. It seems to me that it's just as easy to accept that the competitive liberalization of non-EU preferential agreements could also contribute positively to the multilateral negotiating dynamic.

Economic Benefits of a Free Trade Agreement

This chapter has looked briefly at the studies done in Australia concerned with the potential economic benefits of an FTA, and I think there are clearly more reasons to side with the CIE analysis (2001) than with the ACIL report (2003). DFAT might have given the CIE some unrealistic assumptions to work from, but those assumptions are not impossible. For its part, ACIL clearly started with a big chip on the shoulder against any FTA and that attitude probably poisoned the outcome. Gilbert's study (2003) might not see big gains for either side (although he does not treat

---

18. See the Global Trade Opinion Polls at www.iibel.adelaide.edu.au/hot/.

services, which figured so importantly in the CIE study), but it also does not find the FTA affecting either country negatively.

Leaving aside the studies, it is clear that the majority of those in the business community in both countries are strongly supportive of an FTA. Companies know there are gains to be made in enhanced movement of personnel, elimination of duplicate product testing, potential rationalization of existing labeling requirements, and a more secure environment for investment and movement of capital. FTAs are also valuable because they gradually implement institutional mechanisms that can be important tools for resolving business problems or discussing additional trade liberalization. In addition, there is a good chance that difficult problems and barriers will be significantly modified if not eliminated. There really do not appear to be any important economic downsides to this agreement, given that the two countries are already relatively open to each other in most key sectors.

Australia asked for this negotiation. In fact, Australia started asking for this negotiation quite some time back. Ambassador Zoellick has long believed that it is in the interests of both countries to conclude an FTA. The recent war in Iraq complicated public debate on the issue, at least in Australia. Some commentators openly expressed the view that Australia would be given economic benefits through the FTA as a dividend of the country's participation in the coalition. I have sought to dissuade people from perpetuating this position. I have made the point that even if the Bush administration wants to reward Australia in this way, that wish won't carry much water with those facing a loss of protection in their market and a consequent reduction in profitability. Sensitive political issues will come up on Capitol Hill, and members of Congress are going to support an FTA only if they believe it's a good deal for the United States. Of course, Canberra is also committed to the negotiation of a good deal.

There are plenty of indications that the Australia-US FTA can be a successfully negotiated, economically meaningful agreement of benefit to both countries. The two governments are committed to pursuing a "large" agreement in a relatively short time frame. Reliable economic studies support the prospect of mutual gains. And in both countries, the mainstream business community appears strongly supportive of the FTA and eager to get on with an integration process. In Australia, early skepticism over the benefits of an FTA seems to be changing in favor of broader support. Reportedly, 56 percent of respondents to a March 2003 poll said they would support an FTA, against only 22 percent opposed to a deal.[19]

Of course, that's not all there is to the story. In this case, there will be considerable opposition to a "full-scope" FTA from vested interests in both countries, and some will continue to argue against an FTA on more political

---

19. Hawker Briton UMR research poll, carried out March 28–30, 2003, for political lobbyists and reported in "Vaile Wants Food Aid in FTA Terms," *Australian Financial Review*, April 8, 2003.

grounds. All of these factors will keep things interesting for the negotiators and the newspapers. As of this writing, the question is not whether a good deal can be done, but rather whether it can be done by the end of 2003.

References

ACIL Consulting. 2003. *A Bridge Too Far? An Australian Agricultural Perspective on the Australia/United States Free Trade Area Idea.* Canberra: ACIL Consulting, www.rirdc.gov.au/reports/GLC/ACIL-ABridgeTooFar.pdf (February).

AASC (Australia APEC Study Centre). 2001. *An Australia-USA Free Trade Agreement: Issues and Implications.* Melbourne: Monash University. www.apec.org.au/docs/usfta.pdf (August).

Australia United States Free Trade Agreement Business Group (AUSTA). 2003a. AUSTA Submission to the Australian Senate. www.austa.net (March).

Australia United States Free Trade Agreement Business Group (AUSTA). 2003b. AUSTA Submission to the Department of Foreign Affairs and Trade. International Trade Strategies. www.austa.net (January).

CIE (Centre for International Economics). 2001. *Economic Impacts of an Australia-United States Free Trade Area.* Canberra: Centre for International Economics. www.intecon.com.au/reports_list.htm (June)

CIE (Centre for International Economics). 2002. *Cleaning Up the Act: The Impacts of Changes to the Sugar Industry Act 1999.* Canberra: Centre for International Economics. www.intecon.com.au/reports_list.htm (December).

Department of Foreign Affairs and Trade, Australia (DFAT). 1997. *Closer Economic Relations: Background Guide to the Australia-New Zealand Economic Relationship.* Canberra: Government of Australia.

Department of Foreign Affairs and Trade, Australia (DFAT). 2003. *Advancing the National Interest: Australia's Foreign and Trade Policy White Paper.* Canberra: Government of Australia. www.dfat.gov.au/ani (February).

Garnaut, Ross. 2003a. Australian Security and Free Trade with America. Paper presented at the conference on US and Australian Free Trade Agreement: National Interest or Vested Interest, sponsored by the Australian Business Economists, Sydney (February 27).

Garnaut, Ross. 2003b. Requiem for Uldorama: A Plain but Useful Life. Paper presented at the IIBE&L Trade Conference on New Horizons in International Trade, Adelaide (June 5).

Gilbert, John. 2003. CGE Simulations of US Bilateral Free Trade Agreements. Background paper prepared for the conference Free Trade Agreements and US Trade Policy, sponsored by the Institute for International Economics, Washington (May 7–8).

Kalirajan, K. 2000. Restrictions on Trade in Distribution Services. *Productivity Commission Staff Research Paper.* Canberra: AusInfo (August).

Nguyen-Hong, D. 2000. Restrictions on Trade in Professional Services. *Productivity Commission Staff Research Paper.* Canberra: AusInfo (August).

Stoeckel, Andrew, and Lee Davis. 2003. *Australia-United States Free Trade Agreement: Comments on the ACIL Report.* Canberra: Centre for International Economics. www.intecon.com.au/reports_list.htm (March).

US Trade Representative, Office of (USTR). 2003a. *National Trade Estimates Report on Foreign Trade Barriers.* www.ustr.gov/reports/nte/2003/index.htm.

US Trade Representative, Office of (USTR). 2003b. *United States-Chile Free Trade Agreement.* www.ustr.gov/new/fta/Chile/final/index.htm (June 6).

US Trade Representative, Office of (USTR). 2003c. *United States-Singapore Free Trade Agreement.* www.ustr.gov/new/fta/Singapore/final/index.htm (May 6).

Appendix 5.1
Australia–New Zealand Closer Economic Relations (CER) and Issues Relating to New Zealand in an FTA with the United States

At the outset of this chapter, I noted that I believed the chances for a New Zealand–US FTA were relatively remote and therefore planned to concentrate on a strictly bilateral Australia-US FTA. Nevertheless, there are some issues worth reviewing, if only briefly.

CER entered into force in 1983 and has been hugely successful in integrating the economies of Australia and New Zealand.[20] Through three general reviews of CER's operation, it was progressively widened and deepened. Apart from eliminating tariffs and quantitative restrictions on trade in goods and extensively liberalizing trade in services, CER replaced the use of antidumping actions with competition policy instruments and has moved far into "domestic" policy measures in other areas as well. CER embodies agreements on industry assistance, technical barriers to trade, and harmonization of regulatory barriers to trade, such as the setting of food safety standards. CER has by all accounts been a huge success that has linked the two partners so closely that it is not unusual in 2003 to read serious discussion of monetary union.

The extent to which New Zealand exporters might benefit *directly* (through CER) from an Australia-US Free Trade Agreement is hard to assess in the absence of knowing what rules of origin would apply in the new FTA. CER origin rules specify that in order for merchandise trade to qualify for free movement, the last process of manufacturing and at least 50 percent of the value of the product should be in expenditures associated with materials, labor and factory overheads, or inner containers originating in the area. In the case of the US FTA with Singapore, origin rules go on for pages and appear complex. However, apart from the numerous product-specific rules of origin, the United States seems to have settled basically on an approach that requires either that the good be "wholly obtained or produced entirely in the territory" of Singapore or that it undergo such additional processing in Singapore as to bring about a "change in tariff classification" of the product in question (USTR 2003c, chapter 3).[21] On the face of it, the application by the United States to Australia of Singapore's FTA origin rules could complicate the operation of CER, given the integration of the trans-Tasman economies. It would seem that about the only New Zealand–origin goods that would make it to the United States under the FTA would be those further processed in Aus-

---

20. Background information on the CER is summarized from DFAT (1997).

21. To be considered wholly obtained or produced entirely in Singapore, less than 10 percent of the adjusted value of the good must be from non-Singapore sources.

tralia enough to undergo a change in tariff classification. Many products would likely fail the 90 percent plus content test of the Singapore-US deal. Whether Australian industries and the negotiators in Canberra would be happy with such a scenario is not known, but it is likely to be an interesting and complicated aspect of the negotiations, given the CER context.

In the main body of the chapter, I briefly noted that the CIE study (2001) had found *indirect* benefits to New Zealand of an FTA between Australia and the United States. These arise in part because, as the Australian economy expands as a result of the positive impact of the FTA, New Zealand benefits from increased demand in the Australian market. To the extent that the Australia-US FTA liberalized dairy trade, New Zealand would gain there as well, mainly because it would pick up dairy sales in Japan and elsewhere as Australian dairy exporters diverted some portion of exports to a more profitable American market (CIE 2001, 26). It should also be noted that Gilbert's study (2003) finds a welfare loss for New Zealand in the case of a US-Australia FTA owing to a deterioration in New Zealand's terms of trade.

Notwithstanding the letter from Senator Grassley and his colleagues, it is unlikely that the United States will soon enter into free trade agreement negotiations with New Zealand or that Washington would negotiate a CER-wide FTA with both Canberra and Wellington simultaneously. I am assuming that New Zealand's continued policy with respect to the visits of nuclear-powered and -armed ships and the Clark government's statements made during the war in Iraq will stand in the way of the American administration's willingness to put trade relations with New Zealand on the same footing as those with Australia. This may be good news for Australia, not only because its exporters will not have to compete directly in the US market with New Zealanders but also because it could be more difficult for the United States to liberalize certain agricultural restrictions if it had to contend with imports from both countries. New Zealand creates no difficulties in the sugar sector but it is an important exporter of both beef and dairy products. Over the longer term, an inevitably sequenced approach might actually work to New Zealand's benefit if, through a good experience with increased imports from Australia, American agricultural interests come to believe that they could also live with more beef and cheese from New Zealand.

6

US Free Trade Agreements with ASEAN

DEAN A. DeROSA

After two years of negotiations, in early 2003 the United States successfully concluded a free trade agreement with Singapore. Following on US free trade agreements with only five countries previously—Canada, Mexico, Israel, Jordan, and Chile—the agreement with Singapore is the first comprehensive US bilateral free trade agreement with an Asian country, and it is widely regarded as a possible prototype for US free trade agreements with additional US trading partners in the Asia Pacific region. In this connection—and in a vein similar to the United States's Enterprise for America Initiative launched in 1990 that led to negotiation of NAFTA and, most recently, the US-Chile FTA—in November 2002 the United States announced the Enterprise for ASEAN Initiative (EAI). This initiative provides a road map for members of the Association of Southeast Asian Nations (ASEAN), in addition to Singapore,[1] to pursue a free trade agreement with the United States.[2] It requires an ASEAN country interested in pursuing a free trade agreement with the United States to be a member of the World Trade Organization. It also requires the country

---

Dean A. DeRosa is a visiting fellow at the Institute for International Economics.

1. The negotiations of the US-Singapore FTA began before November 2002—that is, the US-Singapore FTA was negotiated outside the EAI.

2. Ten countries presently make up ASEAN: Brunei, Cambodia, Indonesia, Laos, Malaysia, Myanmar, the Philippines, Singapore, Thailand, and Vietnam. Papua New Guinea is an associate member of the group.

to sign a trade and investment facilitation agreement (TIFA) with the United States, under which senior US and partner country officials form a joint council to identify and discuss ways to eliminate regulatory barriers to trade and foreign investment between the two countries, as a precursor to negotiations of a bilateral FTA.[3]

The ASEAN countries form a diverse but economically (and politically) important bloc of 10 developing Asian countries, led principally by Singapore and the so-called ASEAN-4: Indonesia, Malaysia, the Philippines, and Thailand. With the exception of high-income Singapore, the ASEAN members are chiefly low- and middle-income countries (table 6.1).

Singapore and the ASEAN-4 rose to prominence during the 1970s because of their relative labor abundance combined with their gradual adoption of outward-oriented economic policies, following in the footsteps of the so-called newly industrialized countries of East Asia (i.e., Hong Kong, Korea, Singapore, and Taiwan).[4] Broadly speaking, these factors contributed importantly to attracting foreign direct investment (FDI) in internationally competitive, labor-intensive manufacturing in these countries. It also contributed to their remarkable export performance and economic growth, up until the 1997–98 Asian financial crisis and the advent of increasing competition for international trade and FDI from emerging-market economies in other parts of Asia (mainly China), Latin America, and Eastern Europe.

ASEAN was founded in 1967, mainly with the objective of promoting political security in Southeast Asia in the face of insurgent elements within the region (Wanandi 2001). Today, political security issues remain important in the ASEAN countries, compounded in some measure by the enlargement of the bloc during the late 1990s from 6 members to the present 10, as the new members—Cambodia, Laos, Myanmar, and Vietnam—are for the most part low-income countries with comparatively limited experience with political and economic freedom. Cohesion of the bloc also continues to be important because of pressures from globalization and the mutually recognized need of countries in the bloc to often adopt common positions in their external relations, both economic and political, with major countries in the Asia Pacific region and the rest of the world.

Economic cooperation to promote growth and economic development in Southeast Asia has also long been an important objective of ASEAN,

---

3. All ASEAN countries—except Cambodia, Laos, Myanmar, and Vietnam—are members of the WTO. Cambodia is expected to accede in late 2003. To date, Brunei, Indonesia, the Philippines, Singapore, and Thailand have signed a TIFA with the United States, leaving Malaysia as the only major ASEAN country not to have signed a TIFA. By design, TIFA discussions are wide-ranging and provide an important foundation of common understanding and objectives for formal negotiation of a bilateral FTA with the United States.

4. See World Bank (1993). For a contrarian's view of East Asian growth and export performance, see, e.g., Krugman (1994).

Table 6.1 Basic economic indicators, 2000

Country	Population (millions)	Area (thousands of kilometers squared)	Human develop-ment index	Per capita income (US dollars)	Average 1990–2000 GDP growth (percent)	Structure production (1997, percent of GDP) Agri-culture	In-dustry	Ser-vices	Merchandise exports United States (millions of dollars)	World (millions of dollars)	Merchandise imports United States (millions of dollars)	World (millions of dollars)	FDI (inward stock) United States (millions of dollars)	World (millions of dollars)
ASEAN														
Brunei	0.3	5	n.a.	n.a.	2.2	3	46	51	n.a.	3,552	n.a.	1,111	n.a.	n.a.
Cambodia	12.0	177	n.a.	265	4.7	51	15	35	n.a.	1,327	n.a.	1,525	n.a.	n.a.
Indonesia	212.1	1,890	0.684	723	4.2	16	44	40	8,489	62,103	3,393	33,511	8,514	60,638
Laos	5.3	231	n.a.	324	6.3	53	21	26	n.a.	323	n.a.	500	n.a.	n.a.
Malaysia	22.2	330	0.782	4,035	7.0	11	45	44	20,152	98,153	13,668	82,195	7,400	54,315
Myanmar	47.7	658	n.a.	n.a.	6.1	59	10	31	n.a.	1,520	n.a.	2,371	n.a.	n.a.
Philippines	75.7	300	0.754	988	3.3	19	32	49	11,406	38,066	5,325	31,384	2,735	12,688
Papua New Guinea	5.1	453	n.a.	678	4.3	31	35	35	n.a.	2,096	n.a.	1,151	n.a.	n.a.
Singapore	4.0	1	0.885	22,959	7.8	0	35	65	23,891	137,932	20,270	134,630	25,634	89,250
Thailand	62.8	513	0.762	1,945	4.2	11	39	50	14,706	68,961	7,291	61,923	6,635	24,165
Vietnam	78.5	325	n.a.	399	7.3	26	32	42	n.a.	14,448	n.a.	15,636	n.a.	n.a.
Others														
Australia	19.1	7,741	0.939	20,298	4.1	3	27	70	6,249	63,128	14,897	74,265	35,364	113,610
China	1,252.90	9,560	0.726	862	10.3	19	50	31	52,162	249,195	22,375	225,096	9,861	346,694
Japan	127.1	378	0.933	37,494	1.3	2	34	65	144,009	478,156	72,514	379,530	59,441	54,303
Korea	46.7	99	0.882	9,782	5.7	5	43	52	37,806	171,826	29,286	160,479	8,914	42,329
New Zealand	3.8	271	0.917	13,441	3.0	8	28	65	1,880	12,716	2,425	13,951	3,854	31,960
Taiwan	22.2	36	n.a.	13,946	6.4	4	50	46	30,800	121,000	17,500	100,000	7,821	27,924
Canada	30.8	9,971	0.94	22,778	2.9	3	33	65	240,645	275,183	169,068	262,721	128,814	194,321
Chile	15.2	757	0.831	4,638	6.8	8	35	56	3,243	19,293	3,297	18,535	9,451	42,933
European Union	368.4	3,158	0.921	21,646	2.1	3	30	67	213,392	2,283,980	188,691	2,287,240	601,761	2,376,244
Mexico	98.9	1,958	0.796	5,811	3.1	6	29	66	147,686	166,455	140,288	191,904	37,332	91,222
United States	283.2	9,364	0.939	34,637	3.5	2	25	73	147,991	771,991	140,288	1,238,200	n.a.	1,238,627

n.a. = not available

Sources: IMF, *Direction of Trade Statistics* (2002) US Department of Commerce, Bureau of Economic Analysis, *Foreign Direct Investment (Historical Estimates),* www.bea.doc.gov; UN Conference on Trade and Development, *World Investment Report* (2002) UN Development Program, *Human Development Report* (2002) and World Bank, *World Development Indicators* (2002).

albeit secondary to that of political security (DeRosa 1995; see also Akrasanee 2001). Today, this cooperation finds its principal expression in the ASEAN Free Trade Area (AFTA), under which Singapore and the ASEAN-4 have pledged to reduce tariffs on intrabloc trade in substantially all goods (including primary agriculture) to the range of 0 to 5 percent by 2003—with exceptions for important sensitive sectors in each country (e.g., autos and auto parts in Malaysia) and continued enforcement of nontariff barriers (NTBs) on intra-ASEAN trade in other sensitive products.

Notwithstanding their mutual efforts to expand ASEAN markets through regional integration arrangements, the major ASEAN countries have also been active members in both the Asia Pacific Economic Cooperation group (APEC) and the World Trade Organization. But the recent slow movement of both APEC and WTO plans for expanding multilateral trade and investment on a nondiscriminatory basis, including under the Doha Development Agenda, or the Doha Round, has led economic policymakers in ASEAN to entertain alternative possibilities for expanding the bloc's regional and multilateral trade relations. These possibilities prominently include establishing free trade agreements not only with the United States under the EAI but also with other major trading countries in the Asia Pacific region and Europe (Ariff 2001).

An additional motivation for ASEAN to seek more rapidly to expand trade and investment relations in Southeast Asia is the emergence of China in the global economy and the country's accession to the WTO in December 2001. As the largest labor-abundant, low-wage country in the world, China attracted a particularly large share (between 20 and 30 percent) of FDI in developing countries during the 1990s; it is increasingly the major competitor of ASEAN producers in global export markets for basic labor-intensive manufactures. For their part, the ASEAN countries are interested in gaining preferential access to China's potentially huge market for goods and services, especially for higher-valued manufactures and other products in which producers in China are not yet internationally competitive and in which ASEAN producers are increasingly looking to specialize in line with the growth of both their labor costs and the skills of their workers. In November 2002, the ASEAN heads of state signed a framework agreement with China that envisions completely free trade between ASEAN and China by 2010, following on an early harvest of initial preferential tariff reductions to be negotiated beginning in 2003 (ASEAN 2002). For lack of leadership and consensus among the ASEAN countries, but also because of uncertainty on the part of Japan and Korea about expanding trade in agriculture and other sensitive issues, the ASEAN Plus Three (APT) plan—a bold plan to establish a large free trade area among ASEAN, China, Korea, and Japan—has failed to make significant headway to date (Pangestu 2003).

Preferential access to the US market under US FTAs with the ASEAN countries individually, or possibly under a single agreement, might offer producers in major ASEAN countries advantages similar to a free trade agreement with China. Indeed, the potential economic gains from an FTA with the United States might be more advantageous to ASEAN producers because of the greater size of the US economy than the Chinese economy, and the greater disparity in wage rates and labor skill levels between the ASEAN countries and the United States than between the ASEAN countries and China.[5]

US interest in pursuing FTAs with the ASEAN countries might be ascribed to similar economic and geopolitical motivations, including "competitive liberalization," which foresees the wide spread of regional and bilateral preferential trade agreements as ultimately bringing about multilateral trade liberalization on a nondiscriminatory basis.[6] Indeed, the remainder of this chapter seeks to identify more clearly the interests not only of the ASEAN countries but also of the United States in pursuing FTAs in Southeast Asia. It should be emphasized, however, that based on both the public pronouncements of US trade officials and their formal proposals for broad market access and other concessions under the Doha Round, US economic and geopolitical interests in pursuing FTAs with the ASEAN countries are driven in no small part by a fundamental concern to advance multilateral trade liberalization. Thus, of analytical interest here is whether US pursuit of FTAs with the ASEAN countries may be considered a stepping-stone to the avowed US objective of achieving more liberal world trade on a nondiscriminatory basis. Additionally, I seek to assess in both quantitative and qualitative terms the prospective economic benefits of US FTAs with the major ASEAN countries, and thereby to provide a possible basis for selecting those ASEAN countries after Singapore with which the United States might most beneficially enter into negotiations for a free trade agreement.

These analytical objectives are pursued in the remaining five sections of this chapter. After a section providing an overview of the recent dimensions of US-ASEAN bilateral trade and foreign direct investment, the following section reviews US and ASEAN trade, investment, and social frictions that might be addressed by US-ASEAN FTAs. I then assess the prospective economic benefits to the United States and its ASEAN trading

---

5. Assessing the relative economic advantages of US-ASEAN free trade agreements versus the new ASEAN-China free trade area or the APT plan is more difficult; to clarify the picture to some degree, one might turn to quantitative analysis by a world economic model such as the GTAP model, discussed below.

6. See, most recently, C. Fred Bergsten, 2002, "A Competitive Approach to Free Trade," Financial Times, December 5, 2002, and Bergsten (2002). See also Baldwin (1995) and Andrianmananjara (2000).

Table 6.2 United States and ASEAN trade with selected Asia-Pacific countries and the world, 2000 (millions of US dollars)

Exporting country	Indo-nesia	Ma-laysia	Philip-pines	Singa-pore	Thai-land	ASEAN-5	ASEAN	China
Indonesia	0	2,269	693		1,299	4,261	4,809	4,402
Malaysia	1,131	0	1,142	22,848	3,344	28,464	29,485	5,480
Philippines	115	1,991	0	3,358	1,098	6,562	6,644	1,677
Singapore	3,789	11,763	2,115	0	3,416	21,083	25,114	5,060
Thailand	1,109	3,176	846	5,801	0	10,932	13,005	4,381
ASEAN-5	6,143	19,198	4,795	32,007	9,158	71,301	79,058	21,000
Brunei Darussalam	16	4	0	266	490	776	776	61
Cambodia	1	17	1	75	8	101	142	59
Laos	1	0	0	1	76	78	184	6
Myanmar	22	70	2	110	256	460	464	125
Vietnam	303	455	157	820	331	2,066	2,246	929
Papua New Guinea	7	12	19	22	32	92	92	201
ASEAN	6,494	19,756	4,974	33,300	10,350	74,874	82,962	22,382
China	2,022	3,237	768	7,116	3,377	16,520	18,662	0
Hong Kong	342	2,264	1,217	3,516	883	8,222	9,255	9,429
Korea	2,083	3,663	2,351	4,822	2,165	15,084	17,266	23,207
Taiwan[a]	1,280	2,840	2,620	3,850	2,150	12,740	14,335	2,540
India	525	725	166	1,076	620	3,112	3,376	1,353
Japan	5,397	17,331	6,027	23,189	15,315	67,259	69,974	41,512
APT	15,996	43,987	14,120	68,426	31,208	173,737	188,865	87,101
Australia	1,694	1,593	816	2,298	1,160	7,560	8,514	5,024
New Zealand	228	300	171	192	196	1,087	1,207	638
ANZCERTA	1,922	1,893	987	2,490	1,356	8,648	9,721	5,662
United States	3,393	13,668	5,325	20,270	7,291	49,947	50,548	22,375
Canada	638	379	202	480	344	2,043	2,091	3,751
Mexico	30	141	26	388	123	707	710	488
NAFTA	4,061	14,188	5,553	21,138	7,758	52,698	53,348	26,614
APEC[b]	23,578	65,085	24,494	99,234	43,014	255,405	274,734	131,156
European Union	4,166	8,870	2,979	15,248	6,300	37,563	39,393	30,847
World	33,511	82,195	31,384	134,630	61,923	343,644	367,097	225,096

APT = ASEAN Plus Three (China, Korea, and Japan)

a. Taiwan trade data are for 1999.
b. Excludes Chile, Peru, and Russia.

Note: Bold row heads indicate US+ASEAN member countries. Papua New Guinea is an associate member of the ASEAN.

Sources: IMF, *Direction of Trade Statistics*, 2002; and Taiwan Ministry of Economic Affairs, Board of Foreign Trade, www.trade.gov.tw.

partners of forging FTAs, drawing on simulation results using the GTAP (Global Trade Analysis Project) model. The next section considers domestic economic reforms, mainly in the ASEAN countries, that might be spurred by the proposed US-ASEAN FTAs, and further how the external economic and political relations of the FTA partner countries might be affected. Finally, the concluding section summarizes the findings of the study with a view to identifying those ASEAN-4 countries with which the next US-ASEAN free trade agreements might yield the greatest economic benefits for the United States and, in so doing, might best advance the current US trade strategy of competitive liberalization.

| | | | | | | | Euro- | |
Korea	Japan	APT	ANZCERTA	United States	NAFTA	APEC	pean Union	World

Korea	Japan	APT	ANZCERTA	United States	NAFTA	APEC	European Union	World
5,287	16,371	30,869	1,956	11,097	12,277	47,930	10,098	66,692
4,878	14,490	54,333	3,056	25,990	29,318	94,733	15,917	121,308
1,815	7,190	17,326	372	14,216	15,902	37,883	7,968	48,359
3,723	6,426	40,323	2,598	19,630	21,331	76,657	15,730	106,234
1,631	10,595	29,612	1,991	17,161	18,956	55,303	12,174	75,895
17,333	55,072	172,463	9,974	88,096	97,783	312,505	61,886	418,488
492	1,653	2,982	166	408	409	3,559	161	3,734
2	52	256	2	861	874	1,150	311	1,483
1	12	203	1	10	11	216	109	341
23	119	731	11	487	532	1,322	359	2,083
322	2,637	6,135	1,412	860	1,017	8,974	3,738	14,309
117	349	759	950	39	39	1,758	311	2,095
18,291	59,895	183,529	12,515	90,760	100,666	329,484	66,875	442,532
12,799	55,156	86,617	6,679	106,215	117,725	306,277	59,354	398,674
1,261	1,668	21,613	818	11,861	13,436	38,127	17,556	64,873
0	20,454	60,927	3,138	40,911	48,976	130,231	22,676	178,119
2,580	11,500	30,955	2,011	30,800	33,410	92,324	17,885	121,000
985	2,637	8,351	548	11,034	12,278	24,179	11,567	47,831
31,828	0	143,314	11,358	149,520	168,917	379,390	82,086	512,038
62,918	135,504	474,387	33,690	387,406	436,285	1,145,382	230,992	1,531,363
5,959	14,774	34,271	3,086	6,693	8,173	48,650	8,778	68,470
702	2,194	4,741	2,858	2,186	2,752	11,077	2,384	14,941
6,661	16,969	39,013	5,944	8,878	10,925	59,727	11,162	83,411
29,286	72,514	174,723	17,323	0	309,356	533,343	188,691	851,306
2,108	8,689	16,638	1,431	229,191	233,609	254,078	18,083	282,037
378	2,388	3,964	362	135,080	143,607	148,669	6,516	163,482
31,772	83,591	195,325	19,116	364,271	686,572	936,090	213,290	1,296,825
105,165	249,049	760,103	61,566	801,859	1,179,210	2,268,962	490,105	3,093,564
15,791	46,813	132,843	18,620	223,295	266,840	450,342	1,324,140	2,199,820
160,479	379,530	1,132,202	88,215	1,238,200	1,692,825	3,221,399	2,287,240	6,612,400

US-ASEAN Trade and Foreign Investment

Merchandise Trade. US-ASEAN merchandise trade amounted to about $141 billion in 2000, or about 2 percent of world trade (table 6.2). Of this amount, US exports to the ASEAN countries accounted for about $51 billion (6 percent of total US exports and 14 percent of total ASEAN imports), while ASEAN exports to the United States accounted for about $91 billion (21 percent of total ASEAN exports and 7 percent of total US imports).

US exports to ASEAN constitute a small share of US exports to the world but a substantial share of ASEAN imports from the world (14 percent), second only to intra-ASEAN imports (23 percent) and ASEAN imports from Japan (19 percent). Conversely, ASEAN exports to the United States constitute the largest share of ASEAN exports to the world (21 percent), followed by intra-ASEAN exports (19 percent) and ASEAN exports to the European Union (15 percent), but only a small share of US imports from the world. Thus, US-ASEAN trade in merchandise is very asymmetric. US trade is much more important to ASEAN than vice versa, and the ASEAN bloc enjoys a large trade surplus with the United States (in 2000, about $40 billion).

With respect to the individual ASEAN countries, in 2000 US exports to ASEAN were bound principally for Singapore ($20 billion) and Malaysia ($14 billion), the two highest income ASEAN countries (on a per capita basis), while ASEAN exports to the United States originated principally from Malaysia ($26 billion), Singapore ($20 billion), and Thailand ($17 billion).

The commodity composition of US-ASEAN trade revealed in the top 10 commodity exports and imports of the United States with Singapore and the ASEAN-4 countries appears to follow the prediction of traditional comparative advantage theory (tables 6.3 and 6.4). That is, the relatively human capital– and physical capital–abundant United States tends to export advanced-technology and capital-intensive goods—aircraft, heavy equipment, and chemicals—to the ASEAN countries; in turn, the relatively labor-abundant ASEAN countries (with the exception of high-income Singapore) tend to export labor-intensive goods and other light manufactures—electrical machinery, apparel, and furniture—to the United States. In keeping with Singapore's relatively high income and education levels, leading US imports from Singapore—certain heavy equipment, chemical products, optical equipment, and printed materials—are more skill- and technology-intensive than those from the lower-income ASEAN countries. Finally, differences in natural resource abundance also appear to be a source of comparative advantage. Among the leading exports of the United States to Indonesia, the Philippines, and Thailand are certain oilseeds (mainly soybeans) and certain cereals (mainly wheat, corn, and rice). Similarly, among the leading imports of the United States from the ASEAN countries are fruit preparations from the Philippines (mainly pineapple preparations and juices), and fresh and processed shrimp, prawn, and tuna from Thailand.

Trade in Services. The United States accounted for about 33 percent of combined exports and imports of services in total world trade in services in 2000, while the ASEAN countries accounted for a smaller but still sizable share, about 10 percent (table 6.5). The United States is a net exporter of services to the world ($71 billion), to ASEAN-5 countries combined ($7 billion), and to the ASEAN countries individually. Among the ASEAN countries, only Singapore is a net exporter of services to the world ($6 billion).[7]

---

7. In 2000 Singapore's net imports of services from the United States amounted to $2.2 billion, or about 35 percent of total net service imports by the ASEAN countries from the United States.

Table 6.3 Principal US commodity exports to ASEAN countries and the world, 2000–01

2001 rank	Harmonized System category	2000 Millions of US dollars	2001 Millions of US dollars	2001 Percent of total
Indonesia				
1	84. Nuclear reactors, boilers, machinery	526.4	408.2	16.7
2	12. Oil seeds and oleaginous fruits	164.1	245.4	10.1
3	23. Residues and prepared animal feed	111.2	218.1	8.9
4	52. Cotton, including yarns and fabrics	157.3	196.1	8.0
5	85. Electrical machinery and equipment	188.8	177.1	7.3
6	10. Cereals	121.4	122.6	5.0
7	29. Organic chemicals	149.7	117.1	4.8
8	88. Aircraft, spacecraft, and parts thereof	38.7	104.7	4.3
9	38. Miscellaneous chemical products	111.5	74.7	3.1
10	28. Inorganic chemicals	44.5	69.8	2.9
Malaysia				
1	85. Electrical machinery and equipment	6,009.5	4,339.7	50.7
2	84. Nuclear reactors, boilers, machinery	1,506.1	1,418.5	16.6
3	88. Aircraft, spacecraft, and parts thereof	262.5	589.0	6.9
4	90. Optical and precision instruments	606.0	476.1	5.6
5	98. Special classification provisions, NESOI	207.4	172.4	2.0
6	39. Plastics and articles thereof	225.6	168.2	2.0
7	29. Organic chemicals	140.0	130.3	1.5
8	69. Ceramic products	111.2	105.3	1.2
9	38. Miscellaneous chemical products	81.8	81.0	0.9
10	24. Tobacco and manufactured tobacco	61.5	78.8	0.9
The Philippines				
1	85. Electrical machinery and equipment	5,281.5	4,799.6	64.7
2	84. Nuclear reactors, boilers, machinery	635.8	457.9	6.2
3	10. Cereals	299.6	278.0	3.7
4	90. Optical and precision instruments	373.3	260.1	3.5
5	98. Special classification provisions, NESOI	196.1	181.0	2.4
6	23. Residues and prepared animal feed	196.4	161.9	2.2
7	39. Plastics and articles thereof	201.0	133.5	1.8
8	87. Vehicles, other than railway	92.9	70.9	1.0
9	12. Oil seeds and oleaginous fruits	91.6	62.5	0.8
10	73. Articles of iron or steel	52.8	61.4	0.8
Singapore				
1	84. Nuclear reactors, boilers, machinery	4,767.7	4,087.8	25.9
2	88. Aircraft, spacecraft, and parts thereof	831.5	3,519.2	22.3
3	85. Electrical machinery and equipment	5,004.6	3,366.4	21.3
4	90. Optical and precision instruments	1,311.0	963.7	6.1
5	98. Special classification provisions, NESOI	553.6	550.1	3.5
6	39. Plastics and articles thereof	645.7	537.8	3.4
7	27. Mineral fuels, mineral oils, and waxes	310.6	475.1	3.0
8	29. Organic chemicals	396.6	350.6	2.2
9	38. Miscellaneous chemical products	354.1	278.0	1.8
10	87. Vehicles, other than railway	90.3	122.2	0.8
Thailand				
1	85. Electrical machinery and equipment	2,556.5	1,852.0	32.4
2	84. Nuclear reactors, boilers, machinery	936.9	936.0	16.4

(table continues next page)

Table 6.3 Principal US commodity exports to ASEAN countries and the world, 2000–01 *(continued)*

2001 rank	Harmonized System category	2000 Millions of US dollars	2001 Millions of US dollars	2001 Percent of total
Thailand *(continued)*				
3	88. Aircraft, spacecraft, and parts thereof	531.7	560.7	9.8
4	90. Optical and precision instruments	224.0	187 1	3.3
5	39. Plastics and articles thereof	158.6	171.6	3.0
6	29. Organic chemicals	194.0	161.3	2.8
7	98. Special classification provisions, NESOI	157.7	148.9	2.6
8	87. Vehicles, other than railway	132.6	142.6	2.5
9	12. Oil seeds and oleaginous fruits	148.2	131.0	2.3
10	70. Glass and glassware	87.1	130.5	2.3
World				
1	84. Nuclear reactors, boilers, machinery	143,165.0	129,293.0	19.4
2	85. Electrical machinery and equipment	122,314.0	100,187.0	15.0
3	87. Vehicles, other than railway	58,693.0	55,882.0	8.4
4	88. Aircraft, spacecraft, and parts thereof	39,940.0	42,810.0	6.4
5	90. Optical and precision instruments	42,542.0	41,105.0	6.2
6	39. Plastics and articles thereof	27,343.0	25,968.0	3.9
7	98. Special classification provisions, NESOI	21,721.0	22,644.0	3.4
8	29. Organic chemicals	20,090.0	18,856.0	2.8
9	27. Mineral fuels, mineral oils, and waxes	13,158.0	12,576.0	1.9
10	30. Pharmaceutical products	10,344.0	12,294.0	1.8

NESOI = not elsewhere specified or indicated

Source: US International Trade Commission, http://dataweb.usitc.gov.

US-ASEAN bilateral trade in services is dominated by travel and transport receipts. However, a substantial share of service exports to the United States by Singapore and Malaysia is accounted for by business and other professional services—28 percent and 20 percent, respectively. US exports of services not related to travel and transport are especially important to Indonesia (royalties and licensing fees), Malaysia (business services), and Singapore (royalties, licensing fees, and business services). The high profile of US royalties and licensing fees for Indonesia and Singapore reflects the strong demand in these countries for US-provided technologies, either related or unrelated to US FDI in the two countries.

Notably, ASEAN exports of services to the United States amount to about 20 percent and 30 percent of Thai and Philippine merchandise exports to the United States, respectively. Similarly, for both Indonesia and Singapore US exports of services amount to about 20 percent of US exports of merchandise. Thus, trade in services is a prominent and important element of US economic relations with these ASEAN countries, on par with the relative importance of US trade in services with Japan but not as extensive as US trade in services with the European Union.

Table 6.4 Principal US commodity imports from ASEAN countries and the world, 2000–01

2001 rank	Harmonized System category	2000 Millions of US dollars	2001 Millions of US dollars	Percent of total
Indonesia				
1	85. Electrical machinery and equipment	1,614.9	1,660.7	16.7
2	62. Apparel, not knitted or crocheted	1,500.0	1,596.2	16.1
3	84. Nuclear reactors, boilers, machinery	834.9	757.6	7.6
4	64. Footwear, gaiters and the like	731.2	724.7	7.3
5	61. Articles of apparel, knitted or crocheted	558.7	606.6	6.1
6	94. Furniture	506.2	505.2	5.1
7	40. Rubber and articles thereof	516.5	431.7	4.3
8	27. Mineral fuels, mineral oils, and waxes	555.5	429.0	4.3
9	44. Wood and articles of wood	452.7	365.1	3.7
10	42. Articles of leather	296.2	311.1	3.1
Malaysia				
1	85. Electrical machinery and equipment	12,295.2	10,246.8	46.1
2	84. Nuclear reactors, boilers, machinery	8,364.4	7,560.2	34.0
3	40. Rubber and articles thereof	610.3	532.2	2.4
4	94. Furniture	506.5	446.6	2.0
5	61. Articles of apparel, knitted or crocheted	396.6	412.6	1.9
6	62. Apparel, not knitted or crocheted	404.9	371.6	1.7
7	90. Optical and precision instruments	298.4	350.2	1.6
8	27. Mineral fuels, mineral oils, and waxes	483.6	315.1	1.4
9	98. Special classification provisions, NESOI	204.4	286.7	1.3
10	44. Wood and articles of wood	257.2	207.7	0.9
The Philippines				
1	85. Electrical machinery and equipment	6,896.7	4,668.9	41.3
2	84. Nuclear reactors, boilers, machinery	2,682.7	2,402.8	21.3
3	62. Apparel, not knitted or crocheted	1,186.8	1,175.5	10.4
4	61. Articles of apparel, knitted or crocheted	690.4	699.6	6.2
5	42. Articles of leather	349.1	334.6	3.0
6	94. Furniture	336.5	287.9	2.5
7	98. Special classification provisions, NESOI	95.7	169.5	1.5
8	20. Preparations of vegetables, fruit, nuts	153.5	151.6	1.3
9	90. Optical and precision instruments	129.3	142.9	1.3
10	15. Animal or vegetable fats and oils	189.3	139.9	1.2
Singapore				
1	84. Nuclear reactors, boilers, machinery	10,366.1	8,198.0	55.0
2	85. Electrical machinery and equipment	4,762.1	2,955.5	19.8
3	98. Special classification provisions, NESOI	1,161.1	1,016.1	6.8
4	29. Organic chemicals	634.9	821.2	5.5
5	90. Optical and precision instruments	713.5	728.9	4.9
6	61. Articles of apparel, knitted or crocheted	264.9	233.6	1.6
7	27. Mineral fuels, mineral oils, and waxes	318.6	188.4	1.3
8	49. Printed books, newspapers, pictures	120.4	125.0	0.8
9	99. Special import reporting provisions, NESOI	116.0	93.9	0.6
10	88. Aircraft, spacecraft, and parts thereof	58.7	72.9	0.5
Thailand				
1	85. Electrical machinery and equipment	3,834.0	3,015.2	20.6
2	84. Nuclear reactors, boilers, machinery	2,938.2	2,522.8	17.2

(table continues next page)

Table 6.4 **Principal US commodity imports to ASEAN countries and the world, 2000–2001** *(continued)*

| | | 2000 | 2001 | |
| | | Millions of | Millions of | Percent |
2001 rank	Harmonized System category	US dollars	US dollars	of total
Thailand *(continued)*				
3	61. Articles of apparel, knitted or crocheted	1,013.6	992.1	6.8
4	03. Fish and crustaceans, mollusks	1,019.6	867.0	5.9
5	71. Pearls, precious stones and metals	877.7	850.1	5.8
6	62. Apparel, not knitted or crocheted	825.8	846.5	5.8
7	16. Edible preparations of meat, fish	793.3	737.5	5.0
8	40. Rubber and articles thereof	633.9	556.3	3.8
9	42. Articles of leather	374.2	381.5	2.6
10	90. Optical and precision instruments	363.8	377.3	2.6
World				
1	87. Vehicles, other than railway	164,767.0	160,583.0	14.2
2	84. Nuclear reactors, boilers, machinery	179,439.0	160,030.0	14.1
3	85. Electrical machinery and equipment	184,992.0	153,682.0	13.6
4	27. Mineral fuels, mineral oils and products	121,580.0	113,191.0	10.0
5	98. Special classification provisions, NESOI	34,618.0	35,367.0	3.1
6	90. Optical and precision instruments	36,099.0	34,606.0	3.1
7	29. Organic chemicals	34,050.0	34,233.0	3.0
8	62. Apparel, not knitted or crocheted	32,735.0	31,656.0	2.8
9	61. Articles of apparel, knitted or crocheted	26,357.0	26,816.0	2.4
10	71. Pearls, precious stones and metals	29,886.0	26,132.0	2.3

NESOI = not elsewhere specified or indicated

Source: US International Trade Commission, http://dataweb.usitc.gov.

Foreign Direct Investment. During the 1990s, China attracted a very high share of the FDI flows in developing countries from multinational corporations headquartered in the United States, European Union, and Japan, possibly to some disadvantage of the ASEAN countries and other erstwhile recipients of substantial annual FDI inflows. Yet the stock of US long-term capital invested in the ASEAN countries remains very high (table 6.1). In 2000, it amounted to about $50 billion, compared to $10 billion for China. Thus, US business interests retain a vital investment stake in the ASEAN economies, especially Singapore ($26 billion) but also the ASEAN-4 economies ($7 to $8 billion each in Indonesia, Malaysia, and Thailand). For their part, the ASEAN countries have a clear interest in maintaining if not improving the attractiveness of their economies—especially with regard to their trade, taxation, and other economic policies—to outward-oriented multinational corporations in the United States and elsewhere as they compete both with China and with emerging-market economies worldwide for foreign investment.

Trade, Foreign Investment, and Social Frictions. Bilateral free trade agreements offer opportunities for negotiations on a range of sensitive trade and other economic issues between countries, more so than

Table 6.5 World trade in services, 2000

	Exports						Imports					
	To United States						From United States					
				Structure						Structure		
Country	To world (millions of US dollars)	Total (millions of US dollars)	Percent of merchandise trade	Travel and transport (percent)	Royalties and licensing fees (percent)	Business and other services (percent)	From world (millions of US dollars)	Total (millions of US dollars)	Percent of merchandise trade	Travel and transport (percent)	Royalties and licensing fees (percent)	Business and other services (percent)
ASEAN-5												
Indonesia	29,746	4,178	14	90	1	9	32,998	7,090	19	54	20	26
Malaysia	13,649	329	2	80	0	20	16,614	1,107	5	39	12	48
Philippines	3,935	1,536	29	86	0	14	6,066	1,625	14	67	5	27
Singapore	26,960	2,297	11	72	1	28	21,300	4,472	19	26	24	50
Thailand	n.a.	3,701	21	91	1	8	n.a.	4,686	10	53	14	33
Others												
Australia	17,893	3,282	22	71	3	26	17,620	5,426	87	49	13	37
China	30,146	2,754	12	85	0	15	35,858	4,731	9	44	9	47
Japan	68,303	17,556	24	55	23	22	115,686	34,313	24	51	21	28
Korea	5,060	433	13	72	1	27	14,755	1,106	13	51	5	44
New Zealand	4,270	1,163	48	93	0	7	4,449	1,265	67	68	6	26
Taiwan	13,785	904	12	87	0	13	15,329	1,165	8	40	11	49
Canada	36,287	17,130	10	63	6	31	41,306	23,465	10	48	10	42
Chile	3,843	709	22	81	0	19	4,336	1,406	43	67	4	29
European Union	463,945	74,828	40	59	9	32	467,515	91,377	43	43	19	39
Mexico	13,563	10,999	8	81	1	18	16,720	14,104	10	49	7	44
United States	272,110	—	—	—	—	—	201,060	—	—	—	—	—
World	1,454,883	202,060	16	65	8	27	1,454,883	277,478	36	48	14	38

n.a. = not available

Sources: US Commerce Department, Bureau of Economic Analysis, *Survey of Current Business*, 2002, www.bea.doc.gov/bea/pubs.htm; World Bank, *World Development Indicators*, 2002.

multilateral trade negotiations under the auspices of the 146-member WTO or even negotiations among comparatively smaller numbers of countries under the auspices of regional organizations for economic co-operation. Nonetheless, bilateral free trade agreements remain importantly founded on concerns for border measures restricting trade, beginning with familiar ad valorem tariffs and a variety of nontariff measures enforced against merchandise imports.

Merchandise Trade

Tariffs and Nontariff Barriers. US-ASEAN trade relations are circumscribed by not only import tariffs but also numerous nontariff barriers to imports, including administered protection measures such as antidumping and countervailing duty actions. These barriers to trade are summarized in table 6.6, based on information compiled by the UN Conference on Trade and Development (UNCTAD) about restrictions on imports enforced by the United States and the major ASEAN countries.

The protection statistics in table 6.6 are disaggregated by the 21 sections of the Harmonized System (HS) for coding international trade in commodities and manufactures. They summarize the range and average level of ad valorem tariffs applied to imports on a most favored nation (MFN) basis, the average frequency of nontariff barriers, and the number of national tariff lines that are applied on MFN, free, and (for developing countries and least-developed countries) preferential bases. Each of these measures is not without shortcomings. For instance, tariff averages can mask significant tariff peaks, and nontariff barriers included in the NTB frequency measure can vary significantly with regard to their degree of restrictiveness (Laird 1997).

The United States maintains the lowest average level of applied tariffs, just over 3 percent. ASEAN average tariff levels are appreciably higher but still in the moderate range of 8 to 12 percent; the exceptions are Singapore, which traditionally has been a (virtually) duty-free city-state, and Thailand, whose average applied tariff stands at just over 18 percent.[8] Notably, neither the United States nor the ASEAN-4 apply additional charges to imports, unlike some other countries that enforce customs surcharges, licensing fees, and other special taxes on imports (see UNCTAD 2003).

Broadly speaking, the United States and ASEAN countries tend to apply higher-than-average tariffs on imports of foods, beverages, and tobacco

---

8. Thailand's comparatively high tariff levels might be viewed as a particular obstacle to successful free trade negotiations with the United States. As seen in the quantitative analysis below, however, higher protection levels in Thailand imply greater economic gains for US exports under a US-Thailand FTA than prospective US free trade agreements with the other major ASEAN countries.

Table 6.6 Trade and protection in the United States and ASEAN countries, circa 2000

Country/Harmonized System section	Applied tariff and paratariff measures (percent)				National tariff lines (number)			
	MFN tariff range	Tariff average	Total charges	Nontariff barriers (percent)	MFN	Zero	GSP	LDC
United States								
I. Animals and animal products	0.0–26.0	2.1	2.1	99.1	502	140	39	274
II. Vegetable products	0.0–30.0	2.3	2.3	52.0	507	135	203	338
III. Fats and oils	0.0–19.0	1.9	1.9	7.1	66	18	20	47
IV. Foods, beverages, and tobacco	0.0–350.0	18.5	18.5	57.3	725	131	259	460
V. Mineral products	0.0–7.0	0.2	0.2	5.7	184	151	18	33
VI. Chemical products	0.0–13.0	2.2	2.2	24.8	1,665	496	758	1,169
VII. Rubber and plastics	0.0–14.0	3.2	3.2	10.5	353	83	239	266
VIII. Hides and leather	0.0–20.0	3.4	3.4	43.2	156	38	65	77
IX. Wood and wood articles	0.0–18.0	1.8	1.8	28.2	186	114	58	68
X. Pulp and paper products	0.0–7.0	0.4	0.4	0.0	223	95	128	128
XI. Textiles and apparel	0.0–33.0	7.6	7.6	35.1	1,545	92	86	86
XII. Footwear and accessories	0.0–48.0	5.7	5.7	5.2	168	34	27	27
XIII. Stone and ceramic products	0.0–38.0	3.6	3.6	2.6	299	106	128	177
XIV. Precious stones and metals	0.0–14.0	2.2	2.2	0.0	104	47	53	57
XV. Base metals and products	0.0–15.0	2.3	2.3	8.8	982	186	437	780
XVI. Machinery and electrical equipment	0.0–15.0	1.5	1.5	21.8	1,437	799	564	638
XVII. Transport vehicles and equipment	0.0–25.0	2.5	2.5	46.8	238	121	77	117
XVIII. Optical and scientific equipment	0.0–16.0	2.0	2.0	2.9	530	188	209	281
XIX. Arms and ammunition	0.0–6.0	0.9	0.9	100.0	37	22	13	15
XX. Miscellaneous manufactures	0.0–32.0	2.4	2.4	18.5	277	131	124	141
XXI. Works of art	0.0–0.0	0.0	0.0	7.1	7	7	0	0
All products	0.0–350.0	3.2	3.2	27.5	10,191	3,134	3,505	5,179
Indonesia								
I. Animals and animal products	0.0–20.0	4.5	4.5	94.1	273	32	0	0
II. Vegetable products	0.0–20.0	5.0	5.0	94.6	262	53	0	0
III. Fats and oils	0.0–10.0	4.3	4.3	97.7	70	20	0	0

(table continues next page)

Table 6.6 Trade and protection in the United States and ASEAN countries, circa 2000 (continued)

Country/Harmonized System section	Applied tariff and paratariff measures (percent)			Nontariff barriers (percent)	National tariff lines (number)			
	MFN tariff range	Tariff average	Total charges		MFN	Zero	GSP	LDC
Indonesia (continued)								
IV. Foods, beverages, and tobacco	0.0–170.0	17.1	17.1	21.6	315	37	0	0
V. Mineral products	0.0–20.0	4.1	4.1	2.5	180	42	0	0
VI. Chemical products	0.0–170.0	6.6	6.6	9.8	1,024	221	0	0
VII. Rubber and plastics	0.0–25.0	12.0	12.0	3.9	354	14	0	0
VIII. Hides and leather	0.0–20.0	8.5	8.5	0.0	96	45	0	0
IX. Wood and wood articles	0.0–15.0	9.1	9.1	0.0	269	171	0	0
X. Pulp and paper products	0.0–20.0	5.2	5.2	6.7	188	53	0	0
XI. Textiles and apparel	0.0–20.0	12.4	12.4	4.0	1,196	17	0	0
XII. Footwear and accessories	0.0–20.0	16.7	16.7	0.0	75	1	0	0
XIII. Stone and ceramic products	0.0–20.0	7.0	7.0	0.5	184	3	0	0
XIV. Precious stones and metals	0.0–20.0	9.8	9.8	3.8	66	16	0	0
XV. Base metals and products	0.0–30.0	8.0	8.0	10.0	826	101	0	0
XVI. Machinery and electrical equipment	0.0–20.0	5.4	5.4	1.5	1,028	548	0	0
XVII. Transport vehicles and equipment	0.0–80.0	5.5	5.5	8.1	215	70	0	0
XVIII. Optical and scientific equipment	0.0–20.0	8.6	8.6	0.0	274	31	0	0
XIX. Arms and ammunition	0.0–20.0	9.9	9.9	0.0	35	16	0	0
XX. Miscellaneous manufactures	0.0–20.0	15.5	15.5	0.0	182	5	0	0
XXI. Works of art	0.0–20.0	10.3	10.3	0.0	14	2	0	0
All products	0.0–170.0	8.8	8.8	17.1	7,126	1,504	0	0
Malaysia								
I. Animals and animal products	0.0–25.0	1.9	1.9	55.9	288	211	0	0
II. Vegetable products	0.0–829.0	2.6	2.6	53.9	275	266	0	0
III. Fats and oils	0.0–30.0	2.4	2.4	8.3	167	98	0	0
IV. Foods, beverages, and tobacco	0.0–1,772.0	81.4	81.4	12.2	435	176	0	0
V. Mineral products	0.0–115.0	1.6	1.6	9.7	199	159	0	0
VI. Chemical products	0.0–164.0	4.7	4.7	11.7	1,197	977	0	0
VII. Rubber and plastics	0.0–191.0	18.1	18.1	4.1	627	179	0	0

	Range								
VIII. Hides and leather	0.0–25.0	5.7	5.7	0.0	105	63	0	0	0
IX. Wood and wood articles	0.0–40.0	11.6	11.6	3.4	319	176	0	0	0
X. Pulp and paper products	0.0–40.0	6.4	6.4	6.4	253	100	0	0	0
XI. Textiles and apparel	0.0–288.0	14.9	14.9	2.4	1,091	188	0	0	0
XII. Footwear and accessories	0.0–43.0	21.0	21.0	2.3	85	7	0	0	0
XIII. Stone and ceramic products	0.0–60.0	17.1	17.1	0.0	200	48	0	0	0
XIV. Precious stones and metals	0.0–20.0	2.5	2.5	11.5	61	41	0	0	0
XV. Base metals and products	0.0–38.0	7.1	7.1	7.2	1,052	438	0	0	0
XVI. Machinery and electrical equipment	0.0–290.0	6.1	6.1	8.3	1,215	688	0	0	0
XVII. Transport vehicles and equipment	0.0–200.0	7.7	7.7	8.0	389	97	0	0	0
XVIII. Optical and scientific equipment	0.0–35.0	1.6	1.6	1.0	283	240	0	0	0
XIX. Arms and ammunition	0.0–55.0	15.6	15.6	97.1	21	3	0	0	0
XX. Miscellaneous manufactures	0.0–173.0	14.6	14.6	7.4	235	53	0	0	0
XXI. Works of art	0.0–30.0	4.5	4.5	0.0	10	2	0	0	0
All products	0.0–1,772.0	11.9	11.9	14.8	8,507	4,210	0	0	0

The Philippines

	Range								
I. Animals and animal products	3.0–60.0	9.2	9.2	0.0	235	0	0	0	0
II. Vegetable products	3.0–65.0	8.5	8.5	2.8	220	0	0	0	0
III. Fats and oils	3.0–20.0	5.9	5.9	0.0	46	0	0	0	0
IV. Foods, beverages, and tobacco	3.0–65.0	12.0	12.0	0.0	221	0	0	0	0
V. Mineral products	3.0–10.0	3.2	3.2	3.3	157	0	0	0	0
VI. Chemical products	0.0–20.0	4.5	4.5	3.5	764	5	0	0	0
VII. Rubber and plastics	0.0–15.0	6.3	6.3	0.6	213	2	0	0	0
VIII. Hides and leather	3.0–15.0	7.2	7.2	0.0	83	0	0	0	0
IX. Wood and wood articles	0.0–20.0	9.0	9.0	0.0	70	5	0	0	0
X. Pulp and paper products	3.0–15.0	6.1	6.1	0.9	168	0	0	0	0
XI. Textiles and apparel	0.0–20.0	11.6	11.6	0.3	820	2	0	0	0
XII. Footwear and accessories	3.0–15.0	10.1	10.1	0.0	53	0	0	0	0
XIII. Stone and ceramic products	0.0–15.0	8.4	8.4	0.0	145	1	0	0	0
XIV. Precious stones and metals	3.0–15.0	5.5	5.5	1.9	58	0	0	0	0
XV. Base metals and products	0.0–20.0	5.5	5.5	0.7	534	3	0	0	0
XVI. Machinery and electrical equipment	0.0–20.0	4.4	4.4	0.0	859	95	0	0	0
XVII. Transport vehicles and equipment	3.0–30.0	5.8	5.8	6.8	166	0	0	0	0
XVIII. Optical and scientific equipment	0.0–10.0	4.2	4.2	0.7	242	21	0	0	0

(table continues next page)

Table 6.6 Trade and protection in the United States and ASEAN countries, circa 2000 (continued)

| | Applied tariff and paratariff measures (percent) | | | Nontariff barriers (percent) | National tariff lines (number) | | | |
Country/Harmonized System section	MFN tariff range	Tariff average	Total charges		MFN	Zerc	GSP	LDC
The Philippines (continued)								
XIX. Arms and ammunition	3.0–15.0	13.4	13.4	61.8	17	0	0	0
XX. Miscellaneous manufactures	3.0–20.0	9.7	9.7	1.6	147	0	0	0
XXI. Works of art	10.0–10.0	10.0	10.0	0.0	7	0	0	0
All products	0.0–65.0	7.6	7.6	4.0	5,225	134	0	0
Singapore								
I. Animals and animal products	0.0–0.0	0.0	0.0	54.9	219	213	0	0
II. Vegetable products	0.0–0.0	0.0	0.0	45.1	215	304	0	0
III. Fats and oils	0.0–0.0	0.0	0.0	97.8	48	48	0	0
IV. Foods, beverages, and tobacco	0.0–5.0	0.3	0.3	6.1	261	193	0	0
V. Mineral products	0.0–50.0	0.1	0.1	0.0	174	151	0	0
VI. Chemical products	0.0–0.0	0.0	0.0	30.2	785	779	0	0
VII. Rubber and plastics	0.0–5.0	0.1	0.1	0.4	229	224	0	0
VIII. Hides and leather	0.0–5.0	0.5	0.5	23.3	81	71	0	0
IX. Wood and wood articles	0.0–0.0	0.0	0.0	0.0	72	72	0	0
X. Pulp and paper products	0.0–0.0	0.0	0.0	15.8	151	151	0	0
XI. Textiles and apparel	0.0–5.0	0.7	0.7	0.9	968	340	0	0
XII. Footwear and accessories	0.0–5.0	0.8	0.8	2.3	56	49	0	0
XIII. Stone and ceramic products	0.0–0.0	0.0	0.0	0.0	136	136	0	0
XIV. Precious stones and metals	0.0–5.0	0.1	0.1	0.0	54	52	0	0
XV. Base metals and products	0.0–5.0	0.0	0.0	0.0	523	522	0	0
XVI. Machinery and electrical equipment	0.0–5.0	0.0	0.0	1.6	831	829	0	0
XVII. Transport vehicles and equipment	0.0–45.0	1.9	1.9	7.2	147	123	0	0
XVIII. Optical and scientific equipment	0.0–0.0	0.0	0.0	1.0	228	228	0	0
XIX. Arms and ammunition	0.0–0.0	0.0	0.0	100.0	17	17	0	0
XX. Miscellaneous manufactures	0.0–5.0	0.8	0.8	4.6	158	135	0	0
XXI. Works of art	0.0–0.0	0.0	0.0	7.1	8	8	0	0
All products	0.0–50.0	0.2	0.2	19.0	5,361	4,945	0	0

Thailand

I. Animals and animal products	0.0–65.0	39.4	39.4	69.2	270	26	0	0
II. Vegetable products	0.0–65.0	39.6	39.6	80.5	248	2	0	0
III. Fats and oils	10.0–30.0	15.0	15.0	97.8	90	0	0	0
IV. Foods, beverages, and tobacco	0.0–65.0	30.6	30.6	41.3	272	3	0	0
V. Mineral products	0.0–20.0	3.3	3.3	15.6	202	2	0	0
VI. Chemical products	0.0–40.0	11.8	11.8	42.1	947	55	0	0
VII. Rubber and plastics	0.0–50.0	22.3	22.3	1.6	272	14	0	0
VIII. Hides and leather	0.0–40.0	14.7	14.7	0.0	117	20	0	0
IX. Wood and wood articles	0.0–60.0	18.5	18.5	9.3	141	1	0	0
X. Pulp and paper products	0.0–30.0	11.5	11.5	0.0	163	6	0	0
XI. Textiles and apparel	1.0–60.0	21.3	21.3	10.1	967	0	0	0
XII. Footwear and accessories	10.0–40.0	25.8	25.8	2.3	70	0	0	0
XIII. Stone and ceramic products	0.0–35.0	19.5	19.5	8.9	164	2	0	0
XIV. Precious stones and metals	0.0–20.0	7.7	7.7	5.8	78	32	0	0
XV. Base metals and products	0.0–30.0	12.9	12.9	0.6	646	2	0	0
XVI. Machinery and electrical equipment	0.0–40.0	11.1	11.1	4.1	1,317	3	0	0
XVII. Transport vehicles and equipment	0.0–80.0	12.7	12.7	3.8	230	15	0	0
XVIII. Optical and scientific equipment	0.0–20.0	9.7	9.7	0.3	274	17	0	0
XIX. Arms and ammunition	0.0–30.0	28.2	28.2	0.0	32	1	0	0
XX. Miscellaneous manufactures	5.0–40.0	16.9	16.9	2.3	161	0	0	0
XXI. Works of art	0.0–20.0	10.0	10.0	28.6	12	6	0	0
All products	0.0–80.0	18.2	18.2	20.2	6,673	207	0	0

MFN = most favored nation
GSP = General System of Preferences
LDC = less developed country

Notes: Tariff data refer to 2000 for the United States, Indonesia, the Philippines, and Thailand. NTB data refer to 1999 for the United States and Indonesia, 1998 for the Philippines, 1996 for Malaysia, 1994 for Thailand, and 1992 for Singapore.

Source: UNCTAD, Trade Analysis and Information System (TRAINS), version 8.0, spring 2001, www.unctad-trains.org.

(Section IV). Beverages and tobacco are common excise items worldwide; demand for them is often considered very inelastic (albeit overall, and not necessarily on an import basis). Among processed foods, on the other hand, there are a number of sensitive trade items in both the United States and individual ASEAN countries, as discussed further below; these include sugar, processed meats, fruits, and vegetables.

For the United States, other sensitive sectors revealed by the protection statistics in table 6.6 include agriculture, textiles and apparel, and footwear. Agriculture is covered widely by nontariff barriers, especially in meats and other animal products, including dairy products (applied across 99 percent of national tariff schedule lines in the category); vegetable products, including fresh fruits and vegetables (52 percent); and cereals (52 percent). US imports of textiles and apparel and of footwear are subject to higher than average tariffs and extensive NTBs; in the case of textiles and apparel, these reflect Multi-Fiber Arrangement (MFA) quotas expected to be phased out by 2005. The NTB statistics for the United States also suggest that imports of certain machinery and electrical equipment, as well as labor-intensive miscellaneous manufactures, are subject to quantitative restrictions and other nontariff barriers (including administered protection measures) at higher than average frequency.

For the ASEAN countries, other sensitive import sectors revealed by the protection data in table 6.6 appear to be more numerous than in the United States, especially for Indonesia, Malaysia, and Thailand. Although there is no appreciable tariff protection in Singapore, the country appears to apply NTBs to imports frequently for meat and animal products, vegetable products, fats and oils, and chemical products.[9] Owing to recent trade reforms, the Philippines enforces mainly only tariff protection against imports, and then at very modest levels—generally less than 8 percent. Tariff peaks, however, are apparent for certain animal and vegetable products, as well as for transport vehicles and equipment.

In Indonesia, Malaysia, and Thailand, the frequency of NTBs in agriculture is relatively high; in Thailand they apply in addition to chemicals. Moreover, relatively high tariffs protect a number of sectors beyond the aforementioned processed foods, beverages, and tobacco. In Indonesia and Thailand, these include rubber and plastics, footwear, and miscellaneous manufactures. In Malaysia, other high-tariff sectors include rubber and plastics, footwear, and stone and ceramic products. Finally, not unlike in the Philippines, tariff peaks are apparent for transport vehicles and equipment, especially in Malaysia but also in Indonesia and Thailand, re-

---

9. In addition to providing for duty-free trade between the United States and Singapore, the US-Singapore FTA specifies that most nontariff barriers on trade between the two countries will be eliminated, consistent with the provisions of GATT Article XI, which permits restrictions on trade mainly in connection with standards or regulations for the classification, grading, or marketing of trade goods.

flecting the long-standing interest of ASEAN countries in developing a regional auto production and parts industry.[10]

Administered Protection. Further insight into sensitive trade and other issues surrounding US-ASEAN economic relations can be gained by considering administered protection investigations and actions undertaken by the United States and ASEAN countries against one another during recent years, especially antidumping and subsidy and countervailing investigations. Information about the volume of such activities since the mid-1990s is reported by the WTO in connection with its implementation of the Uruguay Round agreements on antidumping measures and on subsidy and countervailing measures (table 6.7).[11]

Table 6.7 indicates that antidumping and countervailing investigations and remedies applied by the United States against the ASEAN countries, and vice versa, since 1995 have been relatively few compared with the numbers applied globally to the ASEAN countries. For instance, although exports from Indonesia and Thailand faced more than 15 antidumping investigations in the United States on a combined basis between January 1995 and June 2002, the number of antidumping investigations against them during the same period worldwide exceeded 150.

Among the ASEAN countries, Indonesia appears to have been affected most by recent US-administered protection activities, with 13 antidumping investigations and 4 countervailing investigations initiated against its exports to the United States, and with duties applied in 50 percent of the cases for which investigations were started. The other major ASEAN countries appear to have attracted far fewer US-administered protection investigations, albeit with remedies applied by the United States at equal or higher rates than for Indonesia. Administered protection actions by the ASEAN countries against the United States have been virtually nil.

As emphasized by the Office of the US Trade Representative (USTR 2003), US concerns about administered protection and nontariff barriers in the ASEAN-4 center mainly on agricultural commodities and products— especially rice, corn, and poultry—that frequently face nonautomatic licensing requirements, state trading and special sanitary controls, and requirements for special labeling, testing, and (in Indonesia and Malaysia) halal certification. In Malaysia and the Philippines, domestic motor vehicle and auto parts manufacturers are favored by requirements for local content and by excise taxes on autos based on engine displacement rather than value. In the Philippines and Thailand, customs regulations are al-

---

10. Notably, the United States imposes NTBs at high frequency on imports of transport vehicles and equipment (47 percent). These barriers relate principally to US auto emission and safety regulations, applied equally to US-produced vehicles.

11. For background on the WTO agreements on antidumping and on subsidies and countervailing measures, see Schott (1994).

Table 6.7 Antidumping and countervailing investigations and measures, January 1995–June 2002

	Importing country						
Exporting country	United States	Indonesia	Malaysia	Philippines	Singapore	Thailand	World
Antidumping initiations							
United States	—	1	0	0	n.a.	0	105
Indonesia	13	—	3	1	n.a.	1	83
Malaysia	3	1	—	2	n.a.	0	38
Philippines	1	0	0	—	n.a.	0	4
Singapore	0	2	1	0	n.a.	0	26
Thailand	4	2	5	1	n.a.	—	74
World	279	43	22	15	n.a.	12	1,979
Antidumping measures							
United States	—	0	0	0	0	0	62
Indonesia	7	—	3	1	0	1	37
Malaysia	2	0	—	1	1	0	20
Philippines	1	0	0	—	0	0	1
Singapore	0	0	0	0	—	0	9
Thailand	5	0	2	0	0	—	44
World	185	14	11	8	2	3	1,161
Countervailing initiations							
United States	—	n.a.	n.a.	n.a.	n.a.	n.a.	3
Indonesia	4	—	n.a.	n.a.	n.a.	n.a.	9
Malaysia	0	n.a.	—	n.a.	n.a.	n.a.	2
Philippines	0	n.a.	n.a.	—	n.a.	n.a.	1
Singapore	0	n.a.	n.a.	n.a.	—	n.a.	1
Thailand	2	n.a.	n.a.	n.a.	n.a.	—	7
World	59	n.a.	n.a.	n.a.	n.a.	n.a.	147
Countervailing measures							
Indonesia	2	—	n.a.	n.a.	n.a.	n.a.	5
Malaysia	0	n.a.	—	n.a.	n.a.	n.a.	3
Philippines	0	n.a.	n.a.	—	n.a.	n.a.	2
Singapore	0	n.a.	n.a.	n.a.	—	n.a.	—
Thailand	1	n.a.	n.a.	n.a.	n.a.	—	3
United States	—	n.a.	n.a.	n.a.	n.a.	n.a.	1
World	34	n.a.	n.a.	n.a.	n.a.	n.a.	84

n.a. = No antidumping/countervailing initiations or measures reported for WTO member country.

Source: WTO, *WTO Trade Topics* (Anti-Dumping, and Subsidies and Countervailing Measures), 2003. www.wto.org/english/tratop_e.htm.

leged to be complicated, nontransparent, and inconsistently applied. Finally, none of the ASEAN-4 is party to the WTO Government Procurement Agreement. In practice, government procurement decisions are often arbitrary, and foreign suppliers are not able to compete effectively for government contracts without taking on local partners.

Trade in Services

With expansion of merchandise trade in Southeast Asia, demand for trade in services has grown apace. However, the roots of barriers to trade in services are frequently internal policies, social institutions, and local practices that are less transparent than tariffs and other, more familiar border measures restricting trade in goods.

From the ASEAN perspective, notwithstanding the general openness of the US services sector and the generally low level of regulation in the United States by global standards, there are some significant US barriers to expanded trade in services. For instance, US maritime laws have traditionally restricted ASEAN and other foreign-flag carriers from transporting cargo between US ports. And some US requirements for providing professional services or operating financial services firms might still appear onerous or less than transparent to individual professionals and service firms in Southeast Asia. Most important, especially for low-income ASEAN countries, US immigration laws—not unlike those in most other high-income countries—prohibit general immigration of unskilled labor to the United States to meet the high US demand for the services of low-wage labor.

From the US perspective, notwithstanding that individual ASEAN countries have made modest commitments to liberalize some aspects of their services trade under the General Agreement on Trade in Services (GATS), barriers to expanded trade in services remain high in most ASEAN countries—including Singapore, where selected sectors such as media services (broadcasting, cable, and newspapers) and legal services remain sheltered from foreign competition. Indeed, the USTR has amassed a considerable list of service sectors in the major ASEAN countries in which greater progress might be made to allow improved and wider entry by US professionals and service firms, including in telecommunications; wholesale, distribution, and retail service activities; accounting, financial, and legal services; transportation and coastal shipping; and architectural and engineering services. A recurrent problem in many if not most of these ASEAN service sectors, from the US perspective, is the frequent requirement that service professionals be ASEAN nationals or trained in local institutions, or that service firms be predominantly owned by ASEAN interests.

Foreign Direct Investment

Foreign direct investment has been particularly important to the growth and economic development of several ASEAN countries, especially Malaysia, Singapore, and Thailand. Indeed, the impressive export performance by these countries during the 1980s and early 1990s reflected their early relative openness to FDI as well as to imports. However, with the advent of other emerging-market countries and especially China during the 1990s, the FDI policies of the ASEAN countries have come under new scrutiny. ASEAN policymakers are focusing on whether remaining government controls and regulations on foreign investment require more thoroughgoing liberalization in order to make the ASEAN-4 more attractive as host countries for outward-oriented FDI (Felker and Jomo 2000).

By most accounts, the foreign investment policies of Singapore are among the most liberal in the world, except with respect to investment in certain service sectors including broadcast media and domestic retail banking (see, e.g., O'Driscoll, Feulner, and O'Grady 2003). The Enterprise for ASEAN Initiative seeks to promote more liberal policies and an enhanced general environment for greater FDI in the other ASEAN countries.

Recent USTR reports on foreign trade barriers provide an indication of the major issues that the United States sees with respect to the policies of ASEAN countries toward foreign investment. These include vestiges of past discretionary policies toward FDI such as domestic content requirements, limitations on foreign ownership shares, and export earnings requirements. The most entrenched of these appear to survive in investment regulations supporting the auto and auto parts sector in Malaysia and the Philippines. In addition, Indonesia and the Philippines maintain a negative list system by which some sectors still bar FDI. Notably, Thailand appears to engage in these traditional practices restraining FDI least frequently among the ASEAN-4, in line with its efforts following the 1997 Asian financial crisis to attract higher levels of outward-oriented foreign investment.

Finally, an overarching problem emphasized by recent USTR reports is widespread lack of protection for intellectual property rights in the ASEAN-4 countries, seen most prevalently in rampant optical disc piracy in these countries, as well as piracy of other copyrighted materials such as videotapes and films.

ASEAN FDI is comparatively limited, and importantly oriented to investment in other ASEAN and Asian developing countries. Thus, widespread complaints have not been lodged against the United States in connection with any limitations it may impose on FDI in the United States by ASEAN commercial interests.

Social and Other Frictions

The recent trend in multilateral and especially regional trade negotiations has been to incorporate talks to liberalize "behind-the-border measures" in addition to familiar border measures inhibiting trade; these are intended to promote deeper integration among trading partners by harmonizing a broad range of domestic economic policies and regulations that, at the limit, would facilitate a common market or economic union between countries (see Lawrence 1996; Burfisher, Robinson, and Thierfelder 2003). Progress in addressing so-called new agenda issues at the multilateral level has been limited thus far; two of those trade-related areas, of particular interest to vocal political groups in the United States but also to the European Union and Japan, are the environment and labor standards. Other sensitive and new agenda issues include intellectual property rights, competition policy, electronic commerce, trade facilitation, and capacity building.

In many cases, countries' sensitivity to these issues runs along a North-South fault line, as emerged with particular force during the Seattle WTO summit in December 1999. However, since the Doha Development Agenda was adopted in late 2001 and the current US administration succeeded in passing the US Trade Act of 2002, the United States has sought to address some of the most contentious of these issues in "softer" terms than during the late 1990s. It has also begun addressing many of them in bilateral FTAs—including the TIFA discussions that precede FTA negotiations—where the environment for negotiations with individual trading partners might be more conducive to finding common ground on sensitive issues. The recently negotiated US-Chile and US-Singapore FTAs seem to indicate that this US strategy is proving successful, and may be laying important groundwork for future regional and multilateral trade negotiations. For instance, by emphasizing the consistency of US and partner country labor laws and regulations with "core" labor rights and employment practices established by the International Labor Organization (ILO), the United States has been able to forge acceptable labor rights chapters in both recent FTAs. Similar success has been met in forging FTA chapters on trade-related environmental issues, as negotiators have focused on identifying possible trade-related environmental issues of mutual concern to the United States and the two FTA partners, for further study and possible remedial policy action.

Finally, in the political realm, the current US trade agenda clearly calls for promoting FTAs with trading partners that recognize the importance of international security measures and that are committed to combating terrorism.

As strongly performing emerging-market economies with a growing middle class of entrepreneurs and wage earners, Singapore and the ASEAN-4 (with the possible exception of Indonesia) have promulgated domestic labor laws of some sophistication and have increasingly come to face environmental issues—the latter brought home with particular force after the 1997 forest fires in Indonesia that spread haze and air pollution to wide parts of Southeast Asia—more squarely as individual nations and as a bloc. Thus, the ASEAN-4 should be as amenable as Chile and Singapore to cooperatively exploring labor and environmental issues in FTA negotiations with the United States, so long as the negotiations on these issues do not raise their concerns about new forms of protectionism that could stifle ASEAN trade and economic development (see, e.g., Sussangkarn 1997).

Other new agenda issues might prove more troublesome in FTA negotiations between ASEAN countries and the United States. For instance, aside from any possible continued debate over protecting patent rights of multinational pharmaceutical companies that produce anti-AIDS and other advanced drugs, the ASEAN-4 might be sensitive to likely US insistence on greater enforcement of their national laws and WTO commitments to protect intellectual property rights. However, with regard to international terrorism, the ASEAN countries have taken a more public stand with the United States condemning international terrorism, especially in the wake of the September 11 attacks and the October 12 nightclub bombings in Bali in 2002. Moreover, both regional security and international security remain very high on the agenda of the ASEAN countries, not unlike when the bloc was formed in 1967.

Given the political cohesion of strong landholding interests in ASEAN-4 countries, a particularly important area of interest to the ASEAN-4 in FTA negotiations with the United States is likely to be liberalization of agricultural trade. Indeed, the ASEAN-4 are all members of the Cairns Group of agricultural exporting countries, which has been an effective proponent of agricultural trade reform since the Uruguay Round.[12] Thus ASEAN interests in greater access to US markets for sugar, fresh fruits, certain processed foods, and even some cereals (e.g., Thai rice) are likely to be strongly emphasized in free trade negotiations with the United States; the countries will seek to win elimination of tariffs and quantitative controls on their agricultural exports to the United States if not total freedom from US farm programs whose distorting effects on world trade in agriculture might be fully addressed only in multilateral negotiations that include the European Union.

Finally, a second possibly important area of interest to the ASEAN-4 is textiles and apparel. Though MFA restrictions are to be lifted by 2005, elimination of remaining US tariffs on textiles and apparel under an FTA with the United States would be very desirable to ASEAN exporters of these products, especially as they face growing international competition from China's similar exports. Recognition of this interest might be expected to emanate not only from producers of textile and apparel products but also possibly from ASEAN labor groups whose members would

---

12. The remaining Cairns Group members include several existing or prospective US FTA partners: Australia, Canada, Chile, Costa Rica, Guatemala, New Zealand, and South Africa. Although the Cairns Group supports special and differential treatment for developing countries in multilateral trade negotiations on agriculture, it has not taken a formal position on its members pursuing free trade in agriculture through preferential, bilateral trade agreements.

particularly benefit from preferential access for ASEAN exports to the US market for textile products.

Trade- and Foreign Investment–Related Benefits

Assessing the basic economic benefits of FTAs between the United States and the major ASEAN countries involves analyzing the impacts of removing not only tariffs and nontariff barriers to bilateral merchandise trade but also regulatory barriers to bilateral trade in services and foreign direct investment, many of which may lie embedded in national economic policies and institutional practices rather than in border measures. The economic impacts of removing tariff restrictions are the most amenable to quantitative analysis using applied economic models of world trade and economic activity. By comparison, the impacts of removing nontariff barriers and other restrictions against trade in goods and services, and against long-term foreign investment, remain more difficult to analyze quantitatively and are treated only qualitatively here.

With regard to tariff protection, traditional economic theory suggests that trade and other economic benefits will depend importantly on the extent of net trade creation under a bilateral FTA—that is, on the extent to which preferential free trade between FTA partners results in the expansion of trade by internationally competitive producers, improving the economic welfare of consumers in the partner countries and improving the efficiency of resource use in the partner countries if not also the world economy at large.[13] Thus, a priori, some uncertainty surrounds whether FTAs are economically beneficial; this uncertainty may be compounded by assumptions concerning the structural form and parameter values of the applied economic models used to assess them. It should also be noted that although bilateral (and regional) FTAs can have significant spillover effects on third countries and on the world economy at large, partner countries pursue FTAs for their own national gain with no necessary regard for excluded countries, unless they fear offsetting or detrimental retaliation.

The main quantitative analysis presented here relies on simulation results using the GTAP world model (Gilbert 2003). However, before those

---

13. When *trade diversion* occurs, an FTA results in expansion of trade by inefficient producers whose exports expand solely because of their margin of preference. In simple economic models, such diversion generally results in economic gains for inefficient FTA exporters but reduced economic welfare for FTA importers and the world at large. See, for instance, Schiff and Winters (2003). In models suggested by the "new trade theory," consideration is additionally given to the impact of forces that go beyond efficiency gains from reallocating resources according to comparative advantage, forces such as especially imperfect competition and scale economies. For further discussion, see DeRosa (1998b); Burfisher, Robinson, and Thierfelder (2003).

results are discussed, estimates of the gross trade impacts of US-ASEAN FTAs using the so-called gravity model approach, in combination with recent econometric estimates by Andrew K. Rose of the mean sensitivity of bilateral trade flows to regional trade arrangements, are considered (DeRosa 2003; Rose 2003).

Based on econometric analysis, gravity model results carry statistical significance derived from real-world observation and scientific testing. To the extent that the regional trade agreements underlying the econometric estimates incorporate liberalization of both tariffs and nontariff barriers to bilateral trade, and also possibly liberalization of barriers to FDI, the gravity model results may have the additional advantage of capturing broader trade impacts than do applied analyses using world economic models that fail to incorporate liberalization of nontariff barriers to trade in goods and services and of barriers to FDI.

Unfortunately, the gravity model estimates presented here do not differentiate between trade creation and trade diversion effects. Accordingly, they should be interpreted as gross trade impacts—that is, upper-bound estimates of potential trade creation associated with prospective US-ASEAN free trade agreements.

Gravity Model Results

The gravity model estimates of the impacts of prospective US-ASEAN FTAs on merchandise trade are presented in table 6.8 (panel 2 and panel 3), along with US-ASEAN trade flows for base year 2000 (panel 1). Reflecting the asymmetry in US-ASEAN trade noted above, trade with the United States and intra-ASEAN trade make up about 60 percent of ASEAN trade with the world, while ASEAN trade makes up only about 15 percent of US trade with the world. Also as before, US exports to ASEAN are destined chiefly for Singapore, Malaysia, and Thailand, and US imports from ASEAN originate chiefly from Malaysia, Singapore, and Thailand.

Panel 2 of table 6.8 presents gravity model estimates of the trade impacts of US FTAs with the major ASEAN countries individually. Relative to 2000 exports, the prospective US free trade agreements would add most to total exports by the Philippines (44 percent) and by Malaysia and Thailand (about 30 percent). Exports of Indonesia and Singapore expand by much less in proportional terms: 21 percent and 17 percent, respectively. On a combined basis, the prospective US-ASEAN FTAs would add about 15 percent ($118 billion) to overall US merchandise exports—led by expanded US exports to Singapore ($44 billion), Malaysia ($30 billion), and Thailand ($16 billion).

From an economic welfare perspective, the contribution of the FTAs to US and ASEAN imports is arguably more important than their contribution to US and ASEAN exports. The individual FTAs contribute most to expanding imports of Malaysia and the Philippines (20 percent), and

Table 6.8 Gravity model estimates of the trade impacts of US-ASEAN FTAs (millions of dollars)

Exporting country	United States	ASEAN	Indonesia	Malaysia	Philippines	Singapore	Thailand	World	Percent
Panel 1. US-ASEAN trade, 2000 (Base)									
United States	—	49,947	3,393	13,668	5,325	20,270	7,291	771,991	12.9
ASEAN	88,096	77,864	6,143	19,198	4,795	38,569	9,158	405,215	60.2
Indonesia	11,097	10,823	—	2,269	693	6,562	1,299	62,103	52.7
Malaysia	25,990	28,464	1,131	—	1,142	22,848	3,344	98,153	84.5
Philippines	14,216	6,562	115	1,991	—	3,358	1,098	38,066	71.8
Singapore	19,630	21,083	3,789	11,763	2,115	—	3,416	137,932	44.8
Thailand	17,161	10,932	1,109	3,176	846	5,801	—	68,961	56.6
World	1,238,200	343,643	33,511	82,195	31,384	134,630	61,923	—	—
US-ASEAN (percent)	14.2	59.9	46.8	63.3	47.5	72.4	41.4	—	—

Exporting country	United States	ASEAN	Indonesia	Malaysia	Philippines	Singapore	Thailand	Trade increase	Percent change
Panel 2. Trade under US-ASEAN FTAs									
United States	—	108,959	7,402	29,817	11,616	44,218	15,905	118,023	15.3
ASEAN	192,178	77,864	6,143	19,198	4,795	38,569	9,158	104,083	25.7
Indonesia	24,209	10,823	—	2,269	693	6,562	1,299	13,111	21.1
Malaysia	56,696	28,464	1,131	—	1,142	22,848	3,344	30,706	31.3
Philippines	31,013	6,562	115	1,991	—	3,358	1,098	16,796	44.1
Singapore	42,823	21,083	3,789	11,763	2,115	—	3,416	23,193	16.8
Thailand	37,437	10,932	1,109	3,176	846	5,801	—	20,276	29.4
Trade increase	208,165	59,011	4,009	16,148	6,291	23,948	8,614	—	—
Percent change	16.8	17.2	12.0	19.6	20.0	17.8	13.9	—	—

(table continues next page)

Table 6.8 Gravity model estimates of the trade impacts of US-ASEAN FTAs (millions of dollars) *(continued)*

Exporting country	Importing country							World	Percent
	United States	ASEAN	Indonesia	Malaysia	Philippines	Singapore	Thailand	Trade increase	Percent change
Panel 3. Trade under US-ASEAN FTAs extended to intra-ASEAN trade									
United States	—	108,959	7,402	29,817	11,616	44,218	15,905	118,023	15.3
ASEAN	192,178	169,857	13,401	41,881	10,461	84,137	19,978	288,070	71.1
Indonesia	24,209	23,610	—	4,949	1,511	14,316	2,834	38,686	62.3
Malaysia	56,696	62,094	2,466	—	2,491	49,841	7,296	97,966	99.8
Philippines	31,013	14,314	250	4,342	—	7,326	2,396	32,301	84.9
Singapore	42,823	45,991	8,265	25,661	4,614	—	7,452	73,010	52.9
Thailand	37,437	23,847	2,419	6,928	1,846	12,655	—	46,107	66.9
Trade increase	208,165	242,999	18,525	61,513	17,623	115,085	30,254	—	—
Percent change	16.8	70.7	55.3	74.8	56.2	85.5	48.9	—	—

Notes: Trade increase denotes change in US-ASEAN trade relative to base level of US-ASEAN trade. Percent change denotes change in US-ASEAN trade relative to base US and ASEAN trade with the world.

Source: Based on DeRosa (2003).

Singapore (18 percent). Imports of Indonesia and Thailand expand by much less in proportional terms: 12 percent and 14 percent, respectively. On a combined basis, the prospective US-ASEAN FTAs would add nearly 17 percent ($208 billion) to overall US merchandise imports—led by expanded US imports from Malaysia ($57 billion), Singapore ($43 billion), and Thailand ($37 billion).[14]

The trade impacts given by the gravity model might be still larger in magnitude if the US FTAs were to induce the individual ASEAN countries to adopt free trade agreements among themselves, owing to the pressure of competitive liberalization. As noted in the first section of this chapter, the ASEAN countries have pledged to reduce tariffs on substantially all intra-ASEAN trade to between 0 and 5 percent by 2003 in conjunction with the ASEAN Free Trade Area. However, this commitment has not been fully honored to date, especially with respect to sensitive sectors still heavily protected by the ASEAN-4 and to eliminating NTBs on intrabloc trade (Pangestu 2003).

A series of US FTAs with the major ASEAN countries might be sufficient to tilt commitment within ASEAN to extending the FTAs to all intra-ASEAN trade, in effect forming an ASEAN-US free trade area. This scenario leads to considerable magnification of the previous trade impacts. The spread of FTAs between each pair of ASEAN countries causes expansion of ASEAN trade by about 70 percent (relative to 2000 trade levels). The exports of the individual ASEAN countries expand between 53 percent (Singapore) and 100 percent (Malaysia), while the imports of these countries expand by between 49 percent (Thailand) and 86 percent (Singapore). These are remarkable increases and, within the framework of the gravity model, they indicate that the spread of US bilateral FTAs regionally can significantly magnify the economic impacts of US bilateral FTAs with individual trading partners in Southeast Asia. This finding may be particularly important to ASEAN policymakers as they seek to enhance their export performance in the face of continued globalization, enlargement of other regional trade arrangements (e.g., the Free Trade Area of the Americas, or the FTAA), and the emergence of China as an economic power.

GTAP Model Results

The GTAP model is a publicly available computable general equilibrium (CGE) model of world trade and production that has come into partic-

---

14. These very large trade impacts point to the possibility of a considerable worsening of the US merchandise trade balance with the ASEAN countries as a bloc ($90 billion) and individually (e.g., Malaysia, $27 billion; Thailand, $21 billion). To the extent that these trade balance impacts are not offset by changes in US and ASEAN trade balances with third countries (or by induced international capital flows), they might imply significant depreciation of the US dollar vis-à-vis ASEAN currencies.

ularly wide use during recent years (Hertel 1997). The model was employed to quantify the impacts of US FTAs with Singapore and each of the ASEAN-4 individually, in addition to several other prospective partners in US bilateral FTAs (see Gilbert 2003). For each agreement, tariffs on all bilateral trade between the United States and the prospective FTA partner were reduced to zero, including bilateral trade in agriculture for which tariff-equivalent measures are specified in the GTAP model to represent price-raising measures that protect domestic agriculture. Nontariff barriers are not otherwise represented in the GTAP model, and accordingly the impact of their possible elimination under US bilateral FTAs is not captured in the model simulations. Finally, trade in services and possibilities for liberalizing border measures and internal policies restricting international trade in services were not explicitly considered, again because such measures are not incorporated in the basic GTAP model (Dimaranan and McDougall 2002).

Table 6.9 provides a summary of the economywide impacts found by the GTAP model under prospective US FTAs with each of the five ASEAN countries for the United States, the FTA partner country, prominent Asian countries, the European Union, and the world. Among the economywide variables highlighted in table 6.9 are changes in imports and exports, tariff revenue, and GDP. Also included among the diagnostic statistics is equivalent variation, expressed in US dollars. This measure provides an indication of the change in national economic welfare associated with each free trade agreement. Essentially, it measures the change in real income attributable to efficiency changes in the use of productive resources and to possible terms-of-trade effects. Broadly speaking, allocative efficiency increases when trade liberalization leads to greater trade creation than trade diversion, while possibly improved terms of trade that arise from preferential trading arrangements also add to national economic welfare.

Impacts on FTA Countries

The trade impacts found in the GTAP model analysis are much smaller in magnitude than those found in the gravity model analysis. The GTAP results suggest that elimination of import tariffs on bilateral trade under US-ASEAN FTAs would increase total exports by between only 1 percent (Malaysia) and 5 percent (Philippines) for the ASEAN-4, and substantially less than 1 percent for the United States and Singapore. Of course, unilateral trade liberalization by the United States and ASEAN countries would result in significantly greater increases in total exports, but still by no more than about 10 percent for the ASEAN-4 and about 4 percent for the United States. Singapore's total merchandise exports would expand by only 0.1 percent because the city-state is essentially a duty-free trade zone.

Table 6.9 GTAP model simulation results: Economywide impacts of US-ASEAN FTAs

	United States		FTA partner		Other ASEAN		China		Korea		Japan		European Union		World	
	FTA	UTL	FTA	UTL	FTA	UTL*	FTA	UTL*	FTA	UTL*	FTA	UTL*	FTA	UTL*	FTA	UTL*
US-Indonesia FTA																
Import value (percent change)	0.22	−0.26	4.95	8.01	n.a.	n.a.	n.a.	n.a.	n.a.	n.a.	n.a.	n.a.	n.a.	n.a.	n.a.	n.a.
Export value (percent change)	0.24	3.86	4.29	4.87	−0.03	0.30	−0.11	1.55	−0.01	0.97	−0.02	0.78	−0.02	0.26	0.05	0.91
Tariff rev. (millions of $ change)	−1,189	−25,093	−335	−3,918	n.a.	n.a.	n.a.	n.a.	n.a.	n.a.	n.a.	n.a.	n.a.	n.a.	n.a.	n.a.
Nominal GDP (percent change)	−0.02	−1.17	2.75	−0.32	n.a.	n.a.	n.a.	n.a.	n.a.	n.a.	n.a.	n.a.	n.a.	n.a.	n.a.	n.a.
Equivalent variation (millions of $)	−179	−9,279	1,313	1,169	−96	1,318	−295	2,999	−45	1,473	−278	1,440	−286	1,967	−200	7,153
US-Malaysia FTA																
Import value (percent change)	0.15	−0.26	1.87	8.61	n.a.	n.a.	n.a.	n.a.	n.a.	n.a.	n.a.	n.a.	n.a.	n.a.	n.a.	n.a.
Export value (percent change)	0.15	3.86	1.37	5.35	−0.06	0.87	−0.04	1.63	−0.02	0.49	−0.01	0.93	−0.01	0.27	0.03	0.97
Tariff rev. (millions of $ change)	−400	−25,093	−658	−4,846	n.a.	n.a.	n.a.	n.a.	n.a.	n.a.	n.a.	n.a.	n.a.	n.a.	n.a.	n.a.
Nominal GDP (percent change)	0.03	−1.17	0.46	2.67	n.a.	n.a.	n.a.	n.a.	n.a.	n.a.	n.a.	n.a.	n.a.	n.a.	n.a.	n.a.
Equivalent variation (millions of $)	392	−9,279	248	87	−91	2,316	−70	3,192	−30	663	−127	2,034	−140	2,107	−62	6,384
US-Philippines FTA																
Import value (percent change)	0.19	−0.26	5.82	9.63	n.a.	n.a.	n.a.	n.a.	n.a.	n.a.	n.a.	n.a.	n.a.	n.a.	n.a.	n.a.
Export value (percent change)	0.22	3.86	5.05	9.97	−0.06	0.48	−0.06	1.59	−0.04	0.53	0.00	0.83	−0.02	0.26	0.04	0.93
Tariff rev. (millions of $ change)	−662	−25,093	−504	−2,836	n.a.	n.a.	n.a.	n.a.	n.a.	n.a.	n.a.	n.a.	n.a.	n.a.	n.a.	n.a.
Nominal GDP (percent change)	0.01	−1.17	3.06	−2.99	n.a.	n.a.	n.a.	n.a.	n.a.	n.a.	n.a.	n.a.	n.a.	n.a.	n.a.	n.a.
Equivalent variation (millions of $)	224	−9,279	907	−828	−75	1,493	−157	3,155	−50	745	−204	1,922	−211	2,261	−1	5,743
US-Singapore FTA																
Import value (percent change)	0.05	−0.26	0.47	0.09	n.a.	n.a.	n.a.	n.a.	n.a.	n.a.	n.a.	n.a.	n.a.	n.a.	n.a.	n.a.
Export value (percent change)	0.05	3.86	0.45	0.05	−0.01	0.80	−0.01	1.55	−0.01	0.50	0.00	0.74	0.00	0.28	0.01	0.86
Tariff rev. (millions of $ change)	−306	−25,093	−29	−230	n.a.	n.a.	n.a.	n.a.	n.a.	n.a.	n.a.	n.a.	n.a.	n.a.	n.a.	n.a.
Nominal GDP (percent change)	−0.01	−1.17	0.66	−0.25	n.a.	n.a.	n.a.	n.a.	n.a.	n.a.	n.a.	n.a.	n.a.	n.a.	n.a.	n.a.
Equivalent variation (millions of $)	−81	−9,279	343	21	−52	1,648	−47	3,075	−7	656	−11	1,640	−35	2,074	−31	5,264
US-Thailand FTA																
Import value (percent change)	0.38	−0.26	4.68	15.63	n.a.	n.a.	n.a.	n.a.	n.a.	n.a.	n.a.	n.a.	n.a.	n.a.	n.a.	n.a.
Export value (percent change)	0.40	3.86	3.46	9.70	−0.08	0.62	−0.10	1.64	−0.05	0.59	−0.05	1.00	−0.02	0.29	0.06	1.03
Tariff rev. (millions of $ change)	−982	−25,093	1,531	−7,918	n.a.	n.a.	n.a.	n.a.	n.a.	n.a.	n.a.	n.a.	n.a.	n.a.	n.a.	n.a.
Nominal GDP (percent change)	0.07	−1.17	0.72	−5.34	n.a.	n.a.	n.a.	n.a.	n.a.	n.a.	n.a.	n.a.	n.a.	n.a.	n.a.	n.a.
Equivalent variation (millions of $)	824	−9,279	780	−126	−196	1,689	−255	3,159	−56	737	−369	2,777	−338	2,289	−358	7,013

FTA = bilateral free trade agreement; UTL = unilateral trade liberalization on a nondiscriminatory basis; UTL* = combined unilateral trade liberalization by US and ASEAN country partner; Other ASEAN = an aggregate of the four ASEAN countries not included in the US bilateral FTA with the indicated FTA partner; n.a. = Simulated value of variable not compiled in GTAP model results

Source: Gilbert (2003).

It is also noteworthy that the GTAP results indicate that under unilateral trade liberalization the Philippines, Thailand, and the United States would all experience lower, not higher, economic welfare. This results from terms-of-trade losses under unilateral trade liberalization, attributable to relatively inelastic demands for differentiated trade goods in the GTAP model following the so-called Armington assumption, under which similar traded goods produced in different countries are assumed to be imperfect substitutes for one another (Armington 1969).[15]

Finally, the GTAP results indicate that the individual ASEAN countries, and the United States itself, benefit from pursuing a US bilateral FTA. As measured by equivalent variation, economic gains for the ASEAN countries under the US FTAs range between $1,313 million (Indonesia) and $248 million (Malaysia).[16] In each case, the detailed simulation results indicate that allocative efficiency improves (suggesting that net trade creation occurs) but that positive terms-of-trade effects arising from preference margins for ASEAN exporters in the US market contribute most to the reported welfare gains.[17] Unfortunately, the magnitude of these positive terms-of-trade effects is at some risk if the United States pursues FTAs simultaneously with not only the ASEAN countries but also trading partners in other regions. GTAP simulation results for such a scenario (not reported in table 6.9) indicate that although the welfare gains of the individual ASEAN countries remain positive, they become considerably smaller (Gilbert 2003). For instance, the total welfare gain of Thailand under a US free trade agreement declines from $780 million to $428 million.[18]

For the United States, the greatest economic gain occurs under the US FTA with Thailand ($824 million), followed by the US FTAs with Malaysia ($392 million) and the Philippines ($224 million). In each of these cases, the US welfare gain is attributable to substantial terms-of-trade gains, not unlike those enjoyed by the ASEAN partners to the agreements. The simulated US welfare gains under the US FTAs with Indonesia (–$179 mil-

---

15. The Armington assumption of less-than-perfect substitution in demand for similar trade goods raises the prospect that unilateral trade liberalization will reduce economic welfare for some countries, namely, for those countries in the GTAP model for which an "optimal" tariff regime could be pursued at a somewhat higher average import tariff in the absence of tariff retaliation by their major trading partners.

16. All values reported for the GTAP simulation results are in 1997 dollars, where 1997 is the base period for the current version of the model.

17. In simple world trade models that assume that similar traded goods produced in different countries are essentially homogeneous, these terms-of-trade gains would have their reflection in forgone tariff revenues in the FTA partner country if no trade creation occurs, and so would be counted as an additional economic loss to the FTA partner country. See, for instance, Schiff and Winters (2003).

18. The ASEAN country most adversely affected by proliferation of US bilateral FTAs is Malaysia. Its total welfare gain under a US FTA falls from $248 million to zero.

lion) and Singapore (–$81 million) are negative because the average levels of protection against US exports to Indonesia and Singapore are substantially less than against US exports to the other three ASEAN countries, leaving (negative) terms-of-trade effects similar to those encountered under US unilateral trade liberalization to dominate.[19]

Detailed GTAP results for changes in the sectoral pattern of exports are presented in table 6.10. They indicate that the prospective US-ASEAN FTAs would considerably expand bilateral US-ASEAN exports in important and, in some cases, sensitive product categories.[20] ASEAN-4 exports to the United States would particularly expand in nongrain crops, processed food products, and textiles and apparel. For Indonesia, exports to the United States might also expand significantly in certain machinery. For Malaysia, they might also expand significantly in transportation equipment. For the Philippines, they might also expand significantly in a wide variety of categories: metals and metal products, chemicals, motor vehicles and transportation equipment, and machinery. For Singapore, exports to the United States might also expand significantly in chemical products. And finally, for Thailand exports to the United States might also expand significantly in metals, metal products, and miscellaneous manufactures.

With respect to US bilateral exports to the ASEAN countries, the detailed GTAP results in table 6.10 indicate that the prospective US FTAs would significantly expand US exports to individual ASEAN countries in a number of product categories: nongrain crops (Malaysia, Singapore, and Thailand), animal products (Malaysia, the Philippines, and Thailand), forestry and fisheries products (Thailand), processed food products (Indonesia, the Philippines, Singapore, and Thailand), textiles and apparel (ASEAN-4), motor vehicles (ASEAN-4), and miscellaneous manufactures (Indonesia, the Philippines, and Thailand).

The changes in the regional pattern of exports under the prospective US-ASEAN FTAs are reported in table 6.11. They reveal that the expansion of ASEAN exports to the United States would divert exports to the United States from competing countries widely but most prominently from excluded ASEAN-4 countries, China, Korea, Taiwan, and the Central American countries as a bloc. The expansion of US exports to the ASEAN countries would also divert exports from competing countries, including in some instances Japan and the European Union, except under the US FTAs with Indonesia and Singapore. In those cases, as noted previously,

---

19. Of course, if the United States pursues FTAs simultaneously with the ASEAN countries and countries in other regions as mentioned previously in the text, then US welfare gains become dependably positive in the aggregate. See Gilbert (2003).

20. The discussion that follows in the text refers to GTAP model results indicating large *proportional* increases of exports in product categories. If changes in bilateral trade were measured in absolute terms, increases of exports in other product categories might also be found to be important.

Table 6.10 GTAP model simulation results: Changes in sectoral pattern of exports (percent change)

| | US-Indonesia FTA | | | | US-Malaysia FTA | | | | US-Philippines FTA | | | | US-Singapore FTA | | | | US-Thailand FTA | | | |
| | United States | | Indonesia | | United States | | Malaysia | | United States | | Philippines | | United States | | Singapore | | United States | | Thailand | |
Category	Total	To Indonesia	Total	To United States	Total	To Malaysia	Total	To United States	Total	To Philippines	Total	To United States	Total	To Singapore	Total	To United States	Total	To Thailand	Total	To United States
Grains	0.0	19.6	-7.3	-5.7	-0.2	10.0	1.9	24.1	1.6	54.3	-3.9	0.2	0.0	0.7	-1.3	2.0	-0.3	4.0	-4.5	7.7
Other crops	1.0	34.4	21.4	104.9	2.8	210.0	11.4	143.2	0.3	66.0	-2.7	25.8	0.2	34.1	2.6	125.0	0.7	134.5	14.3	109.3
Animal products	0.2	43.1	-10.7	-8.1	-0.2	103.4	0.1	6.1	0.1	132.9	-7.9	-4.9	0.0	1.0	-1.7	1.3	1.1	111.4	-4.3	-2.0
Forestry and fisheries	0.2	5.3	-4.3	-2.9	0.1	3.9	-1.9	-0.9	0.0	24.4	-10.4	-7.6	0.0	0.0	-0.3	0.3	0.6	463.9	-4.6	-2.9
Processed food products	0.7	107.7	-1.4	40.1	0.2	67.8	4.7	49.6	0.8	99.5	25.5	70.5	0.3	26.5	3.0	62.6	1.4	289.0	8.8	55.3
Lumber	0.6	60.7	-4.6	14.1	0.3	76.5	-0.8	10.2	0.5	93.7	-3.9	2.5	0.0	0.6	-0.2	7.9	0.1	77.1	-1.5	9.9
Pulp and paper products	0.2	20.7	-4.4	1.5	0.2	30.0	-1.6	2.4	0.2	28.4	-1.6	5.4	0.0	0.7	-0.9	-0.1	0.1	39.2	-2.1	1.4
Textiles and apparel	1.1	137.4	34.8	123.7	0.3	170.3	27.3	145.1	1.2	208.0	76.4	126.9	0.1	4.3	31.2	152.5	1.2	290.1	38.4	132.2
Coal, oil, and gas	0.3	32.1	-1.9	-0.4	0.0	9.9	-0.7	1.3	0.0	16.9	-4.1	-4.3	0.0	0.0	-0.9	-1.0	-0.2	18.7	-1.4	2.7
Petroleum and coal prods.	0.1	17.7	-1.5	7.7	0.1	90.5	-0.3	8.4	0.0	11.1	-0.2	-0.2	0.0	-0.1	0.0	9.4	0.0	31.0	-0.8	8.7
Chemicals	0.3	42.9	-4.5	0.4	0.1	21.4	3.4	13.2	0.1	33.3	0.5	17.8	0.0	0.6	1.0	20.1	0.7	72.6	-1.8	8.1
Metals	0.2	62.1	-7.4	-1.8	0.3	48.4	-1.4	11.8	0.0	39.5	-5.6	19.4	0.0	-0.1	-1.2	14.1	0.1	52.9	-4.4	16.3
Metal products	1.2	83.4	-1.6	11.8	0.5	70.8	-1.2	10.4	0.5	47.9	0.3	19.1	0.0	0.5	0.0	19.4	2.6	155.3	0.1	15.4
Electronic equipment	0.3	58.8	-2.7	4.3	0.1	2.1	0.8	4.7	0.4	15.8	2.9	5.2	0.1	0.4	0.4	2.6	0.2	19.6	-2.2	3.4
Motor vehicles	0.3	600.4	-13.1	0.5	0.6	1,101.5	-1.8	13.5	0.5	537.4	2.2	16.8	0.0	0.3	-0.9	13.4	2.0	1,592.9	-0.2	15.1
Transportation equipment	0.0	2.6	-4.2	8.5	-0.2	1.5	-1.6	34.0	-0.1	45.0	-2.4	17.0	0.0	0.1	-0.7	7.1	-0.2	10.5	-11.2	9.2
Machinery NEC	0.1	26.8	1.9	16.9	0.1	23.7	-0.4	11.1	0.1	30.5	4.8	17.4	0.0	0.4	0.5	16.3	0.4	72.4	-0.5	15.9
Manufactures NEC	0.5	200.2	-5.4	4.5	0.2	52.8	0.6	8.0	0.3	113.6	-4.4	0.8	0.0	0.5	-0.9	10.4	0.1	108.6	2.4	20.0
Services	0.0	4.2	-6.8	-6.8	-0.1	1.4	-2.4	-2.3	0.0	4.8	-7.7	-7.7	0.0	0.9	-1.2	-1.2	-0.3	2.0	-3.7	-3.6

FTA = bilateral free trade agreement; NEC = not elsewhere classified

Source: Gilbert (2003).

Table 6.11   GTAP model simulation results: Changes in regional pattern of exports (percent change)

Country/region	US-Indonesia FTA			US-Malaysia FTA			US-Philippines FTA			US-Singapore FTA			US-Thailand FTA		
	Total	To United States	To Indonesia	Total	To United States	To Malaysia	Total	To United States	To Philippines	Total	To United States	To Singapore	Total	To United States	To Thailand
Indonesia	4.29	48.92	0.00	-0.05	-0.22	-2.37	-0.06	-0.62	0.38	-0.01	-0.19	0.32	-0.10	-0.72	-4.21
Malaysia	-0.04	-0.23	0.16	1.37	10.61	0.00	-0.07	-0.16	-0.24	-0.01	-0.25	0.29	-0.04	-0.06	-3.02
Philippines	-0.07	-0.62	2.85	-0.06	-0.25	0.14	5.05	27.10	0.00	-0.03	-0.21	0.38	-0.09	-0.39	-3.37
Singapore	-0.01	-0.12	1.44	-0.08	-0.24	-0.59	-0.07	-0.12	-0.53	0.45	6.15	0.00	-0.10	-0.06	-4.08
Thailand	-0.04	-0.65	1.49	-0.04	-0.15	-1.41	-0.05	-0.37	-0.10	0.00	-0.18	0.27	3.46	31.77	0.00
Total ASEAN	0.60	6.33	1.30	0.29	2.39	-0.78	0.47	3.88	-0.28	0.14	1.61	0.54	0.56	5.72	-3.70
China	-0.11	-1.00	2.07	-0.04	-0.21	-0.89	-0.06	-0.53	3.51	-0.01	-0.18	0.67	-0.10	-0.59	-3.76
Korea	-0.01	-0.48	4.08	-0.02	-0.16	-0.32	-0.04	-0.25	0.80	-0.01	-0.17	0.44	-0.05	-0.16	-4.18
Taiwan	-0.03	-0.36	3.26	-0.03	-0.15	-0.56	-0.03	-0.22	4.41	-0.01	-0.16	0.50	-0.06	-0.09	-5.00
Japan	-0.02	-0.03	-1.16	-0.01	0.02	-1.73	0.00	0.07	-3.21	0.00	-0.11	0.34	-0.05	0.28	-7.61
Australia	0.00	-0.27	1.19	-0.02	0.07	-2.97	-0.01	-0.07	-1.10	0.00	-0.05	0.01	-0.04	-0.01	-5.53
New Zealand	0.00	-0.40	0.65	-0.03	0.05	-3.37	-0.03	-0.25	-1.05	0.00	-0.07	-0.26	-0.05	-0.42	-6.67
Central America	-0.14	-1.25	3.64	-0.03	-0.22	1.12	-0.08	-0.62	4.77	-0.02	-0.15	0.25	-0.10	-0.81	-0.59
Chile	-0.02	-0.52	0.09	-0.02	0.04	-3.52	-0.02	-0.11	0.91	0.00	-0.06	-0.06	-0.04	-0.22	-3.29
Rest of South America	-0.03	-0.44	2.31	-0.01	-0.01	-1.16	-0.01	-0.14	0.72	-0.01	-0.06	0.32	-0.03	-0.18	-5.75
Canada	-0.04	-0.11	2.86	-0.02	-0.03	0.09	-0.04	-0.06	0.64	-0.01	-0.04	0.51	-0.02	-0.03	-1.19
United States	0.24	0.00	32.96	0.15	0.00	18.75	0.22	0.00	29.99	0.05	0.00	0.97	0.40	0.00	62.41
Mexico	-0.03	-0.13	3.30	-0.02	-0.04	-0.56	-0.02	-0.07	2.51	-0.02	-0.05	0.48	-0.01	-0.05	-2.70
Total NAFTA	0.16	-0.08	28.45	0.10	0.00	17.10	0.15	-0.03	27.16	0.03	0.00	0.94	0.28	0.00	56.57
European Union	-0.02	-0.20	0.96	-0.01	-0.01	-0.56	-0.02	-0.08	1.58	0.00	-0.08	0.47	-0.02	-0.02	-3.51
World	0.05	0.23	4.89	0.03	0.15	1.84	0.04	0.19	5.69	0.01	0.06	0.52	0.06	0.39	4.66

FTA = bilateral free trade agreement

Source: Gilbert (2003).

US exporters would enjoy only very narrow margins of preference in the two countries.

Political Economy Considerations

A number of the sectors in which trade is sharply affected by the prospective US-ASEAN FTAs are "sensitive" in either the United States or the ASEAN countries. From a political economy perspective, this could make it difficult for economic authorities in the United States and partner countries to win approval for the agreements.

In the ASEAN countries, double-digit and even triple-digit (percentage) surges in US bilateral exports of sensitive agricultural commodities, processed foods, textiles and apparel, and motor vehicles would meet with political opposition from affected landowners, food producers, manufacturers, and even possibly organized labor in sheltered sectors such as motor vehicles. This opposition would be particularly strong if the surges in US exports to ASEAN partner countries resulted in the expansion of overall imports in sensitive trade categories (i.e., trade creation) and significantly lower domestic prices.

Similar political resistance should be expected in the United States among affected resource owners, manufacturers, and organized labor in response to surges in ASEAN exports to the United States in the sensitive categories of agricultural commodities, processed foods, and textiles and apparel. Again, the fierceness of resistance would be largely contingent on the degree to which surges in ASEAN exports to the United States increased overall imports and put significant downward pressure on US prices in the affected sectors. However, so long as only one or two US-ASEAN free trade agreements go forward, political opposition to the agreements might be stronger in the ASEAN countries than in the United States because US exports under FTA preferences have a greater capacity to significantly affect the comparatively small ASEAN markets.[21]

Of course, broader political economy factors surround prospective US-ASEAN FTAs than simply the economic interests of exporters and producers of domestic substitutes in the ASEAN countries and in the United States. Agriculture is a prime case in point. Notwithstanding possible deadlocked WTO negotiations in agriculture, domestic coalitions in favor of agricultural trade liberalization in Southeast Asia and the United States are oriented principally toward the Doha Round negotiations; they might be reluctant to support lesser trade deals involving agriculture, especially if the deals threaten to unravel or weaken domestic coalitions supporting the WTO

---

21. Political resistance in the United States to US FTAs would naturally be expected to mount as more and more FTAs are struck with partner countries in ASEAN or elsewhere, raising the combined capacity of exporters in the FTA partner countries to significantly reduce US prices of sensitive products.

agricultural trade talks. Particularly for the United States, this reluctance might also manifest itself in a willingness to incorporate fundamental US agricultural reforms in bilateral free trade agreements only if the US reforms are to be implemented over a long period of time. Such implementation would certainly not take place before still-possible reforms to agriculture are negotiated in the Doha Round, where the United States would look to use its agriculture reform bargaining chip to greater advantage than in negotiations of bilateral FTAs with the ASEAN-4 or other individual countries.

ASEAN Structural Adjustment

Finally, given the importance of structural adjustment issues to the ASEAN countries, it is interesting to consider the impacts of the US-ASEAN FTAs on factor returns.

The GTAP model incorporates five primary factors of production: two agriculture- and resource sector–specific factors—land and natural resources; and three factors that are assumed to be mobile across all domestic sectors—physical capital, unskilled labor, and skilled labor. The GTAP model results for these primary factors, presented in table 6.12, indicate some interesting patterns under both US bilateral FTAs and unilateral trade liberalization.

For the United States, bilateral FTAs with Malaysia and the Philippines tend to raise returns to US landowners (between roughly 0.5 percent and 1.0 percent), but to have little effect on returns to US owners of other primary factors. Presumably, this outcome reflects the relatively strong derived demand for the services of agricultural land in connection with the two US-ASEAN free trade agreements. In contrast, US unilateral trade liberalization has an opposite impact on returns to land, sharply reducing the land rental rate by about 2.5 percent. At the same time, it also raises the return to natural resources (e.g., forestry, fisheries, and mineral and petroleum resources) by nearly 2.5 percent, but results in only small increases in factor rewards for both unskilled labor and skilled labor and for physical capital (0.2 percent to 0.3 percent).

For the ASEAN countries, changes in factor returns are more pronounced. The US-ASEAN FTAs sharply reduce returns to natural resources in most ASEAN countries, especially Indonesia (9.0 percent) and Malaysia (3.1 percent). In Malaysia and the Philippines, factor returns to land are also sharply reduced, by 4.0 percent and 2.6 percent, respectively. Returns to physical capital, however, are generally higher under the US FTAs, especially in the Philippines, Malaysia, and Thailand (between 1.4 and 2.1 percent). Labor benefits appreciably too, especially unskilled labor. In the ASEAN-4, the wage rate of unskilled labor increases by between 1.0 percent in Indonesia and 2.7 percent in the Philippines, while the wage rate of skilled labor follows a similar pattern of increases across countries but at somewhat more moderate rates of increase.

Table 6.12 GTAP model simulation results: Impacts of US-ASEAN FTAs on factor returns (percent change)

Factor	United States		FTA partner	
	FTA	UTL	FTA	UTL
US-Indonesia FTA				
Land	−0.02	−2.56	0.61	−4.31
Unskilled labor	0.01	0.23	1.03	2.74
Skilled labor	0.02	0.30	0.79	3.10
Capital	0.02	0.24	0.94	2.95
Natural resources	0.21	2.43	−8.97	−4.27
US-Malaysia FTA				
Land	0.66	−2.56	−3.98	−7.69
Unskilled labor	0.01	0.23	1.53	7.37
Skilled labor	0.01	0.30	1.52	8.08
Capital	0.01	0.24	1.49	7.61
Natural resources	−0.07	2.43	−3.05	−3.83
US-Philippines FTA				
Land	0.79	−2.56	−2.56	−11.80
Unskilled labor	0.01	0.23	2.67	3.70
Skilled labor	0.01	0.30	1.71	4.30
Capital	0.01	0.24	2.13	4.19
Natural resources	−0.07	2.43	−0.75	−0.04
US-Singapore FTA				
Land	0.04	−2.56	1.52	0.73
Unskilled labor	0.00	0.23	0.65	0.47
Skilled labor	0.00	0.30	0.51	0.48
Capital	0.00	0.24	0.48	0.48
Natural resources	0.00	2.43	−2.10	0.41
US-Thailand FTA				
Land	0.21	−2.56	0.41	−6.62
Unskilled labor	0.02	0.23	1.83	5.04
Skilled labor	0.03	0.30	1.43	6.41
Capital	0.02	0.24	1.40	5.85
Natural resources	−0.17	2.43	−2.56	−2.60

FTA = bilateral free trade agreement
UTL = unilateral trade liberalization on a nondiscriminatory basis

Source: Gilbert (2003).

Unilateral trade liberalization, however, provides the sharpest increases in wage rates across the ASEAN-4, and notably provides relatively greater returns to skilled labor than to unskilled labor—by margins nearly as great as a full percentage point. For instance, in Malaysia the wage rate for skilled labor increases by 8.1 percent, while the wage rate for unskilled labor increases by 7.4 percent; in Thailand the wage rate for skilled labor increases by 6.4 percent, while the wage rate for unskilled labor increases by 5 percent. Given that a country's own trade liberalization is usually the dominant and major component of the impacts on the country of multilateral trade liberalization, these results suggest that nondiscriminatory, multilateral trade liberalization would provide greater support than US FTAs for structural adjustment in the ASEAN-4, by not only increasing wage incentives for skilled workers but also increasing effective demand for domestic production of skilled-labor-intensive goods.[22]

Impacts on Third Countries

The GTAP results also provide insight to the potential global impacts of US-ASEAN FTAs that arise from the diversion of trade under the prospective US-ASEAN free trade agreements.[23] The third-country impacts found by the GTAP model are summarized in table 6.9; they cover the international trade, import tariff revenues, aggregate output, and economic welfare of the four major ASEAN countries excluded from each US bilateral agreement, other major Asian countries (China, Korea, and Japan), the European Union, and the world as a whole. Also included in table 6.9 are the combined impacts on these countries of nondiscriminatory trade liberalization undertaken by the United States and each FTA partner.

The simulation results tabulated in table 6.9 reveal what might be expected. Total exports of the countries excluded from the US-ASEAN free trade agreements decline in value modestly (generally by less than 1 percent), and economic welfare in these countries and in the world as a whole is adversely affected, especially in two cases: the US-Thailand FTA (world welfare falls by $358 million) and the US-Indonesia FTA (world welfare falls by $200 million). The negative impact on economic welfare in the excluded ASEAN countries (combined) is very substantial in the case of the US-Thailand FTA ($196 million), but generally less than $100 million in connection with the remaining four US-ASEAN FTAs considered in the GTAP analysis. Among the excluded countries outside Southeast Asia, Japan and the European Union are most adversely affected by the prospective US FTAs, especially those with the ASEAN-4. In the case of the US-Thailand FTA, economic welfare in Japan falls by $369 million and in the European Union by $338 million. China also loses significantly: the US-Indonesia FTA results in a $295 million loss in economic welfare, and the US-Thailand FTA results in a $255 million loss.[24] For Korea, the pro-

---

22. It is also notable that nondiscriminatory trade liberalization tends to sharply reduce returns to land as well in the ASEAN-4, reflecting the relatively high levels of agricultural protection in these countries currently.

23. Because traded goods in the GTAP model are differentiated according to their country of production, diversion of trade in the model can have important spillover effects on third countries—much more marked than in simpler world trade models that assume that similar trade goods produced by different countries are homogenous.

24. China's economy is much smaller than the economy of either Japan or the European Union. Therefore, relative to GDP, the economic losses simulated by the GTAP model for China are substantially greater than those simulated for Japan or the European Union.

spective US-ASEAN FTAs with the ASEAN-4, considered individually, result in smaller welfare losses—between $30 million and $56 million.

Economic welfare gains of the excluded countries identified in table 6.9 under nondiscriminatory trade liberalization in the United States and its FTA partners are several orders of magnitude greater than the economic welfare losses just reviewed. For instance, while China's economic welfare would fall by nearly $300 million under a US-Indonesia FTA, its economic welfare would rise by ten times this amount ($3,000 million) if the United States and Indonesia were to eliminate their import tariffs on a nondiscriminatory basis. Unfortunately, according to the GTAP results, the net economic gains to the world from nondiscriminatory trade liberalization by the United States and Indonesia ($7,153 million) are insufficient to "buy off" the US economic loss ($9,279 million) under such a scenario. At the same time, however, it should be clear that this situation would change if the United States were to pursue FTAs with more than a single ASEAN country and with countries outside Southeast Asia. In that case, the opportunity costs to the world economy of not successfully completing the Doha Round would begin to rise steeply, while the opportunity cost to the United States of pursuing nondiscriminatory trade liberalization (as part of a successful multilateral trade negotiation) would begin to fall steeply.

Other Economic Impacts

To this point, the economic benefits of prospective US FTAs with the ASEAN countries have been examined principally with respect to changes in international trade and follow-on changes in output, employment, and economic welfare given by simulations of the GTAP model. Additional economic impacts of US-ASEAN FTAs should be anticipated, though their quantification lies beyond the scope of most applied economic models and they are hence treated qualitatively here. The most prominent of these impacts concerns prospects for greater trade in services and foreign direct investment.

Greater trade in services and FDI might be expected to follow directly from impacts of the US-ASEAN FTAs on bilateral trade flows. As trade expands, trade-related services (e.g., for transportation and insurance) should be expected to expand in favor of both the United States and its ASEAN FTA partners. Similarly, certain FDI might expand proportionally with increased bilateral trade flows—for instance, with respect to the establishment of overseas sales and service facilities. However, the economic benefits (and possible economic costs) of such expanded FDI becomes increasingly difficult to allocate between the United States and its ASEAN FTA partners, especially when possibilities for greater technology transfer and diffusion, improved labor and management skills and training, enhanced total factor productivity, and other economic benefits from higher FDI in the ASEAN countries are recognized (see Moran 1998, 2001; see also DeRosa 1998a). Expanded FDI also raises the prospect of dynamic effects on the ASEAN economies and the United States: that is, additional economic effects that occur with a discernible time trend adding to, or possibly subtracting from, growth of output and employment beyond the short run.

But by far the most important additional economic impacts of the prospective US FTAs with the ASEAN countries would not be those arising from the simple expansion of US-ASEAN trade on a preferential basis. They would instead come from the expected expansion of trade in services and FDI induced by FTA liberalization of the economic policies that directly inhibit both forms of international economic intercourse. Indeed, the past experience of ASEAN countries and the broader general experience of emerging-market economies with globalization during the 1990s suggest that in adopting more open policies toward trade in services and especially FDI, the ASEAN countries will attract greater export-oriented foreign investment that will potentially further economic growth, the modernization of the services economy, and the transfer (and diffusion) of higher levels of technology, know-how, and labor and management skills. In this way, the robust export performance of the ASEAN countries might be maintained if not improved by their participation in US-ASEAN FTAs. Attracting greater foreign investment in domestic service sectors and outward-oriented goods sectors might also be expected to smooth the adjustment of the ASEAN-4 economies especially and their labor force to the production and export of higher-valued products in the face of increasing competition from lower-wage emerging-market countries such as China and even from less-developed countries in ASEAN, such as Vietnam and Laos.[25]

Finally, it should be cautioned that US-ASEAN FTAs might also significantly divert potential trade in services and FDI from the ASEAN countries and even from the United States, in which case net economic benefits could be substantially smaller than expected. Under preferential FTAs, US service providers and multinational corporations might face reduced competition in ASEAN partner countries from service providers and multinational firms in the European Union or Japan that could offer potentially greater benefits for the ASEAN countries. And even the United

---

25. If the United States concludes FTAs with each of the major ASEAN countries, then the distribution as well as magnitude of induced US FDI in the ASEAN region becomes an interesting question. The issue of possible investment diversion induced by US FTAs with the ASEAN countries is addressed further in the text below. It is worth emphasizing here that if the United States were to conclude FTAs with each of the major ASEAN countries, then the possibility of inefficient allocation of invested resources by US multinational corporations in the ASEAN region would be reduced, with concomitant avoidance of economic distortions to the ASEAN economies themselves.

States might benefit more under nondiscriminatory liberalization of its remaining barriers to trade in services and FDI, if preferential arrangements with ASEAN countries divert more competitive or beneficial trade in services and FDI from other emerging-market countries such as Korea, Hong Kong, Poland, or Russia.

Implications for Domestic Economic Reforms

Trade agreements provide a potential means of advancing not only trade policy reforms but also more general economic policy reforms in the countries party to the agreements. Moreover, they can help in important ways to "inoculate" agreed-to reforms from domestic backsliding, or even reversal, under political pressure from domestic interest groups that oppose the reforms: economic reforms etched in bilateral or multilateral trade agreements tend to carry additional respect, if for no other reason than because partner countries might retaliate if a country reneges on its international commitments. This method of advancing economic reforms, of course, has been a feature of recent multilateral and especially recent regional trade negotiations. It might also be an additional important benefit of proposed US bilateral FTAs, not only with less-developed countries but also with more-developed countries that are willing to liberalize their domestic economic policies on a reciprocal basis with the United States beyond the depth of economic policy reforms heretofore found possible in multilateral or regional trade negotiations.

With the enlargement of ASEAN in the late 1990s to include the so-called CLMV countries (Cambodia, Laos, Myanmar, and Vietnam), the bloc has become largely made up of low-income countries still in transition to predominantly private sector–oriented, market-b sed economies. Should US FTAs be extended to the CLMV countries (upor their membership in WTO and after implementation of a TIFA with the United States), possibilities for incorporating requirements for major domestic policy reforms—most likely in support of economic reform programs agreed on with bilateral donors and the Bretton Woods institutions, but also possibly in increasingly prominent areas of trade facilitation and capacity building—would be particularly extensive and would add significantly to the more familiar types of economic benefits emphasized in the previous section.

More immediate interest attaches to the possibility that prospective US FTAs might bring to the FTA negotiating table, and subsequently lock in, important economic reforms in Singapore and the ASEAN-4. With respect to behind-the-border economic policies, the recently concluded US-Singapore FTA emphasized improved access to service sectors in both the United States and Singapore; development of mutually acceptable standards for licensing and certification of professional service providers, especially in architecture and engineering; and increased protection for intellectual property rights in both countries, including through Singapore's accession to WIPO (World Intellectual Property Organization) treaties on copyright protection and stronger government measures against circumvention of international copyrights.[26] Clearly, these reforms, if fully implemented, should be expected to make Singapore a location more attractive to US service firms and individual professionals, and also a location more attractive to FDI by knowledge-intensive US industries such as the electronic chip, medical equipment, and pharmaceutical industries.[27]

Prospective US FTAs with the ASEAN-4 countries would do well to lock in similar economic policy reforms. However, as lower-income countries, the ASEAN-4 face similar but somewhat more basic challenges than Singapore does. As discussed previously, their primary challenge is to adjust their economies to internationally competitive production of higher-value-added goods and exports, in line with the increasing wage levels and, in many cases, increasing skill levels of their national workforce. In this connection, US FTAs with the ASEAN-4 would be especially beneficial if they were to promote thoroughgoing liberalization of foreign investment policies in these countries so that their foreign investment regime might become as open as that of Singapore with regard to such elements as treatment of foreign investors (equivalent to that of nationals); range of sectors open to FDI; and absence of local equity, employment, or content requirements. Such reforms to foreign investment policies would be expected to lead to greater outward-oriented FDI in the ASEAN-4, particularly that investment which is most appropriate to promoting desired structural adjustment in these countries. Given the discussion of current foreign investment policies above, of the four Thailand at present seems to be both most cognizant of the need for further liberalization of its foreign investment policies and the farthest along in beginning such liberalization.

Implications for External Economic and Political Relations

The major ASEAN countries are widely regarded as relatively open, outward-oriented developing countries, by virtue of their high trade-to-GDP ratios if not always their low protection levels. They are also widely

---

26. Tommy Koh, "US-Singapore Free Trade Agreement," speech organized by the Institute of Policy Studies, American Chamber of Commerce, and Foreign Correspondents Association, Singapore, February 25, 2003.

27. Something of an open question is the extent to which these economic policy reforms are effectively extended not only to US service providers and foreign investors but also to competing foreign service providers and investors interested in entering the Singapore marketplace. Notably, Mexico took decisive steps to generalize many of its NAFTA foreign investment reforms. See Hufbauer and Schott (1993).

counted as among the most active developing-country members of both the WTO and APEC. Arguably, the outward orientation of the ASEAN countries even extends to ASEAN preferential trade and investment arrangements under AFTA and the ASEAN Investment Area (AIA),[28] which many ASEAN trade and other economic experts regard as having promoted rather than hindered ASEAN acceptance of wider, more liberal regional and multilateral trade and foreign investment rules and reforms (Ariff 2001). Thus, the ASEAN countries have been outwardly content to pursue closer economic relations among themselves through discriminatory trade and investment practices, while at the same time also supporting wider regional and multilateral trade and investment reforms that would ultimately erode their intrabloc preferences under AFTA and AIA.

Since the 1997 Asian financial crisis and the failure of both ASEAN and APEC to respond effectively to the crisis, a sense has emerged that the two organizations have in some measure lost their vision for promoting greater economic prosperity (Tay and Estanislao 2001). Also, after the 1999 WTO debacle in Seattle and in the face of very uncertain progress of the Doha Round, the ASEAN countries remain guarded in their expectations for a successful outcome to the current WTO negotiations. Against this backdrop, the ASEAN countries have acted more unilaterally than in the past, first to safeguard their economies (and tariff revenues), and subsequently to begin unilateral economic reforms to recapture their economic growth and export performance. Efforts to reform crony capitalism were begun in Indonesia and the Philippines, along with trade policy reforms. Efforts to liberalize foreign investment policies were begun in Thailand (and to some extent Malaysia). And efforts to establish bilateral FTAs were initiated by Singapore and Thailand, mainly with Australia, Japan, New Zealand, and the United States but also with Mexico and Canada (Rajan, Sen, and Siregar 2001; Nagai 2002; Lloyd 2002). During this period the ASEAN bloc as a whole, largely in response to the diversion of FDI flows to China, also initiated free trade discussions with China, Japan, Korea, Australia, and New Zealand (regarding a proposed ASEAN-ANZCERTA free trade area) and with China, Korea, and Japan (regarding a proposed APT free trade area).[29]

---

28. The ASEAN Investment Area, established in 1998, provides a framework for FDI incentives and benefits for qualifying "ASEAN investors," subject to lists of temporary and sensitive sectors excluded from foreign investment until 2010. The agreement also provides for the opening of all sectors to foreign investment by investors outside of ASEAN after 2020 (ASEAN Secretariat 1998).

29. In July 2003, the European Union proposed a new plan for trade and investment cooperation with the ASEAN countries, termed the Trans-Regional EU-ASEAN Trade Initiative (TREATI). Among a number of features that resemble elements of the US Enterprise Initiative for ASEAN, the new plan envisions negotiation of a free trade agreement between the European Union and the ASEAN on a "WTO-plus" basis following a successful outcome of the Doha Round of multilateral trade negotiations (http://europa.eu.int).

Of these bilateral and regional free trade initiatives, to date those initiated by Singapore have most successfully come to fruition (Lloyd 2002). With bilateral FTAs already signed by Singapore with both Australia and New Zealand, among other countries,[30] the new US-Singapore FTA in combination with the new US-Chile FTA goes partway toward realizing the sometimes-proposed Pacific-5 free trade area among Australia, Chile, New Zealand, Singapore, and the United States.[31] With regard to ASEAN as a whole, however, thus far the bloc has balked at forming a free trade area either with ANZCERTA (Australia-New Zealand Closer Economic Relations Trade Agreement) or with the North Asian countries under the APT proposal, owing to general uncertainties (including fear of possibly being overwhelmed by China's giant economic size), the bloc's current institutional malaise, and perhaps the prospect of establishing a series of US FTAs under the new Enterprise for ASEAN Initiative.[32]

Notwithstanding Singapore's avowed official support for the Doha Round and the ASEAN bloc, the country's recent series of bilateral free trade deals has raised some concerns among other ASEAN members; they are worried about their prospects for successfully negotiating FTAs with the United States and other countries in the wake of Singapore's unilateral trade initiative, and possibly for effectively carrying out multilateral trade negotiations in the Doha Round. Singapore is economically the strongest ASEAN country, but unlike its ASEAN partners it is not an agriculture-exporting country. Thus, in striking independent bilateral trade deals, Singapore may lessen the ability of its ASEAN partners to benefit from Singapore's economic prominence and importance in trade negotiations with nonmember countries, particularly as they seek more effective agricultural trade reforms vis-à-vis Japan, the European Union, and the United States.

Of course, it might be argued that in striking independent bilateral FTAs, Singapore has, at the margin, pushed the ASEAN-4 to becoming still more active members in the Cairns Group, and so may have increased overall support for the Doha Round in general and for the negotiations on agriculture in particular. Investigation of this issue must await not only further passage of time but also details about the nature, extent, and time horizon for implementing possible agriculture reforms in US FTAs yet to be negotiated with individual ASEAN-4 countries themselves.

---

30. The other countries are Canada and Mexico. See Lloyd (2002).

31. If in addition the United States concludes an FTA individually with both Australia and New Zealand, then the envisioned P-5 free trade area will climb from 50 percent to 70 percent completion.

32. On the recent hesitancy of ASEAN countries to pursue preferential tariff reductions with China alone under the early harvest provisions of the new ASEAN-China FTA, see Gutierrez (2003).

More generally, it is not clear whether a proliferation of bilateral FTAs by Singapore and the ASEAN-4 with the United States, Japan, and other major trading partners (including the European Union and China) might weaken the ASEAN bloc's interest in pursuing wider regional or multilateral trade negotiations on an MFN basis. In the near term, before a broad range of other countries strike similar FTAs with the major ASEAN trading partners, the ASEAN bloc might well benefit more from its bilateral trade accords than from nondiscriminatory trade liberalization. Over a longer time horizon, however, the countries whose trade is diverted and welfare reduced by ASEAN FTAs—mainly China but also Japan, Korea, and other emerging-market countries—would be compelled to act in their own defense. They might seek their own FTAs with major hub countries such as the United States and European Union, if none were already in place, or they might pursue successful completion of the Doha Round more actively. Such pursuit of FTAs by these countries with the major hub countries would increasingly diminish the economic gains of ASEAN countries from their own FTAs with the hub countries. And if successfully concluded, the Doha Round could achieve significant reductions in trade restrictions across the board that would mostly erode FTA margins of preference enjoyed not only by the ASEAN countries but also by other FTA partners with the major hub countries.

Less-developed countries that are not likely to become partners in FTAs with the major hub countries, including the CLMV countries in ASEAN, might be disenfranchised to some extent by this process in the near term. Those less-developed countries that are not WTO members may have little recourse as the global trading system is increasingly defined by discriminatory FTAs. And those that are WTO members may lack either the voice in the organization or the technical capacity to mount effective support for successful completion of the Doha Round if the higher-income countries choose mainly to pursue FTAs.

From the perspective of the United States, US FTAs with the ASEAN countries clearly further the current US trade policy agenda that emphasizes the so-called competitive approach to global trade liberalization. They also clearly advance major US commercial interests in a number of new or particularly difficult trade agenda areas (e.g., intellectual property rights, trade in services, and FDI) in Southeast Asia. Moreover, from a geopolitical standpoint, US FTAs with the ASEAN countries have the virtue of maintaining an important US presence in Asia should APEC, and its previously avowed vision of "open regionalism," continue to falter or should an East Asian free trade area emerge from the current (mainly exploratory) discussions among the ASEAN countries, China, Korea, and Japan. However, if competitive liberalization ultimately emerges as a potent force for advancing nondiscriminatory trade liberalization worldwide, then US-ASEAN FTAs might contribute not only to invigorating the Doha Round but also to the APEC goal of achieving free trade in the Asia Pacific region by 2010 to 2020.

Finally, it should be recognized that in widely pursuing bilateral FTAs, the United States is creating vested interests among US businesses, including US exporters and US multinational firms that would directly benefit from the new preferential trading arrangements. US import-competing firms might also benefit, to the extent that they are able to safeguard if not improve overall US protection afforded by the rules of origin that necessarily must accompany the US FTAs.[33] Thus, even though global competitive pressure for multilateral liberalization might dominate the creation of new US vested interests in bilateral free trade agreements, US trade policymakers must take care in planning and pursuing FTAs with the ASEAN countries, and with other perspective FTA partners, to minimize or at least contain the possible downside risks of the current US trade strategy.

US Prospects for FTAs with Individual ASEAN Countries

Singapore, which had already signed a number of bilateral free trade agreements, was the first ASEAN country to take advantage of a US willingness to negotiate a bilateral FTA; and the Enterprise for ASEAN Initiative announced by President Bush in 2002 provides a road map for other ASEAN countries interested in pursuing an FTA with the United States. But Singapore is something of a special case. It is a high-income city-state with a relatively well-educated population, strong political as well as economic affinity to the United States, and virtually no agricultural sector. These factors probably contributed to the seeming ease—aside from the thorny issue of short-term capital controls—with which the US-Singapore FTA negotiations were concluded.

The US-Singapore FTA required two years to negotiate. US FTAs with additional ASEAN countries might be completed more quickly if the US agreements with Chile and Singapore can be used successfully as prototypes. Conversely, US commitments to simultaneously pursue FTA negotiations with other countries around the world and the need to grapple with such particularly sensitive issues as agriculture, autos, or intellectual property rights might stretch out the negotiations. Nonetheless, the United States and individual ASEAN-4 countries should look to finalizing their FTAs well in advance of the conclusion of the FTAA negotiations and the Doha Round negotiations (both effective mid-2007, when the current US trade negotiating authority expires), so that trade and other economic

---

33. On the importance of rules of origin in preferential trading arrangements, see Krishna and Krueger (1995) and Scollay (1997).

gains under the US-ASEAN FTAs can be enjoyed for an appreciable period before regional or multilateral agreements to liberalize trade may erode them.

The analysis here suggests that the ASEAN-4 countries would enjoy substantial economic gains from individual FTAs with the United States. These would derive not only from the elimination of tariff and other barriers to bilateral trade with the United States but also from reforms to bilateral trade in services and FDI, and even the possibility of reforms to domestic economic policies that affect economic efficiency (and structural adjustment), economic welfare, and growth. The ASEAN-4 certainly recognize these potential benefits, and to date only Malaysia has yet to conclude a TIFA with the United States—the final stepping-stone to becoming eligible to negotiate an FTA with the United States under the EAI.

Notwithstanding these positive elements, some ASEAN observers have raised concerns about possible fragmentation—affecting not only ASEAN economic cooperation within Southeast Asia but also the bloc's potential for combined leverage in external economic relations vis-à-vis China, other APEC countries, and even the Cairns Group and WTO—if additional ASEAN countries follow Singapore's lead in establishing an individual FTA with the United States. If such fragmentation is a real prospect, then the ASEAN-4 might consider jointly approaching the United States about negotiating a common FTA. Doing so might also significantly invigorate the ASEAN Free Trade Area and new ASEAN Investment Area, through the pressure of competitive liberalization.

US interest, however, lies principally in moving forward with negotiations of FTAs with the ASEAN-4 individually, in the belief that bilateral FTA negotiations would be more fruitful and less prone to delay. A prime issue for the United States is selecting the one or two ASEAN countries with which to next enter into FTA negotiations. By way of conclusion, I consider this issue on two broad grounds: geopolitical and economic.

Geopolitical and Security Grounds: Indonesia and the Philippines

If promoting some combination of geopolitical and regional security is the United States' main criterion in selecting its next ASEAN partners in negotiating FTAs, then the two lowest-income countries among the ASEAN-4, Indonesia and the Philippines, might be chosen. The economic benefits that a preferential trade agreement with the United States would bring to these two countries, both of which remain plagued by insurgent domestic elements with reputed ties to international terrorism, could increase political stability and regional security in Southeast Asia. Indeed, according to the GTAP analysis of prospective US-ASEAN FTAs undertaken for this study, economic welfare in Indonesia and the Philippines under a US

FTA would improve by $1,313 million and $907 million, respectively—more than economic welfare in Singapore or the remaining ASEAN-4 countries would improve under a US FTA (see table 6.9).[34] Also, from an economic development perspective, scope for incorporating and locking in major domestic economic policy reforms in a US FTA would likely be greatest in these two ASEAN countries.

Malaysia might also be considered a candidate for one of the next ASEAN bilateral FTAs with the United States on geopolitical grounds (assuming that Malaysia implements a TIFA in the near future). Specifically, a successfully negotiated US-Malaysia FTA could help to ameliorate the strained political and economic relations between Malaysia and the United States frequently evident in regional and multilateral forums in recent years.

Economic Grounds: Malaysia and Thailand

US trade relations seem frequently to be dominated by political economy rather than geopolitical and security considerations. If the United States looks mainly to its own prospective economic gains in choosing the next one or two ASEAN partners for an FTA, it will naturally pay more attention to the two highest-income ASEAN-4 countries, Malaysia and Thailand. After Singapore, these two countries are certainly the two largest ASEAN trading partners of the United States and, historically, are among the most important host countries in Southeast Asia for US foreign direct investment. Moreover, unlike Singapore, they currently maintain among the highest barriers to US exports (if not also US FDI) in ASEAN. Finally, not unlike Chile, both countries would offer US negotiators a prime environment for pursuing new agenda issues in trade and foreign investment liberalization with middle-income, emerging-market countries of particular interest to many US exporters and multinational firms.

The GTAP analysis of prospective US-ASEAN FTAs undertaken for this study supports these contentions in the main (see table 6.9). Among possible ASEAN-4 partners, a US FTA with Thailand yields the largest gain in economic welfare for the United States ($824 million), followed at some distance by a US FTA with Malaysia ($392 million). These economic gains to the United States are not particularly large, especially in comparison

---

34. Though simulated economic welfare gains for the United States under FTAs with Indonesia (–$179 million) and the Philippines ($224) are disappointing, the GTAP analysis considers only the elimination of tariffs on US bilateral trade with the two countries. The elimination of nontariff barriers under the prospective US FTAs with Indonesia and the Philippines, coupled with other possible agreed-to reforms to economic policies in both countries, might imply substantially greater gains in economic welfare for the United States than found by the GTAP model.

with the magnitude of the US economy (about $8 billion in 2000).[35] However, it should be understood that these gains are small because they are computed with respect to FTAs with individual US trading partners, not the world at large. When the present results are compared to results in the same GTAP analysis for prospective US FTAs with a variety of countries worldwide, the US welfare gain under the prospective US-Malaysia FTA is comparable to that for a US-Chile FTA ($415 million). Also, the US welfare gain under the prospective US-Thailand FTA is greater than the US welfare gain under a prospective US-Taiwan FTA ($760 million) or prospective US-Australia FTA ($468 million), and second only to US gains under prospective US FTAs with Brazil ($2,780 million) and Korea ($2,694 million).[36] Finally, with regard to potential spillover effects on countries excluded from prospective US-ASEAN FTAs, the GTAP model results indicate that a US-Thailand FTA would lead to the greatest reduction in world economic welfare and thereby would advance competitive pressures for global trade liberalization by the greatest degree.

This study favors choice of the next ASEAN country for negotiation of a US FTA on economic grounds, specifically those that most effectively advance US economic interest and, not coincidentally, the current US strategy of competitive liberalization. Coupled with Thailand's own interest in pursuing a free trade agreement with the United States (expressed more strongly and widely than Malaysia has done) and with Thailand's greater willingness, as recently perceived, to discuss liberalization of FDI and new agenda trade issues in FTA negotiations with the United States and other countries, the foregoing results point to Thailand as the most appropriate next ASEAN partner for a US bilateral free trade agreement.[37]

Of course, this conclusion should not lead to Malaysia and the other remaining ASEAN-4 being shunted aside. As the United States's Enterprise for ASEAN Initiative recognizes, it remains very much in the US economic and geopolitical interests to expand US-ASEAN economic relations as broadly as possible. Such expansion would include continued progress in forging closer US economic relations with the ASEAN-4 countries,

---

35. Although not directly comparable, a second quantitative analysis undertaken for this study employing the so-called gravity model approach to estimating the trade impacts of preferential trade agreements suggests that the GTAP model may underestimate the effects of prospective US-ASEAN FTAs by a very large factor.

36. Gilbert (2003). In addition to Singapore and the individual ASEAN-4 countries, the countries considered as prospective partners in US bilateral FTAs in the Gilbert analysis using the GTAP model are Australia, Botswana, Brazil, Chile, Korea, Morocco, New Zealand, Taiwan, and other Southern African Customs Union countries as a bloc.

37. Also, as noted above, under proliferation of US FTAs worldwide, the GTAP analysis finds that the trade-related gain in economic welfare of Thailand remains as high as $428 million, while the trade-related gain in economic welfare of Malaysia falls to zero.

through timely negotiation of additional bilateral FTAs with the major ASEAN countries. It also would include a continued US effort to curry ASEAN-wide support for a successful outcome to the Doha Round of multilateral trade negotiations. Indeed, the analysis here suggests that in pursuing free trade area agreements with the ASEAN countries and simultaneously diverting trade of the excluded countries, the United States may be more effectively working toward a successful outcome to the Doha Round indirectly, by increasing global competitive pressure for multilateral trade liberalization.

References

Akrasanee, Narongchai. 2001. ASEAN in the Past Thirty-Three Years: Lessons for Economic Co-operation. In *Reinventing ASEAN,* ed. Simon S. C. Tay, Jesus P. Estanislao, and Hadi Soesastro. Singapore: Institute for Southeast Asian Studies.

Andrianmananjara, Soamiely. 2000. Regionalism and Incentives for Multilateralism. *Journal of Economic Integration* 15, no. 1: 1–18.

Ariff, Mohamed. 2001. Trade, Investment, and Interdependence. In *Reinventing ASEAN,* ed. Simon S.C. Tay, Jesus P. Estanislao, and Hadi Soesastro. Singapore: Institute for Southeast Asian Studies.

Armington, Paul A. 1969. A Theory of Demand for Products Distinguished by Place of Production. *IMF Staff Papers* 16, no. 1: 159–78.

Association of Southeast Asian Nations (ASEAN). 2002. *Framework Agreement on Comprehensive Economic Co-operation Between the Association of South East Asian Nations and the People's Republic of China.* www.aseansec.org/13196.htm (November 4).

Association of Southeast Asian Nations (ASEAN) Secretariat. 1998. *Framework Agreement on the ASEAN Investment Area.* www.aseansec.org/2280.htm (October 7).

Baldwin, Richard. 1995. *A Domino Theory of Regionalism.* NBER Working Paper 4364. Cambridge, MA: National Bureau of Economic Research.

Bergsten, C.F. 2002. A Renaissance for US Trade Policy? *Foreign Affairs* 81, no. 6: 86–98.

Burfisher, Mary E., Sherman Robinson, and Karen Thierfelder. 2003. Regionalism: Old and New, Theory and Practice. Paper presented at the conference Agricultural Policy Reform and the WTO: Where Are We Heading? sponsored by the International Agricultural Trade Research Consortium (IATRC), Capri, Italy (June 23–26).

DeRosa, Dean A. 1995. *Regional Trading Arrangements among Developing Countries: The ASEAN Example.* Research Report 103. Washington: International Food Policy Research Institute.

DeRosa, Dean A. 1998a. Foreign Trade and Investment Policies in Developing Asia. *Asian Development Review* 16, no. 2: 96–134.

DeRosa, Dean A. 1998b. *Regional Integration Arrangements: Static Economic Theory, Quantitative Findings, and Policy Guidelines.* Policy Research Working Paper 2007. Washington: World Bank. Available at www.worldbank.org/html/dec/Publications/Workpapers/wps2000series/wps2007/wps2007.pdf (August).

DeRosa, Dean A. 2003. Gravity Model Calculations of the Trade Impacts of US Free Trade Agreements. Background paper prepared for the conference Free Trade Agreements and US Trade Policy, sponsored by the Institute for International Economics, Washington (May 7–8).

Dimaranan, Betina V., and Robert A. McDougall. 2002. Data Base Summary: Protection and Support. In *Global Trade, Assistance, and Production: The GTAP 5 Data Base,* ed. Betina V. Dimaranan and Robert A. McDougall. West Lafayette, IN: Center for Global Trade Analysis, Purdue University.

Felker, Greg, and K.S. Jomo. 2000. *New Approaches to Investment Policy in the ASEAN 4*. Asian Development Bank Institute, Japan. www.adbi.org/para2000/papers/Jomo.pdf.

Gilbert, John P. 2003. CGE Simulation of US Bilateral Free Trade Agreements. Background paper prepared for the conference Free Trade Agreements and US Trade Policy, sponsored by the Institute for International Economics, Washington (May 7–8).

Gutierrez, Jason. 2003. Plan for ASEAN-China "Early Harvest" before FTA Meets Members' Resistance. *International Trade Reporter*, April 3, 604.

Hertel, Thomas W., ed. 1997. *Global Trade Analysis: Modeling and Applications*. Cambridge: Cambridge University Press.

Hufbauer, Gary Clyde, and Jeffrey J. Schott. 1993. *NAFTA: An Assessment*. Rev. ed. Washington: Institute for International Economics.

Hufbauer, Gary Clyde, and Jeffrey J. Schott. Forthcoming. *NAFTA: A Ten-Year Appraisal*. Washington: Institute for International Economics.

Krishna, Kala, and Anne O. Krueger. 1995. Implementing Free Trade Areas: Rules of Origin and Hidden Protection. In *New Directions in Trade Theory*, ed. Alan Deardorff, James Levinsohn, and Robert Sterns. Ann Arbor: University of Michigan Press.

Krugman, Paul. 1994. The Myth of Asia's Miracle. *Foreign Affairs* 73, no. 6: 62–78.

Laird, Samuel. 1997. Quantifying Commercial Policies. In *Applied Methods for Trade Policy Analysis: A Handbook*, ed. Joseph F. Francois and Kenneth A. Reinert. Cambridge: Cambridge University Press.

Lawrence, Robert Z. 1996. *Regionalism, Multilateralism, and Deeper Integration*. Washington: Brookings Institution.

Lloyd, P.J. 2002. *New Regionalism and New Bilateralism in the Asia-Pacific*. Institute for Southeast Asian Studies, Singapore, Visiting Researchers Series 3. www.iseas.edu.sg/vr32002.pdf (May).

Moran, Theodore H. 1998. *Foreign Direct Investment and Development: The New Policy Agenda for Developing Countries and Economies in Transition*. Washington: Institute for International Economics.

Moran, Theodore H. 2001. *Parental Supervision: The New Paradigm for Foreign Direct Investment and Development*. Policy Analyses in International Economics 64. Washington: Institute for International Economics.

Nagai, Fumio. 2002. *Thailand's Trade Policy: WTO Plus FTA?* Institute of Developing Economies APEC Study Center, Working Paper Series 01/02 6. www.ide.go.jp/Japanese/Apec/Publish/pdf/apec13_wp6.pdf (March).

O'Driscoll, Gerald P., Edwin J. Feulner, and Mary A. O'Grady, eds. 2003. *2003 Index of Economic Freedom*. Washington: Heritage Foundation; New York: Dow Jones. Available at www.heritage.org/research/features/index.

Pangestu, Mari. 2003. Responding to Regionalism: Towards a Common ASEAN Vision. Paper presented at Trade Forum Meetings, Pacific Economic Cooperation Council, Washington (April 22–23).

Rajan, Ramkishen S., Rahul Sen, and Reza Siregar. 2001. *Singapore and Free Trade Agreements: Economic Relations with Japan and the United States*. Singapore: Institute for Southeast Asian Studies.

Rose, Andrew K. 2003. Which International Institutions Promote International Trade? Mimeo, Haas School of Business, University of California, Berkeley.

Schiff, Maurice, and L. Alan Winters. 2003. How Trade Blocs Increase Trade and Competition. In *Regional Integration and Development*. Washington: World Bank.

Schott, Jeffrey J. 1994. *The Uruguay Round: An Assessment*. Washington: Institute for International Economics.

Scollay, Robert. 1997. Preferential Rules of Origin, Regional Trading Arrangements, and APEC. *Asia-Pacific Economic Review* 3, no. 2: 28–36.

Sussangkarn, Chalongphob. 1997. ASEAN beyond AFTA: Initiatives in Labor Market Cooperation and Integration. *TDRI Quarterly Review* 12, no. 3 (September): 3–8.

Tay, Simon S.C., and Jesus P. Estanislao. 2001. The Relevance of ASEAN: Crisis and Change. In *Reinventing ASEAN*, ed. Simon S. C. Tay, Jesus P. Estanislao, and Hadi Soesastro. Singapore: Institute for Southeast Asian Studies.

UN Conference on Trade and Development (UNCTAD). 2003. UNCTAD Coding System for Trade Control Measures. *Trade Analysis and Information System*. www.unctad-trains.org.

US Trade Representative, Office of (USTR). 2003. *2003 National Trade Estimate Report on Foreign Trade Barriers*. www.ustr.gov/reports/nte/2003/index.htm.

Wanandi, Jusuf. 2001. ASEAN's Past and the Challenges Ahead: Aspects of Politics and Security. In *Reinventing ASEAN*, ed. Simon S. C. Tay, Jesus P. Estanislao, and Hadi Soesastro. Singapore: Institute for Southeast Asian Studies.

World Bank. 1993. *The East Asian Miracle: Economic Growth and Public Policy*. New York: Oxford University Press.

7

Korea-US Free Trade Revisited

INBOM CHOI AND JEFFREY J. SCHOTT

Two years ago, we published an analysis of the costs and benefits of negotiating a bilateral free trade agreement (FTA) between South Korea and the United States (Choi and Schott 2001). Neither government had proposed such an initiative, but it was under active discussion by business leaders and academics in both countries. The study concluded that

- economic welfare gains for both countries would be significant, if all sectors—including agriculture—were covered by the obligations;

- deep-rooted political opposition to specific reforms existed in both countries;

- the FTA would generate substantial trade diversion, particularly affecting suppliers in Japan and China; and

- an FTA could induce a series of counterbalancing initiatives among other East Asian countries in response to the expected discrimination in the US and Korean markets.

For the United States, the main benefits of the FTA would derive from modest welfare gains (resulting primarily from improved terms of trade); from the likely catalytic effect of the Korea-US accord on trade liberalization in the region as Taiwan, the Association of Southeast Asian Nations

Inbom Choi, former visiting fellow at the Institute for International Economics, is the chief economist at the Federation of Korean Industries. Jeffrey Schott is a senior fellow at the Institute for International Economics.

(ASEAN), and possibly Japan sought comparable pacts; and from the support the trade initiative could give to promoting growth and stability on the Korean peninsula. For Korea, the FTA would induce much larger welfare gains as the country implemented domestic economic reforms pursuant to its FTA obligations (such reforms are needed in any event but would be hard to enact in the face of strident political opposition in Korea absent a payoff of US concessions that improve access for Korean exporters to the US market); would counter trade diversion suffered by Korean exporters as a result of other US preferential trade pacts (especially the North American Free Trade Agreement, or NAFTA); and would provide additional incentives for foreign investors in the Korean economy. These findings led us to recommend that "if the United States and Korea want to maximize both welfare gains and political comity in the Asia-Pacific region, the preferred trade strategy should be to concurrently pursue trade reforms bilaterally, in APEC [the Asia Pacific Economic Cooperation forum] and in WTO negotiations" (Choi and Schott 2001, 79–82).

Over the past two years, the trade environment has changed significantly, creating new opportunities but also posing irksome new challenges to prospective Korea-US negotiations. First, the launch of the Doha Round negotiations in the World Trade Organization (WTO) in November 2001 revived prospects for global trade reforms that had been dormant since the failed Seattle WTO ministerial in 1999. The passage of US trade promotion authority (TPA) in August 2002 provided US officials with the congressional mandate and negotiating flexibility needed to pursue comprehensive trade agreements in bilateral, regional, and multilateral forums (provided the agreements cover broad-ranging rights and obligations and produce balanced results in certain import-sensitive sectors). That authority already has been applied to ratify and implement FTAs negotiated with Singapore and Chile, and could be used to facilitate a Korea-US FTA. Indeed, the US International Trade Commission has already been asked by Congress to study the economic implications of a comparable agreement with Korea; it issued conclusions (USITC 2001) in September 2001 similar to those reported by Choi and Schott (2001).

Second, the international trade environment has become more unsettled, especially from a Korean point of view. The Doha Round is traversing rough shoals, with talks threatening to stall on the contentious issue of agricultural reform. While Korea studies its FTA options, its competitors in East Asia have begun to negotiate. Most prominent among the new initiatives is the China-ASEAN free trade talks. The prospect of a broad "10 plus 1" pact has in turn provoked Japan to pursue a comparable initiative; in addition, Japan launched FTA negotiations with Mexico in late 2002. Discussions among the even broader grouping of ASEAN and Northeast Asian countries, the "10 plus 3," seem far removed from concrete trade negotiations—though the prospect of such a regional trading powerhouse excites the imagination of many Korean policymakers. Whether China wants any part of that game is another story. More ominously, the flare-up of North-South tensions on the Korean peninsula raises the political risk premium of investment in Korea; conversely, however, that threat also reinforces interest in deepening trade ties as part of a broader strategy to strengthen economic and political stability in the region.

Third, developments in the bilateral economic relationship also have generated mixed signals about the desire to move into FTA negotiations. On the one hand, there have been important US investments in the Korean economy, including the purchase of Daewoo by General Motors. On the other hand, some trade disputes, notably over steel, have become more contentious. Perhaps more telling is the rapid growth in Korea-China trade, which stands in stark contrast to the basically flat growth rates of Korea-US trade over the past two years. In sum, the decision to launch FTA negotiations between the United States and Korea now involves a much more complicated calculus than it did just two years ago.

This chapter offers a reappraisal of the economic and political benefits and costs of pursuing a bilateral Korea-US FTA. It examines the current status of bilateral trade and investment, as well as the range of trade frictions that could be resolved by an FTA—but that at the same time pose practical obstacles to such a negotiation. We then analyze the potential benefits of an FTA, drawing on both computable general equilibrium and gravity models to suggest parameters of the potential trade and welfare gains for each country. The next section addresses the potential costs of an agreement, in terms both of trade diversion from other suppliers in East Asia and of possible distractions from ongoing WTO negotiations. We conclude with near-term prospects for trade negotiations and policy recommendations.

Bilateral Trade and Investment

Among all the countries with which the United States is either negotiating or seriously considering an FTA, Korea is the one with which it has the most extensive trade relationship. Two-way merchandise trade totaled $56 billion in 2002, with the United States running a bilateral trade deficit of $14 billion. In addition, bilateral trade in services reached almost $11 billion in 2001. Agricultural products in 2002 accounted for less than 5 percent of total trade but represented 11.6 percent of US exports to Korea (see tables 7.1 and 7.2). Overall, Korea ranked as the United States' seventh-largest trading partner in 2002.

The United States remains Korea's most important trading partner, accounting for 20.2 percent of Korean exports and 15.1 percent of Korean imports in 2002. To be sure, trade with China (including Hong Kong) is growing rapidly; in fact, China edged out the United States as Korea's largest export market in 2002. Imports from the United States still exceed those from China, but Chinese suppliers are catching up quickly at the ex-

Table 7.1   US trade with Korea, 1995–2002 (millions of dollars)

Product	1995	1996	1997	1998	1999	2000	2001	2002
US exports to Korea								
Agriculture	2,946	3,231	2,305	1,761	2,261	2,252	2,264	2,449
Share of total (percent)	12.0	12.7	9.5	11.0	10.3	8.6	10.8	11.6
Total merchandise	24,480	25,430	24,290	15,980	22,040	26,300	20,900	21,150
US imports from Korea								
Agriculture	176	176	183	155	180	203	224	248
Share of total (percent)	0.7	0.8	0.8	0.7	0.6	0.5	0.6	0.7
Total merchandise	24,030	22,530	22,940	23,700	31,150	39,830	34,920	35,280
US trade volume with Korea (exports plus imports)								
Agriculture	3,122	3,407	2,488	1,916	2,441	2,455	2,488	2,697
Share of total (percent)	6.4	7.1	5.3	4.8	4.6	3.7	4.5	4.8
Total merchandise	48,510	47,960	47,230	39,680	53,190	66,130	55,820	56,430
US trade balance with Korea (exports minus imports)								
Agriculture	2,770	3,055	2,122	1,606	2,081	2,049	2,040	2,201
Total merchandise	450	2,900	1,350	−7,720	−9,110	−13,530	−14,020	−14,130

Note: "Agriculture" is defined as chapters 1–24 in the Harmonized Schedule.

Source: US International Trade Commission Trade Database, http://dataweb.usitc.gov.

pense of both US and Japanese companies (see table 7.3). Japan remains the leading source of imports, but the Japanese share of the Korean market has steadily eroded from a peak of 41 percent in 1971 to less than 20 percent for the past few years. These dramatic shifts in market share explain in part Korea's growing interest in a regional trade pact with China at the same time that it continues to study potential FTAs with Japan and the United States.

Over the past decade, manufactured goods have accounted for about 60 percent of US exports of goods and services to Korea (mainly electrical machinery and equipment, aircraft, scientific equipment, and organic chemicals), and 80 percent of Korean exports to the United States (primarily autos, telecommunications equipment, semiconductors, computers and parts, and apparel). Interestingly, 30 percent of total Korea-US trade in 2002 was in Harmonized Tariff Schedule chapter 85: electrical machinery and equipment (mainly semiconductors and computers and parts). In the case of computer chips trade, the two countries show a clear pattern of intraindustry trade: the United States exports high-tech processors and chips, and Korea mainly exports memory chips.

Indeed, Korea's intraindustry trade has steadily increased over the years, with the extent of such trade with the United States somewhat less than that with its other global trading partners. This trend has important implications, since a given expansion of intraindustry trade is generally

Table 7.2 US-Korea trade by major product, 2001–02
(millions of dollars, percent of total)

Industry	2001		2002	
	Value	Share	Value	Share
US imports from Korea				
Agricultural and food products	223.4	0.6	247.4	0.7
Minerals and chemicals	1,077.4	3.1	832.3	2.4
Textiles and apparel	1,383.5	4.0	2,032.2	5.8
Goods related to transportation	7,095.5	20.3	7,528.7	21.3
Other manufactured goods	24,395.4	69.9	23,879.2	67.7
Special categories	742.0	2.1	764.0	2.2
Goods subtotal	34,917.2	100.0	35,283.8	100.0
Services	3,765.0	n.a.	n.a.	n.a.
Total	38,862.2	n.a.	n.a.	n.a.
US exports to Korea				
Agricultural and food products	2,264.4	10.9	2,449.4	11.6
Minerals and chemicals	2,412.1	11.6	2,572.6	12.2
Textiles and apparel	304.8	1.5	271.9	1.3
Goods related to transportation	3,050.6	14.6	2,756.8	13.1
Other manufactured goods	12,423.8	59.7	12,624.2	59.9
Special categories	371.8	1.8	406.6	1.9
Goods subtotal	20,827.5	100.0	21,081.5	100.0
Services	7,121.0	n.a.	n.a.	n.a.
Total	27,948.5	n.a.	n.a.	n.a.

n.a. = not available

Sources: US International Trade Commission Trade Database, http://dataweb.usitc.gov; the Office of Textile and Apparel, http://otexa.ita.doc.gov; and the US Department of Commerce Bureau of Economic Analysis, www.bea.doc.gov.

thought to pose fewer adjustment problems and subsequently fewer trade conflicts than intraindustry trade.

In addition to its role in trade, the United States has been the largest source of foreign direct investment in Korea (see table 7.4). The stock of US FDI in Korea reached $10 billion by year-end 2001 and should be valued even higher when flows related to the recent purchase of Daewoo by General Motors are included in the statistics.[1] That investment exemplifies an important shift in US corporate involvement in the Korean economy. In the past, US investors usually took minority stakes in joint ventures because of restrictions on fully owned subsidiaries or majority-owned companies. Liberalization of investment laws and regulations since the 1997 economic crisis has helped to encourage more substantial

---

1. General Motors Group (including GM, Suzuki, and Shanghai Automotive Industry Corp.) holds a 67 percent share in GM Daewoo Auto & Technology Company. The remainder is held by Daewoo Motors Creditors Committee. General Motors (US) paid $251 million for its 42.1 percent share of the new company in October 2002 (correspondence from GM Corporation, May 2003).

Table 7.3 Korea's major trading partners, 1995–2002
(share of trade in percent)

Country	1995	1996	1997	1998	1999	2000	2001	2002
Exports to								
United States	19.3	16.7	15.9	17.3	20.6	21.9	20.8	20.2
Japan	13.6	12.1	10.9	9.3	11.1	11.9	11.0	9.3
China	7.3	8.8	10.0	9.0	9.6	10.7	12.1	14.7
China + Hong Kong	15.9	17.3	18.6	10.1	15.9	17.0	18.4	20.9
Imports from								
United States	22.5	22.2	20.8	21.9	20.8	18.3	15.9	15.1
Japan	24.2	21.0	19.2	18.0	20.1	19.9	18.9	19.6
China	5.5	5.7	7.0	6.9	7.4	8.0	9.4	11.4
China + Hong Kong	6.1	6.5	7.6	7.5	8.1	8.8	10.3	12.6

Source: Korean Customs Department, www.customs.go.kr/hp/homepage/eng/index05.htm.

US investments; the GM deal and the purchase by Newbridge Capital of Korea First Bank are the most ambitious of these.[2] Locking in those reforms and complementing them with the types of investor protections included in the Singapore and Chile FTAs with the United States would be high priorities for US negotiators of an FTA with Korea.

Bilateral Trade Frictions

Any trade relationship as sizable as that between the United States and Korea will naturally provoke a number of bilateral frictions. Such disputes highlight both the problem areas in the trade relationship and some of the most significant opportunities to expand trade, if an FTA can remove existing legal and regulatory obstacles. Both countries publish annual laundry lists of complaints by their domestic industries covering trade barriers, discriminatory standards, and tax and procurement policies, among other areas.[3] In addition, the American Chamber of Commerce in Korea releases an annual report on bilateral trade relations.

The United States has an extensive litany of complaints about Korean trade and regulatory practices that impede trade and investment by US firms. The list compiled by the Office of the US Trade Representative extends 24 pages in its 2003 report on foreign trade barriers—longer than that for any other country in the FTA queue and exceeded only by the lists for Japan, China, and the European Union! The good news is that a num-

---

2. Completion of the long-standing negotiation of a bilateral investment treaty, which continues to be stalled over disputes regarding Korean screen quotas, could boost FDI even more.

3. The US Congress requires the US Trade Representative to issue an annual *National Trade Estimate Report on Foreign Trade Barriers*. In the spirit of reciprocity, the Korean Foreign Ministry publishes an annual *Foreign Trade Environment* report that reviews foreign trade policies and practices that are considered detrimental to Korean export interests.

Table 7.4 FDI stock in Korea, 1995–2002 (millions of dollars)

Indicator	1995	1996	1997	1998	1999	2000	2001	2002
Stock of US FDI in Korea	5,557	6,508	6,467	7,365	7,474	8,968	10,524	12,192
Stock of world FDI in Korea	9,451	12,422	12,526	19,043	32,143	37,106	40,767	43,689
US share (percent)	58.8	52.4	51.6	38.7	23.3	24.2	25.8	27.9
Stock of US FDI in world	699,015	795,195	871,316	1,000,703	1,215,960	1,316,247	1,383,225	1,520,965
Share in Korea (percent)	0.8	0.8	0.7	0.7	0.6	0.7	0.8	0.8

Sources: The US Department of Commerce Bureau of Economic Analysis, www.bea.doc.gov; and UNCTAD, *World Investment Report,* Geneva, various issues.

ber of problems have either been mitigated by the implementation of Uruguay Round tariff reforms or resolved through bilateral agreements (including the long-running dispute over Korean beef imports). The bad news is that many more problems remain, affecting billions of dollars of bilateral trade.[4]

The most enduring and prominent problems involve the auto sector, semiconductors, and agriculture. Restrictions on the import and sale of autos in Korea remain a source of major concern for US firms. Tariffs on autos (8 percent) are about the same as the average levies on manufactured goods, but the sale of American cars is further constrained by sales taxes (based on engine displacement) that burden large vehicles (primarily imports) much more than small, domestically produced cars. As a result, auto imports account for less than 1 percent of domestic consumption in Korea. Past disputes over semiconductors also seem to be heating up, as subsidies provided by the Korean government to help restructure its industry provoke new countervailing duty (CVD) complaints in the United States. In April 2003, the US Commerce Department issued a preliminary determination that imports from Hynix Semiconductor are liable to CVDs of more than 50 percent (*Financial Times,* April 2, 2003, 15). Other US concerns involve such areas as screen-time quotas, burdensome regulations in financial service sectors, and pharmaceutical pricing practices (see USTR 2003, 239–63).

In agriculture, Korea still maintains very restrictive access to its rice market. Other farm imports face an average tariff of 62 percent, though tariffs on forestry and fishery products are not bound in the WTO and thus can be increased at any time without violating Korean trade obligations. Some products of export interest to the United States (e.g., oranges)

---

4. Choi and Schott (2001, table 3.4) estimated that bilateral disputes covered $1.85 billion in US imports from Korea, and $2.5 billion in US exports to Korea in 1999. These figures include the now-resolved beef dispute but do not take into account the recent US steel import restraints.

are subject to tariff-rate quotas with overquota tariffs of 60 percent. In addition, customs clearance red tape and sanitary and phytosanitary certification requirements continue to plague importers of US farm products.

Koreans' main concerns are that the United States uses antidumping (AD) actions and countervailing duties overzealously and in contravention of WTO obligations, and that it maintains high tariffs on some products of major export interest to Korea. The tariff peaks protect a number of textiles, apparel, footwear, and luggage products. Despite those high levies, Korean exports totaled about $400 million in 1999, or 10 percent of total US imports of these products (see Choi and Schott 2001, table 3.1). Exporters of these products would be a major beneficiary of a bilateral FTA, though the value of the FTA preferences would depend on whether US tariff reforms are extended on a most favored nation basis, as proposed in the Doha Round.

The problem with antidumping actions is harder to reconcile, either in a bilateral FTA or in WTO negotiations. As of April 2003, there were 23 US antidumping and CVD measures in effect against Korean exporters. US antidumping and countervail orders against Korean firms represent only 6.7 percent of all current US orders (compared to Korea's 3 percent share of total US imports). Interestingly, all but five of these orders involve iron and steel products, and almost all US orders implemented during the past decade are against iron and steel products (see table 7.5). It is only a slight exaggeration to say that Korea really does not have an antidumping problem with the United States; rather, it has a big steel trade problem.

The steel trade problem involves both AD and CVD cases and US safeguard measures. Korean producers, which were affected by US safeguard actions against line pipe imports in February 2000, were a major target of the broader US steel safeguards in March 2002.[5] As a result, the volume of Korean steel exports to the United States in 2002 fell 16 percent from 2001 levels (and about 40 percent from their peak in 1998), with most of the losses coming from flat and long steel products that were subject to immediate 30 percent tariffs. However, the US protection was attenuated in part by product exclusions from the safeguard measures.[6] Korea brought and won complaints in the WTO against both safeguard actions (though the latest decision is under appeal).

---

5. The 2000 safeguard measure imposed a tariff-rate quota that allowed each non-NAFTA supplier to export 9,000 short tons of line pipe to the United States; overquota imports were subject to a 19 percent tariff. As a result, Korea's exports in 2000 fell by two-thirds from their 1999 levels. Korea filed a WTO complaint, but by the time the case was fully adjudicated and Korea and the United States had reached a mutually acceptable settlement, the line pipe safeguard was only six months away from its scheduled expiration.

6. POSCO—the principal Korean steel producer—was the largest beneficiary of the product exclusions to the global steel safeguard, in part so it could supply unfinished steel to a mill owned by US Steel in California.

Table 7.5 US antidumping and countervailing duty cases against Korea (in effect as of April 2003)

Product	Industry	Date ordered
US antidumping orders		
Malleable cast-iron pipe fittings	Iron/steel	May 1986
Top-of-the-stove stainless steel cooking ware	Miscellaneous	January 1987
Industrial nitrocellulose	Chemicals	July 1990
Polyethylene terephthalate (PET) film	Chemicals	June 1991
Circular welded nonalloy steel pipe	Iron/steel	November 1992
Welded ASTM A-312 stainless steel pipe	Iron/steel	December 1992
Stainless steel butt-weld pipe fittings	Iron/steel	February 1993
Corrosion-resistant carbon steel flat products	Iron/steel	August 1993
Oil country tubular goods	Iron/steel	August 1995
Stainless steel wire rod	Iron/steel	September 1998
Stainless steel plate in coils	Iron/steel	May 1999
Stainless steel sheet and strip	Iron/steel	July 1999
Carbon steel plate	Iron/steel	February 2000
Polyester staple fiber	Miscellaneous	May 2000
Structural steel beams	Iron/steel	August 2000
Steel concrete reinforcing bar	Iron/steel	September 2001
Stainless steel angle	Iron/steel	May 2001
Stainless steel bar	Iron/steel	March 2002
US countervailing duties		
Top-of-the-stove stainless steel cooking ware	Miscellaneous	January 1987
Corrosion-resistant carbon steel flat products	Iron/steel	August 1993
Stainless steel sheet and strip	Iron/steel	August 1999
Carbon steel plate	Iron/steel	February 2000
Structural steel beams	Iron/steel	August 2000

Summary:

Total orders		Steel orders	
Total US orders in effect	341	Total US orders on steel in effect	193
US orders against Korea	23	US orders against Korea on steel	18
Korean share of orders (percent)	6.7	Korean share of orders on steel (percent)	9.3
Korean share of US goods imports, 2002 (percent)	3.1	Korean share of US steel imports, 2002 (percent)	5.3

Sources: US International Trade Commission, www.usitc.gov; USITC Trade Database, http://dataweb.usitc.gov; and US Census Bureau, FTD Steel Imports Trade Data, www.census.gov/foreign-trade/Press-Release/steel_index.html.

Bilateral Disputes in the WTO

Since the WTO entered into force in January 1995 with its new dispute settlement procedures, the United States and Korea have filed 12 cases—6 by each country—involving bilateral trade problems. Not surprisingly, the US cases have involved problems with nontariff agricultural protectionism, which generally have been settled in favor of the US side (either by mutual agreement or by WTO panel ruling). One other case dealt with procurement problems associated with the construction of the new

Inchon airport, and the WTO panel ruled that the matter fell beyond Korea's obligations in the WTO government procurement agreement. The Korean cases dealt with problems with the conduct of US antidumping and safeguard investigations, and the WTO panels generally supported Korea's complaints (see table 7.6).

These cases provide further evidence that antidumping actions and agriculture continue to pose the most enduring obstacles to bilateral trade and the negotiation of an FTA. Neither issue can likely be fully resolved in the context of a bilateral agreement. But precedents from NAFTA and other FTA negotiations suggest that some special treatment under US laws could be provided to FTA partners (as is now done for safeguards cases in NAFTA), and targeted agricultural reforms could be implemented (if accompanied by compensatory domestic income transfers).

Potential Benefits of a Korea-US FTA

Korea and the United States could derive many potential economic and noneconomic benefits from a bilateral FTA. Economic benefits include expansion of trade and associated welfare gains, more secure access to the other market, and other long-run dynamic effects stemming from increased investment and incentives to implement additional economic reforms. Noneconomic benefits include better management of bilateral economic relations between the two governments and the strengthening of their political and security relationship.

Expansion of Trade Between Korea and the United States

To the extent that border and regulatory barriers distort trade and investment flows and thus impede growth, one should expect an FTA to increase trade between the partner countries. How much? To set parameters on the possible aggregate trade effects, we deployed both gravity and computable general equilibrium (CGE) models.

Results from the gravity model analysis show that although the two countries already are very much integrated in trade, bilateral trade expansion is still possible. The analysis also shows that for the last several years of the 1990s, trade integration between Korea and the United States weakened. Perhaps some exports lost their competitiveness and therefore lost market share in the other market. Or perhaps some exports fell because trade barriers rose, or some exporters decided to sell their products elsewhere because of continuing barriers to bilateral trade. Whatever the explanation, the underperformance of the two countries' bilateral trade implies that the United States and Korea have some room for improvement through an FTA.

Table 7.6 Korea-US trade disputes brought to the WTO (as of April 2003)

Consultation requested	Case number	Filed by	Subject of dispute	Status of case
April 1995	WT/DS3	United States	Korean measures concerning testing and inspection of agricultural products	Consultations pending. Although the case is dormant, US farm groups still complain about Korean practices.
May 1996	WT/DS41	United States	Korean requirements on shelf-life products	In July 1995, the parties reached a mutual settlement.
May 1997	WT/DS84/1	United States	Korean internal taxes imposed on certain alcoholic beverages	Korea lost the panel decision (September 1998) and the appeal (February 1999), so it amended its tax law (January 2000).
July 1997	WT/DS89/1	Korea	US AD duties on Korean color TV receivers	Korea withdrew the complaint (September 1999) after the US revoked the AD duties.
August 1997	WT/DS99/1	Korea	US AD duties on Korean dynamic random access memory semiconductors (DRAMs)	The US lost the panel decision (January 1999) and claimed to have implemented the panel recommendations (January 2000). The DSB agreed, at Korea's request, to reconvene the panel (April 2000), but Korea asked the panel to suspend its work (September 2000). The case may heat up again, as the US imposed a preliminary CVD against Korean DRAMs in April 2003.
February 1999	WT/DS161/1	United States	Korean measures restricting imports of beef	Korea lost the panel decision (July 2000) and the appeal (December 2000). In response, Korea eliminated its quotas on imported beef in 2001 and will reduce its tariffs on imported beef by 40 percent by 2004.

(table continues next page)

183

Table 7.6   Korea-US trade disputes brought to the WTO (as of April 2003)   *(continued)*

Consultation requested	Case number	Filed by	Subject of dispute	Status of case
February 1999	WT/DS163	United States	Procurement practices at a Korean airport	The panel found in May 2000 that the issue fell outside the Agreement on Government Procurement. The US did not appeal, and the DSB adopted the panel report in June 2000.
July 1999	WT/DS179	Korea	US AD duties on Korean stainless steel	The panel report (adopted February 2001) found that certain US practices in AD cases were inconsistent with the WTO. The US has revised its methodology.
June 2000	WT/DS202/1	Korea	US safeguards on imports of line pipe	The US lost the panel decision (October 2001) and the appeal (February 2002), though the Appellate Body weakened some of the panel's findings. The US settled the dispute by permitting Korea to export more line pipe from September 2002 through February 2003, when the safeguard expired.
June 2001	WT/DS234	Korea	US Byrd Amendment	The US lost the panel decision (September 2002) and the appeal (January 2003). The Bush administration proposed that the Byrd Amendment be repealed, but that proposal currently has insufficient support in the US Senate.
March 2002	WT/DS251	Korea	US steel safeguard	In May 2003, the panel ruled the US measures violated WTO obligations; the Appellate Body upheld the bulk of that ruling in November 2003.

DSB = Dispute Settlement Body

Sources: WTO Dispute Settlement Gateway, www.wto.org/english/tratop_e/dispu_e/dispu_e.htm; World Trade Online, www.insidetrade.com; and WorldTradeLaw.net, www.worldtradelaw.net.

To understand the potential economic impact of a preferential trading arrangement between the United States and Korea, we performed an analysis using the GTAP (Global Trade Analysis Project) model. In our analysis, we simulated the formation of a free trade agreement under the assumption that all tariffs (or only nonagricultural tariffs) are removed between the United States and Korea. One of the findings from this analysis is that Korea and the United States could expect a significant increase in their bilateral trade volume as a result of forming an FTA. In the case of full liberalization including agriculture, US exports to Korea would increase by 46 percent in the medium run and 49 percent in the long run, while US imports from Korea would increase by 26 percent and 30 percent, respectively. John Gilbert (2003) also confirms the same result of trade expansion, showing that US exports to Korea would increase by 48 percent and US imports from Korea would increase by 23 percent as a result of a Korea-US FTA.

Welfare Improvement

Increased bilateral trade does not necessarily mean that there are net welfare gains in both economies; if welfare losses due to trade diversion exceed the gains from bilateral trade expansion, then the countries could be worse off. In fact, our analysis shows that the formation of an FTA would lead to a significant trade diversion for Korea and the United States. Overall, however, the trade pact would be welfare enhancing for both countries (even in the case of partial liberalization excluding agriculture). The absolute welfare gains are evenly allocated across both economies, in the range of $1.5 billion to $8.9 billion for the United States and $1.7 billion to $10.8 billion for Korea.[7] As the much smaller economy, Korea obviously has proportionally more to gain. Thus, net welfare gains would range from 0.02 percent to 0.13 percent of GDP for the United States and from 0.38 percent to 2.41 percent of GDP for Korea. It is important to note that these results are probably lower-bound estimates of the impact of an FTA: the model does not capture service protection data, which may be a major potential source of welfare gains.

The welfare gains from a Korea-US FTA derive from different effects in the two economies. In the US case, most of the gains are from improvements in the terms of trade. These improvements reflect the benefits of export expansion into the Korean market. Allocative efficiency gains or losses are small, reflecting the relatively low distortion levels in the US economy. In contrast, terms-of-trade effects are less significant for Korea and in some cases are negative. Negative terms-of-trade effects indicate a

---

7. These figures are expressed in 1995 dollars as generated by the model. For details of the analysis, see Choi and Schott (2001).

cost from trade diversion being imposed on the Korean economy. For Korea, the largest gains come from improvements in allocative efficiency—essentially the Vinerian trade creation effect: the benefit associated with replacing inefficient domestic production with imports. This result suggests that Korea has less to gain from an FTA with the United States than from unilateral liberalization. In fact, Gilbert (2003) shows that allocative efficiency gains for Korea are three times greater from unilateral free trade than from an FTA with the United States, and that the total welfare gain is 67 percent higher.

Another important finding is that the potential gains of a Korea-US FTA are reduced by more than half for both economies if agriculture is excluded from the agreement. This result reflects both the importance of agricultural market access for the United States and the potential efficiency gains from agricultural trade reform in Korea.

More Secure Market Access

Another key economic benefit from an FTA is gaining more secure access to the other market. This objective is particularly important for Korea, since shipments to the United States account for about 20 percent of total Korean exports (equivalent to about 7 percent of Korean GDP).

To secure better access to the US market, Korean trade officials place priority on the development of FTA disciplines on contingent protection measures, just as the Canadians did in their FTA negotiations in the 1980s. Canadian manufacturers were particularly concerned that the imposition of antidumping and countervailing duties made access to the US market uncertain and created disincentives for investment in Canada.[8] Korea finds itself in a comparable situation; indeed, many Korean exports already have their access to the US market inhibited by antidumping and countervailing duties and by safeguard measures. One difference, however, is that Canada and Mexico now get preferential treatment from the United States in safeguard cases (though not in AD or CVD cases) under special rules that apply to NAFTA signatories.[9] As a result, Canada and Mexico were exempted from recent US steel safeguards. Korea obviously would like similar protection for its exporters.

Long-Run Dynamic Effects

To this point, we have dealt primarily with tariff liberalization, but an FTA would cover a broader array of trade reforms. In addition to eliminating

---

8. See Schott and Smith (1988) for more discussion of the Canada-US FTA.

9. However, these preferences are now being challenged in the WTO dispute settlement system.

tariffs, an FTA would also cover a wide range of nontariff barriers and other economic issues, including investment, standards, rules of origin, government procurement, intellectual property rights, and competition policy. A liberalized investment regime and service trade would unleash higher efficiency and productivity, generating faster growth for both economies. Therefore, an FTA would have a positive, long-run dynamic effect. For example, increased direct investment from the United States and new industrial alliances would enable many Korean firms to benefit from technology transfer. Many US firms could also benefit from strategic alliances with Korean firms, permitting them to use Korea as a base for further expansion of their activities in China and other Asian markets.

For Korea, there is an additional important benefit. An FTA with the United States would likely accelerate Korea's ongoing domestic reform program and stimulate economic growth. Japan also seems to have this benefit of an FTA in mind in its bilateral FTAs with Mexico and Korea.

Better Management of Economic Relations

Forming an FTA would result in a better economic relationship between the two countries by reducing bilateral trade frictions and reinforcing trade and investment linkages. Since an FTA would not only eliminate tariffs but also lower nontariff barriers, it would lessen many trade frictions between the two governments. This outcome is especially important in the bilateral trade in autos, a source of long-standing discord between the United States and Korea (as noted earlier). In addition, an FTA would increase investment, which in turn would generate increased trade through US affiliate companies, as a substantial share of US trade takes place between parent and subsidiary. Expanding intraindustry trade and investment would subsequently create vested interests in both countries for good relations.

Strengthening Security Ties

Aside from the economic benefits of an FTA, the United States and Korea have another common interest that an FTA could reinforce: a strong security relationship. The two countries have been close military allies for the past 50 years. Forming an FTA not only would bring them much closer in their economic relations but also could improve the climate for cooperation on political and security issues.

Indeed, political objectives often have driven US participation in FTA negotiations. The US-Israel FTA was the first and clearest example of this motive. Congressional support for NAFTA arguably hinged on broad concerns about immigration and US security interests and democracy in Central America. Similarly, US support for trade preferences under the

Caribbean Basin Initiative (CBI) was tied to the goal of resolving the migration and drug trafficking problems in that region. More recently, the US-Jordan FTA, signed in October 2000, seeks inter alia to strengthen the economic foundation for Jordan's participation in the peace process in the Middle East.

Strengthening the political and security relationship could turn out over time to be a much more important benefit of a Korea-US FTA than the consequent economic gains. The trade pact could be particularly valuable as a show of US support for peaceful relations in Northeast Asia and as a means of ensuring that South Korea has the means to advance that process. Recently, Korea-US relations have been under strain caused by the rising anti-American sentiments in Korea and differences between the two countries on the policy responses to the North Korean nuclear threat. Such tensions elevate the political risk of doing business in Korea and thus tend to damp investment (at least in the short run). Moving forward on an FTA could help to offset these negative factors. Indeed, many APEC countries, including Korea, seek to deepen trade ties with the United States as part of a strategy to ensure continued US military engagement in the region.

Effects on Regional Integration

Should a Korea-US FTA be implemented, it is generally expected that the increase of US exports to Korea would exceed the increase of Korean exports to the United States, since US trade barriers are much lower than those of Korea. As a result, the US trade deficit with Korea should be reduced. At the same time, some of the increase in US exports to Korea would come at the expense of Japanese products currently imported into Korea. Thus, while Korea's trade balance with the United States would worsen, its trade balance with Japan would improve.

Our GTAP model simulations confirm these effects of a Korea-US FTA on bilateral trade balances. Although the improvement in a bilateral trade balance does not significantly affect the overall economy, it is important politically and can influence Korean trade policy for better or worse. Korean officials believe that a reduction in their trade deficit with Japan and in the trade surplus with the United States would help them, respectively, to manage protectionist pressures at home against dominant Japanese firms and to mitigate US protectionism directed against competitive Korean exports. Korea has often been under trade pressure because of its chronic trade surplus with the United States. At the same time, a chronic and severe trade deficit with Japan has at times led Korea to try to artificially divert Japanese imports under the "import source diversification system." An FTA with the United States could enable Korea to "naturally" divert the source of imports from Japan to the United States, thereby realigning its trade imbalances with both countries. From the point of view of Korean trade officials, it would kill two birds with one stone.[10]

But that is only part of the story. If a Korea-US FTA were realized, many economies besides Japan (including Taiwan, China, Mexico, Australia, New Zealand, and Canada) would be affected by trade diversion in some sectors (see below). Therefore, a Korea-US FTA would have significant implications for the Asia-Pacific region; indeed, it could promote a bandwagon effect that would prompt other countries to pursue bilateral FTAs in the region, especially with the United States. That is what Singapore is trying to do with its web of bilateral FTAs. Basically, it is attempting to cobble together a core group of FTAs to revive progress toward a regional FTA as envisaged by APEC leaders a decade ago. A Korea-US FTA thus could accelerate the APEC process toward free and open trade and investment in the region by the Bogor target dates of 2010 and 2020.

Potential Costs of a Korea-US FTA

An FTA between the United States and Korea would have some associated political costs for both countries as well as economic costs for US and Korean trading partners due to trade diversion, especially for neighbors in the Asia-Pacific region. It could also have negative implications for the WTO and the Doha Round.

Political Costs of Domestic Adjustments

While an FTA between the United States and Korea would yield economic benefits for both partners, each country would have individual winners and losers from closer trade integration and each would have to change long-standing policies that protect politically powerful industries from foreign competition. Simply put, the benefits from trade would be distributed unevenly among various sectors of the economy, and those facing stiffer competition would likely object vocally.

For Korea, the biggest loser would be the agricultural sector. Thus, as in the Uruguay Round of multilateral trade negotiations, the most vociferous opposition to an FTA with the United States (and to the Doha Round as well) would likely come from agricultural interests. Korea's farm sector is heavily subsidized and not competitive, but it still wields substantial clout in national politics. Korean farmers have disproportionate representation in the National Assembly, even though agriculture, forestry,

---

10. However, Korea and Japan agreed in October 2003 to negotiate an FTA to be concluded by 2005. Such a pact would mitigate the discriminatory effect of a Korea-US FTA on Japanese exports to Korea.

and fishing now account for only 5 percent of GDP and involve only 11 percent of the Korean population (down from 48 percent in 1970). However, because of the rapid urbanization and industrialization of the past 30 years, many in the urban population still have family members residing in agricultural areas and thus support farm protection and subsidies. Over time, however, as the agricultural population continues to decline, these ties—and the political power they lend to the farm sector—are likely to weaken. Only 6 percent of young workers (aged 20–24) are in farming today, and almost 70 percent of the agricultural workforce is more than 50 years old.

Over the near term, agriculture will continue to pose the largest obstacle to free trade talks. Yet without some liberalization of agricultural protection, Korea may become isolated in international trade talks, and Korean industries and exporters may lose the chance to lower foreign barriers affecting their products. Changing demographics suggest that Korea could mitigate at least some of the domestic opposition to farm reforms by switching from trade protection to income support for Korean farmers. Indeed, this is the direction taken by European policy aimed at internal reform of the region's common agricultural policy. If the European Commission is successful in its reform agenda, then Korea (and Japan) would be isolated in opposition in the WTO to farm trade reform.

There is some indication that Korean officials are slowly moving in the same direction as the Europeans. Faced with unexpectedly strong opposition by farmers to the Korea-Chile FTA, the Korean government is proposing a trade adjustment assistance (TAA)–type program for Korean farmers to be included in its FTA implementation bill. However, if such subsidies are large enough to mollify the opposition of Korean farmers, they could very well pressure a government budget already under considerable strain.

For the United States, the main losers from an FTA with Korea would be some manufacturing industries, notably textiles and apparel, steel, and electronics. Just like their counterparts in Korea, these US industries would ask for more subsidies and import relief via antidumping and safeguard measures. From Korea's point of view, support for an FTA with the United States depends significantly on whether a prospective trade pact can deal with problems arising from the use of antidumping actions, countervailing duties, and safeguard measures. Reforms in these areas are particularly important for the steel and electronics industries, which as noted earlier have been frequently targeted by the United States.

US political resistance to an FTA with Korea could surface in two ways: opposition to revisions in US antidumping law and to tariff cuts on textiles and apparel, and indifference about a deal with a relatively small economic payoff. The former could generate strong resistance to a bilateral trade pact; the latter would likely present only a modest barrier to the start of prospective negotiations. Antidumping cases are considered by many US industries as the first and best line of defense against foreign unfair trade practices. Thus, many members of the US Congress, including strong protrade advocates, might not continue to support US trade reforms if antidumping actions are not in the trade policy toolbox. In addition, US industry would probably strongly contest the granting of tariff preferences to Korean textile and apparel exporters in a bilateral FTA. To be sure, such benefits were granted, albeit grudgingly, to Mexico in NAFTA, and more recently to Caribbean and African producers in the US Trade and Development Act of 2000. But a Korea-US FTA would attract more opposition from US industry for two reasons: the Korean textile and apparel industry is not integrated with US firms, and many of the Korean firms are highly competitive.

The wild card in this area is what happens in the Doha Round. The United States has proposed the elimination of all industrial tariffs by 2015 and a sharp interim reduction in peak tariffs (including those on textiles and apparel) by 2010. If US objectives are even partially satisfied in the WTO talks, US industry will likely respond to the new trade liberalization by demanding greater use of contingent protection measures. Such actions in turn could exacerbate the already strident disputes over antidumping and countervailing duties.

Trade Diversion

The United States and Korea are, respectively, the largest and the seventh-largest trading economies in the world (with Japan, the European Union, Canada, China, and Hong Kong in between). An FTA between the United States and Korea would have a sizable impact on and numerous implications for other countries, especially those in the Asia Pacific, that trade heavily with the United States, Korea, or both. With the formation of an FTA, partner countries' exports to each other's markets would increase, in part at the expense of reduced imports from third countries that do not enjoy the duty-free benefits of FTA partners. This trade diversion effect would be a major concern and cost for countries that are competing with the United States and Korea and that would lose market share in the US and Korean economies.

Which countries might be vulnerable to trade diversion caused by a Korea-US FTA? A look at the import market shares of each country provides a first-order approximation of countries at risk. In the Korean market, Japan and China are the second- and third-largest exporters, after the United States. In the US market, Canada, Japan, Mexico, the European Union, and China are the major exporters, followed by Korea.

How vulnerable is trade from these countries? The analysis of export similarity indices (ESIs)—the similarity in the structure of export commodities in comparison to that of the other FTA partner countries—

indicates that if a Korea-US FTA is formed, Japan and Germany would be the most likely to suffer from trade diversion in the Korean market, and Taiwan, Japan, and Mexico would be most likely to suffer from trade diversion in the US market. Overall, Japan and Taiwan would be most affected—particularly Japan, because it exports so much to both the United States and Korea (see Choi and Schott 2001, chapter 5).

The results of sectoral analysis using the revealed comparative advantages (RCAs) of major competing countries indicate that Japan would probably experience a fall in exports, mostly in the chemical and machinery sectors, with the exception of power-generating and office machines; Germany, in chemicals and general industrial machines; and Canada, China, Australia, and New Zealand, in agricultural, food, and raw materials exports. In the US market, Taiwan would probably suffer from trade diversion mostly in textile fibers and in office and electrical machinery; Japan, in rubber products and office and telecommunications machines; Mexico, in textile fibers, telecommunications, and electrical machinery; the European Union, in steel products; and Australia and New Zealand, in textiles, fibers, and steel products. Thus, different countries would feel different trade diversion effects in different sectors.

The preceding discussion of trade diversion, of course, focuses on the short-run direct impact of a Korea-US FTA. In the long run, trade diversion would depend on investment, income, and other effects. Nonetheless, the simulation results of the GTAP model generally confirm the expected trade diversion, even in the long run. For example, the simulation results show that Korea increases imports from the United States but imports less from all other regions. However, the pattern is not so clear in the case of US imports. Expansion of US income tends to result in increases in imports from Japan and in some cases from ASEAN countries, Australia, and New Zealand.

Possible Negative Impact on WTO Negotiations

The pursuit of an FTA between Korea and the United States need not divert attention away from the WTO negotiations. However, a prospective FTA could have adverse effects on current WTO talks.

First, pursuing an FTA with the United States would highlight the need to reform Korean agricultural policies and would thus provoke domestic lobbies in Korea to even stronger resistance against trade liberalization. The farm lobby does not discriminate between FTAs and multilateral negotiations; it dislikes them all. Inciting additional domestic opposition to any trade liberalization accord could make it even harder for Korea to engage in the Doha Round.

Second, if the process of multilateral liberalization stalls, then FTAs might be given prominence as defensive or fallback strategies. While a

Korea-US FTA could catalyze other trade pacts through a process of competitive liberalization, as noted above, it could also incite countries to offset the discrimination against their trade by imposing new contingent protection measures, creating new discriminatory trading blocs, or both. Either way, the WTO process would suffer.

Prospects and Recommendations

Balancing the costs and benefits of a Korea-US FTA involves a complex calculus of economic and political factors. Econometric models suggest that both countries will gain from a bilateral agreement at the expense of other important trading partners, especially the European Union, China, and Japan. For the United States, the potential gain is very small in relation to its $10 trillion economy. Gilbert (2003) calculates the US welfare gain at 0.03 percent of GDP, generated primarily from terms-of-trade effects associated with preferential treatment in the Korean market. For Korea, the potential income gain is more significant. Gilbert (2003) forecasts welfare gains of almost 0.4 percent of GDP, resulting primarily from increased efficiency of Korean industries induced by domestic reforms. However, these welfare gains would be substantially reduced if the FTA excludes important sectors like agriculture.

Both the United States and Korea have important economic stakes in the Asia-Pacific region that would be affected by a prospective FTA. The same holds true if Korea proceeds with FTA talks with Japan or China or both. Given the complementary pattern of trade among East Asian countries, FTAs in the region will likely generate significant trade diversion and thus encourage the negotiation of parallel agreements to counter the discrimination from other pacts. In short, "competitive liberalization" is likely to thrive in the APEC region (Bergsten 1996).

In fact, Korea, China, and Japan are already involved in this process of competitive liberalization. While China and Japan separately pursue an FTA with ASEAN, Korea may be forced to follow suit to protect its market share and trading interests in the region. Preliminary talks already have begun with Singapore and Thailand on a bilateral basis.

Studies have shown that Korea would gain more from having an FTA with China and Japan together than from a bilateral FTA with either China or Japan. In fact, one of the major policy goals of the current Korean administration under President Roh Moo-hyun is to build Korea as the economic hub of Northeast Asia—especially as a business center (distribution and financial). Thus, Korea has a strong interest in pursuing a Northeast Asian (Korea-China-Japan) FTA.

Given the current economic status of Korea, China, and Japan, however, we are not likely to see a Northeast Asian FTA between these big trading nations in the near future. First of all, China is not ready for an FTA with a more advanced economy such as Japan or Korea. It already is having some problems in implementing the extensive reforms to which it committed in its protocols of accession to the WTO, and thus is not likely to be ready in the near future for the even deeper liberalization and deregulation required by an FTA. Second, Japan and Korea are not ready to open their markets to increased agricultural imports from China. Witness the strong resistance by their agricultural lobbies to FTAs with Singapore and Chile—neither of which is really known as an agricultural powerhouse.

The most likely development in this region over the next several years would be a bilateral FTA between Korea and Japan. The two countries have been toying with this idea for the past five years, and they plan to launch negotiations soon. Japan seems to be more eager to start this undertaking while Korea prefers to form a three-way Northeast Asian FTA.

Despite the economic and noneconomic benefits cited above, the short-term prospect for an FTA between Korea and the United States is not very good. The biggest problem remains the agricultural sector in Korea. Attempts by the Korean government to mute the opposition of farm groups by establishing a program to compensate farmers harmed by FTA reforms have met strong political resistance, and it is not clear whether the implementation bill will pass the National Assembly. The Roh administration doesn't seem to want to take on this domestic political fight. Indeed, when asked about the possibility of a Korea-US FTA during his visit to Washington in May 2003, President Roh admitted that the resistance of the agricultural sector would make it difficult for Korea to pursue *any* FTA.

The recent rise in nationalism in Korea could also work against a potential FTA between the United States and Korea. Recall that this was a central argument against the launching of Korea-US FTA negotiations in the late 1980s (see USITC 1989). Fifteen years later, the problem persists. Any attempt to negotiate an FTA between Korea and the United States would unavoidably involve the politically sensitive issue of agricultural-sector reform in Korea, which in turn would likely exacerbate anti-American sentiments in Korea among farmers, students, and even some businessmen.

Nevertheless, the two countries must not lose sight of either the substantial economic benefits that could accrue from an FTA or the positive spillovers on political and security relations. Thus, Korea and the United States should pursue an FTA as an important long-term goal. Several steps should be taken now to better prepare for launching FTA talks in the future.

First, the two countries should increase their efforts to wrap up their negotiations for a bilateral investment treaty (BIT), which has been deadlocked for the last few years because of the dispute over Korea's movie screen quota. Both sides should consider stepping back from their original demands. The United States should accept an increase in the quota for foreign content providers rather than insist on its complete elimination. Korea should drop its protectionist position and agree to such liberalization. Given the rapid improvement in the competitiveness of the Korean movie industry in recent years, the practical impact on Korean industry of increased foreign competition should be relatively minor. For the last couple of years, the market share of Korean movies has been higher than the current screen quota ratio (40 percent). If the Korean movie industry insists on further protection, the government could offer some type of nonprice subsidy or safeguard protection. In any event, it is strongly recommended that the two countries try to sign a BIT as soon as possible. The Korea-US BIT would be the first step toward an FTA between the two countries.

Second, the general public in Korea is not very well informed about what an FTA would mean for Korea. Their perceptions are shaped by what they read in the newspapers about an FTA's negative impact on the Korean agricultural sector and what they see in TV news programs about farmers' street demonstrations against any such agreement. It therefore is important for the general public to be more educated and informed about a possible FTA, particularly about its benefits to other sectors in the economy and to consumers. In this respect, some actions taken by the US-Korea Business Council are encouraging. In early 2003, the council established a joint task force to draw up active strategies to promote the successful negotiation of both a BIT and an FTA between the two countries. But more attention needs to paid to focusing the public debate in Korea itself on the benefits of as well as the adjustments required in pursuing freer trade policies, including through FTA and WTO accords.

Third, both governments should work to contain the rise in anti-American sentiments in Korea. To some degree, these feelings, which are not deeply rooted in the society, have been manipulated for political ends by certain groups using the unfortunate accidental death of two schoolgirls killed by a US armored vehicle in 2002 to fan public ire. The two governments should take additional steps to prevent tragedies of this type from adding fuel to anti-American sentiment in Korea. For example, they could establish a joint investigative team to review all such incidents in the future. Such reviews would be more credible in the eyes of the Korean public than the findings of US military tribunals.

In sum, there is a strong economic rationale for moving forward with negotiations on a comprehensive free trade agreement between Korea and the United States—but only if agricultural reforms are an integral part of the deal. Whether the two countries can muster the political support for dismantling barriers in sensitive sectors is unclear, however. The decision may turn on how much farm reform is conceded in the WTO's Doha Round and on what other Asia-Pacific trading partners do to deepen regional trade ties. The outcome of the WTO ministerial in Cancún in September 2003 is not encouraging in the first regard, as it demonstrated Korea's reluctance to negotiate agricultural reforms. If WTO negotiations get back on track, then Korean officials will have to decide whether they can support that deal—and, if so, whether they can go further by offering more open access to FTA partners. If China and Japan, as well as the

ASEAN countries, expand their network of bilateral and regional FTAs, can Korea stand aside? And if those East Asian pacts discriminate against US exporters, can US trade officials stand aside—or do they insist on bilateral deals of their own? Over time, and perhaps sooner rather than later, we believe that the two countries will move toward free trade for both economic and political reasons.

References

Bergsten, C. Fred. 1996. *Competitive Liberalization and Global Free Trade: A Vision for the Early 21st Century*. Working Paper 96-15. Washington: Institute for International Economics. www.iie.com/publications/wp/1996/96-15.htm.

Choi, Inbom, and Jeffrey J. Schott. 2001. *Free Trade Between Korea and the United States?* POLICY ANALYSES IN INTERNATIONAL ECONOMICS 62. Washington: Institute for International Economics.

Gilbert, John. 2003. CGE Simulation of US Bilateral Free Trade Agreements. Background paper prepared for the conference Free Trade Agreements and US Trade Policy, sponsored by the Institute for International Economics (May 7–8).

Schott, Jeffrey J., and Murray G. Smith. 1988. *The Canada–United States Free Trade Agreement: The Global Impact*. Washington: Institute for International Economics.

US International Trade Commission (USITC). 1989. *The Pros and Cons of Entering into Negotiations on Free Trade Area Agreements with Taiwan, the Republic of Korea, and ASEAN, or the Pacific Rim Region in General*. Report to the Senate Committee on Finance. Publication 2166. Washington: USITC.

US International Trade Commission (USITC). 2001. *US-Korea FTA: The Economic Impact of Establishing a Free Trade Agreement (FTA) Between the United States and the Republic of Korea*. Investigation No. 332-425, Publication 3452. Washington: General Printing Office. www.usitc.gov/wais/reports/arc/w3452.htm (September).

US Trade Representative, Office of (USTR). 2003. *2003 National Trade Estimate Report on Foreign Trade Barriers*. www.ustr.gov/reports/nte/2003/index.htm.

8

US-Taiwan Free Trade Agreement Prospects

NICHOLAS R. LARDY AND DANIEL H. ROSEN

In Asia and elsewhere, the United States is contemplating many free trade agreements, for both economic and noneconomic reasons. This chapter explores the prospect of a US-Taiwan FTA, focusing primarily on its economic implications.[1]

A possible US-Taiwan FTA differs from other pairings because current political realities make it difficult for Taiwan to join in "competitive liberalization" in the Asia Pacific. Political objections from the People's Republic of China, rooted in the complex history of China and Taiwan since 1949, make its neighbors hesitant to begin negotiations with Taiwan.[2] A US-Taiwan FTA therefore might be significant primarily because it could facilitate Taiwan's further integration into the global economy.

Taiwan meets many of the criteria set by US trade policy leaders for deciding which countries should be given high priority as potential partners in FTAs. Taiwan is democratic; US-Taiwan economic relations are significant; the government is willing to negotiate on a broad spectrum of issues; and Taiwan enjoys political support within both US political parties in Washington. An FTA could promote further domestic eco-

Nicholas R. Lardy is a senior fellow and Daniel H. Rosen a visiting fellow at the Institute for International Economics.

1. In a forthcoming policy analysis to be published by the Institute for International Economics, we will examine more closely such an FTA's geopolitical context.

2. A review of this history is outside the scope of the analysis here. For the US Congressional Research Service backgrounder on Taiwan, see Dumbaugh (2001); the most recent book-length treatment of Taiwan's 20th-century history is Roy (2003).

nomic reform within Taiwan, provided its justification is economic and not simply political. Because US-Taiwan trade is already quite open, Taiwan's economic success would be better served through further integration with Asia, including mainland China, rather than with the United States. Other states in the region, however, are reluctant to enter into bilateral trade negotiations with Taiwan. A US-Taiwan FTA might help to overcome this reluctance. The effects of a US FTA are not necessarily all positive for Taiwan or its neighbors, *but on balance they might offset losses that would occur if everyone else in Asia negotiates FTAs while Taiwan is left on the sidelines.*

The introduction of this chapter provides background on the Taiwanese economy and US-Taiwan economic relations. We then examine, in turn, the quantitative evidence on the likely impact of a US-Taiwan FTA and a qualitative analysis of the FTA (with a focus on key sectors). The final section draws conclusions.

Taiwan's Economy

For the past five decades Taiwan has been one of the world's most successful economies. Its long-term growth—just over 8 percent annually in real terms—has been more rapid than that of any other economy, propelling its GDP above $280 billion by 2002. In the process, the structure of the economy has been transformed. Agriculture initially was the most important sector, but by the early 1970s its share of output fell to under 10 percent; it now accounts for less than 2 percent of GDP. Manufacturing expansion drove Taiwan's growth for three decades, from the early 1950s into the early 1980s, when its contribution to output peaked at a little more than two-fifths. In the past decade services have become the major source of growth and now account for two-thirds of GDP.

Although in the early 1950s Taiwan restricted imports to promote the development of the industrial sector, by the end of the decade it began to adopt trade and exchange rate policies that transformed it into a major trading economy. Exports grew annually by an astounding 25 percent and 30 percent, respectively, in the 1960s and 1970s, making Taiwan a leading trading economy by 1980.

Trade expansion continued in the 1980s even after Taiwan lost its membership in the United Nations and related bodies such as the World Bank. Following its entry into the World Trade Organization (WTO) in 2002, its leaders decided to further enhance Taiwan's international economic status by seeking to negotiate FTAs with several of its trading partners, including the United States. That China has directly and indirectly signaled strong opposition to Taiwan's negotiating FTAs is, from a US perspective, not a deterrent.

Table 8.1 Value of US-Taiwan trade, 1985–2002
(millions of dollars)

Year	Exports	Imports	Balance
1985	4,699.8	16,396.3	−11,696.5
1986	5,524.2	19,790.8	−14,266.6
1987	7,412.7	24,621.8	−17,209.1
1988	12,129.1	24,713.9	−12,584.8
1989	11,334.6	24,312.7	−12,978.1
1990	11,490.8	22,665.9	−11,175.1
1991	13,182.4	23,023.0	−9,840.6
1992	15,250.3	24,596.0	−9,345.7
1993	16,167.8	25,101.5	−8,933.7
1994	17,108.8	26,705.8	−9,597.0
1995	19,289.6	28,971.8	−9,682.2
1996	18,460.2	29,907.3	−11,447.1
1997	20,365.7	32,628.5	−12,262.8
1998	18,164.5	33,124.8	−14,960.3
1999	19,131.4	35,204.4	−16,073.0
2000	24,405.9	40,502.8	−16,096.9
2001	18,121.6	33,374.5	−15,252.9
2002	16,950.9	29,447.6	−12,496.7

Source: US Census Bureau, www.census.gov/foreign-trade/balance/
c5830.html.

US-Taiwan Economic Relations

Taiwan is an island a little larger in area than Maryland and a little larger in population than Texas. Relative to Taiwan's size, US-Taiwan economic relations have taken on disproportionate importance, due to the countries' long-standing political and security relationship. Taiwan is the eighth-largest trading partner of the United States, ranking just ahead of North Atlantic Treaty Organization allies Italy and France, and just behind South Korea. Taiwan's per capita income in 2002 purchasing power parity terms was $18,000.

Both the United States and Taiwan are "industrial" democracies, though both are services dominated—services are 80 percent of GDP for the United States, 66 percent for Taiwan. The trend away from industry and toward services in Taiwan has been unwavering since the mid-1980s. In the last 10 years, labor-intensive manufacturing has shifted out of Taiwan (largely to China), much as it left the United States in earlier decades, and today Taiwan is an information technology powerhouse.

Table 8.1 shows US trade with Taiwan from 1985 to 2002. The United States currently exports goods and services valued at about $17 billion to Taiwan (only Japan exports more) and imports more than $29 billion from Taiwan. The United States is now Taiwan's second-largest export market after mainland China. The United States has long maintained a trade deficit with Taiwan—$12.5 billion in 2002, well below historic highs. Two-way trade has declined almost 30 percent since 2000: information technology trade sagged more than most sectors in the downturn in high-tech manufacturing and brought Taiwanese exports down, while a good deal of indigenous Taiwanese manufacturing and manufacturing by foreign-invested enterprises in Taiwan migrated to mainland China. US agricultural exports to Taiwan dropped by $1 billion between 1995 and 2001 as well, from $3.3 billion to $2.3 billion (USITC 2002a).

The stock of US foreign direct investment (FDI) in Taiwan stood at $7.7 billion at the end of 2000, with a flow of $1.1 billion that year. Also in 2000, $186 million of Taiwanese investment to the United States contributed to a stock of $3.2 billion, while $2.6 billion flowed from Taiwan to mainland China.[3] The flow of US FDI into China was $4.4 billion in 2000.

The United States and Taiwan have a significant record of economic disputes, as is typical when countries have sizable trading relationships. The Office of the US Trade Representative (USTR) is critical of the continuing sales of counterfeit goods and other intellectual property problems in Taiwan, which Taiwanese authorities have been lax in deterring. Among other areas of dispute that stand out in the 2003 *National Trade Estimate Report* are access to agricultural markets and telecommunications (USTR 2003a). The US-Taiwan Business Council highlights seven issues Taiwan must address before FTA negotiations can begin: reform of financial institutions, tightened protection of intellectual property rights (IPR), strengthened anticorruption efforts, rice import quotas, unfair agricultural goods labeling requirements, lack of openness in the telecommunications market, and problems in the health care market, including market-restricting regulatory reforms and lack of IPR protection for pharmaceuticals. Another US business advocacy group, the American Chamber of Commerce in Taipei, publishes an annual *Taiwan White Paper*, which details key problems affecting US firms. In it, the chamber documents industry-specific concerns that businesspeople often deem more pressing than an FTA (American Chamber of Commerce 2003).

Trade Barriers and Concerns

Trade barriers between Taiwan and the United States are modest. Taiwan's nominal average tariff is currently 7.1 percent and is to be further lowered as part of its WTO commitments, to 4.2 percent by 2007. Even after Taiwan has fully implemented its WTO obligations, tariff peaks will remain in certain product areas. Three models (discussed below) forecast that the removal of those tariffs, particularly on agriculture and vehicles, would lead to major gains in US exports following enactment of an FTA.

---

3. The $2.6 billion figure, supplied by the Ministry of Economic Affairs in Taipei, substantially understates the magnitude of investment by Taiwanese firms in China.

US nominal average tariffs are an even lower 2.8 percent, with peaks in agriculture (poultry and juice) and various goods (apparel and textiles; steel and steel products, including fasteners; and trucks). The removal of apparel and textile tariffs is responsible for the bulk of gains in Taiwanese exports under an FTA. Taiwan also has nontariff barriers (NTBs) to the imports of agriculture and vehicles. Likewise, the United States uses NTBs in addition to tariffs in certain agricultural sectors.

Some matters already negotiated but not implemented must be addressed before FTA talks can begin. The USTR has effectively ruled out any discussion of an FTA with Taiwan until concerns over what it regards as Taiwan's failure to implement its WTO obligations are addressed. The key actions include protecting intellectual property rights, liberalizing telecommunications, and improving market access for agricultural products (USTR 2003a).

Broader Context of US-Taiwan Relations

The value of US-Taiwan economic relations cannot be separated from their unique foundation in security and political concerns. The United States' security interest in Taiwan dates from the Cold War, and it expressed its commitments to Taiwan in the Taiwan Relations Act of 1979. As a proponent of democratization, the United States continues to view Taiwan as an important model of democratic transition in a region where less liberal philosophies have generally held sway. Taiwan's recent human rights record stands out positively, and Taiwan has been supportive of US security interests.

National security and foreign policy considerations should argue in favor of arrangements that further sustain Taiwan's economic welfare. The question is whether an FTA would in fact strengthen Taiwan—the issue we now address.

Quantitative Analyses

This chapter draws on three quantitative assessments of a possible US-Taiwan FTA. The US International Trade Commission (USITC) assessed US-Taiwan FTA prospects in general and sectors of interest in particular (USITC 2002a). The USITC model considers the elimination of tariff barriers and quotas, but not other nontariff barriers more difficult to convert into tariff equivalents. Taiwan's Chung-Hua Institution for Economic Research (2002) also did a GTAP (Global Trade Analysis Project) assessment, summarized below. The Chung-Hua report uses a similar methodology, though it provides more detail on services. Finally, John Gilbert (2003) estimated the effects of a US-Taiwan FTA alongside 12 other US FTAs currently under negotiation or discussion. All use the GTAP 5 computable general equilibrium model to estimate trade regime changes.[4] The overview of quantitative effects presented below is based on the USITC study except where otherwise specified.

Total Welfare Gains and GDP

The USITC estimates that the total US welfare gains from an FTA with Taiwan—assuming that all the anticipated sectoral effects come to pass— would be $200 million. This is trivial relative to US GDP of $7.95 trillion in the 1997 baseline.[5] For Taiwan the gains are somewhat greater in both absolute and relative terms: $1 billion in total welfare gains, or 0.3 percent of 1997 GDP, which is 100 times more significant in percentage terms than the US gain. Table 8.2 summarizes welfare effects from the studies we consider.

According to the USITC estimate, for both the United States and for Taiwan, welfare gains result from improvement in terms of trade rather than from allocative efficiency gains.[6] The USITC estimates that US allocative efficiency gains are zero—terms-of-trade gains make up the whole welfare gain; the pattern is much the same in Gilbert. The distribution of welfare gains for Taiwan is similar in both studies, though in Gilbert the allocative efficiency effects for Taiwan are slightly negative. In contrast, the Chung-Hua study predicts much larger gains for both Taiwan and the United States, attributing them largely to improvements in allocative efficiency. Indeed, in the case of the United States the Chung-Hua study estimates that the terms-of-trade effect is negative.

Because the absolute impact on the United States of an FTA with Taiwan would be so modest, the USITC assumed that it would not induce US total factor productivity (TFP) gains. Given the more significant impact on Taiwan, it estimated that TFP in Taiwan might increase by 0.38 percent should an FTA be enacted by 2005.[7] If that were the case, then the modest

---

4. The GTAP Web site is www.gtap.agecon.purdue.edu. These three studies are hereafter cited in the text only by their names (USITC, Gilbert, and the Chung-Hua study).

5. USITC (2002a) finds $200 million in welfare gains for the United States, or 0.003 percent of 1997 GDP. Gilbert (2003) yields a higher result: $760 million, or 0.01 percent of GDP.

6. "Terms of trade" refers to the prices of a country's exports relative to the prices of its imports. If the tariff changes following enactment of an FTA have the effect of making a given amount of a country's exports worth a greater amount of the country's imports, then the country's terms of trade are said to improve. "Allocative efficiency" refers to how well an economy's available resources (factors, or inputs) are assigned to production. By reducing distortions in a country's trade environment, an FTA might improve its allocative efficiency.

7. The TFP gains for 2009 and 2013 of 0.35 percent and 0.30 percent, respectively, are predicated on the assumption that an FTA is not implemented until those dates; the USITC is not *adding* those gains to the earlier TFP gains.

Table 8.2 Welfare gains predicted by the US-Taiwan FTA studies (millions of 1997 dollars)

Study	United States	Taiwan
USITC		
Allocative efficiency	0	0
Terms of trade	200	1,200
Total welfare	200	1,000
Gilbert		
Allocative efficiency	108	−23
Terms of trade	653	1,066
Total welfare	760	1,043
Chung-hua Institution		
Allocative efficiency	1,550	1,629
Terms of trade	−480	1,004
Total welfare	1,070	2,633

Sources: USITC (2002a), Gilbert (2003), Chung-hua Institution (2002).

$1 billion Taiwanese welfare gains could increase to $4.2 billion—the equivalent of a 1.5 percent increase in GDP. This TFP component for Taiwan is not quantitatively derived in the USITC report, and it is contingent on the basic gains in welfare predicted by the model. Liberalizing service trade by eliminating NTBs could conceivably produce enough additional gains for the United States to improve total factor productivity, although probably not by very much. This possibility is discussed below in light of the Chung-Hua report (which addresses nonquota NTBs, a more important factor in limiting service trade).

Trade Effects

Bilaterally, the USITC study forecasts an increase in US exports to Taiwan of 16 percent, or roughly $3.5 billion annually, under an FTA. US imports from Taiwan are expected to increase by 18 percent, or $7.0 billion; thus the bilateral trade deficit of the United States with Taiwan increases by $3.5 billion.

US exports globally would increase 0.2 percent over base-year levels, or by $2.4 billion; globally US imports would rise only $3.2 billion—less than half of the value of the increased imports from Taiwan alone. In this model, Taiwanese imports displace imports from other countries in the US market for one of two reasons. First, with the advantage of tariff-free entry into the United States, Taiwan firms may displace the goods of more efficient producers elsewhere. This is referred to as trade diversion. Second, under an FTA, the mix of imported inputs needed by the United States to make finished goods may change, and Taiwan may be the most efficient producer of these goods. This displacement effect is reflected in

Table 8.3   US and Taiwan sectors benefiting most from bilateral export growth, 2005 (millions of 1997 dollars)

United States		Taiwan	
Sector	Growth	Sector	Growth
Other machinery and equipment	868	Textiles, apparel, and leather	3,104
Motor vehicles, parts	629	Other machinery and equipment	836
Other foods	520	Metals and metal products	666
Electronic equipment	307	Electronic equipment	599
Chemicals, rubber, plastic	300	Other transportation equipment	504
Other transportation equipment	199	Chemicals, rubber, plastic	414
Vegetables, fruits, nuts	164	Other foods	182

Source: USITC (2002a).

the USITC forecast that a US-Taiwan FTA would increase the global US trade deficit by only $800 million, not by the $3.5 billion added to the bilateral deficit with Taiwan. Similarly, Taiwan's *global* exports increase by 2 percent or $2.8 billion and imports by 2 percent or $2.6 billion, for an increased net surplus of $200 million.

Would the US-Taiwan FTA create more trade than it diverted? As table 8.3 shows, the preponderance of Taiwanese export growth is in a single commodity group—textiles and apparel—in which poorer economies might seem to be lower-cost producers; this result gives us reason to question the balance-of-trade creation and diversion in the Taiwan FTA case (see below). Gilbert's simulation also indicates trade diversion. His expected reduction in US tariff revenue from trade with third parties under a Taiwan FTA is $281 million—the second largest for the United States (after Indonesia) among the 13 FTAs he looks at. In Taiwan, tariff revenue in trade with the non-US world falls by $498 million. While nonmember tariff revenues decline in a US-Taiwan FTA, tariff revenues from members' trade decline more. Gilbert predicts that total American exports to Taiwan rise by $6.6 billion, and exports to the rest of the world fall by $2.4 billion; imports from Taiwan rise by $7.2 billion, while imports from the rest of the world fall by $2.3 billion. The biggest percentage declines in value of exports to the United States and Taiwan occur for China (–0.16 percent) and for the Philippines, Central America, Indonesia, and Singapore (all between –0.15 and –0.10 percent).

As Gilbert notes (2003, 5), "Negative terms-of-trade consequences of an FTA for non-member economies are another measure of trade diversion, since the changes in trading prices reflect the reduction in imports by members from non-member sources." His study includes terms-of-trade effects for other countries and regions resulting from a US-Taiwan FTA: as is true of other FTAs he examines, they are negative. In our next section, we look at the textiles and apparel sector and conclude that diversion is indeed predominantly responsible for Taiwan's export gains. This outcome would be mitigated (but not eliminated) by fuller inclusion of service trade induced by removal of NTBs, as suggested by the Chung-Hua study.

Sectoral Effects

Though the welfare and trade (global and bilateral) effects of a US-Taiwan FTA are very modest—indeed, almost insignificant in the case of the United States—some sector-specific effects would be more pronounced. In terms of exports to Taiwan for the United States, motor vehicle and parts exports increase by almost 400 percent ($629 million) and by a bit more than 100 percent in fish, processed rice, and other foods. The largest winner in dollar terms is "other machinery and equipment,"[8] at $868 million or 17 percent. Though US exports to the world in this sector rise $709 million, that is only a 1 percent increase on a global basis. In just a handful of sectors is the increase in exports to Taiwan equivalent to as much as a 1 percent increase globally, and only in vegetables, fruits, and nuts is the $164 million increase as much as a 2 percent worldwide export gain. Table 8.3 ranks winners on both sides based on growth in bilateral exports.

In a few Taiwanese sectors, the increase in bilateral exports due to the FTA would exceed 100 percent, but their baselines are insignificantly low. The exception is textiles and apparel, where the 126 percent increase in exports to the United States generating $3.1 billion would be a 21 percent increase on *global* 2001 exports of $14.7 billion. More is said about this sector below because it is the main source of Taiwanese gains and because impending changes in global textile trade make the analysis of benefits for Taiwan complicated. The other big bilateral winners for Taiwan, with over $400 million in export gains, are other machinery and equipment ($836 million), metals and metal products ($666 million), electronic equipment ($599 million), other transportation equipment ($504 million), and chemical, rubber, and plastic products ($414 million). In none of these sectors is the increase in total US imports from the world greater than 1 percent.

Table 8.4 ranks the most affected sectors in the United States by *output* in 2005. Sectoral output gains greater than 0.1 percent occur only in a single grouping: vegetables, fruits, and nuts; and output losses greater than 0.1 percent occur only in a single grouping: textiles, apparel, and leather. These are small effects.

Table 8.5 orders winners and losers by an FTA's effects on the bilateral trade balance, not just on exports, producing a different ranking. When an

---

8. This is a broad commodity category in the GTAP model: it includes computer and office equipment, engines and turbines, communications equipment, appliances, and a variety of other manufactures.

Table 8.4   US sectors most affected by sectoral output, 2005
(percent)

Increased output		Decreased output	
Sector	**Output**	**Sector**	**Output**
Vegetables, fruits, nuts	0.3	Textiles, apparel, and leather	−0.4
Fishing	0.1	Other crops	−0.1
Other foods	0.1	Processed rice	−0.1
Motor vehicles, parts	0.1	Other manufactures	−0.1
Electronic equipment	0.1		
Other machinery and equipment	0.1		

Source: USITC (2002a).

Table 8.5   US sectors most affected by US-Taiwan bilateral trade balance, 2005 (millions of 1997 dollars)

Contributors to surplus		Contributors to deficit	
Sector	**Sector X−M**	**Sector**	**Sector X−M**
Motor vehicles, parts	441	Textile, apparel, and leather	−3,187
Other foods	322	Metals and products	−629
Services	175	Other transportation equipment	−332
Vegetables, fruits, nuts	163	Electronic equipment	−303
Meat products	56	Other manufactures	−174
Livestock	28	Chemicals, rubber, plastic	−141

X = exports
M = imports

Source: USITC (2002a).

FTA is viewed through this lens, support could come from US motor vehicle and parts producers, service industry interests, and those engaged in numerous food and agricultural categories. The sectors facing the most import pressure are textiles and apparel, metal and metal products industries, nonvehicle transportation equipment manufacturers, electronic equipment manufacturers, those in the general category "other manufacturers," and the chemical and rubber industries. In the sectoral output table, textiles and apparel saw the biggest impact—a 0.4 percent decline. This hit is evident in the bilateral trade figures as well: no other industry comes close to losing $3.2 billion.

Table 8.6 shows global trade balance changes, which differ in several ways. The category "other machinery and equipment," which is a mere $2 million gainer in bilateral terms, here becomes a $249 million story. Electronic equipment manufacturing swings from $300 million in new deficits bilaterally to $42 million in export gains net of imports on a worldwide basis. Most dramatically, the service industry moves from the third-biggest gainer to the second-biggest loser in global terms—a shift of more

Table 8.6　US sectors most affected by global trade balance, 2005
(millions of 1997 dollars)

Contributors to surplus		Contributors to deficit	
Sector	Sector X–M	Sector	Sector X–M
Motor vehicles, parts	369	Textiles, apparel, and leather	996
Other foods	335	Services	353
Other machinery and equipment	249	Metals and metal products	296
Vegetables, fruits, nuts	123	Wood paper products	84
Electronic equipment	42	Other transportation equipment	79
Coal, gas, etc.	27	Other manufactures	59

X = exports
M = imports

Source: USITC (2002a).

than half a billion dollars. Finally, the $3 billion textile and apparel loss suffered by the United States bilaterally is reduced to $1 billion on a worldwide basis.

Chung-Hua Institution Report

The aggregate results of the Chung-Hua Institution study (2002) are broadly similar to those of the US International Trade Commission.[9] At the sectoral level, however, there are some important differences.

The Chung-Hua model estimates total welfare gains to a free trade area of $2.6 billion for Taiwan and $1.07 billion for the United States. These numbers are substantially larger than the estimate of the USITC, presumably because the Chung-Hua study models an elimination not only of tariff barriers and quotas but of other nontariff barriers as well. For Taiwan a substantial portion of the welfare gain is due to improvements in terms of trade, whereas for the United States the Chung-Hua model estimates that the terms-of-trade effect is adverse.

Under a free trade agreement bilateral trade expands, with Taiwan and the United States increasing their exports to each other by $6.4 billion and $3.4 billion, respectively. These estimates are almost identical to those of the USITC. US global imports and exports are estimated to increase very slightly—about one-third and two-fifths of a percentage point, respec-

---

9. The Chung-Hua study estimates four scenarios. Scenario 1 is based on free trade in goods; 2 adds to that a 25 percent mutual reduction in the tariff equivalent of the bilateral barriers to trade in services; 3 adds to scenario 2 the assumption that there are productivity gains of 0.5 percent in each productive sector in the Taiwan economy; and 4 adds to scenario 2 the assumption that there are productivity gains of 1.0 percent in each productive sector of the Taiwan economy. Except where elsewhere specified, we cite the results from scenario 1, which is the most directly comparable with the USITC study in its methodology and assumptions.

tively. Despite the slightly larger boost to US exports than imports in percentage terms, the initial large US global trade deficit will lead to an additional increase in the deficit of about $230 million. The global trade effects for Taiwan are several times larger, and its positive trade balance in this model will increase by $340 million.

The Chung-Hua Institution's estimate of the FTA's effect on the composition of exports and imports, and thus on the production structure in each country, is also similar to that of the USITC. It predicts that Taiwan's exports of garments will increase by 152 percent or $3.3 billion, all going to the United States. To achieve this increase, domestic production of garments must rise by 63 percent, which in turn requires an upsurge in textile production of $1.7 billion or 8.6 percent. On the other hand, the effects on US exports and domestic production structure are quite modest. The biggest gain is in the export and production of autos, estimated to be up $1.6 billion and $1.4 billion, respectively. (The estimates of the Chung-Hua Institution for autos are much higher than those of the USITC study.) The largest US losses are in production of garments and textiles, which drop by $1 billion and $500 million, respectively.

Quantitative Effects Relative to Other FTAs

The economic gains described in the preceding section are modest. It is useful to compare them to the expected effects of other FTAs now contemplated by the United States. Table 8.7 presents a range of forecasts for a US-Taiwan FTA alongside forecasts for FTAs with South Korea, Singapore, and New Zealand. Because each of these results was obtained from the GTAP 5 model, they are comparable to a degree (though the scope, initial assumptions, industry disaggregation, and time dimensions may differ).

Even in proportion to the difference in their GDPs ($300 billion for Taiwan versus $446 billion for South Korea in 1997, the baseline numbers in the GTAP model[10]), the effects of a US-Korea FTA far surpass those of a US-Taiwan FTA. Most significant, the former agreement leads to $20 billion in increased exports to South Korea and US welfare gains of that magnitude. The first reason for the difference is that initial Korean trade barriers are greater—in many cases considerably higher—than Taiwanese barriers (in 12 of 18 categories). Second, the size of the South Korean economy is almost half again as large as Taiwan's. Both these factors are associated with greater potential for gains in allocative efficiency and in welfare from trade creation. (More gains from a particular FTA do not mean that that partner economy is "better"; on the contrary, they may well

---

10. Both the $300 billion for 1997 noted here and the $280 billion for 2002 given for Taiwan's GDP earlier in the text are nominal figures. Despite a modest decline in Taiwan's real GDP in 2001, real GDP in 2002 was substantially higher than in 1997.

Table 8.7 Welfare and trade effects predicted by FTA studies for US and partner

Study/ FTA partner	USITC: Taiwan Percent	USITC: Taiwan Billions of US dollars	Gilbert: Taiwan Percent	Gilbert: Taiwan Billions of US dollars	Chung-hua: Taiwan Percent	Chung-hua: Taiwan Billions of US dollars	USITC: Korea Percent	USITC: Korea Billions of US dollars	Gilbert: Korea Percent	Gilbert: Korea Billions of US dollars	Gilbert: Singapore Percent	Gilbert: Singapore Billions of US dollars	Gilbert: New Zealand Percent	Gilbert: New Zealand Billions of US dollars
Welfare effects														
Total welfare, United States[a]	0.0	0.20	0.01	0.76		1.07	0.23	19.62	0.03	2.69	0.00	-0.08	0.00	0.02
Allocative efficiency[a]		0.00		0.11		1.55				-0.17		-0.02		0.01
Terms of trade[a]		0.20		0.65		-0.48				2.86		-0.06		0.01
Total welfare, partner	0.3	1.00	0.35	1.04		2.63	0.69	3.85	0.37	1.64	0.43	0.34	0.25	0.16
Allocative efficiency		0.00		-0.02		1.63				1.74		0.04		0.01
Terms of trade[a]		1.20		1.07		1.00				-0.10		0.30		0.15
Global trade effects														
US exports	0.2	2.40	0.49	4.20	0.39	3.20	0.8	7.40	0.78	6.7	0.05	0.43	0.05	0.43
US imports	0.2	3.20	0.48	5.00	0.35		1.0	12.50	0.69	7.1	0.05	0.51	0.04	0.41
US trade balance[a]		-0.80				-0.23		-5.10						
Partner exports	2.0	2.80	2.88	3.90	1.75	3.41	3.5	8.00	3.57	5.33	0.45	0.57	1.44	0.25
Partner imports	2.0	2.60	3.71	4.12	2.86		6.2	10.60	5.79	9.18	0.47	0.64	2.13	0.35
Partner trade balance[a]		0.20				0.34		-2.60						
Bilateral trade effects on United States														
Exports to partner	16.0	3.50	29.28	6.60		3.40	54.0	19.20	48.16	14.57	0.97	0.20	17.50	0.47
Imports from partner	18.0	6.60	19.89	7.20		6.40	21.4	10.30	23.39	6.08	6.24	1.42	33.64	0.74
Balance with partner[a]		-3.50						8.90						

a. Negative numbers indicate increased deficit.

Sources: USITC (2002a), Gilbert (2003), Chung-Hua Institution (2002). John Gilbert generously supplied data for South Korea, Singapore, and New Zealand omitted from his final draft.

indicate that it has been a more protected and thus a poorer trading partner, on which liberalization will have a much greater effect.)

Regional Quantitative Modeling and Implications for Taiwan

There is reason to wonder whether shifting trade patterns in East Asia are adequately captured by US-Taiwan FTA analyses. The region is very dynamic, and assumptions vary as to the baseline trends from which the future of Asia will unfold. Different GTAP models focusing on different questions can help to illuminate the context of changing trade in the Asia Pacific within which a US-Taiwan FTA would take place.

A GTAP modeling exercise by the Asian Development Bank Institute (ADBI) looks at the effect of Chinese economic development on East Asian trade patterns to 2020 (Roland-Holst 2002). The ADBI model shows an increase in Chinese exports to the world, resulting merely from WTO implementation, of $374 billion over the non-WTO baseline by 2020, and an increase in imports of $257 billion (1997 dollars). The exports go primarily to the developed world (25 percent to the United States), and the imports come primarily from newly industrialized economies (NIEs) of Asia, including Taiwan and South Korea (28 percent).

To what extent are Chinese imports and exports *constrained* by the agreed schedule of tariff reductions (in the model)? That is, is the revealed level of Chinese trade protection already much lower than the bound levels, as has been the case in the past? In many sectors Chinese tariffs are indeed lower than bound levels, as discussed in the following section with regard to textiles and apparel. These factors could throw into question the projected benefits for the United States and Taiwan from an FTA. Even in agriculture, Chinese comparative advantage is mounting in labor-intensive, higher-value crops, and better Taiwanese integration in the region would mean shifting further out of agriculture (Rosen, Rozelle, and Huang, forthcoming).

Further, the USITC study does not anticipate two hypothetical shocks considered in the ADBI study that would further augment Chinese imports and exports, and hence divert trade effects from a US-Taiwan FTA. (Again, it is worth looking at the side effects of China on Taiwan and the United States because Taiwan is so intimately connected to patterns of Chinese trade, and because the benefits of a US-Taiwan FTA are often couched in terms of the US-Taiwan-China value chain.) The first of these is an AFTA (ASEAN, or Association of Southeast Asian Nations, Free Trade Area) + PRC scenario (a pan-Asian free trade agreement), which would increase the sum of Chinese exports and imports from the $631 billion added to the baseline from WTO implementation to only $645 billion. In the second, a "global trade liberalization" scenario, the number rises more dramatically to $828 billion. As this chapter was prepared for press, significant steps toward an ASEAN + China arrangement were announced. China will allow Southeast Asian nations lower agricultural tariffs in an "early harvest" of benefits starting January 2004, en route to manufacturing tariff cuts within the proposed free trade area starting in 2005. With these commitments China demonstrates seriousness and leadership on regional trade, while the global agenda flounders.

The ADBI study predicts that China will be Asia's largest importer by 2005 and largest exporter by 2010, and that it will simultaneously run structural trade *surpluses* with western members of the Organization for Economic Cooperation and Development (the United States and the European Union in the ADBI model) and trade deficits with East Asia.[11] US Trade Representative Robert Zoellick recently pitched the Free Trade Area of the Americas (FTAA) initiative as a tool to help countries such as Mexico compete with China for the US market.[12] This thinking probably informs support for a Taiwan FTA as well. But if the ADBI model is right, Taiwan is among the countries with the greatest incentive to focus on supplying China; an FTA with the United States is less urgent in that scenario, and could be a distraction from more critical policy initiatives.

Analysis: How Dependable Is the Quantitative Evidence?

The GTAP 5 model relies on 1997 economic data. To update it, USITC inserted into the model parameters for the lower trade barriers in Taiwan and China required by their WTO accessions. All other trade barrier data for countries and regions remain as in 1997. One might well ask, however, if other tariff changes that have occurred elsewhere since 1997 might affect the expected new flows between Taiwan and the United States. The Caribbean Basin Initiative (CBI), Andean Trade Preferences Act (ATPA), and African Growth and Opportunity Act (AGOA) all date from this period, and all pay significant attention to textiles and apparel.

The shortcomings of the GTAP model in dealing with nontariff barriers have significant implications for the results of the exercise in the service sector as well. USITC does not disaggregate services at all, nor does Gilbert; the Chung-Hua study does to a greater extent. The GTAP baseline data do not include trade barriers in services because of the perceived difficulty of estimating values correctly; therefore, the shock of freeing up service trade—though qualitatively estimated by USITC to be significant—is missing from their results.

---

11. See Roland-Holst (2002, 30). Unlike the western OECD nations, Japan is in near balance in its China trade. The Asian NIEs see exports to China rise $73 billion over the baseline in 2020, while imports rise just $38 billion. ASEAN is a slight winner in this scenario.

12. Statement of USTR Zoellick before the US Senate Finance Committee, March 5, 2003, www.ustr.gov/speech-test/zoellick/2003-03-05-testimony-finance.pdf.

Qualitative Analysis

This section offers a qualitative check on the forecasts made by economic models. While the total welfare effects of a US-Taiwan FTA may be small, specific sectors may enjoy or suffer concentrated gains or losses. We examine the sector expected to deliver 90 percent of Taiwan's global export gains (textiles and apparel); two sectors forecast to benefit US exports most importantly (agriculture and autos); one characteristic US loser (industrial fasteners); and one ought-to-be-winner for the United States that underperforms in the USITC report, probably because of shortcomings in the model (services). Finally, we discuss the cross-cutting issue of intellectual property protection.

Textiles and Apparel

Textiles and apparel loom so large in all estimates of the effects of a US-Taiwan FTA that they warrant further examination and analysis. Table 8.8 summarizes the estimates of the US International Trade Commission and the Chung-Hua Institution for Economic Research of the increase in Taiwan's textile and apparel production and exports.[13] For exports, the table shows the estimated increase in exports both bilaterally to the US market and globally.

The forecast increases of Taiwanese textile and apparel exports to the United States under an FTA are $3.1 billion and $3.9 billion, respectively, in the USITC and Chung-Hua studies. In each study textiles and apparel account for most of the estimated increase in Taiwan's exports to the United States. Textiles and apparel are even more important from the perspective of Taiwan's global export expansion resulting from an FTA. The sectoral breakdown available in the Chung-Hua study makes it clear that the increase, both global and bilateral, is made up overwhelmingly of increased apparel exports. The estimated expansion of production of textile and apparel—particularly the latter—is so large that it pulls resources out of the production of other goods, reducing both their output and exports. Thus the USITC and the Chung-Hua Institution estimate, respectively, that the global expansion of textile and apparel exports will account for

---

13. The two studies are not fully comparable because the USITC sectoral breakdown aggregates textiles, apparel, and leather goods into a single category while the Chung-Hua study treats textiles and apparel separately. Since the economics of textile and apparel production are quite different—the former is much more capital intensive than the latter—separate treatment of the two sectors seems more appropriate. Leather, which is a much smaller industry than either textiles or apparel, appears to be included in the category "other manufactures" in the Chung-Hua study.

Table 8.8   Estimated increases in Taiwan's textile and apparel production and exports

Model	Garments		Textiles		Total	
	Millions of dollars	Percent	Millions of dollars	Percent	Millions of dollars	Percent
Production						
USITC	n.a.	n.a.	n.a.	n.a.	n.a.	8
Chung-hua	3,280	63	1,665	8.6	4,945	n.a.
Global exports						
USITC	n.a.	n.a.	n.a.	n.a.	2,476	11
Chung-hua	3,227	152	260	2	3,560	n.a.
Exports to United States						
USITC	n.a.	n.a.	n.a.	n.a.	3,104	126
Chung-hua	3,281	n.a.	613	n.a.	3,894	n.a.

Memorandum: Estimated increase in all Taiwan's exports

	Global	To United States
USITC	2,831	6,645
Chung-hua	3,405	6,422

n.a. = not available

Sources: USITC (2002), Chung-Hua Institution (2002).

almost 90 percent and more than 100 percent of the projected expansion of Taiwan's global exports under a US FTA (see table 8.8).[14]

Global trade in textile and apparel is grossly distorted by the quantitative restrictions imposed under the Multi-Fiber Arrangement, due to be phased out pursuant to the Agreement on Textiles and Clothing negotiated in the Uruguay Round. As shown in table 8.9, Taiwan's share of the global market in apparel is expected to fall by about three-quarters, from its initial 1.5 percent down to 0.4 percent; China's share is expected to increase dramatically, from its initial 18.9 percent to 45.9 percent. The decline in Taiwan's share of the US apparel market is even sharper, from an initial 3.8 percent down to 0.3 percent. Both Taiwan and China are expected to increase their share of world trade in textiles, however.

Under the multilateral liberalization that will eliminate textile and apparel quotas at the beginning of 2005, Taiwan is forecast to lose about three-quarters of its existing global market share in apparel but to gain a substantial additional share of the global market for textiles. Its estimated increase in apparel exports, when an FTA with the United States is combined with the phaseout of MFA quotas, would thus appear to be entirely

---

14. The Chung-Hua study estimates that global exports of textiles and apparel will increase by $3.56 billion, 104 percent of the estimated increase of $3.41 billion in Taiwan's total exports.

Table 8.9   Textile and apparel trade of Taiwan and China: Estimated effects of the MFA phaseout (percent)

	Share of US market				Share of global market			
	Apparel		Textiles		Apparel		Textiles	
Year	China	Taiwan	China	Taiwan	China	Taiwan	China	Taiwan
1997	13.5	3.8	8.1	5.2	18.9	1.5	10.8	6.1
2007	20.5	0.3	22.0	3.8	45.9	0.4	18.9	10.0

MFA = Multi-Fiber Arrangement

Source: Ianchovichina and Martin (2001). We are indebted to Dr. Martin for supplying the data for Taiwan, which, while generated in the model used, were not reported in the published article.

at the expense of lower-cost producers, most notably China. The reason is that even after the MFA quotas on apparel are eliminated, the United States will continue to restrict imports of apparel by relatively high tariffs—typically 16 to 17 percent (the average US manufacturing tariff is only 2.8 percent). In a bilateral FTA with the United States, Taiwan's apparel producers will escape this import tariff while China, India, and many other lower-cost producers will not. Thus all the export gains Taiwan would achieve under a bilateral FTA with the United States come at the expense of other lower-cost producers of apparel, suggesting that trade diversion dominates trade creation in a US-Taiwan FTA.

In addition, a bilateral FTA with the United States would cause domestic resources in Taiwan to be reallocated away from sectors of comparative advantage to apparel, in which Taiwan has a comparative disadvantage in production.[15] This shift would not be good for Taiwan itself.

Finally, Taiwan's gains in this sector could be fleeting. Either further multilateral trade liberalization or the establishment of FTAs between the United States and other lower-cost garment producers would undermine Taiwan's gains. We are thus left with the following question: Should Taiwan reallocate resources out of sectors in which it has a true global comparative advantage in order to reap modest and probably transitory gains

---

15. These reallocation effects are reminiscent of (though distinct from) the "Dutch disease" phenomenon, in which booming exports in one sector (usually though not always an extractive industry export like oil) make production in other desirable industries too costly. In the mid-1980s the appreciation of Taiwan's currency threatened to undermine its competitiveness in labor-intensive goods. To avoid a total loss in these industries, Taiwan invested in China, distributing labor-intensive activities there while keeping value-added work at home. A similar transfer now taking place in higher-tech industries would likely be augmented by a textiles miniboom. But it is not clear that Taiwanese leaders want to encourage further migration of manufacturing to China with its lower wages. See Lin (1996) for an analysis of Taiwan and the Dutch disease.

from the production and export of a product in which it is not globally competitive?

Agriculture

Agriculture should yield mutual gains in a US-Taiwan FTA, especially if areas where tariff peaks and technical barriers exist are included in the agreement. In Taiwan, agriculture has shrunk today to less than 1.9 percent of the economy; agriculture is not an area of comparative advantage for Taiwan, which runs a growing trade deficit in agriculture and expects this trend to continue. For those 800,000 Taiwanese households still involved in agriculture, 70 percent of income comes from nonagricultural activities (USITC 2002a, 2-9); they thus resemble Japanese hobby-farmers, who maintain farms more to qualify for entitlements than as a primary vocation.

Major US export winners are sellers of goods for which current tariffs in Taiwan are high, including citrus (25 to 50 percent tariffs), deciduous fruit (19 percent), fish and shellfish (25 percent), poultry (25 percent under the quota, prohibitive above), beef and pork (15 percent), and processed food (12 percent). Overall, a 0.3 percent sectoral output gain is predicted in the vegetables, fruits, and nuts category—the greatest sectoral gain for the United States. Bilaterally, all but two of the agricultural categories examined by USITC enjoy net trade gains (oil seeds and processed rice decline trivially); globally, 7 of the 13 categories enjoy net trade gains, while the others decline slightly.

Taiwan has a rice import quota of 145,000 metric tons and tariffs of 20 to 30 percent for processed rice products within the quota, while apparent annual consumption is 1.4 million metric tons (USITC 2002a, 4-2). Imports are not permitted outside the quota. Although the USITC report shows little absolute growth in US exports in rice, including this sensitive sector would enhance economic welfare for Taiwan. For its part, the United States maintains high protection of sugar, with absolute quotas on imports. If these were removed, Taiwanese sugar exports to the United States could leap: despite Taiwan's low competitiveness in sugar, prices are so inflated in the protected US market that it could profit with preferential access. However, in the just-completed US-Singapore FTA, US sugar imports remain an exception to free trade, with very small tariff rate quotas of 15 to 22 metric tons for 10 years.[16] One imagines that a similar carve-out of sugar would be sought by US interests in a Taiwan negotiation.

---

16. That Taiwan is not a major sugar-exporting nation will not deter American sugar industry interests from seeking to exclude sugar—and probably processed foods containing sugar—from a potential US-Taiwan FTA, as they did in the US-Singapore negotiation (see American Sugar Alliance 2002).

Because Taiwan has thus far taken a permissive stand on genetically modified foods, this issue is unlikely to present a major stumbling block to negotiating an FTA. More generally, the USITC report noted (and the US-Taiwan Business Council highlighted) that there are inconsistencies in the labeling requirements imposed by the Taiwanese government regarding the bulk packaging of food and beverages. To the extent that these inconsistencies are definable technical barriers to trade, FTA negotiations would likely address them and thus facilitate US exports to Taiwan in this sector.

Motor Vehicles and Parts

The motor vehicles and parts sector is the big export winner for the United States in an FTA with Taiwan, according to the GTAP models. US exports to Taiwan rise by $441 million in 2005, and by $369 million worldwide in the USITC study.[17] Though reflecting only 0.1 percent output growth in the sector overall, this increase is significant in the US-Taiwan FTA context.

US-Taiwan motor vehicle trade has been shrinking for some years, a contraction due less to Taiwanese trade protection than to shifting market trends. Japanese and South Korean vehicles have taken US market share, apparently by better anticipating the tastes of Taiwanese consumers regarding interior detailing, size, and style. Discussions with two major US auto manufacturers revealed uncertainty as to whether US duty-free treatment in vehicles would be enough to offset this trend. Taiwanese view autos imported from the United States as being of lower reputation and quality, and this problem extends even to Japanese-brand vehicles manufactured in the United States. Another issue is whether the Taiwanese market is served more naturally by the rapidly proliferating assembly lines in mainland China. At present, however, production costs at these Chinese facilities remain higher than in the United States (by as much as 30 percent, according to the chief global economist for General Motors). Furthermore, vehicles are among the 25 percent of all products currently banned from importation into Taiwan from the mainland; the economics are thus secondary until Taiwan dismantles these import bans, an action they are under some pressure from major automakers to take.

Yet even after Taiwan applies most favored nation (MFN) auto treatment to China, significant tariffs and quotas will remain (under the WTO, Taiwan is permitted to maintain auto quotas until 2011). Under an FTA, US exports would enjoy an exception to these tariffs, and that preference combined with the advantageous US cost of production could bolster US exports serving the Taiwanese vehicle market for some years—if we as-

---

17. In the Chung-Hua study, US bilateral exports increase $1.4 billion, more than three times as much as the USITC estimate.

sume that other countries do not negotiate similar preferential access to the Taiwanese market. If Taiwan joined an ASEAN + 3 FTA or signed an FTA with Japan, then the US advantage would be eliminated (as it would in other product areas). The bottom line is that the US sector that will enjoy the greatest gains, according to the economic models, is hampered by a three-way tug-of-war between market forces, consumer preferences, and preferential trade arrangements. Major US firms in this industry cannot be relied on to fight hard for such an agreement, unless they clearly grasp how Taiwan fits into their global production and supply chains (for instance, through liberalization of Taiwanese prohibitions on auto imports from mainland China).

Fasteners

Representatives of the US fastener industry filed hearing statements strongly opposing a US-Taiwan FTA—at least one that does not exclude metal fasteners. They argue that existing duties on Taiwanese fasteners are not enough to protect US industry; free trade in the sector therefore would be prima facie bad. They observe that protection upstream from them in the US steel industry increases their input costs, making them less competitive (they fail to note that a similar regime for fasteners would simply put the same input cost disadvantage on US manufacturing downstream from them). Most provocatively, they suggest that for the fasteners industry free trade with Taiwan would de facto mean free trade with mainland China.

This raises the question of rules of origin. Responding to this US hearing filing, the Taiwan Industrial Fasteners Institute responded that Taiwan would uphold the terms of the FTA on transshipment, but in any case "Taiwan . . . does not permit fastener imports from Mainland China" (USITC 2002b). Taiwanese industry asserts that industrial fasteners, like products composing 25 percent of Taiwan's tariff code (such as autos, discussed above), cannot be imported into Taiwan from China.

Services

As we note in the quantitative analysis, the GTAP modeling used to estimate the effects of a US-Taiwan FTA does not forecast service trade well, because it does not build in initial barriers. The Chung-Hua study, by contrast, does include a second scenario that models a one-quarter reduction in barriers to trade in services. In that scenario, the total welfare gains to the United States are about 40 percent larger than in the baseline scenario. In terms of production effects, the output of services in the United States expands by $2 billion versus $1.5 billion in the baseline scenario; the largest share and proportionately largest gains are in industrial and financial services.

Service industries ought to provide US businesses with some of their best opportunities in Taiwan if reforms lower barriers to trade. This prediction is supported both by the attempt to model service liberalization in the Chung-Hua report and by anecdotal evidence. Financial services and telecommunications services are considered in the discussion below because they are areas of US comparative advantage and of observed Taiwanese weakness.

In a number of service industries, Taiwan's WTO entry led to the scheduling of market openings that should be well in place. In insurance, for example, US interests applaud the commitments made by Taiwan and are more concerned with implementing them than with negotiating new arrangements in an FTA. Many other service-sector issues are regulatory in nature or deal with competition policy, areas unlikely to be directly addressed in a bilateral FTA.

Financial and Insurance Sectors

US industry has lately emphasized a number of negotiating goals in FTAs, including the removal of bans on 100 percent ownership, national treatment, regulatory transparency, elimination of economic needs tests, and improvements in the dissemination of permits and in the processing of financial information. The models for these objectives are the US-Singapore and US-Chile FTAs. The 2003 *National Trade Estimate Report* from the USTR reports that Taiwan has reformed its financial sector significantly in recent years, in some respects more quickly than required (USTR 2003a, 362). Most remaining issues have to do with financial reforms rather than national treatment or market access, and such reforms are not the subject of FTAs.

Within financial services, insurance is often a focus of US negotiators. Sources at US firms consulted for this study indicated that Taiwan has made considerable progress on insurance-sector market access as part of WTO accession and that an FTA negotiation would not provide a major opportunity for US industry. One US insurance representative pointed out that Taiwan not only accepted the "model schedule" for insurance put forth by the United States for WTO accession, but was the first to embrace extended commitments under the schedule, including regulatory procedures for product approval. In short, Taiwan is considered to be in the vanguard in its commitments to market access for international insurance, and thus an FTA with Taiwan is not a priority for this industry.

Telecommunications

Not all Taiwanese commitments in telecom made in WTO accession talks have been fully implemented, and industry and USTR both identify barriers to market access. These are largely problems of regulations and competition policy. The American Chamber of Commerce in Taipei points to foreign ownership caps, dominant carrier regulations, and the independence of the regulator as priority issues (American Chamber of Commerce 2003). In Type I telecom services (basic service), a 60 percent direct plus indirect ownership cap for foreigners exists, and the chairman of such businesses must be a Taiwanese citizen (though a requirement that half the board of directors and supervisors be Taiwanese has been dropped).

Because the USITC US-Taiwan FTA study does not model these barriers or the effects of removing them, its results probably understate the gains to the US telecom industry (and Taiwanese consumers) should they be dismantled. The US-Singapore FTA, which addresses interconnection, resale of services, regulatory procedures, and nondiscriminatory access to the market, would probably provide a benchmark on procompetitive telecom policy for talks with Taiwan.

Crosscutting Issues

Intellectual Property Rights

The USTR identifies the treatment of intellectual property rights in Taiwan as a "serious and contentious issue" for the United States (USTR 2003a, 361). Despite considerable changes in Taiwanese law and in enforcement action in the run-up to WTO accession, Taiwan is on the Special 301 Priority Watchlist for IPR. In 2003, the USTR acknowledges actions by Taiwanese authorities, but reports no results. Only 10 other economies are on the Priority Watchlist. As mentioned at the start of this chapter, the USTR has ruled out FTA negotiations with Taiwan until existing WTO and bilateral commitments are fulfilled, those regarding IPR in particular.[18]

The *National Trade Estimate Report* calls attention to IPR-infringing facilities, pharmaceutical counterfeiting, trade-dress (the distinctive packaging and representation of a product) infringements, and inadequate judiciary and bureaucratic processes for redress of IPR problems. It also cites (USTR 2003a, 361) an International Intellectual Property Alliance (IIPA) estimate that weak Taiwanese IPR regimes cost US businesses more than $750 million in 2002 (mostly in entertainment software)—a sum almost four times greater than the US welfare gains estimated by the USITC study ($200 million) and the largest loss claimed by IIPA save that for China (this is illustrative only—revenue and welfare are not comparable). Even if this estimate is overstated, as US industry claims regarding IPR have been in the past, the problem is significant. The USTR asserts that the US-Singapore FTA made significant progress on IPR in the areas of trademarks, copy-

---

18. The United States has had a trade and investment facilitation agreement (TIFA) with Taiwan since the late 1990s. Official US policy has been not to elevate TIFA talks to the higher level required to facilitate FTA negotiations until existing Taiwanese commitments are implemented. Of course, if strategic considerations should trump standing modalities, then these limitations could be surmounted.

rights, patents and trade secrets, and prevention of the export of infringing goods, including transshipped goods, to the United States. This success has raised the bar for FTA talks; but the USTR is insisting on major improvement in IPR by Taiwan *before* FTA negotiations can be considered.

Rules of Origin

Taiwan enjoys bipartisan support in Washington, and the effects of freer trade with Taiwan per se are not so great that they should generate concerted opposition from protectionist Americans. Objection on narrow grounds is likely only in a few industries, such as fasteners, where losses would be concentrated. However, the argument that "free trade with Taiwan is de facto free trade with China," though lacking merit, may be echoed by the numerous groups suspicious of China: interests opposed to free trade, security hawks, anti-Communist pundits, and members of Congress nostalgic for bygone annual MFN battles. The "China issue" will arise in debate over free trade with Taiwan, and will inevitably heighten the attention paid to rules of origin language in any FTA. As noted above, the irony is that Taiwan, despite its massive exports to China, prohibits the import of more goods of Chinese origin than does any other economy.

Rules of origin in a US-Taiwan FTA could be expected to follow the model set out in the recently concluded US-Singapore and US-Chile FTAs. These are by no means simple. In the US-Singapore agreement the rules of origin annex runs 284 pages, with textiles and apparel as well as agriculture getting very detailed treatment (USTR 2003b). Many of the rules are clearly crafted to manage the effects of "free trade" to ensure that something other than a truly level playing field is created between the parties. In the case of Taiwan, no less than Singapore, those sectors expected to see the greatest adjustment (hence benefits) between the two parties would probably see the most battles by lawyers over rules of origin.

Another consideration is that if the Washington proponents of a US-Taiwan FTA are those who take a hawkish position on China, then they might insist on inserting a special rule of origin designed to limit any gains to China. As noted throughout this chapter, the more an FTA distracts Taiwan from better integration with the economy of the region, which includes China, the less well it will serve Taiwan's interests in the long run. Therefore any special rules of origin designed to reduce Chinese content in US imports from Taiwan should be examined closely.

Conclusions

This analysis has demonstrated that the overall welfare effects of a US-Taiwan FTA are modest, especially for the United States. In absolute terms, however, the gains to the United States are larger than for all but two of the other prospective FTAs examined by Gilbert.[19] An FTA between the United States and Taiwan would appear to be mostly trade diverting, not trade creating. The biggest reason by far for this outcome is the gains Taiwan would enjoy in textile and apparel exports. To achieve those gains, sunrise industries in Taiwan would likely have to compete with sunset industries more vigorously for resources. Gains in textiles and apparel could be transitory and would even have adverse consequences for Taiwan's long-term economic growth and welfare, because they are concentrated in industries Taiwan cannot sustain in the medium term.

Setting aside for the moment the danger of misallocating resources within Taiwan, a US FTA would partially offset diversion away from Taiwan that would occur if the United States concluded FTAs with many other Asian newly industrialized economies and if politics with China prevented Taiwan from joining in competitive liberalization. Gains from a US-Taiwan FTA alone will not bolster Taiwan's long-term economic welfare and cannot fully offset losses from failure to join in Asian integration. But as noted at the outset, other nations in the Asia-Pacific region have said that negotiating economic arrangements with Taiwan would be easier if the United States broke the diplomatic impasse and did so first. Thus, a US-Taiwan FTA could lead the way to the deeper Asian economic integration that is most likely to support long-term Taiwanese welfare. (Of course, if Beijing withdrew its diplomatic pressure on other Asian nations not to negotiate economic arrangements with Taiwan, then the importance of a US-Taiwan FTA in this regard would be moot.) Failing the ability of a US-Taiwan FTA to facilitate regional economic opportunities for Taiwan, at the bare minimum a US-Taiwan FTA could deliver a modicum of economic gains (diversionary or otherwise) to offset a fraction of the losses from sitting out regional integration.

References

American Chamber of Commerce. 2003. *2003 Taiwan White Paper*. http://amcham.com.tw/publications_services.php (May).
American Sugar Alliance. 2002. On the Negotiation of the U.S.-Singapore Free Trade Agreement. *Archives: Papers & Testimony*. www.sugaralliance.org/archives/index.htm (May 24).
Chung-Hua Institution for Economic Research. 2002. *A Report on the Estimated Economic Effects of a Free Trade Agreement between Taiwan and the United States*. Taipei.
Dumbaugh, Kerry B. 2001. *Taiwan: Recent Developments and US Policy Choices*. CRS Issue Brief for Congress. Report IB98034. Washington: Congressional Research Service. www.

---

19. The two economies are South Korea and Thailand, which Gilbert (2003, table 2) credits with $2.7 billion and $820 million in equivalent variation (EV) gains to the United States, compared with $760 million for Taiwan.

ncseonline.org/nle/crsreports/international/inter-72.cfm?&CFID=9741131&CFTOKEN= 89268373#_1_3 (May 4).

Gilbert, John. 2003. CGE Simulation of US Bilateral Free Trade Agreements. Background paper prepared for the conference Free Trade Agreements and US Trade Policy, sponsored by the Institute for International Economics (May 7–8.)

Ianchovichina, Elena, and Will Martin. 2001. Trade Liberalization in China's Accession to WTO. *Journal of Economic Integration* 16, no. 4 (December): 421–45.

Lin, Justin Yifu. 1996. Dutch disease, Taiwan success, and China Boom. In *Three Chinese Economies: China, Hong Kong and Taiwan: Challenges and Opportunity*, ed. Linda Fung-Yee Ng and Chyau Tuan. Hong Kong: Chinese University Press.

Roland-Holst, David. 2002. An Overview of PRC's Emergence and East Asian Trade Patterns to 2020. *ADBI Research Paper*, no. 44 (October). Tokyo: ADBI.

Rosen, Daniel, Scott Rozelle, and Jikun Huang. Forthcoming. *China's Evolving Interest in Global Agricultural Trade*. Washington: Institute for International Economics.

Roy, Denny. 2003. *Taiwan: A Political History*. Ithaca, NY: Cornell University Press.

US International Trade Commission (USITC). 2002a. *US-Taiwan FTA: Likely Economic Impact of a Free Trade Agreement Between the United States and Taiwan*. Investigation No. 332-438, Publication 3548. Washington. www.usitc.gov/wais/reports/arc/w3548.htm (October).

US International Trade Commission (USITC). 2002b. Brief filed by the Taiwanese Fastener Association, docket 332-TA-438. Washington.

US Trade Representative, Office of (USTR). 2003a. Taiwan. In *2003 National Trade Estimate Report on Foreign Trade Barriers*. www.ustr.gov/reports/nte/2003/taiwan.pdf.

US Trade Representative, Office of (USTR). 2003b. *United States-Singapore Free Trade Agreement*. www.ustr.gov/new/fta/Singapore/final.htm (May 6).

IV

NEW INITIATIVES
IN LATIN AMERICA

9

The US–Central America Free Trade Agreement: Opportunities and Challenges

JOSÉ M. SALAZAR-XIRINACHS AND JAIME GRANADOS

In a speech in Washington at the Organization of American States (OAS) on January 16, 2002, President George W. Bush announced his administration's objective to explore a free trade agreement (FTA) with the five countries that are members of the Central American Common Market in the following terms:

> Today I announce that the United States will explore a free trade agreement with the countries of Central America. My administration will work closely with Congress toward this goal. Our purpose is to strengthen the economic ties we already have with these nations; to reinforce their progress toward economic and political and social reform; and to take another step toward completing the Free Trade Area of the Americas [FTAA].

Earlier, in April 2001, US Trade Representative Robert Zoellick had initiated dialogue with the Central Americans on this possibility; and following President Bush's announcement, a number of technical meetings and consultations took place during 2002, leading to formal initiation of the negotiations on January 8, 2003.

The idea of an FTA between the United States and Central America is not new, however. In fact, Central Americans had been making the case

José M. Salazar-Xirinachs is the director of the Trade Unit at the Organization of American States, and Jaime Granados is coordinator of technical support to the Free Trade Area of the Americas negotiations, Inter-American Development Bank, Washington. The views expressed here are those of the authors and not those of the Organization of American States or the Inter-American Development Bank.

for a free trade agreement with the United States for a number of years, but a window of opportunity had not opened before. Despite the broad access to the US market that began in 1984 with passage of the Caribbean Basin Economic Partnership Act, the North American Free Trade Agreement (NAFTA) has evoked concerns among the Central Americans about the possible effects of this agreement on trade and investment diversion. After NAFTA entered into force in January 1994, Central American and other Caribbean Basin Initiative (CBI) countries lobbied strongly for "NAFTA parity"—that is, for leveling the playing field by providing them the same conditions of access to the US market that Mexico obtained in NAFTA. By 1996–97 there was a sense of frustration with the failure to obtain NAFTA parity and this, coupled with the shortcomings of unilateral preferences and the fact that Central America was already deeply engaged in and quite committed to the FTAA negotiations, led to a rethinking of the trade relationship with the United States.

During President Clinton's visit to Costa Rica in May 1997, the Central American governments made the first formal proposal for a reciprocal free trade agreement between Central America and the United States. The Central American presidents proposed two main trade policy actions: enhanced CBI, or "NAFTA parity," in the short term, and initiation of negotiations for a full-fledged free trade agreement in the long term.[1] Clinton declined, in part due to his lack of fast track trade negotiating authority. The initiative was put on a back burner.

The purpose of this chapter is to analyze the opportunities and benefits as well as the costs and risks—in both economic and political terms—that a prospective FTA with the United States presents to the countries involved. In the following sections, we review some of the asymmetries between the parties, review the objectives and motivations of each party, discuss the main negotiating issues and challenges, comment on the politics in Central America of the Central American Free Trade Agreement (CAFTA), and outline the main policy challenges for Central America. Before our concluding remarks, we briefly consider the importance of capacity building for CAFTA to succeed.

The Parties at a Glance:
Basic Economic Indicators and Asymmetries

Although the large asymmetries between the United States and the Central American countries are obvious enough, it is nonetheless important to review them briefly. It is possible to distinguish three types of asymme-

---

1. See "Gobierno insistirá en TLC con EE.UU." *La Nación* (Costa Rica), April 20, 1997; "Discreto avance comercial," *La Nación*, May 8, 1997; "Socios y amigos," *La Nación*, May 9, 1997; www.nacion.com.

tries: those related to the economy, to institutions, and to objectives and motivations. The main economic ones are as follows (see table 9.1):

- The population of the five Central American countries (33.2 million) is 11.7 percent of that of the United States.

- The territory of Central America is 4.5 percent that of the United States.

- The combined GDP of Central America is only 0.5 percent of the US GDP.

- The per capita income of Central America in 2000 was on average $1,822—that is, 1/19th that of the United States ($34,637).

- There is significant variation in per capita income between the Central American countries themselves: Costa Rica has the highest ($3,940), and Nicaragua the lowest ($473). While agriculture contributes only 2 percent to the GDP of the United States, it contributes on average 17 percent to the GDP in Central America, ranging from a relatively low 9 percent in Costa Rica and El Salvador to as high as 23 percent in Guatemala and 32 percent in Nicaragua.

- Thirty-six percent of the labor force in Central America is employed in agricultural activities compared with only 2 percent in the United States.

- As for trade, 50 percent of Central American exports go to the United States, and 45 percent of imports originate in the United States; in contrast, Central America as a whole accounts for only around 1 percent of US exports and imports (table 9.2).

- The United States ranks first in the 2002 Growth Competitiveness Index calculated by the Global Competitiveness Report; Costa Rica ranks 43rd, El Salvador 57th, and Guatemala, Nicaragua, and Honduras occupy places 70, 75, and 76, respectively.

- The US ranks sixth in the world in terms of the Human Development Index calculated by the UN Development Program, while Costa Rica is 43rd and the other Central American countries rank below the hundredth position.

These figures suggest that there are not only abysmal economic asymmetries between the United States and Central American countries but some important differences among the Central American countries themselves. These differences can also be appreciated by looking at the readiness indicators calculated by Jeffrey Schott (2001).

There are also significant institutional asymmetries. Some of them pertain to the capabilities of trade-related institutions such as those in charge

Table 9.1 Central America and the United States: Fundamental economic indicators

Country	Population (millions)	Area (thousands of square kilometers)	2001 GDP (millions of US dollars)	Average 1990–2000 GDP growth (percent)	2000 per capita income (US dollars)	Structure of production 2001 (percent of GDP) Agri-culture	Indus-try	Ser-vices[a]	2000 Imports from world (millions of US dollars)	2000 Exports to world (millions of US dollars)	Inflation average 1990–2002 (percent annual)	Inflation average 2001 (percent annual)	2000 HDI[b] Index	2000 HDI[b] Rank	2002 GCI[c] Index	2002 GCI[c] Rank	2002 NRI[d] Index	2002 NRI[d] Rank
Costa Rica	4.0	51	16,108	5.3	3,940	9	29	62	7,304	7,651	16.3	10.9	0.8	43	4.19	43	3.57	49
El Salvador	6.4	21	13,739	4.7	2,104	9	22	59	5,642	3,646	9.9	1.4	0.7	104	3.85	57	3.17	63
Guatemala	11.7	109	20,496	4.1	1,668	23	19	58	5,294	3,801	14.0	8.9	0.6	120	3.20	70	2.63	73
Honduras	6.6	112	6,386	3.2	924	14	32	55	3,344	2,512	16.6	8.8	0.6	116	2.98	76	2.37	81
Nicaragua*	5.2	130	2,529	3.5	473	32	23	45	1,945	962	13.3	4.6	0.6	118	2.99	75	2.44	79
Central America average/total	33.9	423	59,258	4.16	1,822	17	25	56	23,529	18,572	14	3	—	—	—	—	—	—
United States	285.3	9,364	10,065,265	3.5	34,637	2	25	73	1,238,200	771,991	3	3	0.9	6	5.93	1	5.79	2

* Excludes years 1990 and 1991.

HDI = Human Development Index
GCI = Growth Competitiveness Index
NRI = Networked Readiness Index

a. For Nicaragua, figures for 2000.
b. Total of 173 countries ranked.
c. Total of 80 countries ranked.
d. Total of 82 countries ranked.

Sources: World Bank World Development Indicators 2002 and 2003; UNDP Human Development Report, 2002; Global Competitiveness Report 2002–2003; World Economic Forum, The Global Information Technology Report 2002–2003; Boletín Estadístico SIECA, 2002.

Table 9.2   Relative importance of CAFTA countries for each other as trading partners, 2000 (percent share)

Country	Share of total US exports	Share of total US imports	US share of total exports	US share of total imports
Costa Rica	0.3	0.3	50.9	49.1
El Salvador	0.2	0.2	34.2	23.7
Guatemala	0.2	0.2	39.6	36.0
Honduras	0.3	0.3	46.6	55.4
Nicaragua	0.0	0.0	24.2	37.8
Central America	1.2	1.0	41.7	42.9

Sources: US International Trade Administration, *US Foreign Trade Highlights* (August 27, 2002); IDB, Data INTAL.

of negotiations, customs, technical standards, sanitary and phytosanitary issues, intellectual property, government procurement, financial-sector supervision, and also labor and environmental issues. Perhaps even more important are differences in institutions such as the branches of government that protect property rights, the rule of law, and democracy. One of the most important conclusions of development economics in the 1990s was the recognition that institutions play a crucial role in growth and development. In this light, institutional asymmetries have two implications for CAFTA. First, one of the main benefits of CAFTA will be to promote a "second generation of reforms" in Central America to improve institutions in all these areas, so that their quality may gradually approach that of institutions in developed countries. Second, as long as many of these institutional deficiencies remain they will continue to constitute an important obstacle to attracting investment, promoting business, and benefiting from the agreement. As stressed below in the discussion of policy challenges, doing its homework in terms of institutional upgrading must be one of Central America's priorities if its countries are to benefit from CAFTA.

The asymmetries of the third kind, related to the objectives and motivations of the parties, merit discussion at greater length.

Opportunities and Benefits: Objectives and Motivations

US Motivations: The Case for CAFTA from a US Perspective

US motivations and objectives in CAFTA are a complex mix of economic, trade policy, security, and political and strategic objectives, as summarized in box 9.1. Some of these objectives are direct and explicit, while others are more implicit and indirect. First and foremost, CAFTA is part of

Box 9.1 US objectives, motivations, and benefits in CAFTA

Trade policy related

- take a positive step toward completing the FTAA
- signal US commitment to free trade
- create a "success case" of an FTA with smaller economies

National security related

- strengthen efforts to control drug traffic
- curb money laundering and prevent terrorism
- reduce immigration

Political and strategic

- promote economic, political, and social reform in Central America
- promote political stability and democracy in the region
- signal US commitment to Latin America

Economic

- increase US exports to the region
- improve global competitiveness in key sectors

the broader US strategy of "competitive liberalization" as well as of supporting democratic developments in the Western Hemisphere and building economic alliances with countries crucial to US national security (see Zoellick 2002).

Trade Policy–Related Objectives

CAFTA is not only a building block to the FTAA but also an example of USTR Zoellick's "competitive liberalization" strategy of pursuing trade negotiations at the multilateral, regional, and bilateral levels under this three-tiered approach. If the World Trade Organization (WTO) or even the FTAA does not make progress, the United States is determined to move forward by other paths. This openness to negotiate bilaterally radically changes the structure of incentives for other countries and regions: it opens up new scenarios, raising the possibility that certain countries will be excluded or be the last to enjoy the benefits of a trade agreement with the United States. The US administration has argued that this tends to increase the incentives to complete the FTAA and has conceived this strategy as a key element in providing an alternate route, if one proves necessary, to complete the FTAA.[2]

---

2. There is no doubt that from a US perspective the strategy of competitive liberalization increases leverage. However, from a Latin American perspective the strategy lessens the scope of coalitions negotiating the FTAA and puts tremendous stress on the remaining countries to get in line after Chile and Central America.

In the initial months of his tenure as USTR, Ambassador Zoellick referred on numerous occasions to the impasse in US trade policy after NAFTA while bilateral agreements proliferated in Latin America and the world, and the negative implications of this situation.[3] Coming just after the agreement with Chile, the negotiation with Central America sends an important signal of US willingness and ability to move forward in trade—particularly at a time when this ability has been put in doubt by a number of negative developments, including measures to protect US steel, the 2002 Farm Bill, and some of the conditions included in recent trade promotion authority (TPA) legislation.

Finalizing an agreement with the Central American economies could set a positive precedent by showing how smaller economies can reach a modern trade agreement with the United States and benefit from such integration.[4] However, there are also risks in this precedent-setting approach, which will be discussed below.

National Security

Efforts to block drug traffic in other countries of Latin America had the unintended consequence during the 1990s of encouraging drug trafficking operations in Central American countries increased. The closer economic and political partnership with Central America promoted by CAFTA will facilitate collective efforts to control the trade in drugs. Similarly, closer economic and political partnership between the United States and Central America will help to strengthen collective efforts to curb money laundering and prevent Central American countries from being used by international terrorist networks.

The number of legal immigrants from Central America increased from 134,640 in the period 1971–80 to 468,088 in 1981–90 and then to 526,915 in 1991–2000.[5] During that last decade, as many immigrants entered the

3. As Zoellick wrote in a *New York Times* op-ed piece, "Each agreement without us may set new rules for intellectual property, emerging high-tech sectors, agriculture standards, customs procedures or countless other areas of the modern, integrated global economy—rules that will be made without taking account of American interests. The price for inaction will eventually be paid by American workers and consumers" ("Falling Behind on Free Trade," April 14, 2002).

4. Even though by many indicators Chile's economy is small in comparison to that of the United States, in terms of income per capita, several indicators of size, level of development, and social conditions the Central American economies are in a different category—much closer to those in the Caribbean (though also different from them in significant ways).

5. US Department of Justice, Immigration and Naturalization Service, 2001 Statistical Yearbook of the *Immigration and Naturalization Service* (available at www.immigration.gov). To put these figures in a broader perspective: 9.1 million people came to the United States from all countries in the world in that decade, of whom 50 percent (4.5 million) came from the Americas. In turn, of this number, 2.3 million people came from Mexico, nearly 1 million from all the Caribbean, slightly over half a million from Central America, and another half million from South America.

United States from a region with a total population of only 33 million people as from all the South American countries combined, whose total population exceeds 200 million. To the extent that CAFTA generates growth and employment opportunities in Central America, it would tend to reduce the region's contribution to the total immigration flows into the United States. That the Central American country whose economic performance in the past two decades has been relatively strong, Costa Rica, is the one whose contribution to immigration is by far the smallest clearly indicates the close link between higher economic growth and standards of living and lower rates of emigration.

Political and Strategic Objectives

Promoting progress in Central America toward economic, political, and social reform was one of the objectives mentioned by President Bush in his OAS speech announcing CAFTA. NAFTA showed the importance of free trade agreements not just to lock in economic reforms but also to promote democracy. The democracy promotion effects of an FTA with Central America can be very significant. Because of their deep reach into domestic regulation in areas such as competition policy, government procurement, customs, and administrative transparency, FTAs are important mechanisms to improve political as well as market fundamentals. The FTA with Central America can be a powerful instrument to bring prosperity to the region and prevent scenarios of increased poverty and instability that would threaten US security interests.

During 2001 and 2002, concerns grew over the worsening economic and political conditions in Latin America and the Caribbean—starkly highlighted by the crisis in Argentina, which was at its worst in 2001. There were widespread perceptions that the US response to the crisis in Argentina had not been forthcoming enough. More generally, the high hopes for continued progress toward more democratic politics, higher growth and employment, and reduced poverty had gradually dissipated in Latin America (Hakim 2001; Shifter 2003). In addition, after September 11, 2001, Latin Americans feared that more urgent worries elsewhere and the new focus on fighting terrorism would lead the United States to indifference toward and disengagement from their region. In this context, sending a strong message that the Bush administration has not abandoned its policy of partnership with Latin America and that backsliding in the area of economic reforms should be avoided was useful and timely.[6]

---

6. It is no coincidence that President Bush's speech at the OAS on January 16, 2002, combined comments on the situation in Argentina with the announcement of the desire to explore an FTA with Central America. This speech and Ambassador Zoellick's presentation—also at the OAS, in February 2002—concretely reassert US policy toward and commitment to Latin America. In his speech, President Bush restated the Summit of the Americas vision that "The future of this hemisphere depends on the strength of three commitments: democracy, security, and market-based development," and that "These commitments are inseparable."

Economic Objectives

Although the combined GDP of Central America totals $56 billion, slightly lower than that of Chile alone, Central America is not an insignificant market for the United States. US exports to the region amounted to nearly $10 billion in 2002, making the region the third most important market for US exports in Latin America, after Mexico and Brazil.[7] Given Central American countries' propensity to import from the United States, and given that the region has higher tariffs on US exports than vice versa, CAFTA has the potential to increase US exports to a degree that is significant relative to the size of the economies of the region.

The investment side of the equation is perhaps more interesting. Investments in Central America are key for the global competitiveness and global sourcing efforts of some US industries, including mostly textiles and apparel but increasingly many others. For instance, investments by Procter and Gamble, Abbott Laboratories, and a number of high-tech firms in Costa Rica tellingly demonstrate that the mutual benefits of US involvement in the region include but can go well beyond unskilled-labor-intensive activities; with ever greater frequency, they incorporate higher levels of skills and participation in more sophisticated manufacturing processes.[8]

Even though for a number of US business sectors CAFTA is a "commercially significant" agreement, the economic importance of Central America in the broader picture of US business and trade should not be overstated. Therefore, it is reasonable to think that from the US public-policy perspective of "competitive negotiations," geopolitical and security objectives and motivations dominate for this particular agreement. But the politics of CAFTA in the United States is a complex subject that lies beyond the scope of this chapter.

Central American Motivations: The Case for CAFTA from a Central American Perspective

Central American governments, business leaders, academics, and others that favor CAFTA have pointed out a number of potential economic, developmental, trade policy, and political benefits the agreement might bring, summarized in box 9.2 and examined in greater detail below.

---

7. This figure is larger than the sales to Russia, India, and Indonesia combined. Or within the Americas, it is as much as the exports to Chile, Colombia, and Argentina combined, and not far behind the exports to Brazil of $15.8 billion in 2001.

8. For the case for CAFTA from a US business perspective, see Emergency Committee for American Trade (2003), particularly the November 19, 2002, testimony of Jerry Cook, vice president of international trade, Sara Lee Knit Branded Apparel, on behalf of the Business Coalition for US-Central America Trade.

Box 9.2   Central American objectives, motivations, and benefits in CAFTA

Trade policy related

- reduce uncertainty by locking in market access to its main trading partner and largest market in the world
- insure against the risks of a protracted FTAA negotiation

Economic and developmental

- promote exports
- attract investment
- diversify imports, with benefits for both consumers and productivity
- improve institutions and market economy fundamentals
- promote policy reform
- increase bilateral and multilateral aid flows

Political

- improve social conditions and democracy
- overcome local resistance to further economic and political reform

---

Trade Policy–Related Objectives

In the realm of trade policy, a key motivation is to seek to protect market access from the uncertainties inherent in unilateral programs such as CBI, a worry exacerbated by recent protectionist pressures in the United States. The reality of this threat was underlined in the recent TPA negotiations when political pressures led to commitments to remove the access to the United States for textile and apparel products dyed and finished in the region—access granted to Central America under the Caribbean Basin Trade Partnership Act (CBTPA) of 2000—by hardening the applicable rule of origin. Under CAFTA, such actions would be much more difficult to undertake, a change that would benefit investors and exporters from Central America by removing uncertainty regarding access rules and conditions in the US market.

The number of players and the accompanying proliferation of sensitivities ensure that the FTAA is an ambitious and complex negotiation, and its precise outcome remains uncertain. Some doubt that the FTAA will be concluded by the target date of January 2005. CAFTA will bring the Central American countries enhanced and more secure access to the market of their principal trade partner, without their having to wait for the conclusion of the FTAA negotiations and its entry into force.

Economic and Developmental Benefits

The fundamental objective of CAFTA is to develop the Central American engines for economic growth. Given the limited size of the regional mar-

Table 9.3 Share of the main 5, 10, and 15 CAFTA products exported to the United States (percent)

Country	Year	5	10	15
Costa Rica	2001	19.93	29.56	30.78
El Salvador	2000	23.49	31.42	35.70
Guatemala	2000	26.17	29.09	30.98
Honduras	2000	38.65	42.25	44.76
Nicaragua	2001	18.03	22.33	38.82

Source: IDB, Hemispheric Database, 2003.

ket and the near exhaustion of import substitution opportunities during 30 years of trying this strategy, Central Americans realize that these engines will be fueled by increased and more diversified exports and by investment resulting from integration with the largest markets in the world. As table 9.3 shows, despite some export diversification in the 1990s, Central American countries still present an export portfolio dominated by a relatively small number of product lines. (See appendix 9.1 for the detailed list of products for each country.)

A free trade agreement with the United States has the potential to boost growth in all the areas in which Central America does business with the world, and with the United States in particular. Simplifying somewhat, these include

- Traditional exports such as coffee, beef, bananas, and sugar.

- Nontraditional agricultural exports such as ornamental plants, melons, pineapples, shrimp, gourmet coffee, and many other products.

- Exports of industrial parts and components. This is one of the most promising lines of business expansion, which will mutually benefit the US and the Central American economies. For instance, Central America is a very attractive location for electronic assembly and manufacturing, such as that done at the Intel plant in Costa Rica. As the case of Intel demonstrates, these types of investments have a very large positive impact on host countries, raising the general level of training, developing local suppliers, and providing both a model for other investments and a nucleus around which they can cluster (see Rodriguez-Clare 2001).

- Services exports from tourism to call centers and from educational to medical services. The increased presence of US service providers in Central American economies will also be a major force in promoting the region's modernization and increased international competitiveness.

- Textile and apparel trade has long been at the center of trade policy concerns between Central America and the United States and may provide large benefits in addition to those conferred by the CBTPA of 2000.

A fundamental point to stress is that despite the importance of the textile and apparel sectors in the short to medium term, in the longer term CAFTA has the potential to promote growth and development in Central America by creating incentives that go well beyond the labor-intensive, relatively low-skilled processes that the Central American countries have until now undertaken in that sector. CAFTA represents an extraordinary opportunity for Central America to climb the ladder of comparative advantage by developing activities that demand higher levels of skills and greater value added and by allowing its mostly small and medium-sized enterprises to increasingly participate more actively in global sourcing networks.

Recent studies have found that access to a wide range of imports at internationally competitive prices can have a large positive impact on economywide productivity. This is so in part because of the economywide production and organizational efficiencies induced by competitive pressures and by the incorporation of best practices, and in part because of the role of imports as a vehicle to access new technologies, including computers, information and telecommunications technologies, automated production lines, and other capital equipment and intermediate goods (Stiglitz and Yusuf 2001).

One of the main conclusions of development economics in the 1990s was the recognition of the crucial role of institutions in growth and development.[9] It can be argued that one of the major benefits of an FTA with the United States will be to trigger a second generation of reforms in Central American countries by upgrading a wide array of institutions, from those most obviously and directly related to trade and globalization (such as customs, standards, and certification-setting bodies; regulatory agencies for the financial and other sectors; competition policy agencies; government procurement processes; etc.) to institutions related to labor markets and environmental policies. In addition, CAFTA will create incentives and a sense of urgency for countries to accelerate policy reform in a number of key areas (to address price distortions and service-sector inefficiencies, for instance), as well as to improve such market economy fundamentals as property rights, the rule of law, and the judicial system.

The likelihood of achieving several of the main economic and developmental benefits discussed above will increase to the extent that the co-

---

9. See Kuczynski and Williamson (2003, 11). Easterly and Levine (2002) conclude that the level of institutional development is the only variable that reliably predicts how developed a country is. According to these results, institutions trump policies in explaining cross-country differences in income per capita.

operation exercise being carried out in parallel with the negotiations succeeds in mobilizing sufficient human and financial resources to the region, thereby providing a benefit in and of itself. During 2002, even before the negotiations were officially launched, Central American governments and the US government agreed to put in place a trade-related cooperation exercise to accompany the negotiations. With the support of the Inter-American Development Bank (IDB), the OAS, the Economic Commission for Latin America and the Caribbean (ECLAC), and the United States Agency for International Development (USAID), each country prepared a National Trade Capacity Building Action Plan to define, articulate, and prioritize needs grouped in three major areas: preparation for negotiations, implementation of the agreement, and transition to free trade and competitiveness.[10] Since January 2003, when negotiations formally started, each negotiating round has involved (in addition to the five negotiating groups) the Group on Cooperation, where donors meet multilaterally and bilaterally with countries so that they can respond to the needs identified by countries and better coordinate their giving. It is too early to tell what additional mobilization of resources this exercise will achieve. So far, it has certainly helped to focus and prioritize needs and to set an agenda for the mix of trade and other developmental homework that countries should undertake to implement and benefit from CAFTA. Putting together the trade and aid components is one of the innovative aspects of CAFTA, which recognizes the close and complex relationship between free trade, the challenges of implementation, and the broader developmental challenges posed by an FTA between such unequal trade partners.

Political Benefits

Finally, many Central Americans believe that an FTA with the United States may have positive political and social impacts. Clearly, however, there are some well-justified fears that if the transition is not gradual, if concessions by Central America are not matched by significant additional access to the US market in key sectors in which Central America has comparative advantage, and if Central American societies do not do their homework in setting up social policies and safety nets, then the economic, social, and political systems of the region could be put under extreme stress by this agreement.

Given both the large effort at unilateral trade liberalization and policy reform undertaken by Central America in the past decade and the current economic and social conditions, the next stage of policy reform in the re-

---

10. These action plans are publicly available at the Web sites of the US Trade Representative (www.ustr.gov) and the OAS Trade Unit's Foreign Trade Information System (www.sice. org), as well as those of each Ministry of Trade of the individual Central American countries.

gion will be facilitated under a reciprocal negotiation with a major trading partner or partners that will end with clearly identified winners whose gains from additional market access granted by those trading partners will offset the resistance of local losers hurt by increased imports and competition. For CAFTA to provide an incentive for change, the negotiation will have to lead to clear mercantilist gains. This benefit goes to the heart of the negotiating and political economy challenges discussed in later sections.

What can be concluded from these different profiles of priority objectives and motivations? How will the asymmetries in economic structures, on the one hand, and in political objectives, on the other, interact to enable the parties to arrive at not only a mutually satisfactory CAFTA agreement in the short term but also an economic relationship that all consider fully satisfactory in the longer term?

These are not questions that are easily answered. However, it seems important for both parties to reflect on the following propositions:

- For the United States, CAFTA is first and foremost a means to achieve "competitive negotiations," in accordance with its geopolitical and security objectives. Its commercial interest in CAFTA, while not negligible, is relatively modest. For Central America, in contrast, the objectives of CAFTA are overwhelmingly economic and developmental.

- The achievement of the US geopolitical and security objectives depends critically on Central Americans achieving their economic objectives, a task that in turn requires significant and balanced progress in both trade and aid. If the economic and developmental benefits expected by Central Americans fail to materialize, if the transition costs are too high, and if the stress on the Central American economic and political systems proves to be excessive, then emigration to the United States could increase instead of diminish, popular resistance during the implementation of CAFTA could destabilize instead of consolidate the fragile Central American democracies, and CAFTA will certainly not become a model that others in Latin America and the Caribbean will wish to emulate. In the light of these considerations, a US policy of quickly extracting the maximum number of concessions could even backfire.

- On the other hand, Central Americans must consider that the economic and developmental benefits of CAFTA will not be achieved if many sectors or areas are excluded from high levels of trade discipline and, most important, if the countries of the region do not do the type of economic and social policy homework discussed below.

We will come back to these fundamental issues after commenting briefly on the main challenges in each of the relevant negotiating areas.

Key Negotiating Issues and Challenges

Space constraints allow us to discuss only the most salient issues and challenges posed by the CAFTA trade negotiations, and in general terms.

Market Access: Tariffs and Nontariff Measures

Tariff profiles of the six countries show some similarities and some divergences (table 9.4). The US nominal average tariff is much lower than that of any Central American country, but the Central American tariffs are not very high. The US import tariff applied to Central American exports is 0 percent for all products that qualify for CBI or other preferential treatment. On average, 61 percent of Central American exports actually enter the US duty-free under these unilateral programs; however, there are important differences among the countries.[11] After having undergone trade reform in the 1980s and 1990s, the Central American countries do not, broadly speaking, provide very high levels of tariff protection, at least when compared with historical levels (especially during the peak of the import substitution industrialization phase in the 1960s and 1970s). There are sectors in which each party in this agreement shows comparative advantages and comparative disadvantages.[12] The challenge in this negotiation, as in many trade negotiations, is to maximize opportunities for market access at the lowest possible internal political cost. Both the United States and Central America have tariff peaks in agricultural products that are not only politically very sensitive but also in areas of mutual interest for gaining market access (table 9.5), giving rise to deep underlying tensions in these negotiations.

It is very likely that the tariff elimination programs will result in a series of baskets accommodating the goods according to political, commercial, and fiscal criteria, probably in that order of importance. In this regard, Central American negotiators should have no major difficulties in securing US recognition of the clear economic asymmetries that pervade this agreement. Since most Central American exports enter duty-free to the United States while US exports to Central America pay customs tariffs, the expected tariff elimination scheme will necessarily imply a higher burden of liberalization for Central America, thereby following the typical pattern in North-South agreements. Notwithstanding any built-in asymmetric reciprocity and whatever the possible political importance of longer tariff transition periods, in the case of Central America such longer

---

11. By country, the proportions of duty-free imports are Costa Rica, 84 percent; Honduras, 67 percent; El Salvador, 58 percent; Guatemala, 50 percent; Nicaragua, 47 percent (USTR 2001).

12. For an analysis of opportunities and challenges in agriculture and agribusiness in Costa Rica and El Salvador, see Monge, González, and Monge (2002).

Table 9.4   CAFTA countries' tariffs by Harmonized System section, 2000

Section and description	Costa Rica			El Salvador		
	Average MFN	Maximum	Imports	Average MFN	Maximum	Imports
I. Live animals; animal products	19.6	162.0	44,443	12.1	40.0	118,674
II. Vegetable products	9.7	49.0	234,613	9.8	40.0	193,055
III. Animal or vegetable fats and oils and their cleavage products; prepared edible fats; animal or vegetable waxes	8.3	30.0	10,645	7.7	15.0	70,687
IV. Prepared foodstuffs; beverages; spirits and vinegar; tobacco and manufactured tobacco substitutes	15.2	162.0	174,599	14.3	40.0	239,158
V. Mineral products	4.1	49.0	512,241	2.9	15.0	611,530
VI. Products of the chemical or allied industries	1.4	14.0	686,256	1.9	15.0	468,472
VII. Plastics and articles thereof; rubber and articles thereof	5.0	14.0	437,487	4.5	15.0	232,273
VIII. Raw hides and skins, leather, fur skins, and articles thereof; saddlery and harness; travel goods; handbags and similar containers; articles of animal gut (other than silkworm gut)	8.9	14.0	25,598	9.1	15.0	13,459
IX. Wood and articles of wood; wood charcoal; cork and articles of cork; manufactures of straw; basketware and wickerwork	8.3	14.0	23,803	7.3	15.0	26,286
X. Pulp wood or other fibrous cellulosic material; recovered (waste and scrap) paper or paperboard	4.6	14.0	329,778	4.5	15.0	189,631
XI. Textiles and textile articles	9.2	49.0	768,195	17.8	25.0	1,008,743
XII. Footwear, headgear, umbrellas, walking sticks, whips, riding crops, and parts thereof; prepared feathers and articles made thereof	11.2	14.0	41,755	15.0	20.0	37,643
XIII. Articles of stone, plaster, cement, asbestos, mica, or similar materials; ceramic products; glass and glassware	6.7	14.0	78,103	6.5	15.0	76,689
XIV. Natural or cultured pearls, precious or semiprecious stones, precious metals, metals clad with precious metal; imitation jewelry	7.4	14.0	29,787	8.2	20.0	4,182
XV. Base metals and articles of base metal	3.4	14.0	427,998	3.3	15.0	252,653
XVI. Machinery and mechanical appliances; electrical equipment; sound recorders and reproducers, television image and sound recorders; accessories of such articles	2.2	14.0	1,936,046	2.3	15.0	755,384
XVII. Vehicles, aircraft, vessels, and associated transport equipment	4.6	14.0	376,477	6.2	30.0	251,065
XVIII. Optical, photographic, cinematographic, measuring, checking, precision, medical, or surgical instruments	3.1	14.0	131,704	4.2	25.0	71,568
XIX. Arms and ammunition; parts and accessories thereof	9.6	14.0	705	30.0	30.0	2,930
XX. Miscellaneous manufactured articles	10.6	14.0	100,818	10.9	30.0	80,335
XXI. Works of art, collectors' pieces, and antiques	4.0	9.0	862	20.0	30.0	206

a. Tariff year for Honduras is 1999.

Source: IDB, Hemispheric Database.

Guatemala			Honduras[a]			Nicaragua			United States		
Average MFN	Maximum	Imports	Average MFN	Maximum	Imports	Average MFN	Maximum	Imports	Average MFN	Maximum	Imports
9.9	15.0	99,096	13.4	50.0	92,285	10.2	180.0	38,737	12.2	236.6	15,027,158
9.8	20.0	165,505	12.0	50.0	113,134	7.7	55.0	79,407	3.9	163.8	13,409,122
7.2	15.0	63,717	10.1	50.0	18,355	6.5	10.0	40,159	4.2	19.1	1,383,572
11.0	20.0	281,642	14.7	60.0	263,572	8.5	55.0	116,692	13.3	350.0	20,505,853
3.7	15.0	705,058	4.4	20.0	393,276	3.4	10.0	325,220	0.5	13.1	121,403,851
2.0	15.0	639,263	2.8	18.0	365,851	1.4	10.0	231,799	4.4	12.7	70,342,814
4.5	17.0	308,621	5.0	20.0	167,307	3.4	10.0	89,570	3.8	14.0	29,069,556
9.1	15.0	13,694	10.7	18.0	5,829	6.1	10.0	4,177	4.9	20.0	8,627,544
7.8	15.0	11,373	8.7	18.0	18,153	4.5	10.0	4,368	2.3	18.0	15,923,564
4.7	15.0	274,426	5.0	20.0	145,723	2.7	10.0	64,731	0.8	6.8	22,254,225
17.6	24.0	143,315	14.8	30.0	143,704	6.2	15.0	49,058	10.0	34.9	74,612,355
17.9	27.0	22,390	19.5	55.0	19,022	8.5	10.0	14,326	13.5	58.4	17,474,614
6.4	15.0	65,776	7.9	18.0	44,506	3.5	10.0	33,314	5.0	38.0	11,870,097
8.2	20.0	7,627	9.2	20.0	1,426	5.1	10.0	276	3.0	13.5	29,809,194
3.2	15.0	387,156	3.9	18.0	198,917	2.0	10.0	131,755	2.7	24.5	56,673,155
2.6	15.0	1,085,934	3.6	20.0	508,219	1.6	10.0	247,311	1.6	15.0	364,410,413
7.8	20.0	514,250	9.4	35.0	310,254	4.8	15.0	179,690	2.6	25.0	185,947,897
4.1	20.0	73,590	5.1	20.0	45,659	2.8	10.0	25,296	2.7	31.8	40,830,084
20.0	20.0	3,756	18.2	20.0	4,013	9.4	10.0	1,103	1.3	5.7	836,390
10.8	20.0	78,839	14.5	50.0	51,703	7.0	10.0	39,965	3.3	40.2	45,922,572
11.1	20.0	251	16.4	20.0	227	5.0	5.0	265	0.0	0.0	5,860,919

Table 9.5 United States and Central America: Tariff peaks
(by Harmonized System chapter)

Chapter number	Description	Most favored nation	Maxi- mum	Imports	Country
US tariff peaks more than 50 percent					
4	Dairy produce; birds' eggs; natural honey; edible products of animal origin, not elsewhere specified or included	21.3	116.6	1,035,394	
12	Oil seeds and oleaginous fruits; miscellaneous grains, seeds, and fruit; industrial or medicinal plants; straw and fodder	6.4	163.8	822,860	
17	Sugars and sugar confectionery	16.6	159.3	1,489,288	
18	Cocoa and cocoa preparations	13.8	108.9	1,404,323	
19	Preparations of cereals, flour, starch, or milk; pastry cooks' products	18.1	253.5	1,775,215	
20	Preparations of vegetables, fruit, nuts or other parts of plants	8.9	131.8	2,604,900	
21	Miscellaneous edible preparations	14.5	102.4	1,240,015	
22	Beverages, spirits, and vinegar	3.7	57.1	8,027,408	
23	Residues and waste from the food industries; prepared animal fodder	4.7	98.0	615,516	
24	Tobacco and manufactured tobacco substitutes	51.0	350.0	1,129,986	
64	Footwear, gaiters, and the like; parts of such articles	17.4	58.8	14,855,456	
Central American tariff peaks more than 50 percent					
2	Meat and edible meat offal	16	180	3,563	Nicaragua
4	Dairy produce; birds' eggs; natural honey; edible products of animal origin, not elsewhere specified or included	53	88	17,307	Costa Rica
10	Cereals	20	55	36,260	Nicaragua
16	Preparations of meat, of fish or of crustaceans, molluscs or other aquatic invertebrates	29	162	4,984	Costa Rica
17	Sugars and sugar confectionery	19	55	8,144	Nicaragua
21	Miscellaneous edible preparations	14	88	39,038	Costa Rica
24	Tobacco and manufactured tobacco substitutes	10	55	30,453	Nicaragua

Source: IDB, Hemispheric Database, 2003.

transition periods by themselves will be insufficient for structural adjustment: they must be accompanied by other internal measures. We will comment further on this issue below.

That Central America has maintained a common external tariff (CET) during the past 10 years benefits both parties, procedurally and substantially, in a negotiation such as this. By the same token, any imperfections in the CET suggest complications in the negotiations. The problem here is that in the Central American CET, as in every CET in the Western Hemisphere, there are many imperfections; these are linked to different sources in each of the five Central American countries. Such sources include fiscal problems, the need for faster unilateral liberalization, the imposition of temporary protective tariffs, Uruguay Round tariffication resulting in different tariff levels in key agricultural commodities, intraregional acts of political retaliation, and so forth (see Granados 2001). Regardless of the legal, political, or economic justifications for these imperfections, the fact is that they make it difficult for the Central American delegations to define a common negotiating position, while at the same time creating strategic opportunities for US negotiators. Many of the features of the resulting tariff elimination programs will take shape as a function of these problems.

Another source of potential concern for both US and Central American negotiators is the issue of export-processing zones (EPZs). It has been the policy of the United States that some tax and fiscal incentives typically found in EPZs, such as tariff deferrals or exemptions, be phased out either on entrance into force of the free trade agreement or within a specific period.[13] Among other things, this serves to avoid trade deflection. The challenge here is that a considerable amount of the total exports from Central American countries come from EPZs.[14] Therefore, any provision to this effect in CAFTA would have an important impact on Central America. Furthermore, if WTO provisions banning export subsidies by 2008 are factored into the picture, we must conclude that EPZs, as they are known today in Central America, are likely to change substantially in the next 5 to 10 years.[15]

---

13. NAFTA Article 303, for example, mandates that Mexico introduce important changes into its *maquila* regime by 2001—that is, seven years after the entry into force of the agreement. Basically, Mexico can no longer engage in duty-free importation of inputs from third countries that are to be incorporated in goods to be further exported duty-free to the other NAFTA countries. In the US-Chile FTA (USTR 2003), Article 3.8 grants Chile eight years to adopt somewhat similar obligations.

14. In the year 2000, the specific percentages, by country, were Honduras, 55 percent; Costa Rica, 51.1 percent; El Salvador, 48.8 percent; Nicaragua, 21.8 percent; and Guatemala, 6.5 percent (figures from Zonas Francas of the Americas Committee).

15. For a more thorough analysis of these issues, see Granados (2003). During the Doha Ministerial Conference in November 2001, the ministers decided in essence to sympathetically consider requests from certain developing countries to possibly allow export incentives typically found in EPZs to extend five years beyond the 2003 deadline originally negotiated during the Uruguay Round, a decision that will benefit Central American countries.

Broadly speaking, Central American countries have eliminated most nontariff measures (NTMs), either because they are meeting conditions set by international financial institutions or because they are following WTO disciplines. There are no quotas (except in the case of tariff rate quotas, or TRQs, resulting from the Uruguay Round Agreement on Agriculture in some countries, notably Costa Rica), and they apply only ad valorem duties. The range of measures that typically are labeled nontariff is larger in the case of the United States, many of them so designed in response to tremendous internal lobbying pressures. As a result, there are quotas for a vast array of products that the Central American countries are interested in exporting, such as textiles and clothing, dairy products, sugar, beef, peanuts, tobacco, and cotton.[16] Many products are subject to specific tariffs as well. In addition, in practice the technical and sanitary procedures at best make market access cumbersome and at worst turn into access barriers.[17] Finally, Central American traders face the difficult challenge of dealing with US distribution channels, which is the private dimension of international trade relations.

A set of transparent and clear rules of origin should be negotiated in this agreement. Central American countries have experience with NAFTA-like rules of origin, since they have negotiated similar disciplines with other trading partners such as Mexico and Canada. As a result, many of the approaches that the United States will seek in the CAFTA origin regime will be familiar and acceptable to Central American countries. The substantial question here is whether those rules will take into account the particularities of the Central American region or simply replicate the structure of US industrial protection. Central American countries are generally not well endowed with rich sources of raw materials. Their levels of value added tend to be low. Therefore, for CAFTA to be a meaningful source of trade opportunities for Central American countries, flexible and softer rules of origin will be required in many sectors, such as textiles and clothing. The rules of origin should not be crafted so as to neutralize concessions made to gain market access.

It is not at all unreasonable to suggest that the agreement should have an adequate mechanism to ensure safeguards. Again, Central American–US asymmetries in industry and agriculture are so wide that Central American producers and industrialists are likely to require clear and transparent safeguard rules to guarantee them adequate opportunities to adjust. The ability to impose safeguards should be maintained during the transition period at least. A public hearing to listen to consumers and other downstream users of the imported good should also be part of the disciplines.

---

16. Agricultural products with TRQs account for 24 percent of US tariff lines. See Gibson et al. (2001).

17. For an analysis of these issues, including perceived technical and sanitary barriers in the United States and other countries, see Roberts, Josling, and Orden (1999).

Table 9.6 Employment in agriculture in CAFTA countries
(in thousands, and percent of workforce)

	1990		1995		2000	
	Number	Share of workforce (percent)	Number	Share of workforce (percent)	Number	Share of workforce (percent)
Costa Rica	264	26	252	22	252	17
El Salvador	620	40	801	41	912	40
Guatemala	942	39	1,334[a]	44	1,727[a]	48
Honduras	688	47	766	43	853	38
Nicaragua	442	39	497	40	712	43
Central America	2,956	38	3,650	38	4,456	38
United States	3,429	3	3,592	3	3,457	2

CAFTA = Central American Free Trade Agreement

a. Estimate.

Sources: ILO, Laborsta; World Bank, *World Development Indicators, 2002–2001;* Comisión Económica para América Latina, Información Básica del Sector Agropecuario, Subregión Norte de América Latina y el Caribe, 1990–2001, LC/MEX/L.549, December 2002.

Agriculture

As table 9.6 shows, in 2000 on average 38 percent of the labor force in Central America (some 4.5 million people) was employed in and making a living from agriculture, in comparison to only 2 percent in the United States (3.5 million). If the linkages and indirect effects of agricultural activities with other commercial and industrial activities are taken into account, it is clear that a very significant part of the economic activity of Central America is connected to agriculture.

As in many developing economies, this large agricultural sector in Central America is characterized by an important degree of dualism. A number of modern, mostly export-oriented, dynamic, and internationally competitive agribusiness clusters, with significant participation of foreign capital, coexist with large segments of highly protected agricultural activities oriented toward the domestic food markets. The latter in turn contain some relatively modern agricultural clusters (dairy, poultry) as well as a large number of small and subsistence farmers (maize, beans, rice, and other products). The modern sectors and clusters are not threatened by CAFTA; on the contrary, they will tend to be winners if they gain additional access to the US market. The traditional, domestic market–oriented sectors represent a major social, political, and developmental challenge, particularly in the transition to free trade, because economically they are very sensitive to international competition, and politically they are as a rule highly organized and proactive.

As development proceeds, the long-term trend is clearly that part of the rural population becomes increasingly engaged in nonfarm activities. Experience elsewhere in the world shows that the process of economic development involves a structural change toward manufacturing and tertiary activities, as the demand for food grows at a slower rate than the demand for nonfood goods and services, and as economies diversify away from their concentration on natural resource–based activities into more productive knowledge- and skill-intensive activities. It is also in the interest of countries to promote this change because over time agricultural commodity prices tend to decrease.

This process is not painless, however, and it has taken decades to complete in many now-developed countries. One of the most difficult policy challenges is thus how to influence and manage this transformation. If adjustment is too fast, inducing rural-urban migration, and if the new high-productivity jobs in manufacturing or services cannot absorb the influx, then the agricultural transition will increase unemployment and expand the ranks of the poor working in the informal sector.

Policies on two fronts will influence the speed, costs, and benefits of the agricultural adjustment process. On the external front are the transition periods negotiated for specific sectors and products and the treatment given to the agricultural sensitivities. On the internal front, the process of agricultural transformation induced by trade liberalization needs to be carefully managed; such management includes making the necessary investments in rural development, education, communications, transportation infrastructure, export diversification, and sanitary and phytosanitary measures to protect the safety of food. Ultimately, each country must find the right balance and pace for its rural transformation process, facing the challenge of increasing modernization via new investments in large, highly integrated agribusinesses while preserving a space for the small and medium-sized producers, including family farms, engaged in production for both export and the domestic food market.

Given this asymmetry in the importance and role of the agricultural sectors in the economies of the United States and Central America, the agricultural negotiations are viewed very differently by the parties involved. For the United States, they mostly remain a trade negotiation, with relatively little potential to influence domestic production and employment structures—and even so the subject is highly sensitive. For the Central American countries, these negotiations have the potential to affect their production, employment, and development in fundamental ways over the next few years.

In the United States, agricultural trade has been made subject to special treatment by TPA legislation. Consultation and coordination channels between the USTR and Congress have gained a higher profile. More precise deadlines, procedures, and requirements have been established when agricultural goods are the focus of negotiations. These changes, of course, will give Congress—and by implication farm lobbying groups—a better chance to influence policy outcomes in ongoing trade negotiations.

US farm policy has historically been to provide intensive support to farmers, aiding both production and exportation. US farmers have a wide set of benefits at their disposal, many of which are decoupled measures—that is, they provide no incentive to increase production and therefore have a less distorting impact on trade. Many observers argue, however, that a number of these measures are indeed trade distorting. The recently approved Farm Bill of 2002 not only maintained but in some respects enlarged some of the existing benefits.[18] US support concerned with export competition (that is, excluding other programs focused on commodities, crops, and conservation) includes direct export subsidies, export credit, food aid, generic market development programs, market access programs, and other programs using foreign currency (Hathaway forthcoming). Central American farmers enjoy far fewer benefits, if any. There is therefore a striking difference between farm programs in the United States and those in Central American countries.

The US administration has given indications that in fact many of these programs, especially those with trade-distorting effects, may be negotiated down.[19] This by itself demonstrates a very positive attitude. But for the United States the preferred venue for such bargaining is the WTO Doha Development Agenda and not regional FTA negotiations. The reason for this preference is understandable: because the European Union and Japan—the two major world agriculture subsidizers—are absent from regional negotiations, the United States is reluctant to negotiate away domestic support, export subsidies, and, in general, any instrument of agricultural policy that may distort trade.

Here new difficulties arise in attempting to strike a balanced CAFTA agreement. If this agreement does not address the thorny aspects of domestic support and export subsidies (the US-Chile FTA did not address these issues either), is Central America going to liberalize its tariff protection for agricultural products without having any guarantees as to the direction, depth, and scope of the WTO exercise regarding domestic support and export subsidies? Is there going to be any relationship between the Central American tariff phaseout calendars for agricultural goods and any likely dismantling of US domestic support and other export subsidies on commodities relevant for Central American countries? Does the timing of the two negotiations lend itself to the kind of synchronicity needed for the Central American countries to reach a reasonable comfort zone? It is doubtful that the Doha Round will finish before the US CAFTA negotiations. Therefore, the governments of Central America should be prepared to address many of these issues with utmost political care and technical

---

18. For a summary of the provisions, see Farm Bill Conference Summary (2002).

19. See US position regarding agricultural negotiations in the WTO as presented on the USTR Web site, www.ustr.gov.

creativity. Since not all of the US programs will have an impact on Central American agriculture, as they may be geared toward products that are not of interest to Central American countries or are not trade distorting, Central American authorities should try to focus their attention on issues of real relevance to their task at hand. They should avoid discussions based on broad principles, many of which may not be relevant for the dynamics of trade between the United States and Central America.

It is interesting to reflect on the likely outcome of this negotiation and its broader implications. From the US standpoint, the size of the Central American economies and their agricultural sectors may make the size of the concessions needed to please the countries in the region fairly negligible. At the same time, those countries also have their own internal political difficulties when it comes to liberalizing agriculture and ensuring that adequate conditions for the adjustment, including safety nets, are in place. Long phaseout periods and transitional TRQs in many sensitive products may be part of a solution. In addition, adjustment assistance should be part of the deal, not only because it will be needed for the transition to free trade but also, more immediately, because it will be needed to secure smoother passage for the agreement through Central American congresses.

One relevant question is what kind of precedent any CAFTA agricultural package might set for other negotiations, such as the FTAA or WTO.[20] For one thing, it would signal US willingness to achieve genuine free trade in agricultural products, at least in the long run. This is very positive—but perhaps it is not as strong a signal as it first appears. Although Chile and Central America are important producers of certain farm products, broadly speaking they do not represent the kind of threat to US producers posed by other, much larger partners inside and outside the Western Hemisphere; thus the real test for the United States is yet to come. A related question is whether US farm groups will voice opposition to the US-Chile FTA or to CAFTA as a matter of principle, viewing the agreements as precedent setting, or will save their political capital for negotiations that may present a more direct danger to them.

In essence, there are still too many questions not yet answered. Agriculture will be a difficult issue in CAFTA. For some Central American countries—not all—agriculture may be a deal breaker. Judging by the US-Chile FTA, the United States seems willing to phase out agricultural tariffs in the long run. Except for progress in export subsidies, not much is to be expected regarding domestic support and other measures that may have an effect equivalent to export subsidies. Not all US programs

---

20. In a groundbreaking negotiation, the United States and Chile were able to agree to total free trade in agricultural products, phased in over 12 years. There are TRQs in the transition period. (Sugar is an issue resolved by what resembles the NAFTA solution rather than crystal-clear free trade.) See USTR (2003); see also informational documents from Chilean trade authorities at www.direcon.cl.

will have an impact on Central American agricultural production and trade. Nevertheless, those programs that do should be carefully looked at in the negotiations in order to engineer appropriate mechanisms to achieve the right balance between the United States and Central America. Finally, given the lack of synchronicity between CAFTA and the WTO, there seems to be limited opportunity for fruitful cross-fertilization between these two forums.

Services

As table 9.1 shows, services are a key component of the six CAFTA economies. Of course, from an export point of view, they are more important still to the United States. The United States clearly enjoys a comparative advantage in tradable services in areas such as telecommunications, finance, transportation, various professions, and entertainment. Central American countries may lack comparative advantage in almost all of these sectors but they do have comparative advantages in others, including tourism, software programming, telemarketing, bilingual call centers, and those professional services for which the consumer may travel to the country of the provider (especially in some areas of health care, such as dentistry, plastic surgery, and ophthalmology).[21]

With few exceptions, Central American countries are relatively open to foreign service providers, as they see the competitive provision of services as key to achieving nationwide systemic competitiveness and a sound regulatory environment.[22] However, both sides maintain restrictions on a number of service activities, some of which are politically very sensitive—for example, professional services and maritime transportation in the United States, telecommunications and insurance services in Costa Rica, and professional services in all of the Central American countries.

A very important question in this negotiation is whether the agreement, in complying with the General Agreement on Trade in Services (GATS), Article V, will seek only to consolidate the legal status quo in substantially all service sectors, thereby temporarily freezing opportunities for market access for US providers at their current level, or whether the United States will in addition try to open up some of the most entrenched existing market access barriers in areas of US interest. Here the United States will have to make a decision—one that, again, will be carefully scrutinized by negotiators from other countries for its precedent-setting implications for the FTAA as well as for other "competitive liberalization" sequences. It is

---

21. Other cross-border services, such as Spanish-English translation services making use of the Internet, are also on the rise in Central America.

22. For some interesting opinions on financial services in Central America in light of free trade negotiations with the United States, see Camacho (2003).

very likely that any final chapter on services will base its market access disciplines on a negative list approach, and that many reservations and exceptions will be insisted on both by the United States and by Central American countries.

For some countries, a difficult negotiating issue is the extent and intensity with which the United States may seek to open up state monopolies in areas of interest. This is a particularly sensitive topic for Costa Rica, where insurance and telecommunications services remain state monopolies and where previous attempts at deregulation have failed (Monge 2000). CAFTA confronts this country with a tough choice: to give in to majority public opinion and to powerful domestic groups that have a history of fighting fiercely for keeping those monopolies (most notably, but not exclusively, trade unions), or to embrace CAFTA as an opportunity to move toward a more open and competitive provision of telecommunications and insurance services. The latter would certainly help to overcome one of the most intractable developmental bottlenecks facing the country as it attempts to move fully into the information age and the knowledge-based economy.[23] Costa Rica has expressed its intention to avoid liberalization commitments in CAFTA in these areas.[24] While this decision avoids a domestic political confrontation,[25] it also misses an opportunity to address an important area where modernization is needed; moreover, to succeed in holding this position Costa Rica may be forced to pay a high price in concessions in other negotiating areas and objectives of interest.

Investment

Investment is, to a large extent, a win-win area in this agreement, as it may be in the FTAA. The US interest is to furnish US investors with a set of rules that provide stability and predictability, guarantees for nondiscriminatory treatment, an effective and expeditious dispute settlement mechanism, and a liberal environment for repatriating capital and profits. For Central American countries, the main interest is also to furnish those conditions to attract US investors. In fact, Central American countries ex-

---

23. Modernization of telecommunications infrastructure has been diagnosed as one of the main challenges for sustainable human development in Costa Rica. See Estado de la Nación (2001). See also the ranking of Central American countries in the Networked Readiness Index (NRI), as calculated by the World Economic Forum and reproduced in table 9.1.

24. See Costa Rican position in Costa Rica, Ministry of Foreign Trade (2003, 23, 26).

25. This issue is very divisive. Polls indicate that the majority of the people do not support privatization or competition. Others blame the rent-seeking behavior of trade unions and bureaucrats coupled with popular misconceptions and ignorance about the challenges posed by new technologies (e.g., broadband Internet) and complacency born of having benefited for many years from no-longer-sustainable welfare policies in a paternalistic state.

pect that one of the main benefits of CAFTA will be precisely increased foreign direct investment, mostly from the United States.

As explained further in a later section, it is important for Central American policymakers and leaders to realize that these expectations will materialize only if extensive internal efforts—which typically fall outside the scope of an FTA—are made in many other areas of their economies, institutions, and regulatory systems, such as improving physical infrastructure, raising levels of education, strengthening the rule of law, defending property rights, reducing poverty, increasing flexibility in the labor market, putting in place adequate taxation systems, and protecting the environment. Cooperation in building trade capacity can be enormously helpful for Central American countries seeking to make progress in all these areas.

In CAFTA the United States may seek changes to its traditional investment agreement model, epitomized by NAFTA's Chapter XI. Chief among those aspects possibly open to revision are the questions of the settlement of disputes between investors and states, indirect expropriation ("tantamount to expropriation"), and procedural amendments to allow more participation of civil society in the dispute settlement process. For years, nongovernmental organizations and other interests—not only in the United States but also in Central America (see, e.g., Gitli and Murillo 2001)—have argued against NAFTA-type provisions, sometimes overstating their point. In the United States these groups were successful in shaping the policy preferences in the TPA. As a result, the US-Chile FTA sets new guidelines for handling these issues. On the controversial topic of indirect expropriation, for example, that agreement develops a careful understanding as to how to interpret the question in the light of overriding public policy objectives. It is highly likely that a similar approach will be suggested by the United States in the CAFTA negotiations.

Of interest in the investment talks will be whether the Central American countries are able to negotiate disciplines to prevent the most negative effects of speculative investment flows. Traditionally, the United States has been active in promoting a regulatory framework in which portfolio capital can freely flow in and out of the partner country. As will be discussed in more detail below, recent literature expresses concerns that such an approach may prevent developing countries from reacting promptly and effectively in the face of sudden, destabilizing flows of speculative capital. Attention in the investment negotiations should be devoted to this issue.

Intellectual Property

As in any North-South trade negotiation, matters of intellectual property (IP) are likely to prove complex and controversial. During the past 10 years, Central American countries have signed on to several intellectual property agreements of varying kinds: not only to the Agreement on Trade-Related Aspects of Intellectual Property Rights (TRIPs)—the current multilateral standard—but to NAFTA-type rules in the agreements negotiated with Mexico and Canada. CAFTA, however, is bound to go beyond these standards, since it is very unlikely that the United States will be satisfied with simply replicating them. On the contrary, the United States is seeking to adopt IP rules in different trade forums that take into account new technologies and US interests. The US-Chile text, for instance, provides evidence for the emergence of a new US-led standard. This text will probably be the US road map for CAFTA and for the FTAA; it is therefore taken as the basis for the comments in this section.

The US-Chile FTA contains several interesting features. It extends IP protection into new areas not included in North-South trade agreements currently in effect, enforced by a strong dispute settlement mechanism. The text mandates that the two countries will adhere to certain international IP conventions in specified time frames and that they will make efforts to conform to others.[26] The text develops further the obligations existing in TRIPs and NAFTA regarding transparency and cooperation; it also provides protection in cutting-edge areas such as domain names on the Web and limitations on liability for Internet service providers. The US-Chile agreement expands many of the obligations existing in NAFTA or TRIPs related to patents, trademarks, well-known marks, copyrights and related rights, satellite signals, and border measures. Many of these provisions can be found in US law and in World Intellectual Property Organization treaties and recommendations, but not under trade agreements subject to strong dispute settlement provisions.

Establishing a suitable legal and institutional domestic framework to make possible adequate enforcement of new rules such as these is not at all easy in the Central American countries. That difficulty has been recognized in the US-Chile FTA agreement, which allows Chile to implement many of the obligations over periods of two, four, and five years (see USTR 2003, Article 17.12). If this is the approach adopted in the case of Chile—a country widely recognized as exemplary in its public policies and institutional development—could something less be expected in the case of CAFTA? The answer in our view is no. The Central American countries can be reasonably sure that the United States will request the

---

26. International IP conventions are now adhered to by CAFTA countries as follows: Patent Cooperation Treaty (Costa Rica, Nicaragua, United States), International Convention for the Protection of New Varieties of Plants (Nicaragua, United States), Trademark Law Treaty (United States), Convention Relating to the Distribution of Program-Carrying Signals Transmitted by Satellite (Costa Rica, Nicaragua, United States), Patent Law Treaty (none), Hague Agreement Concerning the International Deposit of Industrial Designs (none), and Protocol Relating to the Madrid Agreement Concerning the International Registration of Marks (none).

same substantial level of obligation, particularly in the new context of competitive negotiations and the associated precedent-setting logic. Longer transition periods and more efforts at capacity building and co-operation may be agreed on and definitely needed in Central America, given that the United States can be expected to try to raise the bar high.

Government Procurement

Government procurement (GP) is an area in which finding an internal balance of concessions is quite challenging. On the one hand, with a few exceptions Central American countries are very open and nondiscriminating regarding the foreign origin of the goods and services procured by government entities.[27] On the other hand, the ability to compete effectively in US procurement markets is limited by several factors, including distance, language, culture, lack of specific knowledge of US procedures, and lack of competitiveness of potential suppliers vis-à-vis US suppliers.

If GP obligations in existing trade agreements are any predictor for CAFTA, the prospects in this area do not look very encouraging for Central American countries from the narrow mercantilist viewpoint of trade negotiators. Again, it is highly probable that the US-Chile FTA shows the shape of what the United States will seek in CAFTA: relatively high thresholds, exclusions of state- and county-level procurement opportunities, and exceptions for the set-aside programs for small and minority businesses. In brief, it may block the niches where potential Central American suppliers might have an opportunity of ever winning a bid. The US-Chile agreement may be a groundbreaking exercise insofar as it enhances the material scope of the concessions—it may be Government Procurement Agreement (GPA) plus, or NAFTA plus—but a CAFTA agreement along similar lines does not necessarily ensure any benefits to potential Central American suppliers, who suffer from a tremendous supply-side asymmetry.

Perhaps the analysis of GP issues should focus not on mercantilist expectations but rather on the institutional development aspects of this set of disciplines. Bringing about more transparent, predictable, and nondiscriminating GP rules may ultimately (at least in theory) deliver economic benefits and competitiveness to the Central American countries. In addition, exposing public-sector markets to the forces of free trade may also generate considerable gains in a group of countries chronically affected by fiscal deficits, thereby benefiting the public at large. Finally, as a positive externality, this set of rules may generate momentum for creating truly regional procurement markets in Central America—an alien concept so far, but one with great potential to facilitate growth and business, particularly for the small and medium-sized Central American suppliers.

---

27. For the exceptions, see IDB (2003).

Labor and the Environment

Labor and environmental issues have always been divisive topics in trade negotiations, and CAFTA is no exception. Mostly because of its domestic politics, the United States has been pressing for their incorporation in trade agreements since NAFTA. While it has had little success in the multilateral context, the United States has managed to include these issues in FTAs with small partners: Jordan, Chile, and Singapore. In the WTO, only matters pertaining to the environment will be on the table (and then only some aspects of it); responsibility for the global governance of labor issues was explicitly assigned to the International Labor Organization (ILO). In negotiations for the FTAA, Latin American and Caribbean countries have, in protracted discussions, systematically rejected the introduction of language on either environmental or labor issues.[28]

There are important differences in the approaches, procedures, and dispute settlement mechanisms in US trade agreements with Mexico, Canada, Chile, Jordan, and Singapore. But TPA requirements instituted in 2002 prescribe a series of policy guidelines for addressing the issues in US trade agreements. In very broad terms, the two most important questions are whether the labor and environmental provisions will be contained in the agreements proper or in "side agreements" and whether any breach of the obligations will trigger trade, monetary, or other sanctions. The answers suggested by the US-Chile agreement (which by law has to follow TPA guidelines) are that labor and environmental provisions will be within the agreement and subject to dispute settlement procedures equivalent to those applicable to the core trade disciplines, with the potential of having both monetary and (very subtle and implicit) trade sanctions.[29]

The issues are difficult for Central American countries—not because they would "race to the bottom" in labor or environmental standards to promote trade or attract investment, but because of the complex problems normally associated with low levels of development and the lack of strong domestic institutions and of law enforcement capacities. Everything seems to indicate that to comply with TPA guidelines, CAFTA is very likely to include labor and environmental provisions similar to those found in the US-Chile FTA. If so, the most important (but certainly not the only) issues are to determine the nature of the institutions established for labor and environmental cooperation and to allocate resources to build capacity and to domestically enforce labor and environmental laws.

NAFTA's environmental institutions have been partly responsible for the deepening of technical cooperation on environmental protection be-

---

28. For a description and analysis of the arguments in favor of and against introducing labor provisions into trade agreements, see Salazar-Xirinachs and Martinez-Piva (2003).

29. Regarding labor in the US-Chile FTA, see Elliott (forthcoming 2004).

tween the United States and Mexico (see Gilbreath 2003; Torres 2002). This experience strongly suggests that here institutional design, more than the threat of sanctions, is the key to achieving results. It is also clear that enforcement of environmental and labor laws is resource intensive. Therefore, Central American countries will need substantial technical and financial assistance to cope with the type of commitments they are about to undertake in these areas in CAFTA.

Meeting the agreement's labor standards may at first appear to be a less onerous task, as Central American countries have already agreed to many ILO conventions.[30] But the commitments they may be taking on in CAFTA obligate them to create better conditions to fully comply with core labor rights, under the threat posed by effective dispute settlement procedures. Achieving those conditions will in some cases require the attainment of a more advanced stage of economic and institutional development. The challenge for Central American countries will therefore be enormous.

Treatment of Asymmetries

The treatment of asymmetries in free trade agreements is a hotly debated topic. Central Americans are not talking about special and differential treatment as understood in the General Agreement on Tariffs and Trade (GATT)/WTO system. Instead, CAFTA will most likely take a number of different approaches to these asymmetries:

- The negotiations will lead to differential treatment in transition periods and to technically creative ways of dealing with specific issues on a country-by-country, sector-by-sector, and product-by-product basis.

- A major trade-related capacity-building exercise has already been begun in three main areas: preparation for negotiations, implementation of the agreement, and transition to free trade and competitiveness. It is too early to assess the extent of its benefits (see the section on capacity building, below).

- Most certainly other aspects of differential treatment will emerge from the negotiations over the rules and disciplines of the agreement.

Other Issues

Unfair Trade Practices

To date, Central American countries have been little affected by antidumping or countervailing duty actions in the United States. One reason

---

30. As of April 2003, Costa Rica has ratified 50 ILO conventions; El Salvador, 25; Guatemala, 72; Honduras, 22; Nicaragua, 59; and the United States, 14 (ILO 2003).

is that their levels of export subsidization are very low and progressively diminishing as a result of unilateral policies and WTO commitments. Second, Central American countries do not produce the kind of industrial commodities that are more likely to be involved in these proceedings, such as steel products and electronics and other high-technology goods. Third, the low volume of Central American exports to the United States relative to those from the rest of the world means that goods are not normally exported in such quantities as to cause or threaten to cause statutory injury to domestic production.

But there is no reason to believe that this situation is permanent. On the contrary, given the expected increases of exports to the United States, certain products such as garments will probably become subject to claims of dumping in that market. Therefore, it is in the best long-term interest of Central American countries to achieve better discipline regarding unfair trade practices, particularly dumping. But because these issues are very contentious in the United States, CAFTA, as the US-Chile FTA demonstrated, is very unlikely to be a forum for addressing and finding effective solutions to them. Some doubt that even the FTAA could make progress in negotiating better disciplines in this area. At the end of the day Central American countries may have to turn to the WTO, where the issues are currently being discussed, for a meaningful negotiation of trade remedy rules.

Dispute Settlement

The quality of dispute settlement procedures is also now key to any trade agreement. In general, it is expected that the CAFTA, like other recent agreements, will have strong and effective procedures for settling disputes among the parties. Meaningful trade commitments need a rules-based framework backed by clear, expeditious, and not too costly dispute settlement mechanisms. Such procedures are especially necessary for those Central American countries with less capacity to initiate actions or to defend themselves. It is worth observing that the dispute settlements that currently exist in the WTO, NAFTA, and other modern trade agreements, which rely exclusively on trade sanctions to retaliate and to restore the balance of rights and obligations, by their very nature are implicitly biased in favor of the more powerful party. Trade-based sanctions do not have the same economic effect on countries of different sizes. In other words, if the United States breaches its obligations under CAFTA and it does not want to modify its behavior, which country will suffer more from the retaliatory action prescribed in the agreement, the United States or the aggrieved Central American party? Perhaps some kind of monetary fines (a notoriously sensitive issue in the United States), appropriately designed to take into account asymmetries, would lead to a more balanced approach to enforcing agreements between large and small economies. This issue warrants further careful thought.

It can only be hoped that the six CAFTA countries fully realize the importance of designing fair rules and of following them in today's interdependent world.

The CAFTA Endgame

Wrapping up the CAFTA negotiation presents the United States and Central America with fundamental problems.

For the United States the basic dilemma is the following: while textiles and apparel, clothing, footwear, leather, food, and agriculture are sectors particularly sensitive to being opened up, these are precisely the areas with the largest potential benefits for Central America. Moreover, as argued earlier, the United States' ability to accomplish its geopolitical and security objectives depends critically on Central American countries' achieving their economic objectives: only an agreement that creates additional access to the US market and concrete growth opportunities for Central America will manage to increase employment and standards of living, promote further economic and social reform, and consolidate the fragile democracies of the region.

If concessions to provide Central America market access prove to be politically impossible for the United States, the result will be not only to put at risk the United States' own geopolitical and security goals but also to present the Central Americans with a stark choice:

- On the one hand, they can keep insisting on a genuine mercantilist balance of reciprocal concessions, only to find that US reluctance leads to their gains and losses not adding up. Following this path would lead to frustration, protracted negotiations, and even potentially to the talks' derailment.

- On the other hand, they can internalize to some extent the political-economy restrictions of the United States, giving more weight to a logic of investment and growth that holds that even in the absence of attractive mercantilist concessions, other growth, investment, and policy-signaling effects tip the balance in favor of signing a less liberalizing, or less ambitious, agreement. But would simply turning the existing level of unilateral access to the US market into a reciprocal agreement be a sufficient payoff from this negotiation?

Central Americans must also realize that the reciprocal nature of this agreement makes it very likely that the price for recognition of their political sensitivities will be the United States' insistence on its own exclusions and reserves in areas of interest to Central America. It is here that the complex array of objectives and motivations of each party described above must be balanced to wrap up the CAFTA negotiation.

Table 9.7   Profiles of winners and losers in Central America

Winners: CAFTA supporters	Losers: CAFTA detractors
Consumers	Traditional or other specific agriculture and agribusiness activities (depending on the nature of the reciprocal agricultural liberalization schedules)
Exporters, including small and medium enterprises oriented toward exports	
Bankers and financial operators	Traditional (import substitution) industrialists
Import traders	
	Small and medium enterprises oriented toward the domestic market
Tourism sector and tourism operators	
Large regional groups	Agricultural subsistence and very low skilled workers
Highly skilled workers, women	
	Trade unions in some public enterprises
Low-skilled workers, women	
Nontraditional agriculture	
Traditional agriculture/agribusiness (depending on specific market access opportunities)	

Source: Adapted from Colburn and Sanchez (2000).

Winners, Losers, and the Politics of CAFTA in Central America

By its nature, any healthy process of economic modernization and transformation generates sectors and activities that grow (winners) and sectors and activities that decline or disappear (losers).[31] To ease the process of adjustment and reduce its costs, governments may establish mechanisms to compensate losers and may create incentives to smooth the transition.

One of the mechanisms by which CAFTA will promote modernization and increase productivity in the Central American economies is precisely an acceleration of the process of economic transformation. Table 9.7 identifies the main winners and losers from such transformation in Central American countries. Though its characterizations are general and thus tend to oversimplify a complex reality, it provides some insight into the

---

31. The biological metaphor is appropriate: just as a healthy living organism generates new cells to replace dying ones, so a healthy economic system generates new, more productive, more competitive activities and firms to replace uncompetitive, inefficient businesses and activities. Joseph Schumpeter called this engine of innovation and growth that drives capitalist competition the process of "creative destruction."

nature of the economic changes, and associated political challenges, that will be brought by CAFTA in Central American societies.

If CAFTA is comprehensive, winners would include the 33 million Central American consumers, who would benefit in multiple ways from lower prices and wider choice; exporters, including small and medium-sized enterprises (SMEs) linked to export operations; bankers and financial operators (although the increased competition in the financial sector might reduce profits and rents for some of the existing groups); import traders; tourism-sector businesses, where Central American countries have unique natural, ecological, and historical attractions and comparative advantages; large regional business groups able to enter into strategic alliances with US companies to penetrate the US market and to marginally service the Central American market; highly skilled workers, who will find expanded job opportunities with modern national and international business firms; low-skilled but semiliterate workers, particularly women, who could find jobs in labor-intensive manufacturing assembly operations that have expanded significantly with the CBI and most likely will experience a new wave of expansion with CAFTA; nontraditional agriculture in numerous product lines where Central American countries are quite competitive; and, finally, traditional agriculture and agribusiness activities (sugar, beef, poultry, and dairy), assuming that manages to open significant opportunities for market access in the United States. Most groups in the winners' column of table 9.7 see CAFTA as an opportunity; they believe that if the negotiations go reasonably well, the benefits as discussed above will overwhelmingly exceed the costs.

The list of potential losers includes traditional or other agricultural and agribusiness activities, if Central America liberalizes some of its own sensitive sectors in the face of continued US subsidization of agriculture while gaining no significant additional market access in the United States; traditional—that is, import substitution—industrial activities, many of which have already gone through substantial adjustment and rationalization with the trade liberalization of Central American economies so far, but which will not be able to survive the transition to full free trade with the United States; SMEs oriented toward the domestic market that either are in niches that will be hit by import competition or new competitive players, or do not manage to link up to expanded local and global sourcing networks; and agricultural subsistence and very low skilled workers who might not be able to take advantage of the new opportunities opened by modern economic activities, even in the labor-intensive manufacturing that requires a minimum of knowledge. Also in this list are some trade union leaders and members in a number of public enterprises that—probably wrongly—think that their jobs are threatened and thus perceive themselves as potential losers.

A number of dissenting voices in Central America have raised objections to or reservations about CAFTA. Those that perceive themselves as losers argue that the costs are higher than the benefits and that there is no way for many industrial and agricultural sectors to survive US competition. Others oppose CAFTA for ideological reasons; they fear that it will lead to greater concentration of economic activities in the hands of a few, mostly foreigners, with reduced opportunities for Central American nationals, or that it will erase or dilute Central American cultural traditions. Still others think that such an agreement is the way to go in the long term but assert that Central America is not yet ready in one or more areas, such as its infrastructure, competitive conditions, efficiency of public services, or entrepreneurship. Some believe strongly in "food security" and fear that the agricultural and rural way of life in Central America will be severely disrupted and threatened by CAFTA. In some countries, particularly Costa Rica, most of the population feels strongly that some "strategic" services should be produced and distributed by the public sector (e.g., telecommunications, energy, fuel, and drinking water) and would oppose CAFTA if its ratification would mean changing the status quo in these sectors.[32]

This profile of winners and benefits on the one hand, as well as of losers and objections on the other, explains why CAFTA was generally well received by many sectors of Central American society while others have expressed concerns or outright skepticism. The agreement's detractors include some very well organized and influential groups that pose a major political challenge to Central American governments and leaders. A more detailed analysis of the politics of CAFTA in Central America is beyond the scope of this chapter.

Central American governments are aware that these politics are very complex and that only a policy of transparency and participation, combined with a major investment in public education and debate as well as success in the negotiations, will make it possible to persuade doubters of the benefits of this agreement and to respond to their objections, fears, and concerns.

The Central American Policy Agenda to Fully Benefit from CAFTA

Since the Central American Common Market was launched, no project has had greater potential than CAFTA to promote growth, create employment, reduce poverty, and improve standards of living in Central America. But CAFTA will not achieve this transformation in and of itself. For its hopes and promises to materialize, Central American countries have a lot of homework to do, and they must see CAFTA as part of a much broader

---

32. For an inventory of these objections and some arguments in response, see Lizano and González (2003).

set of development policies. In other words, countries must "mainstream" CAFTA into their development strategies. This section presents a five-part policy agenda to summarize what we see as the policy challenges that must be a priority for Central America if it is to fully take advantage of the developmental opportunities opened up by CAFTA for higher growth, reduced poverty and better income distribution.

Macroeconomic Policy and "Crisis Proofing"

First, an appropriate macroeconomic policy framework is essential to reduce Central America's vulnerability to international shocks and crises. Reduced vulnerability and volatility are in turn essential elements for sustaining a reasonable rate of growth and for improving the distribution of income. To achieve such a framework, Central America should adopt most of the elements of "crisis proofing" recommended by Pedro-Pablo Kuczynski and John Williamson (2003). To do so:

- The chronic fiscal deficits and the high levels of domestic debt that characterize most countries in the region must be reduced.

- An exchange rate regime must be adopted that is sufficiently flexible to allow external competitiveness to be improved through currency depreciation when there is a sudden stop in capital inflows or other balance of payments difficulties. This system has indeed served Costa Rica very well since the early 1980s, and is a key element of the country's export success.

- Countries should also give serious thought to maintaining an instrument (such as a variation of the Chilean encaje) to avoid overvaluation if capital inflows threaten to become excessive. In El Salvador, remittances are a major contribution to foreign-exchange earnings, but they also represent a risk if they are allowed to support an artificially high exchange rate that would damage the competitiveness of Salvadoran exports.

- The flexible exchange rate regime should be complemented with a monetary policy based on targeting a low rate of inflation.

- Prudential supervision of the banking system should also be strengthened.

- Every effort should be made to increase domestic savings in both the public and private sector, by reforming domestic pension systems, developing the emerging capital markets, and taking other measures.

In addition, a very important policy issue is the fiscal impact of CAFTA and the tax reform that must accompany the agreement. As table 9.8

Table 9.8   Central America's reliance on
             taxes on trade (percent of current
             tax revenue)

Country	3-year average, 1999–2001
Costa Rica	6.4
El Salvador	10.2
Guatemala	12.7
Honduras	16.1
Nicaragua	10.3

Source: Schott and Kotschwar (2002).

shows, most countries in the region derive a substantial share of current revenues from taxes on international trade. Because imports from the United States represent around 50 percent of their total imports, CAFTA will erode between 3 percent and 8 percent of total tax revenue in these economies during the transition period to free trade. There is a great deal of work to be done by Central American countries on tax reform to replace this lost revenue.

Institutional Upgrading and Building

As stated above, one of the major benefits to Central American countries of an FTA with the United States will be to trigger a second generation of reforms by upgrading a wide array of institutions, from those most obviously and directly related to trade and globalization—such as customs, standards- and certification-setting bodies, regulatory agencies for the financial and other sectors, competition policy and government procurement agencies, and the like—to institutions related to labor markets and environmental policies.

Some of the institutional upgrading is directly linked to the requirements of implementing the CAFTA agreement itself. Michael Finger and Philip Schuler (2002) have estimated the costs of implementation of trade agreements in three areas (customs valuation, sanitary and phytosanitary standards, and intellectual property) using World Bank project data. They show that these investments require the purchasing of equipment and software, the hiring and training of specialized personnel, systems development, and other steps to upgrade the institutions and systems of developing countries to industrial-country standards. Depending on each country's existing capacities, the requisite investment may be on the order of tens of millions of dollars.

Improving compliance with international labor and environmental standards first and foremost needs substantive investments in institutional capacities and in a variety of specific projects. Even more broadly, depending on its specific situation, each Central American country needs to invest in improving market-economy fundamentals in areas such as property rights, the rule of law, the judicial system, and corporate governance and social responsibility. Only by working to improve the quality of all these institutions and of economic governance mechanisms will Central American countries manage to attract sufficient investment to grow and take full advantage of the new market access opened up by CAFTA.

The trade-cooperation nexus established during CAFTA's negotiation phase is a major opportunity for Central Americans to mobilize resources to upgrade and build the institutions they need to benefit from free trade with the world's largest market and most competitive economy. However, this exercise has resulted in too many initiatives too widely dispersed across many areas. Although many small incremental changes can make a significant contribution, it is possible that the Central Americans will seek, as part of the negotiation, that priority be placed on significant institution building and on the resources to finance them. And if they do, how will the United States respond to such a request?

The Challenge of Competitiveness and Productive Development

As is true of many small, developing economies, the economies of Central America are held together almost entirely by micro, small, and medium-sized enterprises and businesses. Most workers are found in the extremes: in microenterprises with fewer than 20 employees and in medium- to large-sized firms (by Central American standards) with more than 150 employees. This profile suggests a certain duality in the industrial structure of the region, where a modern sector coexists with many family and informal businesses (see Fedepricap 1996).

A number of studies have identified the main obstacles for the competitiveness of Central American SMEs. These include deficiencies in infrastructure (electricity, telephone, Internet, roads, ports, and airports); limited access to credit (high interest rates, bureaucratic procedures, collateral-based eligibility criteria in banking institutions, and lack of venture capital); insufficient knowledge of modern management, administrative, and marketing techniques; an insufficient degree of e-readiness, that is, of using information and telecommunications technologies for doing business; deficiencies in support services such as quality verification, specialized laboratories, diffusion of technological information, and product and process design; and scant investment in research and development. Factors such as these explain the low ranking of Central American countries in the competitiveness indices of the World Economic Forum (Fedepricap 1996, INCAE 1996, Monge and Céspedes 2002).

A competitive model that would enable the region to take advantage of CAFTA would necessarily have to incorporate SMEs, not just large businesses and groups, and apply appropriate policies to tackle these different weaknesses. Given the lessons from the "picking winners" type of industrial policies in Asia (Noland and Pack 2003) and the limits imposed by the WTO on the use of certain instruments (Pangestu 2002), the right approach for the region will be comprehensive rather than targeting specific sectors. Hence, the main elements of a productive modernization policy should include enhancing the efficiency of basic infrastructure and services, improving human capital, reducing procedural constraints to doing business, promoting the diffusion of technological information and the use of e-business, encouraging venture capital, and promoting a well-networked national and regional system of innovation based on a technologically supportive infrastructure that accelerates the introduction of best practices in the region. In some cases, these policies could converge in the context of facilitating the growth of industrial clusters à la Porter. Upgrading on all these different fronts is the key for Central America to make a successful transition from a reliance on natural resources and unskilled, labor-intensive activities to the knowledge economy.

Central American countries must overcome the so-called neoliberal or old Washington Consensus view that macroeconomic stabilization and trade liberalization are sufficient for development: they must recognize that establishing and strengthening such programs is not only a necessary but a legitimate role for government. Most Central American countries have a long way to go to establish or strengthen their institutional and human capacities to put such policies in place. In a positive step in this direction, the third part of the National Strategies for Trade Capacity Building (being developed as part of the cooperation exercise in parallel with the CAFTA negotiations) is adjusting to free trade and developing competitiveness. In the light of the discussion above, the importance of this parallel capacity-building initiative needs no further emphasis.

The agricultural sector requires special attention. As suggested above, the process of agricultural transformation that CAFTA will bring to Central America must be carefully considered and managed; such management includes making the necessary investments in rural development, education, communications, transportation infrastructure, export diversification, and sanitary and phytosanitary and food safety capacities.[33] This is by itself a huge challenge for Central American countries, given the current status of these areas.

---

33. For an analysis of NAFTA's implications for agriculture and the challenges of agricultural adjustment, particularly in Mexico, see Veeman, Veeman, and Hoskins (2002); Yunes-Naude (2002); and Appendini (2003).

Table 9.9 Central America: Poverty and indigence indicators, 1990–99

	1990	1994	1997	1999
Percent below poverty line				
Costa Rica	26.2	23.1	22.5	20.3
El Salvador	n.a.	54.2	55.5	49.8
Guatemala	69.1	n.a.	n.a.	60.5
Honduras	80.5	77.9	79.1	79.7
Nicaragua	n.a.	73.6	n.a.	69.9
Latin American average	48.3	45.7	43.5	43.8
Percent below indigence line				
Costa Rica	9.8	8.0	7.8	7.8
El Salvador	n.a.	21.7	23.3	21.9
Guatemala	41.8	n.a.	n.a.	34.1
Honduras	60.6	53.9	54.4	56.8
Nicaragua	n.a.	48.4	n.a.	44.6
Latin American average	22.5	20.8	19.0	18.5

n.a. = not available

Note: Two income-based indicators of poverty are included in this table—poverty line and indigence line. The poverty line for each country is estimated based on the cost of a basic basket of goods that includes the minimum to cover food and nutritional requirements as well as nonfood needs. The indigence line takes into account only food requirements. Indigents (or the extremely poor) are defined as those persons living in households whose incomes are so low that even if they use them entirely to buy food, they will not adequately satisfy the minimum nutritional requirements of all household members.

Source: UN, Economic Commission for Latin America and the Caribbean, *Social Panorama of Latin America, 2001–2002.*

Social Policy, Safety Nets, and Adjustment Assistance

As table 9.9 shows, during the 1990s all Central American countries experienced a slight reduction in poverty. However, with the exception of Costa Rica, the proportion of poor people continues to be extremely high, much higher than the Latin American average: in 1999, 79.7 percent in Honduras, 69.9 percent in Nicaragua, 60.5 percent in Guatemala, and 49.8 percent in El Salvador. The proportion of persons living under the indigence line is also extremely high. In addition, high rates of income inequality remain deeply entrenched in the region.

CAFTA represents an opportunity to boost growth and reduce poverty, but it may also make the social situation worse under two scenarios: in the short to medium term, if the costs of adjustment that attend trade liberalization are not matched by new investment and employment creation; and in the longer term, if the agreement accelerates the transition in some Central American economies away from their predominantly agrarian nature and increases rural-urban migration without creating enough new jobs in highly productive services and industries. Unlike in developed industrial economies, in Central America new jobs must be created not just to absorb workers displaced by trade-related adjustments but also, more fundamentally, to improve the acute poverty and unemployment already existing in the region.

Thus, for Central American economies, CAFTA poses both the familiar issue of trade adjustment assistance and the much more basic issue of using social policy to address underlying structural problems. Given the inability of economic reforms and social policies in the region so far to significantly reduce poverty and inequality, it seems obvious that this area requires some rethinking. Efforts will have to be renewed in the new stage of economic and social development, as new stresses are induced in the region by CAFTA.

It is beyond the scope of this chapter to delve more deeply into this important policy area. We wish only to signal the importance of social policies in the post-CAFTA stage of economic development in Central America.[34]

Deepening Regional Integration

What would be the impact of the FTA on regional integration in Central America? Despite years of economic integration, significant trade areas have not yet been negotiated by these countries. In this respect, CAFTA confronts Central Americans with a choice between a hub-and-spoke configuration—that is, the disciplines and the market access concessions of CAFTA would apply bilaterally between each Central American country and the United States, but not among Central American countries[35]—and a common generic agreement, in which the disciplines do not just apply bilaterally but also are binding for the Central American countries among themselves.

There are important reasons to prefer the generic route rather than the hub-and-spoke configuration:

- A hub-and-spoke pattern would tend to fragment and undermine the Central American Common Market (CACM), because there is the risk that Central American countries would apply some rules among themselves and a different set of rules with their principal trading partner.

---

34. Much has been learned about social policy in Latin America in the past decade. Birdsall and Székely (2003) provide a recent review of lessons learned and a persuasive rethinking of what needs to be done in the future. They propose an approach based on three main components: the mainstreaming of poverty reduction and the equity objective into the traditional macroeconomic and trade policies, so as to reduce volatility and protect poor people's assets; policies and programs to increase their assets (in addition to investing in education, health, and increased schooling, put greater emphasis on poor people's access to land, credit, and financial markets); and policies to increase the return on their assets, which is mainly their own labor.

35. Central Americans have negotiated such bilateral agreements with Mexico, Chile, and the Dominican Republic.

- A hub-and-spoke design for CAFTA would also entail the risk of making market access less secure among Central American countries than between them and the United States. For instance, in the recent past some Central American countries have raised tariffs against other Common Market members, in some cases for political and not economic reasons. Making CAFTA-like commitments binding among the members of the CACM would discipline such measures.

- Such commitments would give US and other multinationals as well as Central American companies the security of knowing that there will be no backsliding in the level of free trade among Central American countries in such areas as tariffs, nontariff barriers, and rules of origin, thereby encouraging trade and investment. This security is important if the region is to become a platform for operations and sourcing. A similar logic applies to investment protection. This would give an additional incentive to growth by improving the "investment quality" of the region as a whole, positioning it—rather than just individual countries—as a platform of operations for global sourcing and promoting freer trade and business facilitation regionwide.

Determining whether it is desirable and feasible to apply this logic across the board would require further reflection, but there do seem to be important gains associated with having government procurement, technical barriers to trade, sanitary and phytosanitary standards, investment, and other key disciplines apply and be binding among Central American countries as well as bilaterally with the United States. Whether this should done as part of CAFTA or in parallel instruments among Central American countries is a major issue to be decided. Under this approach, of course, the CACM rules would still remain in place wherever they exceed CAFTA's standards. In essence, the CAFTA negotiations present a golden opportunity for Central American countries to deepen their own economic integration.

The Capacity-Building Pillar of Free Trade Between the United States and Central America

In the long term CAFTA will be judged, among other criteria, by whether its fostering greater economic integration with the United States will help Central American countries to reduce the large gaps in levels of income and standards of living between them and rich countries. In other words, it will be judged on whether this path to globalization will help in promoting "economic convergence."

The accelerated process of economic development that CAFTA will induce has a number of costs—or, more precisely, requires a big push in public goods and public investment: investment in capacity building to implement the agreement; investment to facilitate not only trade adjustment but, as suggested above, broader social policies; the costs of developing international competitiveness; and the costs of dealing with the financial implications of lowering tariffs. Of course, these are the main challenges of financing development in Central America over the next few years with or without CAFTA, but CAFTA will make them more urgent. In addition, as argued in the previous section, since free trade alone will not suffice to meet Central America's development challenges, Central Americans must avoid the risk of having CAFTA trigger priorities and policies that, in the absence of broader progress, might not be the "right" sequencing for development. Once CAFTA is approved, the rest of the development homework cannot be postponed.

A number of distinguished economists think that for economic convergence and integration to occur, these arrangements themselves or parallel efforts must incorporate substantial transfers of resources from the richer countries and regions to the poorer ones to close the gaps in infrastructure, education, institutions, and elsewhere.[36] This claim raises a number of important issues for CAFTA:

- Will the trade-cooperation nexus established in CAFTA be sufficient to mobilize the resource transfer to Central America necessary to do the homework outlined in the previous section?

- How will the resources mobilized by the United States, as a partner in this agreement, compare in magnitude to those mobilized by other bilateral donors and multilateral agencies?

- Given that NAFTA created a North American Development Bank, as well as a number of cooperation commissions in key areas, what institutions should be created to sustain aid and resource transfer efforts to Central America?

- Are Central Americans underestimating the challenge of financing the domestic tasks outlined in the previous section?

Given US and Central American objectives and asymmetries in size and level of economic development, the foundations for a win-win outcome from free trade must include both a world-class trade agreement and a no less impressive capacity-building component.

---

36. See Lopez-Calva and Lustig (forthcoming 2004) and literature cited therein. Of course, aid and international resource transfers will not do much good if the internal redistributive mechanisms (tax policy, social policy) are not working and if no social safety nets are in place.

Concluding Remarks

Only rarely do small economies have the opportunity to engage and sustain the interest of a large global power and economy in a modern trade negotiation. Many political, economic, and other circumstances must converge and synchronize for this to happen. Central Americans are aware that they have a window of opportunity that they must capitalize on.

A free trade agreement between the United States and Central America has the potential to generate significant benefits for both parties in the negotiation. The United States is motivated by a complex mix of economic, trade policy, security, and strategic objectives. CAFTA is part of the broader US strategy of "competitive liberalization," as well as of building economic alliances with countries that are critical to US national security and to promoting democracy in the Western Hemisphere.

From the point of view of Central America, CAFTA is a unique and extraordinary opportunity to boost growth and development. Indeed, it has the greatest potential for transformation of any project in recent history, both in terms of its benefits (growth, employment, poverty reduction, standards of living, institution building, modernization) and its costs (agricultural transition, rural-urban migration, job dislocation).

Given the large economic, social, and institutional asymmetries between the parties, the negotiation of CAFTA poses huge challenges for both parties.

A key negotiating challenge for the United States will be to strike a balance between the trade negotiators' basic mercantilist instincts to extract maximum concessions and set precedents in competitive liberalization and the broader interests of national security (drugs, terrorism, immigration), as well as political-strategic objectives of promoting political stability, democracy, and economic reform in the region. Yet, as noted above, for the United States to achieve these broader goals, Central Americans must achieve their economic objectives: a firm economic foundation is required for social and political reform and stability. The United States will do more than put at risk its own geopolitical and security objectives if it does not concede market access to Central America, for it will leave Central Americans an unattractive choice: either to continue to insist on genuine reciprocal concessions (thereby ensuring frustration and perhaps even leading to a breakdown in the talks) or accept a less liberalizing, less ambitious agreement—which may do little to further their economic objectives.

The key negotiating challenges facing Central Americans include the development of broad-based national consultations, regional coordination in defining common negotiating positions and strategies, and the need to maintain discipline in the midst of the heterogeneous conditions of the region, the differences in sensitivities, and the multiple pressures and trade-offs inherent to the broad and complex agenda of US-Central

American relations. Central Americans should also develop and fund an effective strategy to garner as much support as possible for their case in the United States.

For the hopes and promises of CAFTA to materialize, Central American countries have a lot of homework to do, and they must see CAFTA as part of a much broader set of development policies. In other words, countries must mainstream CAFTA into their development strategies. These broader policies include (1) an appropriate macroeconomic framework that reduces the vulnerability of Central American economies to international shocks and crisis; (2) a big push, supported by US and other bilateral and multilateral aid, for institutional upgrading and capacity building—the CAFTA trade-cooperation nexus must not be allowed to fail; (3) the putting in place of aggressive policies to promote productive modernization and competitiveness; (4) rethought and renewed efforts in the area of social policies not just to facilitate trade adjustment but to attack the underlying structure of poverty and inequality; and (5) the determination to design CAFTA or complementary commitments in such a way that not a hub-and-spoke configuration but rather a solid single-market economy is promoted in Central America, thereby turning the region into a competitive platform for regionwide investments, operations, and sourcing.

And for the hopes and promises of CAFTA to materialize, the United States also faces a challenge. It must deliver not only trade concessions but fresh aid and cooperation to Central Americans to make possible their big push to invest in public goods, build the necessary institutions, and apply the appropriate policies. If this happens, CAFTA will represent a new paradigm in North-South trade negotiations and governance, in which trade and aid complement each other in developmentally beneficial ways. This developmental bar must be placed high for CAFTA to be the road map for economic relationship between small developing and developed countries in the 21st century. Otherwise, in 10 years, we will be discussing why the revised new Washington Consensus failed to live up to its promise.

Appendix 9.1

List of the 15 main product lines exported from Central America to the United States

Chapter number	Description

Costa Rica

8	Edible fruit and nuts; peel of citrus fruit or melons
84	Nuclear reactors, boilers, machinery, and mechanical appliances; parts thereof
62	Articles of apparel and clothing accessories, not knitted or crocheted
85	Electrical machinery and equipment and parts thereof; sound recorders and reproducers, television image and sound recorders and reproducers, and parts and accessories of such articles
61	Articles of apparel and clothing accessories, knitted or crocheted
90	Optical, photographic, cinematographic, measuring, checking, precision, medical, or surgical instruments and apparatus; parts and accessories thereof
3	Fish and crustaceans, molluscs and other aquatic invertebrates
9	Coffee, tea, maté, and spices
20	Preparations of vegetables, fruit, nuts, or other parts of plants
6	Live trees and other plants; bulbs, roots, and the like; cut flowers and ornamental foliage
7	Edible vegetables and certain roots and tubers
40	Rubber and articles thereof
71	Natural or cultured pearls, precious or semiprecious stones, precious metals, metals clad with precious metal, and articles thereof; imitation jewelry; coin
42	Articles of leather; saddlery and harness; travel goods, handbags, and similar containers; articles of animal gut (other than silkworm gut)
39	Plastics and articles thereof

El Salvador

61	Articles of apparel and clothing accessories, knitted or crocheted
62	Articles of apparel and clothing accessories, not knitted or crocheted
9	Coffee, tea, maté, and spices
85	Electrical machinery and equipment and parts thereof; sound recorders and reproducers, television image and sound recorders and reproducers, and parts and accessories of such articles
63	Other made-up textile articles; sets; worn clothing and worn textile articles; rags
3	Fish and crustaceans, molluscs and other aquatic invertebrates
17	Sugars and sugar confectionery
27	Mineral fuels, mineral oils, and products of their distillation; bituminous substances; mineral waxes
22	Beverages, spirits, and vinegar
52	Cotton
64	Footwear, gaiters, and the like; parts of such articles
34	Soap, organic surface-active agents, washing preparations, lubricating preparations, artificial waxes, prepared waxes, polishing or scouring preparations, candles and similar articles, modeling pastes, "dental waxes" and dental preparations with a basis of plaster
48	Paper and paperboard; articles of paper pulp, of paper, or of paperboard
7	Edible vegetables and certain roots and tubers
76	Aluminum and articles thereof

Guatemala

9	Coffee, tea, maté, and spices
8	Edible fruit and nuts; peel of citrus fruit or melons
27	Mineral fuels, mineral oils, and products of their distillation; bituminous substances; mineral waxes
34	Soap, organic surface-active agents, washing preparations, lubricating preparations, artificial waxes, prepared waxes, polishing or scouring preparations, candles and similar articles, modeling pastes, "dental waxes" and dental preparations with a basis of plaster

(Appendix continues on next page)

List of the 15 main product lines *(continued)*

Chapter number	Description

Guatemala *(continued)*

7	Edible vegetables and certain roots and tubers
17	Sugars and sugar confectionery
6	Live trees and other plants; bulbs, roots, and the like; cut flowers and ornamental foliage
12	Oil seeds and oleaginous fruits; miscellaneous grains, seeds, and fruit; industrial or medicinal plants; straw and fodder
3	Fish and crustaceans, molluscs and other aquatic invertebrates
48	Paper and paperboard; articles of paper pulp, of paper, or of paperboard
24	Tobacco and manufactured tobacco substitutes
76	Aluminum and articles thereof
42	Articles of leather; saddlery and harness; travel goods, handbags, and similar containers; articles of animal gut (other than silkworm gut)
61	Articles of apparel and clothing accessories, knitted or crocheted
84	Nuclear reactors, boilers, machinery, and mechanical appliances; parts thereof

Honduras

9	Coffee, tea, maté, and spices
49	Printed books, newspapers, pictures, and other products of the printing industry; manuscripts, typescripts, and plans
8	Edible fruit and nuts; peel of citrus fruit or melons
3	Fish and crustaceans, molluscs and other aquatic invertebrates
44	Wood and articles of wood; wood charcoal
24	Tobacco and manufactured tobacco substitutes
61	Articles of apparel and clothing accessories, knitted or crocheted
94	Furniture; bedding, mattresses, mattress supports, cushions, and similar stuffed furnishings; lamps and lighting fittings, not elsewhere specified or included; illuminated signs, illuminated nameplates, and the like; prefabricated buildings
26	Ores, slag, and ash
7	Edible vegetables and certain roots and tubers
62	Articles of apparel and clothing accessories, not knitted or crocheted
84	Nuclear reactors, boilers, machinery, and mechanical appliances; parts thereof
20	Preparations of vegetables, fruit, nuts, or other parts of plants
17	Sugars and sugar confectionery
71	Natural or cultured pearls, precious or semiprecious stones, precious metals, metals clad with precious metal, and articles thereof; imitation jewelry; coin

Nicaragua

3	Fish and crustaceans, molluscs and other aquatic invertebrates
9	Coffee, tea, maté, and spices
2	Meat and edible meat offal
8	Edible fruit and nuts; peel of citrus fruit or melons
71	Natural or cultured pearls, precious or semiprecious stones, precious metals, metals clad with precious metal, and articles thereof; imitation jewelry; coin
69	Ceramic products
15	Animal or vegetable fats and oils and their cleavage products; prepared edible fats; animal or vegetable waxes
24	Tobacco and manufactured tobacco substitutes
38	Miscellaneous chemical products
7	Edible vegetables and certain roots and tubers
17	Sugars and sugar confectionery
44	Wood and articles of wood; wood charcoal
4	Dairy produce; birds' eggs; natural honey; edible products of animal origin, not elsewhere specified or included
76	Aluminum and articles thereof
21	Miscellaneous edible preparations

Note: The chapter numbers refer to the Harmonized Tariff Schedule; the categories are listed in order of volume of exports to the United States.

References

Appendini, Kirsten. 2003. The Challenges to Rural Mexico in an Open Economy. In *Mexico's Politics and Society in Transition*, ed. Joseph S. Tulchin and Andrew D. Selee. Boulder, CO: Lynne Rienner Publishers.

Birdsall, Nancy, and Miguel Székely. 2003. Bootstraps, Not Band-Aids: Poverty, Equity, and Social Policy. In *After the Washington Consensus: Restarting Growth and Reform in Latin America*, ed. Pedro-Pablo Kuczynski and John Williamson. Washington: Institute for International Economics.

Camacho, Arnoldo. 2003. Impacto en los sistemas financieros del Tratado de Libre Comercio de Centroamérica con los Estados Unidos. Memorandum prepared for the Inter-American Development Bank, Washington.

Fedepricap (Federation of Private Entities of Central America and Panama). 1996. *Inventario y análisis de la situación de la mediana empresa productiva en Centroamérica*, Programa de Apoyo a Iniciativas Regionales para Centroamérica, SOGEMA, Canadian Corporation, May.

Colburn, Forrest, and Fernando Sanchez. 2000. *Empresarios centroamericanos y apertura económica*. San Jose, Costa Rica: EDUCA.

Costa Rica, Ministry of Foreign Trade. 2003. Tratado de Libre Comercio entre Centroamérica y los Estados Unidos: Posición nacional, San Jose. www.comex.go.cr.

Dutta, Soumitra, Bruno Lanvin, and Fiona Paua, eds. 2003. *The Global Information Technology Report, 2002–2003: Readiness for the Networked World*. New York: Oxford University Press.

Easterly, William, and Ross Levine. 2002. *Tropics, Germs and Crops: How Endowments Influence Economic Development*. Center for Global Development Working Paper 15. Available at www.nyu.edu/fas/institute/dri/Easterly/Research.html (October).

Elliott, Kimberly Ann. Forthcoming 2004. Labor Standards and the Free Trade Area of the Americas. In *The FTAA and Beyond: Prospects for Integration in the Americas*, ed. Antoni Estevadeordal, Dani Rodrik, Alan Taylor, and Andrés Velasco. David Rockefeller Center, Harvard University Press.

Emergency Committee for American Trade. 2003. ECAT Positions. www.ecattrade.com/statements.

Estado de la Nación, 8th Report. 2001. www.estadonacion.or.cr.

Farm Bill Conference Summary. 2002. agriculture.senate.gov/Briefs/2002FarmBill/conframe.htm (April 20).

Finger, Michael, and Philip Schuler. 2002. Implementation of WTO Commitments: The Development Challenge. In *Development, Trade and the WTO: A Handbook*, ed. Bernard Hoekman, Aaditya Mattoo, and Philip English. Washington: World Bank.

Gibson, Paul, Johan Wainio, Daniel Whitley, and Mary Bohman. 2001. *Profiles of Tariffs in Global Agricultural Markets*. Agricultural Economic Report 796. Washington: US Department of Agriculture, Economic Research Service. Available at www.ers.usda.gov/publications/aer796 (January).

Gilbreath, Jan. 2003. *Environment and Development in Mexico: Recommendations for Reconciliation*. Washington: CSIS Press.

Gitli, Eduardo, and Carlos Murillo. 2001. La diferencia entre tener o no un acuerdo de inversiones con los Estados Unidos. Centro Internacional de Política Económica para el Desarrollo Sostenible (CINPE), Heredia, Costa Rica.

Granados, Jaime. 2001. *La integración comercial Centroamericana: Un marco interpretativo y cursos de acción plausible*. INTAL-ITD, Occasional Paper 8. www.asies.org.gt/ca/documentos/Jaime%20Granados/integracion_comercial_CA.pdf (May).

Granados, Jaime. 2003. *Zonas Francas y otros regímenes especiales en un contexto de negociaciones comerciales multilaterales y regionales*. INTAL-ITD-STA, Occasional Paper 20. www.iadb.org/intal/publicaciones/Granados_DD20.pdf (January).

Hakim, Peter. 2001. The Uneasy Americas. *Foreign Affairs* 80, no. 2 (March–April): 46–61.

Hathaway, Dale. Forthcoming 2004. US–Central American Free Trade Agreement: Main Impacts on Agricultural Products. In *Agricultural Liberalization in the FTAA and WTO*. Washington: Inter-American Development Bank.

INCAE (Central American Institute for Business Administration). 1996. *Competitiveness in Central America: Preparing Companies for Globalization*. Costa Rica: INCAE.

Inter-American Development Bank (IDB). 2003. National Legislation, Regulations, and Procedures Regarding Government Procurement in the Americas. alca-ftaa.iadb.org/eng/gpdoc2/INTRO.htm (April).

International Labor Organization (ILO). 2003. ILOLEX; Database of International Labour Standards. www.ilo.org/ilolex/english.

Kuczynski, Pedro-Pablo, and John Williamson, eds. 2003. *After the Washington Consensus: Restarting Growth and Reform in Latin America*. Washington: Institute for International Economics.

Lizano, Eduardo, and Anabel González. 2003. *El Tratado de Libre Comercio entre el Istmo Centroamericano y los Estados Unidos de América—Oportunidades, desafíos y riesgos*. BID-INTAL, Occasional Paper 9. www.iadb.org/intal/Publicaciones/intalDD9_Lizano.pdf (March)

Lopez-Calva, Luis, and Nora Lustig. Forthcoming 2004. Inclusive Trade: Strengthening the Sources of Convergence within the FTAA. In *The FTAA and Beyond: Prospects for Integration in the Americas*, ed. Antoni Estevadeordal, Dani Rodrik, Alan Taylor, and Andres Velasco. Cambridge, MA: Harvard University Press.

Monge, Ricardo. 2000. La economía política de un intento fallido de reforma en telecomunicaciones. In *Los Retos Políticos de la Reforma Económica en Costa Rica*, ed. Ronulfo Jiménez. San Jose, Costa Rica: Academia de Centroamérica.

Monge, Ricardo, and Oswald Céspedes. 2002. *Costa Rica: Hacia la Economía Basada en el Conocimiento*. Comisión Asesora en Alta Tecnología de Costa Rica. San Jose, Costa Rica: Fundación CAATEC.

Monge, Ricardo, Claudio González, and Francisco Monge. 2002. Efectos Potenciales de un Tratado de Libre Comercio entre USA y Centroamérica sobre el sector agropecuario y agroindustrial de Costa Rica y El Salvador. Background paper prepared for a larger report on lessons from NAFTA and other free trade agreements. World Bank, Washington.

Noland, Marcus, and Howard Pack. 2003. *Industrial Policy in an Era of Globalization: Lessons from Asia*. Washington: Institute for International Economics.

Pangestu, Mary. 2002. Industrial Policy and Developing Countries. In *Development, Trade, and the WTO: A Handbook*, ed. Bernard Hoekman, Aaditya Mattoo, and Philip English. Washington: World Bank.

Roberts, Donna, Timothy Josling, and David Orden. 1999. *A Framework for Analyzing Technical Barriers to Trade in Agricultural Markets*. Technical Bulletin 1876. Washington: US Department of Agriculture, Economic Research Service. Available at www.ers.usda.gov/publications/tb1876 (March).

Rodriguez-Clare, Andrés (Office of the Chief Economist, Inter-American Development). 2001. Costa Rica's Development Strategy Based on Human Capital and Technology: How It Got There, the Impact of INTEL, and Lessons for Other Countries. Report prepared for UNDP *Human Development Report* of 2001 when author was chief of economic advisers to the president of Costa Rica.

Salazar-Xirinachs, J.M., and J.M. Martinez-Piva. 2003. Trade, Labor Standards, and Global Governance: A Perspective from the Americas. In *International Economic Governance and Non-Economic Concerns: New Challenges for the International Legal Order*, ed. Stefan Griller. New York: Springer-Verlag.

Schott, Jeffrey. 2001. *Prospects for Free Trade in the Americas*. Washington: Institute for International Economics.

Schott, Jeffrey, and Barbara Kotschwar. 2002. *Readiness Indicators for Central America, 2002 Update*. Washington: Institute for International Economics.

Shifter, Michael. 2003. Introduction: Latin America in the New Century. In *Latin America in a Changing Global Environment*, ed. Riordan Roett and Guadalupe Paz. Boulder, CO: Lynne Rienner Publishers.

Stiglitz, Joseph, and Shadid Yusuf. 2001. The East Asian Miracle at the Millennium. In *Rethinking the East Asian Miracle*, ed. Joseph Stiglitz and Shadid Yusuf. Washington: World Bank; Oxford: Oxford University Press.

Torres, Blanca. 2002. The North American Agreement on Environmental Cooperation: Rowing Upstream. In *Greening the Americas: NAFTA's Lessons for Hemispheric Trade*, ed. Carolyn Deere and Daniel Esty. Cambridge, MA: MIT Press.

USTR (US Trade Representative, Office of). 2001. Fourth Report to Congress on the Operation of the Caribbean Basin Economic Recovery Act. www.ustr.gov/reports/2002cbi-final.pdf (December 31).

USTR (US Trade Representative, Office of). 2003. United States–Chile Free Trade Agreement. www.ustr.gov/new/fta/Chile/final/index.htm (June 6).

Veeman, Michele, Terrence S. Veeman, and Ryan Hoskins. 2002. NAFTA and Agriculture: Challenges for Trade and Policy. In *NAFTA in the New Millennium*, ed. Edward J. Chambers and Peter H. Smith. La Jolla, CA: Center for U.S.–Mexican Studies, University of California, San Diego; Edmonton: University of Alberta Press.

Yunes-Naude, Antonio. 2002. Lessons from NAFTA: The Case of Mexico's Agricultural Sector. Report to the World Bank, Washington.

Zoellick, Robert. 2002. Globalization, Trade, and Economic Security. Remarks at the National Press Club. Available at www.ustr.gov/speech-test/zoellick/zoellick_26-npc.PDF (October 1).

10

Brazil: FTA or FTAA or WTO?

ALBERT FISHLOW

Brazil is the great current question mark as US trade strategy moves toward implementing its current strategy of "competitive liberalization."[1] That phrase is a good description of current policy. It conveys the ultimate intent of liberalization but stresses that national policy, in a variety of forms, is needed to get to that end.

This process is not a sudden innovation. Rather, it has emerged with increasing clarity over the past decade. The United States has moved away from its former insistence on multilateralism and on the General Agreement on Tariffs and Trade (GATT), now the World Trade Organization (WTO), as the unique forum of trade negotiation. First, it fully embraced regionalism, after earlier experiments with Canada and Israel, when it accepted the North American Free Trade Agreement (NAFTA) in 1992 and, two years later, provided decisive support for the extension of free trade throughout the Western Hemisphere at the Miami summit. This was the state of affairs from the end of the Clinton administration to the beginning of bilateral negotiations. And despite finally gaining approval of new "fast-track" authorization—trade promotion authority (TPA), as it is now called—the Bush administration has committed itself much more fully to

---

Albert Fishlow is a professor of international and public affairs at Columbia University and director of the Center for Brazilian Studies and of the Institute for Latin American Studies there.

1. US Trade Representative Robert Zoellick has argued the case for bilateral agreements as "a speedy route to free trade" (*Financial Times*, November 19, 2002). Fred Bergsten (1996) had earlier argued the case for open regionalism—a mode that others have embraced, as this volume suggests. On the other side, WTO officials and other economists have continued to defend multilateralism.

such a bilateral strategy, moving actively in the direction earlier signaled by its predecessor in signing trade pacts with Jordan and Vietnam. Most recently, it has completed and signed bilateral free trade agreements (FTAs) with Singapore and Chile. Trade negotiations are under way with the Southern African Customs Union, Morocco, Australia, and Central America (to include in 2004 the Dominican Republic). That makes for quite a burden for US Trade Representative Robert Zoellick and company, in addition to the continuing Doha Round of multilateral negotiations.

To be sure, the United States is hardly the only FTA practitioner. The European Union has been even more prominently engaged in this process. It moved actively toward Eastern Europe after the fall of the Berlin Wall and toward the Maghreb and other parts of Africa; most recently, it has sought to make its influence felt in Latin America and Asia. Developing nations have been vigorously pursuing these negotiations in recent years. Overall, more than half of all regional agreements reported to the GATT and the WTO have emerged since 1995. Almost half of reported global trade emerges in such free trade groups.

Within that new international setting, Brazil now has a new government, and one unlike its predecessors. The victory of the Workers' Party, the PT (Partido dos Trabalhadores), has brought to power the Brazilian left. Luiz Inácio Lula da Silva won a stunning victory in the presidential election of October 2002, with some 60 percent of the popular vote—counted accurately, as Brazilians always like to note, within hours of closure of the polling booths. His party, although it controls only about a fifth of the seats in Congress, has succeeded in achieving a working majority in both the Chamber of Deputies and the Senate. This was the fourth time Lula had run, and many had anticipated that policy in Brazil—a country afflicted by limited economic growth, the persistence of extreme income inequality, and insufficient attention to social policy—would take a radical turn. That certainly was the expectation of the markets, as well as the fervent hope of many of Lula's supporters.

The immediate surprise has been the turn in the exact contrary direction. Six months into Lula's administration, the new finance minister, Antonio Palocci, and the new central bank president, Henrique Meirelles, have begun to regain the confidence of Brazil's lenders. As a consequence, the risk premium of Brazil has descended from about 2300 basis points after the election of Lula to something in the range of 700 points. In addition, the exchange rate has moved from a level close to 4 to about 3 reais to the dollar, where it seems to have stabilized. Trade finance, at least in the form of short-term capital, has begun to flow again, although foreign direct investment (FDI) still remains scarce, as investors have as yet failed to react positively. At current magnitudes of $4 billion in the first seven months of 2003, net FDI is well below inflows in recent years and now trails foreign investment in Mexico.

The International Monetary Fund (IMF) has reviewed and enthusiastically continued its pact with Brazil, hastily signed in August 2002 prior to the election. Indeed, the new government, early on, committed itself to an even larger and continuing fiscal surplus of 4.25 percent of GDP. Reserves have begun to creep upward: the trade surplus is projected to reach as much as $18 billion by the end of 2003. Under these circumstances, despite the hesitancy of foreign investors noted above, the current account deficit has rapidly declined to less than 1 percent of GDP; in previous years, this key statistic had often hovered above 4 percent and regularly climbed higher.

One inevitable consequence of Brazil's tight monetary and fiscal policy has been continued anemic economic performance. Growth continues to remain below acceptable levels, given the country's high, and increasing, rate of unemployment—almost 13 percent officially and higher in fact—and the social unrest manifested in the urban centers of Rio de Janeiro and São Paulo. The projections are not optimistic: the Central Bank recently reduced its estimate of GDP growth for this year to 1.5 percent, and it is even more cautious about the longer term. Next year growth is expected to improve, but to still remain below the target rates of 4 to 5 percent that had been promised in the election campaign.

A potential political struggle inside (and outside) the government has been avoided only because of Lula's unwavering support of Palocci's approach. But the stage has been set for those divisions to emerge more starkly as the Congress takes up constitutional amendments to address the recurrent deficit emanating from the social security system for public employees (now consuming more than 5 percent of GDP) and the complicated structure of taxes (now running at more than 35 percent of GDP). Lula must cope with disappointed federal workers and the judiciary, as well as with unhappy governors who resist the loss of their constitutionally guaranteed claim on resources. At this early stage, however, the results are quite favorable. The pension reform has gone through much as it had been initially presented. Future retirees will eventually be faced with a defined contribution rather than a defined benefits scheme.

Equally relevant, but until now subordinated to the central problem of economic performance, is the question of Brazil's foreign policy—more specifically, its position on negotiations about the Free Trade Area of the Americas (FTAA). Brazil is now co-chair, along with the United States, of the final phase of the negotiations. Like the Doha Round, these regional talks are also scheduled to terminate by the beginning of 2005. Time is beginning to run out on both.

Unlike Lula's economic policy, the issue of freer trade has yielded no dramatic surprise. Indeed, regarding international relations, from the very beginning Lula and the PT had defined a rather straightforward anti-American, antiglobalization policy. After all, it was the PT that had organized the World Social Forum in Pôrto Alegre to counteract the World

Economic Forum in Davos, Switzerland. During his most recent campaign, Lula was not alone among the candidates in directly opposing Brazilian accession to the FTAA. In December 2002, he provided petroleum to a Venezuela racked by the strike of the national oil producer, PDVSA (Petroleos de Venezuela). And his breakfast meeting on inauguration day with Fidel Castro and Hugo Chavez hardly went unnoticed by the American right. But that initial position, too, has shown considerable moderation, adding to the unhappiness of the Brazilian left. Lula has met twice with President Bush in Washington, most recently in June 2003, along with joint sessions held by 10 cabinet ministers. The final communiqué hinted at a new special relationship.

But the trade issue still remains unresolved. USTR Zoellick held meetings in Brasília in May, preparatory to the Bush-Lula meeting on June 20. The next FTAA ministerial meeting is scheduled for November in Miami; by then, only a year away from the negotiation's scheduled conclusion, it will be clearer whether there will be a hemispheric agreement or merely a wider series of bilateral initiatives. In the interim will be held the Cancun WTO ministerial meeting, and in such forums Brazil has already taken a leadership role. It may give a much better idea of how Mercosur (Mercado Comun del Cono Sur) negotiations with the European Union are evolving, as well as an indication of how much progress Brazil has made with its South American neighbors. Already, the European Union has indicated some greater responsiveness, and Lula's recent visit to London emphasized Brazil's longtime connection with Europe.

The intent of this chapter is to anticipate the consequences of these important events now unfolding. The structure is a play in three acts. In the first section, I elaborate the historical Brazilian position on international trade, emphasizing the strong, and continuing, Brazilian preference for advance at the multilateral level. There I also discuss the parallel strategy of strengthening Mercosur and of extending it to a South American Free Trade Area. The latter was designed as the logical counterpoint to NAFTA, and as a venue in which Brazilian leadership could play a leading role. Building on this discussion, I then elaborate on some of the additional elements introduced by the Lula administration. Necessarily, because it looks ahead, this analysis can hardly be definitive. And I conclude, even more speculatively, by examining the possibility of a bilateral arrangement between Brazil (or Mercosur) and the United States, adding to the regional spaghetti bowl—a result that might appear attractive in the midst of continuing delays in progress on the broader multilateral agenda.

The Past

Brazil has long pursued its destiny as an important component of the international environment. Since the end of World War II, Brazilian foreign

Table 10.1   Brazilian income and trade, 1950–2002

	GDP			Exports		
	Total (billions of dollars)	Per capita (dollars)	Growth (percent)	Growth (percent)	Percent of world trade	Percent of GDP (2000 base)
1950–64	66.4	1,033	6.6	2.7	1.5	4.6
1965–73	152.4	1,694	10.0	8.3	0.9	5.4
1974–80	318.1	2,885	5.8	8.1	1.0	5.4
1981–94	388.1	2,778	2.0	6.0	1.1	6.9
1995–2002	595.1	3,594	2.3	5.7	0.9	9.1

Sources: Comisión Económica para América Latina y el Caribe (CEPAL); and Brazil's Ministério do Desenvolvimento, Indústria e Comércio Exterior.

policy has evolved in five consecutive stages. Table 10.1 provides information on the performance of the economy during each stage.

In the first of these periods, the country, under civilian leadership from 1950 to 1964, progressively moved away from closely paralleling the United States to actively participating in the nonaligned movement in the early 1960s. Initially, Brazil anticipated strong US external support for its development efforts as a response to its aid during the war, both with its military and with a supply of raw materials. But that was not to be, and Brazil drifted away as the Cold War monopolized US attention. The economy's rapid growth through import substitution enhanced Brazil's independence. At the initiation of the Alliance of Progress that pattern was broken, but only briefly. Janio Quadros's more independent foreign policy—he awarded the Cruzeiro do Sul to Che Guevara in 1961—was followed by João Goulart's explicit appeal to internal nationalism and populism as well as his active engagement with the nonaligned nations.

A second, and intense, relationship with the United States ensued after the Brazilian military intervened in March 1964. The new foreign minister defined the objectives clearly: "to defend the security of the continent against aggression and subversion, whether external or internal; to strengthen all the ties with the United States, our great neighbor and friend of the North; to broaden our relations with Western Europe and the Western community of nations."[2] This new policy of concentricity replaced the internationalism of the earlier flirtations with nonalignment with a focus on the hemisphere. But above all, the strategy once again saw the United States as a close and ongoing ally.

For a time thereafter, Brazil's engagement with the United States was obvious: it was the second-largest site of official American foreign presence in the world. External investment was welcomed. Rising inflation gave way to stabilization, participation in the euro-dollar market, mushrooming exports, and the eventual Brazilian "miracle," with rates of ex-

2. Foreign Minister Vasco Leitão da Cunha, as quoted in Fishlow (1978–79, 393).

pansion in the early 1970s of more than 10 percent a year. In that world, still another tack was taken in international policy: to assert a new independence, an opposition to any impediments that would limit the attainment of the *grandeza* that finally appeared within reach. After all, as such rates of expansion continued, Brazil would soon be the envy not merely of its Latin American neighbors but even of Spain and Portugal. Lending flowed after the first oil crisis of 1973; thus, even in its aftermath, Brazil's economy managed to expand at a still-significant though diminished rate of 6 percent a year. Yet the country was substantially dependent on imports of petroleum, and when the second shock came in 1979, a growing nightmare soon replaced the previous dreams.

The debt crisis of the early 1980s was the decisive factor in the next period. Thereafter, the military government, even after Delfim Netto was recalled to manage the economy, could not restore the expansion. By that time, internal matters—the return to civilian government in 1985 and a search (alas unsuccessful) for a new, noninflationary basis for economic growth—had become dominant. External policy fell somewhat by the wayside, with the important exception of a new emphasis on regionalism. Mercosur and the new focus of engagement with neighbors in a democratizing South America date to this period in the later 1980s, when the Reagan administration had little time for Brazil. How little was displayed in the presidential trip to Latin America in 1986, when Reagan stood in São Paulo and erroneously referred to the country he was visiting as Bolivia! On the other hand, it might as well have been. After failed attempts at controlling spiraling inflation, poor economic performance, and finally, in 1993, impeachment of the president, Brazil saw the first period in a century when per capita income failed to increase.

A fifth phase began when Fernando Henrique Cardoso, after being elected as president, successfully implemented the *Real* Plan. Brazil had finally confronted and halted its inflationary upsurge. This time, unlike the failed Cruzado Plan of 1986, macroeconomic policy worked correctly, as income rose and price increases slowed dramatically. But all was not to be sweetness and light. Despite the extensive privatization, mounting government deficits—together with severe recurrent international crises—necessitated sharp devaluation of the *real* in early 1999. That potentially positive adjustment, too, was subsequently confounded in 2000 by the Argentine crisis, an internal energy shortage, and a recession in the United States.

As a consequence, in Cardoso's second term Brazilians saw little progress on fundamental reforms in taxation, social security, the financial system, and so on. The average annual rate of growth declined from 2.5 percent in the first four years to just 2 percent in the second. What had started so gloriously turned into utter political rejection in the campaign of 2002.

These increasing internal macroeconomic difficulties had external consequences. Brazil's strong commitment to Mercosur was complicated by

Table 10.2 Mercosur trade (percent of total exports)

	1990	1995	1999	2000	2001	2002[a]
Argentina	14.8	32.1	30.3	31.8	28.4	22.4
Brazil	4.2	13.2	14.2	14.0	10.9	5.4
Paraguay[b]	39.5	57.4	41.5	63.4	52.4	50.4
Uruguay	35.1	46.2	44.0	42.9	39.1	33.3
Mercosur	8.8	20.6	19.9	21.1	17.2	11.4

Mercosur = Mercado Comun del Cono Sur

a. Data are for first nine months of 2002, except for Paraguay, where they refer to first six months.

b. Data for Paraguay have been corrected to exclude reexports.

Source: CEPAL (2002, 159).

the devaluation of the *real* and the increase in protection required to reduce the burgeoning Brazilian trade deficit. The Argentine recession and eventual financial crisis struck another decisive blow. But much earlier, in 1997, actual intrazonal trade had peaked, and the absence of continuous advance had led to increasing dissatisfaction. For that reason the regional experiment, despite the strong current political commitment, demands closer attention.

The experience of more than a decade of relationships among Argentina, Brazil, Paraguay, and Uruguay may be quickly summarized.[3] From Mercosur's formal start in March 1991 with the Treaty of Asuncion up to the present time, three separate periods may be distinguished (see table 10.2).

The initial phase was one of preparation: an attempt to establish a zone of free trade before the later move to a common market scheduled to occur at the end of 1994. Given the mounting problems in Brazil—this was the era of Fernando Collor de Mello's impeachment and of the inability of his successor, Itamar Franco, to control raging inflation—we can hardly be surprised that relatively limited progress was made toward actually achieving free trade. But it was also the period when intrazonal exchange expanded greatly relative to trade with the outside world. Indeed, from its low starting values, such commerce grew more rapidly in this first interval than subsequently. And the number of products liberalized was substantial, even though the countries retained control over key areas—automobiles, textiles, sugar, and the like—not to mention the areas of capital goods and information technology, which were treated separately. The exceptions, excluding automobiles and sugar, totaled about 25 percent of trade by the end of this initial period.

---

3. A number of general discussions of Mercosur and its evolution are now available. See IDB (2002), which offers an analysis as well as an extensive bibliography.

Alexander Yeats of the World Bank was quick to criticize this first period of expansion as inefficient (Yeats 1998).[4] His point was that much of the growth in intrazonal trade occurred in uncompetitive, capital-intensive products. In other words, the rise in exchange between Argentina and Brazil, a good part of it in the protected automobile sector, was trade diverting rather than trade creating. Had trade occurred on a nondiscriminatory basis, the Mercosur countries could have purchased more from those outside the region and would have wound up better off.

The appearance of this piece motivated a range of responses,[5] but there were two basic criticisms. First, Yeats's focus was on member country exports rather than imports, which show much less difference between the rate of expansion of regional and external trade. This was a period of reduction of tariffs and the beginning of a new policy of openness, when import growth was viewed as important in curbing inflation. Second, the potential economies inherent in the new patterns of specialization would take time to be fully realized. To some degree, as a result of much slower subsequent growth—and indeed a reversal in Mercosur expansion—this debate became irrelevant. But it revealed a sensitive issue that has never quite disappeared. Later works continue to deal with this question, in different ways.

As the Protocol of Ouro Prêto successfully concluded in December 1994, a second phase of movement to a common external tariff was supposed to proceed, building on the expansion of trade that had taken place during the first period. But this new stage encountered real problems: the decline of Argentine national income in 1995 with Mexico's Tequila crisis and, more significantly, the effect on Brazil of the Asian and Russian financial crises. One result of these disturbances was the decision to increase Mercosur's common tariff in December 1997 from 14 percent to 17 percent. Additionally, the lists of national exceptions grew as each of the four members added more. As table 10.2 reveals, intrazonal trade advanced much more slowly after 1995. Nevertheless, formal efforts to liberalize services and other areas of commerce continued.

The devaluation of the *real* in January 1999 and the subsequent slowing of growth within the group set in motion a reversal. Not only did trade among the countries of the group decline but also relations between Brazil and Argentina became progressively more difficult. When Domingo Cavallo resumed his position as finance minister of Argentina in 2001, he both called for a return to the initial idea of a free trade area instead of a common market and unilaterally raised Argentine tariffs on consumer goods to 30 percent and reduced those on capital goods to zero. Even in the

---

4. A version of this article appeared a year earlier as a Policy Research Working Paper.

5. For a summary of the dispute from the standpoint of Yeats's critics, see IDB (2002, 41); for a treatment that extends the basis for questioning Mercosur, see Schiff and Winters (2003, 212, 217–20).

midst of such problems, however, Mercosur hosted its first meeting with the chiefs of government of Europe in 1999, seeking to secure an agreement that would parallel the negotiations of the FTAA. And President Cardoso invited the presidents of all the South American countries to Brasília in the following year to discuss the potential advantages of coordinating their policies.

Mercosur is currently in crisis, a situation made much worse by the domestic difficulties faced by its members. Argentina (and Uruguay) experienced an extraordinary 10.5 percent decline in income in 2002; that same year, Argentina, Uruguay, and Brazil had to resort to the IMF for extensive additional resources. Yet the member states are faced with impending, and important, trade negotiations with deep consequences for Mercosur. Already the new Brazilian and Argentine presidents have begun to grapple with this reality. Early indications, such as the grouping of the countries in other negotiating forums (e.g., those of the Doha and FTAA meetings), are that this regional focus is far from irrelevant. Indeed, given skepticism about possible results in the Cancun and Miami meetings, Mercosur appears to have taken on a new priority.

Historically, Brazil has regarded the multilateral track as more important. That circumstance in part reflects a distribution of trade with the major world markets that has always been fairly well balanced. It also results from the preferences of Brazil's Foreign Office. That leadership role has hardly gone unchallenged. Finance has objected in the past, and successfully. But most recently, the victory over Canada in the WTO dispute between the aircraft manufacturers Bombardier and Embraer provided a new forward impetus. So, too, did the significant Brazilian role in achieving a successful launch of the Doha Round after the WTO failure in Seattle.

In particular, Brazil's positions on three major parts of the WTO agenda were quite important to the final document that emerged in Doha. First, and ever more important as Brazilian exports of agricultural products have been recently increasing, was its insistence on a major reduction of the barriers to such trade faced by developing countries. Here there was apparent consistency with the United States, which like the other developed countries provides its own farmers with agricultural subsidies but of relatively smaller size. Moreover, as the European Union expands toward the east, the issue is not merely French resistance but also the anticipated entry of such important agricultural producers as Poland, Hungary, and others. In Asia, Japan and South Korea are equally hesitant to burden their diminishing agricultural sectors.

Table 10.3, which provides a measure of the international distribution of support to agriculture and the size of that support relative to national income before and after the Uruguay Round, suggests two important points. First, the expenditures of the European Union are comparatively large but have declined relative to those of the other countries included. In particular, the United States' total support increased even while its

Table 10.3 Total agricultural subsidies

	1986–88		2000	
	Total (billions of dollars)	Percent of GDP	Total (billions of dollars)	Percent of GDP
European Union	109.7	2.6	102.4	1.4
United States	68.1	1.4	92.1	0.9
Japan	58.2	2.4	68.2	1.4
South Korea	14.2	10.0	22.8	5.0
OECD	302.1	2.3	321.1	1.3

Source: OECD, Agricultural Policies in OECD Countries 2002, 176.

share declined. Second, the outlays by both Japan and South Korea exceed the relative contribution of their agricultural sectors to national income. While the corresponding barriers to free trade are now relatively smaller than they were before the Uruguay Round, they remain large enough to severely limit international trade. Agricultural subsidies now total $1 billion a day, a sum far exceeding the amount available for economic development assistance.[6]

The major reduction in trade-distorting subsidies proposed by the United States would accelerate their relative decline following the Uruguay Round agreement. Europe has been reluctant to accept, but has recently begun to shift its position. Brazil and the United States would be more closely allied on this issue were it not for the subsidy increases voted by the US Congress in the 2002 Farm Bill and the American quotas and high tariffs that directly handicap key Brazilian exports such as sugar, orange juice, and tobacco.

Much more fundamental has been the United States' insistence that such farm subsidy issues be treated only in the multilateral setting and not in the FTAA negotiations. Brazil's rapid current growth in agricultural exports—a class of goods, basic and processed, that accounts for almost 30 percent of the country's total sales abroad—makes this issue an especially important one, and not only in its dealings with the United States. Europe, which receives a larger share of such products from Brazil, is also a major current target in the Doha Round and in the Mercosur-EU negotiations.

A second advance at Doha had been US acquiescence in discussion of antidumping and similar protective provisions enacted by sections 201 and 301 of the Trade Act of 1974. This acceptance stands in dramatic contrast to the continuing imposition of these sanctions. Data compiled by the WTO show that the United States has brought 257 actions against imports

---

6. To be sure, these gross data do not differentiate between consequences of domestic policies that distort trade and those that redistribute income. But they do measure the extent to which agricultural interests make their voices heard.

since 1995, more than any other country, and that steel products account for one-third of the measures taken by all members (WTO, *Annual Report* [2003], 23). The increased protection imposed by the United States in 2002 for the benefit of the steel industry—recently ruled illegal, in a decision now under appeal—especially riled Brazil, less because of the severity of its effects (Russia, Europe, and South Korea felt them much more) than because it involved an industrial sector in which Brazil had gained a comparative advantage. If export emphasis, not agriculture alone, is to be an important part of future Brazilian policy, then such additional sectors as steel, automobiles, cell phones, and the like become central.

Here, too, the US position is clear as far as the FTAA is concerned: there is no need to take up this issue during those negotiations; only at the multilateral level can any progress occur. Brazil's reaction is to argue that such matters as government purchases and foreign investment should similarly be excluded from FTAA concern and left exclusively to the multilateral arena. This position, of course, goes very much counter to United States efforts to ensure that any FTAA treaty be WTO-plus in its provisions in these areas. In this matter, unlike in agriculture, Brazil's interests appear to clearly differ from those of the United States, leaving no easy solution.

Such difficulty is especially characteristic of the third issue addressed at Doha: the exemption of certain medicines from the rules that have applied to intellectual property rights since the Uruguay Round. Brazil and South Africa were quite eager to substitute generic alternatives for the treatment of AIDS; India, as a potential supplier, was equally interested. Drugs targeting malaria and tuberculosis were also included. Needless to say, pharmaceutical firms in the United States (and Europe) were appalled. But this dramatic gain was essential to the satisfactory conclusion of the Doha meeting, and it was a source of great Brazilian satisfaction. Indeed, in subsequent negotiations, international firms, faced with the threat of generic substitutes, have agreed to significantly reduce the price of AIDS medications. Brazil's approach to AIDS has received wide and quite favorable notice.

Ironically, events in the world's wealthiest country helped to shift the balance toward relaxing patent protection. The US anthrax scare in the aftermath of the terrorist attacks of September 11 caused a huge demand for Cipro—and supplies of the patented drug were inadequate as well as expensive. The United States quickly secured a major reduction in price from Bayer. That decision, so soon after Doha, provided dramatic support for the position of the developing countries. Similar gains are now being sought in other fields where important health advances have occurred. And as reimbursement for prescription drugs under Medicare has suddenly emerged as a major issue in the United States, their high costs—particularly in contrast with the prices for the same drugs under the national Canadian system—have become a matter of daily comment. That may help to explain the recent agreement to allow exports of generic drugs to poor countries, as Brazil has sought.

Such substantial Brazilian gains at Doha, although widely promoted nationally, did little to help the political ambitions of the government's candidate, former minister of health José Serra, in the presidential elections of 2002. Worried about rising inflation and internal debt, reduced access to foreign capital, and slower growth, as well as increasing crime in urban areas and mounting unemployment, Brazilians wanted change. As noted earlier, in the runoff Luiz Inácio Lula da Silva, the candidate of the Workers' Party, won a convincing victory; at the same time, the PT gained a leading but far from a majority position in congressional elections.

The Present

In the run-up to the election and immediately after, Brazilian markets reflected the worries of the domestic and the international business communities. The exchange rate dropped considerably, moving to a value of 4 reais to the dollar; to counter the uncertainty, domestic interest rates were progressively raised in the last months of the Cardoso administration to 26 percent; inflation rose, especially prices of international goods; and there was even much talk of the inevitable rescheduling of the domestic debt that would have to take place.

To the surprise of many, the new government, guided by Finance Minister Antonio Palocci, has responded to the crisis by imposing even tighter monetary and fiscal policies. Simultaneously, the Workers' Party has taken on the task of pushing through Congress many of the needed changes that they had earlier opposed: greater independence of the central bank, reform of the social security provisions for public employees, revisions in the tax system, and modernization of the labor laws. The results have included impressive real appreciation of the exchange rate and the beginnings of interest rate reduction that should accelerate over coming months.

Such continuity in domestic economic policy has been accompanied by continuity in the foreign sphere. We therefore can focus on the three elements that define current international economic policy.[7]

The first is the strengthening of Mercosur and the continuation of efforts to extend it to a free trade area within South America. It is essential to appreciate that the benefits of this relationship, seen from the context of Brazil, go beyond simple economics.

> Mercosur is a fundamentally *political* decision that is realized as a consequence of *economic* actions. . . . Mercosur emerges as an exercise of convergence of interests between countries situated, in general terms, at the *same level of economic and social development*, despite differences in their size. . . . In sum, Mercosur is a modest con-

---

7. In a recent speech Celso Amorim, the minister of foreign affairs, sets out the current Brazilian position in greater detail; see Amorim (2003).

struction of integration that functions as a condominium, with relative permeability and association between its present few members.[8] (Almeida 2002, 31; emphasis his)

There is little doubt that Lula's election has led to even greater Brazilian commitment to this objective than had been seen earlier. The recent election of Néstor Kirchner as Argentine president—defeating Carlos Menem, who earlier had argued for direct Argentine economic integration with the United States—reinforces the Brazilian position. There has been a new emphasis on the four members of Mercosur presenting a unified front in negotiations, first with the Andean countries, then with the European Union, and finally with the United States. And, not least important, Brazil is able to exercise leadership in this venue.

The second element is negotiations within the WTO. Here, as with the FTAA and the pact with the European Union, the focus is primarily economic. But these forums now are drawing greater Brazilian interest as a result of the rapid increase in exports achieved in the past year. For the first time in some 30 years, it is genuinely possible that exports may spark a domestic recovery. The agricultural sector is making a strong contribution as well. And in such a world, in the words of Foreign Minister Celso Amorim, the "policies and practices of the developed countries with their billion-dollar subsidies and arbitrary recourse to measures of commercial protection penalize the more efficient producers instead of recognizing them" (Amorim 2003, 2).

Clearly the Brazilian preference is to focus on the WTO, particularly given the recent entry of China and potential accession of Russia, as the source of the real benefits. The WTO's importance has been heightened by its recent finding that US safeguards on steel products were illegal, a case in which Brazil was among the complainants. In this forum, Brazilian skill and knowledge have begun producing results. As a consequence, the role of the Foreign Office has been enhanced; at the same time, the claims of Brazil for a permanent seat on the UN Security Council have been strengthened.

The Doha Round offers an opportunity for more than progress on the questions of agricultural subsidies and antidumping restrictions; it also may make possible a revision of the Agreement on Trade-Related Aspects of Intellectual Property Rights (TRIPs) reached in the Uruguay Round—and not merely, as the United States insists, as it pertains to drugs used to treat HIV-AIDS, malaria, and tuberculosis. Additionally, Brazil, in conjunction with other developing nations, seeks a modification of the Trade-Related Investment Measures (TRIMs) accord to permit a national policy of greater industrial promotion, particularly in high-technology spheres. Finally, it strongly prefers to negotiate on such matters as services, invest-

---

8. Translations are mine throughout.

ments, governmental purchases, and intellectual property rights within the WTO rather than to open these subjects to the United States' WTO-plus strategy in negotiating the FTAA.

The FTAA, accordingly, comes last in Brazilian priorities—behind even the negotiations with the European Union. In those, at least, Brazil sees itself making no additional concessions beyond those already under discussion in the Doha Round. And there as well, Brazil sees the possibility of applying a little "competitive liberalization," in the manner of the United States. In the discussions surrounding the FTAA, Mercosur has already responded to the US decision to differentiate among CARICOM (the Caribbean Common Market), the countries of Central America, the Andean Community, and Mercosur by refusing to submit offers for tariff reductions in services; nor have any of the four countries in the group presented a formal position on investments or governmental purchases. Increasingly, Brazil seems to favor a minimal FTAA rather than any strategy that foresees replication of the NAFTA and US-Chile agreements.

This stance has great domestic appeal, and not merely to the supporters of the PT. Much of the industrial sector (though not all) concurs. Brazilian calculations of the benefits that could be anticipated from successful conclusion of the FTAA negotiations seem consistently to indicate limited, and unequally distributed, benefits. In particular, Brazil is not a clear beneficiary. Thus Marcelo de Abreu reports computable general equilibrium results showing Brazilian exports to the United States increasing 9 percent while corresponding imports rise 23 percent, figures consistent with other partial equilibrium estimates by himself and others (Abreu, forthcoming).

But a review of other recent quantitative models demonstrates a lack of consensus (see Castilho 2002). Much depends on the specific conditions imposed—dynamic versus static, inclusion of nontariff barriers, degree of disaggregation, demand elasticities utilized, base year of the study, and so forth. The selection reported here in table 10.4—limited to the 1999–2001 period—contains five studies. All presume full liberalization, either within the FTAA or with the European Union, and some with both. They thereby provide apparent upper-bound estimates of the practical consequences of trade integration. On the other side, comparison of the initial calculations and actual results of NAFTA show a tendency toward understatement of the changes in trade that resulted, because such advances in commercial policy have been associated with new reasons for gains in investment and productivity.

The results presented in table 10.4 clearly suggest that the FTAA should not lead to Brazilian imports exceeding exports. Only one study predicts such an outcome, and there the deviation is virtually zero. Second, and somewhat surprisingly given that Brazil exports relatively more agricultural products to Europe than to the United States, the orders of magni-

Table 10.4 Results of econometric studies of the impact on Brazil of the FTAA (percent change)

	FTAA					FTAA and European Union	
	Study 1	Study 2	Study 3	Study 4	Study 5	Study 1	Study 5
Total imports	12.7	7.0	29.5	6.2	8.0	25.9	10.9
Total exports	17.5	14.0	38.0	10.0	7.3	35.7	8.4
GDP	7.0	n.a.	0.5	4.0	4.5	13.3	4.5

Studies: 1. Wanatuki and Monteagudo (2001); 2. Carvalho and Parente (1999); 3. Roland-Holst and van der Mensbrugghe (2001); 4. Diao, Diaz-Bonilla, and Robinson (2001); 5. Tourinho and Kume (2002).

Source: Castilho (2002, 23).

tude of benefits are quite similar in both markets. While the size of total trade is similar, one would expect the differences in composition to have had greater effect. Third, the consequence of liberalization of trade both with the European Union and with the United States appears dramatically different in the two relevant studies (Wanatuki and Monteagudo 2001; Tourinho and Kume 2002): in one, the addition of the European Union makes little difference; in the other, the changes caused by each liberalization separately are in effect added to create a much larger total.

Thus it is not obvious that the reduction of Brazilian protection under the FTAA will lead to especially great difficulties. Certain sectors will be harmed initially, but many of these have already adjusted to the much greater level of imports that have flowed into Brazil in recent years as tariffs have been lowered. The reality will likely be far different from what those violently opposed to the agreement envision. This, of course, brings us to the central point. Policymakers in Europe have been far more willing than those in the United States to support Brazil politically, and to accept Lula. Bush's recent efforts at conciliation represent a major change in US policy, and they may lead to much better relations than have been experienced in the past few years. But more than rhetoric will be needed to achieve any gains.

We may therefore conclude that Brazilian policy on international trade has changed little. Its domestic economic recovery has enabled Brazil to express its external preferences more effectively now than in the past, and much of the current restatement of policy reflects that new ability. The foreign minister makes this case clearly when he maintains that

> the route of credibility that the Brazilian economy has entered, the commitment to fight poverty and hunger, the attention given to human rights, and the consolidation of democracy are factors that trace a picture of international respectability and enormously help the external action of the government in its various directions, including that of foreign trade. (Amorim 2003, 5)

The Future

Brazil has thus far performed well as the final phases of its three separate trade negotiations approach. All—the Doha Round, the FTAA, and the Mercosur treaty with the European Union—are scheduled to conclude at the beginning of 2005. Moreover, its international position has been much strengthened by the effective leadership demonstrated over the first six months of Lula's presidency. His acceptance reaches far beyond the domestic sphere: abroad in Europe he has been equally effective, most recently winning Tony Blair's open support for a permanent Security Council position.

In the Doha Round, Brazil has had an opportunity to clarify its position over the past year.[9] Agriculture has been chosen as the premier area for significant concessions, and recent export performance only enhances its importance. But beyond that, there is a well-defined Brazilian stand on industrial products, services, review of the TRIPs and TRIMs agreements, and so on. On the Singapore issues, which include discussions on investment, government purchases, competition policy, and easing of commercial restrictions (i.e., trade facilitation), Brazil is neutral. It wishes to see what gains can be achieved before announcing potential concessions here.

The still-tenuous European and US agreement on agriculture seemingly had provided the impetus at the WTO ministerial in Cancun in September 2003 to avoid what all would regard as disaster. Alas, it contributed to breakdown and one directly confronting the United States and Brazil. That inability to reach consensus left the Doha Round in total disrepair, awaiting further negotiations in Geneva.

That conclusion was directly responsible for a different resolution at the FTAA discussion in Miami in November, where Brazil and the United States agreed to a short statement postponing any substantive decision until continuing rounds of meetings in 2004. The compromise signaled stalemate. The United States is free to negotiate bilaterally with a number of additional countries in the region, those that are prepared to accept FTAs equivalent to the earlier agreement with Chile. Brazil and Mercosur were deliberately not among the chosen. They will await the continuing FTAA meetings to see whether any minimal regionwide framework evolves.

This lack of consensus has occurred despite the apparently closer relationship with the United States that Brazil has achieved in recent months. Lula and Bush have met twice, the last including separate sessions between 10 Brazilian ministers and their US counterparts, and the final joint statement was very positive; it began, "The United States and Brazil resolve to create a closer and qualitatively stronger relationship between

---

9. For a good summary, see Filho (2003, 6–7).

our two countries. It is time to chart a newly purposeful direction in our relationship . . . in order to promote hemispheric and global cooperation" ("Joint Statement" 2003). American Ambassador Donna Hrinak foresaw such an outcome before the meeting itself: "Brazil and the US are jointly assuming responsibility for leading the hemisphere toward free trade and integration" (quoted in *Brazil News*, June 2003, 2).

Yet in reality, Brazilian enthusiasm about the FTAA seems not quite to match this positive news emanating from Washington. First of all, the current second-ranking figure at Itamaraty, Ambassador Samuel Pinheiro, is well known for his negative views on the FTAA; they had led, after all, to his demotion by the previous foreign minister, Celso Lafer. Before Zoellick's visit to Brazil in May, Pinheiro wrote, in an article on the PT Web site, "Brazilian society ought to mobilize in defense of preserving the sovereign right of Brazil to have a development policy . . . that a future FTAA would come to prevent definitively and legally" (quoted in *Estado de São Paulo* Web site, May 28, 2003).

In an interview published in *Isto É* on July 5, 2003, Rubens Barbosa, currently Brazil's ambassador to Washington, was almost as disapproving, declaring that the FTAA could not be concluded without the simultaneous conclusion of the Doha negotiations. Moreover, he directly criticized the United States for the failure to allow discussion of antidumping legislation and subsidies, indicating that Brazil's response was to eliminate intellectual property and investment from the FTAA. And finally, Foreign Minister Amorim, in an article appearing in the *Fôlha de São Paulo* on July 8, 2003, wrote:

> President Lula approved the blueprint of the Brazilian position on FTAA negotiations. . . . [It] can be described as follows: 1) the substance of the themes of access to the goods market, and in limited form, for services and investments, would be treated in a 4 + 1 negotiation between Mercosul and the United States; 2) the FTAA process would focus on some basic elements, such as resolution of controversies, special and differential treatment for developing countries, compensation funds, sanitary rules, and commercial trade facilitation; 3) the more sensitive themes that would represent new obligations for Brazil, such as the normative part of intellectual property, services, investments, and governmental purchases, would be transferred to the WTO[.][10]

This was exactly the position subsequently put forth by Brazil at the vice ministerial meeting in El Salvador held shortly thereafter. There was, as a consequence, little advance. Indeed, in the words of one newspaper, "On one side, there is Brazil, which, with the support of the Mercosur countries, disagrees with the present structure of the negotiations. On the other, there are the other 30 beneficiaries of the project, who did not see any benefit in the adoption of the new Brazilian architecture" (*O Estado de São Paulo*, July 16, 2003).

---

10. "Tendencias e Debates," *Fôlha de São Paulo*, July 8, 2003.

This does not sound as though there is much prospect of a definite advance. The positions that have been taken are unlikely to shift in a brief span of time.

The same statement also applies on the US side of the negotiations. Trade issues generally move slowly in presidential election years. NAFTA was an exception that came about as a consequence of Mexican insistence in moving forward. And with the electoral loss of the incumbent 1992, one may doubt the capability even of USTR Zoellick to push matters along in 2004. Given all the bilateral discussions already on the US agenda, a more realistic assessment is that both the Doha Round and the FTAA will have their deadlines extended. That very much seems to be the expectation in Washington, and a decision will be made very soon.

In these circumstances, why not a bilateral pact between the United States and Brazil, or, much more probably, with Mercosur? In principle, this arrangement would suit Brazilian interests quite well. It would allow Brazil to bypass the WTO-plus requirement that the United States currently insists on in its FTAA negotiations; it is consistent with the differentiation of tariff offers among groups of Latin American countries thus far made by the United States; and it provides greater leverage in the simultaneous discussions under way with the European Union to permit initial concessions—to be extended in the Doha Round—in agriculture. Not least, it enables the Lula government to extract an important, and early, diplomatic victory in its international trade negotiations that equals its earlier advance in domestic economic policy.

The more difficult problem is to provide a rationale for US compliance, which would seemingly contradict the basic tenets of its current policy, as reiterated most recently at the El Salvador meeting. But that negotiating position does not take into account the probability that an additional delay will occur. By embracing a strategy of bilateral advance with Brazil and Mercosur, the United States would transform the postponement of the FTAA and the Doha Round from a negative to a positive signal, indicating that the present policy of continued growth of trade is alive and well.

Such a strategy is consistent with the many additional discussions now in progress. A separate agreement with Central America is certainly likely to emerge, adding those countries to NAFTA; why not a more limited advance with Mercosur at the same time? Moreover, to the extent that such an advance enables Mercosur to achieve some agricultural concessions from the European Union, that step would signal potential future gains for the United States in the multilateral discussions.

The cost—added complication in the existing spaghetti bowl of trade associations—is minor relative to the benefits of achieving a real, closer US relationship with Brazil and South America. That achievement could later turn out to be a very positive element in the ongoing Doha discussions, as well as in addressing the broader hemispheric agenda involving drugs, money laundering, immigration, corruption, judicial standards, and so forth.

Such an arrangement, moreover, preserves and indeed enhances Mercosur's identity, which is very much in need of updating. Earlier expectations have gone unmet. The new leaders of Brazil and Argentina both see this relationship as central to their foreign policy. A partial agreement with the United States could provide a positive impulse to renegotiation among the four countries. After the devaluations of Brazil's and Argentina's currencies, and the great reduction in trade among them, a new basis is required if the commercial relationship is to keep pace with the closer political interactions of the last year.

At root, continuing Brazilian expansion over the next decade requires substantial revision in the role of foreign trade. For too long, rhetoric about the need to take advantage of surging international commerce—which has grown at about twice the rate of national product over the past half century—has been accompanied by far too little action. The immediate interests of the domestic market have always dominated, translating into protection and subsidies in one form or another. Brazil should now be exporting just about twice the percentage of GDP—10 percent—it has currently achieved. If it is to attain that goal, it will have to be just as aggressive in the range of internal economic policies it follows as in the international policies it promulgates.

Though there seems to be virtual consensus in Brazil at the present time favoring such an increase in exports, two challenges remain. First, Brazil must be able to sustain an emphasis on the external market once domestic demand recovers. Second, it must be able to match the regular rise in exports with corresponding increases in imports, rather than seeking to protect the internal market. Meeting these challenges would irrevocably alter the future.

Logic, internal economic policy, and foreign relations do not always intersect. Here at last is an issue where they do. Brazil has already defined its conditions in a way that makes such a bilateral, or 4 + 1, arrangement a natural approach to continuing progress toward freer and greater trade. What remains to be seen is the ultimate US response. It would seem far better to incorporate Brazil within expanding and freer, hemispheric trade than to punish it with isolation.

References

Abreu, Marcelo Paiva de. Forthcoming. The Political Economy of Economic Integration in the Americas: Latin American Interests. In *FTAA and Beyond: Prospects for Integration in the Americas*, ed. Antoni Estevadeordal, Dani Rodrik, Alan Taylor, and Andres Velasco. Cambridge, MA: Harvard University Press.

Almeida, Paulo Roberto de. 2002. *Mercosur em sua primera decada (1991–2001): Uma avaliacão politica a partir do Brasil.* INTAL-ITD-STA Document 14. Buenos Aires: INTAL.

Amorim, Celso. 2003. As transformações na ordem mundial e as posições multilateral e regional do Brasil. Speech presented at the XV Forum Nácional, Rio de Janeiro (May 20–22).

Bergsten, C. Fred. 1996. Globalizing Free Trade. *Foreign Affairs* 75, no. 3 (May–June): 105–20.

Carvalho, Alexandre, and Andreia Parente. 1999. *Impactos comercias da área de livre comércio das Américas.* Texto para Discussão no. 635. Brasília: Instituto de Pequisa Econômica Aplicada.

Castilho, Marta R. 2002. *Impactos de acordos comerciais sobre a econômia Brasileira: Resenha dos trabalhos recentes.* Texto para Discussão no. 936. Rio de Janeiro: Instituto de Pequisa Econômica Aplicada.

Comisión Económica para América Latina y el Caribe (CEPAL). 2002. *Panorama de la inserción internacional de América Latina y el Caribe, 2001–2002.* Santiago: CEPAL.

Diao, Xinshen, Eugenio Diaz-Bonilla, and Sherman Robinson. 2001. Scenarios for Trade Integration in the Americas. Paper presented in the seminar Impacts of Trade Liberalization on Latin America and the Caribbean, sponsored by CEPII and the IDB, Washington (November 5–6).

Filho, Clodoaldo Hugueney. 2003. A nova rodada de negociações multilaterais da OMC. Paper presented at the XV Fórum Nacional, Rio de Janeiro (May 20–22).

Fishlow, Albert. 1978–79. Flying Down to Rio: Perspectives on US-Brazil Relations. *Foreign Affairs* 57, no. 2 (winter): 387–405.

Inter-American Development Bank (IDB). 2002. *Beyond Borders: The New Regionalism in Latin America.* Washington: Inter-American Development Bank; Baltimore: distributed by Johns Hopkins University Press.

Joint Statement between the United States of America and the Federative Republic of Brazil. 2003. www.whitehouse.gov/news/releases/2003/06/20030620-11.html (June 20).

Roland-Holst, David, and Dominique van der Mensbrugghe. 2001. Regionalism versus Globalization in the Americas: Empirical Evidence on Opportunities and Challenges. Paper presented in the seminar Impacts of Trade Liberalization on Latin America and the Caribbean, sponsored by CEPII and the IDB, Washington (November 5–6).

Schiff, Maurice, and L. Alan Winters. 2003. *Regional Integration and Development.* Washington: World Bank.

Secretario do Itamaraty ataca Alca em artigo para site do PT. 2003. *O Estado de S. Paulo.* www.estado.estadao.com.br (May 28).

Tourinho, Octávio Augusto Fontes, and Honorio Kume. 2002. Os impactos setoriais de acordos de comercio: analise com um modelo CGE da econômia brasileira. Instituto de Pequisa Econômica Aplicada, Rio de Janeiro. Photocopy.

Wanatuki, Mazakazu, and Josefina Monteagudo. 2001. Regional Trade Agreements for Mercosur: The FTAA and the FTA with the European Union. Paper presented in the seminar Impacts of Trade Liberalization on Latin America and the Caribbean, sponsored by CEPII and the IDB, Washington (November 5–6).

Yeats, Alexander. 1998. Does Mercosur's Trade Performance Raise Concerns about the Effects of Regional Trade Arrangements? *World Bank Economic Review* 12, no. 1 (January): 1–28.

V

NEW INITIATIVES IN
AFRICA AND THE MIDDLE EAST

11

Egypt, Morocco, and the United States

AHMED GALAL AND ROBERT Z. LAWRENCE

The political importance of the Middle East to the United States is evident from the willingness of the United States to wage a war in Iraq, the political capital some US administrations have invested in resolving the Palestinian-Israeli conflict, and the amount of aid extended to such countries as Egypt and Israel. It is not surprising, therefore, that political rather than economic considerations have driven US free trade agreements (FTAs) in the Middle East. This is true of the agreements that the United States has already implemented (with Israel and Jordan), as well as agreements that are being contemplated with other countries in the region and with the region as a whole. Indeed, it can be argued that FTAs between the United States and Middle Eastern countries are fundamentally about potentially large political (and consequently economic) gains for the United States, while the potential gains to the countries themselves are mostly economic in nature (and consequently political).[1]

Nonetheless, it is risky, even for the United States, to focus on politics alone. The history of the Middle East, like that of many other regions, is replete with failed regional economic integration initiatives that were purely politically motivated and not supported by the necessary economic measures. In the long run, not only did these initiatives fail to pro-

Ahmed Galal is executive director and director of research for the Egyptian Center for Economic Studies (ECES) in Cairo and Robert Z. Lawrence is a senior fellow at the Institute for International Economics. They are the authors of Building Bridges: An Egypt-US Free Trade Agreement *(Brookings Institution Press, 1998).*

1. See Gresser (2003) for the case that freer trade would support the war against terror.

vide economic benefits, but their failures ultimately led to disillusion, disappointment, and a loss of credibility that inflicted political damage as well. Exacerbating this problem is the tendency over time for people to take the political gains for granted; to offset these, increasing economic benefits are required.

Thus, even those interested in the political benefits of FTAs must appraise their economic basis. The key questions relate to the (static) benefits that result from trade creation, the losses from trade diversion, and the dynamic benefits that result if the agreement stimulates productivity growth and investment, enhances policy credibility, and reinforces domestic economic reforms and institutional development. The answers to these questions will depend heavily on the form these agreements take and on the other policies that accompany them. Of particular importance is whether the agreements focus simply on border barriers (shallow integration) or include investment, services, and other rules and institutions (deeper integration); whether the agreements are seen as sufficient in themselves or are used to leverage domestic economic reforms. Moreover, even if the net benefits are positive, a crucial issue is whether they detract from or complement multilateral liberalization that could be even more beneficial.

An appraisal of FTAs between the United States and Egypt and the United States and Morocco is also timely. In a commencement address at the University of South Carolina on May 9, 2003, President George W. Bush proposed "the establishment of a US–Middle East free trade area within a decade." US Trade Representative Robert Zoellick amplified the point in remarks before the World Economic Forum meeting in Jordan on June 23, 2003, describing the regional FTA with the United States as representing a goal that will be achieved by a series of cumulative measures that include (1) actively supporting World Trade Organization (WTO) membership of "peaceful countries that seek it," (2) increased use of the Generalized System of Preferences (GSP), (3) negotiation of trade and investment facilitation agreements (TIFAs) that often precede FTAs, (4) bilateral investment treaties (BITs), (5) bilateral FTAs such as those currently being negotiated with Morocco and planned with Bahrain, (6) the extension of these agreements to include neighboring countries, and, (7) ultimately, their extension to the whole region.

At the time of this writing, the United States has not announced negotiations for an FTA with Egypt, but Egypt is often mentioned as a potential FTA candidate. Accordingly, the first section of this chapter considers some key economic and political characteristics of Egypt as a potential FTA partner. The next section considers the likely impact of an Egypt-US FTA. The United States and Morocco have already begun negotiations for a free trade agreement. The final sections of the chapter mirror the Egyptian analysis with a similar discussion of Morocco as a partner and of the likely economic impact of a US-Morocco FTA. Some brief conclusions and comparisons are then provided.

Egypt as a Potential Partner

If the United States were to select its FTA partners based on relative political importance in their regions, Egypt would arguably top the list among Arab states. If the selection criteria were derived from the potential of boosting economic reforms in partner countries with ample demonstration effects as a reform model, Egypt would undoubtedly qualify. And if the choice were based on the potential of the partner country to take full advantage of an agreement, Egypt seems reasonably well positioned, assuming that the FTA is accompanied by further domestic reforms and additional trade liberalization. Below is a brief discussion of what makes Egypt a viable political and economic FTA partner to the United States.

Key Political Characteristics

Egypt is the largest Arab country, with 66 million inhabitants, or 23 percent of the regional population. It has played a key role in shaping the politics of the region in recent decades. Most notably, Egypt has hosted the Arab League since its inception in 1945, led the region's efforts toward resolving the Palestinian-Israeli conflict, and began fighting Islamic extremists decades before September 11. Although the process is incomplete, Egypt has been undergoing a democratic transition over the past couple of decades. Changes have included adopting a multiparty system, increasing the freedom of the press, and strengthening the role of civil society. Egypt has also been a cultural hub for Arab countries, providing most of the movies, books, and TV programs produced in Arabic. Furthermore, some 2 million Egyptians are currently working in neighboring countries in various professions.

For these reasons, Egypt came to be seen by many of its neighbors as a country to emulate. Over the past half century, Egypt led the liberation movement from colonial powers, offered the region a vision of Pan-Arabism and Arab socialism, and more recently embraced a model of gradual political and economic liberalization. That many Arab countries adopted similar ideas after Egypt did lends credence to the view that Egypt's influence extends beyond its borders. Accordingly, support given to the reform movement in Egypt through various measures, including a well-designed FTA with the United States, could lead to a positive demonstration effect throughout the region.

Key Economic Characteristics

Although Egypt is a developing country with a per capita income of about $1,530, its economy is diversified; industry and mining account for 33 percent of GDP, agriculture for 16 percent, and services for 50 percent. Egypt is also reasonably well endowed with relatively cheap and skilled labor, abundant historical sites and other tourism attractions, and moderate natural resources (oil and natural gas). Water is available from the Nile. These characteristics suggest that Egypt could take advantage of more open markets abroad, provided domestic policies are aligned to promote exports.

As a destination for imports and a potential location for foreign direct investment (FDI), Egypt offers a relatively large market. The size of that market depends not only on its large population and a GDP of about $100 billion, but more significantly on the proximity of Egypt to Europe (with which Egypt has concluded an industrial tariff-free pact) and its central location in the Arab world (among countries with which Egypt is also an FTA partner). With an enlarged market, Egypt has the potential to serve as an export base for FDI in industries with substantial economies of scale.

Current State of Reform

Comparative advantage can be stifled, however, by policy-induced distortions. In this regard, Egypt has made significant progress on policy in recent years, although the reform process remains incomplete. It partially departed from its inward-looking and state-led development strategy, which had lasted for decades, in 1974. However, the real shift to a market-based and private-sector-led strategy came in 1991, when Egypt initiated far-reaching reforms in the tradition of the Washington Consensus. One consequence of these reforms is that the private sector now accounts for 70 percent of total investment and 73 percent of GDP, compared with 41 percent and 62 percent, respectively, in 1990–91.

Several studies have assessed the stabilization program of the 1990s, concluding that it was one of the most successful in the developing world (e.g., Subramanian 1997). The program included the unification and devaluation of the Egyptian pound, financial-sector and capital account liberalization, and a drastic reduction in the fiscal deficit (from 20 percent in 1990–91 to 1 percent in 1997–98).[2] Inflation came down to a single digit, and the economy grew at an average rate of 5 percent for most of the 1990s.

---

2. For other measures of structural change, see Dasgupta, Keller, and Srinivasan (2002).

The estimated stabilization reform index[3] (given in figure 11.1) shows that Egypt not only has caught up with several reforming countries in the region but also fares well in comparison to other developing countries.

Structural reforms were also initiated in the early 1990s, but this effort remains work in progress. The reforms included trade liberalization, privatization of state-owned enterprises, and various improvements in the business environment. The trade liberalization effort is elaborated below. The cumulative proceeds from privatization amounted to 4.7 percent of GDP in 2001. As for the business environment, investment laws were changed to allow foreign participation without restrictions, protect ownership rights, and guarantee repatriation of profits. A stronger intellectual property rights law has also been passed, along with a money-laundering law. More recently, the parliament approved a new labor law that accords firms greater flexibility in return for workers' right to strike and engage in collective bargaining. In addition, a new income tax law, about to be submitted to parliament, will reduce the corporate tax rate to 30 percent. At the sectoral level, reforms were carried out in telecommunications and electricity to encourage private-sector participation, to increase competition where possible, and to regulate the monopolistic segments of the market.[4]

Notwithstanding these reforms, the estimated structural reform index[5] (shown in figure 11.2) indicates that Egypt lags behind a sample of MENA (Middle East and North Africa) countries as well as other developing countries. Furthermore, the reform process has slowed down in recent years. An FTA with the United States could boost economic reform and

---

3. The index is a composite of current account balance, fiscal balance, inflation rate, and exchange rate premium. The four elements are given equal weights. All data are normalized using the formula

$$Xjt = \frac{(W - Vjt)}{(W - B)}$$

where

Xjt	is the normalization value j for year t.
Vjt	is the value of variable for country j in year t.
B	is the best value for all countries and all years.
W	is the worst value of all countries and years.

4. The private sector was awarded two licenses to provide mobile phone services, and a new telecommunications law was passed in 2002.

5. This index is a composite of trade policy (measured by unweighted average tariffs), tax policy (measured by highest marginal corporate and individual tax rates), exchange rate overvaluation (measured by deviation from purchasing power parity), and privatization (measured by cumulative privatization proceeds as share of GDP). The four elements are given equal weight, with the weight for the tax policy equally divided between individual and corporate tax rates. All data are normalized using the formula in footnote 3.

Figure 11.1 Economic stabilization in Egypt versus different regions

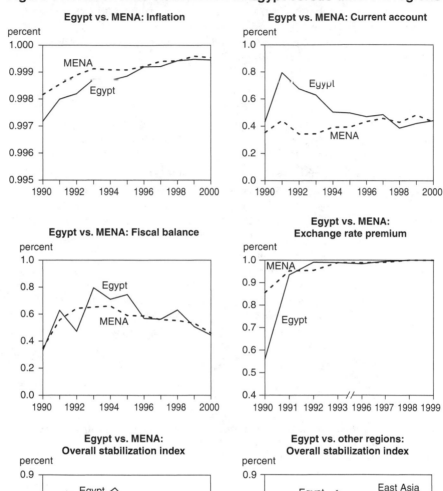

Note: MENA includes Egypt, Jordan, Morocco, and Tunisia. Latin America includes Argentina, Bolivia, Brazil, Chile, Colombia, Mexico, Peru, and Venezuela. South Asia includes India and Pakistan. East Asia and Pacific includes China, Indonesia, Korea, Malaysia, the Philippines, and Thailand.

Figure 11.2 Structural reform in Egypt versus different regions

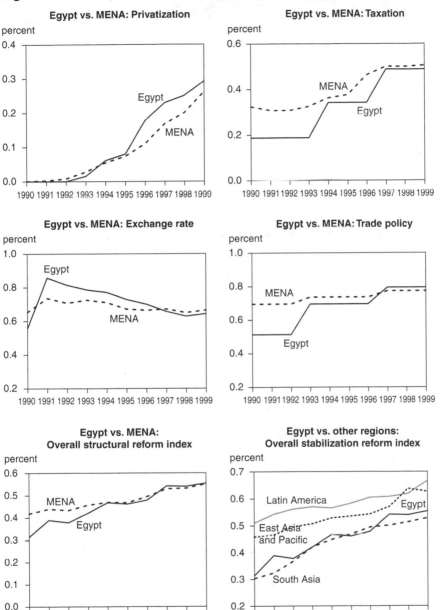

Note: MENA includes Egypt, Jordan, Morocco, and Tunisia. Latin America includes Argentina, Bolivia, Brazil, Chile, Colombia, Mexico, Peru, and Venezuela. South Asia includes India and Pakistan. East Asia and Pacific includes China, Indonesia, Korea, Malaysia, the Philippines, and Thailand.

enable the Egyptian economy to attract FDI, improve efficiency, and generate much-needed productive jobs for a growing labor force.

Trade Patterns and Policies

Egypt's trade deficit averaged 10 percent of GDP over the past three years. This deficit was financed mainly by revenues from tourism, workers' remittances, and the Suez Canal. Exports averaged about 6.6 percent of GDP over the period between 1996–97 and 2001–02. The European Union and the United States are Egypt's most important trading partners. During 1990–91 to 2000–01, the European Union and the United States averaged 39 and 23 percent of Egypt's imports, and 33 and 31 percent of its total exports, respectively. Currently both the European Union and the United States are subject to the same Egyptian tariff rates. However, Egypt has signed an association agreement with the European Union that will eliminate tariffs on EU exports within 12 years. Unless a similar agreement is reached with the United States, US exports will be seriously disadvantaged.

The modest export performance in Egypt is due to the prevailing incentive structure, which makes it more profitable for producers to sell at home rather than abroad. According to a recent study (Galal and Fawzy 2001), the bias stems from lack of competitiveness of the exchange rate, relatively high tariff rates on imports, high corporate taxation, and low efficiency of trade logistics.

In recent years, there have been significant trade reforms. Most notably:

- *Nominal and effective protection.* Maximum tariff rates were reduced successively from 70 percent in 1994 to 43 percent in 2002, excluding alcoholic beverages, cars, whole poultry, textiles, and clothing (Refaat 2003). As a result, both nominal and effective rates of protection came down (table 11.1). The dispersion rates also fell during the same period, albeit modestly.

- *Nontariff barriers to trade.* The import ban list that covered 210 items in 1990 currently includes only poultry parts and some textile products. The ban on ready-made garments was replaced in 2002 by specific tariffs, which translate into an average ad valorem equivalent of 627 percent. Egypt also adopted the World Trade Organization (WTO) agreement on customs valuation in July 2001. Reforms of customs administration are under way.

- *Exchange rate.* Egypt unified, devalued, and kept fixed the exchange rate in 1991 to curb inflation and increase the competitiveness of Egyptian exports. The fixed regime was abandoned in favor of an interme-

Table 11.1 Levels of protection in the Egyptian economy, 1994–2002

Sector	Nominal protection (percent)		Effective protection[a] (percent)	
	1994	2002	1994	2002
Economywide protection[b]				
Average protection	22.0	18.9	23.3	18.5
Dispersion	13.3	11.1	16.6	14.7
Protection by economic sector				
Agriculture	8.3	7.6	7.9	7.2
Mining and quarrying	9.4	7.2	7.4	5.2
Crude oil	14.3	14.3	13.0	11.0
Industry	25.1	21.4	27.1	21.4
Food industries	8.8	7.9	6.6	1.5
Textiles	34.5	32.9	40.4	38.4
Clothes and leather footwear	68.9	516.6	81.1	674.1
Wood and wood products	12.5	12.7	11.5	12.0
Paper and printing	16.7	15.6	15.9	15.0
Leather and leather products	44.4	37.4	52.3	43.6
Rubber products	35.8	28.3	39.5	31.0
Chemical industries	11.4	10.7	9.6	6.9
Basic metal industries	19.9	15.3	21.0	12.0
Nonmetal industries	25.4	20.2	27.9	19.6
Mining and extraction	19.9	15.1	19.5	11.1
Transport devices	46.7	39.3	53.4	44.6

a. Using input/output tables, 1998–99.
b. The reported averages exclude garments, beverages, and tobacco because of their exceptionally high tariffs.
Source: Refaat (2003).

diate regime in January 2001, but the new regime was never put to the test. Policy inconsistency gave way to a floating regime in January 2003 (figure 11.3).

Despite these reforms, the Egyptian economy remains more protected than its competitors' economies. If Egypt's commitments under its trade pacts with the European Union and Arab countries are supplemented by further commitments under a US FTA, the Egyptian economy will become much more open than it is today.

Impact of an FTA Between the United States and Egypt

The argument made at the outset of this chapter is that the impact of a prospective FTA between Egypt and the United States ought to be measured against both economic and political objectives, given the nature of

Figure 11.3 Nominal and real exchange rate indices in Egypt, 1991–2003

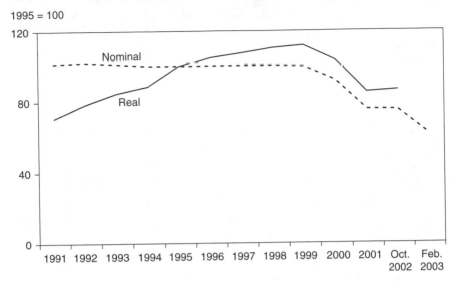

Note: Nominal and real exchange rates are expressed in terms of US dollars per Egyptian pound. Increases in indices reflect appreciation of the pound.

Sources: IMF, *International Financial Statistics,* different issues; data from EFG-Hermes; and authors' calculations.

the Middle East region and US interests. The starting point for subsequent analysis is that the interest of the United States in the Middle East revolves around an improved relationship with the Arab world, regional stability, and a reliable supply of oil, besides the usual economic gains from trade and investment. Egypt's interest lies presumably in achieving higher economic growth and greater capacity for job creation through trade and investment rather than aid, coupled with additional gains that will result from resolving the region's conflicts. A discussion of both dimensions follows, starting with the likely economic impact.

Likely Economic Impact

The expected static economic gains from an FTA between the United States and Egypt were estimated by Bernard Hoekman, Denise Konan, and Keith Maskus (1998), Robert Lawrence (1998), and more recently Dean DeRosa (2003). Hoekman, Konan, and Maskus used a general equilibrium model to estimate the impact of both shallow and deep integration agreements (the results are reported in table 11.2). The analysis took into account Egypt's trade pacts with the European Union and Arab coun-

Table 11.2   Impact of US FTA on welfare in Egypt and on bilateral trade flows

	EMA, AFTA, and no US FTA	EMA, AFTA, and shallow US FTA	EMA, AFTA, and deep US FTA
Impact on welfare			
(percent of GDP)	0.99	1.26	1.84
Trade impacts			
Trade creation			
(millions of dollars)	252	342	450
Trade diversion			
(millions of dollars)	233	197	170
Average weighted tariff	4.1	2.7	2.6
Trade flows (percent growth)[a]			
Exports to European Union	3.2	2.8	31.8
Imports from European Union	38.2	29.3	47.3
Exports to United States	−7.0	17.5	51.3
Imports from United States	−14.3	21.9	38.8
Exports to Arab countries	44.4	45.8	41.4
Imports from Arab countries	33.3	26.7	29.4

EMA = Euro-Mediterranean Agreement
AFTA = Arab Free Trade Agreement

a. Relative to 1996 base.

Source: Hoekman, Konan, and Maskus (1998).

tries. Drawing on the results of this study, Lawrence estimated the impact of an agreement on the United States, using partial equilibrium analysis and information about traded commodities, the prevailing trade barriers in 1996, and an import elasticity of 2.0 to 3.0. Finally, DeRosa estimated the impact of an FTA between the United States and Egypt, using a gravity model that estimates the typical impact of an FTA on bilateral trade. The main results of these studies are discussed below.

- According to Hoekman, Konan, and Maskus (1998), the expected static economic gains to Egypt from an FTA with the United States are positive but small in absolute terms. A shallow FTA involving the elimination of barriers to trade on the border would expand net trade (trade creation minus trade diversion) by $145 million in 1996 prices. A deep FTA would expand net trade by $280 million in 1996 prices. Deep integration produces better results because it entails increased efficiency and better allocation of resources due to increased competition, lower cost of services, and lower transaction costs. DeRosa (2003) finds larger numbers. His model predicts an increase of Egyptian exports to the United States from $895 million to $1,953 million, an increase of $1 billion or 118 percent.

- For the United States, the expected static economic gains are larger in absolute terms than the expected gains for Egypt, but these gains are very modest relative to the US economy. According to Hoekman, Konan, and Maskus (1998), the increase in US exports to Egypt is expected to be 21.9 percent under a shallow FTA, and 38.8 percent under a deep FTA (table 11.2). Furthermore, Lawrence (1998) finds that an FTA with Egypt would cause a modest increase in employment in the United States because of trade expansion. DeRosa (2003) again finds a much larger impact. His model predicts an increase in US exports to Egypt from $3,729 million to $8,135 million.

- Without an FTA agreement, both Egypt and the United States are expected to be worse off. According to Hoekman, Konan, and Maskus (1998), the Egyptian economy would suffer from trade diversion as a result of the agreements with the European Union and Arab countries. For the United States, the "opportunity cost" would be in the neighborhood of $1.5 billion. To the extent that current US aid to Egypt (about $2 billion a year) is tied to imports from the United States, phasing out economic aid will further diminish US exports to Egypt.

DeRosa's estimates (2003) are probably exaggerated for both Egypt and the United States. Egyptian exporters currently face relatively low barriers to enter US markets, outside of textiles and apparel (table 11.3). But the abolition of quotas on imports of textiles and clothing in 2005 mandated by WTO obligations will increase the competition facing Egyptian products in the United States from low-cost developing countries and countries enjoying preferential US treatment. With respect to the United States, the removal of trade barriers in Egypt, which currently average 18 percent (table 11.4), is likely to increase US exports to Egypt. But US exporters will also face greater competition from the European Union over the next 12 years, as Egyptian tariffs are gradually reduced to conform with the Euro-Med Agreement (EMA).

By the same token, the estimates of Hoekman, Konan, and Maskus (1998) are probably too low. They start from a low level of Egyptian exports for reasons that are at least in part related to the prevailing disincentives for Egyptian producers wishing to export. If Egypt adopts reforms to increase the competitiveness of its producers and to improve incentives to export, Egyptian exports are expected to increase. Greater access to the US market through an FTA would offer an outlet for this increase in exports by more than the mere removal of trade barriers in the United States would suggest.

Moreover, if the Egypt-US FTA is structured along the lines of the North American Free Trade Agreement (NAFTA), further dynamic gains can accrue to Egypt. Domestic reforms would improve both resource allocation and productivity. In addition, the agreement could help to mobilize capital inflows from the United States and elsewhere to Egypt. Currently the level of FDI inflow to Egypt is very modest, amounting to about $277 mil-

**Table 11.3   Egyptian exports to the US and bound tariff rates
in the US market by 2-digit Harmonized System
classification**

HS code	Category	Average exports 2000–01 (millions of dollars)	Bound tariff rates (percent)
62	Articles of apparel and clothing accessories, not knitted	249.6	10.0
61	Articles of apparel and clothing accessories, knitted	147.0	11.5
27	Mineral fuels and oils and products of distillation	142.7	0.5
31	Fertilizers	36.9	0.0
52	Cotton, yarns, and woven fabrics	53.0	7.9
57	Carpets and other textile floor coverings	45.1	2.9
98	Special-classification provisions	65.2	
63	Made-up textile articles	25.3	6.2
72	Iron and steel	17.2	0.3
94	Furniture; bedding, cushions, etc.	24.1	1.9
97	Works of art, collectors' pieces, and antiques	14.9	0.0
29	Organic chemicals	5.7	3.3
28	Inorganic chemicals	3.3	2.2
20	Preparations of vegetables, fruit, nuts	5.5	7.4
12	Oil seeds and oleaginous fruits	4.9	1.3
82	Tools, cutlery, spoons of base metal; parts	4.4	3.5
09	Coffee, tea, maté, and spices	3.1	0.03
25	Salt, sulfur, earths and stone, plastering materials	2.8	0.2
99	Special import-reporting provisions	2.9	
73	Articles of iron or steel	3.0	1.2
84	Nuclear reactors, boilers, and parts	2.7	1.3
17	Sugars and sugar confectionery	3.2	2.3
07	Edible vegetables and certain roots and tubers	1.9	2.4
33	Essential oils, perfumery, cosmetic preparations	1.8	1.6
54	Manmade filaments, yarns, and woven fabrics	1.9	9.7
39	Plastics and articles	1.5	4.4
95	Toys, games, and sports equipment; parts	1.3	1.4
68	Articles of stone, plaster, cement, asbestos	1.6	1.3
49	Printed books and other printed products	0.8	0.0
60	Knitted or crocheted fabrics	2.1	9.9
19	Preparations of cereals, flour, starch, or milk	0.5	4.3
70	Glass and glassware	1.1	4.6
	Others	11.9	
	Total exports/average tariffs (unweighted/weighted)	888.2	3.5/5.9

Sources: Institute for International Economics FTA Project database; OECD (2000).

lion in 2000–01. The association between FDI and deep FTAs was seen in Mexico, where NAFTA stimulated a large amount of FDI. To be sure, although Egypt does not enjoy Mexico's geographic advantages, a similar increase in FDI could occur in Egypt if it becomes more attractive to foreign investors. With increased FDI, the Egyptian economy could benefit from the transfer of modern technical and managerial techniques, as well as market access. For the US investors, Egypt could offer access to cheap labor and an attractive location.

Table 11.4   Egyptian imports from the US and applied tariffs in Egypt by 2-digit Harmonized System classification

HS code	Category	Average imports 2000–01 (millions of dollars)	Applied tariff rates 2002 (percent)
88	Aircraft, spacecraft, and parts	730.9	5.0
10	Cereals	813.7	1.0
84	Nuclear reactors, boilers and parts	425.4	10.9
39	Plastics and articles	183.9	18.6
87	Vehicles, other than railway or tramway rolling stock, and parts	222.5	40.9
85	Electrical machinery and equipment and parts	196.5	19.0
89	Ships, boats and floating structures	69.0	11.2
90	Optical, photographic, cinematographic equipment and parts	92.5	11.9
23	Residues from the food industries; prepared animal feed	97.2	8.1
98	Special-classification provisions	80.4	
93	Arms and ammunition and parts	151.5	25.9
12	Oil seeds and oleaginous fruits; miscellaneous grains	40.2	12.4
27	Mineral fuels, mineral oils and products of their distillation	47.1	11.2
94	Furniture; bedding, cushions, etc.	23.8	35.8
55	Manmade staple fibers, including yarns and woven fabrics	16.4	40.7
15	Animal or vegetable fats and oils and their cleavage products	25.2	14.5
02	Meat and edible meat offal	28.0	35.1
29	Organic chemicals	24.9	9.7
48	Paper and paperboard; articles of paper pulp	23.7	24.0
73	Articles of iron or steel	26.4	25.0
47	Pulp of wood or other fibrous cellulosic material	22.1	5.0
30	Pharmaceutical products	18.4	8.7
28	Inorganic chemicals	10.2	11.8
38	Miscellaneous chemical products	18.2	11.7
74	Copper and articles	6.0	17.4
08	Edible fruit and nuts; peel of citrus fruit or melons	8.1	35.2
32	Tanning or dyeing extracts; tannins and derivatives	9.4	18.9
44	Wood and articles of wood; wood charcoal	9.2	21.7
40	Rubber and articles	6.1	17.2
83	Miscellaneous articles of base metal	4.7	26.9
82	Tools, cutlery, spoons of base metal and parts	5.0	16.0
86	Railway or tramway locomotives and parts	5.3	6.7
	Others	78.1	
	Total imports/average tariffs (unweighted/weighted)	3,519.3	18.0/11.3

Sources: Institute for International Economics FTA Project database; authors' calculations based on Egypt's applied tariff schedule for 2002.

Political Impact

Unlike the potential economic gains from FTAs, the political ramifications of an FTA between Egypt and the United States are difficult to identify, let alone measure accurately. But this difficulty is by no means a convincing reason for ignoring such benefits. Below is a brief discussion of the possible political impact of a US-Egypt FTA.

The starting point is the observation that the relationship between the United States and the Muslim/Arab world has deteriorated in the aftermath of September 11. The perception is widespread in Arab countries—especially in the wake of the war in Iraq—that the United States is targeting them for the sake of oil. Complicating the picture further is another widespread perception: that US foreign policy is one-sided in dealing with the Palestinian-Israeli problem. On the other hand, some in the United States claim that the discontent does not follow from US policies toward the region: rather, it grows out of local conditions and the lack of progress in these countries.

Whatever the roots of the negative perception of the United States in the region, confidence-building measures are needed on both sides to bring about better relations and a more peaceful and prosperous Middle East. An FTA with a country like Egypt could be a step toward achieving this goal. Clearly, the single act of ratifying an FTA would not by itself change the image of the United States in the Muslim/Arab world. Nor would it be the cornerstone on which Egypt's sustainable growth and prosperity is built. The most an FTA could do is to demonstrate a US commitment to countries that are willing to reform their economies. For Egypt, such an agreement would also help to smooth the transition from aid to trade and bring about a more sustainable economic relationship between the two countries.

If an FTA with Egypt materializes, along with progress in areas such as resolving the Palestinian-Israeli conflict and the situation in Iraq, the gains could be enormous for all parties. One way to judge the size of the potential gains is to review what actually happened in the past. A more peaceful and prosperous Middle East might have saved the United States a war in Iraq. It might have prevented the two oil shocks in the mid-1970s and early 1980s. Egypt might have avoided several wars since 1948, saving some of the resources allocated to defense and enabling policymakers to focus their attention on domestic reforms. And if Egypt were doing even better than it is doing today, other countries in the region would perhaps have followed suit.

Morocco as a Potential Partner

The history of Morocco has been deeply affected by its geographic location at the crossroads between Africa, the Middle East, and Europe.[6] The patterns of Morocco's international and economic relations today con-

---

6. The list of foreigners who have ruled Morocco includes the Phoenicians, Romans, Vandals, Visigoths, Byzantine Greeks, Arabs, French, and Spanish. This section draws heavily on the profile of Morocco issued by the US State Department (2002).

tinue to reflect that physical position. Morocco also has long had a close relationship with the United States.[7] Both countries have, more recently, shared interests in trying to bring about peace between Israelis and Palestinians, containing Iraqi aggression, and combating terrorism. As befits its role as a moderate Arab state, Morocco has been active in the search for peace in the Middle East, encouraging negotiations and urging moderation on both sides.[8] Morocco was one of the first Arab states to condemn Iraq's invasion of Kuwait, and it sent troops to defend Saudi Arabia and aid the efforts to repulse Saddam Hussein. Morocco was also vocal in denouncing the attacks of September 11 and it has assisted the United States in the war against terrorism. However, Morocco has not been supportive of the recent US war with Iraq.

Several features of Morocco's international dealings are contentious and hamper its relations with its neighbors. There are tensions between Morocco and Spain and other EU members over immigration and drug smuggling. Morocco also has a long-standing dispute over jurisdiction of the western Sahara territory that lies between Morocco and Mauritania.[9] This friction stands in the way of North African regional economic integration.

Key Political Characteristics

Morocco also occupies the crossroads between monarchy and a full-fledged democracy. Morocco is a constitutional monarchy, in which ultimate authority rests with the king, currently Mohammed VI, who assumed the throne in July 1999. The king is also head of the military and the country's religious leader. He appoints the prime minister, following legislative elections. He also directly appoints the five most senior cabinet positions, and may at his discretion terminate the tenure of any minister, dissolve the parliament, and call for new elections or rule by decree.

---

7. According to the US State Department (2002), "Moroccans recognized the Government of the United States in 1777. Formal U.S. relations with Morocco date from 1787, when the two nations negotiated a treaty of peace and friendship. Renegotiated in 1836, the treaty is still in force, constituting the longest unbroken treaty relationship in U.S. history."

8. In 1986, then-King Hassan II invited then-Israeli Prime Minister Shimon Peres for talks. Following the Oslo Agreement between Israel and the Palestinians in 1993, Morocco increased its economic and political ties with Israel; in 1994, both parties opened liaison offices. These offices were closed in 2000, however, in response to renewed violence between the Israelis and Palestinians.

9. In 1991, after a long period of hostilities, the United Nations brokered a cease-fire between Morocco and the Polisario; it remains in effect. In addition, the UN also proposed that the area be given autonomy under Moroccan sovereignty—a position agreed to by Morocco, the United States, France, and the United Kingdom. However, because of opposition from Spain, Algeria, and the Polisario, a final settlement has not occurred. In addition, Russia and China continue to seek a UN-organized referendum that would enable the territory's inhabitants to determine their future.

Morocco's system of proportional representation has generated a large number of parties that span the political spectrum. In 2002, after parliamentary elections, the king named not an elected member of parliament but Driss Jettou, a technocrat with no political party affiliation, to head the government. This marked a shift from the previous left-wing coalition government that had served since 1999, although the coalition assembled by Jettou is said to be not very different from its predecessor (EIU 2003). The leading opposition party, with 13 percent of the seats, is the Islamist PJD (Justice and Development Party).[10] Moreover, the low participation in the election has given rise to speculation that support for radical Islamism is considerably higher. This possibility explains why faster economic growth and efforts to reduce unemployment deserve a high priority on Morocco's economic policy agenda.

Key Economic Characteristics

Morocco is a midsized, middle-income developing country. In 2002, its GDP was about $40 billion; with a population of 29.6 million, per capita income was $1,350. Agriculture continues to play an important role—typically accounting for between 14 percent and 20 percent of output (depending on rainfall) and employing about 40 percent of the workforce. Morocco has substantial deposits of phosphates and phosphate derivatives, as well as mines producing lead, silver, and copper. It also has a large fishing industry and a large public sector. While Morocco has a modern manufacturing sector with significant output of clothing and textiles, a considerable share of its output is from traditional craft industries. According to a recent study, almost a fifth of Moroccan GDP originates in traditional craft industries that produce ceramics, metalware, woodcrafts, traditional clothing, footwear, and textiles including rugs.[11] The sector produces almost entirely for the domestic market and tourism, generating almost no exports.

Morocco has been successful in maintaining monetary stability and low inflation but less successful in stimulating economic growth. In the 1960s and 1970s, Morocco's growth performance was strong, but more recently growth has been insufficient either to significantly improve living standards or to provide employment opportunities for the expanding labor force. It is estimated that in 2001, for example, the overall unemployment rate stood at almost 13 percent while urban unemployment was over 20 percent (IMF 2003).

---

10. Morocco's largest Islamist group, Al-Adl Wal-Ihsane (Justice and Charity), did not have political party status and took no part in the elections. According to the EIU (2003, 1), "Its absence from the ballot and the fact that the turnout was a meager 52 percent appear to be related: a significant proportion of the 48 percent who did not vote probably stayed at home because of their non-participation."

11. This figure is based on a Unesco study cited by the EIU (2003).

Table 11.5 Principal Moroccan trade partners, 2000

	Exports			Imports	
Country	Share (percent)	Total (millions of dollars)	Country	Share (percent)	Total (millions of dollars)
France	34	2,491.0	France	24	2,771.3
Spain	13	963.5	Spain	10	1,138.4
United Kingdom	10	712.7	United Kingdom	6	711.6
Italy	7	529.5	United States	6	643.5
Germany	5	369.2	Saudi Arabia	5	573.1
India	4	310.9	Germany	5	562.8
Japan	4	283.8	Italy	5	546.3
United States	3	253.9	Iraq	4	475.2
Belgium	3	209.6	Iran	3	357.4
Netherlands	2	124.1	China	2	268.0
Brazil	1	68.9	Sweden	2	255.9
All others	15	1,114.7	All others	28	3,229.7

Source: UNSD (2003).

Morocco has typically run a merchandise trade deficit offset by earnings from tourism and remittances from expatriates abroad. Moroccan merchandise trade is focused on the European Union. In 2000, for example, the European Union accounted for 58 percent of imports and about 75 percent of exports. France was by far its most important trading partner (24 percent of imports and 34 percent of exports), followed by Spain (10 percent of imports and 13 percent of exports) (tables 11.5 and 11.6).

The United States is a relatively minor trading partner. In 2000, US exports of $253.9 million and imports of $643.5 million accounted for 3 and 6 percent of Moroccan exports and imports, respectively. The pattern of trade is quite predictable and reflects resource endowments and levels of development. US imports are concentrated in phosphates, fish and prepared vegetables, mineral fuels and oils, and textiles and clothing; US exports are concentrated in agricultural products (maize and wheat), aircraft, and machinery (see table 11.7).

Reform and Trade Liberalization

In the 1980s, Morocco was an inward-looking, highly regulated economy with considerable state participation. Over time, numerous measures have been taken to enhance the role of the domestic and international markets. Yet the process has slowed down over the past few years under the government dominated by the Socialist Union of Popular Forces and remains incomplete.[12] As indicated in figures 11.4 and 11.5, and judged by

---

12. Morocco currently is 68th out of 156 countries in terms of the Index of Economic Freedom developed by the Heritage Foundation (O'Driscoll, Feulner, and O'Grady 2003); it ties with Tunisia and Saudi Arabia. Its overall score of 2.95, based on 10 equally weighted criteria, places it just in the "mostly free" category and just out of the "mostly unfree" category.

Table 11.6 Principal Moroccan trade products, 2000

	Exports			Imports	
Category	Share (percent)	Total (millions of dollars)	Category	Share (percent)	Total (millions of dollars)
Articles of apparel, accessories, not knitted or crocheted	22	1,666.2	Mineral fuels, oils, distillation products, etc.	18	2,039.2
Fish, crustaceans, molluscs, aquatic invertebrates	10	766.2	Electrical, electronic equipment	12	1,412.7
Electrical, electronic equipment	10	760.8	Nuclear reactors, boilers, machinery, etc.	9	1,068.4
Articles of apparel, accessories, knitted or crocheted	10	710.9	Cereals	6	730.6
Inorganic chemicals, precious metal compounds, isotopes	7	507.7	Vehicles other than railway, tramway	4	491.9
Other commodities	41	3,020.0	Other commodities	50	5,790.5

Source: UNSD (2003).

both the stabilization and structural reform measures, Morocco's performance is fairly typical for a MENA country.

The liberalization of both trade and investment has played an important role in Morocco's reform efforts. Tariffs have been reduced and the tariff system has been simplified. Reference prices for textiles, clothing, and appliances as well as several quantitative restrictions have been eliminated. Nonetheless, Morocco still has high most favored nation (MFN) tariffs (average 33.9 percent) and a fairly restrictive regime of nontariff barriers (see table 11.8). In the General Agreement on Trade in Services, Morocco's few commitments are typical for a developing country.

Morocco has undertaken additional liberalization commitments regionally. Like Egypt, it has concluded an association agreement that will lead to free trade in industrial products with the European Union by 2012. The EU agreement is incomplete, particularly with respect to services, agricultural products, and investment.[13] Morocco has a similar agreement

13. For a discussion of the welfare effects of this agreement, see Page and Underwood (1997). They report that since Moroccan nonagricultural exports were already entering the EU market duty-free, the expected gains from the agreement came primarily from lower prices to consumers due to Moroccan trade barriers being reduced. A troubling feature of the agreement was related to the phasing in of these tariff reductions. In particular, relatively rapid increases in tariffs on inputs actually raised effective protection in the short run, thereby generating small welfare losses.

Table 11.7 Moroccan bilateral trade with the United States, by product category, 2000

	Exports			Imports	
Category	Share (percent)	Total (millions of dollars)	Category	Share (percent)	Total (millions of dollars)
Articles of apparel, accessories, not knitted or crocheted	28	60.7	Aircraft, spacecraft, and parts thereof	22	143.8
Salt, sulphur, earth, stone, plaster, lime, and cement	24	60.0	Cereals	21	135.4
Meat, fish, and seafood food preparations	9	23.2	Nuclear reactors, boilers, machinery, etc.	11	69.3
Mineral fuels, oils, distillation products, etc.	9	21.6	Mineral fuels, oils, distillation products, etc.	8	48.8
Vegetable, fruit, nut, etc. food preparations	8	19.9	Tobacco and manufactured tobacco substitutes	7	43.0
Other commodities	23	58.5	Other commodities	32	203.2

Source: UNSD (2003).

with the European Free Trade Association (EFTA). It has also signed preferential arrangements with Algeria, Guinea, Iraq, Libya, and Mauritania. Egypt, Jordan, Morocco, and Tunisia last year agreed to set up a free trade zone ahead of the 2010 target for ending trade barriers in the Euro-Mediterranean area. The zone would also "be open to other Arab countries" such as Algeria, Libya, Mauritania, Syria, Lebanon, and Palestine. In addition, Morocco belongs to the Community of Sahel-Saharan States (COMESSA), which seeks to consolidate economic and commercial integration among member states.[14] The government has also taken numerous unilateral measures to liberalize and attract foreign investment.[15]

---

14. Members of COMESSA include Burkina Faso, Central African Republic, Chad, Djibouti, Egypt, Eritrea, Gambia, Libya, Mali, Morocco, Niger, Nigeria, Senegal, Somalia, Sudan, and Tunisia. Algeria is not a member.

15. In November 1989, it abrogated a 1973 law requiring majority Moroccan ownership in a wide range of industries. In 1993 Mobil Oil was allowed to buy back a 50 percent share of a major oil-producing subsidiary it had previously owned. The government does not screen FDI and provides favorable treatment on foreign exchange for foreign investors. Investment is permitted in all sectors except agricultural land and sectors reserved for the state (e.g., phosphate mining). There are no performance requirements. In 1991, Morocco signed a BIT with the United States that provided for MFN treatment and international arbitration for expropriation; in 1995, Morocco drafted a new foreign investment code that provides some tax breaks on income for investment in certain regions, in crafts, and in export industries.

Figure 11.4 Economic stabilization in Morocco versus different regions

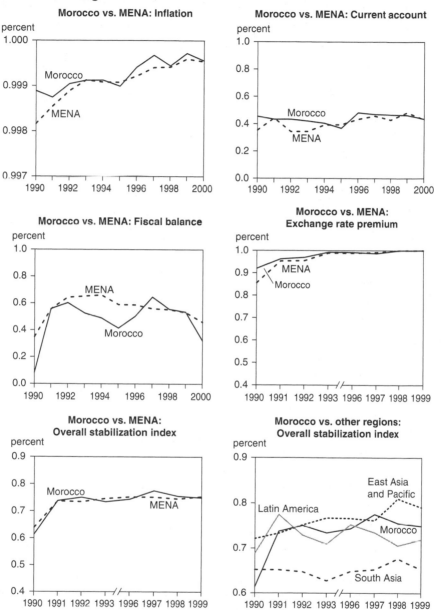

Morocco vs. MENA: Inflation

Morocco vs. MENA: Current account

Morocco vs. MENA: Fiscal balance

Morocco vs. MENA: Exchange rate premium

Morocco vs. MENA: Overall stabilization index

Morocco vs. other regions: Overall stabilization index

Note: MENA includes Egypt, Jordan, Morocco, and Tunisia. Latin America includes Argentina, Bolivia, Brazil, Chile, Colombia, Mexico, Peru, and Venezuela. South Asia includes India and Pakistan. East Asia and Pacific includes China, Indonesia, Korea, Malaysia, the Philippines, and Thailand.

Figure 11.5 Structural reform in Morocco versus different regions

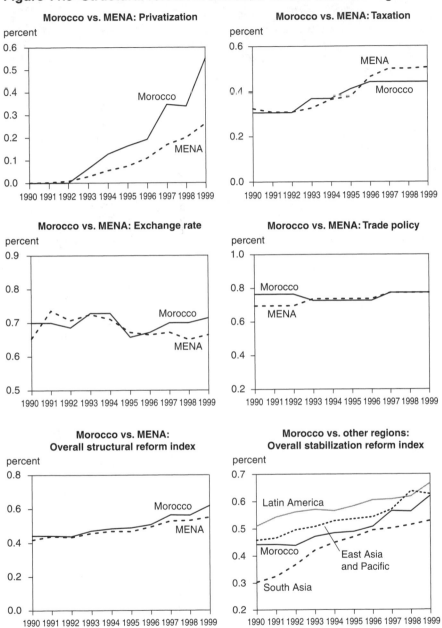

Note: MENA includes Egypt, Jordan, Morocco, and Tunisia. Latin America includes Argentina, Bolivia, Brazil, Chile, Colombia, Mexico, Peru, and Venezuela. South Asia includes India and Pakistan. East Asia and Pacific includes China, Indonesia, Korea, Malaysia, the Philippines, and Thailand.

Table 11.8 Moroccan average rates of tariff protection, by major trade categories, 2000–01

Category number	Category	Tariff (percent)
0	Food and live animals	2.5
1	Beverages and tobacco	50.0
2	Crude materials, inedible, except fuels	25.0
3	Mineral fuels, lubricants, and related materials	17.5
4	Animal and vegetable oils and fats	50.0
5	Chemicals	32.5
6	Manufactured goods	32.5
7	Machinery and transport equipment	2.5
8	Miscellaneous manufactured articles	50.0
9	Commodities and transactions not classified according to kind	2.5

Note: These tariffs held for the same classifications (Standard International Trade Classification Revision 1) in both years, 2000 and 2001. However, the tariffs varied greatly when different categories were used. For instance, the average tariff on "food and beverages" is 2.5 percent—the same as "food and live animals," but much less than "beverages and tobacco" in the above table.

Source: World Bank, WITS (World Integrated Trade Solution) database, 2003.

In sum, Morocco stands at a crossroads in several respects: it has close political linkages with the United States, Europe, Africa, and the Middle East. It is in transition from an autocratic monarchy to a more full-fledged democracy. It is shifting from an economy that is highly controlled to one based on free-market principles, and it is in the process of making itself the hub of a set of preferential trade agreements. These are crucial attributes of Morocco as an FTA partner for the United States.

Impact of an FTA Between the United States and Morocco

The Moroccan Perspective. The analysis of Morocco's general economic characteristics and its relationship with the United States does not immediately suggest that the United States is the ideal candidate for a free trade agreement for Morocco. From a Moroccan perspective the immediate economic benefits are questionable; the case for an agreement rests partly on its less certain potential dynamic benefits.

After all, Morocco's primary international economic focus has been Europe. Its widely spoken foreign languages (French and to a lesser degree Spanish), history, and geographic location all suggest that Europe, to use the parlance of trade theorists, is Morocco's "natural" trading partner. By contrast, Morocco and the United States do not have a particularly close economic relationship. The United States accounts for only 5 percent of Moroccan trade, and US foreign investment is small. In addition, most of the goods Morocco currently exports to the United States are not subject to high tariffs—many of these actually enter duty-free, in part because US tariffs are already low for minerals and some agricultural products.[16] The disparities in tariff rates explain why an FTA has very different implications for tariff revenues in the two countries. John Gilbert's computable general equilibrium analysis (2003) reports that by implementing a free trade area, Morocco would lose a total of $293 million and the United States just $10.9 million [17]

Under such circumstances, it is quite possible that giving US exports tariff-free access to the Moroccan market could result in substantial trade diversion. Although Moroccan consumers might enjoy lower prices, these gains could be more than offset for the economy as a whole because tariff revenue would be lost and goods would be purchased from the United States rather than from more efficient sources. In addition, it is possible that Morocco could experience declines in its terms of trade, since its tariff reductions would be much larger than those of the United States. In fact, according to simulations undertaken for the conference that occasioned this volume, the trade impact of a US FTA would *reduce* Moroccan incomes by about $93 million (in 1997 dollars)—0.26 percent of GDP—of which $25 million is estimated to result from reduced efficiency and $68 million from reductions in terms of trade (Gilbert 2003).

While this conclusion is a good starting point for thinking about the agreement's economic impact, there are economic considerations that could mitigate these effects and others that could exacerbate them. We consider each in turn.

First, the conclusions are sensitive to assumptions made about other Moroccan tariffs, with respect both to the European Union and to other trading partners. In particular, the simulations take tariffs on the European Union, EFTA, and other regional trading partners as given. In fact, the tariffs on industrial products with Europe are scheduled to be eliminated by 2012, a change that will surely reduce the trade diversion from the US-Morocco FTA. Indeed, the FTA with the United States can be seen as a measure that offsets trade diversion due to Morocco's FTA with the European Union. Moreover, if Morocco were to complement its US FTA with more reductions in its MFN tariffs, the impact of this diversion could be reduced and even eliminated—though such considerations also point to the need for policies to deal with the budgetary implications of these measures.

---

16. According to Gilbert (2003), US tariffs exceed 4 percent in crops besides grains (13.9 percent), processed food products (11.5 percent), and textiles and apparel (11.8 percent). By contrast, Moroccan tariffs are generally between 15 and 25 percent and are as high as 71 percent for processed foods.

17. Gilbert (2003) estimates that Morocco would lose $115 million from revenues currently collected on US products and an additional $177 million as a result of purchasing additional US products rather than those of other trading partners.

Second, there could also be gains due to liberalization of services and investment that have not been modeled.[18] These could be significant. In its goals for the FTA negotiations, the Coalition of US Service Industries is seeking general disciplines to improve policy transparency and strengthen intellectual property protection, as well as sectoral provisions for market access and national treatment for a number of modes of delivery.[19] These could provide additional benefits, especially if Morocco extends the measures unilaterally to other trading partners or uses such a prospect to obtain additional benefits from other trading partners, particularly Europe.[20]

Third, regional trade agreements can stimulate domestic regulatory reform, improve administrative procedures, raise domestic standards, remove bureaucratic red tape, and improve the rule of law. If such steps are taken, they confer benefits not only on international trade and investment but also on other forms of economic activity. In addition, agreements can serve to improve investor expectations.

When countries have long histories of intervention in trade and investment, their unilateral action is often greeted with skepticism. Locking in economic reform could reduce risk premiums and thereby enhance investment and economic growth. There could be additional benefits not captured in the static framework if trade liberalization reduces the price of capital goods, stimulates domestic investment, enhances the transfer of technology through foreign investment, and stimulates productivity growth through enhanced competition.

Fourth, Morocco is thwarted in some of its efforts in the European market. It faces restrictions on exporting citrus fruits, fresh vegetables, horticultural products, and apparel.[21] Striking an agreement with the United States could give Morocco greater leverage in negotiations currently under way with the European Union to improve its market access in agricultural products. Just as the United States has been motivated by the Euro-Med agreements to act defensively to match preferences granted to

---

18. As indicated above, Morocco already has a bilateral investment treaty with the United States and liberal investment rules. To stimulate additional investment, it would have to take additional measures to improve its general business environment.

19. These include e-commerce, telecommunications services, banking and financial services, insurance, audiovisual and computer services, education, energy, environmental services, express delivery, and tourism (see Vastine 2002).

20. In their simulations of an FTA between the European Union and Egypt, for example, Hoekman, Konan, and Maskus (1998) found very large gains when service liberalization was included.

21. The French external trade minister, François Loos, is reported to have pointed to an "incompatibility" in Morocco's conducting free trade negotiations with the United States and with the European Union at the same time. That the European Union has concluded an FTA with Mexico has apparently escaped his attention.

European competitors, so Europe could be similarly motivated to match preferences granted to the United States in services, investment, and particularly agricultural products.

Finally, Morocco's strategy in being willing to sign FTAs with a multitude of trading partners resembles the approach used by other prolific FTA negotiators. While economists are fond of pointing out that preferential trading arrangements are in general second-best to multilateral free trade, they often fail to notice that for a single country, the best outcome would be to have no domestic barriers together with preferential access in all other markets. It appears that countries such as Chile, Mexico, and Singapore are headed in this direction; and while it is far behind these three countries in eliminating its domestic barriers, Morocco could be trying to move toward such an outcome.

There are, however, other considerations that suggest the gains could actually be lower than projected in the model. One is the possibility that agriculture will not be fully liberalized. NAFTA, for example, contained some noteworthy exceptions, such as Canadian dairy and poultry products (see Miller 2002). A second potential complication is the impact of the FTA rules of origin, particularly for textiles.[22] The United States has generally insisted on highly restrictive rules of origin—so-called fiber-forward rules—for clothing products to qualify for duty-free access. By forcing Moroccan clothing manufacturers to use high-cost domestic or US inputs, these rules could seriously affect Moroccan export competitiveness. A report issued by the American Chamber of Commerce (2002) suggests that this concern is not simply academic. Describing the recent cutbacks in the production of Jordache denim jeans in Morocco, it notes: "The high price of local fabric is a key issue. J.R.A. [J.R.A. Morocco, the Jordache group] believes that Jordache New York could not justify continued imports of finished goods from Morocco—even with an FTA—if the high cost of using local fabric (required to satisfy the rules of origin) negated its benefits."[23]

Major sectors of Moroccan agriculture currently enjoy high rates of tariff protection. A third concern, therefore, relates to the adjustment challenges posed by eliminating these tariffs on US exports. According to Gilbert's simulations (2003), the real returns to owners of land, that is, farmers, could be reduced by as much as 4 percent as a result of such an arrangement. By contrast, owners of natural resources would see their incomes rise by 4 percent; the incomes of skilled labor and unskilled capital would each rise by about 1 percent. Morocco faces the challenge of pro-

---

22. Both these elements have been troubling features of other US preferential arrangements, in particular NAFTA. For an excellent analysis of NAFTA exceptions, see Miller (2002).

23. Morocco's role as a regional hub could be improved if the rules of origin allowed for cumulating with other countries in the Middle East.

viding a rural social safety net program in the short run, and alternative activities and agricultural income supports in the long run.

A fourth, more general challenge relates to implementation. It takes considerable administrative capacity to negotiate and implement an agreement of the type envisaged.[24] Ensuring compliance with new rules in areas such as intellectual property, customs, competition, environmental protection, worker rights, and government procurement will require that skills and resources be upgraded across the board. Actions by the private sector to avail itself of new market opportunities could entail additional costs. Agricultural producers may have to first meet new rules on food safety and additional sanitary and phytosanitary requirements. Similarly, potential exporters of manufactured goods will have to meet US safety and design standards and labeling requirements. Meeting these requirements could lead to additional positive spillovers to the rest of the economy, but in the short run they will entail additional costs not captured by the economic simulations. Nathan Associates (2003) has estimated that a reasonable package would require between $39.5 and $48.3 million in additional resources—a considerable increase over the aid given to Morocco in 2002 (according to the US Agency for International Development data, Morocco's repayments actually exceeded its receipts from the United States).

It is common to hear the slogan "trade, not aid." However, as trade agreements become deeper, and as their implementation demands enhanced domestic capacity, this becomes a false choice. Trade and aid are complements in agreements between developed and developing countries, not substitutes. Without appropriate and adequate aid, the benefits from trade are unlikely to be realized. US Trade Representative Robert Zoellick has declared that the Bush administration intends to target ongoing development assistance and trade-related technical assistance to help Morocco to follow through on the commitments it will make as part of the FTA.

In sum, for Morocco to benefit from an FTA with the United States, it needs to accompany the agreement with complementary policies, such as

- extending the bilateral tariff reductions to those placed on other trading partners;

- using the agreement to accelerate domestic reforms that improve the overall business environment;

- using the agreement as a means of making these reforms more credible;

---

24. For an extensive appraisal of these requirements, see Nathan Associates (2003).

- using the agreement to increase its bargaining leverage with the European Union, and to improve its market access, particularly in agricultural products; and

- improving its capacity to implement and take advantage of the agreement.

The US Perspective. The simulations undertaken for this conference indicate positive effects from the removal of high tariff barriers. According to Gilbert (2003), measured in 1997 dollars, the United States benefits to the tune of $178 million as exports increase by 88 percent. Most of the welfare gain stems from improvements in America's terms of trade. Moreover, since Europe has already signed an agreement to give it preferential access, for the United States an FTA with Morocco can be seen as a defensive measure against an important competitor. In addition, the agreement helps to underscore American willingness to move to free trade with all partners who are willing to reciprocate.

Nonetheless, the primary US objectives are political, although their realization is subject to considerable uncertainty. An optimist would point to several potential benefits. First, the agreement could enhance Morocco's reform process, both improving its institutions and governance and stimulating its economic growth. Prosperity based on a market system could enhance political stability and make possible the emergence of a more full-fledged democracy. Second, growth based on trade and foreign investment would cement the friendly relations between Morocco and the West. Third, prosperity would also help to reduce the conditions of despair that have created a breeding ground for terrorists; and fourth, the example of a successful Morocco could serve to catalyze similar changes in neighboring countries.

However, it should be pointed out that none of these outcomes is assured. First, the economic effects of a US FTA are relatively small, and there is no guarantee that the required complementary policies will be adopted. If they are not, the immediate economic impact of the agreement could actually reduce welfare in Morocco. Second, a movement toward greater democracy without the necessary preconditions could actually enhance the power of Islamic fundamentalists—Algeria being a telling example of such an outcome. Third, a larger foreign presence could help to stimulate more xenophobic political responses and be viewed as even more threatening by such fundamentalists. Fourth, since Morocco remains on the periphery of the Middle East and has fairly distinctive characteristics, its success might have little precedent-setting value for the region. By contrast, as we will argue below, successful reform in a more pivotal country such as Egypt could prove to be a much more powerful impetus toward change.

In agreeing to negotiate with Morocco, the United States is signaling its willingness to negotiate FTAs with partners in the Middle East besides Israel and its neighbors. But there is a danger that by negotiating these agreements separately and crafting deals to meet individual cases, it could be creating a crazy-quilt set of agreements that introduce costly complexity into its trading relationships. It is important, particularly if the goal is eventually to produce a single regional FTA, that the component agreements be designed to allow easy docking.

Conclusions and Final Comments

Under both FTAs considered in this chapter, the United States could enjoy positive economic benefits, although these are unlikely to be perceptible in an economy of its size. Egypt would derive positive benefits from a US-Egypt FTA. By contrast, the (static-efficiency) economic benefits of a US FTA covering only goods trade could be negative for Morocco. These conclusions are sensitive to the scope of agreement. Simulations indicate, for example, that Egypt would benefit more from a deep agreement that includes services and investment than one confined to merchandise trade. Since these sectors are to be included in the US-Morocco FTA, the sign of the economic impacts for Morocco could be reversed.

The magnitudes of the economic benefits for both Egypt and Morocco will ultimately depend on their agreement's more dynamic effects. These will in turn largely reflect the other policy measures they adopt and the additional aid they receive. Especially important will be their ability to mitigate trade diversion by lowering other external barriers, their ability to use an agreement to enhance domestic reform, and their ability to enhance domestic implementation capacity.

By serving as an anchor for reform, a free trade agreement can affect the probability that complementary measures will be adopted. Negotiators should be mindful of this potential when deciding on the content of the agreement. In particular, they should insist on including the relevant institutional changes in its terms. In addition, mechanisms for conditionality and monitoring should be incorporated and the agreements phased in with suitable time provided to ensure effective implementation.

On the political front, it is no coincidence that countries with which the United States has had the most conflict—including Cuba, Iraq, Libya, North Korea, and Iran—have been among the most controlled economies, the least integrated with the global economy, and the least democratic. But we cannot say with certainty that political gains will follow free trade agreements. Their political implications are far more difficult to analyze than the economic, not simply because we are economists by profession but also because the causal relationships are tenuous.

Nevertheless, successful economic reform is likely to enhance prosperity and employment opportunities and thus help to create societies that are less fertile breeding grounds for terrorism. The demonstration effect of success could also have positive spillover, pressuring those in the region more resistant to change to emulate their neighbors. To the extent that the United States is party to such a process, its image would improve. America's involvement would help dispel perceptions that its regional interests are simply strategic rather than tied to promoting the welfare of all who reside in the region.

It is certainly plausible that free markets, participation in international economic agreements and institutions, improved governance, and greater harmony with the United States could go together. Freer markets and the rule of law are natural complements to good governance. Regimes are far more able to confer rents and preferences on political allies when the economy is centrally controlled and regulated than when it is based on free-market principles. Favoritism and nepotism are less likely when firms profit from improvements in efficiency and in meeting consumer needs rather than by obtaining permits and licenses. Similarly, when a particular government is subject to binding international rules and requirements of transparency, its capacity to provide special favors will be more constrained.

Moreover, countries that do not allow their own citizens access to the rule of law and economic freedom will certainly be unwilling to accord such freedoms to foreigners. Conversely, if foreigners are allowed to compete freely in the domestic market, it becomes difficult to prevent citizens from doing likewise. That is why international agreements and domestic reform are complementary activities, particularly when the agreements entail deep economic integration and cover domestic rules and institutions.

Yet this same logic suggests that actually implementing and obtaining compliance with agreements could be difficult. A formal agreement will not necessarily be effectively implemented if economic reform threatens the political control of the government in power. In addition, it is important that the rules themselves be appropriate to the country's social and political conditions. There are dangers that such agreements could actually create greater domestic instability and harm external relations if they are perceived to be unfair and to have been imposed from without.

In short, the choice of Morocco as an FTA partner for the United States appears to be driven more by the availability of an opportunity than by compelling economic or strategic considerations. Morocco has long had a close political relationship with the United States, but its economic ties with the United States are weak—and its economic future will be driven far more by its relationships with Europe and its neighbors. From a political standpoint, its influence in the region is likely to be moderate.

Although not yet chosen as a partner, Egypt could offer favorable opportunities. Egypt's pivotal role in the Middle East, the importance of its continuing progress in economic reforms, its relationship with the United States, and its influential role in the region all suggest that an Egypt-US FTA should be given priority. Ultimately, however, in the case of both FTAs, the political gains to be reaped, like the potential economic gains, will depend on factors beyond the agreements themselves. While the economic gains will require the adoption of complementary policies by Morocco and Egypt, the political gains for the United States will depend on its success in restoring the prosperity and independence of Iraq and in ensuring an equitable resolution of the Israeli-Palestinian conflict.

References

American Chamber of Commerce in Morocco. 2002. Written Comments to the Office of the United States Trade Representative on the Proposed U.S.-Morocco Free Trade Agreement. www.amcham-morocco.com/downloads/ustrfta.pdf (November 22).

Dasgupta, Dipak, Jennifer Keller, and T.G. Srinivasan. 2002. Reform and Elusive Growth in the Middle East—What Has Happened in the 1990s? Photocopy. World Bank, Washington.

DeRosa, Dean. 2003. Gravity Model Calculations of the Trade Impact of US Free Trade Agreements. Background paper prepared for the conference Free Trade Agreements and US Trade Policy, sponsored by the Institute for International Economics, Washington (May 7–8).

EIU (Economist Intelligence Unit). 2003. Country Report: Morocco.

Galal, Ahmed, and Samiha Fawzy. 2001. *Egypt's Export Puzzle*. Policy Viewpoint 9. Cairo: Egyptian Center for Economic Studies. www.eces.org.eg.

Gilbert, John. 2003. CGE Simulation of US Bilateral Free Trade Agreements. Background paper prepared for at the conference Free Trade Agreements and US Trade Policy, sponsored by the Institute for International Economics (May 7–8).

Gresser, Edward. 2003. *Blank Spot on the Map: How Trade Policy Is Working Against the War on Terror*. Policy Report. Washington: Progressive Policy Institute. www.ppionline.org/documents/Muslim_Trade_0203.pdf (February).

Hoekman, Bernard, Denise Konan, and Keith Maskus. 1998. An Egypt-US Free Trade Agreement: Economic Incentives and Effects. In *Building Bridges: An Egypt-US Free Trade Agreement*, ed. Ahmed Galal and Robert Z. Lawrence. Washington: Brookings Institution.

IMF (International Monetary Fund). 2003. Morocco: Statistical Appendix. IMF Country Report 03/163 (June): 14. Washington: IMF.

Lawrence, Robert Z. 1998. Is It Time for a US–Egypt Free Trade Agreement? A US Perspective. In *Building Bridges: An Egypt–US FTA*, ed. Ahmed Galal and Robert Z. Lawrence. Washington: Brookings Institution.

Miller, Eric. 2002. *The Outlier Sectors: Areas of Non-Free Trade in the North American Free Trade Agreement*. Washington: Inter-American Development Bank.

Nathan Associates. 2003. Assessment of Morocco's Technical Assistance Needs in Negotiating and Implementing a Free Trade Agreement with the United States. Arlington, VA. Photocopy.

O'Driscoll, Gerald P., Edwin J. Feulner, and Mary A. O'Grady, ed. 2003. *2003 Index of Economic Freedom*. Washington: Heritage Foundation; New York: Dow Jones. www.heritage.org/research/features/index.

OECD (Organization for Economic Cooperation and Development). 2000. Tariffs and Trade: OECD Query and Reporting System. CD-ROM version.

Page, John, and John Underwood. 1997. Growth, the Maghreb, and Free Trade with the European Union. In *Regional Partners in Global Markets: Limits and Possibilities of the Euro-*

Med Agreements, ed. Ahmed Galal and Bernard Hoekman. Egyptian Center for Economic Studies. London: Centre for Economic Policy Research.

Refaat, Amal. 2003. Trade-Induced Protection in Egypt's Manufacturing Sector. Working Paper no. 85. Egyptian Center for Economic Studies. www.eces.org.eg.

Subramanian, Arvind. 1997. *The Egyptian Stabilization Experience: An Analytical Retrospective.* ECES Working Paper Series 18. Cairo: Egyptian Center for Economic Studies. www.eces.org.eg.

UNSD (UN Statistics Division). 2003. Comtrade Database. unstats.un.org/unsd/comtrade.

US State Department. 2002. Background Note: Morocco. www.state.gov/r/pa/ci/bgn/5431.htm (January).

Vastine, Robert (president, Coalition of Service Industries on the US-Morocco Free Trade Agreement). 2002. Statement before the Trade Policy Staff Committee, Office of the United States Trade Representative (November 21). www.uscsi.org/publications/papers/moroccof.pdf.

12

Competitive Liberalization and a US-SACU FTA

J. CLARK LEITH AND JOHN WHALLEY

The conference that gave rise to this volume was devoted to the analysis of actual and potential regional trade initiatives proposed by the United States over the past year or so for various parts of the world. The broad rubric for this set of initiatives is "competitive liberalization," the idea that a sequence of barrier-reducing preferential initiatives undertaken by the United States and the European Union in competition one with another for smaller regional markets can serve to spur global trade growth and also sow the seeds for a successful conclusion to the World Trade Organization (WTO) Doha Round in 2007 by partially reducing some barriers first (see C. Fred Bergsten, "A Competitive Approach to Free Trade," *Financial Times,* December 4, 2002; and Zoellick 2002). These latest bilaterals stand in contrast to preferential trade arrangements in the 1980s and 1990s such as the Canada-US Trade Agreement and the North American Free Trade Agreement (NAFTA), which were typically initiated by the smaller parties seeking security of access (or insurance, to paraphrase Perroni and Whalley 2000). A counterargument to claims for the likely success of this new competitive thrust in moving multilateral liberalization forward is that by establishing margins of preference in large markets for midsized entities, coalitions of groups of countries that would otherwise

J. Clark Leith is professor of economics at the University of Western Ontario. John Whalley is director of the Centre for the Study of International Economics Research (CSIER) at the University of Western Ontario, professor of economics at the University of Warwick, and coauthor of The Trading System after the Uruguay Round *(Washington: Institute for International Economics, 1996).*

lose margins of preference may be created in opposition to new multilateral liberalization. There is no theoretical reason why competitive liberalization will achieve its stated aim—but, on the other hand, it might. The proof of the pudding, in our view, will be in the eating.

Here we discuss a possible US bilateral arrangement with the Southern African Customs Union (SACU), which consists of South Africa, Botswana, Lesotho, Namibia, and Swaziland, assessing both its potential contribution to the overall US strategy and the impacts on SACU countries. Thus far, in addition to NAFTA, four US agreements have been concluded: with Israel (1985), Jordan (2001), Chile (2003), and Singapore (2003). Several others seem slated to follow, with partners including Morocco, Australia, ASEAN (the Association of Southeast Asian Nations), and Central America. We assume that the United States has consciously decided to negotiate with the whole of SACU rather than only with South Africa. The Europeans, in contrast, have two separate agreements—one with South Africa and the other with the African, Caribbean, and Pacific (ACP) countries under the Cotonou Agreement, which includes the smaller SACU members: Botswana, Lesotho, Namibia, and Swaziland (BLNS). It is important to note that SACU is for now only a customs union; it does not cover key noncommodity trade issues such as services, investment, intellectual property, and other areas. If these are substantively included in a US agreement (they are effectively not, save competition policy, in the earlier EU–South Africa agreement), there will need to be a prior internal SACU negotiation. Also, constraints on government capacity to participate are a major factor because expertise is limited and because several SACU members must address other urgent policy issues. Whether the United States should also seek wider humanitarian goals when negotiating (such as by offering a waiver of drug patent rights for treatment of AIDS) is yet another issue.

We assume, for now, that a US-SACU agreement would likely follow the broad contours of the recently signed Singapore and Chile agreements (although in practice there will of course be differences). These are NAFTA-esque in incorporating duty-free trade in goods (following transitional arrangements), with extremely complex NAFTA-like rules of origin in textiles and apparel, autos, and many other areas, as well as related provisions covering intellectual property, investment protection, temporary entry of businesspersons, and bilateral dispute settlement. The agreements go well beyond NAFTA in the coverage of services, as well as competition policy.

We suggest that SACU's interest, while that of five countries collectively, will likely be dominated by the interests of its most powerful member, South Africa. These interests are multifaceted. South African trade policy was for many years highly protectionist, in part because of anti-apartheid sanctions, and focused on trade with small, local hinterland market economies with transportation routes through South Africa. This

Table 12.1   South African trade with selected regions, 2000 (percentage shares)

Region	Exports	Imports
Asia	18.7	24.6
European Union	34.2	39.8
NAFTA	12.5	12.9
SADC	10.0	1.4

NAFTA = North American Free Trade Agreement
SADC = Southern African Development Community

Source: Cassim et al. (2002, table 6.6).

policy focus has changed substantially in recent years with liberalization in South Africa, first under WTO negotiations (Uruguay Round), and later under the 1999 bilateral free trade agreement (FTA) between the European Union and South Africa. South Africa is already liberalizing.

As table 12.1 indicates, South African exports to the European Union and to Asia are considerably larger than to NAFTA, and exports to the region are also large. Trade with NAFTA is not the dominant South African interest it might seem from the outside. Also, given the high unemployment rates in South Africa, any trade agreement perceived to exacerbate this problem may face fierce and perhaps insurmountable domestic opposition.

In this chapter we make six points relating to the evaluation of such an arrangement's impacts and possible benefits to the two sides. First, the gains in terms of conventional trade policy lie in improved access for SACU to a large North American market; for the United States the SACU market is much less significant. The asymmetry in size is partially offset by a substantial (if now diminished) asymmetry in initial barriers, which are considerably higher in SACU. However, if multilateral elimination of nonagriculture tariffs in the WTO were to occur in 2015 as per the latest US proposal at the Doha Round, such benefits to SACU members would be temporary. A SACU–US FTA, coming on top of the South Africa–EU FTA, might also speed the reduction of SACU's most favored nation (MFN) trade barriers, better preparing the SACU producers for multilateral free trade in nonagricultural goods. But the reduction of trade barriers also means reduction of tariff revenue, an important consideration for some of the smaller SACU members that makes the development of alternative revenue sources (such as a value-added tax) all the more urgent. Potential complexities in rules of origin are another key issue.

Second, a potentially important benefit for SACU may be in access in the textiles and apparel sector that is free from quotas under the Multi-Fiber Arrangement, or MFA (and the trade regime that eventually replaces it). In recent years, apparel exports from SACU to the United States have grown rapidly, encouraged in part by the African Growth and Opportunity Act (AGOA) and some elements of the MFA phaseout, but some products still remain restrained by quotas. Potential benefits here may be significant for SACU, as well as for US fiber producers under the "yarn forward" rules of origin in textiles and apparel. Hence not only the possibility of multilateral tariff elimination but also the certainty of MFA elimination in 2005 enter.

Third, the implementation of an extensive agreement covering services, intellectual property, and competition policy poses special problems for SACU. SACU does not address these matters. The smaller countries are still in the process of developing updated competition policy statutes; intellectual property regimes are in process as well, designed for compliance with the WTO's Agreement on Trade-Related Aspects of Intellectual Property Rights (TRIPs); and financial institutions are regulated under national authorities in each SACU country. While these are all issues included in the Doha Round agenda, their possible inclusion in a likely more immediate bilateral arrangement with the United States may give rise to complexities and inconsistencies. Perhaps most important, if the US-Chile and US-Singapore arrangements are a guide, requested liberalization may well be highly asymmetric and in some areas (such as banking and insurance) involve larger (and even in some areas unilateral) concessions on the SACU side.

Fourth, the prior completion of a bilateral FTA between South Africa and the European Union in 1999 and the EU-ACP Cotonou agreement covering the smaller members of SACU are further factors involved in a US-SACU negotiation. The United States will want to restore its competitive position in SACU markets, giving SACU some negotiating room. The form and content of the two bilateral relationships—US-SACU and EU-SACU—will raise issues with their joint operation. The EU arrangements sidestep the most significant noncommodity trade issues likely to be raised by a US negotiation.

Fifth, the multicountry nature of SACU, combined with the fact that it covers only trade in goods, may cause problems. SACU will have to agree both on how to treat issues such as services, intellectual property, investment, temporary entry of businesspersons, and competition policy and on how to expand its coverage of these issues before it can negotiate bilaterally with the United States. This raises the issues of negotiating capacity and institutional infrastructure. SACU's relationship with the wider Southern African Development Community (SADC) grouping in the region, which contains 14 countries, as well as individual SACU members' bilateral arrangements with Zimbabwe, will also likely need some adjustments as a result.

Finally, although a US-SACU arrangement will focus on considerations of commercial policy, it clearly has wider implications for US foreign policy in the region in terms of humanitarian and developmental objectives. Even if the benefits of such an arrangement were to accrue more than proportionately to SACU (which, given the services situation, is by no means clear), it still fits within wider US aid and development objectives in Africa. These were the motives behind the recent US initiative for the Africa Growth and Opportunity Act. A bilateral US-SACU arrangement complements this undertaking, and promises somewhat more permanence than the time-limited and unilateral AGOA. But key developmental issues may almost certainly be raised in a bilateral negotiation: How will poverty in southern Africa be affected? What about the rights of companies holding the patents for AIDS drugs? How will growth be affected? ·

Thus, overall, while we see a bilateral US-SACU FTA as highly negotiable, especially if it is limited in its services and related provisions, it may offer SACU only temporary and relatively small benefits if US MFN tariffs are already low. In contrast, liberalization in noncommodity trade areas, and the associated regulatory reform within SACU members, may be more significant. The prior EU–South Africa arrangement provides added US incentives to pursue a bilateral agreement, but in its own way it also complicates things. Complexities arise with the overlapping regional arrangements already existing in the region, as well as with the entrance of foreign-policy issues and domestic SACU macro policy concerns. But both the reduction of barriers to goods trade and liberalization of other areas are likely to have the potential of promoting growth and reducing poverty in SACU. Such a thrust is also clearly in the foreign-policy interest of the United States.

What Is SACU?

The Southern African Customs Union is a grouping of five countries (Botswana, Lesotho, Namibia, South Africa, and Swaziland) that maintain a common external tariff to third countries. Most trade goes through South Africa, which dominates the grouping economically and accounts for a large majority of the region's GDP.

While the SACU arrangement dates from 1910, it has been renegotiated on various occasions, with the most substantial changes made in 1969 and 2002. The renegotiation completed in 2002 was initiated in November 1994, shortly after the launching of the Government of National Unity in South Africa. The five members of SACU are also all members of the 14-member Southern African Development Community, and several members of SACU have long-standing bilateral trade arrangements with other countries of the region. Furthermore, these arrangements are evolving independently of the proposed US-SACU free trade agreement. Also important to the background are the bilateral EU-South African trade and cooperation agreement of 1999 and the long-standing EU-ACP agreement that covers the smaller members of SACU, which we take up below.

The basic elements of SACU are a common external tariff, common excise duties, and a compensation (or revenue) distribution formula between members. The latest treaty both changed the compensation formula and introduced new governance and administration arrangements (Kirk and Stern 2003). The SACU compensation formula had previously transferred revenues to the smaller members on the basis of shares of the value of their imports from all sources (including elsewhere in SACU) plus their consumption of excisable goods. All the revenues from the common external tariff and the common excise duties on third-country imports were paid into the South African Treasury; and after payments made to the smaller members, South Africa retained the residual balance (Hudson 1981).[1] Before the implementation of the Uruguay Round tariff cuts, that arrangement undercompensated the smaller members relative to what they would have received had the tariff been directly applied to their third-country trade (Leith 1992), but in later years it may have overcompensated them for the net costs of the common external tariff. The new formula simply divides up the revenue collected from the common external tariff, on the basis of shares of intra-SACU trade.

In addition, the distribution of the common excise duties switched to a sharing on the basis of shares of GDP adjusted at the margin to favor the poorer members. The new formula means that any reduction in the customs pool due to lower average tariffs or duty-free access under the EU-SA and the proposed US-SACU bilateral arrangements will be of concern to those members that rely heavily on this revenue source—Lesotho and Swaziland, and to a lesser extent Namibia.

New SACU institutional arrangements under the latest treaty also create a secretariat to manage the affairs of SACU; a SACU tariff board to replace the South African Board of Tariffs and Trade, which previously set and adjusted the common external tariff; and an independent ad hoc tribunal to arbitrate disputes. These institutions are still being established. At the time of writing the head of the secretariat has yet to be named, and the process for amending the common external tariff has yet to be determined. A US-SACU agreement would thus be negotiated in a period when SACU itself is in institutional flux.

The new SACU agreement also raises for the first time the possibility of establishing common policies in a limited number of areas beyond tariffs and excise duties. There is a commitment to harmonize product and technical standards, and to apply product standards and technical regulations in accordance with the WTO. Members have agreed to develop common policies and strategies on industrial development. Regarding agricultural policies, members have agreed to cooperate with each other, with the aim

---

1. The old formula also amplified the share of imports plus excisable consumption to compensate the smaller members for the disadvantages that they faced, such as lack of fiscal discretion, and contained minimum and maximum provisions.

of ensuring coordinated development of agriculture. Each is committed to having a competition policy (but for most of the smaller members that remains to be achieved) and to cooperating in the enforcement of laws and regulations governing competition. Finally, members are committed to developing SACU-wide policies to address unfair trade practices between members. The new agreement does not set out the nature or details of these common policies. Much remains to be done, and the capacity among the smaller members for policy development on intra-SACU issues is severely limited, given other very pressing policy questions that they must address. All of this evolution will also complicate a US-SACU negotiation.

The Content of a Possible US-SACU Arrangement

Predicting the outcome of a bilateral trade negotiation is always difficult, but gaining a rough sense of what a US-SACU agreement could look like is clearly germane to any evaluation of both its impact and the interests of the parties to such an arrangement. Our assumption is that a US-SACU agreement would broadly follow the contours of the already-negotiated US-Singapore and US-Chile deals, since such an agreement would be seen from the US side as fitting into its broad strategy of "competitive liberalization."[2] As SACU is one of the more heavily protected significant markets around the world, from a US standpoint such an agreement would have the explicit objective of restoring the US market position in the southern African market, given the 1999 EU–South African Free Trade Agreement and the Cotonou Agreement (discussed below).

The assumption on the US side is that the United States would negotiate on its own and independently of its NAFTA partners. There is nothing in the structure of NAFTA that precludes such independence. We see the following elements as likely to be part of the package that could emerge.

Trade in Goods

We would anticipate that all duties between the United States and SACU would be removed on a bilateral basis. The majority of tariff line items (say 85 percent, as in the Chile agreement) would become duty-free upon signing. The remainder would be phased out over a 5- to 10-year implementation period.

---

2. Our interpretation of these agreements is based primarily on the US Trade Representative's summaries (2002a, 2002b) and the reports of the US Advisory Committee for Trade Policy and Negotiations (2003a, 2003b). The lengthy texts of the US-Chile and US-Singapore agreements are now publicly available. See the USTR Web site, www.ustr.gov.

Rules of origin, as in NAFTA, would most likely apply. These would likely be extremely complex and detailed. Not only would they involve a two-way test of significant transformation (perhaps 50 percent of manufacturing content) and a change in tariff nomenclature on reexport, but many detailed product and sectoral prisons would certainly apply. Paul Brenton (2003) points out that the Singapore-US agreement in draft form contains 240 pages of text on rules of origin with bewildering detail (see box 12.1). A SACU arrangement would almost certainly encounter similar problems, as such rules are used as trade exclusion devices. In the two critical areas of textiles and apparel and autos and auto parts, NAFTA rules of origin would likely apply. For the first, these would involve duty-free treatment only for apparel items made from US or SACU fibers, and US-SACU yarn and yarn processing (the so-called yarn forward rule). For the second area, where SACU exports have been growing rapidly in recent years, the 60 percent NAFTA local content rule for duty-free treatment would most likely apply.

In agriculture, if the Chile agreement sets a precedent, duty-free treatment will eventually arrive, but it will be phased in differentially across the two country groupings. In the US-Chile agreement, Chilean agricultural duties disappear after a 4-year period, while bilateral US duties disappear in 12 years. Bilateral export subsidies will likely be banned, and a bilateral agricultural safeguard mechanism (snapbacks) installed. The treatment of sugar will be of particular interest to Swaziland and the South African province of KwaZulu-Natal. If the agreement follows the pattern of that with Chile, the United States will insist on SACU's not replacing sweeteners exported to the United States with lower-priced imports from elsewhere. Similarly, wine may be a contentious issue.

For the United States, the opportunity is to gain improved market access to a much smaller but more heavily protected southern African market. For southern Africa, it is improved access to the large US market, with the added benefit of being quota-free in textiles and apparel if content rules are met, should whatever trade regime that takes effect post-MFA (beginning in 2005) continue to have some form of quotas.

Trade in Services

There has been a substantial amount of attention paid in the recent literature to the impact of liberalizing services in developing countries. From econometric work, Aaditya Mattoo, Randeep Rathindran, and Arvind Subramanian (2001) have claimed large growth effects in developing countries (1.5 percentage points a year) from certain forms of service trade liberalization. Using an FTAP (a version of the GTAP, or Global Trade Analysis Project) model, Philippa Dee and Kevin Hanslow (2000) have produced calculations that show very large gains as a percentage of

Box 12.1 Men's and boys' woolen overcoats: Rules of origin in proposed Singapore-US FTA

To quote Paul Brenton (2003, 29–31): "The rules of origin for clothing products in the proposed Singapore–US FTA provide an example of how complex the rules can become and how difficult they must be for producers to satisfy and prove compliance. The following example is for men's or boys' overcoats made of wool:

620111 A change to subheading 620111 from any other chapter, except from heading 5106 through 5113, 5204 through 5212, 5307 through 5308 or 5310 through 5311, Chapter 54 or heading 5508 through 5516, 5801 through 5802 or 6001 through 6006, provided that:

(a) the good is both cut and sewn or otherwise assembled in the territory of one or more of the Parties, and
(b) the visible lining fabric listed in Note 1 to Chapter 62 satisfies the tariff change requirements provided therein.

The requirements of Note 1 are that

Chapter Rule 1: Except for fabrics classified in 54082210, 54082311, 54082321, and 54082410, the fabrics identified in the following sub-headings and headings, when used as visible lining material in certain men's and women's suits, suit-type jackets, skirts, overcoats, carcoats, anoraks, windbreakers, and similar articles, must be formed from yarn and finished in the territory of a Party: 5111 through 5112, 520831 through 520859, 520931 through 520959, 521031 through 521059, 521131 through 521159, 521213 through 521215, 521223 through 521225, 540742 through 540744, 540752 through 540754, 540761 through 540772 through 540774, 540782 through 540784, 540792 through 540794, 540822 through 540824 (excluding tariff item 540822aa, 540823aa or 540824aa), 540832 through 540834, 551219, 551229, 551299, 551321 through 551349, 551421 through 551599, 551612 through 551614, 551622 through 551624, 551632 through 551634, 551642 through 551644, 551692 through 551694, 600110, 600192, 600531 through 600544 or 600610 through 600644.

There is also a second general rule for the chapter which is applicable,

Chapter Rule 2: Apparel goods of this Chapter shall be considered to originate if they are both cut and sewn or otherwise assembled in the territory of one or more of the Parties and if the fabric of the outer shell, exclusive of collars or cuffs, is wholly of one or more of the following:

(a) Velveteen fabrics of subheading 580123, containing 85 percent or more by weight of cotton;
(b) Corduroy fabrics of subheading 580122, containing 85 percent or more by weight of cotton and containing more than 7.5 wales per centimeter;
(c) Fabrics of subheading 511111 or 511119, if hand-woven, with a loom width of less than 76 cm, woven in the United Kingdom in accordance with the rules and regulations of the Harris Tweed Association, Ltd., and so certified by the Association;
(d) Fabrics of subheading 511230, weighing not more than 340 grams per square meter, containing wool, not less than 20 percent by weight of fine animal hair and not less than 15 percent by weight of man-made staple fibers; or
(e) Batiste fabrics of subheading 551311 or 551321, of square construction, of single yarns exceeding 76 metric count, containing between 60 and 70 warp ends and filling picks per square centimeter, of a weight not exceeding 110 grams per square meter."

Brenton then suggests that "the basic rule of origin stipulates of chapter but then provides a list of headings and chapters from which inputs cannot be used. Thus in effect the overcoat must be manufactured from the stage of wool fibres forward. In addition, Chapter Rule 1 stipulates that the visible lining used must be produced from yarn and finished in either party. This rule may well have been introduced to constrain the impact of the tolerance rule which would normally allow 7 per cent of the weight of the article to be of non-originating materials. In overcoats and suits the lining is probably less than 7 per cent of the total weight. The second chapter rule seems to provide very specific exemptions to the rules of origin for materials which are in short-supply or not produced in the US or in Singapore, see category (c) for example, and reflects firm specific lobbying to overcome the restrictiveness of these rules of origin when the original NAFTA rules of origin were defined."

GDP for certain countries (11 percent for China). Some therefore argue that a focus on services is the key for developing countries in both regional and multilateral liberalization.

However, other studies produce much smaller gains, and data and the representation of barriers in ad valorem form may be problematic. In addition, these studies apply to genuinely multilateral liberalization rather than to the more asymmetric liberalization that may occur in SACU. Nonetheless, this may be the part of a SACU agreement most notable in its positive impacts on SACU members.

If, again, the Chilean precedent is followed, SACU will be asked to take on significant liberalization in the areas of banking, insurance, securities, and other related services. Under the Chilean arrangement, US insurance firms have full rights (with only very limited exceptions) to establish subsidiaries or joint ventures in Chile for all insurance sectors (life, nonlife, reinsurance, brokerage). US banks and securities firms may establish branches and subsidiaries, invest in local firms without restriction, and offer services to Chilean citizens participating in Chile's privatized voluntary savings plans. In telecommunications, US phone companies can interconnect with Chilean networks at nondiscriminatory rates. In e-commerce and digital products, duties are based on physical value (e.g., the disc, not the music). We anticipate these and other components being in a US-SACU agreement, but perhaps with little by way of new liberalization occurring on the US side.

The services area will pose special problems for SACU. First, with no coverage of services in SACU, if SACU is to negotiate as a single entity it will first have to agree on common positions among its members. We must note that currently their agreements do not extend beyond trade and issues directly related to it; there are no SACU-wide arrangements on most of the nongoods trade issues likely to be on the agenda for a US-SACU bilateral agreement.

Second, service sectors in each SACU country are heavily regulated, and if a US-SACU FTA includes services, major changes both within SACU members and between members will be required.

Third, and perhaps most important, the liberalization requested of SACU could well be asymmetric and markedly so in some key sectors, such as banking and insurance. While four of the five SACU members are part of the Rand Monetary Area,[3] whose currencies are irrevocably fixed to the South African rand, the licensing of banks and banking supervision in each SACU member is handled by each country's central bank under its national legislation. The same applies to insurance and other financial

---

3. The exception is Botswana, which established its own independent currency in 1976; it has since accumulated more than $5 billion in foreign-exchange reserves.

services such as mutual funds. In most cases the national legislation requires incorporation and capitalization in the country. The emphasis has been on maintaining solvent financial institutions to protect depositors' and policyholders' interests. Any proposal to establish free trade in banking and other financial services between SACU and the United States would require significant modification of current practices in these critical areas, in different ways, in each SACU country.

Investment

Major bilateral protection of investors along the lines of the NAFTA agreement will likely be proposed. These may include rights to establish, acquire, and operate investments in either region on an equal footing, as well as rights to due process protection and fair market value compensation in the event of expropriation. Local content rules on inputs to be used by investors will likely be banned. None of these provisions currently applies under the SACU treaty. Some SACU members have investment promotion schemes that are biased in favor of citizen entrepreneurs.

Intellectual Property

Here existing (or yet to be implemented) WTO levels of intellectual property protection will likely be enhanced in several ways, as in the Chile agreement. There will be protection for copyrighted works in digital form, expanded protection for patents and trade secrets, and stronger penalties for piracy and counterfeiting.

SACU currently does not deal with issues of intellectual property rights, and in some of the countries, which have lagged in implementing WTO disciplines, there are effectively only limited (or no) intellectual property regimes. Coming into compliance in this area will again pose tough challenges and require major change for some SACU members.

Competition Policy

SACU members will likely be requested (as in the Chile agreement) to install and maintain laws that prohibit anticompetitive business behavior and regulate state-owned enterprises. At present, laws governing competition in SACU members are focused not so much on ensuring open markets as on preserving certain activities threatened by outside competition. The new SACU agreement requires members to have competition policies. Whether the laws of individual countries can conform with the range of commitments mandated by the US-Chile agreement is an open question.

Government Procurement

The Chile agreement in effect extends WTO procurement agreements to all regional and municipal governments in both countries; a US-SACU agreement could take a similar form. Compliance may require that domestic preference in government procurement—in place in several SACU members—be abandoned; it could be particularly problematic for South Africa, with its separate provincial jurisdictions.

Customs Procedures

Information sharing and transparency provisions would likely apply in the area of customs. There are no formal common customs procedures currently in SACU, but in practice the nations cooperate considerably in dealing with fraud and similar matters. Plans are afoot to create a common customs declaration form to be used for intra-SACU trade to document each transaction for each of the exporting and importing countries.

Temporary Entry of Personnel

If the Chilean model is followed, NAFTA-style temporary entry visas will also apply. They are unrestricted for entry to Chile, but on the US side they are limited to holders of four-year degrees and subject to a numerical cap. SACU, we presume, could be asked to enter into similar arrangements.

Labor and the Environment

On both labor and the environment, given the flux on these issues in the WTO, the likely content of a US-SACU bilateral agreement is less clear. Worker rights as set out in the International Labor Organization will probably be reaffirmed, and there will likely be joint environmental projects, as in the Chile agreement. Special procedures for settling cases involving environmental disputes could be devised. Some form of environment impact assessment might also be agreed on.

Dispute Settlement

Bilateral dispute settlement as in the Chile agreement may be adopted. An important new feature could be the imposition of fines to enforce rulings. Given the thrust to establish new FTAs, pressures on the United States from the potentially high number of bilateral dispute panels could become a factor. If NAFTA teaches us anything, it is that bilateral dispute resolution arrangements will not fully restrain the United States from using antidumping and countervailing duties to protect specific sectors.

In sum, a US-SACU agreement could involve bilateral free trade in goods (with rules of origin, especially in textiles and apparel and in autos), asymmetric liberalization in services, bilateral investment protections, strengthened intellectual property arrangements, arrangements on competition policies, and a series of related measures in other areas. Bilateral preferential access in goods would be temporary if it were eventually superseded by the WTO's elimination of nonagriculture tariffs in the Doha Round in 2015, as the United States has proposed.

Issues in Noncommodity Trade Areas

In many ways, it is the noncommodity trade areas of a US-SACU agreement that offer simultaneously the greatest potential benefits to both parties and also the greatest challenges. SACU members will face many difficulties, not the least of which is that SACU is an agreement covering only trade in goods. At present, SACU negotiating capability in these areas is extremely limited. In the WTO it is accepted that negotiating capacity in these areas must be developed in lower-income countries. Similar issues now arise in preferential trade agreements. These and other issues have recently been explored by Aaditya Mattoo and Carsten Fink (2002).

Another central issue in this area is the extent to which potential commitments by SACU are fairly balanced, both in reality and in the perceptions of others. If the broad deal is understood effectively as a bilaterally accelerated removal of tariffs on goods—tariffs that anyway (under current US WTO proposals) would largely disappear by 2010 and would be totally gone by 2015—in return for large and mainly unreciprocated liberalization in nontrade areas by SACU, such a deal may well be rejected by SACU as showing insufficient balance.

In services it is likely that commitments will be sought by the United States across a wide range of sectors. If the Chile agreement is taken as a guide, some degree of two-way commitment could be demanded in a list of peripheral services, including computer and related services, audiovisual services, construction and engineering, tourism, advertising, express delivery, professional services (architects, engineers, accountants), distribution services, adult educational training, and environmental services. However, the core services of banking, insurance, and telecommunications could well be areas where mainly SACU commitments alone would apply. These would make it possible for various services—among them insurance and banking, brokerage, retirement income advice, and management—to cross borders.

In investment, the focus will likely be on investor guarantees, somewhat similar to Chapter 11 arrangements in NAFTA. Arrangements pertaining to intellectual property would be strengthened and extended into new areas, including digital content. An especially significant set of issues will likely pertain to drugs and patent protection related to social calamities, as discussed recently in the WTO. SACU will no doubt raise issues connected with AIDS-related medications.

South Africa's post-apartheid policy thrust has been to open up markets to competition, and the smaller SACU members have all been developing new competition policies harmonized with the South African approach. These approaches may not be compatible with the US approach. However, allowing freer entry of US firms to compete with local firms might provide a major benefit to SACU consumers.

Negotiating new bilateral rules on labor migration poses special difficulties; any liberalization on the US side will likely be restricted numerically and in other ways, as in the Chile agreement. The parallel development of US-SACU dispute resolution mechanisms may also prove challenging. SACU's new agreement, for instance, contains an untried provision under which the council of ministers refers disputes to ad hoc tribunals.

We see these noncommodity trade issues as perhaps the most significant quantitatively for both SACU and the United States (even though few or no studies exist to test that view), and the hardest to negotiate. There is both a limited capacity on the SACU side to negotiate and a perceived (if not actual) one-sidedness to this part of any negotiated arrangement.

Third Parties

Any new bilateral preferential trade agreement will potentially affect third parties with which there are existing preferential trading arrangements. In the case of SACU, members are involved in preferential trading arrangements with two important third parties: the European Union and the Southern African Development Community.

The EU–South Africa and the EU-ACP (Cotonou) Agreements

One motive for the United States to establish trade and related agreements in many parts of the world is undoubtedly competition with either earlier or proposed EU initiatives made in the same markets.[4] The idea is to restore a level playing field for US exporters where EU preferential agreements exist. It is thus likely that the EU–South African agreement of

---

4. The Congressional Research Service report on FTAs (Cooper 2003) notes that the European Union has FTAs with a number of countries; similarly the CRS report explicitly points to the existence of Canada-Chile and Mexico-Chile FTAs, and the Japan-Singapore FTA.

1999 has been one factor in the United States' identifying SACU as a target for a US bilateral FTA negotiation.

Following its change in government, South Africa had hoped to be included in the European Union's agreements with former colonies: the African, Caribbean, and Pacific countries. The asymmetrical nature of the then EU-ACP agreement, which provided ACP countries with preferential access to the EU market while not requiring the reverse, was particularly attractive to South Africa. Arguing that certain aspects of the South African economy resemble those of a developed country, the European Union developed a two-track arrangement with South Africa: while putting in place a free trade agreement between the European Union and South Africa (signed in 1999) and including South Africa in the renewed arrangement with the ACP, the Cotonou Agreement (2000), it explicitly excluded South Africa from the trade arrangements of the Cotonou Agreement and from access to the soft loan European Development Fund.[5]

The FTA portion of the EU–South African agreement covers 90 percent of bilateral trade, but it has some important exceptions. Separately negotiated agreements cover the entry into the European Union of wines and spirits, as well as the products of fisheries (still in process). South Africa continues to restrict entry of various industrial items, including motor vehicles and some textiles. In addition, provisions allow for safeguards when imports cause injury to a national industry.

Several trade-related issues, such as competition policy, intellectual property rights, free movement of capital, and technical barriers to trade, are covered; but significantly, core services (banking, insurance, telecommunications, and transportation) are not. Generally the language is couched in terms of objectives, with "consultations" and "close cooperation" as the mechanisms. In both the EU-SA and the Cotonou agreements, the European Union includes a reference to the importance of democratic principles, human rights, and the rule of law. Each party is free to employ "appropriate measures" unilaterally if the other violates those principles.

From a US point of view, a US-SACU agreement would redress the trade advantage currently enjoyed by EU exporters over US exporters in the South African market, as well as give preferences to US exporters in the rest of the SACU markets. The prior EU–South Africa agreement thus seems to be playing a clear role in driving forward a US-SACU agreement. But in the key areas of autos and textiles, different trade rules will apply. It is very likely that the United States would seek preferred access to the still highly protected SACU auto market. Yet if multilateral elimination of nonagricultural tariffs are achieved by 2015, all such effects will be temporary.

---

5. The Cotonou Agreement also includes a provision for phasing in reciprocal trade concessions, commencing in 2008.

Also, it is important to highlight the sharp differences in architecture between the US and EU approaches. The European Union negotiates de facto separately with South Africa and other SACU countries, recognizing their differences. The EU agreement explicitly states the wider humanitarian goals that underlie wider foreign policy, and proceeds to link them to trade. The EU agreement does not deal centrally with service and key nontrade issues. If the US objective were only to compete with the European Union, it might do the same. So perhaps the strategy is to go beyond the European Union into new areas, to establish a new US advantage. And perhaps the EU response will be to renegotiate, seeking also to extend into new areas. All these issues await resolution, but the need to consider the interplay between these agreements is obvious.

The Southern African Development Community

The five members of SACU all belong to the 14-member Southern African Development Community, and most SADC members have signed an FTA protocol,[6] effective September 2000, that envisions almost complete intra-SADC free trade by the year 2012. Hanging over the SADC FTA is a complex set of rules of origin, which differ across different types of goods (Flatters 2002). Rules of origin are not an issue within SACU, given the common external tariff.[7] Hence, the potential for inconsistencies between the protection of goods originating within SACU and goods originating elsewhere is substantial.[8] It is perhaps for this reason that in mid-2002, the SADC executive secretary proposed that SADC move to a customs union. This complex combination of actual and proposed preferential trading arrangements is illustrated in figure 12.1. Several SACU members also have bilateral free trade agreements with regional nonmembers, including Zimbabwe, Malawi, and Mozambique.

This overall picture—as both the United States and the European Union engage in a series of bilateral preferential arrangements—is what Ronald Wonnacott (1996) calls a "hub-and-spoke" system: the hubs in this case are the United States and the European Union, and the spokes are the individual countries or regions that have or are considering preferential bi-

---

6. Angola, the Democratic Republic of the Congo, and the Seychelles have not yet signed the SADC trade protocol.

7. Rules-of-origin issues arising from the EU-SA FTA are avoided by the European Union's treating all SACU-origin inputs as South African for purposes of calculating origin and the BLNS's being content to purchase lower-priced goods that enter duty-free through South Africa.

8. A further wrinkle is that two members of SACU (Namibia and Swaziland) also belong to the Common Market for Eastern and Southern Africa (COMESA), although they cannot grant duty-free entry to COMESA-origin goods.

Figure 12.1 Overlapping trade relationships between SACU, the United States, SADC, and the European Union

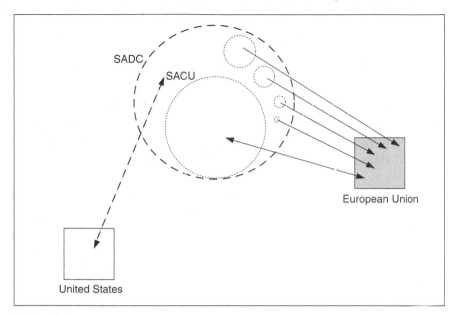

SACU = Southern African Customs Union
SADC = Southern African Development Community

lateral trading arrangements with each hub. While such competition be-tween the European Union and the United States may hasten the ultimate goal of multilateral free trade, the significant effects that may occur in the interim need to be included in any evaluation of the FTAs' impact. For each spoke of an existing preferential arrangement, the addition of an-other spoke will reduce its margin of preference in the hub. This effect applies particularly to the non-SACU members of SADC in their rela-tionship with SACU. Furthermore, the individual spokes could gain by collectively rather than individually dealing with the hub. For this reason, SACU clearly has an interest in coordinating its negotiations in concert with other US bilateral partners.

Within this context of preexisting preferential trading arrangements in southern Africa, new institutions barely under way, and a substantial un-finished agenda of intra-SACU policy development, the proposed US-SACU FTA poses challenges to SACU to both determine and promote the interests of its members in any negotiations. It is in part because of all these complexities, limited intra-SACU coverage across nontrade areas, complex bilateral agreements, limited negotiating capacity in some of the smaller SACU countries, and the need for a prior SACU negotiation that an obvi-ous fundamental question arises. From the point of view of all the parties to the proposed SACU-US FTA, might not a dual-track arrangement—between the United States and South Africa and the United States and BLNS, much like the relationship between the European Union and South Africa and between the European Union and BLNS (under the Cotonou Agreement)—be simpler, easier, and quicker to negotiate? The economic impacts for the United States would be much the same, but the complexities would be much reduced. Alternatively, an asymmetric treatment of the smaller or poorer SACU members, allowing them a longer period of adjustment, might be contemplated. We put such issues to one side, given the stated US aim of bilaterally negotiating with SACU, and turn now to assessing the impacts of a US-SACU arrangement.

The Impacts of a US-SACU Arrangement

Evaluating the impact of a possible US–SACU arrangement involves an assessment of the initial barriers to flows of goods and services and the levels of intellectual property protection used by the two parties; the relative sizes of the potential markets, as well as the sizes of current and potential flows; and the strength of possible negative effects of trade and service diversion. Once these possible impacts are known, then an evaluation of the narrower commercial policy incentives to participate is possible for the two parties. This discussion puts to one side, for the moment, whether there is also a humanitarian, developmental, and implicit aid objective for the United States, possibly making a contribution to a rebuilding of African society worthwhile even if the balance of commercial advantage goes against the United States. Because other initiatives are already under way, including the US AGOA of 2000, evaluation of a bilateral agreement must take into account a changing trade policy environment.

The principal trade flows in the bilateral US-SACU relationship are set out in table 12.2. The United States now runs a substantial merchandise trade deficit with SACU, the outcome of rapid growth of SACU exports to the United States in recent years combined with stagnant US exports to SACU.[9] US imports from SACU are dominated by platinum (for catalytic converters) and diamonds, which are already largely duty-free, but SACU exports of autos and auto parts, as well as apparel, are growing rapidly. US exports of manufactures to SACU face tariffs that are still moderately high, although they have come down substantially in recent years (see table 12.3).[10] Service trade flows, for now, are probably small, but data are not readily available.

---

9. A large part of the change is probably due to the dramatic real depreciation of the rand against the dollar.

10. The IMF (2002) reports that the average unweighted tariff rate in 1990 was 30 percent.

Table 12.2 US-SACU trade flows in goods (millions of dollars)

HTS code	HTS category	1996	1997	1998	1999	2000	2001	2002
Imports from SACU								
7110	Platinum	744	754	1,006	1,002	1,529	1,534	1,173
7102	Diamonds	105	163	163	144	342	474	517
87	Motor vehicles and parts	46	57	76	120	150	359	573
61 and 62	Apparel	143	180	205	241	321	441	603
72	Iron and steel	338	306	467	393	462	289	302
26	Ores, slag, and ash	274	282	330	340	269	243	248
84	Mechanical appliances	79	72	91	121	154	253	235
	Other	741	899	912	1,027	1,252	1,178	1,108
	Total	**2,470**	**2,713**	**3,250**	**3,388**	**4,479**	**4,771**	**4,759**
Exports to SACU								
84	Mechanical appliances	793	756	763	578	541	540	501
88	Aircraft	162	178	733	400	609	631	317
87	Motor vehicles and parts	260	264	286	147	238	457	287
85	Electrical machinery and equipment	239	238	284	199	198	200	160
90	Optical instruments	149	157	168	155	148	153	150
	Other	1,509	1,408	1,356	1,148	1,214	1,142	1,139
	Total	**3,112**	**3,001**	**3,590**	**2,627**	**2,948**	**3,123**	**2,554**
	Bilateral balance	642	288	340	(761)	(1,531)	(1,648)	(2,205)

HTS = Harmonized Tariff Schedule codes
SACU = Southern African Customs Union

Source: US International Trade Commission, Tariff and Trade DataWeb, www.dataweb.usitc. gov, 2003.

Our evaluation of the impact of a US-SACU agreement follows from what we have already set out. While labeled a "free trade agreement," the reality of such an arrangement is more complex. The label suggests that its central element is trade in goods, but much more is involved in this case (services, investment, intellectual property, labor mobility, dispute settlement, and other areas). Also, post–Uruguay Round formal tariff barriers are already low,[11] save for remaining tariff peaks in textiles and apparel, though they are significantly higher on the SACU than on the US side. These tariffs facing SACU exports may in any case be phased out through multilateral negotiation in the WTO Doha Round. More significant access issues for SACU pertain to contingent protection—that is, antidumping and countervailing duties. These are governed by a US quasi-judicial process that is unlikely to be affected by a bilateral US-SACU arrangement.

In contrast, major barriers remain in the services area, where domestic regulation segments markets in banking, insurance, telecommunications, and transportation. This segmentation occurs both across US-SACU relations and within SACU. While bilateral flows of services between the

11. See also, however, Burfisher, Robinson, and Thierfelder (2003), whose discussion of the effects of regional trade agreements stresses new trade theory considerations.

Table 12.3   SACU tariff structure, 2000 and 1997

Sector	Number of lines, 2000	Imports, 2000 (percent)	Weighted average, 2000	Unweighted average, 2000	Unweighted average, 1997
Agriculture	295	0.8	1.4	4.2	5.6
Gas	2	0.0	0.0	0.0	0.0
Manufacturing	5,479	84.7	8.6	6.7	15.6
Mining	107	14.5	0.0	1.2	1.4
Total	**5,883**	**100.0**	**7.3**	**6.5**	**15.1**

SACU = Southern African Customs Union

Note: The source indicates that the tariff data refer to South Africa. However, because there is a common external tariff, and because many of the goods destined for the Botswana, Lesotho, Namibia, and Swaziland (BLNS) markets pass through South Africa, the data are a reasonable representation of SACU's tariffs.

Source: Cassim et al. (2002, table 3.11).

United States and SACU are still small relative to goods flows (lack of data is a major problem here), the barriers thrown up by licensing and other restrictions are sizable. The key, if the Chile agreement is a guide, is that the United States will likely seek what is in many ways one-sided liberalization: that is, freer entry for US service providers to SACU markets with little reciprocal improvement of access to US service markets. It may be that SACU providers cannot in fact compete in US markets, but unless improved access is offered this hypothesis will never be tested.

In addition, liberalization offered in other nonmanufactures areas of trade is also highly asymmetric in the Chilean case. Short-term permits are unconstrained for professionals entering Chile, but are to be numerically capped for those entering the United States. Agricultural liberalization occurs over a period of 4 years on the Chilean side, but over 12 years on the US side. Investment protections are designed for US investors in Chile, rather than for Chilean investors in the United States.

Thus, one could view the US-Chile agreement as primarily an asymmetric package to lower nonmanufactures trade barriers. If a US-SACU negotiation takes this direction, it may be similarly judged by those on the SACU side. SACU exporters in textiles might gain by being quota-free in the US market, but depending on what follows the elimination of MFA in 2005, this removal of quotas may be worth less than first appears. Given the relative scarcity of service arrangements in SACU, to be plunged into effectively unilateral liberalization in services (which did not occur with the EU-SA agreement of 1999) may be hard for SACU to deal with institutionally and politically, even if there are substantial benefits to domestic consumers.

The more direct impacts that may follow on trade and other bilateral flows are at this point unfortunately conjectural at best. Aaditya Mattoo, Devesh Roy, and Arvind Subramanian (forthcoming) assess the impacts of AGOA as surprisingly small, and attribute this result to the restrictions pertaining to rules of origin. Jagdish Bhagwati (2002) suggests that most benefits for smaller entities such as SACU from such arrangements could potentially be achieved by unilateral liberalization without the trade diversion costs of regional agreements, although his analysis neglects the access benefits to US markets. Paul Collier and Jan Willem Gunning (1999), who discuss the reasons for poor African growth, do not put access barriers high on their list. Paul Brenton and M. Manchin (forthcoming) highlight the role of rules of origin in making EU agreements work, something that also may apply to a US-SACU arrangement.

Trade liberalization and the removal or lowering of trade barriers are generally viewed by economists as good; and economic theory clearly suggests that as the smaller partner, SACU should benefit disproportionately from a US-SACU arrangement. Theory also suggests that there is likely to be trade diversion where existing barriers are high, such as in services. But the combination of an FTA with temporary and small barriers in the large market and all the add-on diversions does not guarantee that such an arrangement will be welfare enhancing. Also, such an arrangement may be so broad that it will prove impossible to negotiate with the whole of SACU at this time of flux. Simpler alternatives may need to be explored.

Developmental Implications for Southern Africa and Concluding Remarks

In our view, the political reality is that debate in both SACU and the United States on a US-SACU FTA cannot be delinked from wider foreign-policy and developmental issues, nor perhaps should it be. Some of the key questions raised may include the following: Would a proposed US-SACU FTA contribute to the development of the southern African region? Would it contribute to a reduction of poverty in the region? if so, in what ways? Will unemployment rates in South Africa and in SACU grow with liberalization?

It is widely acknowledged that successful development depends on good policies (Burnside and Dollar 2000). Among the "good policies" usually credited for successful development is the alignment of domestic prices with world market prices, usually achieved by movement toward freer trade. Such a policy stance also limits the power of domestic monopolies and the power of specific interests to capture transfers from the rest of society, thereby forcing entrepreneurs to continuously pursue the innovation on which productivity growth depends. Empirical work that draws on both developing and mature economies offers evidence that trade has a significant and positive effect on growth (Frankel and Romer 1999), although Mattoo, Roy, and Subramanian (forthcoming) argue the size of the effect is uncertain. This suggests that the US-SACU FTA, and a fortiori in combination with the EU-SA FTA, could bring substantial development benefits to the region by hastening the process of trade and market liberalization.

Major caution is in order, however, regarding even this qualified claim of benefit. First, the poverty effects in SACU of an FTA with the United States may be negative. While in general it is reasonable to presume, after Jagdish Bhagwati and T. N. Srinivasan (2002), that trade promotes growth and that growth reduces absolute poverty, the opposite outcome is possible in the current circumstances of SACU. Given the distortions in both the goods markets and the factor markets of SACU, as well as the partial nature of any US-SACU trade liberalization, it would be too facile to presume a positive effect on the poor. Furthermore, the region's comparative advantage is based on natural resources, while natural resources and capital appear to be complementary inputs.[12] In these circumstances, a movement toward freer trade will very likely reduce demand for labor in a labor market that is already exhibiting significant evidence of unemployment.[13] Thus for poverty reduction to result from trade liberalization, the distortions giving rise to the unemployment must also be tackled. This link between liberalization and unemployment is likely to be a central issue in the debate within SACU on an agreement.

Second, as Collier and Gunning (1999) contend, nontrade issues are the more critical in explaining Africa's slower growth performance. Of particular significance is the development of institutions. William Easterly and Ross Levine's recent work (2002) argues that once one controls for institutions, the effect of good policies on growth disappears. If that is the case, we need to be concerned about the effectiveness of SACU's regional and national institutions. This concern applies not only to the new policies and programs being negotiated and then administered, such as the proposed US-SACU FTA, but also to existing national economic institutions.

South Africa, over the twentieth century, developed effective institutions that reflected the wishes of the governing interests. As the governing interests changed in the 1990s, the institutions were largely maintained— both by the Government of National Unity and by the African National Congress–led government. Unlike the changeover in Zimbabwe in 1980, that in South Africa kept the experience base of existing institutions intact. Consequently, today's economic institutions remain both effective and largely attuned to the wishes of the new governing interests.

Botswana, which has maintained both institutional and political continuity since its independence in 1966, is similarly reasonably well positioned to negotiate and administer a new arrangement, and then to reap the growth benefits from the increased openness that results. Namibia, which has been independent for a far shorter period (since 1990), and Lesotho and Swaziland, which have ongoing constitutional turmoil, are less well equipped institutionally.

---

12. Alleyne and Subramanian (2001) show that South Africa's exports are capital intensive.

13. The IMF (2002) cites South Africa's official unemployment rate for 2001 as 28.8 percent.

The new SACU is only now commencing to build its institutions. While the new institutions will be able to draw on the experience base of SACU's members, the institutions themselves have yet to develop. SACU policies dealing with industrial development, competition, and "unfair" trade practices face a significant gestation period. Yet such SACU policies may be a prerequisite for coming to terms with the United States on many of the nontrade issues that the United States will likely seek to include in any agreement. The need for considerable patience on the part of all parties to the negotiation is clear. The United States will need to be patient with the need for SACU to develop policy positions, and SACU will need to be patient with a potentially overstretched US trade representative.

The promise of substantial American funding for technical assistance announced at the time of US Trade Representative Robert Zoellick's January 2003 visit to South Africa may be of some help in the institution-building process. However, unless that technical assistance is perceived by the SACU governments and the new SACU institutions as working to promote their interests, rather than simply pushing the agenda of the donor (as has happened all too often with donor-funded advice), it will do little to promote the agreement as benefiting all parties. Another nontrade issue that is likely to be on the table is the matter of capital controls. As Sidney Weintraub's chapter in this volume makes clear, capital controls were prohibited in the Chile and Singapore agreements at the insistence of the US Treasury.[14] Chile, in particular, had been relatively successful for several years at avoiding the disruptive effect of "hot money" on the real side of the economy. On more than one occasion in the past, South Africa has used the financial rand to separate the exchange rate for current account transactions from the exchange rate for capital account transactions, allowing real adjustment to a major capital flow to be made gradually over months, not days. The governments of the countries of southern Africa may not be willing to give up this degree of freedom in dealing with international financial disturbances.

On balance, however, we believe that since the principal impact of a US-SACU FTA will be to align SACU prices more closely with world prices, the effect on the region is likely to be positive. Such an agreement may also provide the opportunity for SACU member governments to launch much-needed regulatory reform, which is particularly important in unleashing the forces of "creative destruction" (Aghion and Howitt 1992). To be seen to be pressing a growth-promoting agenda is clearly in the foreign-policy interests of the United States. Furthermore, this thrust is likely to coincide with the new governing interests in South Africa, which are less beholden to the import-substitution sector that was built up under apartheid. The rest of SACU has a fundamental interest in freer

---

14. Chile is allowed to impose restrictions for 12 months on certain types of speculative capital, as long as those restrictions do not substantially impede capital transfers.

trade with the rest of the world, as the bulk of consumer goods are protected by the common external tariff and most exports sell on the world, not regional, markets. If this change in incentives can be accompanied by a reduction of factor-market distortions, especially in South Africa, and by effective SACU institution building, then the development benefits for the region will begin to flow.

References

Advisory Committee for Trade Policy and Negotiations. 2003a. The US-Chile Free Trade Agreement. Washington: Office of the US Trade Representative.

Advisory Committee for Trade Policy and Negotiations. 2003b. The US-Singapore Free Trade Agreement. Washington: Office of the US Trade Representative.

Aghion, Philippe, and Peter Howitt. 1992. A Model of Growth Through Creative Destruction. *Econometrica* 60, no. 2 (March): 323–51.

Alleyne, Trevor, and Arvind Subramanian. 2001. *What Does South Africa's Pattern of Trade Say About Its Labor Market?* IMF Working Papers 01/148. www.imf.org/external/pubs/ft/wp/2001/wp01148.pdf (July).

Bhagwati, J.N. 2002. The Poor's Best Hope. *The Economist*, June 22, 24–26.

Bhagwati, Jagdish, and T.N. Srinivasan. 2002. Trade and Poverty in Poor Countries. *American Economic Review* 92, no. 2 (May): 180–83.

Brenton, Paul. 2003. Notes on Rules of Origin with Implications for Regional Integration in South East Asia. www.iadb.org/intal/foros/LAbrenton_paper.pdf.

Brenton, Paul R., and M. Manchin. Forthcoming. Making EU Trade Agreements Work: The Role of Rules of Origin. *World Economy*.

Burfisher, Mary E., Sherman Robinson, and Karen Thierfelder. 2003. Regionalism: Old and New, Theory and Practice. Paper presented at the conference Agricultural Policy Reform and the WTO: Where Are We Heading? sponsored by the International Agricultural Trade Research Consortium (IATRC), Capri, Italy (June 23–26).

Burnside, Craig, and David Dollar. 2000. Aid, Policies, and Growth. *American Economic Review* 90, no. 4 (September): 847–68.

Cassim, Rashad, Donald Onyanso, and Dirk Ernst van Seventer. 2002. The State of Trade Policy in South Africa. Trade and Industrial Policy Strategies, South Africa (March).

Collier, Paul, and Jan Willem Gunning. 1999. Why Has Africa Grown Slowly? *Journal of Economic Perspectives* 13, no. 3: 3–22.

Cooper, William H. 2003. *Free Trade Agreements: Impact on US Trade and Implications for US Trade Policy*. Congressional Research Service, Report RL 31356. Washington: Congressional Research Service, Library of Congress. Available at www.fpc.state.gov/documents/ organization/9674.pdf (April 9).

Dee, Philippa, and Kevin Hanslow. 2000. Multilateral Liberalization of Services Trade. Productivity Commission Staff Research Paper. Ausinfo, Canberra.

Easterly, William, and Ross Levine. 2002. *Tropics, Germs, and Crops: How Endowments Influence Economic Development*. NBER Working Paper 9106. Cambridge, MA: National Bureau of Economic Research.

Flatters, Frank. 2002. SADC Rules of Origin: Undermining Regional Free Trade. Paper presented at the Trade and Industrial Policy Strategies Annual Forum, South Africa, September 9–11. Available at qed.econ.queensu.ca/pub/faculty/flatters/writings/ff_sadc_roo_tips_forum.pdf.

Frankel, Jeffrey A., and David Romer. 1999. Does Trade Cause Growth? *American Economic Review* 89, no. 3 (June): 379–98.

Hudson, Derek J. 1981. Botswana's Membership in the Southern African Customs Union. In *Papers on the Economy of Botswana*, ed. Charles Harvey. London: Heinemann.

IMF (International Monetary Fund). 2002. South Africa, Staff Report for the 2002 Article IV Consultations, Washington (June).

Kirk, Robert, and Matthew Stern. 2003. The New Southern African Customs Union Agreement. SADC and the World Bank. Photocopy.

Leith, J. Clark. 1992. The Static Welfare Effects of a Small Developing Country's Membership in a Customs Union: Botswana in the Southern African Customs Union. *World Development* 20, no. 7: 1021–28.

Mattoo, Aaditya, and Carsten Fink. 2002. *Regional Agreements and Trade in Services: Policy Issues*. World Bank Policy Research Working Paper 2052. Washington: World Bank. Available at http://econ.worldbank.org/files/15653_wps2852.pdf (June).

Mattoo, Aaditya, Randeep Rathindran, and Arvind Subramanian. 2001. *Measuring Services Trade Liberalization and its Impact on Trade Growth: An Illustration*. World Bank Working Paper 2655. Washington: World Bank. Available at www.worldbank.org/research/trade/archive.html (August).

Mattoo, Aaditya, Devesh Roy, and Arvind Subramanian. Forthcoming. The Africa Growth and Opportunity Act and Its Rules of Origin: Generosity Undermined? *World Economy*.

Perroni, C., and J. Whalley. 2000. The New Regionalism: Insurance or Liberalization. *Canadian Journal of Economics* 33, no. 1: 1–24.

USTR (United States Trade Representative). 2002a. Free Trade with Chile. *Trade Facts*. Washington: United States Trade Representative.

USTR (United States Trade Representative). 2002b. Free Trade with Singapore. *Trade Facts*. Washington: United States Trade Representative.

Wonnacott, Ronald J. 1996. Trade and Investment in a Hub-and-Spoke System versus a Free Trade Area. *World Economy* 19, no. 3 (May): 237–52.

Zoellick, Robert. 2002. Unleashing the Tradewinds. *The Economist*, December 7, 27–29.

VI

POLICY CONCLUSIONS AND RECOMMENDATIONS

13

Assessing US FTA Policy

JEFFREY J. SCHOTT

As of January 2004, the United States has entered into free trade agreements (FTAs) with Israel, Canada, Mexico, Jordan, Singapore, and Chile. It is currently crafting bilateral FTAs with 12 countries (Australia, Morocco, the 5 Central American countries, and the 5 members of the Southern African Customs Union)—which some also count among the 33 partners in the negotiation of the Free Trade Area of the Americas (FTAA). In addition, the US Trade Representative (USTR) has notified Congress of his intent to open talks with Bahrain, Bolivia, Colombia, the Dominican Republic, Ecuador, Panama, Peru, and Thailand in 2004. Current FTA partners account for more than one-third of total US merchandise trade; upon completion of the new bilateral FTA negotiations and the FTAA, more than 40 percent of US trade will be covered by free trade pacts (see table 13.1).

Besides the current US negotiating partners, there is a lengthy queue of countries seeking to enter bilateral FTA negotiations with the United States. This list includes Uruguay in Latin America, Egypt in the Middle East, and New Zealand, Pakistan, the Philippines, Sri Lanka, and Taiwan in the Asia Pacific region. In addition, some members of Congress and business leaders in both countries have advocated adding South Korea to the negotiating queue. FTAs would cover about 50 percent of US trade if agreements were reached with all these countries as well as those already in train.

This spurt of negotiating activity—in parallel with the Doha Round of multilateral trade negotiations in the World Trade Organization (WTO)—is unprecedented in postwar US trade policy. The benefits and drawbacks of each individual initiative, including their implications for the world

Table 13.1   US FTA partners, current and prospective

Partners	2001 GDP (billions of dollars)[a]	2001 GDP per capita (dollars)	US merchandise trade, 2002 (billions of dollars) Exports to[b]	Imports from[c]	Trade balance	Total two-way trade
Current						
Canada	694	22,343	142.5	210.5	−68.0	353.1
Chile	66	4,314	2.3	3.6	−1.3	5.9
Israel	108	17,024	5.3	12.4	−7.1	17.7
Jordan	9	1,755	0.4	0.4	0.0	0.8
Mexico	618	6,214	86.1	134.1	−48.0	220.2
Singapore	86	20,733	14.7	14.1	0.6	28.8
Subtotal			251.4	375.2	−123.8	626.5
Under negotiation						
Australia	369	19,019	12.3	6.4	5.9	18.7
Bahrain	8	12,189	0.4	0.4	0.0	0.8
Bolivia	8	936	0.2	0.2	0.0	0.3
Brazil	503	2,915	11.2	15.6	−4.4	26.8
CAFTA-5	59	1,758	9.4	11.8	−2.4	21.3
Colombia	82	1,915	3.3	5.4	−2.1	8.7
Dominican Republic	21	2,494	4.1	4.2	−0.1	8.3
Ecuador	21	1,632	1.5	2.1	−0.6	3.6
Morocco	34	1,173	0.6	0.4	0.2	1.0
Panama	12	4,163	1.3	0.3	1.0	1.6
Peru	54	2,058	1.4	2.0	−0.5	3.4
South Africa	113	2,620	2.4	4.2	−1.8	6.7
Thailand	115	1,874	4.5	14.8	−10.3	19.3
Subtotal			52.7	76.8	−15.1	120.4
Prospective						
Egypt	98	1,511	2.8	1.3	1.5	4.2
South Korea	422	8,917	21.2	35.3	−14.1	56.4
New Zealand	50	13,101	1.7	2.3	−0.5	4.0
Pakistan	59	415	0.7	2.3	−1.6	3.0
Philippines	71	911	7.0	11.0	−4.0	17.9
Sri Lanka	16	836	0.2	1.8	−1.6	2.0
Taiwan	282	12,572	16.8	32.1	−15.3	48.8
Uruguay	19	5,522	0.2	0.2	0.0	0.4
Subtotal			50.5	86.2	−35.8	136.7
United States	10,065	35,277	629.6	1,154.8	−525.2	1,784.4

CAFTA = Central American Free Trade Agreement

a. In current US dollars.
b. US domestic exports.
c. US imports for consumption.

Sources: For GDP, World Bank *World Development Indicators* 2003; Council for Economic Planning and Development Yearbook, Taiwan (2003); Central Bank of Nicaragua statistics (2002), www.bcn.gob.ni/; and IADB country homepages (2003), www.iadb.org/exr/country/eng/. For trade, USITC Trade Dataweb, http://dataweb.usitc.gov.

trading system, have been examined in the preceding chapters of this book. In this concluding chapter, I assess the US policy to date—including the criteria for selecting FTA partners—and offer recommendations on how the FTA strategy should be recast to meet US economic and foreign policy objectives and to complement ongoing negotiations in the Doha Round.

US FTA Strategy

The United States has global trading interests. Throughout the postwar period, it has been a leader of the multilateral trading system and the *demandeur* of all nine rounds of GATT and WTO negotiations.

For the past two decades, however, bilateral FTAs have been pursued both to complement and to cajole progress at the multilateral level. In the 1980s, frustration following the acrimonious GATT ministerial meeting of November 1982 led then-USTR William Brock to pursue bilateral options with Israel and later Canada (Schott 1983). As Howard Rosen explains in chapter 3, talks with Israel served as a convenient pilot project for the new FTA policy—offering a large political payoff with little economic consequence or impact on the GATT system. The Canada–US FTA advanced the policy dramatically by reinforcing the extensive economic integration already occurring in the North American market and by suggesting alternative negotiating options if a new GATT round was not launched (Schott and Smith 1988). This message was reiterated and amplified with the start of the NAFTA negotiations in 1991 after the GATT ministerial in Brussels in December 1990 failed to conclude the Uruguay Round (Hufbauer and Schott 1992, 42–43).

After the bitter NAFTA ratification debate and the lapse of "fast-track" trade negotiating authority in mid-1994, US trade policy refocused on "Big Emerging Markets" that potentially offered substantial growth opportunities for US exporters and investors. Two superregional initiatives were launched during this period, involving Asia Pacific and Western Hemisphere countries. US officials found willing partners among the developing countries in the Western Hemisphere and launched the FTAA process at the Summit of the Americas in Miami in December 1994. That meeting came three weeks after the United States and its partners in the Asia Pacific Economic Cooperation (APEC) forum committed at the APEC Summit in Bogor, Indonesia, to the ambitious goal of free trade and investment in the region by 2010–20. After early successes in pushing the conclusion of the Uruguay Round and later the WTO Information Technology Agreement, the APEC free trade initiative bogged down.[1] FTAA

---

1. APEC members never committed to a traditional FTA negotiation, but instead sought progress towards free trade through a process of "concerted unilateralism" (Bergsten 1996).

negotiations began in 1998, though US participation was initially hobbled by the lack of a congressional negotiating mandate until the reauthorization of fast-track authority—renamed "trade promotion authority," or TPA—in the summer of 2002.

Despite the fast-track interregnum, the FTAA talks proceeded—albeit sluggishly. The United States began bilateral FTA negotiations with Jordan and later Singapore and Chile, as a number of other developing countries sought to join the FTA queue. The US–Jordan FTA was implemented under regular legislative procedures, but the other FTA partners had to wait until new US trade authority was enacted before their deals could be consummated. The explanation for this activity may have more to do with the changing approaches to trade negotiations by developing countries than with new US trade strategies.

Traditionally, trade officials have tried to deflect demands for reform of their own trade barriers, acceding to the minimum change needed to complete a trade pact. But over the past decade or so, developing countries engaged in FTAs have turned such negotiating strategies on their head. Instead of limiting their own reforms, trade officials have tried to "out-reform" their competitors in an effort both to secure preferential access to key markets and, even more important, to lock in domestic reforms through contractual obligations and thus improve the investment climate in their markets. Mexico and Chile have been the most prolific proponents of this strategy, concluding FTAs with numerous neighbors plus the European Union. It is no exaggeration to say that these FTAs are primarily investment-driven and integrally linked with economic development strategies.

Fred Bergsten (1996) recognized this new negotiating dynamic and called it "competitive liberalization."[2] Increasingly, both developed and developing countries have adopted this approach to their trade policies. The reason is straightforward: FTAs offer opportunities not just to bolster exports but also to reinforce and secure domestic reforms crucial for economic development. These domestic reforms, in turn, make it easier for countries to undertake and sustain the obligations of broader multilateral accords. With TPA in hand, US trade officials have aggressively pursued this strategy—building on NAFTA—to encourage other countries to accelerate the pace of trade reform in bilateral and regional free trade pacts pursued concurrently with the Doha Round of multilateral trade negotiations (Zoellick 2002).

---

2. Bergsten (1996) developed the concept of competitive liberalization in his analysis of negotiating incentives in the Asia Pacific context, building on an earlier analysis by Hufbauer (1989, chap. 6). Since then, the phenomenon has taken root in all regions and has been adopted by USTR Robert Zoellick as the core strategy of US trade policy.

Picking FTA Partners

In response to the numerous requests for FTAs by countries of widely diverse size, income, and geographic proximity to the United States, how do US trade officials pick their negotiating partners? Members of Congress often have suggested that US officials pursue pacts with specific countries but rarely have asked the executive branch to establish selection criteria that would set priorities among their prospective initiatives. Until recently, the selection process has been opaque but uncontroversial—since it was rarely used. That situation obviously has changed. The following sections provide a closer look at US objectives and selection criteria, and how the policy has been implemented to date.

Two introductory points bear mention. First, countries ask the United States to negotiate FTAs for several reasons. Bilateral fast-track authority, as amended by the Trade and Tariff Act of 1984, required that US trading partners take the initiative. For the past 15 years, countries have requested an FTA in response to the Canada–US FTA, and then NAFTA—reflecting concerns about discriminatory treatment against their exporters in the US market. For developing countries, taking the initiative is particularly important to demonstrate the political commitment (or "buy-in") to pursue the requisite reforms in domestic and trade policies that would be required by a free trade pact.

Second, the United States generally has preferred to deal with the European Union, Japan, and now China in the WTO rather than in bilateral FTA negotiations. To be sure, the Clinton administration vetted proposals for a TAFTA, or Transatlantic FTA, on several occasions. Each time, however, the idea was rejected because of skepticism that either side would remove long-standing protectionist measures as well as concerns about the impact on the global trading system if the two elephants of world trade gave each other preferential treatment. Proposals for a US–Japan FTA likewise suffered from serious doubts that Japan would undertake meaningful reform commitments in agriculture or eliminate nontariff barriers to trade. Interestingly, to get around that problem some former Japanese officials have publicly suggested free trade talks only in services (Hatakeyama 2002).

What this means is that picking FTA partners primarily involves US relations with developing countries and is affected by the myriad US political, economic, and security interests with those countries. On the economic front, this means advancing US trade and investment interests abroad by improving access to growing markets and "leveling the playing field" for US firms, workers, and farmers in competition with foreign suppliers, as well as by building alliances in support of US objectives in WTO talks. On the foreign policy front, this means using free trade to promote economic growth and the rule of law, to strengthen the foundations of democratic governance, and to secure support for global efforts against terrorism.

Such goals reflect the strategic vision of trade policy propounded by President Bush (commencement address at the University of South Carolina, May 9, 2003): "Across the globe, free markets and trade have helped defeat poverty and taught men and women the habits of liberty."[3]

While such a "strategic" approach to foreign relations is desirable in theory, in practice US policy often vacillates on how much priority to give commercial policy in overall US foreign policy. Why?

First, with the advance of globalization, economic interactions between nations have become an increasingly important component of foreign relations. Economic aid and economic sanctions are used in turn to promote good relations or to coerce good behavior from foreign governments. Growing commercial ties create a web of interlocking interests, as Henry Kissinger has often said, but they can also create a set of conflicting policy objectives within each country. Should political and security interests trump commercial concerns? In the Cold War era, the obvious answer was yes.[4] In the immediate post–Cold War era, economic interests gained in relative importance. However, the tragedy of September 11, 2001, restored the primacy of security concerns in US international relations.

Second, coordination among executive branch agencies is in short supply; initiatives of State, Defense, Commerce, Treasury, and the USTR often work at cross purposes owing to conflicting directives from Congress and the White House. Some members of Congress and the business community believe that trade should be unfettered and not a handmaiden to foreign policy. At the same time, however, other members have put forward legislation limiting US trade with or financial assistance to countries that violate specified norms of good behavior such as human rights abuses, proliferation of weapons, and support of terrorism and drug trafficking.

Given this cacophony of stated policy goals, it is difficult to formulate a coherent US trade strategy. US trade officials must negotiate on two fronts: at home with domestic lobbies and Congress, and abroad with US trading partners. Often the bargaining at home is more difficult than dealing with other trade officials in Geneva or elsewhere—since the Congress must pass legislation to ratify and implement US participation in trade agreements. In any event, the demands of bi-level negotiations require that all US trade initiatives meet both domestic and international objectives. This conundrum is evident in the USTR's approach to selecting partners for FTA negotiations.

---

3. This statement preceded the announcement of a new Middle East trade initiative that seeks to establish a US–Middle East FTA within a decade; it was part of a speech on US efforts to promote democracy in postwar Iraq.
4. FTAs were less useful for advancing US political goals in the Cold War era. Most developing countries weren't ready for FTAs with industrial powers and, in any event, preferred the GATT process because they didn't have to offer reciprocal trade reforms.

Current US Selection Criteria

In informal comments at "FTAs and US Trade Policy," the IIE conference in early May 2003 that gave rise to this volume, USTR Robert Zoellick discussed 13 factors that he takes into account in determining whether to launch FTA negotiations with a particular country (see *Inside U.S. Trade*, May 9, 2003). On the basis of those remarks, I array current US selection criteria under four broad and somewhat overlapping categories: impact on domestic US politics, economic objectives, level of commitment of the partner country to trade reform, and foreign policy considerations. This ordering does not necessarily reflect US priorities, though passing the domestic politics test undoubtedly is a prerequisite for the launch of new FTA negotiations.

Domestic Politics

The enactment of trade promotion authority in the Trade Act of 2002 has helped to facilitate the Bush administration's pursuit of FTA negotiations. However, that legislation passed the House by an extremely narrow margin; this is worrisome, since members were voting only on procedural rules. When Congress is asked to ratify agreements that could require changes in existing laws and practices that would have an immediate impact on their constituents, the task of securing a majority vote in the House may be much more difficult.[5] Thus, the first set of criteria focuses on whether new FTAs will help to broaden support for US trade initiatives among members of Congress and private-sector interest groups. Three factors seem to guide the process:

- Do members favor helping prospective FTA partners for both economic and political reasons?

- Is there negotiating flexibility to manage—or possibly exempt—the liberalization of products that are especially important for key congressional constituencies?

- Can FTA provisions help to build support among business and farm lobbies as well as groups in civil society that have heretofore been skeptical of trade agreements?

---

5. To be sure, US FTAs with Chile and Singapore passed Congress relatively easily in 2003. Those pacts posed few competitive challenges for US industries and farmers and elicited only mild opposition from organized labor. The Central American Free Trade Area and other FTAs will face a harsher welcome from members of Congress.

The current challenge for US officials is twofold: to convince moderate Democrats in the House that FTAs can help to build stronger bonds with countries in which their constituents have strong interests and that they are part of a broader program of US support for the economic development of the country and its region; and to secure support from Republicans whose constituents favor trade protection. Some members who oppose trade pacts in general may support agreements that involve countries (e.g., those in southern Africa or in Central America and the Caribbean Basin) they have long sought to help for economic and political reasons. However, some members may oppose prospective FTAs unless the US partners accept "special treatment"—for example, lengthy phase-in periods for trade reforms—for sensitive US imports so that trade protection can be maintained for their constituents. Finally, some members may find FTAs more acceptable if the pact promotes greater compliance with national laws and international commitments on labor and the environment, and seeks to resolve long-standing problems in these areas. Yet at the same time, those members will continue to be wary of new trade pacts if they exacerbate US unemployment problems or fail to address the needs of displaced US workers.[6]

Economic Policy Considerations

The next set of criteria involve the "traditional" reasons for pursuing FTAs—that is, advancing US economic interests. In judging candidate countries, the following questions are posed:

- Will the FTA expand US export opportunities and protect the interests of US investors in the partner country?

- Will the pact level the playing field for US exporters by offsetting the preferences that benefit other foreign suppliers under existing FTAs to which the candidate country is a party?

- Will the FTA establish precedents for future negotiations in areas such as services, intellectual property, labor, and the environment that then can be used as building blocks for broader regional and multilateral pacts?

US trade officials tout FTAs as opening new export opportunities for US firms, workers, and farmers.[7] NAFTA clearly contributed to the sharp in-

---

6. Note that TPA would not have passed without the enhanced trade adjustment assistance programs included in the Trade Act of 2002 at the insistence of Senate Democrats.

7. Less convincingly, they also sometimes try to sell the pacts as engines of net US job creation.

crease in regional trade and investment over the past decade; US trade has grown twice as fast with Canada and Mexico as with the rest of the world (see Hufbauer and Schott, forthcoming). Nonetheless, compared with overall US trade, the potential merchandise trade creation from new FTAs should not be oversold: almost all the current candidates are developing countries, and many of them are small economies. Bigger countries could offer larger trade payoffs. In almost every case, however, such gains accrue only if the United States liberalizes barriers protecting import-sensitive sectors such as agriculture, textiles, and clothing—reforms that would raise hackles on Capitol Hill, undercutting the benefits sought in the first set of selection criteria.

This analysis, of course, ignores an important part of US economic relations with its FTA partners. US trade in services with, and US foreign direct investment (FDI) in, several of these countries are substantial (see table 13.2). US companies engaged in these transactions stand to benefit significantly if an FTA can remove investment requirements that discriminate against US firms as well as other regulatory barriers to trade that limit access to the foreign market.[8] In addition, FTAs can be valuable as negotiating laboratories that create precedents for regional and WTO accords, and that help to teach trade negotiators how to deal with evolving problems in the global economy.

Commitment of Partner Country

US officials argue that their FTAs are "state-of-the-art"—with comprehensive coverage (i.e., limited exceptions) and rule-making obligations that go beyond what has been developed in the WTO. While one can debate the relative value of some of the "new" provisions (e.g., the detailed, industry-specific origin rules and constraints on the imposition of short-term capital controls), there is no disagreement that the FTA obligations require significant reforms in both the trade and domestic regulatory practices of the US trading partners. Countries must be committed to an extensive reform program that allows them to participate in new accords developed bilaterally and in the WTO. The third set of criteria for selecting FTA partners thus judges their willingness and ability to change their own policies in order to meet the requirements of a reciprocal free trade pact, and to work cooperatively with US negotiators to pursue positive results in WTO negotiations:

---

8. For example, US services trade with Australia is valued at $8.1 billion, or almost 44 percent of merchandise trade. With Brazil, the services trade is $6.7 billion, or about 25 percent of goods trade. In both countries, the stock of US FDI exceeds $30 billion (see table 13.2).

Table 13.2 Economic ties with FTA partners, current and prospective
(millions of dollars)

Partners	Total trade with the United States, 2002		US foreign direct investment, 2002	Average tariff on US goods (percent)	Military and economic aid, 2001	FTAA/ APEC partner (Y/N)	EU PTA negotiating partner (Y/N)
	Merchandise	Services					
Current							
Canada	353,061	42,708	152,522	4.1	U	Y	N
Chile	5,901	1,876	11,625	7.0	1	Y	Y
Israel	17,741	3,846	5,207	n.a.	4,789	N	Y
Jordan	809	n.a.	n.a.	16.6	336	N	Y
Mexico	220,197	26,969	58,074	18.0	54	Y	Y
Singapore	28,834	7,836	61,361	0.0	0	Y	N
Subtotal	626,542	83,235	288,789		5,181		
Under negotiation							
Australia	18,692	8,138	36,337	4.4	0	Y	N
Bahrain	802	n.a.	n.a.	8.5	0	N	Y
Bolivia	342	n.a.	n.a.	9.2[a]	192	Y	N
Brazil	26,816	6,668	31,715	13.8	25	Y	Y
CAFTA-5	21,269	n.a.	2,263[b]	33.1	287	Y	N
Colombia	8,727	n.a.	3,735	12.0	153	Y	N
Dominican Republic	8,276	n.a.	1,123	9.1	52	Y	N
Ecuador	3,612	n.a.	1,082	11.6	33	Y	N
Morocco	970	n.a.	n.a.	26.1	26	N	Y
Panama	1,594	n.a.	20,003	7.9[a]	8	Y	N
Peru	3,394	n.a.	3,237	13.6	276	Y	N
South Africa[c]	6,682	1,912	3,428	8.2	89	N	Y
Thailand	19,272	1,949	6,883	15.8	22	Y	N
Subtotal	120,448	18,667	107,543		1,161		
Prospective							
Egypt	4,151	n.a.	2,959	17.7	3,005	N	Y
South Korea	56,434	12,094	12,192	8.4	0	Y	N
New Zealand	4,004	n.a.	4,383	3.0	0	Y	N
Pakistan	2,994	n.a.	n.a.	16.5	90	N	N
Philippines	17,943	2,788	4,097	5.3	86	Y	N
Sri Lanka	1,978	n.a.	n.a.	8.5	18	N	N
Taiwan	48,840	9,853	10,091	7.0	0	Y	N
Uruguay	380	n.a.	n.a.	15[a]	0	Y	Y
Subtotal	136,724	24,735	33,722		3,200		
Total	883,715	126,637	430,054		9,541		

n.a. = not available
APEC = Asia Pacific Economic Cooperation
CAFTA = Central American Free Trade Agreement
FTAA = Free Trade Area of the Americas
PTA = preferential trade agreement

a. Data for 2001.
b. Based on latest available data from Costa Rica, Honduras, and Guatemala.
c. Data only for South Africa, which represents the predominant share of the Southern African Customs Union (SACU-5).

Sources: World Bank's World Integrated Trade Solution Database 2003; USITC Trade Dataweb3, http://dataweb. usitc.gov; US Department of Commerce, Bureau of Economic Analysis, *Survey of Current Business*, September 2003; USAID *Greenbook* 2003; and European Commission Bilateral Trade Relations (2003), http://europa.eu.int/ comm/trade/bilateral/index_en.htm.

- How committed is the partner country to implementing and enforcing domestic economic reforms, and to deepening economic integration with its neighbors?

- How committed is the partner country to working with the United States to forge common objectives, and to promote their acceptance, in WTO negotiations?

In essence, these criteria test the readiness of countries to adjust to a more competitive environment in their domestic markets. The willingness to do their "homework" is critical to their participation in FTAs and WTO negotiations. Almost all the prospective FTA partners (except Australia) are developing countries, so there is a legitimate concern about their ability and political commitment to pursue and sustain over time reforms of macroeconomic, trade, and tax and other regulatory policies. In many cases, such initiatives also are linked with ongoing efforts at regional integration with neighboring countries (especially in Central America and southern Africa).

Since an FTA also seeks to promote convergence of interests in more open trade, it follows that FTA partners will have areas of common interest that they should want to advance in the global trade talks. The United States and the other major trading nations can no longer dictate the terms of global trade deals; instead, they need to build coalitions to help to promote consensus among the WTO's 146 member countries. In light of the difficulty in developing such a consensus (as evidenced most recently at the failed WTO ministerial meeting in Cancún in September 2003), FTAs can be used to forge alliances among "like-minded" countries that can contribute to the consensus-building process so necessary for agreement on WTO accords.[9] Note that this suggests that FTAs with key developing countries, including members of the G-20 coalition, could help to move the Geneva process forward in the coming years.

Foreign Policy Considerations

The fourth set of criteria involves two distinct US policy objectives: rewarding friends for their support in international ventures, and demonstrating the global reach—or geographic diversity—of US trade and foreign policy interests. In brief, the USTR bases its decisions on three tests:

---

9. To be sure, FTA preferences also can create disincentives to moving forward with WTO reforms (as noted in chapter 1), if FTA partners try to maintain the value of their trade preferences by slowing or stalling multilateral accords (some AGOA beneficiaries seem to fall into this camp).

- Is the country cooperating with the United States on foreign policy issues?

- Will the FTA contribute to the economic development of the partner country and thus encourage a deepening of democratic processes and the rule of law?

- Would negotiations with the country contribute to a geographic balance of initiatives on each continent?

The first criterion is simply a concrete manifestation of the carrot-and-stick approach to diplomacy that dates back to the days of Thucydides. That said, the application of the policy remains erratic. Australia is honored for its support of the US war against Iraq by an acceleration of the pace of FTA negotiations; New Zealand is shunned for its opposition. While Iraq seems to be the litmus test for many current candidate countries, other international initiatives may also spur or impede trade talks in the future. FTA talks with Bahrain commend that country's role in promoting democratic reform and peace talks in the region, while Egypt is first extolled and then criticized for failing to advance customs and other economic reforms.[10] In the future, will talks with Colombia run afoul of that country's support for the International Criminal Court—despite its backing of the war in Iraq and of the war against drug trafficking?

The second criterion follows a US policy standard since the Marshall Plan sought the reconstruction of postwar Europe. Countries that are prosperous encourage political pluralism and a strengthening of democratic governance. In turn, these countries are more stable politically and better markets for US exporters and investors (though often stronger competitors to US trading interests as well).

The third criterion is meant to signal that US policymakers seek to expand relations and trade opportunities all over the world. Obviously, the clearest way to send this signal is by engaging in multilateral trade negotiations like the current Doha Round. FTAs are meant to offer another way to demonstrate global trading interests. The USTR has launched initiatives in Southeast Asia and the Middle East (e.g., Thailand, Bahrain), and prospectively in South Asia with Sri Lanka, to complement the array of initiatives in Latin America and the Caribbean and in Africa in hopes of establishing building blocks that over time can yield broader regional pacts.[11] But the value of those FTA outposts is exaggerated. If the United

---

10. In addition, Egyptian trade officials drew the ire of US negotiators when they backtracked on support for US initiatives in the WTO on genetically-modified foods and seeds.

11. No central or eastern European countries are on the US list, presumably because those that are "ready" are already in line to join the European Union. The USTR geographic balance sheet also omits countries in Northeast Asia because of their reluctance to reform agriculture.

States wanted regional initiatives that underpinned its global trading interests, the talks would have to be with bigger trading powers. Unfortunately, FTAs with many of the larger countries are either unviable (because the prospective partner is not willing to open its trade) or undesirable (because of the potential impact on the WTO).

Implementation of US Selection Criteria

The four broad categories of selection criteria outlined above capture the complexity of addressing the myriad economic and foreign policy issues at play in US relations with diverse countries in the developing world. Few would criticize the mixture of trade and foreign policy goals; few agree, however, on what priority to give to economic and political factors in determining how to utilize the government's limited negotiating resources. Opinions differ as well both on how the selection criteria have been applied and on whether the United States is negotiating FTAs with the right set of countries.

Some criticize US policy for thinking small and negotiating pacts that cover only modest volumes of trade. These critics fall into two camps: those who want bigger deals in economic terms (e.g., Baucus 2003, US Chamber of Commerce 2003), and those who argue that the US policy is cherry-picking easy-to-do pacts and leaving the tough issues for the WTO— a strategy that they claim diverts attention from, and makes it harder to reach agreements in, the WTO talks (e.g., Guy De Jonquières in chapter 1).[12] In response, US officials defend the policy as maintaining momentum for trade reform, and establishing precedents for broader regional and multilateral initiatives. Conducting parallel talks at the bilateral, regional, and multilateral levels generates the constructive process of competitive liberalization and offers channels for pursuing liberalization in case so-called foot-draggers stall progress in the Doha Round (Zoellick 2002).

In fact, looking at the long list of current and prospective partners reported in table 13.1, both sides are (partly) right. This ambiguous verdict stems from how the FTA policy has been implemented to date.

First, most of the US initiatives have focused on FTAs with trading partners in the Western Hemisphere. The most significant initiative in economic and political terms is NAFTA, which is in its final stages of implementation (see Hufbauer and Schott, forthcoming). In many respects, however, NAFTA is still a work in progress with an ongoing agenda for deepening economic integration in North America.[13] While new NAFTA-

---

12. See also Martin Wolf, "The Abominable No-Men Menacing World Trade," *Financial Times*, September 24, 2003, 13.
13. For a discussion of initiatives that could be taken to further integration in the NAFTA region, see Schott and Hufbauer (2004) and Pastor (2001).

like pacts under development steal the headlines, the continuing work to elaborate the existing agreement remains the most important regional initiative being pursued by the United States.

Second, most of the new FTAs under negotiation involve Latin American countries with which the United States is also negotiating the FTAA.[14] These pacts thus can be seen either as small individual deals or as components of a much bigger regional trade agreement. Brazil, Argentina, Paraguay, Uruguay, Venezuela, and the small Caribbean Basin countries (which already receive extensive trade preferences in the US market) are the only FTAA participants not in the current US FTA queue. Unfortunately, those countries account for more than 50 percent of the total GDP of Latin America and the Caribbean (excluding Mexico).

Whether the Latin American initiatives constitute a big economic deal or not depends on one's assessment of how these pacts will influence the larger South American countries—particularly Brazil—in the negotiation of the comprehensive hemispheric accord.[15] The US strategy seems to be to "surround Brazil" with FTAs with other Latin American countries in order to up the ante of the US–Brazil deal that eventually will be required to construct the FTAA. Alternatively, as I argue below, the United States could try to engage Brazil in FTA talks as a big stepping-stone to the hemispheric FTAA.

Third, trade is clearly subservient to broader political objectives in some of the FTA initiatives. Talks with Morocco and Bahrain make sense as demonstration or pilot projects—following the US–Jordan model—for a Middle East FTA.[16] These pacts aim to set standards for future adherents in the region with which the United States has important, albeit complex, economic and political relations, such as Egypt (and possibly Saudi Arabia and Iraq, once these countries pass muster and join the WTO). The US motivation in these cases is primarily political, though the FTA provisions set out a detailed agenda of domestic economic reform that prospective partners would need to pursue if they wanted a comparable accord.

By contrast, the negotiation with the Southern African Customs Union (SACU) is unlikely to serve as a demonstration project for other countries in sub-Saharan Africa. The United States insisted on negotiating with the five SACU members instead of just South Africa, in part to help to deepen integration efforts among the SACU partners (a similar objective drives

---

14. Many of these countries suffered trade and investment diversion because of NAFTA and therefore have sought "NAFTA parity" to level their playing field with Mexico in competing for US market share.

15. As Albert Fishlow argues in chapter 10, that assessment in turn depends on developments in the Doha Round as well as the evolution of bilateral trade relations between the United States and the Mercosur countries.

16. In May 2003, President Bush proposed a series of trade initiatives—culminating within a decade in an FTA with countries in the Middle East "that demonstrate a commitment to economic openness and reform" (USTR 2003).

US talks with the Central American countries).[17] But unlike the relative parity among CAFTA countries, there is a big gap between South Africa and its regional partners in terms of both economic power and political importance (see chapter 12)—and the gap is even wider with other sub-Saharan countries. Getting the other SACU members to meet the terms of an FTA with the United States will be difficult enough; adding other African countries—through future negotiations that allow them to "dock" onto the existing accord—will be harder still.

The Commission on Capital Flows to Africa (2003) recommended a US–Africa FTA with African countries that establish their own regional FTAs. I believe such an initiative to be too ambitious, though offering the prospect of an FTA with the United States could spur those countries to accelerate free trade initiatives within their own regions, which in turn would help to promote the economic reforms needed to integrate those nations more fully into the world trading system.

Fourth, the FTA with Australia is the outlier in the pack: it is the only current negotiation with a developed country. Bilateral trade is about the same as total US trade with other FTA aspirants such as Colombia, Thailand, and the Philippines. Although the US–Australia pact raises sensitive agricultural problems involving sugar, beef, dairy, and lamb that politicians would like to avoid in an election year, President Bush decided to move forward on an accelerated timetable for the talks as a reward for Australian support of US foreign policy initiatives.

Finally, prospective talks with Thailand (and possibly Sri Lanka) seem designed to establish FTA outposts in Southeast and South Asia. Annual US–Thai trade volume is about $20 billion, and a pact—building on the US–Singapore FTA—would set standards for similar deals with other Association of Southeast Asian Nations (ASEAN) members, once those countries are ready, willing, and able to undertake and enforce the requisite obligations.[18] The United States launched the Enterprise for ASEAN Initiative in November 2002 to guide those preparations, and to spur a process of competitive liberalization among the ASEAN members (which have not yet achieved free trade among themselves despite efforts that span more than three decades).

Overall, the implementation of US FTA strategy gets mixed marks. Much of the US effort to date has been directed toward building big trading pacts (NAFTA, the FTAA) in the Western Hemisphere. Those initiatives seem to fulfill US economic and political objectives in negotiating FTAs, and they broadly complement parallel talks in the WTO. On the other hand, too much effort has been invested in low-risk, low-reward (in both economic and political terms) negotiations with small countries around the globe.

---

17. South Africa also preferred broader negotiations to avoid complaints by its SACU partners that it was proceeding alone on trade (as it previously did with the European Union).
18. Total US–ASEAN merchandise trade exceeded $140 billion in 2002, so an US–ASEAN FTA would be a big deal (as Dean DeRosa discusses in chapter 6).

Lessons from the European Experience?

The European Union has long been the most active participant in regional trading arrangements; indeed, it is the most successful example of economic and political integration among neighboring states, apart from the United States of America! Thus, it is not surprising that policymakers ask whether there are lessons from the European experience that could inform US policy toward FTAs. Some scholars argue that certain aspects of the European approach merit emulation (see, e.g., Pastor 2001). I am more skeptical.

The postwar European efforts at integration have had both strong political and economic dimensions. Countries were willing to cede sovereignty to supraregional authorities as part of the process of creating a more politically unified Europe. Part of the glue of the alliance was transfers mandated by the common agricultural policy. In addition, new entrants received subsidies in the form of regional development grants funded by the richer, northern members as inducements to join the Community. More recently, the association pacts that Brussels concluded with central and eastern European and Mediterranean countries clearly were understood to be way stations to eventual membership in the common political and economic institutions of the evolving European Union.

The above obviously is only a caricature of the process of European integration. However, it suffices to make the simple point that the European experience in its neighborhood has had much broader economic and political goals than those sought in US trade pacts.

The European Union also negotiates with countries that are not geographically proximate. Outside its neighborhood, however, the European Union has been playing catch-up with the United States for the past decade (with the exception of the EU–South Africa FTA). In large measure, it now emulates US initiatives in Latin America and East Asia—though with a somewhat different tactical approach.

In East Asia, the European Union's TREATI (Trans Regional EU–ASEAN Trade Initiative) seems to be cast from the mold of the Enterprise for ASEAN Initiative of the United States. Its strategic priorities cover both political and economic objectives, such as supporting regional stability and the fight against terrorism; promoting human rights, democratic principles, and good governance; and expanding trade and investment with the region.

In Latin America, the European Union negotiates FTAs incrementally and does not have an integrated negotiation like the FTAA. It has concluded pacts with Mexico and Chile, is negotiating with the Mercosur, and is preparing to enter FTA talks over time with the Andean Community and the Caribbean signatories of the Cotonou Agreement (see Schott and Oegg 2001).[19] Its criteria for selecting partners seem largely to be to follow the leader in the region and to focus on the main markets (Chile was supposed to be blended into the Mercosur). European FTA partners also must pass a democracy test (though EU officials seem to apply this standard flexibly in judging prospective partners—particularly those in the Middle East).

Unlike the United States, the European Union has committed not to launch new free trade talks until after the conclusion of the Doha Round. EU trade officials are not on the sidelines, however. Current talks under way with Mercosur and the Gulf Cooperation Council will continue, and those mandated in existing pacts (e.g., Cotonou) presumably also would not be affected by the moratorium. The European Union has some type of preferential trading arrangement with 10 of the current or prospective US FTA partners (table 13.2), though EU negotiators—constrained by their position on farm reform—do not seem to subscribe to the leveraging tactics implicit in the "competitive liberalization" approach of the United States.

Setting FTA Priorities

Does US policy toward FTAs need a major overhaul, or just a tune-up? Some critics of current policy advocate forswearing FTAs (except NAFTA) in favor of working exclusively on the WTO negotiations (e.g., see Richard Cooper's comments in chapter 1). Others want a different lineup of negotiating partners that better fit the commercial policy interests of US–based firms.[20] Ideally, it would be desirable to focus negotiating efforts on the pacts with the biggest economic payoff—that is, to primarily devote attention to the WTO and then to FTAs involving substantial US trade and investment interests that complement and reinforce the multilateral process. In practice, however, each case or situation poses different sets of economic and foreign policy opportunities and challenges—some mutually reinforcing, others conflicting. Trying to establish priorities among the selection criteria that could apply equally to all prospective FTA partners is a futile task.

---

19. EU policy envisages revising trade ties with former colonies gradually under the Cotonou Agreement from one-way preferences to reciprocal FTAs.

20. For example, the US Chamber of Commerce (2003) issued a policy statement on FTAs in February 2003 that recommended FTA talks primarily with larger economies such as the European Union, Japan, Russia, Turkey, and India as well as several others already in the FTA queue. Their selection criteria focused exclusively on economic factors, ignored the political problems that can arise in reforms affecting import-sensitive US industries (especially textiles and apparel), and would severely tax USTR negotiating resources.

The current US approach has several advantages. Most important, it tries to link domestic politics with international initiatives and attempts to build a strong base of domestic support for trade and other foreign policies. Second, it integrates commercial diplomacy and foreign policy, recognizing that economic advances abroad can serve US political interests (especially with nascent or aspiring democracies) and that political alliances help to encourage flows of trade, investment, and people between the partner countries.

However, the US approach also has some drawbacks. First, the advantage gained by integrating trade and foreign policy interests is impeded by inefficient policy coordination within the US government (as noted above). The fact that the USTR has taken the lead in formulating US policy for initiatives that span important geopolitical as well as commercial interests is unusual, to say the least, and probably not sustainable. Second, the diverse set of FTAs has spawned different and complex trading rules, especially regarding origin requirements for some industrial and agricultural products. As I argued in chapter 1, US negotiators need to continue to push for the elimination of industrial tariffs in the Doha Round inter alia to minimize the costs of discriminatory rules of origin in FTAs. Third, the strategy stretches the limited resources of the USTR by engaging with a number of small countries that do not represent political or economic power centers in their region (e.g., Morocco in North Africa, Bahrain in the Persian Gulf, and Sri Lanka in South Asia). These countries may be suitable partners for pilot programs, but they cannot be expected to yield big economic or political payoffs.[21] More critically, such small initiatives divert the attention and resources of US trade officials from WTO negotiations and from other FTAs that are potentially more lucrative.

Considering the broad-ranging negotiating objectives set by Congress in the Trade Act of 2002, USTR operates on a shoestring budget—another example of conflicting US policy objectives. Significant additional funding is unlikely given the soaring US budget deficit, so USTR will need to recast their FTA priorities.

If the United States wants to establish influential outposts in various regions to advance its economic and foreign policy interests, then it should engage other—and bigger—partners in FTA talks. However, before I name names to be pursued in bigger deals, two caveats bear mention.

The bigger the deal in economic terms, the bigger the prospective payoff in terms of increased growth for the US economy. That's why talks with Turkey and South Korea, among others, are favored by companies

---

21. USTR Zoellick (2003) argues that, excluding countries with which an FTA would have adverse effects on the WTO (e.g., China, Japan, and the EU), these small deals combined actually account for a large share of the rest of US merchandise trade. Nonetheless, it is a large proportion of a small volume of trade.

with export or investment interests in those markets (US Chamber of Commerce 2003). However, some of the US gains come from reductions in US trade barriers and subsidies, and thus entail significant US economic adjustments. As a result, these FTAs will provoke opposition from US import-competing farmers and industries (especially steel, textiles, and clothing) that would face greater competition in their home market. In short, "big stakes" FTAs elicit broader political support from potential winners but also more intense opposition from potential losers threatened by the increased competition.

From a political perspective, bigger deals also complicate the calculus for picking FTA partners. Good trade relations can generate substantial political benefits that can be used to forge common approaches to regional problems (e.g., dealing with North Korea). On the other hand, such deals can produce perverse incentives from a trade policy perspective, since the US partner may demand exceptions to trade reform as a payoff for the political alliance.[22]

What needs to be done? First, US officials should seek the biggest bang for the buck in trade negotiations and thus give priority to the WTO. Given the extensive problems evidenced recently in conducting such negotiations, however, the United States should also continue to pursue FTAs that complement the WTO process and provide constructive incentives for advancing global trade reforms. Second, US officials should up the ante on FTAs by selecting partners that can produce big dividends in economic and foreign policy terms—without undercutting the multilateral system.

If one looks at the broad US economic relationship with countries seeking FTAs—including merchandise and services trade, foreign direct investment, and development assistance—a few individual countries stand above the rest (see table 13.2). Most notable are South Korea and Brazil.[23] These countries play crucial roles in regional political stability. FTAs with them would raise contentious and politically difficult problems, but the economic and political gains would be substantial—if the pacts cover substantial reforms in agriculture, industrial goods, and services.

US trade with South Korea is larger than that with any other current or prospective FTA negotiating partner. In 2002, two-way trade in goods and services exceeded $68 billion. As Inbom Choi and I report in chapter 7, an FTA could yield significant welfare gains for both economies, *if* agriculture is included in the deal (otherwise, the gains are cut in half). Such a

---

22. Take, for example, the case of the Philippines. It is an ally in the war on terrorism, but a footdragger on trade reform and unhelpful in the WTO (where it tried to block the US compromise on intellectual property and access to medicines prior to the Cancún ministerial).
23. US–Taiwan trade and investment is also substantial, but negotiating an FTA now would inflame US relations with China. Such talks should be postponed to allow cross-straits ties between Taiwan and China to deepen.

pact would also reinforce political and security relations at a time of increasing tension on the Korean peninsula.

To date, however, officials in both countries have been cautious about moving toward an FTA. Liberalization of long-standing US barriers to South Korean exports of textiles, apparel, and steel would trigger loud rebukes from domestic industries already suffering sharp competition from Chinese suppliers. In South Korea, FTA-induced reforms would provoke even harsher reactions from Korean farmers. Few South Korean politicians have dared cross that constituency; indeed, President Roh declared in May 2003 that his country would not pursue FTAs if they required reform of agricultural policies. As a result of such intransigence on farm reform, US officials have not given serious consideration to a bilateral FTA with South Korea.

Nonetheless, recent trade developments in East Asia may force Korea to soften its resistance to agricultural reforms. In particular, Korea–Japan FTA talks will unleash demands for comparable trade initiatives from countries whose exporters will face new discrimination in both Northeast Asian markets. Indeed, competitive liberalization could explode with a vengeance in East Asia—led by the United States as it seeks to level the playing field with Japan. China, which is rapidly becoming Korea's top trading partner, may follow suit. For both countries, agriculture will be a central focus of their demands. In addition, any prospective deal in the Doha Round will be possible only if the major trading nations, including Korea and Japan, agree to significantly reduce their farm trade barriers. Korean exporters will pay a heavy price if their trade negotiators continue to block progress in the WTO over agriculture.

Changing demographics suggest that Korea could deflect at least some of the domestic opposition to farm reforms by switching from trade protection to income support for Korean farmers. Indeed, this is the direction that European policy seeks to go in its reform of the common agricultural policy. A combination of "decoupled" support for Korean farmers and substantial, albeit incomplete, reform of import barriers could provide a big boost to Korea's economy. Such reforms could be phased in over time to mitigate the economic adjustment pressures and to help to manage the political fallout. Under such conditions, an FTA is doable over the next few years.

Brazil presents different, but equally important, opportunities and challenges. Bilateral US–Brazil trade currently is far below potential due to both trade restrictions and burdensome tax and regulatory policies that create disincentives to trade and investment. Projections from gravity models suggest that a bilateral FTA could quickly stimulate a doubling of trade, increasing US–Brazil merchandise trade to the level of current US–South Korea trade. As in the South Korean case, sensitive trade barriers would have to be reduced, if not eliminated. That means that concrete concessions would have to be offered to expand Brazilian access to the US market for products such as sugar, ethanol, citrus, and steel.[24] Brazil, in turn, would have to improve access to its services markets, bidding on government contracts and coverage and enforcement of intellectual property rights (IPRs). Both countries would need to eliminate their tariffs, including those on sensitive agricultural products as well as on textiles, clothing, and footwear.

For Brazil, it is a propitious time to move forward on the trade front. Brazil needs to offset sluggish domestic demand and propel economic growth. An FTA could complement domestic efforts to push the needed reforms to both domestic economic and trade policies. Brazil's new government has a narrow window to take advantage of its competitive exchange rate, which has dampened protectionist pressures, in order to reduce the notorious "Brazil cost" at home and barriers to Brazilian exports abroad. Success both in the Doha Round and in Western Hemisphere FTAs could be achieved before Lula da Silva faces reelection in late 2006.

For the United States, closer ties with Brazil would reinforce efforts made over several decades to promote economic development and to strengthen democratic processes in the region. Increased trade and investment can help to boost income and employment in both countries, open new channels for political cooperation and cultural exchange, and strengthen prospects for hemispheric integration.

To date, US–Brazil talks have been channeled through the FTAA process. This approach is understandable, since the FTAA is the biggest prize in the US FTA policy—but only if Brazil (which accounts for about 50 percent of South American GDP) is part of the agreement. However, the hemispheric talks have slowed to a crawl amid continuing differences between the United States and Brazil over the scope and coverage of the prospective accord. Brazil has been reticent until recently to put forward even minimal offers on services, procurement, and IPRs. And, of course, agriculture remains a major source of contention—particularly sugar and domestic farm supports.[25] Given the impasse at the FTAA ministerial in Miami in November 2003, US policymakers have opted to move forward with most other Latin American and Caribbean countries, choosing to let Brazil and its Mercosur partners catch up when they are ready to proceed in the FTAA.

To energize the grudging pace of FTAA and WTO talks, an alternative approach to US–Brazil trade relations should be considered. Instead of leav-

---

24. I recognize that US sugar lobbies threaten to block an FTA with Brazil if the pact liberalizes the extensive US protection of their industry. They also are trying to scuttle the CAFTA and US–Australia pacts. Exempting sugar could cause the collapse of key US trade initiatives, and should be avoided.

25. In principle, all farm trade issues are subject to FTAA reforms, although important problems caused by domestic subsidies are not amenable to regional solutions and must instead be handled in the WTO (where the United States and Brazil may have common objectives).

ing a US–Brazil deal for the end of the FTAA process, it might be more productive to move forward with bilateral talks to catalyze the hemispheric process. As Albert Fishlow reports in chapter 10, President Lula da Silva has suggested just such an initiative in talks with President Bush. Such talks could also deepen the understanding of the common interests both countries have in a successful Doha Round, thus encouraging them to work together (instead of at cross purposes, as in Cancún) to craft a big package of WTO accords, including substantial reductions in domestic farm subsidies.

Would South Korea and Brazil agree to enter FTA negotiations with the United States? Admittedly, neither country has indicated a willingness to undertake comprehensive trade reforms. Domestic opposition is substantial and the negotiating payoff—in terms of increased access to the US market—is uncertain. But both countries will have to confront these lobbies in any event in the near future, if they hope to achieve their economic development goals. Thus, a US initiative hopefully would catalyze new reforms.

FTAs with South Korea and Brazil would dramatically alter the profile of US FTA policy. Both are doable, if the US partners are willing to accept a comprehensive free trade deal in return for concrete reforms of sensitive US trade barriers. Both would force US officials to make difficult political decisions but would reward the effort with substantial economic benefits for US firms, workers, and farmers. Both would provide positive "shocks" for the regional and multilateral trade talks by advancing farm reforms in each country. Both should move to the head of the FTA queue.

Do US officials dare advance so aggressively? In fact, they already committed to doing so in proposals put forward in the Doha Round in 2002 that would eliminate industrial tariffs and farm export subsidies and would substantially reduce domestic farm supports. Such changes in US trade measures always will be difficult to sell to Congress, and thus will require a big package of benefits—both economic and foreign policy—to offset the opposition from US constituencies that will lose their subsidies and other trade protection. To succeed in that task, US officials have to think big—and big FTAs should be part of their trade strategy to complement and catalyze world trade reforms.

References

Baucus, Max. 2003. Letter to Zoellick on FTAs (June 11). Text reproduced in *Inside U.S. Trade*, June 13.

Bergsten, C. Fred. 1996. *Competitive Liberalization and Global Free Trade: A Vision for the Early 21st Century*. Working Paper No. 96-15. Washington: Institute for International Economics. www.iie.com/publications/wp/1996/96-15.htm.

Commission on Capital Flows to Africa. 2003. *A Ten-Year Strategy for Increasing Capital Flows to Africa*. Washington. June.

Hatakeyama, Noboru. 2002. Japan's New Regional Trade Policy: Which Country Comes Next After Singapore? Whitman International Lecture, Institute for International Economics, Washington (March 13). www.iie.com/publications/papers/hatakeyama0302. htm.

Hufbauer, Gary Clyde. 1989. *The Free Trade Debate*. Reports of the Twentieth Century Fund Task Force on the Future of American Trade Policy. New York: Priority Press.

Hufbauer, Gary Clyde, and Jeffrey J. Schott. 1992. *North American Free Trade: Issues and Recommendations*. Washington: Institute for International Economics.

Hufbauer, Gary Clyde, and Jeffrey J. Schott. Forthcoming. *NAFTA: A Ten-Year Appraisal*. Washington: Institute for International Economics.

Pastor, Robert A. 2001. *Toward a North American Community: Lessons from the Old World for the New*. Washington: Institute for International Economics.

Schott, Jeffrey J. 1983. The GATT Ministerial: A Postmortem. *Challenge* 26, no. 2 (May/June): 40–45.

Schott, Jeffrey J., and Gary Clyde Hufbauer. 2004. *Prospects for North American Economic Integration: An American Perspective Post-9/11*. The Border Papers. Toronto: C. D. Howe Institute.

Schott, Jeffrey J., and Barbara Oegg. 2001. Europe and the Americas: Toward a TAFTA-South? *The World Economy* 24, no. 6 (June): 745–59.

Schott, Jeffrey J., and Murray G. Smith, eds. 1988. *The Canada-United States Free Trade Agreement: The Global Impact*. Washington: Institute for International Economics.

US Chamber of Commerce. 2003. International Policy Objectives for 2003 and Beyond. Washington (February).

US Trade Representative, Office of (USTR). 2003. Middle East Free Trade Initiative. *Trade Facts*. www.ustr.gov/regions/eu-med/middleeast/2003-06-23-middle-east-factsheet. PDF (June 23).

Zoellick, Robert. 2002. Unleashing the Trade Winds. *The Economist*, December 7, 27–29.

Zoellick, Robert. 2003. Freeing the Intangible Economy: Services in International Trade. Speech to the Coalition of Service Industries, Washington. www.ustr.gov/speech-test/ zoellick/2003-12-02-services.pdf (December 2).

Technical Appendix
Quantitative Estimates of the
Economic Impacts of US Bilateral
Free Trade Agreements

DEAN A. DeROSA AND JOHN P. GILBERT

To support the development of the papers for the Institute for International Economics conference on Free Trade Agreements and US Trade Policy and, more generally, to provide quantitative points of reference for discussions of the economic impacts of US bilateral free trade agreements (FTAs), the Institute commissioned two quantitative background studies by the authors. The first study, undertaken by John Gilbert, was tasked with providing estimates of the trade and economic welfare impacts of prospective US free trade agreements using a prominent computable general equilibrium model of the world economy, the GTAP (Global Trade Analysis Project) model (Gilbert 2003). The second study, undertaken by Dean DeRosa, was tasked with providing estimates of the trade impacts of prospective US free trade agreements using another prominent applied method for investigating the impacts of preferential trading arrangements, the so-called gravity model (DeRosa 2003).

This appendix provides an overview of the general economic framework and findings of the two studies, as set against both the increasing

Dean A. DeRosa is a visiting fellow at the Institute for International Economics. John P. Gilbert is an assistant professor in the department of economics at Utah State University.

prominence of bilateral and regional trading arrangements in the global economy and the basic objectives of the Institute for International Economics conference. The latter include investigating the geopolitical and economic benefits of the prospective US FTAs from the viewpoint of both the United States and FTA partners and identifying likely sensitive trade, foreign investment, or other political or economic issues. Another important objective was to investigate the so-called competitive liberalization hypothesis—that is, whether the pursuit of discriminatory bilateral trading arrangements ultimately leads to multilateral trade liberalization on a nondiscriminatory basis.[1]

Before we turn to the results of the two studies, the next section briefly reviews what trade and other economic impacts are expected to follow from bilateral FTAs according to traditional and new economic theories of international trade and investment.

Traditional and New Theories of Preferential Trade Arrangements

Viner-Meade Theory

Traditional economic theory of preferential trade arrangements is associated principally with the seminal contributions to the "customs union issue" by Jacob Viner (1950) and subsequently James Meade (1955), followed by many others.[2] Traditional economic theory focuses largely, though not exclusively, on the concepts of trade creation and trade diversion under customs unions and other forms of preferential trade arrangements, as introduced by Viner. Essentially, trade creation refers to the possible expansion of a country's total imports on entering into a bilateral or other preferential trade arrangement, leading to an improvement in economic welfare as high-cost domestic output is replaced by lower-cost output produced abroad. However, trade diversion may also occur if high-cost imports from one or more preferential trading partners supplant lower-cost imports from third countries not party to the arrangement, resulting in a diminution of economic welfare for the importing country. On balance, if trade creation effects outweigh trade diversion effects, then the preferential trade arrangement is said to be trade creating on a net basis and the arrangement is generally regarded as economically beneficial.

---

1. See C. Fred Bergsten, "A Competitive Approach to Free Trade," *Financial Times*, December 5, 2002, and Bergsten (2002). See also Baldwin (1995) and Andrianmananjara (2000).

2. See, among others, Lipsey (1970), Lloyd (1982), Robson (1987), and Pomfret (1988).

Viner considered mainly the case of "small" trading countries forming a customs union, whereas Meade's analysis expanded Viner's analysis to consider the more general case in which world relative prices might also be affected by the formation of a customs union—especially when one or more of the union members are "large" trading countries whose trade policies can have appreciable spillover effects on the economies of nonmember countries through the diversion of trade flows and, more fundamentally, the impacts of the diversion of trade on world relative prices.

Spillover effects of preferential trade arrangements on third countries are particularly important today as bilateral and regional FTAs spread rapidly, with implications for the competitive liberalization hypothesis. Under the assumption made in many applied economic models that similar traded goods produced by different countries are imperfect substitutes for one another, spillover effects arising from the diversion of trade under preferential trade arrangements can be significant because imperfect substitution implies that all countries, large and small, can influence world prices in some degree—especially when a major hub country such as the European Union or the United States forges FTAs with a number of partners simultaneously. Under the competitive liberalization hypothesis, these spillover effects would be expected to provide an incentive for adversely affected nonmember countries to retaliate either by forging their own FTAs with countries from which their exports have been diverted or by more strongly supporting multilateral trade liberalization, to reduce if not entirely offset the margins of preference created by the trade-diverting free trade agreements. In the former case, if all adversely affected countries pursue FTAs (on substantially all traded goods) with the country whose imports were originally diverted, then at its limit the process should be expected to approach if not converge to unilateral free trade for the importing country. Moreover, if such bilateral trade liberalization spreads widely, then the process should also be expected to approach multilateral free trade. To be sure, this process involves considerable diversion of trade, but of the sort that may be offsetting in its retaliatory mode and even trade creating if the process leads to de facto unilateral trade liberalization for individual FTA partner countries.

The foregoing discussion, of course, is a simplification that does not take into account the full range of possible political-economy considerations that could hinder the process of competitive liberalization. In particular, the process could create vested interests in new FTAs (in hub countries or partner countries) that might significantly slow if not effectively halt progress toward either unilateral or multilateral trade liberalization. Such political-economy considerations are especially important areas for further analysis and research into bilateral FTAs and the dynamics of their adoption in individual countries.

New Trade Theory and Deeper Integration

Coincident with the new wave of regionalism that emerged during the 1990s and continues today, many economists have sought to provide new understanding of the attractiveness of regional trade arrangements, including bilateral free trade agreements, in the belief that traditional trade theory does not adequately explain the appeal of regionalism today or even the potential benefits of nondiscriminatory trade liberalization itself. As a recent review points out (Burfisher, Robinson, and Thierfelder 2003; see also Panagariya 1999, 2000), the new literature on regional trade and economic integration arrangements forms an eclectic collection of theoretical and applied economic studies of both regional and general trade liberalization under conditions that might be considered extensions of those assumed in the traditional Viner-Meade theory.[3]

Under the rubric of the *new trade theory*, a number of economists have begun to explore the implications of imperfect competition in an increasingly integrated world economy (Helpman and Krugman 1985; Krugman 1995). When there is imperfect competition, natural, technological, or policy-based barriers to market entry by firms give rise to monopolistic profits, often in the presence of increasing returns to scale and production of differentiated goods by competing firms. Under such conditions, regional (and general) trade liberalization can result in procompetitive effects that are substantially larger than predicted by traditional trade theory, providing greater assurance that net trade creation and significant welfare benefits will occur. But also in the presence of imperfect competition, diversion of trade with nonmember countries may still occur under preferential trading arrangements, leaving the spillover effects of such arrangements on third countries no more certain than in traditional models.

Also in recent years, many economists have turned their attention to investigating the implications of so-called *deep integration*, which (following in the footsteps of the Europe 1992 Plan) is an essential feature of many new regional integration arrangements.[4] "Deep integration" refers to possibilities for harmonizing economic policies between countries seeking to forge closer economic relations: the objective is to eliminate administrative and regulatory "trade frictions" restricting expansion of international trade and foreign investment from within countries rather than at

---

3. For further discussion of the issues raised in this section, see, e.g., Baldwin and Venables (1995), DeRosa (1998), and Schiff and Winters (2003).

4. The topic is strongly associated with its extensive description and discussion by Robert Lawrence (1996). Deep integration, however, has antecedents in early analyses of regional integration arrangements: see, e.g., Mikesell (1963).

their borders. These frictions take many forms, including customs clearance procedures, product standards and certification systems, labeling requirements, intellectual property rights enforcement, foreign direct investment (FDI) policies, and prudential supervision and professional licensing systems. In the context of regional integration arrangements among less-developed countries, inadequate or outmoded infrastructure—including networks of roads, railways, and telecommunication systems—might also be targeted for regional improvement or rationalization under deep integration provisions of modern customs unions and free trade area agreements.

Conceptually, eliminating administrative and regulatory frictions inhibiting international trade and foreign investment should be expected to reduce the costs of producing and distributing traded goods (and services) and, hence, to increase economic welfare in the countries seeking to forge these closer relations. However, some uncertainty surrounds the question of whether deep integration undertaken to harmonize national procedures and standards, and to improve regional social infrastructure and communication networks, will spur trade and investment between preferential trade agreement partners significantly more than it does trade and investment with third countries, leaving unclear the magnitude (and even the sign) of possible spillover effects on the world economy.

Although issues raised by the new trade theory and possibilities for deep integration are important and relevant to the new global economy, no applied economic model of the world economy is currently specified to investigate these issues across the wide spectrum of prospective partner countries with which the United States is currently considering bilateral FTAs. Indeed, previous quantitative studies of these issues have been of a one-off variety, using specially formulated, applied economic models calibrated to the circumstances of a comparatively small number of countries.

While we understand that more sophisticated economic models and modes of analysis might be called for in in-depth studies of prospective US bilateral FTAs, in the remainder of this appendix we present the quantitative results found from applying the current GTAP model—which incorporates differentiated traded goods but otherwise is founded principally on traditional, Viner-Meade customs union theory—to a large number of prospective US bilateral FTAs, individually and simultaneously. As mentioned at the outset, we also consider the quantitative results found from applying standard gravity model estimates to the question of the trade impacts of US bilateral FTAs with the same set of prospective partner countries.

GTAP Model Results

This section presents estimates of trade and other economic impacts of US FTAs with a total of 14 prospective partner countries.[5] The estimates are derived from simulations of the standard GTAP model, using the GTAP5 database (Hertel 1997; Dimaranan and McDougall 2002).

The GTAP Model

Computable general equilibrium (CGE) models are numerical models based on general equilibrium theory, built with the objective of turning the abstract models of economic theory into practical tools for policy analysis. A number of features distinguish CGE models from other widely used tools of trade policy analysis. CGE models are multisectoral, and in many cases they are multiregional. The behavior of economic agents is modeled explicitly through utility- and profit-maximizing assumptions. In addition, economywide resource and expenditure constraints are rigorously enforced; as a consequence, distortions in an economic system will often have repercussions beyond the sector in which they occur. Thus, simulations of CGE models are effective at capturing relevant direct and indirect effects of changes in trade policy.[6]

The GTAP model is a publicly available CGE model that is in widespread use and has a structure typical of many CGE models. Both multisectoral and multiregional, it assumes perfect competition and constant returns to scale in all markets and production of all goods. Bilateral trade is handled via the so-called Armington assumption, which treats similar goods produced in different countries as imperfect substitutes in consumption. Production is modeled using nested constant elasticity of substitution (CES) functions, with intermediate goods used in fixed proportions to output. Representative household demand is nonhomothetic; that is, it takes into account changes in commodity demand patterns as incomes rise.

---

5. US bilateral FTAs with Australia, Botswana, Brazil, Chile, Indonesia, Malaysia, Morocco, New Zealand, Philippines, Singapore, Thailand, Taiwan, Korea, and the rest of the Southern African Customs Union (i.e., SACU besides Botswana) are considered, along with a scenario implementing all of the proposed agreements simultaneously. Other proposed FTA partners, such as Egypt, are not available in the GTAP5 database. The economies of the Central American Common Market countries (Costa Rica, El Salvador, Guatemala, Honduras, and Nicaragua) are identified in GTAP in the aggregate, but because this group is based on a constructed input-output database and not on actual data from these countries, the group is not considered as a partner in the present analysis.

6. CGE simulation has become a widely employed tool of trade policy analysis; it is particularly well suited to examining proposed FTAs, where multisectoral reform is to be undertaken in at least two economies simultaneously. For recent surveys of the application of CGE models to regional trade negotiations, see Scollay and Gilbert (2000), Gilbert and Wahl (2002), and Robinson and Thierfelder (2002).

FTA Scenarios

Although the GTAP5 database identifies some 66 regions and 57 sectors, the GTAP simulations presented here use an aggregation of 23 countries and 19 sectors, including 14 prospective partners in US FTAs that can be identified in the GTAP database. Other individual countries and regions included in the aggregation were selected on the basis of the extent of trading relations with the United States. The 19-sector aggregation in table A.1 was chosen on the basis of the prominence of the sectors in US total trade (exports plus imports). Values of the Armington substitution elasticities, also reported in table A.1, are those assumed uniformly for all countries in the standard GTAP database.

Each of the proposed US FTAs is initially simulated independently of the other proposed agreements, and thus the initial simulation results reflect the impacts of each prospective US FTA in isolation.[7] The exception is a second basic scenario in which all 14 proposed agreements are implemented simultaneously, in order to assess their impacts when the United States will have implemented FTAs with several trading partners under its new bilateral trade policy.

In all FTA scenarios, the US bilateral trade agreements are assumed to be implemented "clean," meaning that all import tariffs are reduced to zero in the participating economies, on a preferential basis. All other tariffs (i.e., those applied to nonparticipating economies) are left in place. The tariffs used for the United States and its prospective FTA partners, reported in table A.2, are those in place in the base year 1997.[8] It should be noted that the GTAP database does not currently incorporate information about goods protection afforded by nontariff barriers. Nor does it incorporate information about service protection. Hence, the simulations

---

7. Preexisting bilateral FTAs (mainly EU partnership agreements with such countries as Chile and Morocco) and preexisting regional trading arrangements such as AFTA (the ASEAN Free Trade Area), CER (Closer Economic Relations between Australia and New Zealand), and NAFTA (the North American Free Trade Agreement) are taken into account in the simulation results because the GTAP database incorporates the official tariff preferences of these preexisting trade agreements for their members.

8. GTAP protection data are derived from the Agricultural Market Access Database (AMAD, www.amad.net) in the case of agriculture, and the UN Conference on Trade and Development (UNCTAD) TRAINS database (www.unctad.org/trains) in the case of other merchandise trade. In the case of agriculture, applied rates are used where available, then MFN bound rates. US Department of Agriculture estimates are used in the case of rice to Japan, Korea, and the Philippines. In the case of other merchandise, the rates are generally MFN bound rates. Tariffs are specified on a bilateral basis, with the differences reflecting the differences in the composition of trade at the disaggregate level. Tariff preferences for NAFTA, EU-EFTA (European Free Trade Association), CER, and SACU are included in the database. Other preferences (such as the Generalized System of Preferences) are not. For full details, see Dimaranan and McDougall (2002).

Table A.1 Sectoral aggregation and central values of Armington elasticities

Sector	Items	Armington elasticities	
		Domestic-imported	Imported by source
Grains	Paddy rice, wheat, cereal grains NEC	2.20	4.40
Other crops	Vegetables and fruit, oilseeds, sugar cane/beet, plant-based fibers, crops NEC	2.20	4.40
Animal products	Cattle, animal products NEC, raw milk, wool	2.61	5.47
Forestry and fisheries	Forestry, fisheries	2.80	5.60
Processed food products	Meat products, vegetable oils, dairy products, processed rice, sugar, food products NEC, beverages, and tobacco	2.39	4.71
Lumber	Lumber	2.80	5.60
Pulp and paper products	Paper products, publishing	1.80	3.60
Textiles and apparel	Textiles, wearing apparel, leather products	3.32	6.78
Coal, oil, and gas	Coal, oil, gas, minerals NEC	2.80	5.60
Petroleum and coal products	Petroleum and coal products	1.90	3.80
Chemicals	Chemicals, rubber and plastics, mineral products NEC	2.10	4.07
Metals	Ferrous metals, metals NEC	2.80	5.60
Metal products	Metal products	2.80	5.60
Electronic equipment	Electronic equipment	2.80	5.60
Motor vehicles	Motor vehicles and parts	5.20	10.40
Other transportation equipment	Transportation equipment NEC	5.20	10.40
Machinery NEC	Machinery and equipment NEC	2.80	5.60
Manufactures NEC	Other manufactures NEC	2.80	5.60
Services	Electricity, gas, water, construction, trade and transportation, communication, financial services and insurance, recreation, public services, ownership of dwellings	1.94	3.85

NEC = not elsewhere classified

Source: Dimaranan and McDougall (2002).

Table A.2 Tariffs applied by United States and prospective FTA partners by sector (percent)

Sector	Australia	New Zealand	Korea	Taiwan	Indonesia	Malaysia	Philippines	Singapore	Thailand	Brazil	Chile	Morocco	Botswana	Rest of SACU
								US tariffs on FTA partner imports						
Grains	0.7	1.4	0.9	0.6	0.6	4.9	1.1	0.8	2.7	0.7	0.6	1.9	0.7	1.3
Other crops	9.5	7.6	10.5	16.9	21.1	20.2	7.1	21.0	19.2	18.6	6.3	13.9	8.1	10.0
Animal products	0.9	0.7	0.6	0.6	0.6	0.6	0.7	0.6	0.6	0.6	0.8	0.6	0.6	0.7
Forestry and fisheries	1.2	0.3	0.0	0.3	0.3	0.2	0.4	0.1	0.3	1.1	0.4	0.0	0.0	2.6
Processed food products	12.0	14.5	10.9	12.3	9.6	8.2	13.6	11.1	11.1	18.9	9.3	11.5	9.8	20.4
Lumber	1.6	0.2	1.7	2.0	4.0	2.3	2.3	1.6	2.7	2.1	1.1	2.6	0.0	2.1
Pulp and paper products	0.4	0.3	1.3	1.5	1.8	1.2	2.5	0.3	1.0	0.2	0.0	0.1	0.0	0.0
Textiles and apparel	9.0	4.2	14.0	13.9	14.9	14.7	14.2	15.0	14.2	8.5	12.4	11.8	0.0	11.6
Coal, oil, and gas	0.3	0.0	0.2	6.6	0.3	0.4	0.0	0.0	0.7	0.5	0.2	0.0	0.0	0.2
Petroleum and coal products	2.4	2.4	2.3	1.2	2.4	2.3	0.0	2.4	2.4	2.3	2.4	0.0	0.0	0.0
Chemicals	3.2	2.9	3.9	4.4	1.6	2.7	5.1	4.9	2.8	5.0	2.2	2.8	0.0	4.4
Metals	0.7	3.5	3.7	4.5	1.1	2.4	4.4	2.6	3.8	2.4	1.4	1.4	0.0	1.0
Metal products	3.2	2.4	3.7	4.4	3.6	2.3	3.6	3.5	3.4	3.5	1.9	3.0	0.0	3.3
Electronic equipment	2.3	1.2	0.6	1.1	2.2	1.0	0.6	0.6	1.4	2.7	1.2	0.1	0.0	2.3
Motor vehicles	2.2	1.3	2.4	2.1	1.6	1.5	1.5	1.4	1.5	1.7	1.4	1.3	0.0	1.7
Transportation equipment	0.6	1.3	0.4	5.6	1.4	3.3	2.8	0.9	2.2	1.9	1.3	0.0	0.0	2.2
Machinery NEC	2.6	2.1	2.6	3.1	3.4	2.4	3.5	3.0	3.3	2.2	1.7	3.3	0.0	2.4
Manufactures NEC	1.5	1.5	4.2	3.5	3.1	1.7	1.7	2.0	4.4	4.4	1.9	0.7	0.0	0.4

(table continues next page)

Table A.2 Tariffs applied by US and prospective FTA partners by sector (percent) *(continued)*

Sector	Australia	New Zealand	Korea	Taiwan	Indonesia	Malaysia	Philippines	Singapore	Thailand	Brazil	Chile	Morocco	Botswana	Rest of SACU
								FTA partner tariffs on US imports						
Grains	0.7	1.2	197.2	2.0	3.1	1.9	18.1	0.0	0.0	6.9	11.0	18.1	46.5	43.0
Other crops	2.1	2.6	98.3	9.1	7.0	45.0	12.2	7.6	33.0	7.0	11.0	24.1	21.2	19.5
Animal products	0.7	0.2	10.0	0.3	5.8	14.3	16.6	0.0	16.9	6.0	11.0	22.4	8.3	3.8
Forestry and fisheries	0.2	0.4	4.7	15.2	0.5	0.4	2.4	0.0	37.3	4.9	11.0	9.2	39.6	0.3
Processed food products	5.8	9.2	37.8	27.0	16.8	12.6	16.6	5.4	36.4	16.6	11.0	70.8	64.3	35.8
Lumber	4.6	7.5	5.7	1.2	9.2	11.6	14.1	0.0	11.0	17.3	11.0	28.8	27.9	2.8
Pulp and paper products	2.9	6.1	3.7	2.5	6.0	8.0	9.2	0.0	10.8	9.2	10.8	26.3	26.5	7.4
Textiles and apparel	14.4	8.2	7.1	5.2	10.4	14.6	13.7	0.0	23.1	16.3	11.0	22.6	22.3	21.6
Coal, oil, and gas	0.1	0.8	3.1	4.7	5.0	1.6	2.9	0.0	3.2	0.2	11.0	2.5	8.3	0.1
Petroleum and coal products	0.0	0.3	6.7	7.3	4.0	18.4	3.0	0.0	7.3	4.6	11.0	2.7	23.9	0.0
Chemicals	3.6	3.6	7.4	3.5	8.5	5.5	7.3	0.0	16.0	9.4	11.0	16.5	24.5	4.3
Metals	3.1	5.6	3.6	2.1	9.1	7.7	6.4	0.0	8.3	10.3	11.0	17.3	25.7	5.7
Metal products	6.4	6.8	6.2	8.2	12.6	10.7	8.8	0.0	22.6	16.2	11.0	24.1	81.8	5.7
Electronic equipment	0.9	2.2	8.0	2.7	10.0	0.4	3.1	0.0	3.9	13.7	11.0	8.0	20.5	1.6
Motor vehicles	8.5	9.7	8.4	28.9	21.1	28.2	22.4	0.0	35.7	37.0	11.0	15.4	22.3	18.9
Transportation equipment	0.4	0.7	0.7	1.0	0.2	0.1	3.7	0.0	1.7	1.3	7.5	6.3	22.3	0.4
Machinery NEC	3.9	4.8	7.6	4.3	4.6	4.3	5.3	0.0	11.5	14.6	11.0	12.7	21.9	5.6
Manufactures NEC	3.7	7.3	7.3	4.3	23.4	8.4	15.8	0.0	14.2	18.0	11.0	25.1	29.8	4.7

NEC = not elsewhere classified
SACU = Southern African Customs Union

Source: Dimaranan and McDougall (2002).

should be interpreted as representing the potential impacts of preferential tariff liberalization in merchandise goods only.

In order to provide a benchmark for the implications of the US bilateral FTAs, we consider simulated multilateral trade reform. Under this scenario, all economies in the model are assumed to eliminate all tariffs, on an MFN (most favored nation) basis.

In all of the simulations, factor market equilibrium conditions in the GTAP model allow full mobility of capital and labor (skilled and unskilled) across domestic activities, and hence the implicit time period in the comparative static exercises is the long run (10 to 12 years). Land is treated as imperfectly mobile across agricultural activities, while natural resources such as fisheries and mineral fuels are assumed to be sector-specific factors.

Finally, it should be noted that the competitive assumption of the standard GTAP model used here implies that all agents take prices as given and make zero economic profits in the long run. Alternative models that incorporate imperfect competition would predict larger net gains from trade liberalization as a consequence of economies of scale or procompetitive effects of trade, as discussed in the previous section. Also, the static nature of the GTAP model implies a focus on efficiency effects for a given level of productive capacity. Dynamic CGE models would incorporate growth in productive capacity through capital accumulation as a consequence of trade liberalization or other economic policy reforms, and accordingly would also tend to predict larger net gains in economic welfare. For these well-known reasons, the results presented here should probably be regarded as lower-bound estimates of the trade and other economic impacts of prospective US FTAs on the United States and its FTA partners.

Simulation Results

FTAs Considered Independently. The GTAP simulation results for the 14 US free trade agreements considered independently are presented in table A.3, for several key economywide variables. Export and import changes are given as percentages, evaluated at world prices. Impacts on tariff revenue and the change in economic welfare in equivalent variation (EV) form are presented in 1997 dollars. And finally, the change in economic welfare in equivalent variation form is also presented relative to GDP.

Tariff revenue changes are presented in terms both of the total revenue change and of the changes in revenue obtained from partner and nonpartner sources.[9] The loss in revenue from the partner country reflects the fall in the tariff rate applied to those goods being liberalized. The change in the

---

9. The breakdown into two components extends the approach of Fukase and Martin (2001) for examining trade diversion consequences of preferential reform.

Table A.3 Changes in economywide variables under proposed US FTAs considered individually

Variable	Aus-tralia	New Zealand	Korea	Taiwan	Indo-nesia	Malay-sia	Philip-pines	Singa-pore	Thailand	Brazil	Chile	Morocco	Botswana	Rest of SACU
Impacts on United States														
Total imports														
(percent change)	0.1	0.0	0.7	0.5	0.2	0.2	0.2	0.1	0.4	0.7	0.1	0.0	0.0	0.1
From partner	13.9	33.6	23.4	19.9	48.8	10.8	27.7	6.2	32.2	37.4	18.1	18.2	0.5	18.3
From rest of the world	0.0	0.0	0.1	−0.2	−0.3	−0.1	−0.2	−0.1	−0.1	0.3	0.1	0.0	0.0	0.0
Total exports														
(percent change)	0.2	0.1	0.8	0.5	0.2	0.2	0.2	0.1	0.4	0.8	0.1	0.0	0.0	0.1
To partner	17.6	17.5	48.2	29.3	33.0	18.8	30.0	1.0	62.4	78.2	46.3	88.3	103.5	44.6
To rest of the world	−0.2	0.0	−1.0	−0.3	0.0	−0.1	−0.1	0.0	−0.3	−0.9	−0.1	−0.1	0.0	−0.1
Tariff revenue (millions of 1997 dollars)	−206.9	−180.4	−869.4	−1,442.1	−1,188.7	−400.1	−662.1	−306.2	−982.2	−617.9	−112.3	−10.9	0.9	−109.0
From partner	−182.6	−140.2	−746.8	−1,160.7	−820.0	−337.3	−470.3	−251.3	−744.0	−565.8	−105.1	−15.2	−0.1	−95.4
From rest of the world	−24.3	−40.2	−122.6	−281.4	−368.7	−62.8	−191.8	−54.9	−238.2	−52.1	−7.2	4.3	0.8	−13.6
Equivalent variation (millions of 1997 dollars)	467.8	18.6	2,694.1	760.2	−178.6	391.6	224.4	−81.0	823.8	2,779.9	414.8	178.2	16.8	339.1
Allocative efficiency	71.2	8.2	−165.3	107.6	−48.7	67.7	−42.3	−24.7	105.6	482.8	59.0	10.5	2.3	35.9
Terms of trade	396.6	10.4	2,859.4	652.5	−129.9	323.8	266.7	−56.2	718.2	2,297.1	355.7	167.8	14.5	303.2
Equivalent variation (percent GDP)	0.01	0.0	0.03	0.01	0.0	0.0	0.0	0.0	0.01	0.03	0.01	0.0	0.0	0.0

Impacts on FTA partner countries

Total imports														
(percent change)	1.6	2.1	5.8	3.7	5.0	1.9	5.8	0.5	4.7	9.0	2.8	3.8	0.7	2.7
From United States	17.7	17.7	49.6	29.3	33.6	19.5	30.9	1.0	63.7	78.2	46.5	92.8	107.3	45.1
From rest of the world	-2.7	-1.0	-5.1	-3.0	1.1	-1.1	0.3	0.4	-4.7	-11.6	-9.8	-5.1	-3.6	-3.4
Total exports														
(percent change)	1.1	1.4	3.6	2.9	4.3	1.4	5.1	0.5	3.5	7.8	2.2	4.2	0.3	1.8
To United States	13.2	32.5	22.9	19.6	48.9	10.6	27.1	6.2	31.8	37.4	17.6	18.0	0.5	18.0
To rest of the world	-0.5	-2.9	-0.4	-3.0	-6.0	-0.9	-3.9	-0.8	-3.9	1.4	-0.3	2.9	0.2	-0.1
Tariff revenue (millions of 1997 dollars)	-553.6	-88.6	-7,832.4	-1,462.6	-334.5	-657.7	-503.5	-28.8	-1,530.5	-3,745.4	-621.7	-292.3	-14.1	-439.6
From United States	-435.4	-76.5	-4,467.7	-965.0	-334.6	-402.8	-473.4	-25.3	-826.4	-1,940.1	-443.6	-115.3	-6.5	-232.2
From rest of the world	-118.3	-12.1	-3,364.7	-497.6	0.0	-255.0	-30.1	-3.5	-704.1	-1,805.3	-178.1	-177.0	-7.6	-207.4
Equivalent variation (millions of 1997 dollars)	83.0	161.5	1,637.8	1,042.8	1,313.2	248.3	907.1	342.6	779.7	31.8	-51.4	-92.6	4.6	-36.7
Allocative efficiency	-18.8	11.1	1,739.6	-22.9	308.0	18.8	404.2	41.8	19.0	218.6	-82.5	-24.7	4.7	-40.3
Terms of trade	101.8	150.3	-101.8	1,065.7	1,005.3	229.5	502.9	300.8	760.7	-186.8	31.1	-67.9	0.0	3.7
Equivalent variation (percent GDP)	0.02	0.25	0.37	0.35	0.63	0.23	1.16	0.43	0.49	0.00	-0.07	-0.26	0.10	-0.03

SACU = Southern African Customs Union

Source: GTAP simulation results.

nonpartner revenue reveals the implications of falls in the volume of trade flows not being liberalized, and is an indicator of trade diversion.[10]

The EV measure represents the change in income at constant prices that occurs as a result of the proposed change in trade policy. To give an indication of the significance of the dollar measure relative to total economic activity, the EV is also presented as a percentage of the base-year GDP. The dollar EV measure is further decomposed into allocative efficiency and terms-of-trade effects, following Arnold Harberger's fundamental equation of applied welfare economics (Harberger 1971). In essence, allocative efficiency effects measure the economic implications of reallocation of resources across activities (consumption, production, and trade). The greater the distortions in the economy, the greater the potential allocative efficiency effects of policy reform. Terms-of-trade effects, on the other hand, measure the implications of changes in the prices faced by the economy in international trade. The larger the economy, the greater are the expected terms-of-trade consequences of policy reform. Negative terms-of-trade consequences of an FTA for nonmember economies are another indicator of trade diversion, since the changes in trading prices reflect the reduction in imports by members from nonmember sources. Strong positive terms-of-trade effects for members can reflect both an improvement in economic welfare vis-à-vis nonmembers and the effects of improved access to partner markets (preferential access).

The simulation results in table A.3 for the individual US FTAs are wide-ranging, as one might expect, given the variety of prospective US partner countries and their economic circumstances. It is apparent that the potential trade and welfare impacts of the proposed FTAs for the United States are very small. Indeed, the improvement in US welfare is generally no more than 0.01 percent of GDP, except in the cases of a US-Brazil FTA or US-Korea FTA, for which the improvement in US welfare is 0.03 percent. In dollar terms, US free trade agreements with Brazil ($2.8 billion), Korea ($2.7 billion), Thailand and Taiwan ($0.8 billion), Australia ($0.5 billion), and Chile ($0.4 billion) would contribute most to improving US welfare.

At the same time, the prospective US FTAs are substantially more beneficial to the US partner countries, when the gains in economic welfare are measured relative to GDP. In these terms, the Philippines benefits most (1.2 percent of GDP), followed by Indonesia (0.6 percent), Thailand (0.5 percent), and Korea, Singapore, and Taiwan (0.4 percent). Notably, according to the GTAP simulation results, economic welfare in Chile, Morocco, and SACU (the Southern African Customs Union, mainly South Africa) besides Botswana falls as a result of individual FTAs with the

---

10. Fukase and Martin (2001) identify a third component, the increase in revenues associated with increased trade volumes of liberalized imports. This effect is not present in this study because of the assumption that liberalization is complete (i.e., the post-FTA preferential tariffs are zero).

United States: by 0.1 percent in Chile, 0.3 percent in Morocco, and less than 0.1 percent in the rest of SACU. These results follow from the dominance of trade diversion effects in the US FTAs with the three countries. However, the decline in economic welfare for the three countries should be considered in a somewhat broader context than the present GTAP results—namely, one that recognizes the preexistence of other preferential trading arrangements, such as European Union partnership agreements with Chile, Morocco, and South Africa. To the extent that increased US exports to these countries under US FTAs mainly reduces margins of preference enjoyed by countries under preexisting preferential agreements, the net trade diversion effects reflected in the present GTAP simulation results might be viewed in a more positive light. Conversely, to the extent that the increased US exports add to existing discrimination against third countries that are not party to preexisting preferential trading arrangements, the net trade diversion effects should be considered deleterious to these countries (Chile, Morocco, and the rest of SACU).

FTAs Considered Simultaneously. Table A.4 reveals the impacts of US bilateral FTAs when the agreements are implemented between the United States and a number of partner countries simultaneously. The initial economic gains for partner countries, as indicated in table A.3, are appreciably reduced by the inclusion of many countries as partners in US bilateral FTAs. For instance, the welfare gain of the Philippines is reduced by one-third, from 1.2 percent of GDP to 0.8 percent of GDP. Also, the total US economic gain from the bilateral FTAs rises to 0.1 percent of GDP. In effect, US pursuit of FTAs simultaneously with a wide number of partners reduces the margins of preference in the United States initially enjoyed by export producers in FTA partner countries (and hence reduces trade diversion), while it increases the magnitude of trade creation enjoyed by consumers in the United States.

Tables A.5 and A.6 indicate the corresponding changes in sectoral and regional patterns, respectively, of exports under the US bilateral FTAs. US exports to the world expand in a number of important categories, especially food grains (29 percent), motor vehicles (21 percent), other crops (12 percent), processed foods (11 percent), textiles and apparel (7 percent), and metal products (6 percent). Given the preferential nature of the agreements, US exports to the FTA partners increase by substantially larger margins in the same categories: for instance, by nearly 375 percent in motor vehicles and by more than 100 percent in food grains (165 percent), processed foods (126 percent), and textiles and apparel (109 percent).

Similarly, partner country exports to the United States also expand by very large proportions in some important categories, especially textiles and apparel (98 percent), nongrain crops (82 percent), and processed foods (66 percent). However, reflecting the partner countries' comparatively limited trade liberalization (i.e., only vis-à-vis imports from the

Table A.4 Changes in economywide variables under proposed US FTAs considered simultaneously

Variable	United States	Aus-tralia	New Zealand	Korea	Taiwan	Indo-nesia	Malay-sia	Philip-pines	Singa-pore	Thailand	Brazil	Chile	Mo-rocco	Bo-tswana	Rest of SACU
Total imports (percent change)	3.2	0.8	1.2	5.3	3.1	3.9	1.3	4.6	-0.2	3.9	7.9	2.2	3.2	-0.6	2.0
From partner	19.9	14.1	13.1	46.8	25.6	28.1	15.8	26.2	-2.3	58.4	74.0	42.1	86.2	99.3	39.5
From rest of the world	-0.2	-2.7	-1.2	-5.0	-2.7	0.7	-1.2	-0.2	0.2	-4.7	-11.7	-9.3	-5.1	-4.6	-3.5
Total exports (percent change)	3.4	0.6	0.8	3.1	2.4	3.5	0.8	4.1	-0.2	2.8	7.4	1.7	3.7	-0.8	1.4
To partner	32.4	13.5	31.1	20.6	18.2	42.9	9.6	23.0	5.7	27.9	35.4	16.6	15.7	0.7	16.7
To rest of the world	-3.0	-1.0	-3.4	-0.5	-3.1	-5.6	-1.4	-3.6	-1.5	-3.7	1.3	-0.8	2.6	-0.9	-0.4
Tariff revenue (millions of 1997 dollars)	-6,607.3	-551.8	-89.2	-7,816.5	-1,439.1	-368.2	-664.4	-521.3	-28.0	-1,533.5	-3,736.3	-612.1	-291.6	-16.9	-439.1
From partner	-5,634.9	-435.4	-76.5	-4,467.7	-965.0	-334.6	-402.8	-473.4	-25.3	-826.4	-1,940.1	-443.6	-115.3	-6.5	-232.2
From rest of the world	-972.4	-116.4	-12.8	-3,348.8	-474.1	-33.6	-261.7	-47.9	-2.7	-707.2	-1,796.2	-168.5	-176.3	-10.4	-206.9
Equivalent variation (millions of 1997 dollars)	9,113.6	-235.4	69.9	1,069.2	634.2	963.9	-11.8	610.2	72.3	414.2	-475.5	-114.2	-110.5	0.2	-126.3
Allocative efficiency	8,215.9	-186.1	67.1	-548.5	658.8	739.1	12.9	307.5	64.5	471.3	-451.2	-28.2	-82.9	-2.9	-71.7
Terms of trade	897.7	-49.3	2.8	1,617.6	-24.7	224.7	-24.7	302.7	7.7	-57.0	-24.2	-86.0	-27.7	3.1	-54.6
Equivalent variation (percent GDP)	0.11	-0.06	0.11	0.24	0.21	0.46	-0.01	0.78	0.09	0.26	-0.06	-0.15	-0.32	0.00	-0.09

SACU = Southern African Customs Union

Source: GTAP simulation results.

Table A.5 Changes in the sectoral pattern of exports under proposed US FTAs considered simultaneously
(percent change; exports in millions of 1997 dollars)

| | United States | | | | FTA partners | | | |
| | Initial exports | | Free trade agreement | | Initial exports | | Free trade agreement | |
Sector	Total	To FTA partners	Total	To FTA partners	Total	To United States	Total	To United States
Grains	10,924.9	2,266.0	29.2	164.6	2,984.1	45.0	−1.9	10.5
Other crops	18,663.8	3,672.7	12.2	91.0	15,882.7	2,167.2	8.9	81.5
Animal products	2,939.6	983.6	2.3	21.9	4,811.8	281.6	0.1	8.8
Forestry and fisheries	2,648.2	257.9	2.4	44.1	4,274.2	276.3	−2.2	0.9
Processed food products	30,540.7	3,633.1	10.6	125.5	49,677.9	6,249.9	8.5	65.6
Lumber	9,473.4	812.9	1.4	40.6	19,754.3	3,998.4	−0.2	11.2
Pulp and paper products	19,912.9	3,343.2	1.2	15.6	12,010.7	994.7	−1.3	3.0
Textiles and apparel	20,611.1	1,942.4	7.3	109.1	72,097.7	16,458.4	21.2	98.2
Coal, oil, and gas	6,402.9	1,322.0	1.8	15.1	42,381.0	1,463.8	−0.5	2.2
Petroleum and coal products	6,382.0	1,420.4	2.0	12.6	16,086.2	281.8	−0.3	9.3
Chemicals	96,106.9	19,657.2	2.8	21.5	73,038.8	8,569.1	0.5	14.9
Metals	20,523.8	2,977.2	1.1	23.5	55,182.3	5,932.9	−0.1	12.6
Metal products	13,714.1	2,070.1	6.4	56.7	14,222.3	3,531.5	1.9	20.3
Electronic equipment	109,331.5	33,273.7	3.0	15.7	226,040.0	67,783.3	0.0	3.8
Motor vehicles	56,832.4	3,593.7	20.5	374.3	22,254.1	4,069.0	2.7	31.3
Transportation equipment	45,807.6	12,122.0	−2.9	2.7	14,338.0	1,519.7	1.1	36.9
Machinery NEC	160,560.8	31,786.3	3.7	30.1	83,679.3	14,690.7	0.3	15.5
Manufactures NEC	11,322.0	1,570.6	3.0	43.5	16,044.4	4,294.7	1.7	15.6
Services	210,108.8	28,740.9	−2.5	−1.2	140,788.3	23,551.4	−1.6	−0.5

NEC = not elsewhere classified

Source: GTAP simulation results.

Table A.6 Changes in the regional pattern of exports under US FTAs considered simultaneously (percent change; exports in millions of 1997 dollars)

Region/country	Initial exports			Free trade agreement		
	Total	To United States	To FTA partners	Total	To United States	To FTA partners
USA	852,718.7	—	1,008,342.0	3.4	—	32.4
Canada*	230,948.0	167,579.9	411,535.2	−0.3	−0.1	−3.5
Mexico*	115,223.2	86,241.1	206,690.4	−0.2	−0.1	−6.2
Total NAFTA	1,198,889.9	253,820.9	1,626,568.0	2.4	−0.1	28.5
European Union	2,360,107.4	221,573.8	2,771,685.0	−0.3	0.4	−3.4
Australia*	70,568.7	7,820.7	99,348.7	0.6	13.5	−3.1
New Zealand*	17,027.1	2,068.1	24,584.0	0.8	31.1	−5.6
Japan	490,448.8	127,311.1	763,190.7	−0.1	1.8	−3.2
China	292,748.8	75,785.4	416,218.6	−0.8	−3.1	−2.5
Korea*	149,293.4	25,360.9	203,748.2	3.1	20.6	−2.9
Taiwan*	136,412.6	35,282.1	194,249.3	2.4	18.2	−4.5
Indonesia*	56,894.5	10,613.4	79,828.1	3.5	42.9	−5.8
Malaysia*	95,093.7	18,826.4	146,908.4	0.8	9.6	−2.0
Philippines*	40,994.6	11,848.4	60,261.8	4.1	23.0	−3.5
Singapore*	125,698.3	22,396.0	186,264.7	−0.2	5.7	−2.5
Thailand*	70,707.9	14,558.2	101,636.8	2.8	27.9	−4.6
Total ASEAN	389,389.0	78,242.3	574,899.8	1.6	18.4	−3.1
Brazil*	57,880.7	10,321.5	74,335.5	7.4	35.4	−4.2
Chile*	18,801.1	2,627.2	25,348.1	1.7	16.6	−2.9
Central America	39,265.1	16,104.7	57,783.4	−0.7	−4.6	0.5
Rest of South America	90,590.8	25,061.3	134,632.7	−1.3	0.4	−9.9
Morocco*	8,789.0	764.0	9,933.7	3.7	15.7	0.9
Botswana*	2,912.2	90.7	3,423.6	−0.8	0.7	−6.8
Rest of SACU*	34,388.4	3,582.3	45,318.1	1.4	16.7	−2.3
Rest of world	840,206.9	103,320.5	1,036,218.0	−0.3	−1.0	−1.4
Total world	6,197,719.8	989,137.3	8,061,485.0	0.6	3.2	3.1

* = FTA partners; ASEAN = Association of Southeast Asian Nations; SACU = Southern African Customs Union

Source: GTAP simulation results.

United States), partner exports to the world do not expand appreciably except in the aforementioned categories.

With respect to the changes in the regional pattern of exports (table A.6), total exports of the United States and most FTA partners expand by 2 to 4 percent. The United States expands its total exports to FTA partners by 32 percent, and the FTA partners generally expand their total exports to the United States by similar and in some cases greater proportions (e.g.,

Indonesia's 43 percent). The exports to the world of third countries generally decline by only about 1 percent (China and rest of South America) or less. However, appreciable trade diversion is apparent in the results for exports to the FTA partner countries. Except for exports of the United States, exports of most countries to FTA partner countries, including bilateral exports of FTA partner countries themselves, decline by 2 to 6 percent. This last result again illustrates the degree to which the current US strategy to pursue bilateral FTAs with a wide number of partner countries tends to limit trade diversion in the United States but not trade diversion in the partner countries, so long as the partner countries themselves do not likewise pursue unilateral trade liberalization or a wide number of bilateral FTAs.

The spillover effects of the simultaneous US bilateral FTAs on economic welfare in selected third countries, including China, the European Union, Japan, and Mexico, are presented in table A.7. Also presented in the table are benchmark GTAP results for multilateral free trade undertaken simultaneously by the United States, its 14 FTA partners, and the third countries included in the table.

The spillover effects on economic welfare of the US bilateral FTAs are modest relative to GDP for major countries such as Japan (–0.1 percent) and the European Union (–0.0 percent), but arguably less so for NAFTA partners Canada and Mexico (both –0.2 percent). Spillover effects are also of appreciable magnitude relative to GDP for the Central American countries (–0.7 percent) and China (–0.2 percent). Of course, these results mask possibly sizable impacts on the economic welfare of different groups of consumers and producers within third countries, including large third countries such as EU members and Japan. In these countries, export producers that suffer especially adverse affects might be sufficiently influential politically to unleash competitive liberalization forces within their country that would push more effectively for multilateral trade liberalization on a nondiscriminatory basis. However, the present GTAP results suggest that competitive liberalization forces are likely to be strongest in China and other developing countries excluded from the prospective US free trade agreements—that is, in the countries that are least likely to be effective in promoting multilateral trade liberalization.

Finally, the benchmark welfare effects for multilateral trade liberalization indicate how dramatically better off the world economy would be under multilateral trade liberalization than under widespread US bilateral free trade agreements. The GTAP results indicate that whereas the world economy would lose by $0.4 billion under the US FTAs, it would gain by more than $84 billion under multilateral trade liberalization. This would seemingly provide the latent forces of competitive liberalization worldwide considerable grist for finally winning support for multilateral trade liberalization, whether in a successful outcome to the Doha Round or some other form (including possibly coalescence of FTAs worldwide).

Table A.7 Changes in economic welfare by region under US FTAs and multilateral free trade (millions of 1997 dollars)

Region/ country	Initial GDP	Free trade agreements considered simultaneously		Multilateral free trade	
		Equivalent variation	Equivalent variation (percent GDP)	Equivalent variation	Equivalent variation (percent GDP)
USA	7,945,196.5	9,113.6	0.11	−254.0	0.00
Canada*	631,127.2	−1,021.0	−0.16	1,732.2	0.27
Mexico*	388,824.4	−776.3	−0.20	−514.4	−0.13
Total NAFTA	8,965,148.1	7,316.3	0.08	963.9	0.01
European Union	7,957,957.5	−3,499.6	−0.04	−3,574.7	−0.04
Australia*	392,841.3	−235.4	−0.06	2,803.1	0.71
New Zealand*	65,079.0	69.9	0.11	3,350.8	5.15
Japan	4,255,524.0	−2,041.7	−0.05	15,749.1	0.37
China	994,687.2	−1,926.0	−0.19	5,536.5	0.56
Korea*	445,502.9	1,069.2	0.24	9,638.6	2.16
Taiwan*	299,681.0	634.2	0.21	3,769.4	1.26
Indonesia*	208,833.9	963.9	0.46	2,642.1	1.27
Malaysia*	106,090.4	−11.8	−0.01	1,263.5	1.19
Philippines*	78,356.1	610.2	0.78	−57.3	−0.07
Singapore*	79,822.1	72.3	0.09	2,157.8	2.70
Thailand*	157,779.8	414.2	0.26	2,745.7	1.74
Total ASEAN	630,882.3	2,048.8	0.32	8,751.9	1.39
Brazil*	789,679.9	−475.5	−0.06	5,996.1	0.76
Chile*	76,147.5	−114.2	−0.15	551.4	0.72
Central America	94,053.6	−615.4	−0.65	1,735.2	1.84
Rest of South America	626,100.0	−750.8	−0.12	4,855.1	0.78
Morocco*	34,946.7	−110.5	−0.32	990.0	2.83
Botswana*	4,777.3	0.2	0.00	172.6	3.61
Rest of SACU*	139,050.5	−126.3	−0.09	1,458.4	1.05
Rest of world	3,209,725.0	−1,688.2	−0.05	21,602.5	0.67
Total world	28,981,783.7	−445.1	0.00	84,349.8	0.29

* = FTA partners; ASEAN = Association of Southeast Asian Nations; SACU = Southern African Customs Union

Source: GTAP simulation results.

However, the GTAP results also reveal a possible dark outcome for the world economy, one in which economic interests in the European Union and the United States effectively block competitive liberalization forces. The GTAP results make it clear that both the European Union and the United States are worse off under multilateral free trade than under the US bilateral FTAs, the European Union by only about $0.1 billion but the United States by more than $9.0 billion.

Gravity Model Results

Among the most robust empirical approaches to forecasting bilateral trade flows is the so-called gravity model approach.[11] The basic gravity model consists of the results of ordinary least squares regression pitting bilateral trade flows in a common currency (adjusted for inflation) against the gravitational "mass" of explanatory variables describing the bilateral trading partners, including especially their proximity, combined population, and combined GDP. Most gravity models find that trade between two countries is significantly greater, the greater their combined population and GDP and the shorter the distance between them. Additional explanatory variables also are frequently important. For instance, trading partners that share a common border or a common language are often found to enjoy significantly greater mutual trade.

In recent years, gravity models have been applied widely to assess whether, and to what extent, regional and other forms of preferential trading arrangements result in expanded bilateral trade among member countries. This is typically accomplished by including a dichotomous (0, 1) explanatory variable in the regression equation for each preferential arrangement among two or more trading partners. The econometric results have been impressive, widely supporting the hypothesis that preferential trading arrangements lead to significant expansion of trade between member countries (see, e.g., Frankel 1997).[12]

Gravity model results for preferential trading arrangement variables do not usually differentiate between the effects of trade creation and trade diversion. That is, while they indicate the expected magnitude of expansion in bilateral trade, they typically do not indicate whether the main cause of an increase in mutual trade is trade with internationally competitive producers (trade creation), or trade with noncompetitive producers attributable to margins of preference (trade diversion). Trade creation adds to the economic welfare of the importing country (and the world at large), while trade diversion generally increases only the economic welfare of inefficient exporters (and their home country).

Nonetheless, gravity model estimates of the responsiveness of bilateral trade flows to regional and other preferential trading arrangements might be applied to consider the *gross* trade impacts of proposed US FTAs with partner countries. Specifically, they are interpreted here as an upper bound on the potential magnitude of trade creation.

---

11. The theoretical basis of the gravity model has not been fully appreciated until relatively recently; see, e.g., Anderson (1979), Bergstrand (1985, 1989), and Deardorff (1998).

12. See also Greenaway and Milner (2002) for an extensive discussion of methodological and modeling issues surrounding the econometric results for FTAs using the gravity model.

Methodology and FTA Scenarios

The quantitative analysis here is based on recent gravity model estimates found by Andrew Rose (2003) for bilateral merchandise trade between 178 trading countries during the period 1948–1999.[13] His gravity model regressions find that regional free trade areas tend to add 0.78 to bilateral real trade (measured in log terms) between member countries. In the analysis here, this econometric estimate is applied in combination with IMF *Direction of Trade* data for 2000 for the United States and more than 20 prospective partner countries in diverse regions of the world,[14] to calculate the trade impacts of forming US bilateral free trade agreements.

Three FTA scenarios are considered:

1. US FTAs are established bilaterally with the selected prospective partner countries.

2. US FTAs lead to regional free trade areas among prospective partner countries in the same region and the United States.

3. US FTAs lead to a "multilateral" free trade area among the prospective partner countries worldwide and the United States.

The first scenario corresponds to the simple case of bilateral FTAs struck by the United States with each of the prospective partner countries. The second scenario adds the possibility that prospective FTA partners in the same region will be stimulated by the US free trade agreements in the first scenario to forge bilateral FTAs among themselves, in effect forming regional free trade areas that include the United States as an extraregional member. Finally, the third scenario considers the impacts of forging bilateral FTAs among all prospective FTA partners, in effect forming a multilateral free trade area among the prospective FTA partners and the United States.

---

13. Rose's regression data for annual bilateral trade flows (in US dollars, deflated by the US consumer price index for urban consumers) are drawn from the IMF *Direction of Trade* database, which excludes Taiwan and some centrally planned economies. His regression estimates include year-specific "fixed" effects to account for such factors as the value of the dollar, the global business cycle, the extent of globalization, oil shocks, and so forth.

14. Actual and prospective partner countries in US free trade agreements are Canada and Mexico (NAFTA); Australia and New Zealand (CER, or Closer Economic Relations, countries); Korea, Indonesia, Malaysia, Philippines, Singapore, Taiwan, and Thailand (ASEAN, or Association of Southeast Asian Nations, countries plus Korea and Taiwan); Brazil, Chile, Costa Rica, El Salvador, Guatemala, Honduras, and Nicaragua (CACM, or Central American Common Market, countries plus Brazil and Chile); Egypt, Israel, Jordan, Morocco (MENA, or Middle East and North Africa, countries); and Botswana, Lesotho, Namibia, South Africa, and Swaziland (Southern African Customs Union, or SACU, countries). Of these countries, Canada, Israel, and Mexico enjoyed FTAs with the United States that were substantially in force during 2000.

The three FTA scenarios are grounded partly in fact. For instance, the second scenario may well describe the outcome of proposed US FTAs with the ASEAN (Association of Southeast Asian Nations) countries, CACM (Central American Common Market) countries, and SACU countries, in which members of these existing regional trading arrangements are stimulated, if not compelled, to incorporate their bilateral trade reforms with the United States with one another. However, the possibility that the US FTAs might lead to a multilateral free trade area among the prospective partner countries worldwide and the United States—for instance, as an alternative to an unsuccessful Doha Round—seems more remote, though widespread adoption of FTAs might well lead to some coalescence of them in the long run should the Doha Round fail.

Finally, it should be borne in mind that the single gravity model estimate underlying the quantitative analysis here might not be appropriate to each of the three scenarios. Indeed, while Rose's econometric estimate of the average trade impact of regional trade arrangements worldwide might be appropriate to the second scenario, it might overestimate and underestimate, respectively, the trade impacts of US bilateral FTAs in the first scenario and the multilateral free trade area in the third scenario.

Quantitative Results

The computed trade impacts of the three FTA scenarios are presented in table A.8. The results are derived by applying Rose's estimate of the (proportional) impact of regional free trade areas on bilateral trade to "base" 2000 trade flows among the United States and the prospective partner countries, grouped by regional blocs in the first panel of table A.8. Rose's regression coefficient estimate of 0.78 for the bilateral trade impact of regional free trade areas implies that countries entering into a bilateral free trade agreement can expect their mutual trade to expand by 118 percent in real terms.[15]

The base trade flows in table A.8 account for between about 50 percent (imports) and about 60 percent (exports) of the total international trade of the United States and its prospective FTA partners in 2000. As might be expected, the United States and its prospective FTA partners account for substantially smaller proportions of the total international trade of the MENA (Middle East and North Africa) and SACU countries, whose

---

15. Given the particular log-specification of the regression equation underlying Rose's gravity model, the proportional impact of a free trade agreement on bilateral trade is computed as $[EXP(0.78) - 1] = 1.18$, where EXP is the natural exponential function operator. Rose's gravity model is not explicitly dynamic, so, given that annual data are used to estimate the parameters of his model, the trade impacts presented in table A.8 might be expected to occur over a medium-term period of one to five years.

Table A.8a Gravity model estimates of US FTA–led expansion of bilateral, regional, and "multilateral" trade: Base "multilateral" trade, 2000 (millions of dollars)

Export/import country	United States	NAFTA	CER	ASEAN+	CACM+	MENA	SACU	Base	World	Base/world (percent)
NAFTA	364,271.0	686,572.1	19,115.5	111,423.4	31,778.9	12,098.9	3,978.0	864,966.7	1,296,825.0	66.7
United States	—	309,356.0	17,322.6	104,358.8	26,933.2	11,411.1	3,612.4	472,994.1	851,306.0	55.6
Canada*	229,191.0	233,609.2	1,430.7	5,424.7	1,913.5	657.8	293.4	243,329.4	282,037.0	86.3
Mexico*	135,080.0	143,606.9	362.2	1,639.9	2,932.1	30.0	72.2	148,643.3	163,482.0	90.9
CER	8,878.2	10,924.9	5,944.4	19,190.9	547.5	668.2	802.9	38,078.8	83,410.6	45.7
Australia	6,692.7	8,173.1	3,086.0	17,020.2	452.1	570.5	743.8	30,045.6	68,469.6	43.9
New Zealand	2,185.5	2,751.8	2,858.4	2,170.6	95.5	97.6	59.2	8,033.2	14,341.0	53.8
ASEAN + KO + TA	163,820.9	184,671.9	15,167.8	159,290.3	6,496.8	3,594.3	2,367.6	371,588.7	744,322.8	49.9
Korea (KO)	40,911.0	48,976.0	3,137.9	24,071.5	3,018.2	1,480.4	588.9	81,273.0	178,119.0	45.6
Indonesia	11,097.4	12,276.7	1,956.0	19,125.1	385.4	330.8	225.5	34,299.6	66,692.2	51.4
Malaysia	25,990.0	29,318.4	3,056.4	38,667.5	744.1	345.3	337.2	72,468.9	121,308.0	59.7
Philippines	14,216.4	15,901.5	371.8	11,970.2	193.4	62.7	53.3	28,553.1	48,358.5	59.0
Singapore	19,630.4	21,331.0	2,598.2	29,819.3	361.8	453.9	231.5	54,795.7	106,234.0	51.6
Thailand	17,161.4	18,955.6	1,991.1	15,330.6	380.6	199.1	299.3	37,156.2	75,894.8	49.0
Taiwan (TA)	34,814.3	37,912.7	1,827.9	1,733.6	94.2	39.3	0.8	63,042.2	148,516.3	42.5
CACM + BR + CH	30,179.2	35,479.4	543.5	4,808.9	5,778.6	559.6	366.2	47,536.3	102,679.6	46.2
Brazil (BR)	14,393.1	17,481.7	457.5	2,498.1	1,635.2	511.3	321.3	22,905.1	61,199.2	37.4
Chile (CH)	3,601.8	4,996.6	66.6	1,983.2	1,195.4	30.8	39.2	8,311.8	20,206.7	41.1
Costa Rica	3,717.0	4,050.7	13.7	232.2	628.0	2.3	3.3	4,930.3	8,139.9	60.6
El Salvador	1,952.5	2,086.9	0.7	15.3	813.3	9.5	0.1	2,925.8	3,254.9	89.9
Guatemala	2,743.8	2,956.3	2.8	49.4	819.0	4.9	2.0	3,834.5	4,635.8	81.8
Honduras	3,173.7	3,236.7	1.4	24.6	321.9	0.7	0.0	3,585.3	4,158.9	86.2
Nicaragua	597.3	670.5	0.8	6.1	365.6	0.1	0.3	1,043.4	1,234.3	84.5

MENA	14,334.2	15,293.3	415.8	2,590.3	625.9	304.6	237.2	19,467.1	47,461.9	41.0
Egypt	894.7	926.0	12.3	336.5	40.7	81.1	8.3	1,404.9	6,239.7	22.5
Israel*	12,899.8	13,667.3	291.5	1,885.8	487.3	144.4	222.5	16,698.8	30,860.0	54.1
Jordan	74.5	76.5	4.0	77.5	5.2	65.4	3.6	232.2	1,785.9	13.0
Morocco	465.2	623.5	108.0	290.5	92.7	13.7	2.7	1,131.1	8,576.3	13.2
SACU	4,603.3	5,029.2	585.4	2,748.5	312.3	371.3	0.0	9,046.7	33,729.5	26.8
Botswana	42.0	42.2	0.0	6.5	0.2	1.4	0.0	50.4	778.2	6.5
Lesotho	143.9	148.7	0.0	0.5	0.0	0.0	0.0	149.2	172.4	86.5
Namibia	44.5	87.7	5.7	5.4	0.0	0.5	0.0	99.2	606.3	16.4
South Africa	4,316.8	4,693.1	578.3	2,458.3	311.4	369.5	0.0	8,410.6	31,843.5	26.4
Swaziland	56.1	57.5	1.4	277.8	0.7	0.0	0.0	337.3	329.1	102.5
Base	586,086.8	937,970.9	41,772.4	300,052.3	45,540.0	17,596.9	7,751.8	1,350,684.4	2,309,229.4	58.5
World	1,238,200.0	1,692,825.0	88,216.0	644,126.9	103,628.5	75,632.0	28,567.0	2,632,995.4	—	—
Percent										
(Base/world)	47.3	55.4	47.4	46.6	43.9	23.3	27.1	51.3	—	—

* = Countries with existing FTA with the United States.
ASEAN = Association of South East Asian Nations
CACM = Central American Common Market
CER = Closer Economic Relations (Australia–New Zealand)
MENA = Middle East and North Africa
NAFTA = North American Free Trade Agreement
SACU = Southern African Customs Union

Table A.8b Scenario 1: US FTA expansion of bilateral trade (millions of dollars)

Export/import country	United States	NAFTA	CER	ASEAN+	CACM+	MENA	SACU	Total	Change	Change:base (percent)	Change:world (percent)
NAFTA	**364,271.0**	686,572.1	39,581.7	234,720.5	63,599.7	17,729.3	8,245.9	1,050,449.1	185,482.4	21.4	14.3
United States	—	**309,356.0**	**37,788.8**	**227,655.8**	**58,754.1**	**17,041.5**	**7,880.3**	658,476.5	185,482.4	39.2	21.8
Canada*	**229,191.0**	**233,609.2**	1,430.7	5,424.7	1,913.5	657.8	293.4	243,329.4	0.0	0.0	0.0
Mexico*	**135,080.0**	**143,606.9**	362.2	1,639.9	2,932.1	30.0	72.2	148,643.3	0.0	0.0	0.0
CER	**19,367.5**	21,414.3	5,944.4	19,190.9	547.5	668.2	802.9	48,568.2	10,489.3	27.5	12.6
Australia	**14,599.9**	16,080.3	3,086.0	17,020.2	452.1	570.5	743.8	37,952.9	7,907.2	26.3	11.5
New Zealand	**4,767.6**	5,333.9	2,858.4	2,170.6	95.5	97.6	59.2	10,615.3	2,582.1	32.1	17.3
ASEAN + KO + TA	**357,370.7**	378,221.8	15,167.8	159,290.3	6,496.8	3,594.3	2,367.6	565,138.6	193,549.8	52.1	26.0
Korea (KO)	**89,246.2**	97,311.2	3,137.9	24,071.5	3,018.2	1,480.4	588.9	129,608.2	48,335.2	59.5	27.1
Indonesia	**24,208.7**	25,388.0	1,956.0	19,125.1	385.4	330.8	225.5	47,410.8	13,111.3	38.2	19.7
Malaysia	**56,696.5**	60,024.9	3,056.4	38,667.5	744.1	345.3	337.2	103,175.3	30,706.5	42.4	25.3
Philippines	**31,012.7**	32,697.8	371.8	11,970.2	193.4	62.7	53.3	45,349.4	16,796.3	58.8	34.7
Singapore	**42,823.2**	44,523.8	2,598.2	29,819.3	361.8	453.9	231.5	77,988.5	23,192.8	42.3	21.8
Thailand	**37,437.1**	39,231.3	1,991.1	15,330.6	380.6	199.1	299.3	57,432.0	20,275.7	54.6	26.7
Taiwan (TA)	**75,946.4**	79,044.8	2,056.4	20,306.1	1,413.1	722.0	631.8	104,174.4	41,132.1	65.2	27.7
CACM + BR + CH	**65,835.1**	71,135.3	543.5	4,808.9	5,778.6	559.6	366.2	83,192.2	35,655.9	75.0	34.7
Brazil (BR)	**31,398.1**	34,486.8	457.5	2,498.1	1,635.2	511.3	321.3	39,910.1	17,005.0	74.2	27.8
Chile (CH)	**7,857.2**	9,252.1	66.6	1,983.2	1,195.4	30.8	39.2	12,567.2	4,255.4	51.2	21.1
Costa Rica	**8,108.5**	8,442.2	13.7	232.2	628.0	2.3	3.3	9,321.9	4,391.5	89.1	54.0
El Salvador	**4,259.3**	4,393.7	0.7	15.3	813.3	9.5	0.1	5,232.6	2,306.8	78.8	70.9
Guatemala	**5,985.5**	6,198.1	2.8	49.4	819.0	4.9	2.0	7,076.2	3,241.7	84.5	69.2
Honduras	**6,923.3**	6,986.3	1.4	24.6	321.9	0.7	0.0	7,335.0	3,749.6	104.6	90.2
Nicaragua	**1,303.0**	1,376.2	0.8	6.1	365.6	0.1	0.3	1,749.1	705.7	67.6	57.2

MENA	**16,028.9**	16,988.0	415.8	2,590.3	625.9	304.6	237.2	21,161.8	1,694.7	8.7	3.6
Egypt	**1,951.8**	1,983.1	12.3	336.5	40.7	81.1	8.3	2,462.0	1,057.1	75.2	16.9
Israel*	**12,899.8**	13,667.3	291.5	1,885.8	487.3	144.4	222.5	16,698.8	0.0	0.0	0.0
Jordan	**162.5**	164.5	4.0	77.5	5.2	65.4	3.6	320.2	88.0	37.9	4.9
Morocco	**1,014.8**	1,173.1	108.0	290.5	92.7	13.7	2.7	1,680.8	549.6	48.6	6.4
SACU	**10,042.0**	10,467.9	585.4	2,748.5	312.3	371.3	0.0	14,485.4	5,438.7	60.1	16.1
Botswana	**91.6**	91.8	0.0	6.5	0.2	1.4	0.0	100.0	49.6	98.5	6.4
Lesotho	**313.9**	318.7	0.0	0.5	0.0	0.0	0.0	319.2	170.0	114.0	98.6
Namibia	**97.1**	140.3	5.7	5.4	0.0	0.5	0.0	151.8	52.6	53.0	8.7
South Africa	**9,417.0**	9,793.3	578.3	2,458.3	311.4	369.5	0.0	13,510.8	5,100.2	60.6	16.0
Swaziland	**122.4**	123.8	1.4	277.8	0.7	0.0	0.0	403.6	66.3	19.6	20.1
Total	832,915.3	1,184,799.4	62,238.6	423,349.3	77,360.9	23,227.3	12,019.8	1,782,995.2	432,310.9	32.0	18.7
Change	246,828.5	246,828.5	20,466.2	123,297.0	31,820.9	5,630.4	4,267.9	432,310.3	—	—	—
Change/base (percent)	42.1	26.3	49.0	41.1	69.9	32.0	55.1	32.0	—	—	—
Change/world (percent)	19.9	14.6	23.2	19.1	30.7	7.4	14.9	16.4	—	—	—

* = Countries with existing FTA with the United States.
ASEAN = Association of South East Asian Nations
CACM = Central American Common Market
CER = Closer Economic Relations (Australia–New Zealand)
MENA = Middle East and North Africa
NAFTA = North American Free Trade Agreement
SACU = Southern African Customs Union

Note: Numbers in bold indicate base trade plus bilateral FTA effects.

Table A.8c   Scenario 2: US FTA–led expansion of regional trade (millions of dollars)

Export/import country	United States	NAFTA	CER	ASEAN+	CACM+	MENA	SACU	Total exports	Change	Change/base (percent)	Change/world (percent)
NAFTA	364,271.0	**686,572.1**	39,581.7	234,720.5	63,599.7	17,729.3	8,245.9	1,050,449.1	185,482.4	21.4	14.3
United States	—	309,356.0	37,788.8	227,655.8	58,754.1	17,041.5	7,880.3	658,476.5	185,482.4	39.2	21.8
Canada*	229,191.0	233,609.2	1,430.7	5,424.7	1,913.5	657.8	293.4	243,329.4	0.0	•0.0	0.0
Mexico*	135,080.0	143,606.9	362.2	1,639.9	2,932.1	30.0	72.2	148,643.3	0.0	0.0	0.0
CER	19,367.5	21,414.3	**12,967.5**	27,311.1	547.5	668.2	802.9	63,711.5	25,632.7	67.3	30.7
Australia	14,599.9	16,080.3	6,731.9	22,506.7	452.1	570.5	743.8	47,085.4	17,039.7	56.7	24.9
New Zealand	4,767.6	5,333.9	6,235.6	4,804.3	95.5	97.6	59.2	16,626.1	8,592.9	107.0	57.5
ASEAN + KO + TA	357,370.7	378,221.8	15,167.8	**304,970.1**	6,496.8	3,594.3	2,367.6	710,818.4	339,229.7	91.3	45.5
Korea (KO)	89,246.2	97,311.2	3,137.9	43,841.5	3,018.2	1,480.4	588.9	149,378.2	68,105.2	83.8	38.2
Indonesia	24,208.7	25,388.0	1,956.0	41,181.7	385.4	330.8	225.5	69,467.5	35,167.9	102.5	52.7
Malaysia	56,696.5	60,024.9	3,056.4	73,208.9	744.1	345.3	337.2	137,716.8	65,247.9	90.0	53.8
Philippines	31,012.7	32,697.8	371.8	19,480.0	193.4	62.7	53.3	52,859.1	24,306.0	85.1	50.3
Singapore	42,823.2	44,523.8	2,598.2	55,507.2	361.8	453.9	231.5	103,676.4	48,880.7	89.2	46.0
Thailand	37,437.1	39,231.3	1,991.1	27,453.5	380.6	199.1	299.3	69,554.9	32,398.7	87.2	42.7
Taiwan (TA)	75,946.4	79,044.8	2,056.4	44,297.2	1,413.1	722.0	631.8	128,165.4	65,123.2	103.3	43.9
CACM + BR + CH	65,835.1	71,135.3	543.5	4,096.4	**12,605.8**	559.6	366.2	89,306.9	41,770.6	87.0	40.6
Brazil (BR)	31,398.1	34,486.8	457.5	1,964.4	3,567.2	511.3	321.3	41,308.4	18,403.3	80.3	30.1
Chile (CH)	7,857.2	9,252.1	66.6	1,363.5	2,607.8	30.8	39.2	13,359.9	5,048.1	60.7	25.0
Costa Rica	8,108.5	8,442.2	13.7	641.9	1,370.0	2.3	3.3	10,473.5	5,543.1	112.4	68.1
El Salvador	4,259.3	4,393.7	0.7	33.1	1,774.2	9.5	0.1	6,211.3	3,285.5	112.3	100.9
Guatemala	5,985.5	6,198.1	2.8	65.4	1,786.7	4.9	2.0	8,059.9	4,225.4	110.2	90.2
Honduras	6,923.3	6,986.3	1.4	23.0	702.2	0.7	0.0	7,713.8	4,128.4	115.1	99.3
Nicaragua	1,303.0	1,376.2	0.8	5.1	797.7	0.1	0.3	2,180.1	1,136.7	108.9	92.1

MENA	**16,028.9**	16,988.0	415.8	2,572.6	625.9	**664.5**	237.2	21,504.0	2,036.9	10.5	4.3
Egypt	**1,951.8**	1,983.1	12.3	318.9	40.7	**176.9**	8.3	2,540.1	1,135.2	80.8	18.2
Israel*	**12,899.8**	13,667.3	291.5	1,885.8	487.3	**314.9**	222.5	16,869.4	170.6	1.0	0.6
Jordan	**162.5**	164.5	4.0	77.5	5.2	**142.7**	3.6	397.5	165.3	71.2	9.3
Morocco	**1,014.8**	1,173.1	108.0	290.5	92.7	**30.0**	2.7	1,697.0	565.8	50.0	6.6
SACU	**10,042.0**	10,467.9	585.4	2,748.5	312.3	371.3	0.0	14,485.4	5,438.7	60.1	16.1
Botswana	**91.6**	91.8	0.0	6.5	0.2	1.4	0.0	100.0	49.6	98.5	6.4
Lesotho	**313.9**	318.7	0.0	0.5	0.0	0.0	0.0	319.2	170.0	114.0	98.6
Namibia	**97.1**	140.3	5.7	5.4	0.0	0.5	0.0	151.8	52.6	53.0	8.7
South Africa	**9,417.0**	9,793.3	578.3	2,458.3	311.4	369.5	0.0	13,510.8	5,100.2	60.6	16.0
Swaziland	**122.4**	123.8	1.4	277.8	0.7	0.0	0.0	403.6	66.3	19.6	20.1
Total imports	832,915.3	1,184,799.4	69,261.7	576,419.1	84,188.1	23,587.2	12,019.8	1,950,275.3	599,590.9	44.4	26.0
Change	246,828.5	246,828.5	27,489.3	276,366.8	38,648.1	5,990.3	4,267.9	599,590.9			—
Change/base (percent)	42.1	26.3	65.8	92.1	84.9	34.0	55.1	44.4			—
Change/world (percent)	19.9	14.6	31.2	42.9	37.3	7.9	14.9	22.8			—

* = Countries with existing FTA with the United States.
ASEAN = Association of South East Asian Nations
CACM = Central American Common Market
CER = Closer Economic Relations (Australia–New Zealand)
MENA = Middle East and North Africa
NAFTA = North American Free Trade Agreement
SACU = Southern African Customs Union

Note: Numbers in bold indicate base trade plus regional FTA effects.

Table A.8d Scenario 3: US FTA–led expansion of "multilateral" trade (millions of dollars)

Export/import country	United States	NAFTA	CER	ASEAN+	CACM+	MENA	SACU	Total exports	Change	Change/base (percent)	Change/world (percent)
NAFTA	364,271.0	686,572.1	41,700.0	243,067.1	69,324.7	18,541.9	8,677.8	1,067,883.6	202,916.8	23.5	15.6
United States	—	309,356.0	37,788.8	227,655.8	58,754.1	17,041.5	7,880.3	658,476.5	185,482.4	39.2	21.8
Canada*	229,191.0	233,609.2	3,121.0	11,833.8	4,174.3	1,435.0	640.0	254,813.4	11,484.1	4.7	4.1
Mexico*	135,080.0	143,606.9	790.1	3,577.4	6,396.3	65.3	157.5	154,593.7	5,950.4	4.0	3.6
CER	19,367.5	23,832.4	12,967.5	41,864.3	1,194.5	1,457.6	1,751.6	83,067.9	44,989.1	118.1	53.9
Australia	14,599.9	17,829.4	6,731.9	37,129.1	986.2	1,244.6	1,622.5	65,543.7	35,498.1	118.1	51.8
New Zealand	4,767.6	6,003.0	6,235.6	4,735.2	208.3	213.0	129.1	17,524.1	9,491.0	118.1	63.5
ASEAN + KO + TA	357,370.7	402,856.7	33,088.2	347,487.3	14,172.6	7,840.8	5,164.8	810,610.4	439,021.7	118.1	58.9
Korea (KO)	89,246.2	106,839.8	6,845.1	52,511.4	6,584.2	3,229.5	1,284.7	177,294.8	96,021.8	118.1	53.9
Indonesia	24,208.7	26,781.2	4,267.0	41,720.9	840.8	721.7	491.9	74,823.5	40,524.0	118.1	60.8
Malaysia	56,696.5	63,957.3	6,667.3	84,352.1	1,623.3	753.2	735.6	158,088.8	85,620.0	118.1	70.6
Philippines	31,012.7	34,688.7	811.1	26,112.8	422.0	136.9	116.3	62,287.8	33,734.7	118.1	69.8
Singapore	42,823.2	46,532.9	5,667.9	65,049.9	789.3	990.1	505.1	119,535.3	64,739.6	118.1	60.9
Thailand	37,437.1	41,351.1	4,343.6	33,443.2	830.3	434.3	652.9	81,055.3	43,899.1	118.1	57.8
Taiwan (TA)	75,946.4	82,705.5	4,486.0	44,297.2	3,082.7	1,575.1	1,378.3	137,524.9	74,482.6	118.1	50.2
CACM + BR + CH	65,835.1	77,397.4	1,185.7	10,490.6	12,605.8	1,220.8	798.8	103,699.1	56,162.8	118.1	54.6
Brazil (BR)	31,398.1	38,135.9	998.0	5,449.5	3,567.2	1,115.3	700.9	49,966.7	27,061.7	118.1	44.2
Chile (CH)	7,857.2	10,900.0	145.3	4,326.3	2,607.8	67.1	85.5	18,132.0	9,820.2	118.1	48.6
Costa Rica	8,108.5	8,836.4	30.0	506.6	1,370.0	5.1	7.2	10,755.4	5,825.1	118.1	71.6
El Salvador	4,259.3	4,552.4	1.5	33.5	1,774.2	20.8	0.1	6,382.6	3,456.8	118.1	106.2
Guatemala	5,985.5	6,449.2	6.1	107.7	1,786.7	10.7	4.3	8,364.9	4,530.4	118.1	96.7
Honduras	6,923.3	7,060.8	3.0	53.6	702.2	1.6	0.1	7,821.3	4,236.0	118.1	101.9
Nicaragua	1,303.0	1,462.6	1.8	13.4	797.7	0.2	0.7	2,276.2	1,232.8	118.1	99.9

MENA	16,028.9	17,214.3	562.6	3,422.7	789.6	494.0	254.5	22,737.7	3,270.6	16.8	6.9
Egypt	1,951.8	2,020.0	26.8	734.2	88.8	176.9	18.1	3,064.8	1,659.9	118.1	26.6
Israel*	12,899.8	13,667.3	291.5	1,885.8	487.3	144.4	222.5	16,698.8	0.0	0.0	0.0
Jordan	162.5	166.9	8.7	169.0	11.4	142.7	7.9	506.6	274.4	118.1	15.4
Morocco	1,014.8	1,360.1	235.6	633.8	202.2	30.0	5.9	2,467.6	1,336.4	118.1	15.6
SACU	10,042.0	10,971.1	1,277.1	5,995.8	681.2	810.1	0.0	19,735.2	10,688.5	118.1	31.7
Botswana	91.6	92.1	0.1	14.2	0.5	3.1	0.0	109.9	59.5	118.1	7.6
Lesotho	313.9	324.4	0.0	1.0	0.0	0.0	0.0	325.4	176.3	118.1	102.2
Namibia	97.1	191.3	12.4	11.8	0.0	1.0	0.0	216.5	117.3	118.1	19.3
South Africa	9,417.0	10,237.8	1,261.6	5,362.8	679.3	806.0	0.0	18,347.5	9,936.9	118.1	31.2
Swaziland	122.4	125.5	3.0	605.9	1.4	0.0	0.0	735.9	398.5	118.1	121.1
Total imports	832,915.3	1,218,844.0	90,781.0	652,327.8	98,768.5	30,365.1	16,647.5	2,107,733.9	757,049.5	56.0	32.8
Change	246,828.5	280,873.1	49,008.6	352,275.5	53,228.5	12,768.2	8,895.6	757,049.5	—	—	—
Change/base (percent)	42.1	29.9	117.3	117.4	116.9	72.6	114.8	56.0	—	—	—
Change/world (percent)	19.9	16.6	55.6	54.7	51.4	16.9	31.1	28.8	—	—	—

* = Countries with existing FTA with the United States.
ASEAN = Association of South East Asian Nations
CACM = Central American Common Market
CER = Closer Economic Relations (Australia–New Zealand)
MENA = Middle East and North Africa
NAFTA = North American Free Trade Agreement
SACU = Southern African Customs Union

Note: Numbers in bold indicate base trade plus "multilateral" FTA effects.

exports and especially imports are predominantly oriented to markets in the European Union.[16]

Scenario 1: FTA-Led Expansion of Bilateral Trade. US FTAs with the large number of prospective partner countries in table A.8b (excluding Canada, Mexico, and Israel) result in the expansion of US imports by $247 billion and US exports by $185 billion. Relative to US trade with the world in 2000, the US FTAs result in the expansion of both US imports and exports by about 20 percent.[17]

With respect to the FTA partner countries, imports of the CACM countries plus Brazil and Chile and of the CER (Australia–New Zealand Closer Economic Relations) countries expand the most in proportional terms, 31 percent and 23 percent respectively, because the imports of these countries are sourced mainly from the United States. Similarly, exports expand most in proportional terms for those partner countries whose exports are mainly destined for the United States: the CACM countries (between 50 percent and 90 percent) and the Philippines (35 percent).

Scenario 2: FTA-Led Expansion of Regional Trade. If the US FTAs lead FTA partner countries in the same region to adopt bilateral free trade agreements among themselves, in effect forming a series of regional free trade areas that include the United States as an extraregional member, then trade impacts substantially larger than in scenario 1 result. With respect to imports, the ASEAN countries plus Korea and Taiwan expand their imports by 43 percent, followed by the CACM countries plus Brazil and Chile (37 percent) and the CER countries (31 percent). On a combined basis, the United States and its FTA partners increase their total imports by 23 percent, compared to 16 percent in the first scenario.

With respect to exports, the ASEAN countries plus Korea and Taiwan expand their exports by 46 percent, followed by the CACM countries plus Brazil and Chile at 41 percent. Combined, the United States and its FTA partners increase their total exports by 26 percent, compared to 19 percent in the first scenario.

Scenario 3: FTA-Led Expansion of "Multilateral" Trade. If US FTAs lead the United States and the FTA partner countries worldwide to adopt a

---

16. The base trade data in table A.8 are incomplete for the SACU countries, except South Africa. Also notably, the analysis here assumes that the base trade data already reflect the impact of preexisting US FTAs with Canada and Mexico and with Israel, under NAFTA and the US-Israel FTA respectively.

17. The description of the quantitative results here emphasizes proportional rather than absolute changes in trade. Also, the discussion focuses mainly on changes in trade vis-à-vis the world rather than individual partner countries. Thus, while FTAs everywhere result in the expansion of bilateral trade between FTA partners by 118 percent, the calculated changes in their trade vis-à-vis the world are typically substantially less than this figure.

multilateral free trade area among themselves, then the calculated expansion of trade climbs to especially high levels, except for the NAFTA countries (Canada and Mexico are already the beneficiaries of an FTA with the United States) and the MENA countries (among which Israel is already the beneficiary of an FTA with the United States). With respect to imports, the CER countries expand their imports by 56 percent, followed by the ASEAN countries plus Korea and Taiwan (55 percent) and the CACM countries plus Brazil and Chile (51 percent). On a combined basis, the United States and the prospective FTA partner countries increase their total imports by 29 percent, compared to 16 percent in the first scenario and 23 percent in the second scenario.

With respect to exports, the ASEAN countries plus Korea and Taiwan expand their exports by 59 percent, followed by the CACM countries plus Brazil and Chile, and the CER countries, both at about 54 percent. Combined, the United States and the prospective FTA partner countries increase their total exports by 33 percent, compared to 19 percent in the first scenario and 26 percent in the second scenario.

Conclusion

Although the economic basis of the gravity model is less transparent than that of CGE models such as the GTAP model, gravity model estimates of the trade impacts of US free trade agreements appear to be substantially greater than those produced by the GTAP model. In addition, they give little indication that eventual multilateral trade liberalization brought about by the forces of competitive liberalization might be less attractive to the United States, its prospective FTA partners, or third countries than the currently emerging world of preferential trade arrangements.[18]

Nonetheless, the gravity model results presented here are no less subject to important caveats than the GTAP model results (see, e.g., Anderson and van Wincoop 2003). Among these, in the context of the present study, is the uncertain appropriateness of applying a single gravity model estimate of the mean sensitivity of bilateral trade flows to regional trade arrangements to prospective US FTAs established bilaterally, regionally, and even multilaterally. Moreover, the present gravity model–based results provide no assurance that the expansion of bilateral trade resulting from the prospective US FTAs is predominantly trade creating and hence mainly welfare enhancing for the individual countries considered. Indeed, while the quantitative results presented here may be broadly indicative of the range of impacts that prospective US FTAs might have on

---

18. Gravity model estimates of the trade impacts of FTAs might be still greater, according to recent empirical studies in which the possible endogeneity of tariffs and other protection measures is recognized. See Baier and Bergstrand (2002).

trade and other economic variables, there is considerable need for more in-depth economic research into free trade agreements entered into by the United States and others, including careful political economy analysis of how, and even whether, the forces of competitive liberalization lead to welfare-enhancing outcomes for both the United States and the world as a whole.

References

Anderson, James E. 1979. A Theoretical Foundation for the Gravity Equation. *American Economic Review* 69, no. 1: 106–16.

Anderson, James E., and Eric van Wincoop. 2003. Gravity with Gravitas: A Solution to the Border Problem. *American Economic Review* 93, no. 1: 170–92.

Andrianmananjara, Soamiely. 2000. Regionalism and Incentives for Multilateralism. *Journal of Economic Integration* 15, no. 1: 1–18.

Baier, Scott L., and Jeffrey H. Bergstrand. 2002. On the Endogeneity of International Trade Flows and Free Trade Agreements. Department of Economics, Clemson University, South Carolina, and University of Notre Dame, Indiana.

Baldwin, Richard. 1995. A Domino Theory of Regionalism. *NBER Working Paper* 4364. Cambridge, MA: National Bureau of Economic Research.

Baldwin, Richard E., and A. J. Venables. 1995. Regional Economic Integration. In vol. 3 of *Handbook of International Economics*, ed. Gene Grossman and Kenneth Rogoff. Amsterdam: Elsevier.

Bergsten, C. F. 2002. A Renaissance for US Trade Policy? *Foreign Affairs* 81, no. 6: 86–98.

Bergstrand, Jeffrey H. 1985. The Gravity Equation in International Trade: Some Microeconomic Foundations and Empirical Evidence. *Review of Economics and Statistics* 67, no. 3 (August): 474–81.

Bergstrand, Jeffrey H. 1989. The Generalized Gravity Equation, Monopolistic Competition, and the Factor-Proportions Theory in International Trade. *Review of Economics and Statistics* 71, no. 1 (February): 143–53.

Burfisher, Mary E., Sherman Robinson, and Karen Thierfelder. 2003. Regionalism: Old and New, Theory and Practice. Paper presented at the conference Agricultural Policy Reform and the WTO: Where Are We Heading? sponsored by the International Agricultural Trade Research Consortium (IATRC), Capri, Italy (June 23–26).

Deardorff, Alan V. 1998. Determinants of Bilateral Trade: Does Gravity Work in a Neoclassical World? In *The Regionalization of the World Economy*, ed. Jeffrey A. Frankel. Chicago: University of Chicago Press.

DeRosa, Dean A. 1998. Regional Integration Arrangements: Static Economic Theory, Quantitative Findings, and Policy Guidelines. *Policy Research Working Paper* 2007. Washington: World Bank. Available at www.worldbank.org/html/dec/Publications/Workpapers/wps2000series/wps2007/wps2007.pdf (August).

DeRosa, Dean A. 2003. Gravity Model Calculations of the Trade Impacts of US Free Trade Agreements. Background paper prepared for the conference Free Trade Agreements and US Trade Policy, sponsored by the Institute for International Economics, Washington (May 7–8).

Dimaranan, B., and R.A. McDougall. 2002. Global Trade, Assistance, and Protection: The GTAP5 Database. Center for Global Trade Analysis, Purdue University, West Lafayette, IN.

Frankel, Jeffrey A. 1997. *Regional Trading Blocs in the World Economic System*. Washington: Institute for International Economics.

Fukase, Emiko, and Will Martin. 2001. A Quantitative Evaluation of Vietnam's Accession to the ASEAN Free Trade Area. *Journal of Economic Integration* 16, no. 4: 545–67.

Gilbert, John. 2003. CGE Simulations of US Bilateral Free Trade Agreements. Background paper prepared for the conference Free Trade Agreements and US Trade Policy, sponsored by the Institute for International Economics, Washington (May 7–8).

Gilbert, John, and T. Wahl. 2002. Applied General Equilibrium Assessments of Trade Liberalization in China. *World Economy* 25, no. 5: 697–731.

Greenaway, David, and Chris Milner. 2002. Regionalism and Gravity. *Scottish Journal of Political Economy* 49, no. 5: 574–85.

Harberger, Arnold C. 1971. Three Basic Postulates for Applied Welfare Economics. *Journal of Economic Literature* 9, no. 3: 785–97.

Helpman, Elhanan, and Paul R. Krugman. 1985. *Market Structure and Foreign Trade: Increasing Returns, Imperfect Competition, and the International Economy*. Cambridge, MA: MIT Press.

Hertel, Thomas W., ed. 1997. *Global Trade Analysis: Modeling and Applications*. Cambridge: Cambridge University Press.

Krugman, Paul R. 1995. Increasing Returns, Imperfect Competition, and the Positive Theory of International Trade. In *Handbook of International Economics* (vol. 3), ed. Gene Grossman and Kenneth Rogoff. Amsterdam: Elsevier.

Lawrence, Robert Z. 1996. *Regionalism, Multilateralism, and Deeper Integration*. Washington: Brookings Institution.

Lipsey, Richard G. 1970. *The Theory of Customs Unions: A General Equilibrium Analysis*. London: Weidenfeld and Nicolson.

Lloyd, P. J. 1982. 3x3 Theory of Customs Unions. *Journal of International Economics* 12: 41–63.

Meade, James E. 1955. *The Theory of Customs Unions*. Amsterdam: North-Holland Publishing.

Mikesell, Raymond F. 1963. The Theory of Common Markets as Applied to Regional Arrangements among Developing Countries. In *International Trade in a Developing World: Proceedings of a Conference Held by the International Economic Association*, ed., R. Harrod and D. Hague. New York: St. Martin's Press.

Panagariya, Arvind. 1999. The Regionalism Debate: An Overview. *World Economy* 22, no. 4: 477–511.

Panagariya, Arvind. 2000. Preferential Trade Liberalization: The Traditional Theory and New Developments. *Journal of Economic Literature* 38, no. 2: 287–331.

Pomfret, Richard. 1988. *Unequal Trade: The Economics of Discriminatory International Trade Policies*. Oxford: Basil Blackwell.

Robinson, Sherman, and Karen Thierfelder. 2002. Trade Liberalization and Regional Integration: The Search for Large Numbers. *Australian Journal of Agricultural and Resource Economics* 46, no. 4: 585–604.

Robson, Peter. 1987. *The Economics of International Integration*. London: Unwin Hyman.

Rose, Andrew K. 2003. Which International Institutions Promote International Trade? Haas School of Business, University of California, Berkeley. Photocopy.

Schiff, Maurice, and L. Alan Winters. 2003. *Regional Integration and Development*. Washington: World Bank.

Scollay, Robert, and John Gilbert. 2000. Measuring the Gains for APEC Trade Liberalization: An Overview of CGE Assessments. *World Economy* 23, no. 2: 175–93.

Viner, Jacob. 1950. *The Customs Union Issue*. New York: Carnegie Endowment for International Peace.

About the Contributors

Inbom Choi, former visiting fellow, is the chief economist at the Federation of Korean Industries. He was assistant secretary to the president for economic affairs and the director of international economic policy in the Office of the President of Korea (1995–96). He was also the managing director for programs of the APEC Foundation (1997–98). He has been a research fellow at the Korea Institute for International Economic Policy since 1990. He was also a consultant to the World Bank and a visiting professor at Georgetown University. In 1998 and 1999, he was selected by the Asia-Europe Meeting (ASEM) as one of the Next Generation Leaders of Asia. He is the coeditor of *The Korean Diaspora in the World Economy* (2003) and coauthor of *Free Trade between Korea and the United States?* (2001).

Richard N. Cooper is the Maurits C. Boas Professor of Economics at Harvard University and chairman of the Advisory Committee of the Institute for International Economics. He was the chairman of the National Intelligence Council (1995–97), chairman of the Federal Reserve Bank of Boston (1990–92), undersecretary of state for economic affairs (1977–81), deputy assistant secretary of state for international monetary affairs (1965–66), senior staff economist at the Council of Economic Advisers (1961–63), and professor of economics (1963–77) and provost (1972–74) at Yale University. He is the author, editor, coeditor, or coauthor of *What the Future Holds: Insights from Social Science* (MIT Press, 2002), *Environment and Resource Policies for the World Economy* (Brookings Institution, 1994); *Macroeconomic Policy and Adjustment in Korea, 1970–1990* (Harvard University Press, 1994); *Boom, Crisis, and Adjustment: The Macroeconomic Adjustment in Developing Countries* (World Bank, 1993); *Economic Stabilization and Debt in Developing Countries* (MIT Press, 1992); and *Can Nations Agree? Issues in International Economic Cooperation* (Brookings Institution, 1989).

Guy de Jonquières is world trade editor of the *Financial Times*, responsible for its coverage of international trade policy developments. He is also a principal leader writer on a wide range of issues, including the EU internal market, US-EU relations, and cross-border competition and regulation policies. He has served as an *FT* staff correspondent in Paris, Brussels, Washington, and New York. Previous assignments include information technology industries, the European single market, and consumer industries.

Dean A. DeRosa is a visiting fellow at the Institute for International Economics and principal economist at ADR International Ltd., an economic research and policy consulting firm in Falls Church, Virginia. His previous positions include research fellow at the International Food Policy Research Institute, senior economist at the International Monetary Fund, senior economist at the Asian Development Bank, and international economist at the US Treasury. He is the author of *Regional Trading Arrangements among Developing Countries: The ASEAN Example* (International Food Policy Research Institute, 1995) and author or coauthor of a number of journal articles and published conference papers on international trade, foreign investment, and economic development.

Albert Fishlow is a professor of international and public affairs at Columbia University and director of the Center for Brazilian Studies and of the Institute for Latin American Studies there. He was the Paul A. Volcker Senior Fellow for International Economics at the Council of Foreign Relations until June 30, 1999. He was a professor of economics at the University of California, Berkeley, and dean of international and area studies there; visiting professor at the Yale School of Management; and professor of economics and director of the Center for International and Area Studies at Yale University. He served as deputy assistant secretary of state for inter-American affairs from 1975 to 1976. He is coeditor of *The United States and the Americas: A Twenty First Century View* (Norton, W. W. & Company, Inc., 1999).

Ahmed Galal is executive director and director of research at the Egyptian Center for Economic Studies (ECES) in Cairo. He has also been a staff member of the World Bank since 1984. During this long tenure, he served as industrial economist in Europe, the Middle East, and North Africa; senior then principal economist in the bank's research arm; and economic adviser to the private-sector development department. He has coauthored or coedited several books on a range of issues including privatization, regulation of monopolies, trade, and monetary policy. His works include, among others, *Building Bridges: An Egypt-U.S. Free Trade Agreement* (Brookings Institution Press, 1998) and *Monetary Policy and Exchange Rate Regimes: Options for the Middle East* (ECES, 2002).

John P. Gilbert is an assistant professor in the department of economics at Utah State University, where he specializes in international trade theory and policy. His work focuses on applied general equilibrium analysis of trade policy reforms, in particular those currently occurring in China, East Asia and the Americas. His work has been published in several journals including the *Journal of Comparative Economics*, *Economics Letters*, *World Economy*, *Developing Economies* and *Southern Economic Journal*. He is coauthor of *New Regional Trading Arrangements in the Asia-Pacific?* (2001).

Ben Goodrich is a Ph.D. student at Harvard University and a former research assistant at the Institute for International Economics. He is coauthor of several Institute policy briefs, including *Next Move in Steel: Revocation or Retaliation?* (2003), *More Pain, More Gain: Politics and Economics of Eliminating Tariffs*, *Steel Policy: The Good, the Bad, and the Ugly* (2003), and *Time for a Grand Bargain in Steel* (2002).

Jaime Granados is general coordinator of technical support to the Free Trade Area of the Americas (FTAA) negotiations, Inter-American Development Bank, Washington. He was director of international trade negotiations at the Ministry of Foreign Trade, Costa Rica. He also taught at the School of Diplomacy of the Ministry of Foreign Affairs, Costa Rica. He has published several papers on agricultural trade liberalization in the Western Hemisphere, export-processing zones, the Central American integration process, market access in the FTAA, and FTAA-WTO interactions.

Gary Clyde Hufbauer, Reginald Jones Senior Fellow, was the Marcus Wallenberg Professor of International Finance Diplomacy at Georgetown University (1985–92), deputy director of the International Law Institute at Georgetown University (1979–81), deputy assistant secretary for international trade and investment policy of the US Treasury (1977–79), and director of the International Tax Staff at the US Treasury (1974–76). He has written extensively on international trade, investment, and tax issues, with a particular focus on economic sanctions and NAFTA. He is coauthor or coeditor of *Awakening Monster: The Alien Tort Statute of 1789* (2003), *The Benefits of Price Convergence: Speculative Calculations* (2002), *The Ex-Im Bank in the 21st Century: A New Approach* (2001), *World Capital Markets: Challenge to the G-10* (2001), *NAFTA and the Environment: Seven Years Later* (2000), *Unfinished Business: Telecommunications after the Uruguay Round* (1997), *Flying High: Liberalizing Civil Aviation in the Asia Pacific* (1996), *Fundamental Tax Reform and Border Tax Adjustments* (1996), *Western Hemisphere Economic Integration* (1994), *Measuring the Costs of Protection in the United States* (1994), *NAFTA: An Assessment* (rev. ed. 1993), *Economic Sanctions Reconsidered: History and Current Policy* (2d ed. 1990), and others.

Nicholas R. Lardy, senior fellow, was a senior fellow in the Foreign Policy Studies Program at the Brookings Institution from 1995 to 2003 and also served as interim director of the program in 2001. He was the director of the Henry M. Jackson School of International Studies at the University of Washington from 1991 to 1995. From 1997 through the spring of 2000, he was the Frederick Frank Adjunct Professor of International Trade and Finance at the Yale University School of Management. His publications include *Integrating China into the Global Economy* (Brookings Institution Press, 2002), *China's Unfinished Economic Revolution* (Brookings Institution Press, 1998), *China in the World Economy* (Institute for International Economics, 1994), *Foreign Trade and Economic Reform in China, 1978–1990* (Cambridge University Press, 1992), and *Agriculture in China's Modern Economic Development* (Cambridge University Press, 1983).

Robert Z. Lawrence, senior fellow, is also the Albert L. Williams Professor of Trade and Investment at the John F. Kennedy School of Government at Harvard University. He served as a member of President Clinton's Council of Economic Advisers from 1999 to 2000. He held the New Century Chair as a nonresident senior fellow at the Brookings Institution between 1997 and 1998 and founded and edited the Brookings Trade Forum in 1998. He was a senior fellow in the Economic Studies Program at Brookings (1983–91), a professorial lecturer at the Johns Hopkins School of Advanced International Studies (1978–81), and an instructor at Yale University (1975). He has served as a consultant to the Federal Reserve Bank of New York, the World Bank, the OECD, and UNCTAD. He is the author or coauthor of more than 100 papers and articles on international economics and of several books, including *Crimes and Punishments: Retaliation under the WTO* (2003), *Globaphobia: Confronting Fears about Open Trade* (Brookings Institution Press, 1998), and *Building Bridges: An Egypt-U.S. Free Trade Agreement* (Brookings Institution Press, 1998).

J. Clark Leith is professor emeritus of economics at the University of Western Ontario. He is a fellow at the Economic Policy Research Institute, University of Western Ontario. He was economic consultant to the Botswana Ministry of Finance and Development Planning (1986–88), director of research at the Bank of Botswana (1993–95), and senior policy adviser to the bank (1995–97). He is the author of *Why Botswana Prospered* (forthcoming).

Daniel H. Rosen, visiting fellow, was a member of the National Economic Council staff from 2000 to 2001, where he served as senior adviser for international economic policy. His work has focused on the economic development of East Asia, particularly Greater China, and US economic relations with the region. He is the author of *Behind the Open Door: Foreign Enterprises in the Chinese Marketplace* (1998) and coauthor of *APEC and the New Economy* (2002).

Howard Rosen was minority staff director of the Congressional Joint Economic Committee (1997–2001), executive director of the Competitiveness Policy Council (1991–97), assistant director and research associate at the Institute for International Economics (1982–987), and an economist with the Bank of Israel (1987–89) and the US Department of Labor (1978–81). In 2001, he drafted legislation that became part of the Trade Act of 2002, which significantly reformed and expanded the Trade Adjustment Assistance program. He has also served as a consultant to the Senate Finance Committee, the Agency for International Development, the Inter-American Development Bank, the United Nations Conference on Trade and Development, the Business Roundtable, and Data Resources, Inc.

Renato Ruggiero has been the chairman of Citigroup in Switzerland since February 2003 and vice chairman of Citigroup European Investment Bank since August 2002. He was the director general of the World Trade Organization from 1995 to 1999. From 1987 to 1991, he was Italy's minister for foreign trade. He also served as Italy's minister for foreign affairs from 2001 to 2002 in the second government of Prime Minister Silvio Berlusconi. His other Italian government positions included political adviser to the president of the European Commission, diplomatic adviser of the prime minister, chef de cabinet of two foreign ministers, director general for economic affairs at the foreign ministry in Rome, Italy's permanent representative to the European Community, personal representative of the prime minister for six G7 summits, and chairman of the Executive Committee of the OECD in Paris. He serves on the boards of FIAT and several Italian, European, and American companies.

José M. Salazar-Xirinachs is the director of the Trade Unit at the Organization of American States, Washington. He has taught at the Universidad de Costa Rica, Cambridge University, and Georgetown University. Previous positions include minister of foreign trade of Costa Rica, member of the Board of Directors of the Central Bank of Costa Rica, executive president of the Costa Rican Development Corporation, executive director and chief economist of the Federation of Private Entities of Central America and Panama, and executive director and founder of the Business Network for Hemispheric Integration. He has published numerous papers in specialized journals on trade, integration, and international economics. He is coeditor of *Toward Free Trade in the Americas* (Brookings Institution Press, 2001).

Jeffrey J. Schott, senior fellow, was a senior associate at the Carnegie Endowment for International Peace (1982–83) and an international economist at the US Treasury (1974–82). He is the author, coauthor, or editor of *Prospects for Free Trade in the Americas* (2001), *Free Trade between Korea and the United States?* (2001), *The WTO after Seattle* (2000), *NAFTA and the*

Environment: Seven Years Later (2000), *Launching New Global Trade Talks: An Action Agenda* (1998), *Restarting Fast Track* (1998), *The World Trading System: Challenges Ahead* (1996), *WTO 2000: Setting the Course for World Trade* (1996), *The Uruguay Round: An Assessment* (1994), *Western Hemisphere Economic Integration* (1994), *NAFTA: An Assessment* (rev. ed. 1993), *North American Free Trade: Issues and Recommendations* (1992), *Economic Sanctions Reconsidered* (2d ed. 1990), among others.

Andrew L. Stoler is the executive director of the Institute for International Business, Economics, and Law at the University of Adelaide. He served as deputy director general at the World Trade Organization (WTO) from 1999 to 2002. Before joining the WTO, he spent 10 years in Geneva as the deputy chief of mission, United States Mission to the WTO, Office of the United States Trade Representative (1989–99). He served as the chairman of the Working Party on the Accession to the WTO of Ukraine and as the deputy chairman of the WTO Committee on Regional Trade Agreements. During the Uruguay Round of multilateral trade negotiations, he was the principal US negotiator for a range of WTO agreements, including the Trade Policy Review Mechanism and the Marrakesh Agreement Establishing the WTO. In 1988 and most of 1989, he served as deputy assistant US trade representative for Europe and the Mediterranean in the Washington office of the USTR. From 1982 to 1987, he was the nontariff measure codes coordinator in the Geneva USTR office.

Sidney Weintraub is the William E. Simon Chair in Political Economy and the director of the Americas Program at the Center for Strategic and International Studies. He is also professor emeritus at the Lyndon B. Johnson School of Public Affairs, University of Texas. A member of the US Foreign Service from 1949 to 1975, Dr. Weintraub held the post of deputy assistant secretary of state for international finance and development from 1969 to 1974 and assistant administrator of the US Agency for International Development in 1975. He has also been a senior fellow at the Brookings Institution. He is the author of *Financial Decision-Making in Mexico: To Bet a Nation* (University of Pittsburgh Press, 2000), *Development and Democracy in the Southern Cone: Imperatives for U.S. Policy in South America* (CSIS, 2000), and *NAFTA at Three: A Progress Report* (CSIS, 1997); and coauthor of *The NAFTA Debate: Grappling with Unconventional Trade Issues* (Lynne Rienner, 1994).

John Whalley is a professor of economics at both the University of Warwick, UK, and the University of Western Ontario, Canada. He is also codirector of the Centre for the Study of Globalisation and Regionalisation (CSGR) at the University of Warwick and codirector of the Centre for the Study of International Economic Relations (CSIER), University of Western Ontario. He is a fellow of the Royal Society of Canada and of the Econometric Society. He is a research associate at the National Bureau of Economic Research (NBER) and the joint managing editor of *The World Economy*. He has published widely and is best known for his contributions to applied general equilibrium analysis, trade and tax policy, and environmental issues. He has served on a Canada-US trade dispute panel and been a research director for the MacDonald Royal Commissions in Canada. He is coauthor or coeditor of *Uruguay Round Results and the Emerging Trade Agenda: Quantitative-Based Analyses from the Developmental Perspective* (United Nations, 1998), *Environmental Issues in the New World Trading System* (MacMillan, 1997), and *The Trading System after the Uruguay Round* (Institute for International Economics, 1996).

Acronyms

ACP	African, Caribbean, and Pacific countries
AD	antidumping
ADBI	Asian Development Bank Institute
AGOA	African Growth and Opportunity Act
AFTA	ASEAN Free Trade Area
AMAD	Agricultural Market Access Database
AIA	ASEAN Investment Area
ANZCERTA	Australia–New Zealand Closer Economic Relations (CER) Trade Agreement
APEC	Asia Pacific Economic Cooperation
APT	ASEAN Plus Three Plan
ASEAN	Association of Southeast Asian Nations
ATAP	Agreement on Trade in Agricultural Products
ATPA	Andean Trade Preferences Act
AUSTA	Australia–United States Free Trade Agreement Business Group
BIT	bilateral investment treaty
BLNS	Botswana, Lesotho, Namibia, and Swaziland
BPA	bilateral preferential agreement
CACM	Central American Common Market
CAFTA	Central American Free Trade Agreement
CAP	Common Agricultural Policy
CBI	Carribean Basin Initiative
CBTPA	Caribbean Basin Trade Partnership Act
CER	Closer Economic Relations
CES	constant elasticity of substitution
CET	common external tariff

CGE	computable general equilibrium models
CIT	countries in transition
CLMV	Cambodia, Laos, Myanmar, and Vietnam
COMESA	Common Market for Eastern and Southern Africa
COMESSA	Community of Sahel-Saharan States
CUSTA	Canada-US Trade Agreement
CVD	countervailing duty
EAI	Enterprise for ASEAN Initiative
EC	European Community
EFTA	European Free Trade Association
EMA	Euro-Mediterranean Agreement
EPZ	export processing zone
ESI	export similarity index
EU	European Union
EV	equivalent variation
FDI	foreign direct investment
FSU	former Soviet Union
FTA	free trade agreement
FTAA	Free Trade Area of the Americas
GATS	General Agreement on Trade in Services
GATT	General Agreement on Tariffs and Trade
GPA	Government Procurement Agreement
GSP	Generalized System of Preferences
GTAP	Global Trade Analysis Project
HS	Harmonized System
HTS	Harmonized Tariff Schedule
IIPA	International Intellectual Property Alliance
ILO	International Labor Organization
IMF	International Monetary Fund
IPR	intellectual property rights
LAC	labor advisory committee
MAI	Multilateral Agreement on Investment
MENA	Middle East and North Africa
Mercosur	Southern Cone Common Market
MFA	Multi-Fiber Agreement
MFFTA	most favored FTA
MFN	most favored nation
NAAEC	North American Agreement on Environmental Cooperation
NAFTA	North American Free Trade Agreement
NGO	nongovernmental organization
NTB	nontariff barrier
PTA	preferential trade arrangement
QIZ	qualifying industrial zone
SACU	Southern African Customs Union

SADC	Southern African Development Community
SME	small and medium enterprise
TAFTA	Transatlantic FTA
TAA	trade adjustment assistance
TIFA	trade and investment facilitation agreement
TFP	total factor productivity
TPA	trade promotion authority
TREATI	Trans-Regional EU-ASEAN Trade Initiative
TRIMs	Trade-Related Investment Measures
TRIPs	Agreement on Trade-Related Aspects of Intellectual Property Rights
TRQ	tariff rate quota
USITC	US International Trade Commission
USTR	Office of the US Trade Representative
WIPO	World Intellectual Property Organization
WTO	World Trade Organization

Index

Abbott Laboratories, 233
Abdullah II, 62
ACIL Consulting, 96
ACIL study, 104, 105–06
  criticized, 112
  FTA as distraction, 110
  trade diversion, 109
  WTO negotiations, 110
ACP. *See* African, Caribbean, and Pacific (ACP)
  countries
ADBI. *See* Asian Development Bank Institute
  model
administered protection, 137–38
Africa
  Singapore, exports and origin of imports, 82*t*
  US FTA initiative, 373
Africa Growth and Opportunity Act (AGOA)
  changing environment, 348
  impacts, 350
  textiles to US, 333–34
  US motives, 335
African, Caribbean, and Pacific (ACP) countries
  Cotonou Agreement with EU, 25, 332, 345
  EU former colonies, 345
  South Africa, 345
African National Congress, 352
AFTA. *See* ASEAN Free Trade Area
  effects on China, 210–11
  outward orientation, 162
Agreement on Trade in Agricultural Products
  (ATAP), 54–55

Agreement on Trade-Related Aspects of
  Intellectual Property Rights (TRIPs)
  Brazil, 289
  SACU, 334
Agricultural Market Access Database (AMAD),
  389*n*
agriculture
  ASEAN, 142, 155, 163
  ASEAN-4, 163
  ASEAN Plus Three, 120
  Australia, 96
    US FTA, 97, 373
    WTO, 110
  Brazil, 285–86
    Doha Round, 292
    FTAA, 379
  Central America, 239
    adjustment process, 245–46, 248
    as deal breaker, 248–49
    development of, 264
    employment by country, 245*t*
    problems liberalizing, 248
    TRQs, 244
    winners and losers, 258*t*, 259
  Chile, 84, 85, 89, 248, 248*n*
    Australia and, 99–100
    market access, 99
  China, comparative advantage, 210
  Common Agricultural Policy, 14
    EU subsidies, 285, 286*t*
    Israel, 53, 54–55

Singapore, exports and origin of imports, 82*t*
trade
services, 129*t*
with US, 38*t*, 122*t*–123*t*, 360*n*
with ASEAN, 122*t*–123*t*
US economic ties, 368*t*
US FDI, 38*t*
Canada-US FTA, as alternative negotiating
option, 361
Canada-US Trade Agreement (CUSTA), 37, 40
CAP. *See* Common Agricultural Policy
capital controls
Chile, 87, 90, 353, 353*n*
SACU, 353
Singapore, 87, 90
South Africa, 353
Cardoso, Fernando Henrique, 282, 285
Caribbean Basin Initiative
NAFTA parity, 226
political objectives, 188
US trade with FTAA countries, 39*n*
value of trade preferences diluted, 14
Caribbean Basin Trade Partnership Act (CBTPA),
234
Caribbean Regional Negotiating Machinery, 17
Castro, Fidel, 280
Cavallo, Domingo, 284
Central America. *See also* CAFTA
asymmetries in negotiations with US
economic, 227, 228*t*
institutional, 227, 229
objectives and motivations, 229–38
treatment of, 255
benefits of FTA for, 237–38
bilateral agreements with regional partners,
266*n*
Chile compared, 231*n*
"crisis proofing," 261
economic indicators, 227, 228*t*
exports, 235, 235*t*
government procurement, 253
income distribution, 265
industrial clusters, 264
institutional reform, 236, 262–63
integration with region, 266–67
intellectual property rights, 251–53
investment, 233, 250–51, 267
market access, 234, 249–50
multinational corporations, 267
NAFTA parity, 226
regional pattern of exports per GTAP
simulation, 400*t*
rural-urban migration, 246, 265
small and medium enterprises, 258*t*, 259, 263
social policy, 265–66
social safety nets, 265–66
taxes on trade, 261–62, 262*t*
trade capacity building, 237, 264
trade with US, 227, 229*t*
US interest in, 23, 232

Central American Common Market (CACM)
CAFTA compared, 260
GTAP model, 388*n*
hub-and-spoke pattern vs., 266–67
CET. *See* common external tariff
CGE. *See* computable general equilibrium
models
Chávez Frias, Hugo, 280
Chile. *See also* Chile-US FTA
agriculture trade negotiations, 99–100
capital controls, 87, 353, 353*n*
Central America compared, 231*n*
economic indicators, 80–81, 81*t*, 119*t*
EU deals, 25
GDP, 360*n*
Iraq linkage, 91
lock-in effects, 362
multiple FTAs, 88*n*
as precedent, advantages, 79
regional pattern of exports per GTAP
simulation, 400*t*
salmon mariculture, 89
services, 85
South Korea FTA, 6
trade
services, 129*t*
with US, 38*t*, 82, 360*n*, 368*n*
trade diversion, tomato paste, 22
uniform import tariff, 82
US FDI, 38*t*
US interest, 23
wine phaseout, 85, 89
Chile-US FTA
as asymmetric package, 350
concluded, 39
congressional passage, 365*n*
discrimination, 82*n*
e-commerce, 12*n*, 85, 91
government procurement, 253
intellectual property rights, 252
key elements, 85–88
labor and environmental provisions, 254
as precedent, 338, 340
US motives, 83
China
agriculture, 378. *See also* agriculture, China
ASEAN, 120, 162, 174
ASEAN Plus Three, 120, 174
Australia-US FTA, 108, 111
Australian view, 107
economic indicators, 119*t*
FDI, 128
gas supply, 111
regional economy, 6
regional pattern of exports per GTAP
simulation, 400*t*
South Korea, trade, 175–76, 178*t*
Taiwan, 197–99, 200, 214*n*
Taiwan-US FTA, pressure, 221
textiles and apparel, 142, 213, 214*t*

China—*continued*
  trade, services, 129,
  trade patterns, ABDI model, 210
  trade with ASEAN, 122*t*–123*t*
  trade with US, 175–76
  as threat to developing countries, 10
  unready for FTAs, 193–94
  US-ASEAN FTAs, impact, 157, 157*n*
  WTO accession debate, 11
Chung-Hua report, 201, 202, 207–08, 211
  services, 217
  textiles and apparel, 212–15, 212*n*
CIE study, 102–04, 107
  advocated, 112
  auto exports, 111
  New Zealand benefits, 116
  trade diversion, 109
Cipro, 287
Clinton, Bill
  Central America initiative, 226
  labor and environmental side agreements, 41
  Seattle ministerial, 33
  TAFTA, 363
  US-Jordan FTA, 62, 70
Cold War
  Brazil, 281
  FTAs, 364*n*
  economic interests vs., 364
Colombia
  GDP, 360*t*
  political criterion, 370
  US economic ties, 368*t*
  US trade, 360*t*
COMESA (Common Market for Eastern and
    Southern Africa), 346*n*
COMESSA (Community of Sahel-Saharan States),
    Morocco, 318, 318*n*
Commission on Capital Flows to Africa, 373
Common Agricultural Policy (CAP)
  budgetary cost, 31
  as glue of European integration, 14, 374
common external tariff (CET)
  Brazil, 284
  Central America, 243
  SACU, 335, 336
comparative advantage
  southern Africa, 352
  tradable services, 249
  US-ASEAN, 124
competition policy, with SACU, 334, 337, 341, 344
competitive liberalization
  APEC, South Korea–US FTA, 193
  ASEAN, gravity model, 147
  Australia-US FTA, 97
  background to, 277–78
  CAFTA, 230, 238, 269
  complementary liberalization, 29
  demonstration effect of FTA, 110
  developing countries, 11
  East Asia, 378

FTAA, Brazil, 290
  initiatives summarized, 331–32
  investigating hypothesis, 384
  Latin American perspective, 230*n*
  non-EU preferential agreements, 112
  political-economy considerations, 385
  spillover effects, 385
  Taiwan, 197
  traditional theory, 385
  US FTAs with ASEAN, 164–65
  US strategy, 26–27, 227–228, 371
competitive regionalism, 28
complementary liberalization, G-8, 29
computable general equilibrium (CGE) models,
    106, 147
  features described, 388
  GTAP model, 388–402
  reasons for selecting, 388*n*
concentricity policy, 281
concerted unilateralism, APEC, 361*n*
conditional most favored nation (MFN)
    treatment, 80, 80*n*
Congress, US role of, 364
constant elasticity of substitution (CES), 388
Costa Rica
  agricultural employment, 245*t*
  anti-privatization, 260
  economic indicators, 227, 228*t*
  immigration, 232
  main product lines (list), 271*t*
  poverty and indigence indicators, 265*t*
  state monopolies, 250
  tariffs, 240*t*
  taxes on trade, 262*t*
  trading partners, 227, 229*t*
Cotonou Agreement, 344–45
  Caribbean signatories, 374–75
  members, 332
  revising trade ties, 375*n*
  South Africa excluded, 345
  US competition, 334
countervailing duty (CVD) actions
  ASEAN, 137, 138*t*
  Central America, 255–56
  FTAA, 89
  NAFTA, 47
  SACU, 349
  South Korea, 179–80
Croatia, EU deals, 25
CUSTA. *See* Canada-US Trade Agreement
customs unions
  debates, 3
  in effect or under negotiation, 6–7, 7*t*
  Viner theory, 384–85

Daewoo purchase by GM, 175, 177, 177*n*
dairy sector
  Australia, 100, 104
  Chilean case, 99
  New Zealand gains, 116

investment diversion—*continued*
    Central America's concern over NAFTA, 226
    drawback of FTA, 13–16, 21
investor-state disputes
    Chile, 86
    NAFTA, 47, 48
    Singapore, 86
Iran, trade with Morocco, 316*t*
Iraq, 316*t*, 329
Iraq, war against
    Australia, 42, 113
    linkage to US-Chile FTA, 91
    as litmus test, 370
    New Zealand, 42, 96, 116
Islamic fundamentalists, 326
Islamist PJD (Justice and Development Party),
        315
Israel. *See also* Israel-US FTA
    administrative protection, 54
    agriculture, 53
    balance of payments deficit, 52, 54
    congressional support, 53
    EC, special treatment, 22
    economic conditions, 53
    EU deals, 25
    European Community (EC), 52, 54
    exports, 56*t*, 58, 61
    GDP, 360*n*
    goals in FTA, 52–53
    imports, 56*t*, 58
    trade with US, 38*t*, 58*t*, 360*n*
    US economic ties, 368*t*
    US FDI, 38*t*
Israel-US FTA, 52–53
    agriculture, 54
    conclusions, 73–76
    "elastic" nature, 59–60
    evaluation, 61–62
    foreign policy interests, 51, 62
    lessons from, 62, 75–76
    NAFTA compared, 54
    as pilot project, 361
    political objectives, 187
    recent trade flows, 56–58
    rules of origin, 55
    US-Canada FTA compared, 54
    US goals, 52–53
    what is traded, 58–59
Italy, trade with Morocco, 316*t*
Ives, Ralph, 110

Japan
    agriculture, subsidies, 285, 286, 286*t*
    ASEAN Plus Three, 120
    China, agricultural imports, 194
    Doha Round, 6
    economic indicators, 119*t*
    FTA participation, 9*t*
    Mexico FTA, 6
    Morocco, trade with, 316*t*

motor vehicles and parts, 111
multiple FTAs, 88*n*
regionalism in Asia, 26
regional pacts in effect or under negotiation,
        6–7, 7*t*
regional pattern of exports per GTAP
        simulation, 400*t*
Singapore FTA, 6, 26
South Korea
    FTA in future, 189*n*, 378
    trade, 176, 178*t*, 194
    trade deficit, 188–89
South Korea–Japan FTA, prospect, 194
South Korea–US FTA, effects, 174
Taiwan, motor vehicle trade, 216
trade, services, 129*t*
trade diversion, South Korea–US FTA, 192
trade with US and ASEAN, 122*t*–123*t*
US-ASEAN FTAs, impact, 157
US-Japan FTA, prospect, 363
Jettou, Driss, 315
job dislocations, NAFTA, 43–44, 43*n*
Jones Act, 97, 101
Jordache, 324
Jordan. *See also* Jordan-US FTA
    GDP, 360*n*
    trade with US, 38*t*, 73*n*, 360*n*
    US economic ties, 368*t*
    US FDI, 38*t*
Jordan-US FTA, 62–64
    conclusions, 73–76
    congressional debate, 70
    congressional opposition, 70
    delays, 41
    dispute settlement, 64
    e-commerce, 64
    environment, NAFTA and NAAEC compared,
        68*t*–69*t*
    environmental and labor provisions, 51, 64,
        66–70, 83*n*
    foreign policy interests, 51, 62
    intellectual property rights, 63
    joint committee, 64
    labor, NAFTA compared, 71*t*–72*t*
    lessons from, 73, 75–76
    long-term impact, 73
    precedents, 70
    rules of origin, 66
    safeguard measures, 64
    trade flows, 63, 64–65, 64*t*, 65*t*
    trade preferences to QIZs, 60
    US goals, 62
    US political objectives, 188

Kirchner, Néstor, 289
Kissinger, Henry, 364
Korea. *See* North Korea; South Korea

labor advisory committee (LAC) for trade
        negotiations and trade policy (US), 87*n*

labor and environmental issues
Central America, 254–55, 262–63
displacement of workers, 366
NAFTA debates, 86
SACU, 342
trade promotion authority, 83
US-Chile FTA, 83, 86–87
US domestic politics, 366
US-Jordan FTA, pioneer agreement, 83n
US policy guidelines, 254
US-Singapore FTA, 83, 86–87
labor and environmental side agreements, NAFTA
Clinton, Bill, 41
real purpose, 46
weaknesses analyzed, 45–46
labor issues
ASEAN factor returns, 155, 156t
Chile, 86
Singapore, 86
US-Jordan FTA, 64, 67, 70, 71t–72t
labor rights, Egypt, 303
labor unions, NAFTA, 46
landholding interests, ASEAN, 142
Laos
ASEAN competition, 159, 160
ASEAN membership, 118
economic indicators, 119t
trade, 122t–123t
Latin America
See also CAFTA; FTAA; individual countries; Mercosur
Central American market, 233, 233n
competitive liberalization, 230n
Egypt vs., 304f
EU, 374–75
FTAA vis-à-vis, 372
poverty and indigence indicators, 265t
regional pattern of exports per GTAP simulation, 400t
trade and investment diversion, 372n
learning-by-doing effects, 13
Lesotho, 332, 336, 352
less-developed countries, disenfranchising, 164
line pipe safeguard, 180n
local content rules, 341
lock-in effects of FTAs, 13, 362
Loos, François, 323n
Lula (Luiz Inácio Lula da Silva)
antiglobalization, 279–80
bilateral talks, 380
Brazil on FTAA, 293
Bush relations, 280, 291, 292–93
economic policy, 279
leadership, 292
victory, 278, 288

Malawi, 346
Malaysia
antidumping (AD) actions, 138t

countervailing actions, 138t
economic indicators, 119t
exports, GTAP model, 148, 151
factor returns, 155, 156, 156t
foreign direct investment, 140
gravity model effects, 144, 145t–146t
GTAP model, results, 149t, 152t, 167–68
regional pattern of exports per GTAP simulation, 400t
Singapore, exports and origin of imports, 82t
strained US relations, 167
tariffs, 132t–133t, 136
trade, 122t–123t, 129t
trade and investment agreement with US, 166
US commodity exports to, 125t
US commodity imports from, 127t
US economic gains, 167
US exports to ASEAN, 124
maquiladoras, 60, 243n
market access issue
Brazil, 380
CAFTA, 239–44
Central America, 234, 237, 257, 269
developing countries, 32
industrial markets, 17
SACU, 350
services, US–Central America, 249–50
Southern Africa, 338
South Korea, 186, 380
technical and sanitary procedures as barrier to, 244
Marshall Plan, 370
Mauritania, 314
Meirelles, Henrique, 278
merchandise trade
ASEAN, 130–43, 373n
creation, 367
current and prospective US FTA partners, 360n
Morocco, 316
SACU, 337–38, 348
South Korea, 175, 176, 177t
US-ASEAN, 122t–123t, 123
Mercosur (Southern Cone Common Market)
Brazil, 282–83
crisis, 285
EU deals, 25, 280, 285, 375
identity, 295
political focus, 288–89
trade, by country, 283t
unified negotiating front, 289
US, strategy of bilateral advance, 294
US interest, 23
Mexico. See also NAFTA
economic indicators, 119t
EU deals, 25
foreign direct investment, 15
FTAA interest, 14–15
GDP, 360n
generalizing NAFTA reforms, 161n
immigration, 42, 49

dispute settlement mechanisms, 47–48
FTA as first step, 48–49
job counts, 43–45
labor and environmental side agreements,
45–47
post hoc ergo propter hoc fallacy, 42–43
top leadership essential, 40–42
Mexican insistence, 294
parity with, 226, 372n
political objectives, 187
potential FTAs compared, 37–40
regional pattern of exports per GTAP
simulation, 400t
rules of origin, 22
Trade Adjustment Assistance, 45
trade and investment diversion, 14, 21, 372n
trade increases, 366–67
trade with ASEAN, 122t–123t
trade with South Africa, 333, 333t
trade with US, 122t–123t
Uruguay Round, 31
Uruguay Round conclusion linked, 110
US economy size vs. partners, 52
US-Israel FTA compared, 54
US-Jordan FTA, compared, 67
US-SACU arrangement, 337
as work in progress, 371–72
NAFTA plus, 253
Namibia, 332, 336, 346n, 352
National Strategies for Trade Capacity Building, 264
national treatment for US foreign investment
Chile, 85–86
FTA motives, 83
Singapore, 85–86
natural resources
ASEAN, 124
Central America, 244
Morocco, 315
negotiating process
Australia-US FTA, 98–99, 100
CAFTA, 257, 269
Canada-US FTA, 361
FTAs as negotiating laboratories, 367
learning by doing, 13
limited resources for FTAs, 15–16
SACU, 334, 343
South Korea, 13n
US concessions in Chile and Singapore FTAs,
89–91
neoliberal model, Central America, 264
nepotism, 328
Netherlands, trade with Morocco, 316t
New Zealand. *See also* ANZCERTA
agreements, 7
Australia–New Zealand CER, 115–16
Australia-US FTA, 96
economic indicators, 119t
GDP, 360t
lack of support for US war against Iraq, 42, 96,
116, 370

regional pattern of exports per GTAP
simulation, 400t
Singapore FTA, 163
trade, 122t–123t, 129t, 360t
US economic ties, 368t
New Zealand–US FTA, other FTAs compared,
209t
Nicaragua
agricultural employment, 245t
economic indicators, 227, 228t
main product lines (list), 272t
poverty and indigence indicators, 265t
tariffs, 241t
taxes on trade, 262t
trading partners, 227, 229t
nonaligned movement, 281
nontariff barriers
agriculture, 136
ASEAN, 120, 148
ASEAN-4, 147
Central America, 244
Egypt, 306
Morocco, 317, 321t
Taiwan-US, 201
US-ASEAN summarized, 130, 131t–135t
North American Agreement on Environmental
Cooperation, 67
North American Development Bank, 268
Northeast Asia (Korea-China-Japan) FTA,
193–94
North Korea, 175, 188
North-South FTAs, 14–15

Oceania, Singapore, exports and origin of
imports, 82t
oil shocks, 282, 313
Olso Agreement, 314n
Olso peace process, 60, 62
open regionalism, 164
Oxley, Alan, 107

Pacific-5 free trade area, 163, 163n
Pakistan, 360t, 368t
Palestinian-Israeli conflict, 299
Arab perceptions of US, 313
Egyptian efforts, 301
equitable resolution, 329
Morocco, 314, 314n
Palestinian trade, 60, 62, 74–75
Palocci, Antonio, 278, 279, 288
Panama, 360t, 368t
pan-Arabism, 301
Papua New Guinea, 117n, 119t, 122t–123t
Paraguay, 283–85
patent protection, 287
pension reform, Brazil, 279
Peru, 360t, 368t
Pharmaceutical Benefits Scheme (Australia), 99,
101
pharmaceutical companies, 142, 287

services, special problems, 340–41
trade with US, 38*t*
US FDI, 38*t*
SACU-US FTA
asymmetries, 333
contents of possible, 337
competition policy, 341
customs procedures, 342
dispute settlement, 342
government procurement, 342
intellectual property rights, 341
investment, 341
labor and environment, 342
temporary entry of personnel, 342
trade in goods, 337–38
trade in services, 338, 340–41
as demonstration project, 372–73
developmental implications, 334–35, 351–54
impacts, 348–51
nontrade issues, 353
price alignment, 353
summarized, 343
trade flows, 348, 349*t*
SADC (Southern African Development
Community), 346–48
customs union idea, 346
overlapping trade relationships, 347*f*
relationship with SACU, 334
rules of origin, 346
SACU-US FTA, 346
trade with South Africa, 333, 333*t*
safeguard cases, Canada, 186
safeguard rules, Central America, 244
safeguards, US, on steel products, 289
salmon mariculture, Chile, 89
sanctions, trade-based, 46, 256–57
Saudi Arabia, trade with Morocco, 316*t*
Schumpeter, Joseph, 258*n*
sectoral effects, Taiwan-US FTA, 205–07
security. *See also* Iraq, war against
APEC, 188
ASEAN, 118, 120, 142
Australia-US FTA, 97, 98
Central America, 231–32, 238, 257
Cold War, 5
EU, 26
Indonesia, 166–67
intifada, 60
Philippines, 166–67
post–September 11, 364
South Korea, 175, 187–88
Taiwan, 201
US FTAs, 42
US trade agendas, 141
September 11, 2001
Egypt, 313
Morocco, 314
US policy, 232, 364
Serra, José, 288

Services. *See also* GATS (General Agreement on
Trade in Services)
Australia, 99, 102, 367*n*
Brazil, 367*n*, 379
Central America, 228*t*, 235, 249–50
Central America and US, 249
Chile, 85
comparative advantage, 249
FTA partners' trade in, 367, 368*t*
liberalizing model, developing countries, 338,
340
Morocco, 323, 323*n*
SACU, 334, 340, 343, 349–50
Singapore, 85, 124, 124*n*, 161, 161*n*
South Africa–EU FTA, 345
Taiwan, 198, 199, 206–07, 217–19
US, Latin America and Caribbean, 290
US-ASEAN, 124, 126, 129*t*, 139, 148, 158, 159
US-Jordan FTA, 63
Seychelles, 346*n*
Shadow G-8, 28
shallow integration, 300
Silva, Luiz Inácio Lula da. *See* Lula
Singapore
antidumping actions, 138*t*
ASEAN-4 compared, 161
Australian FTA, 111
Australia-US FTA, 99
bilateral FTAs, 162, 189
Brazil neutrality on issues, 292
capital controls prohibition, 87
countervailing actions, 138*t*
domestic economic reforms, 160–61, 161*n*
economic indicators, 80–81, 81*t*, 119*t*
exports, GTAP model, 148, 151
FDI, 140
free trade initiatives, 163
GDP, 360*n*
gravity model effects, 145*t*–146*t*, 147
GTAP model results, 149*t*, 152*t*
intellectual property rights, 219–20
Japan FTA, 6, 26
middle class, 141
multiple FTAs, 88*n*
position on FTAs, 84
regional pattern of exports per GTAP
simulation, 400*t*
services, 85, 124, 124*n*
as special case, 165
tariffs, 134*t*, 136
telecommunications, 219
trade
services, 124, 126, 129*t*
with US, 38*t*, 124, 125*t*, 127*t*, 360*n*
US economic ties, 368*t*
US FDI, 38*t*
US FTA
concluded, 39
congressional passage, 365*n*

Other Publications from the Institute for International Economics

* = out of print

65 The Benefits of Price Convergence:
Speculative Calculations
Gary Clyde Hufbauer, Erika Wada,
and Tony Warren
December 2001   ISBN 0-88132-333-0
66 Managed Floating Plus
Morris Goldstein
March 2002   ISBN 0-88132-336-5
67 Argentina and the Fund: From Triumph
to Tragedy
Michael Mussa
July 2002   ISBN 0-88132-339-X
68 East Asian Financial Cooperation
C. Randall Henning
September 2002   ISBN 0 88132-338-1
69 Reforming OPIC for the 21st Century
Theodore H. Moran
May 2003   ISBN 0-88132-342-X
70 Awakening Monster: The Alien Tort
Statute of 1789
Gary C. Hufbauer and Nicholas Mitrokostas
July 2003   ISBN 0-88132-366-7
71 Korea after Kim Jong-il
Marcus Noland
January 2004   ISBN 0-88132-373-X

BOOKS

IMF Conditionality* John Williamson, editor
1983   ISBN 0-88132-006-4
Trade Policy in the 1980s* William R. Cline, editor
1983   ISBN 0-88132-031-5
Subsidies in International Trade*
Gary Clyde Hufbauer and Joanna Shelton Erb
1984   ISBN 0-88132-004-8
International Debt: Systemic Risk and Policy
Response*   William R. Cline
1984   ISBN 0-88132-015-3
Trade Protection in the United States: 31 Case
Studies*   Gary Clyde Hufbauer, Diane E. Berliner,
and Kimberly Ann Elliott
1986   ISBN 0-88132-040-4
Toward Renewed Economic Growth in Latin
America* Bela Balassa, Gerardo M. Bueno, Pedro-
Pablo Kuczynski, and Mario Henrique Simonsen
1986   ISBN 0-88132-045-5
Capital Flight and Third World Debt*
Donald R. Lessard and John Williamson, editors
1987   ISBN 0-88132-053-6
The Canada-United States Free Trade Agreement:
The Global Impact*
Jeffrey J. Schott and Murray G. Smith, editors
1988   ISBN 0-88132-073-0
World Agricultural Trade: Building a Consensus*
William M. Miner and Dale E. Hathaway, editors
1988   ISBN 0-88132-071-3
Japan in the World Economy*
Bela Balassa and Marcus Noland
1988   ISBN 0-88132-041-2

America in the World Economy: A Strategy for
the 1990s*   C. Fred Bergsten
1988   ISBN 0-88132-089-7
Managing the Dollar: From the Plaza to the
Louvre*   Yoichi Funabashi
1988, 2nd ed. 1989   ISBN 0-88132-097-8
United States External Adjustment and the World
Economy*   William R. Cline
May 1989   ISBN 0-88132-048-X
Free Trade Areas and U.S. Trade Policy*
Jeffrey J. Schott, editor
May *1989*   ISBN 0-88132-094-3
Dollar Politics: Exchange Rate Policymaking in
the United States*
I.M. Destler and C. Randall Henning
September 1989   ISBN 0-88132-079-X
Latin American Adjustment: How Much Has
Happened?*   John Williamson, editor
April 1990   ISBN 0-88132-125-7
The Future of World Trade in Textiles and
Apparel* William R. Cline
1987, 2d ed. June 199   ISBN 0-88132-110-9
Completing the Uruguay Round: A Results-
Oriented Approach to the GATT Trade
Negotiations* Jeffrey J. Schott, editor
September 1990   ISBN 0-88132-130-3
Economic Sanctions Reconsidered (2 volumes)
Economic Sanctions Reconsidered:
Supplemental Case Histories
Gary Clyde Hufbauer, Jeffrey J. Schott, and
Kimberly Ann Elliott
1985, 2d ed. Dec. 1990   ISBN cloth 0-88132-115-X
                              ISBN paper 0-88132-105-2
Economic Sanctions Reconsidered: History and
Current Policy
Gary Clyde Hufbauer, Jeffrey J. Schott, and
Kimberly Ann Elliott
December 1990   ISBN cloth 0-88132-140-0
                         ISBN paper 0-88132-136-2
Pacific Basin Developing Countries: Prospects for
the Future*   Marcus Noland
January 1991   ISBN cloth 0-88132-141-9
                       ISBN paper 0-88132-081-1
Currency Convertibility in Eastern Europe*
John Williamson, editor
October 1991   ISBN 0-88132-128-1
International Adjustment and Financing: The
Lessons of 1985-1991*   C. Fred Bergsten, editor
January 1992   ISBN 0-88132-112-5
North American Free Trade: Issues and
Recommendations*
Gary Clyde Hufbauer and Jeffrey J. Schott
April 1992   ISBN 0-88132-120-6
Narrowing the U.S. Current Account Deficit*
Allen J. Lenz
June 1992   ISBN 0-88132-103-6
The Economics of Global Warming
William R. Cline/*June 1992*   ISBN 0-88132-132-X

Flying High: Liberalizing Civil Aviation in the Asia Pacific*
Gary Clyde Hufbauer and Christopher Findlay
November 1996   ISBN 0-88132-227-X

Measuring the Costs of Visible Protection in Korea*   Namdoo Kim
November 1996   ISBN 0-88132-236-9

The World Trading System: Challenges Ahead
Jeffrey J. Schott
December 1996   ISBN 0-88132-235-0

Has Globalization Gone Too Far?   Dani Rodrik
March 1997   ISBN cloth 0-88132-243-1

Korea-United States Economic Relationship*
C. Fred Bergsten and Il SaKong, editors
March 1997   ISBN 0-88132-240-7

Summitry in the Americas: A Progress Report
Richard E. Feinberg
April 1997   ISBN 0-88132-242-3

Corruption and the Global Economy
Kimberly Ann Elliott
June 1997   ISBN 0-88132-233-4

Regional Trading Blocs in the World Economic System   Jeffrey A. Frankel
October 1997   ISBN 0-88132-202-4

Sustaining the Asia Pacific Miracle: Environmental Protection and Economic Integration   Andre Dua and Daniel C. Esty
October 1997   ISBN 0-88132-250-4

Trade and Income Distribution   William R. Cline
November 1997   ISBN 0-88132-216-4

Global Competition Policy
Edward M. Graham and J. David Richardson
December 1997   ISBN 0-88132-166-4

Unfinished Business: Telecommunications after the Uruguay Round
Gary Clyde Hufbauer and Erika Wada
December 1997   ISBN 0-88132-257-1

Financial Services Liberalization in the WTO
Wendy Dobson and Pierre Jacquet
June 1998   ISBN 0-88132-254-7

Restoring Japan's Economic Growth
Adam S. Posen
September 1998   ISBN 0-88132-262-8

Measuring the Costs of Protection in China
Zhang Shuguang, Zhang Yansheng, and Wan Zhongxin
November 1998   ISBN 0-88132-247-4

Foreign Direct Investment and Development: The New Policy Agenda for Developing Countries and Economies in Transition
Theodore H. Moran
December 1998   ISBN 0-88132-258-X

Behind the Open Door: Foreign Enterprises in the Chinese Marketplace
Daniel H. Rosen
January 1999   ISBN 0-88132-263-6

Toward A New International Financial Architecture: A Practical Post-Asia Agenda
Barry Eichengreen
February 1999   ISBN 0-88132-270-9

Is the U.S. Trade Deficit Sustainable?
Catherine L. Mann
September 1999   ISBN 0-88132-265-2

Safeguarding Prosperity in a Global Financial System: The Future International Financial Architecture, Independent Task Force Report
Sponsored by the Council on Foreign Relations
Morris Goldstein, Project Director
October 1999   ISBN 0-88132-287-3

Avoiding the Apocalypse: The Future of the Two Koreas   Marcus Noland
June 2000   ISBN 0-88132-278-4

Assessing Financial Vulnerability: An Early Warning System for Emerging Markets
Morris Goldstein, Graciela Kaminsky, and Carmen Reinhart
June 2000   ISBN 0-88132-237-7

Global Electronic Commerce: A Policy Primer
Catherine L. Mann, Sue E. Eckert, and Sarah Cleeland Knight
July 2000   ISBN 0-88132-274-1

The WTO after Seattle   Jeffrey J. Schott, editor
July 2000   ISBN 0-88132-290-3

Intellectual Property Rights in the Global Economy   Keith E. Maskus
August 2000   ISBN 0-88132-282-2

The Political Economy of the Asian Financial Crisis   Stephan Haggard
August 2000   ISBN 0-88132-283-0

Transforming Foreign Aid: United States Assistance in the 21st Century   Carol Lancaster
August 2000   ISBN 0-88132-291-1

Fighting the Wrong Enemy: Antiglobal Activists and Multinational Enterprises   Edward M.Graham
September 2000   ISBN 0-88132-272-5

Globalization and the Perceptions of American Workers
Kenneth F. Scheve and Matthew J. Slaughter
March 2001   ISBN 0-88132-295-4

World Capital Markets: Challenge to the G-10
Wendy Dobson and Gary C. Hufbauer, assisted by Hyun Koo Cho
May 2001   ISBN 0-88132-301-2

Prospects for Free Trade in the Americas
Jeffrey J. Schott
August 2001   ISBN 0-88132-275-X

Toward a North American Community: Lessons from the Old World for the New
Robert A. Pastor
August 2001   ISBN 0-88132-328-4

Measuring the Costs of Protection in Europe: European Commercial Policy in the 2000s
Patrick A. Messerlin
September 2001   ISBN 0-88132-273-3

WORKS IN PROGRESS

Australia, New Zealand,
and Papua New Guinea
D.A. Information Services
648 Whitehorse Road
Mitcham, Victoria 3132, Australia
tel: 61 3 9210 7777
fax: 61-3-9210-7788
email: service@adadirect.com.au
http://www.dadirect.com.au

United Kingdom and Europe
(including Russia and Turkey)
The Eurospan Group
3 Henrietta Street, Covent Garden
London WC2E 8LU England
tel: 44-20-7240-0856
fax: 44-20-7379-0609
http://www.eurospan.co.uk

Japan and the Republic of Korea
United Publishers Services, Ltd.
KenkyuSha Bldg.
9, Kanda Surugadai 2-Chome
Chiyoda-Ku, Tokyo 101 Japan
tel: 81-3-3291-4541
fax: 81-3-3292-8610
email: saito@ups.co.jp
For trade accounts only.
Individuals will find IIE books in
leading Tokyo bookstores.

Thailand
Asia Books
5 Sukhumvit Rd. Soi 61
Bangkok 10110 Thailand
tel: 662-714-07402 Ext: 221, 222, 223
fax: 662-391-2277
email: purchase@asiabooks.co.th
http://www.asiabooksonline.com

Canada
Renouf Bookstore
5369 Canotek Road, Unit 1
Ottawa, Ontario KIJ 9J3, Canada
tel: 613-745-2665
fax: 613-745-7660
http://www.renoufbooks.com

India, Bangladesh, Nepal, and Sri Lanka
Viva Books Pvt.
Mr. Vinod Vasishtha
4325/3, Ansari Rd.
Daryaganj, New Delhi-110002
India
tel: 91-11-327-9280
fax: 91-11-326-7224
email: vinod.viva@gndel.globalnet.
ems.vsnl.net.in

Southeast Asia (Brunei, Cambodia,
China, Malaysia, Hong Kong, Indonesia,
Laos, Myanmar, the Philippines, Singapore,
Taiwan, and Vietnam)
Hemisphere Publication Services
1 Kallang Pudding Rd. #0403
Golden Wheel Building
Singapore 349316
tel: 65-741-5166
fax: 65-742-9356

Visit our Web site at:
www.iie.com
E-mail orders to:
orders@iie.com